The LAW of WORK

Industrial Relations and Collective Bargaining

David J. Doorey

 emond • Toronto, Canada • 2017

Emond Montgomery Publications Limited
60 Shaftesbury Avenue
Toronto ON M4T 1A3
http://www.emond.ca/highered

Printed in Canada.

We acknowledge the financial support of the Government of Canada.   Canadä

Emond Montgomery Publications has no responsibility for the persistence or accuracy of URLs for external or third-party Internet websites referred to in this publication, and does not guarantee that any content on such websites is, or will remain, accurate or appropriate.

Publisher: Mike Thompson
Managing editor, development: Kelly Dickson
Senior editor, production: Jim Lyons
Production supervisor: Laura Bast
Copy editor: Claudia Forgas
Typesetters: Shani Sohn and Christopher Hudson
Permissions editor: Lisa Brant
Proofreader: David Handelsman
Indexer: Paula Pike
Original cartoons: David J. Doorey & Rob Elliott/Swizzle Studio
Cover designers: Stephen Cribbin & Simon Evers
Cover image: © moodboard/Alamy

Library and Archives Canada Cataloguing in Publication

Doorey, David J.
[Law of work (Toronto, Ont.)]
    The law of work : industrial relations and collective bargaining / David J. Doorey, Alison Braley, Scott Walsworth, Chris Rootham.

Includes bibliographical references and index.
ISBN 978-1-77255-166-2 (softcover)

    1. Collective bargaining—Law and legislation—Canada.   2. Labor unions—Law and legislation—Canada.   3. Labor laws and legislation—Canada.   I. Braley, Alison, author   II. Walsworth, Scott, 1976-, author   III. Rootham, Christopher, author   IV. Title.   V. Title: Law of work (Toronto, Ont.)

KE3193.D65 2017   344.7101'89   C2016-907245-2
KF3408.D65 2017

Brief Contents

PART I   THE LAW OF WORK: THEMES, FRAMEWORKS, AND PERSPECTIVES

PART II   INDUSTRIAL RELATIONS AND THE COLLECTIVE BARGAINING REGIME

PART III   THE CANADIAN CHARTER OF RIGHTS AND FREEDOMS AND THE LAW OF WORK

Detailed Contents

PART I THE LAW OF WORK: THEMES, FRAMEWORKS, AND PERSPECTIVES

PART II INDUSTRIAL RELATIONS AND THE COLLECTIVE BARGAINING REGIME

PART III   THE CANADIAN CHARTER OF RIGHTS AND FREEDOMS AND THE LAW OF WORK

Preface

This is a different sort of law book. It was born of frustration with existing legal texts that were, to my mind, unsuitable for the vast majority of people who study the laws that govern work in Canada. Upper-year law school students represent a tiny fraction of Canadians who study work law in post-secondary institutions or for professional purposes. Traditional legal texts are too dense with case law and far too dry for readers who are new to the field. On the other hand, law books written specifically for legal, business, and labour relations practitioners lack broader context and, to quote my favourite law teacher, Harry Arthurs, "often degenerate into the mere recitation of rules and ... contribute neither to genuine interdisciplinary insights nor to greater citizen involvement in the law."

The Law of Work is written as an invitation to non-lawyers and lawyers alike to engage with the fascinating world of labour and employment law in a more accessible and contextual manner than is typical with most legal texts. The book interacts with the popular *Law of Work* blog (http://lawofwork.ca), which follows the same recipe for making the law and industrial relations accessible and engaging. The text moves quickly, using short chapters that cut through huge swaths of historical and contemporary legal developments. For readers or teachers who are interested in a deeper exploration of the subject matter, detailed information can be found in the endnotes of each chapter.

Part I (Chapters 1-4) introduces some key themes, frameworks, and perspectives that inform the parts that follow. The "framework" in Chapter 3 maps the interrelationships that exist throughout the various components of the "law of work" system. This is a descriptive exercise intended to introduce to a new audience what everyone in the field knows: that we cannot understand the laws and norms that govern work in isolation from the broader social, political, cultural, and economic contexts in which they emerge and function. This observation has long guided industrial relations teaching and scholarship.

The framework also emphasizes the interrelationships among the three regimes of work law—the *common law regime*, the *regulatory regime*, and the *collective bargaining regime*. This special volume explores the collective bargaining regime and industrial relations, and is especially useful for courses in industrial relations, collective labour law, labour relations, labour studies, labour law, and labour arbitration. The companion volume (*The Law of Work: Common Law and the Regulation of Work*) explores the other two regimes in detail, and is targeted at courses in employment law and policy. For those instructors who (like myself) prefer to expose students to all three regimes, the full volume including all four parts is also available. *The Law of Work* is the first Canadian text in the field that explores all three regimes in detail, in a comprehensive and coherent format that explores the interrelationships among the regimes.

I am hopeful that this book will mark a welcome new approach to teaching and learning about how our laws govern the labour relationship.

Acknowledgments

Many people contributed valuable research, reviewer feedback, or helpful suggestions during the writing of this book, including Bernie Adell, Eric Tucker, Alison Braley-Rattai, Leah Vosko, Cynthia Estlund, Michael Lynk, Rick MacDowell, Lorne Slotnick, Erin Kuzz, Jim Robbins, Morley Gunderson, Armine Yalnizyan, Rafael Gomez, Andrew Pinto, Chris Sweeney, Mitchell Doorey, Ryan Edmonds, Jim Stanford, the library staff at the Centre for Industrial Relations and Human Resources at the University of Toronto, and The Junction Pigeons.

Thanks are also due to reviewers of various parts of this project: Pnina Alon-Shenker (Ryerson University), Bob Barnetson (Athabasca University), Kathryn Filsinger (Humber College), Jason Foster (Athabasca University), Dan McGarry (Seneca College), and Larry Savage (Brock University).

As noted in the table of contents, several chapters in this volume were written by some of Canada's leading scholars and practitioners in this field (listed below), and their expertise, cooperation, and enthusiasm have been much appreciated. The book is much stronger for their contributions. Special thanks are owed to Harry Arthurs, who is the inspiration for this text. Harry provided helpful suggestions in relation to this project, but more generally has offered unwavering support and encouragement since my law school days two decades ago. I want to thank as well the Emond Publishing team for their hard work and for sharing my vision for the book. In particular, great thanks are due to Mike Thompson and Paul Emond for their enthusiastic support for the project and their many contributions to the book, to my copy editor Claudia Forgas, and to the rest of the team, particularly Kelly Dickson, Laura Bast, Shani Sohn, and David Handelsman. Finally, my greatest thanks are reserved for my wonderful family. I am the luckiest man alive that fate and the alphabet placed me beside my spouse, May Cheng, at the British Columbia call to the bar ceremony nearly 20 years ago. Her boundless positive energy inspires me every day, and this book and my new career as an academic would not have been possible without her. And, of course, to my beautiful children, Amanda and Dylan, who make every day special.

Dedication

This book is dedicated to my brother Stephen Doorey. We miss you.

David J. Doorey
Toronto

For Instructors

For additional information and resources, please visit the accompanying website for this book at **http://www.emond.ca/lawofworkircb**. The Updates tab on the site provides links to the author's *Law of Work* blog, organized to reflect the chapter structure of this book, and featuring breaking news, updates, commentary, and more.

For information on obtaining the teaching resources available to instructors who have chosen this book for their courses, visit the For Instructors tab on the book's website. These resources include PowerPoint slides, a test bank, an image bank, and more. Contact your Emond Publishing representative for more information.

About the Author

David J. Doorey is an associate professor at York University, where he is the Director of the School of Human Resource Management and Academic Director of Osgoode Hall Law School's professional part-time LLM program, specializing in labour and employment law. He is a recipient of the prestigious Dean's Award for Excellence in Teaching at York, and is a regular media commentator on work law and industrial relations. His scholarly articles have been published in leading Canadian and foreign law journals, and he is articles review editor of the *Canadian Labour and Employment Law Journal*. He is a recipient of the Morley Gunderson Prize for Outstanding Contribution to Canadian Industrial Relations from the University of Toronto, and the David Watson Memorial Award from the *Queen's Law Journal* for the law journal article making the most significant contribution to legal scholarship. His popular *Law of Work* blog has been awarded the Fodden Award for the Best Law Blog in Canada and was an inaugural inductee into the Canadian Law Blog Awards "Hall of Fame" in 2016. He was called to the law bars of Ontario and British Columbia in 1997 and practised labour law in both provinces before returning to academia. Professor Doorey was educated at the University of Toronto (BA, MIR), London School of Economics and Political Science (LLM Labour Law), and Osgoode Hall Law School (JD, PhD). He lives in Toronto's west end and in Prince Edward County with his family and Australian Labradoodle, and coaches kids' hockey.

Contributors

Alison Braley-Rattai is an assistant professor in the Department of Political Science at the University of Toronto.

Benjamin Oliphant is a lawyer with Gall Legge Grant & Munroe LLP in Vancouver, and an adjunct professor in the Faculty of Law at the University of British Columbia.

Christopher C. Rootham is a partner with Nelligan O'Brien Payne LLP and teaches at the University of Ottawa.

Scott Walsworth is an associate professor of Industrial Relations at the Edwards School of Business, University of Saskatchewan.

The Law of Work: A Timeline

2010
- *SFL v. Saskatchewan* (2015): SCC recognizes a limited Charter-protected right to strike
- "Gender identity" or "gender expression" added to some human rights statutes (2012–2015)
- *Jones v. Tsige* (2012): Ont. CA recognizes privacy tort of "intrusion upon seclusion"

- *Honda Canada v. Keays* (2008): SCC reforms "bad faith discharge" damages law
- *BC Health Services* (2007): Charter protects collective bargaining
- *Parry Sound* (2003): Labour arbitrators must apply employment-related statutes
- *RWDSU, Local 558 v. Pepsi-Cola Canada* (2002): Secondary picketing is legal per se

2000
- *Dunmore v. Ontario* (2001): Expanded scope of section 2(d) of the Charter
- *McKinley v. BC Tel* (2001): SCC explains test for "summary dismissal"
- The *Meiorin* decision on the BFOR defence to employment discrimination (1999)
- *Vriend v. Alberta* (1998): Sexual orientation read into human rights statutes
- *Wallace v. UGG* (1997): Bad faith in the manner in which an employee is terminated
- *Farber v. Royal Trust Co.* (1997): SCC explains the law of constructive dismissal
- *Weber v. Ontario Hydro* (1995): Expanded jurisdiction of labour arbitrators

NAFTA (1992)
1990
- *Machtinger v. HOJ Industries* (1992): Statutory and common law notices
- *Central Okanagan School District, No. 23 v. Renaud* (1992): The duty to accommodate

Canada–US Free Trade Agreement (1988)
- *CADP v. Alberta* (1990): Duty to accommodate religion
- "Labour Trilogy" decisions (1987): No Charter right to collective bargaining, strike
- First proactive pay equity acts (Manitoba, 1986; Ontario, 1987)
- *RWDSU, Local 580 v. Dolphin Delivery* (1986): Charter and private common law disputes
- *OHRC v. Simpsons-Sears* (1985): "Indirect discrimination" recognized

1980
- *Canadian Charter of Rights and Freedoms* (1982)

- *Wm. Scott & Co. (Re)* (1977): Arbitral test applied in "just cause" for discipline or dismissal cases
- *Canadian Human Rights Act* (1977)

- Federal wage controls legislation for public sector and some private sector workers (1975)
- Occupational health and safety statutes

1970
- Maternity leave laws (early 1970s)
- First duty of fair representation laws (Ontario, 1971)
- Severance pay law (federal, 1970)
- *R. v. Arthurs, Ex p. Port Arthur Shipbuilding Co.* (1967): Summary dismissal without notice
- Federal *Public Sector Staff Relations Act* (1967)
- *Russel Steel* (1966): Reserved management rights doctrine in labour arbitration
- Statutory notice of termination laws (mid to late 1960s)

1960
- *Hersees of Woodstock v. Goldstein* (1963): Secondary picketing is illegal per se
- Ontario *Human Rights Code* (1962)
- *Canadian Bill of Rights* (1960)
- *Bardal v. Globe & Mail Ltd.* (1960): Criteria for assessing "reasonable notice"
- Standard 8-hour day, 40-hour week legislation in some provinces

ILO Equal Remuneration Convention (1951)
- Canadian Labour Congress formed (1956)

1950
- *Female Employees Fair Remuneration Act* (Ontario, 1951)
ILO Convention 98 (1949)
- Fair employment practices laws banning discriminatory hiring (early 1950s)
ILO Convention 87 (1948)
- First racial discrimination laws (Ontario, 1944; Saskatchewan, 1947)
UN Universal Declaration of Human Rights (1948)
- "Rand Formula" award (1946)
- Paid vacation laws (1944–1950)
Second World War (1939–1945)
1940
- PC 1003: Template for modern collective bargaining laws (1944)
American *Wagner Act* (1935)
- *Christie v. The York Corporation* (1940): Discrimination in contract permissible
- *Unemployment Insurance Act* (1940)

- *Carter v. Bell & Sons (Canada) Ltd.* (1936): Termination with "reasonable notice"
- "On to Ottawa Trek" (1935)
- Men's minimum wage, 8-hour day legislated in various provinces
Great Depression (1929–1933)
1930
- Unemployment "relief" camps (1930)
ILO Minimum Wage Fixing Convention (1928)

- *TEC v. Snider* (1925): Provinces have primary jurisdiction over work law
- First minimum wage law for men (BC, 1925)
1920
- First 8-hour day, 48-hour week law (BC, 1923)
ILO Hours of Work Convention (1919)
- Winnipeg General Strike (1919)
ILO formed (1919)
- Early minimum wage laws for females only (1917–1920)
First World War (1914–1918)
- Workmen's compensation legislation (1914–1920)
- Meredith Commission on Workers' Compensation (1913)

1910
- *Industrial Disputes Investigation Act* (1907): Mandatory government conciliation
- *Lord's Day Act* (1906): Prohibited conducting of business on Sundays

- *Railway Labour Disputes Act* (1903): Early labour dispute conciliation law

1900

| 10 | 15 | 20 | 25 | 30 | 35 |

Union density, 1920–present (% of non-agricultural paid employees in unions)

PART I

The Law of Work: Themes, Frameworks, and Perspectives

Canadian Work Law in a Nutshell

I. Introduction

At the beginning of a long journey, it is useful to survey a topographical map of the terrain to come—to study the forest canopy before entering the thicket. We can see patterns from above not apparent from the forest floor. It helps to have a sense of where we are going so that we can anticipate what is to come. Therefore, we will begin our journey by looking down at a map of sorts: a map of *work law*. This map charts the manner in which our legal system regulates labour markets and the buying and selling of labour.

For over a century, legal scholars have studied these laws. In truth, though, scholars have really only been interested in work performed through one specific organizational form: **employment**. Workers can of course sell their labour through arrangements other than employment. I once contracted with a company called High Park Building Services Inc. (or HPBS) to build me a backyard deck. It turned out that HPBS was really just a guy named Jason Phillips who was between jobs and who had set up a company so that he could use his carpentry skills to earn some money. Whether I hired Jason as my employee or contracted with a company called HPBS is crucially important to how the law treats our relationship. If Jason is my employee, then all of the laws that govern employment considered in this text apply to our relationship. But if my contract is with HPBS, maybe none of them do. It's the same work in either case, but the legal regime that applies is fundamentally different.

Whether so much should depend on this fine distinction between employment and *not* employment is one of the great debates in our legal field.[1] We will revisit this debate at various

---

employment: An organizational form through which a person (employee) sells his or her labour power to a buyer of labour (employer) in exchange for value and in which the relationship is governed by an employment contract.

points throughout this text, and we will explore how the law draws the distinction between an employee and a worker who is not an employee in Chapter 2. The reason for mentioning the "employment" versus "not employment" distinction at this early stage is to explain the boundaries of our map of the law of work set out in this chapter. It is a high-level map of how Canadian law governs the employment relationship. It does so through three distinct legal regimes: (1) the common law of employment; (2) regulatory law; and (3) collective bargaining law. In Chapter 3, we will pull back and consider how the law of employment relates more generally to the broader legal system.

This chapter provides an overview of the key components of the legal system that governs employment in Canada, outside of Quebec. Quebec is a special case because its legal system, including much of the law that governs the employment relationship, is based on the French model of civil law rather than the British-based common law system applied elsewhere in Canada. Therefore, while we will occasionally consider cases and regulations originating in Quebec in this text, our focus will be on the legal system that governs the rest of Canada.

II. The Three Regimes of Work Law

As noted above, the system of laws that governs employment in Canada (outside of Quebec) consists of three distinct, yet overlapping regimes:

1. The common law regime (covered in Part II of the companion volume)*
2. The regulatory regime (covered in Part III of the companion volume)
3. The collective bargaining regime (covered in Part II of this text)*

FIGURE 1.1 Mapping the Three Regimes of Work Law

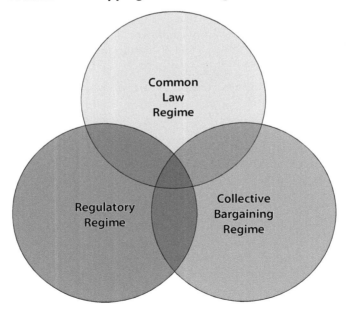

What follows is a brief introduction to each of these regimes. The remainder of the text is devoted to filling in the details.

---

* *The Law of Work: Common Law and the Regulation of Work.* See www.emond.ca/lawofwork.

A. The Common Law Regime

The common law regime comprises both the *law of contracts* and the *law of torts*.

1. The Law of Contracts

The cornerstone of the common law regime is the **contract** and, in particular, **employment contracts** between employers and individual (non-union) employees. A *contract* is a legally binding agreement in which two or more parties make promises to provide benefits to one another. In a typical employment contract, the employee promises to provide labour power in exchange for monetary compensation in the form of a wage paid by the employer, and sometimes other benefits, such as health benefits and pension contributions. The two parties discuss, or negotiate, what the terms of the contract will be and their agreement becomes a contract, a source of legal rules by which the parties are to be governed.

BOX 1.1 » TALKING WORK LAW

Understanding Legal Terminology

In Canada and the United States, the *common law regime* and the *regulatory standards regime* are commonly grouped together under the label *employment law.*

The legal regime that governs collective bargaining processes, by contrast, is usually referred to as *labour law.*

This text uses the terms *work law* and *law of work* synonymously to refer to the entire system of legal rules in all three legal regimes.

While the law of contracts has deep roots in the **common law** system, dating back centuries in Britain, the law of employment contracts dates only from the late 1800s in Canada.[2] Prior to that time, the relationship between buyers and sellers of labour was dealt with under a branch of law known as *master and servant law*, and through a mix of contract, property, criminal, and tort law.[3] The law permitted servants (workers) to recover unpaid wages from their masters (employers) and workers who quit a job to be imprisoned.[4] Legal historians describe master and servant law as a system of rules based on "status," by which they mean that workers were considered subservient to their masters, and therefore subject to their masters' largely unquestioned authority. The master and servant regime was exported from Britain into parts of early Canada, but by the early 1900s it had been largely supplanted by the emerging common law of the employment contract.[5]

"Freedom of contract" is a powerful idea. Its supporters argue that allowing employees and employers to "negotiate" the conditions of employment leads to the fairest and most efficient outcomes for the parties, the economy, and society as a whole. Professor Hugh Collins (Oxford University) summarizes the central arguments in favour of freedom of contract as a means of coordinating employment relations as follows:

---

contract: A legally binding agreement consisting of reciprocal promises between two or more parties.

employment contract: A contract between an employer and an individual employee that defines the conditions under which the employee will provide labour to the employer in exchange for a monetary benefit (wages, salary), and sometimes other benefits (e.g., health benefits). An employment contract may be written or oral.

common law: A system of judge-made rules originating in England around the 12th century, and inherited by Canada as a British colony, that uses a precedent-based approach to case law. Earlier decisions dealing with similar facts or legal issues guide later decisions in an attempt to create legal predictability. However, common law rules can and often do evolve as social values change.

The principle of freedom of contract removes the possibility of workers being treated exactly like commodities, because by giving them the power to choose, the principle ensures the elementary respect for the dignity, autonomy, and equality of citizens. So too the principle ensures a measure of justice and fairness by permitting everyone to seek work without discrimination and obstructions to competition. Furthermore, freedom of contract permits the parties to regulate their own relationship in order to deal with the special difficulties presented by the unique combination of characteristics of the employment relationship. The parties are likely to have the best information about where their interests lie, and therefore they should be permitted to forge a compromise between their competing interests without interference by a paternalistic state.[6]

Occasionally, disputes arise between employers and employees in which one of the parties accuses the other of violating the contract. Those disputes may end up in a courtroom in front of a judge if one party sues the other party for **breach of contract**. If the lawsuit does not settle (most do), a judge will conduct a trial. At the trial, the parties will present a story to the judge in the form of documentary evidence and witness testimonies, recounting versions of what happened leading up to the disagreement. The judge must then decide whether the contract was breached, and, if so, what the guilty party should be ordered to do as a remedy for the breach.

The judge writes a decision that is distributed to the parties and then published in legal case digests and, nowadays, electronic case databases. At that point, the decision becomes part of the *common law of employment contracts*, a large body of legal decisions about employment contracts dating back to the beginning of the employment model in 19th-century Britain. The common law of employment contracts in Canada now comprises hundreds of thousands of decided cases.

BOX 1.2 » TALKING WORK LAW

Law Schools and Libraries in Canada

Sixteen law schools across Canada teach the British-based common law system, four in Quebec teach the French-based civil law system, and two (at the University of Ottawa and McGill University) offer programs in both legal systems. Each law school has its own law library. The largest law library in Canada is housed at Osgoode Hall Law School at York University in Toronto, with over 500,000 legal books. Each province's professional legal body, or "law society," also has a law library. In the past, lawyers needed to visit a law library to conduct research on old cases. Nowadays, much if not all of that legal research can be conducted electronically through the use of both free (CanLII) and fee-based services (LexisNexis Quicklaw).

The exercise at the end of this chapter gives you the opportunity to practise finding common law case law using CanLII (www.canlii.org), which provides free online access to Canadian case law and legislation databases.

The law library at Osgoode Hall Law School in Toronto.
Source: Osgoode Hall Law School.

---

breach of contract: Occurs when a party to a contract violates one or more terms of a legally binding contract.

Lawyers research case law in search of decisions and reasoning that support their arguments. They also must be prepared to **distinguish** cases that do not support their argument—to explain to the judge why a previous decision relied on by their opponent is different from the one they are now dealing with. This process is necessary because the common law system operates on a **precedent**-based system known as *stare decisis*, a Latin phrase meaning, loosely, "to stand by a previous decision." Guided by a desire for the law to be predictable, the principle of *stare decisis* instructs judges to follow the reasoning and outcomes in earlier cases that dealt with the same legal issues and involved similar facts.

If the earlier decision was decided by a *higher level of court* from the same **jurisdiction** (see Figure 1.2 for the levels of Canadian courts), then the reasoning in that decision is a **binding precedent**. This means that a lower court judge who later deals with a lawsuit involving the same, or very similar, factual and legal circumstances must apply the same legal reasoning applied by the higher court, even if he or she does not agree with it. Decisions that are not binding precedents can still have "precedent" value. Since the common law system prefers predictability, judges usually follow earlier decisions, even those that are not issued by a binding higher court, unless they distinguish the facts or legal issues decided in the earlier decision or they rule that the earlier decision was just plain wrong.

2. The Law of Torts

Torts are the second branch of the common law of concern in a text on the law of work. A *tort* is a legal wrong defined by judges to allow a person to recover damages for harm caused by the actions of another person.[7] Torts allow damages to be recovered even when the harm caused does not violate a contract or government **statute**. Many of the torts that are applied in Canada were initially developed years ago by British judges. You have likely heard of some of them, even if you did not know they were called torts: *nuisance, trespass, deceit, negligence, conspiracy, defamation,* and *assault and battery*. All of these torts have potential application to the relationships that structure work in our society. Other less well-known yet important torts with application to work include *intentional infliction of mental suffering* and *negligent misrepresentation*.

The usual remedy for a tort violation is monetary damages, but judges can also order **injunctions** to remedy a tort. An *injunction* is an order to stop doing something unlawful. Injunctions have played an important role throughout history in restricting collective activities of workers, such as strikes and picketing, aimed at winning better working conditions. Judges have applied

---

distinguish: To explain how a prior legal decision dealt with facts or legal issues that are different from the facts or issues in the current case.

precedent: An earlier decision by a judge that dealt with the same, or very similar, facts and legal issues as those before a judge in the current case.

***stare decisis*:** A Latin term meaning "to stand by a previous decision." It is a guiding principle in the common law regime.

jurisdiction: The scope of authority over which a government, court, or expert administrative power has the power to govern.

binding precedent (or binding decision): An earlier decision by a court of higher ranking dealing with the same legal issue in a case that comes before a lower court judge. The lower court judge is required to apply the same reasoning and legal test applied by the higher court.

tort: A type of wrongful act done by one person to another (or to another's property) that judges have recognized as legally actionable. Examples are *nuisance, trespass, negligence,* and *conspiracy*.

statute: A law, or legislation, produced by a government that includes rules that regulate the conduct of business and people. An example is the Ontario *Employment Standards Act, 2000*.

injunction: A legal order issued by a judge prohibiting a person from engaging in a particular course of action, such as breaching a contract, committing a tort, or violating a statute.

FIGURE 1.2   Levels of Canadian Courts

> ### Supreme Court of Canada (SCC)
>
> Sits in Ottawa. Hears final appeals from all jurisdictions in Canada. Court must first grant "leave" (permission) to hear an appeal.

↑

> ### Courts of Appeal
>
> Each province and territory (except Nunavut) has its own Court of Appeal. There is also a Federal Court of Appeal that hears appeals from lower-level federal courts and tribunals.

↑

> ### Courts of First Instance (Lower Courts)
>
> These have different names across the country, and, other than in Nunavut, where there is a unified Court of Superior Justice, the courts of first instance are usually further subdivided into inferior and superior courts, which have jurisdiction over different subject matter. Judges in the inferior courts are appointed by the provinces, whereas superior court judges are appointed by the federal government. Superior courts have general authority to hear most private lawsuits and serious criminal matters, while inferior courts are usually assigned less serious criminal matters, traffic violations, and some specialized subject matters, such as many family law matters. Most (though not all) employment-related matters are heard initially in the superior courts of the jurisdiction in which the legal proceeding is launched.
>
>   Here is a quick overview of provincial and territorial courts of first instance:
>
> | JURISDICTION | INFERIOR COURT | SUPERIOR COURT |
> |---|---|---|
> | Alberta | Provincial Court | Queen's Bench |
> | British Columbia | Provincial Court | Supreme Court |
> | Manitoba | Provincial Court | Queen's Bench |
> | New Brunswick | Provincial Court | Queen's Bench |
> | Newfoundland & Labrador | Provincial Court | Supreme Court |
> | Northwest Territories | Territorial Court | Supreme Court |
> | Nova Scotia | Provincial Court | Supreme Court |
> | Ontario | Ontario Court of Justice | Superior Court of Justice |
> | Prince Edward Island | Provincial Court | Supreme Court |
> | Quebec | Court of Quebec | Superior Court |
> | Saskatchewan | Provincial Court | Queen's Bench |
> | Yukon | Territorial Court | Supreme Court |

torts such as *conspiracy* and *trespass to property* and *economic torts* (a special type of tort that we will consider in Part II) to put an end to strikes, picketing, and other worker protests.[8] Together, the common law rules of contract and tort restrict many activities of trade unions. However, as we will learn in Part II, Canadian governments have intervened in the common law model by passing laws that exempt unions from some of the most restrictive common law rules to enable them to represent workers through collective bargaining.

B. The Regulatory Regime

As noted above, the common law regime is guided by the powerful claim that "freedom of contract" advances individual liberty while producing the most efficient and desirable distribution of skills and resources in a society. On this basis, defenders of freedom of contract argue that the courts and governments should limit their intervention in employment relations to enforcing contracts between employers and individual workers.[9] However, this position has long been the subject of intense debate and dissent.

Most of the time, employers enjoy far superior bargaining power as compared with employees and are able to unilaterally fix the terms of the contract. This "inequality of bargaining power" leaves most employees with a simple choice of whether to accept or not accept the terms the employer offers. No negotiation takes place at all. Think about your job, if you have one. Did you engage in negotiations with your employer at the time you were hired, or did you just accept whatever wage rate and other conditions your employer provided? Employees of Walmart or a manufacturer do not normally negotiate over starting wages or health benefits. Typically, the employers present a standard form employment contract (if they even bother to put anything in writing), and the worker signs it.

Sometimes a person has multiple job possibilities, so he or she may be able to reject a poor offer by one or more employers. However, often, and particularly in periods of high unemployment and for jobs requiring low skills, far more workers are seeking work than there are jobs available. Since most workers require income from work to survive, the option of not accepting a job is often not a realistic one. In most cases, workers need a job far more than an employer needs any particular worker.

The fact that the more powerful party—employers—can almost always fix the terms of the employment contract unilaterally is not a new insight. Adam Smith (1723–1790) knew it, as did Karl Marx (1818–1883), two great thinkers with very different perspectives on the role of markets, law, and work.[10] German sociologist Max Weber (1864–1920) summarized the point as follows:

> The formal right of a worker to enter into any contract whatsoever with any employer whatsoever does not in practice represent for the employment seeker even the slightest freedom in the determination of his own conditions of work, and it does not guarantee him any influence in the process. It rather means, primarily, that the more powerful party in the market, i.e. normally the employer, has the possibility to set the terms, to offer a job "take it or leave it," and given the normally more pressing economic need of the worker, to impose his terms upon him.[11]

The Supreme Court of Canada has recognized that employment contracts are distinguishable from typical commercial contracts by the inherent inequality of bargaining power involved. In the case of *Machtinger v. HOJ Industries*, the court agreed with the following analysis by Professor Katherine Swinton (now a judge in Ontario):

> [T]he terms of the employment contract rarely result from an exercise of free bargaining power in the way that the paradigm commercial exchange between two traders does. Individual employees on the whole lack both the bargaining power and the information necessary to achieve more favourable contract provisions than those offered by the employer, particularly with regard to tenure.[12]

The factual claim that employees usually are the weaker party in the employment contract is not very controversial. However, whether this inequality of bargaining power is problematic and creates a need for legislative intervention to protect employees is one of the great debates in work law policy.[13] We will explore it throughout this text. However, it was important to introduce the debate at this early point in order to understand the origins of the second regime of work law, the regulatory standards regime.

In practice, employers often have not exercised their superior power in a responsible manner deemed acceptable to society. In the early days of industrial capitalism in Canada, for example, before much employment protection legislation existed, working conditions were often horrific, characterized by dangerous practices, long hours, low pay, and verbal and physical abuse at the hands of employers. Consider the following description of working conditions in some late 19th-century Canadian factories, as described by a commissioner in a government inquiry:

> Many children of tender age, some of them not more than nine years old, were employed in cotton, glass, tobacco, and cigar factories. … Some of them worked from six o'clock in the morning till six in the evening, with less than an hour for dinner, others worked from seven in the evening till six in the morning. … The darkest pages in the testimony … are those recording the beating and imprisonment of children employed in factories. Your Commissioners earnestly hope that these barbarous practices may be removed, and such treatment made a penal offence, so that Canadians may no longer rest under the reproach that the lash and the dungeon are accompaniments of manufacturing industry in the Dominion.[14]

The sorts of working conditions described in the preceding passage led governments across Canada to intervene in freedom of contract by enacting legislation (statutes and **regulations**) that regulates working conditions. In fact, there has never been a time in Canada when employment was purely a matter of free contracting; for as long as employment has existed, so too has employment regulation.

Nowadays, employment is among the most regulated of all relationships in society. In Part III of the companion volume, we looked at government legislation that regulates wages and minimum employment standards, immigration and the right to work, health and safety at work, human rights and discrimination, workers' compensation, intellectual property, and pensions, among other forms of legislation. Sometimes this type of government regulation is described as **protective standards regulation** because its central function is to protect employees from employers that may use their superior bargaining power to impose working conditions that fall below what the government believes to be acceptable.[15]

A second type of regulatory standards involves government regulation that, while not specifically aimed at protecting vulnerable employees, nevertheless has important effects on labour markets. For example, vulnerable employees are not the focus of intellectual property regulation. However, that regulation is important in work law because it determines who owns the product of a worker's labour. Constitutional law is not primarily concerned with employment regulation, yet it sets the parameters of a government's ability to regulate work in the first place. Regulation that affects labour markets in important ways is part of the law of work.

---

regulations: Government-made detailed rules introduced as a supplement to, and pursuant to authority created in, a statute. For example, the Ontario *Employment Standards Act, 2000* requires that employers pay at least "the prescribed minimum wage," but does not say what that wage rate is. That Act gives the government the right to introduce regulations (in s. 144), and one regulation (O. Reg. 285/01) sets out the precise amount of the minimum wage.

protective standards regulation: Government regulation designed primarily to protect employees by imposing mandatory standards, such as minimum contract requirements and safety rules.

Regulation is usually enforced by a combination of government inspections and complaints filed by people who believe their statutory rights have been violated. The task of hearing those complaints falls to **expert administrative tribunals**. Tribunals (which are created by statutes) are not the same as courts, although they sometimes function in a similar manner. Governments staff tribunals with experts in the field, who help employers and employees resolve disputes through mediation. When settlements cannot be obtained, tribunals hold hearings and issue legally binding decisions. By assigning authority over employment statutes to expert administrative tribunals, governments also limit the volume of employment-related disputes going to the courts.

For example, one of the busiest administrative tribunals in Canada is the Ontario Labour Relations Board (OLRB), which has authority to interpret several employment-related statutes, including the provincial *Labour Relations Act* and *Employment Standards Act*. The adjudicators are known as *chairs* or *vice-chairs*, and almost all are former practising lawyers in the field. The adjudicators conduct hearings and issue decisions resolving disputes arising under those statutes. Similar tribunals exist in every jurisdiction in Canada. The courts play a smaller role in the regulatory standards regime than in the common law regime. The role of the courts is limited mostly to reviewing tribunal decisions to ensure that the tribunal does not exceed the authority granted it under its constituting statute, a process known as **judicial review**.

C. The Collective Bargaining Regime

The third regime of work law, the collective bargaining regime, is also primarily a response to the imbalance of power in the employment relationship. However, rather than impose mandatory rules ("pay at least the minimum wage," "do not work more than 48 hours in a week," "do not pay women less than men for the same work") like the regulatory standards regime, the collective bargaining regime addresses the inequality of bargaining power by conferring more power on workers so that they can bargain a better deal for themselves. Whereas a single worker acting alone usually lacks sufficient power to bargain with his or her employer over working conditions, a group of workers acting in combination often does have sufficient power to bargain. If those workers, acting as a collective, can withhold their labour (**strike**) as bargaining leverage, then their bargaining power grows substantially.

The collective bargaining regime is concerned with the processes through which workers act collectively in pursuit of higher wages and better benefits and working conditions. Otto Kahn-Freund (1900–1979), who was professor of law at Oxford University, provided a now often-cited justification for labour (collective bargaining) laws:

> In its inception [the employment relationship] is an act of submission, in its operation it is a condition of subordination, however much the submission and the subordination may be concealed by the indispensable figment of the legal mind known as the "contract of employment." The main object of labour [collective bargaining] law has always been, and we venture to say will always be, to be a countervailing force to counteract the inequality of bargaining power which is inherent and must be inherent in the employment relationship.[16]

---

expert administrative tribunals: Decision-making bodies created by a government statute and given responsibility for interpreting and enforcing one or more statutes and any regulations pursuant to that statute.

judicial review: The process through which a decision of an expert administrative tribunal is appealed to a court on the basis that the tribunal exceeded its authority (or jurisdiction) as defined in the statute that created it or that the tribunal's decision was wrong. How much deference a court must give to the expert tribunal's decision is a complex question that is considered in a field of law known as *administrative law*.

strike: Legislation can assign a particular definition to the word *strike*. In Canada, strikes are usually defined to include both (1) a collective refusal by employees to perform work, and (2) a deliberate collective slowdown by workers designed to restrict the output of an employer (commonly known as a *work to rule*).

Whether law *should* encourage or prohibit collective worker action is one of the great enduring legal debates. We will explore these issues in detail in this volume.

The collective bargaining regime comprises three categories of legal rules:

1. Government-made statutory rules regulating the formation and administration of unions, collective bargaining, and industrial conflict, enforced by expert administrative tribunals called *labour relations boards*.
2. Collectively bargained rules found in **collective agreements**. Employers and unions usually negotiate these, although in some cases, collective agreements are imposed in whole or in part by **interest arbitrators**. Collective agreement rules are enforced by either labour boards or expert **labour arbitrators**.
3. Judge-made rules based in common law torts that mostly apply to labour picketing and strikes, which are issued and enforced by the courts.

All three categories of rules function together to create a complex, multi-layered legal model that seeks to balance the sometimes overlapping but often competing interests of workers, employers, suppliers, consumers, the broader society, and the economy in general.

Labour laws erect shields to protect workers who act collectively from some tort and contract law rules that are designed to restrict collective actions. For example, the tort of *conspiracy to injure* prohibits individuals from acting together in order to cause economic harm to another. Until labour laws were enacted to protect collective bargaining rights, workers who sought to bargain as a group and threatened to withhold their labour (strike) in order to pressure their employer were engaged in unlawful conspiracy.[17] The courts would order the collective action to cease, impose fines, and occasionally imprison union organizers or striking workers. Canadian government support for collective bargaining has ebbed and flowed dramatically over the past century, from outright hostility prior to the 1940s to cautious support in the decades following the Second World War.[18] More recently, the prevailing political attitude appears to be shifting back toward hostility.

Once workers are covered by a collective agreement, the legal rules of contract interpretation applied by judges to individual employment contracts in the common law regime, discussed above, no longer apply. The collective bargaining regime replaces the common law of the employment contract for unionized workers. Canadian labour law statutes require that all disputes between unions and employers about the interpretation and application of collective agreements be resolved by labour arbitrators rather than judges. Since the 1940s, labour arbitrators have developed a large body of labour arbitration case law, and many of the rules of interpretation that are applied to collective agreements are different from those applied to individual employment contracts by judges in the common law regime.[19]

III. Chapter Summary

This chapter introduced the three regimes of work law (the laws that regulate the employment relationship in Canada) at a general level, as if we were looking down at a topographical map of the law. We can summarize what we saw as follows:

---

collective agreement: A contract between an employer (or employers) and a trade union (or trade unions) that sets out the conditions of employment for a group of employees.

interest arbitrator: An individual or three-person expert arbitration board tasked with writing the terms of a collective agreement when the union and employer are unable to reach agreement through voluntary collective bargaining.

labour arbitrator: An individual or three-person expert arbitration panel appointed to decide disputes over the application and interpretation of collective agreements.

- The *common law regime* is concerned with legal rules found in employment contracts between individual employees and employers, including rules judges have developed over the years when interpreting those contracts, and with another branch of judge-made legal rules known as *torts*.
- The *regulatory regime* is concerned with rules governing the work relationship—and employment contracts in particular—created by governments and codified in legislation (statutes and regulations). The regulatory regime includes both legislation designed to protect vulnerable employees and legislation that affects labour markets in substantial ways. Those rules are interpreted by expert administrative tribunals created by governments for that purpose.
- The *collective bargaining regime* is concerned with three categories of legal rules. The first category comprises government-made statutory rules that regulate areas including union formation, collective bargaining processes, and industrial conflict. The second comprises collective bargaining rules found in collective agreements, which are bargained by unions (on behalf of employees) and employers (and sometimes employer associations). Labour arbitrators decide collective agreement disputes, guided by a large volume of labour arbitration jurisprudence developed since the 1940s. The third comprises judge-made rules based in common law torts that continue to apply within the collective bargaining regime, particularly in relation to picketing and strikes. It is this regime that is the focus of this volume.

QUESTIONS AND ISSUES FOR DISCUSSION

1. What two branches of law comprise the common law regime?
2. Briefly explain the three regimes of work law. Who (or what) is responsible for resolving disputes that arise under each of the three regimes?
3. What are three levels of courts in Canada?
4. Explain the concept of *stare decisis*.
5. What are some strengths and weaknesses of "freedom of contract" in the context of work law?
6. What three categories of legal rules compose the collective bargaining regime?
7. What is the difference between a "labour arbitrator" and an "interest arbitrator"?

EXERCISE

Throughout this text, we will examine a lot of case law decided by courts and expert administrative tribunals. In the past, accessing case law was difficult and mostly the domain of lawyers. It required visiting a law library and conducting complicated legal research using dense legal reporting books and complex legal research skills honed in law school and years of legal practice.

Today, lawyers and non-lawyers alike can access legal decisions on their computers. While the most thorough legal databases require payment of expensive fees, increasingly legal decisions are being posted on free Internet databases. The Canadian Legal Information Institute (CanLII) is a prime example. It is produced by the various Canadian law societies with the goal of making "Canadian law accessible for free on the Internet."

This text includes a number of exercises that encourage readers to conduct their own legal research using CanLII. To give you a sense of how CanLII works, try the following exercise.

1. Go to the CanLII home page: www.canlii.org.
2. In the search window, type the phrase "wrongful dismissal" in quotation marks. That search should give you over 7,000 legal decisions.

3. Find one decision that sounds interesting to you from the brief description that appears in the search results. Select the link to the decision. Answer the following questions:
   a. What is the name of the case?
   b. What year was the case decided?
   c. In what province did the case originate?
   d. Was the case decided by a court or an expert administrative tribunal?
   e. If it was a court, which court? If it was a tribunal, which tribunal?
   f. Read the case. Can you determine what the dispute was about, and which party won the case?

If this is your first time reading a legal decision, it may be difficult for you to follow what is happening. Do not fear, because that is normal. Reading the law takes a bit of practice because the law uses specialized language. We will decipher this language throughout the text.

UPDATES

Go to emond.ca/lawofworkircb for links to news, author's blog posts, content updates, and other information related to the chapters in this text.

NOTES AND REFERENCES

1. G. Davidov, "The Reports of My Death Are Greatly Exaggerated: Employee as a Viable (Though Overly-Used) Legal Concept," in G. Davidov and B. Langille, eds., *Boundaries and Frontiers of Labour Law* (Oxford: Hart, 2006), 133-52, at 133-34; B. Langille, "Labour Law's Back Pages," in Davidov and Langille, ibid., at 13; and J. Fudge, E. Tucker, and L. Vosko, "Changing Boundaries in Employment: Developing a New Platform for Labour Law" (2003) 10 *Canadian Labour and Employment Law Journal* 329.

2. C. Mummé, *The Indispensable Figment of the Legal Mind: The Contract of Employment at Common Law in Ontario, 1890–1979* (PhD dissertation, Osgoode Hall Law School, 2013), at 83.

3. P. Craven, "The Law of Master and Servant in Mid-Nineteenth Century Ontario," in D. Flaherty, ed., *Essays in the History of Canadian Law*, vol. 1 (Toronto: University of Toronto Press, 1981), 175-211.

4. See, e.g., *An Act to Regulate the Duties Between Master and Servant, and for Other Purposes Therein Mentioned*, S. Prov. Can. 1847, c. 23, S. Prov. Can 1851, c. 11; and Ontario *Master and Servant Act of 1855*, 18 Vict., c. 136.

5. Sir Henry Maine famously wrote that "the movement of the progressive societies has hitherto been a movement from Status to Contract," and the transition from master and servant law to the employment contract model is often considered to be an important part of that story. H.S. Maine, *Ancient Law: Its Connection with the Early History of Society, and Its Relation to Modern Ideas*

(London: J. Murray, 1861), at 170. However, employment contracts have always been heavily regulated and subject to special rules of interpretation developed by common law judges. See Mummé, supra note 2.

6. H. Collins, *Employment Law*, 2nd ed. (Oxford: Oxford University Press, 2009), at 14-15. Leading works advocating the freedom of contract school of employment law and the common law model that supports it include R. Posner, *Economic Analysis of Law*, 5th ed. (New York: Aspen Law and Business, 1998), at chapter 8; M. Friedman, *Capitalism and Freedom* (Chicago: University of Chicago Press, 1962); R. Epstein, "In Defense of Contract at Will" (1984) 51 *University of Chicago Law Review* 947; and R. Epstein, *Simple Rules for a Complex World* (Cambridge, MA: Harvard University Press, 1995), at chapters 8 and 9.

7. Many good books deal with Canadian tort law, including E. Weinrib, *Tort Law: Cases and Materials*, 4th ed. (Toronto: Emond Montgomery, 2014); and A.M. Linden, *Canadian Tort Law*, 6th ed. (Toronto: Butterworths, 1997).

8. See the discussion in H. Carty, *An Analysis of the Economic Torts* (Oxford: Oxford University Press, 2001).

9. See, e.g., Posner, supra note 6, at chapter 11.

10. A. Smith, *An Inquiry into the Nature and Causes of the Wealth of Nations* (London, 1776), vol. 1, at 81: "it is not … difficult to foresee which of the two parties must, upon all ordinary occasions, have the advantage in the dispute, and force the other into compliance with their terms. …

In all such disputes the masters [employers] can hold out much longer." K. Marx and F. Engels, *The Communist Manifesto* (London, 1848), at 347: "In proportion as the bourgeoisie, i.e., capital, is developed, in the same proportion is the proletariat, the modern working class, developed—a class of laborers, who live only so long as they find work, and who find work only so long as their labor increases capital. These laborers, who must sell themselves piecemeal, are a commodity, like every other article of commerce, and are consequently exposed to all the vicissitudes of competition, to all the fluctuations of the market. Owing to the extensive use of machinery, and to the division of labor, the work of the proletarians has lost all individual character, and, consequently, all charm for the workman. He becomes an appendage of the machine, and it is only the most simple, most monotonous, and most easily acquired knack, that is required of him. Hence, the cost of production of a workman is restricted, almost entirely, to the means of subsistence that he requires for maintenance, and for the propagation of his race." See also K. Marx, *Capital* (Hamburg, 1867). For a review of Marx and the application of his work to industrial relations and the law of work, see J. Goddard, *Industrial Relations, the Economy, and Society*, 4th ed. (Toronto: Captus Press, 2011), at chapter 2. See also M. Skousen, *The Big Three in Economics: Adam Smith, Karl Marx, and John Maynard Keynes* (Armonk, NY: M.E. Sharp, 2007).

11. M. Weber, "Freedom and Coercion," in M. Rheinstein, ed., *Max Weber on Law in Economy and Society* (Cambridge, MA: Harvard University Press, 1954), at 188.

12. *Machtinger v. HOJ Industries*, [1992] 1 SCR 986, at 1003.

13. A vast amount of legal literature exists on this debate, dating from the beginning of waged labour. A good summary of some of the leading historical voices in this debate is found in Labour Law Casebook Group, *Labour and Employment Law: Cases, Materials, and Commentary*, 8th ed. (Toronto: Irwin, 2011), at chapter 1. In particular, see the famous exchange between M. Friedman, *Capitalism and Freedom* (Chicago: University of Chicago Press, 1962), at 12-15, and C.B. MacPherson, "Elegant Tombstones: A Note on Friedman's Freedom," in *Democratic*

Theory: Essays in Retrieval (Oxford: Oxford University Press, 1973), 143-56, at 143. Some recent contributions include B. Langille, "Labour Law's Theory of Justice," in G. Davidov and B. Langille, eds., *The Idea of Labour Law* (Oxford: Oxford University Press, 2011), 101-20, at 111; H. Arthurs, "Labour Law After Labour," in Davidov and Langille, 13-29, at 13; and A. Davies, *Perspectives on Labour Law*, 2nd ed. (New York: Cambridge University Press, 2009), at chapter 2.

14. J. Rinehart, *The Tyranny of Work: Alienation and the Labour Process*, 2nd ed. (Toronto: Harcourt Brace, 1987), at 40; and G. Kealey, *Canada Investigates Industrialism* (Toronto: University of Toronto Press, 1973), at 14, 22.

15. S. Bernstein, K. Lippel, E. Tucker, and L. Vosko, "Precarious Employment and the Law's Flaws: Identifying Regulatory Failure and Securing Effective Protection for Workers," in L. Vosko, ed., *Precarious Employment: Understanding Labour Market Insecurity in Canada* (Montreal: McGill-Queen's University Press, 2006), at 203.

16. P. Davies and M. Freedland, *Kahn-Freund's Labour and the Law*, 3rd ed. (London: Stevens, 1983), at 18. This passage was quoted with approval by Chief Justice Dickson of the Supreme Court of Canada in *Slaight Communications Inc. v. Davidson*, [1989] 1 SCR 1038, at part IV.

17. See the British House of Lords decision in *Rookes v. Barnard*, [1964] AC 1129. A discussion of the torts that restrict collective action can be found in Labour Law Casebook Group, supra note 13, at 418-21.

18. L. Panitch and D. Schwartz, *From Consent to Coercion: The Assault on Trade Union Freedoms*, 3rd ed. (Toronto: Garamond Press, 2003); and J. Fudge and E. Tucker, *Labour Before the Law* (Oxford: Oxford University Press, 2001).

19. A number of very good books describe labour arbitration law in Canada, including D. Brown, D. Beatty, and C. Deacon, *Canadian Labour Arbitration*, 4th ed. (Aurora, ON: Canada Law Book, 2006); M. Mitchnick and B. Etherington, *Labour Arbitration in Canada* (Toronto: Lancaster House, 2006); and R. Snyder, *Collective Agreement Arbitration in Canada*, 5th ed. (Markham, ON: LexisNexis, 2013).

CHAPTER 2

The Law of What? Employment, Self-Employment, and Everything in Between

LEARNING OBJECTIVES

After reading this chapter, students will be able to:

- Distinguish between an employee, an independent contractor, and a dependent contractor.
- Explain why this distinction is important in the law of work.
- Explain how the courts, administrative tribunals, and governments (in statutes) distinguish between the different groups of workers.
- Explain the treatment of "unpaid interns" under Canadian employment standards legislation, and discuss how employers often misclassify workers as unpaid interns in order to receive unpaid labour.

CHAPTER OUTLINE

I. Introduction

Samir was a taxi driver in Ottawa. He owned his own car and paid the car's expenses, including the insurance. He did not own the taxi licence that permitted him to use his car as a taxicab, so he rented one. Samir decided what hours to work and where in the city to focus his efforts. He could hire another worker to drive his car when he was not available. He was not paid a wage; his compensation comprised the amount of fares received from customers remaining after paying his expenses.

One of those expenses was a fee paid to a dispatch company called Blue Line Taxi. That fee entitled Samir to pick up customers at designated Blue Line taxi stands in Ottawa, and to use a two-way radio system through which Blue Line assigned customers to taxi drivers. By agreeing to drive his car under the Blue Line Taxi banner, Samir subjected himself to a set of rules prepared by Blue Line relating to dress code and treatment of customers, among other guidelines.

Late one night, on a quiet and dark street, a customer sliced Samir's throat and ran from the car. Samir suffered serious injuries, as well as trauma that prevented him from driving a taxicab again. He was unable to do any job for a long while, and he applied for benefits under workers' compensation legislation, which creates a government-controlled insurance plan to compensate employees injured on the job. However, he was at first denied the benefits because he was found not to be an employee of Blue Line. The adjudicator ruled that Samir was an independent contractor, in business for himself and therefore not covered by workers' compensation legislation. Samir appealed, and the workers' compensation appeals tribunal overturned that decision and found that he was an employee of Blue Line and, therefore, entitled to workers' compensation benefits.[1]

It might seem strange that an issue so important to Samir and his family turns on a narrow, technical legal distinction between employment and *not* employment. Yet the question of

whether a worker is characterized as an employee or a "self-employed" **independent contractor** is a central boundary issue in the *law of work*. Common law judges and governments (through legislation) have developed a complex system of legal rules to regulate the employment relationship. Most of what we will consider in this text relates to those rules, which do not apply to workers who are characterized as independent contractors. Nor do they apply to types of work that are not recognized as being part of the formal labour market at all, such as caring for your children or other family members and other types of unpaid work.

This chapter explores how the courts and governments have drawn boundaries around the employment relationship for the purposes of developing and assigning special legal rules to that relationship. How do we know whether a worker is an "employee" and therefore subject to employment-based legal rules, or something else and excluded from coverage under those legal rules? We will also explore how the courts and governments have sometimes recognized a hybrid category, in between a true employee and a true independent contractor in order to extend the reach of employment-related legal rules.

II. Distinguishing Employees from Independent Contractors

An **employee** is a worker who enters into an employment contract with an employer that involves an exchange of labour for wages (and maybe benefits), and that contract is subject to all of the laws that govern employment contracts. Employment laws are intended to protect employees, and to provide them with various benefits. Many social security rights available to citizens in Canada are also linked to employment status, including employment insurance, the Canada Pension Plan, and (as we saw in the story in the Introduction) workers' compensation benefits. Independent contractors, by contrast, enter into **commercial contracts** to sell their labour in exchange for revenues and the chance of profit. The laws that govern commercial contracts are very different from those that apply to employment contracts, and independent contractors are excluded from employment-related benefits.

The *common law of employment* and the legal rules found in the *regulatory* and *collective bargaining regimes* are concerned almost exclusively with governing the relationship of subordination between employees and employers. The distinction has also been important in determining liability when workers cause damage to others. Judges have held employers liable (in tort law) for damages caused by their employees according to a rule known as **vicarious liability**. A business would rarely be held liable "vicariously" for harm caused by an independent contractor.[2] Since an employee is acting on behalf of the employer and under the employer's control, it is sometimes fair to hold the employer liable for damage caused by its employees.

---

independent contractor: A worker who is in business for himself or herself and who, therefore, is not an employee.

employee: A worker who is in a position of subordination to an employer and subject to rules and entitlements set out in an employment contract.

commercial contract: A contract between two businesses, including a business in the form of an independent contractor.

vicarious liability: A legal rule under which an employer is liable for damage caused to a third party by one or more of its employees.

The historical justification for creating a special legal regime to govern employment was that "employees" are vulnerable and require legal protection and subsidized public benefits, whereas independent business people can look after themselves.[3] The essential characteristics that distinguish an employee from an independent contractor are autonomy and control, which together might be described as "subordination." Employees are workers who sell their autonomy over certain key decisions, such as how and when to work, in exchange for income (wages, benefits) and some measure of job security. Employees agree to be subordinate to their employer.[4] Independent contractors are in business for themselves, and retain more autonomy and control over how and when they perform their work. Whether this rationale for a legal distinction between employees and independent contractors is still appropriate (if it ever was) is considered later in this chapter.

It is not always easy to decide whether an employment relationship exists. In many instances, workers exhibit a mix of autonomy and subordination. Therefore, it was necessary to develop legal tests to distinguish employees from independent contractors. As we will see shortly, governments have often addressed this question by including a definition of "employee" in a statute that governs employment relationships. However, absent a specific statutory definition, we need to look to the common law regime and the tests that judges have applied in deciding whether an employment relationship exists.

A. The Common Law Tests for Distinguishing Between an Employee and an Independent Contractor

Courts have long struggled with the appropriate legal test to distinguish between an employee and an independent contractor. Initially, courts looked primarily at the degree of control exercised over the worker (the "control test"). The Supreme Court of Canada described the control test as follows: "the essential criterion of employer-employee relations is the right to give orders and instructions to the employee regarding the manner in which to carry out his work."[5] However, the control test was criticized for being overly simplistic and soon gave way to a more nuanced "fourfold test," applied in the 1947 case of *Montreal v. Montreal Locomotive Works Ltd.* The court explained the test as follows:

> In earlier cases a single test, such as the presence or absence of control, was often relied on to determine whether the case was one of master and servant, mostly in order to decide issues of tortious liability on the part of the master … . In the more complex conditions of modern industry, more complicated tests have often to be applied. It has been suggested that a fourfold test would in some cases be more appropriate, a complex involving (1) control; (2) ownership of the tools; (3) chance of profit; (4) risk of loss. Control in itself is not always conclusive.[6]

In some cases, judges applied what they called the "organization test," which asks whether the work in question is "an integral part of the business" of the purported employer or only peripheral to that business.[7]

In the 2001 case of *671122 Ontario Ltd. v. Sagaz Industries Canada Inc.*, the Supreme Court of Canada encapsulated these various tests into the following leading statement of the approach judges must take in assessing whether a worker is an employee or an independent contractor:

> *The central question is whether the person who has been engaged to perform the services is performing them as a person in business on his own account.* In making this determination, the level of control the employer has over the worker's activities will always be a factor. However, other factors to consider include whether the worker provides his or her own equipment, whether the worker hires his or her own helpers, the degree of financial risk taken by the worker, the degree of responsibility for investment and management held by the worker, and the worker's opportunity for profit in the performance of his or her tasks.[8] [Emphasis added.]

Ultimately, courts look at the facts and decide whether the worker looks more like an employee or more like an entrepreneur who is in business in his or her own right. The 2008 Ontario Court of Appeal decision in *Braiden v. La-Z-Boy Canada Limited* demonstrates this approach, as Box 2.1 shows.[9]

BOX 2.1 » CASE LAW HIGHLIGHT

Employee or Independent Contractor?

Braiden v. La-Z-Boy Canada Limited
(2008), 294 DLR (4th) 172 (Ont. CA)

Key Facts: Braiden worked for La-Z-Boy for 22 years as a sales representative. In 1996, 15 years into this employment, the employer instructed him to sign a contract that stated that he was an "independent sales and marketing consultant" and not an "employee" of La-Z-Boy. In 1997, Braiden was instructed by La-Z-Boy to incorporate a business, and future contracts would be signed between that company and La-Z-Boy. Braiden worked mostly from a home office, and he paid his own expenses. He was paid solely on the basis of commissions. La-Z-Boy set sales targets and prohibited Braiden from selling other products and from assigning his work for La-Z-Boy to other workers.

In 2003, Braiden's contract was terminated without his having been given "reasonable notice," an entitlement to which he would be entitled if he was an employee, but not if he was an independent contractor. Braiden sued La-Z-Boy for "wrongful dismissal," which is a lawsuit that alleges an employment contract was terminated without "reasonable notice" having been given.

Issue: Was Braiden working pursuant to an "employment" contract, and, if so, did the employer violate that contract?

Decision: Yes and yes. The court referred to the Supreme Court of Canada decision in *671122 Ontario Ltd. v. Sagaz Industries Canada Inc.* for the applicable legal test and concluded as follows:

> In many ways, the question ... — whose business is it?—lies at the heart of the matter. Was the individual carrying on business for him or herself or was the individual carrying on the business of the organization from which he or she was receiving compensation? In my view, given the findings of the trial judge, the answer to that question can only be that Mr. Braiden was carrying on the business of La-Z-Boy.

Braiden was required to work full-time and exclusively for La-Z-Boy. He could not sell other products and his clients were assigned to him by La-Z-Boy. His territory, which products he sold, as well as the quantity and price, and what sales methods were to be used were determined by La-Z-Boy. Finally, the sales work he performed was crucial to La-Z-Boy's business.

Since Braiden was an employee, he was working pursuant to an employment contract. Applying the rules of the common law of employment contracts (discussed in Part II of the companion volume), Braiden was entitled to "reasonable notice" from La-Z-Boy of the impending termination of his contract. In this case, that amounted to 12 months' notice.

In *Braiden*, the contract clearly stated that the worker was *not an employee*, and yet the court ruled that he was. The courts have said that how a contract describes a worker, while relevant, does not determine the worker's status. If it did, then an employer could easily avoid all of its employment law obligations by simply including a term in every employment contract stating that the worker is an "independent contractor."

Box 2.2 presents a tool that helps assess how a court is likely to decide a dispute over whether a worker is an employee or an independent contractor.

BOX 2.2 » Employee or Independent Contractor? The "Scorecard" Approach

The courts are often asked to decide whether a worker is an "employee" or an "independent contractor" because different laws and rules apply to employment contracts than to contracts between two businesses. Although courts apply a variety of legal tests to arrive at a decision on the matter, all of these tests attempt to answer this question: Does the worker look more like an employee or like an entrepreneur in business for himself or herself?

One way to assess this question is to create a scorecard like the one below, based on the facts of the case.

No one of these factors is determinative of the status of the worker. When using this scorecard, consider all of the facts and ask yourself whether, based on the distribution of checkmarks in the scorecard, the worker more closely resembles an independent contractor in business for himself or herself or an employee dependent on the company for income. See the Exercise at the end of this chapter for scenarios to test this approach.

	FACTORS THAT MAKE THE WORKER LOOK MORE LIKE AN EMPLOYEE		FACTORS THAT MAKE THE WORKER LOOK MORE LIKE AN INDEPENDENT CONTRACTOR
	The company sets working hours and assigns work.		The worker has considerable discretion over when and how to perform work.
✓	The company owns the tools needed to do the job.		The worker owns the tools needed to do the job.
	The company controls how the work is done and closely supervises the work.		The worker receives little direct supervision by the company.
✓	The customers/clients are the company's.		The worker has a variety of customers/clients.
✓	The worker works exclusively for the company.		The worker advertises his or her services on the open market.
	The work is performed at the company's premises.		The worker has his or her own office and pays own expenses.
	The worker has no personal assets invested in the company.		The worker has invested his or her own money in the business, so is at risk of loss but could also earn a profit.
✓	The worker must perform assigned tasks himself or herself.		The worker can hire others to perform work.
	Regular employee deductions are made from pay.		The worker issues invoices to the company; no employee deductions are made.

B. "Employment" Status in the Regulatory Regime

Governments can include a specific definition of "employment," "employee," or "employer" in a statute that overrides the common law tests we have just discussed, and indeed they do so regularly. We considered some of the special statutory definitions of "employee" in Part III of the companion volume. Below, we will just introduce the general concept of a statutory definition of "employee."

Sometimes governments *broaden* the definition of "employee" in order to extend coverage under the legislation to a wider segment of workers than might be considered "employees" under common law tests. For example, Canadian collective bargaining legislation broadens the definition of "employee" to include workers who are **dependent contractors**. The BC *Labour*

dependent contractor: A worker whose status falls in between that of an employee and an independent contractor. This worker has more autonomy and independence than a typical employee yet remains economically dependent on one customer for income and is subject to considerable control at the hands of that customer.

Relations Code is typical. It says that, for the purposes of the Code, an "employee … includes a dependent contractor." A dependent contractor is defined in the Code as follows:

> [A] person, whether or not employed by a contract of employment or furnishing his or her own tools, vehicles, equipment, machinery, material or any other thing, who performs work or services for another person for compensation or reward on such terms and conditions that he or she is in relation to that person in a position of economic dependence on, and under an obligation to perform duties for, that person more closely resembling the relationship of an employee than that of an independent contractor.[10]

Governments added the concept of a "dependent contractor" in order to extend the right to collective bargaining to workers who have greater independence than a typical employee, yet remain vulnerable and dependent such that they are in a position of subordination similar to an employee.[11]

Sometimes governments move in the opposite direction and *narrow* the definition of "employee" in order to exclude from certain legislative rules and protections workers who otherwise would be considered "employees." For example, the *Saskatchewan Employment Act* excludes from the definition of employee (among a variety of other workers) any person "whose primary responsibility is to exercise authority and perform functions that are of a managerial character."[12] The people in the excluded jobs might be "employees" if the standard common law tests were applied; however, the effect of the job being excluded from the definition of employee in a statute is to exclude those workers from the legal rules applicable to "employees" in that legislation. For policy reasons, the government does not think that the legal rules in the legislation should apply to these workers.

A particularly controversial statutory narrowing of the definition of "employee" relates to so-called **unpaid interns**. Unpaid interns are workers who perform work for free. Since employment standards legislation in Canada requires employers to pay most employees at least a wage rate equal to the statutory minimum wage (discussed in Part III, Chapter 21 of the companion volume), an unpaid internship would be unlawful unless the worker in question either is not an "employee" as defined in the legislation or is an employee for whom the minimum wage law does not apply. In Ontario, as elsewhere in Canada,[13] a student performing work for a company as part of a practicum for his or her degree program is excluded from coverage under the *Employment Standards Act* (ESA).[14] However, the Ontario ESA also excludes from the definition of "employee" a worker who is "being trained," but not as part of a formal educational program, when *all* of the following conditions are met:

1. The training is similar to that which is given in a vocational school.
2. The training is for the benefit of the individual.
3. The person providing the training derives little, if any, benefit from the activity of the individual while he or she is being trained.
4. The individual does not displace employees of the person providing the training.
5. The individual is not accorded a right to become an employee of the person providing the training.
6. The individual is advised that he or she will receive no remuneration for the time that he or she spends in training.[15]

The purpose of this exclusion is to encourage employers to act as surrogate educational institutions, providing practical training to workers starting out in a field. However, the section has been widely abused by employers seeking unpaid workers. It is extremely difficult for an employer to satisfy all six of the above factors. Consider the decision discussed in Box 2.3 as an example.

---

unpaid intern: A term used to describe a person who performs work for a business or receives training by a business, but who is not paid for that work.

BOX 2.3 » CASE LAW HIGHLIGHT

Are Unpaid Interns "Employees" Under Employment Standards Legislation?

Girex Bancorp Inc. v. Hsieh
2004 CanLII 24679 (Ont. LRB)

Key Facts: Hsieh worked for Girex Bancorp as a software designer without being paid while she was still a student at a technical institute. After Hsieh stopped working for Girex, she filed a complaint under the *Employment Standards Act* for unpaid wages. Girex argued that Hsieh was being trained, within the meaning of section 1(2) of the ESA, and was therefore excluded from the definition of "employee" in the ESA and not entitled to the minimum wage.

Issue: Was Hsieh an "employee" of Girex Bancorp when she performed programming work for the company? If so, was she entitled to damages for unpaid wages?

Decision: Yes and yes. The Ontario Labour Relations Board ruled that not all six conditions in section 1(2) had been met. First, the board found that Hsieh had not actually received any formal training from Girex, so condition 1 was not met. Second, Hsieh was developing software for use by Girex, and so the benefit was primarily to the company and not Hsieh. Third, the work Hsieh did had previously been performed by Girex employees, and the company was attempting to get that same work done for free by Hsieh. In that sense, Hsieh "displaced" employees. Conditions 5 and 6 were met, but the other four conditions were not. Therefore, Hsieh was an employee of Girex and was entitled to $10,000 in unpaid minimum wages and statutory vacation pay.

The use of unpaid internships has been defended on the grounds that it enables young workers to gain much-needed experience and to build career networks that can lead to good jobs in the future. However, unpaid internships have also been criticized for taking away paid jobs, for privileging wealthy workers who can afford to work for free, and for perpetuating the exclusion of young workers from the paid labour market.[16] In recent years, concern has grown about the widespread misclassification of employees as "trainees" (see Box 2.4). "Trainees" are just one of many types of workers who are excluded from statutory definitions of "employees" for one reason or another. A variety of other statutory exclusions from the definition of "employee" are considered in Part III of the companion volume.

BOX 2.4 » TALKING WORK LAW

Abuse of Trainee Exception in the Definition of "Employee" Leads to Government Crackdown

The plight of unpaid interns has captured substantial media attention and caused the Ontario government to inspect businesses that use them more closely, as the following CBC News excerpt describes.

Enforcement action by the Ontario Ministry of Labour has led to the shutdown of unpaid internship programs at two popular magazines—Toronto Life and The Walrus—and the crackdown may not be over.

Following complaints, the ministry carried out inspections at both magazines last December "to determine whether certain publicly posted positions were [Employment Standards Act] compliant," said a government statement.

As a result of those inspections, the ministry issued compliance orders alleging violations of several parts of the act, including minimum wage provisions, holiday pay and vacation pay. It said the interns would have to be paid.

Ontario's Labour Ministry says there are few exceptions to the requirement that interns be subject to the Employment Standards Act. The main exception would be for interns working under a program approved by a college of applied arts and technology or a university, and secondary school students working under an authorized work experience program.

Most of the interns at Toronto Life and The Walrus do not fall into those categories, so most have subsequently been told they no longer have positions at the magazines. The magazines say they simply cannot afford to pay their interns.

"The Ministry of Labour Employment Standards Act inspector has said our four-to-six-month unpaid internships can no longer be offered unless the interns have a formal agreement for a work experience with a vocational school," says a statement published on the website of The Walrus.

The magazine says it is "extremely sorry" that its internship program, which has been running for 10 years, can no longer be offered. It said the program has "assisted many young Ontarians—and Canadians—

in bridging the gap from university to paid work and in, many cases, on to stellar careers." Five interns will lose their jobs next week.

At Toronto Life, the internship program has been running for about 20 years. "We thought the socially responsible thing to do was at least to provide a bridge for those young people who want to get into the magazine world," said Doug Knight, president of St. Joseph Media, which publishes Toronto Life.

Two unpaid interns at Toronto Life are being let go.

Unpaid internships have become a growing flashpoint across the country as businesses of all stripes have been accused of taking advantage of young people desperate for work experience.

By some estimates, there are as many as 300,000 Canadians working as unpaid interns. Some are working in industries that can ill afford to pay them. Some are working as part of a work-experience program affiliated with an academic institution. Others are working in big, profit-making corporations. ...

Ontario's Labour Ministry said it will be launching an "enforcement blitz" this spring, targeting unpaid internships "across a variety of sectors." It isn't yet clear what sectors the government will target.*

---

* Excerpt from "Unpaid Internships at Toronto Life, The Walrus Shut Down by Ontario," *CBC News*, March 27, 2014, http://www.cbc.ca/news/business/unpaid-internships-at-toronto-life-the-walrus-shut-down-by-ontario-1.2589115. Reprinted with the permission of the Canadian Press and CBC Licensing.

C. An "Intermediate Category" Between Employee and Independent Contractor in the Common Law Model

A "dependent contractor" is a category of employee that falls somewhere in between a true employee and a true independent contractor, as demonstrated in Figure 2.1. As we just noted, governments have occasionally introduced this intermediate category into statutes in order to extend the reach of the statute beyond typical employees. Common law judges too have recognized an "intermediate category" of worker in order to extend some entitlements of employees under the common law regime. In particular, judges have found that contractors who are in a position of subordination and economic dependence similar to an employee should be entitled to "reasonable notice" before their contract is terminated, just like employees.[17] A requirement to provide notice before terminating a contract provides workers with a measure of job security, since they will at least be warned before losing their job, which gives the worker time to prepare, such as by seeking a new job.

FIGURE 2.1   Categories of Workers in the Law of Work

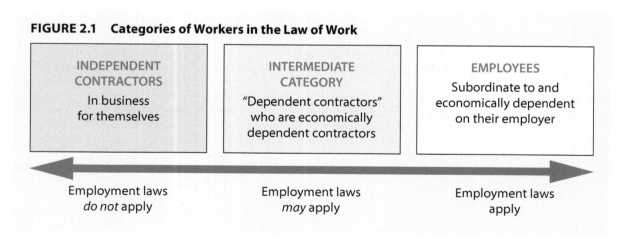

An intermediate category of worker recognizes that a worker might have some autonomy in the manner in which he or she performs work, and may have the external appearance of being self-employed, and yet still be economically dependent and subordinate. This subordination places the worker in a situation more closely resembling an employee than a true independent contractor. In the case of *McKee v. Reid's Heritage Homes*, the Ontario Court of Appeal explained how the courts decide whether a contractor falls into the "intermediate category":

> [T]he proper initial step is to determine whether a worker is a contractor or an employee, for which the *Sagaz* ... analysis [described earlier] ... controls. Under that analysis, the exclusivity of the worker is listed as a *factor* weighing in favour of the employee category ... . The next step, required only if the first step results in a contractor conclusion, determines whether the contractor is independent or dependent, for which a worker's exclusivity is *determinative*, as it demonstrates economic dependence.[18]

So in the common law approach, a "dependent contractor" is a contractor that works exclusively (or almost exclusively) for one customer. "Economic dependence" is key. A dependent contractor is entitled to receive "reasonable notice" before the other party terminates the contract, a right that is read in (implied) by judges into employment contracts. An independent contractor is not entitled to "reasonable notice" of the termination of the contract, unless he or she specifically bargained that requirement into the commercial contract that governs the performance of the work.

III. Is the Distinction Between Employee and Independent Contractor Appropriate?

Our discussion so far demonstrates that the distinction between an employee and an independent contractor is often blurred. This raises questions about the appropriateness of a legal model that links legal benefits and protections to a technical distinction between these two employment categories. The distinction between employees and independent contractors gained significance with the ascendancy of the employment contract model in the mid-20th century, as Professors Judy Fudge (University of Kent), Eric Tucker (York University), and Leah Vosko (York University) explain:

> Despite the fact that the legal concept of employment was of recent vintage and complex heritage, by the end of World War II protective labour legislation—both in its collective bargaining and labour standards versions—was built upon the platform of the contract of employment. This meant that to claim the benefit of most labour legislation, workers had to establish at minimum that there were employees, parties to a contract of employment with an employer rather than self-employed or independent contractors, parties to a contract for service. ... The "contractualization" of the employment relationship was "associated with the gradual spread of social legislation in the fields of workmen's compensation, social insurance, and employment protection."[19]

In fact, during the post–Second World War period, Canadian governments had a very particular form of employment in mind, known as the **standard employment relationship** (SER). The SER existed primarily in large industrial workplaces, applied mostly to men,[20] and was characterized by long-term, steady job security, regular full-time hours, and internal job markets in which workers expected to rise through the ranks of a single employer over their working lives.[21] Canadian labour policy pursued the ideal of the single-income male breadwinner who earned decent pay with benefits in full-time employment, and who was supported by a female spouse performing unpaid domestic work in the home, perhaps supplemented with "pin money" through occasional part-time work. Many of the important social and employment protections enacted since the 1930s were linked directly to the SER.

---

standard employment relationship: A model of employment characterized by stable, long-term job security, full-time hours, decent benefits, and wage rates that rise steadily over time.

Precarious work is contrasted with the SER. It includes part-time, sporadic, temporary, and contingent work, as well as homework. It is characterized by few if any employer-provided benefits, lower wages, and less job security than under the SER model.[22] Many workers who meet the technical legal definition of an independent contractor, and thus who are excluded from all or most of the law's protections for employees, are nevertheless in a situation at least as precarious as that of employees. Until recently, precarious work has received little attention from legislators, courts, and legal academics, who have focused on law's interaction with the SER.[23] However, over the past 30 years, the percentage of workers who enjoy the relative security of the SER model has declined in Canada, as elsewhere. Nearly 40 percent of Canadians today work under other types of work arrangements, including precarious part-time or temporary work, or as **own account self-employed workers**, many of whom struggle to earn enough to live.[24] This growth in precarious work and the move away from the SER model have led to calls to rethink the utility of linking work law protections to an increasingly artificial distinction between employees and independent contractors. For example, many scholars have proposed that statutory protections be linked to precarity of work, rather than just "employment."[25]

IV. Chapter Summary

This chapter introduced the important distinction between "employees" and "independent contractors" in the law of work. The former are governed by a broad range of legal rules targeting employment contracts and are eligible for many employment-related benefits. The latter are in business for themselves and treated in the law as businesses. Governments (through legislation) and the courts (in common law decisions) have sometimes extended the scope of "employees" to include economically dependent contractors who share more in common with employees than they do with independent contractors. Governments have also sometimes used a narrow definition of "employees" in statutes in order to exclude some types of employees from statutory provisions.

QUESTIONS AND ISSUES FOR DISCUSSION

1. What is the difference between an employee and an independent contractor? Why is this distinction important in the law?
2. Describe the test that the Supreme Court of Canada has set down to distinguish between an independent contractor and an employee.
3. What is a dependent contractor, and what is the significance of a court finding that a worker is one?
4. Provide an example of Canadian legislation in which the definition of "employee" was refined to *exclude* a worker who would be considered an employee if the usual common law test for employment status were applied.
5. What is an unpaid intern? What are some reasons for and against making an unpaid internship unlawful?
6. Explain the difference between the standard employment relationship and precarious work. Why have some scholars proposed that precarious work is a better concept than employee versus independent contractor as a means of applying protective work laws?

---

precarious work: Work that is defined by characteristics such as job insecurity; short job tenure; low pay; few benefits; low collective bargaining coverage; and sporadic, limited, or unpredictable work hours.

own account self-employed workers: Independent contractors who have no employees.

EXERCISE

Using the "scorecard" approach described in Box 2.2, read the following three scenarios and indicate whether you think the worker profiled in each would be considered an employee or an independent contractor. After doing the exercise, read the decision to see what the court or expert tribunal actually decided.

Scenario One: The Massage Parlour

"D" performed massages at Sweet City Massage Parlour. She was one of about 20 massage attendants who performed massages out of Sweet City's location. Sweet City provided the rooms, massage tables, oils and ointments, and linens. D paid Sweet City $1 per massage to cover the cost of laundering the linen. D decided what days she worked at Sweet City, although if she did not report for a shift she had agreed to work, she would be fined by Sweet City between $100 and $200. Customers at Sweet City could select from among the massage attendants present, but D could refuse any specific customer. No one from Sweet City supervised how D performed her massages. No wage was paid to D. Her income consisted of about 50 percent of the fees paid for the massages she gave, the other 50 percent going to Sweet City. If no customers showed up, she would earn nothing that shift. D could perform massages at her home or in other locations if she wished, and she could substitute another person to complete a scheduled shift at Sweet City.

Was D an employee or an independent contractor?

Check your answer by reading *Abe Vergara o/a Sweet City v. MNR*, 2004 TCC 263.

Scenario Two: The Massage Therapist

Wang performed massages at the facilities of Active Therapy Clinic (Clinic) on a full-time basis. He was the only licensed massage therapist. His contract permitted him to perform massage services elsewhere, which he did. The contract also described Wang as an "independent contractor" and not an employee of the Clinic. Wang was paid an hourly rate while working at the Clinic. The contract stated that the customers belonged to the Clinic and not Wang. The Clinic fixed the price of a massage, and supplied Wang with all of the necessary equipment and supplies to perform the massages. Wang billed the Clinic every two weeks at the agreed rate for hours worked at the Clinic, plus an amount for harmonized sales tax. Wang was paid by the Clinic without any deductions, and he claimed deductions himself, as a business, when he filed his personal income taxes.

Was Wang an employee or an independent contractor?

Check your answer by reading *Wang v. 1139613 Ontario Limited (Active Therapy & Sports Clinic)*, 2013 CanLII 11224 (Ont. LRB).

Scenario Three: The Forklift Sales Representative

Moseley-Williams worked full-time as a salesperson for a forklift supplier called Hansler. He was expected to work only for Hansler. He was assigned a jurisdiction in which to sell Hansler products, and was required to meet certain requirements set down by Hansler while working. However, he performed his work mostly on his own within those parameters and was often outside of the office meeting and finding new customers. He used few tools beyond a car and phone. Moseley-Williams owned his own car, but Hansler paid him a monthly car allowance and also paid for a business cellphone. Moseley-Williams received a commission, the rate of which was set out in a contract between him and Hansler, and had not invested his money in Hansler. No statutory deductions were made from Moseley-Williams's pay, and his contract described him as an independent contractor.

Was Moseley-Williams an employee or an independent contractor?

Check your answer by reading *Moseley-Williams v. Hansler Industries Ltd.*, 2008 CanLII 57457 (Ont. Sup. Ct. J.).

NOTES AND REFERENCES

1. If you are interested in reading the decision upon which this story relies, you can find it here: *Decision No. 934/98*, 2000 ONWSIAT 3346.

2. See, e.g., *671122 Ontario Ltd. v. Sagaz Industries Canada Inc.*, 2001 SCC 59.

3. G. Davidov, "The Reports of My Death Are Greatly Exaggerated: Employee as a Viable (Though Overly-Used) Legal Concept," in G. Davidov and B. Langille, eds., *Boundaries and Frontiers of Labour Law* (Oxford: Hart, 2006), 133-52, at 133-34; and B. Langille, "Labour Law's Back Pages," in Davidov and Langille, ibid., at 13.

4. B. Langille, "Labour Policy in Canada—New Platform, New Paradigm" (2002) 28 *Canadian Public Policy* 133, at 137.

5. *Hôpital Notre-Dame de l'Espérance and Théoret v. Laurent*, [1978] 1 SCR 605, at 613.

6. *Montreal v. Montreal Locomotive Works Ltd.* (1947), 1 DLR 161 (PC), at 169.

7. The organization test was first applied in the British Court of Appeal case *Stevenson Jordan & Harrison, Ltd. v. Macdonald*, [1952] 1 TLR 101, at 111.

8. *671122 Ontario Ltd. v. Sagaz Industries Canada Inc.*, supra note 3, at para. 47.

9. See also *Belton v. Liberty Insurance Co. of Canada* (2004), 72 OR (3d) 81 (CA) (sales representatives are "employees" even though their contract described them as independent contractors); *Kordish v. Innotech Multimedia Corp.* (1998), 46 CCEL (2d) 318 (Ont. Ct. J. (Gen. Div.)) (a worker can be an employee even if he or she has created a corporation through which work is performed); *Doyle v. London Life Insurance Co.* (1985), 23 DLR (4th) 443 (BCCA); and *Farmers of North America Incorporated v. Bushell*, 2013 SKCA 108.

10. *Labour Relations Code*, RSBC 1996, c. 244, s. 1. The other jurisdictions in Canada similarly include "dependent contractor" in their labour relations statutes.

11. For a discussion of the origins of and justification for the "dependent contractor" definition, see H. Arthurs, "The Dependent Contractor: A Study of the Legal Problem of Countervailing Power" (1965) 16:1 *University of Toronto Law Journal* 89.

12. *Saskatchewan Employment Act*, SS 2013, c. S-15.1, s. 6-1(1)(h).

13. For a nice overview of how the various provinces treat the exclusion and inclusion of student internships, see this summary prepared by the Canadian Intern Association: http://www.internassociation.ca/what-is-the-law/.

14. *Employment Standards Act*, SO 2000, c. 41, s. 3(5)2.

15. Ibid., s. 1(2).

16. See, e.g., the discussion in R. Perlin, *Intern Nation: How to Earn Nothing and Learn Little in the Brave New Economy* (New York: Verso, 2011).

17. A leading early decision recognizing this category was *Carter v. Bell & Sons (Canada) Ltd.*, [1936] OR 290 (CA). More recent cases included: *Marbry et al. v. Avrecan International Inc.* (1999), 171 DLR (4th) 436 (BCCA); *JKC Enterprises Ltd. v. Woolworth Canada Inc.* (1986), 300 AR 1 (QB); *Erb v. Expert Delivery Ltd.* (1995), 167 NBR (2d) 113 (QB); and *McKee v. Reid's Heritage Homes Ltd.*, 2009 ONCA 916.

18. *McKee v. Reid's Heritage Homes Ltd.*, supra note 17, at para. 34.

19. J. Fudge, E. Tucker, and L. Vosko, "Changing Boundaries in Employment: Developing a New Platform for Labour Law" (2003) 10 *Canadian Labour and Employment Law Journal* 329, at 354.

20. J. Fudge and L. Vosko, "Gender, Segmentation and the Standard Employment Relationship" (2001) 22 *Economic and Industrial Democracy* 271.

21. J. Fudge, "The New Workplace: Surveying the Landscape" (2009) 33 *Manitoba Law Journal* 131, at 132; L. Vosko, "Precarious Employment: Towards an Improved Understanding of Labour Market Insecurity," in L. Vosko, ed., *Precarious Employment: Understanding Labour Market Insecurity in Canada* (Montreal and Kingston: McGill-Queen's University Press, 2006), 6.

22. Ibid.; Law Commission of Ontario (LCO), *Vulnerable Workers and Precarious Work* (2013), http://www.lco-cdo.org/en/vulnerable-workers-final-report-sectionII; and K. Stone, *From Widgets to Digits: Employment Regulation for the Changing Workplace* (Cambridge: Cambridge University Press, 2004).

23. J. Fudge, "Reconceiving Employment Standards Legislation: Labour Law's Little Sister and the Feminization of Labour" (1991) 7 *Journal of Law and Social Policy* 73; H. Arthurs, "Charting the Boundaries of Labour Law: Innis Christie and the Search for an Integrated Law of Labour Market Regulation" (2011) 34 *Dalhousie Law Journal* 1; and B. Langille, "Labour Law Is a Subset of Employment Law" (1981) 31 *University of Toronto Law Journal* 200.

24. J. Fudge, supra note 21, at 139. See also L. Vosko, N. Zukewich, and C. Copeland, "Precarious Jobs: A New Typology of Employment" (October 2003) 4 *Perspectives* 16, 19; and LCO, supra note 22, section IV, http://www.lco-cdo.org/en/vulnerable-workers-interim-report-sectionIV.

25. There is a huge literature exploring the challenge to employment and labour law posed by changes to the nature of work and the shift away from the standard employment model in Canada and abroad. Some notable examples include: Stone, supra note 22; Fudge, Tucker, and Vosko, supra note 19; H. Arthurs, "Labour Law as the Law of Economic Subordination and Resistance: A Counterfactual?" (2012) 8:3 *Comparative Research in Law and Political Economy*; H. Collins, "Independent Contractors and the Challenge of Vertical Disintegration of Employment Protection Laws" (1990) 10 *Oxford Journal of Legal Studies* 331; P. Davies and M. Freedland, *Towards a Flexible Labour Market* (Oxford: Oxford University Press, 2007); S. Deakin, "The Comparative Evolution of the Employment Relationship," in G. Davidov and B. Langille, eds., *Boundaries and Frontiers of Labour Law* (Oxford: Oxford University Press, 2006), 89; A. Blackett, "Emancipation in the Idea of Labour Law," in G. Davidov and B. Langille, eds., *The Idea of Labour Law* (Oxford: Oxford University Press, 2011), 420; M. Finkin, "The Death and Transfiguration of Labor Law" (2011-2012) 33 *Comparative Labour Law and Policy Journal* 171; and J. Fudge, "After Industrial Citizenship: Market Citizenship or Citizenship at Work?" (2005) 60 *Industrial Relations* 1.

CHAPTER 3

A Framework for Analyzing the Law of Work

I. Introduction

In Chapter 1, our survey of the topographical map of work law introduced, at a high level of generality, the three legal regimes that comprise the main subject matter of this text—the common law of employment, regulatory standards, and collective bargaining. Dividing the law into these three distinct regimes is a useful way for law professors and lawyers to organize and teach the laws that govern employment in Canada. The first two regimes (common law and regulatory standards) have traditionally been taught in "employment law" seminars using "employment law" texts.[1] The collective bargaining regime, by contrast, has usually been hived off and taught as separate courses in "labour law" and "labour arbitration law," and described in law texts with similar names.[2] As mentioned in Chapter 1, this text uses the labels *work law* and the *law of work* when discussing the entire system of legal rules in all three legal regimes.[3]

However, compartmentalizing the laws that govern employment into the three regimes, while useful for organizing the legal materials, oversimplifies the complexity of the legal framework that governs the employment relationship in Canada. This becomes evident when we zoom in on our map of the law of work. A closer inspection shows a far more complicated terrain, one that cannot be so neatly compartmentalized. Continuing on with our geographical analogy, we see that rivers flow across boundaries; inhabitants move from one part of the map to another, only later to return; some inhabitants function in all three regimes simultaneously. The real world of work law is a far more complex place than our discussion so far has suggested.

We need a way to understand and organize this complexity. This chapter addresses this challenge by developing a conceptual framework for the analysis of the law of work. This framework draws a more complete map of the laws that govern work, as well as the relationship of those laws to the broader economic, legal, political, social, and environmental context in which they evolve and function.

II. Law Is What Law Does

Let's begin with a simple lesson about law. The relationship between a seller and buyer of labour is above all else a human relationship, and human behaviour is complex. People behave as they do for all sorts of reasons, of which formal legal rules are but one. Often, in fact, legal rules in employment contracts and government regulations conflict with other powerful economic, legal, political, social, and environmental forces present in society. When that occurs, something has to give, and sometimes it is the legal rules that are cast aside.

This lesson is demonstrated in the news article excerpt presented in Box 3.1. The excerpt describes the experience of recent immigrants working in Toronto's Chinatown. Some were charged a $400 fee to obtain a job that pays them only $25 per day for ten hours of work, seven days a week. Others earn $4 per hour for a 70-hour workweek. Ontario's government long ago passed a minimum wage law (regulation regime). The same employment standards statute also caps the number of hours employees can work and requires overtime pay at a higher hourly wage rate for hours worked beyond 44 hours in a week.[4]

Systemic violations of labour rights such as those described in Box 3.1 raise complex questions: Why would employees agree to work conditions that violate minimum legal standards? Why does the government bother passing employment standards laws if workers and employers are prepared to agree to conditions falling below the legal minimums? Why do some employers violate these laws? How do those employers get away with such violations? Why isn't the law working?

The excerpt in Box 3.1 reminds us of a fundamental point: we should never assume that people will comply with legal rules. What matters is how a legal rule actually affects behaviour (if it does at all) and not simply what a legal rule says. To paraphrase film character Forrest Gump, "Law is as law does."[5] Non-compliance with legal rules is a big problem in the law of work. A 1997 Labour Standards Evaluation study noted that "about 25% of all federal employers were not in compliance with most [employment standards] obligations … and that 75% of these employers were not in compliance with at least one [employment standards] provision."[6] The latter figure was confirmed by a 2005 Statistics Canada Federal Jurisdiction Workplace Survey of employment practices.[7] As Professor Harry Arthurs (York University) noted in his 2006 study of Canadian labour standards, these numbers likely *understate* non-compliance because they are based on employer self-reporting.[8]

Ignorance of laws is no doubt partially to blame for this non-compliance. Work-related laws can be complicated and difficult to understand. But ignorance of the law is only part of the story. As noted earlier, sometimes a legal rule is sacrificed because it conflicts with more powerful societal rules and norms. Other times a legal rule is knowingly violated because, considering all relevant factors, including the odds of being caught and the penalties for non-compliance, it makes more economic sense to someone to break the law than to comply with it. Economists refer to this type of infraction as an **efficient breach**.[9] Efficient breaches are a common problem with employment regulation because governments lack the resources, capacity, and often the political will to inspect all workplaces, and many employees will not complain for fear of losing their jobs in reprisal. If a government decides to aggressively enforce its legal rules, some employers might respond by fleeing the reach of the law altogether by moving their business (and the jobs) to another jurisdiction. In that case, a law designed to help workers could actually cause their unemployment.

We are beginning to scratch the surface of the complexity we are dealing with when we study the law of work. If we are to make sense of how legal rules come about and why some are effective and others are not, we need a richer framework that can map this complexity. One way

---

efficient breach: A deliberate violation of a contract or government statute owing to the belief that it is more economically efficient to violate the legal rule than to comply with it.

BOX 3.1 » Recent Immigrant Workers in Toronto's Chinatown and Labour Rights Violations

The following *Toronto Star* excerpt describes serious labour rights violations regarding minimum wage, the hours employees can work per week, and overtime.

Sue Zheng was happy to land her first job in Toronto at a manicure salon. But there was a catch: she had to pay a $400 deposit to work there, and receive only $25 a day for 10 hours of work, seven days a week. She took the job anyway.

"I don't know any English and had no idea what my rights were," she explained in Mandarin during an interview ... . "Workers don't have a lot of rights where I came from." Zheng, 40, who arrived in Toronto from Fuzhou, China in 2006, said she was desperate to find work last year after raising two young children. "You just accept what you are given."

Hers is one of numerous stories of abuse and exploitation of immigrant workers uncovered in a survey by the Chinese Interagency Network of Greater Toronto, an umbrella group of 33 social and health service agencies serving the Chinese community.

The survey found fewer than one in five know what the maximum hours of work are in Ontario. Of the 119 people interviewed, 66 per cent were unaware of overtime and holiday pay. And four out of 10 people did not know the current minimum wage or that they were protected by labour laws even if they didn't have a written employment contract. ...

"The problem is newcomers are not familiar with their rights in Canada. They also face the language barrier and don't know the social infrastructure and supports available to them" [said Daniel Yau of the Metro Toronto Chinese and Southeast Asian Legal Clinic].

Zheng said she finally quit the salon job after two months due to exhaustion. She had no idea about her labour rights until she was asked to participate in the July street survey in Chinatown. She has since been put in touch with a legal clinic to try and get back her $400 deposit. ...

More than 500 individuals were approached for the survey, but an overwhelming majority declined to comment for fear they would be seen by their employer and risk losing their job.

"Many of the workers have worked in those kinds of conditions for years and they just don't care about their rights. They just do whatever their bosses order them to do and accept what they pay them. They never challenge," said a disheartened Wei Sun, one of eight volunteers who conducted the survey.

"It's shocking in Canada that these people are working 70 hours a week, with an average hourly wage of $4."

Andy Mark of Toronto's Chinese Canadian National Council said many skilled immigrants put up with poor

Many Asian immigrants to Canada come from countries with few workers' rights, and are vulnerable to exploitation by employers.

working conditions because their foreign credentials are not recognized.

"It is difficult to find jobs in the mainstream job market. They want to keep their jobs. It's simply about survival," Mark said.

Hui-min Li said he worked in a Chinese-run Toronto automobile parts factory for eight years before the company abruptly laid off its workers and moved to Mexico in late 2008. The Shanghai immigrant was owed $8,000 in severance pay.

"It was not unusual for us to work 70 hours a week. We worked from 8 a.m. to 1 a.m. and the boss wouldn't let you go until you finished the work," said Li, who filed a complaint and won his case with the Ontario Labour Relations Board this year.

"Most people don't have knowledge of their rights. Even if they do, they don't dare to fight for their rights because they are not the type to rock the boat."

The survey calls for stronger workplace audits and outreach to educate newcomers about their rights, including incorporating the topic in newcomer English classes.*

---

* Excerpt from N. Keung, "Few Aware of Labour Rights in Toronto's Chinatown," *Toronto Star*, July 23, 2010, http://www.thestar.com/news/investigations/2010/07/23/few_aware_of_labour_rights_in_torontos_chinatown.html. Reprinted with permission of PARS International Corp.

to do this is to treat work law as one of many components, or **subsystems**, present in any complex, multi-faceted society, and to then study how those subsystems interact to produce the rules that govern work. The remainder of this chapter discusses such a framework.

III. A Framework for Analysis of the Law of Work

Treating work law as one of a variety of subsystems operating in society at any given time provides a more realistic depiction of how things actually work. It allows us to see how legal rules relating to the labour relationship are influenced by a whole range of pressures emanating from outside the formal confines of laws targeting the employment relationship. The framework discussed in this section helps us more fully assess the role of law in our society, explain legal rules, and predict the impact of legal rules.[10]

The Law of Work Framework is presented in Figure 3.1. It demonstrates the breadth of our subject, drawing attention to the reality that the law of work is more than the sum of its parts. Every legal rule we encounter in this text is a result of the interaction among a variety of forces; fierce debates; rich histories; reluctant compromises; and, sometimes, violent and bloody clashes. The laws that govern work in any society emerge from this complex milieu. To borrow the words of Professor Arthurs, one of Canada's foremost academics in the field, without paying attention to this broader context, the study of work law will "degenerate into the mere recitation of rules and will contribute neither to genuine interdisciplinary insights nor to greater citizen involvement in law."[11]

A. The Work Law Subsystem

As noted earlier in this chapter, the separation of laws governing employment into three distinct regimes obscures the important interconnections among the three regimes.[12] It presents an incomplete picture of how the laws that govern employment actually function in the real world. To obtain a fuller, more accurate view, we need to step back and view the laws that govern the employment relationship as a distinct subsystem of the broader society in which it functions. This subsystem is presented in the box in Figure 3.1 labelled "The Work Law Subsystem."

1. The Three Regimes of the Work Law Subsystem

The work law subsystem is dominated by the three traditional regimes of work law already introduced. However, now we add some new layers to produce a more complex and realistic depiction of the legal system. For those new to the study of law, or work law in particular, some of the concepts and terms used in the following description of the work law subsystem will be new. Not to worry; as we proceed through this text, we will consider everything that follows in greater detail and consider examples. The purpose of the discussion here is to introduce the main components of the framework.

a. The Common Law Regime

The *key actors* in the common law regime are employers and individual employees. They engage in the *rule-making process* of **negotiation**, and their agreements produce the main *output* of the regime—individual contracts of service. When disputes arise about those contracts, they are sometimes resolved through **civil litigation**, which is the second rule-making process in this

---

subsystem: In legal sociology, a self-contained system within the broader social system that possesses its own rules, norms, and modes of communication. Examples include economic and market; legal; political; social, cultural, and religious; and ecological/environmental subsystems.

negotiation: Discussion between two or more people aimed at reaching an agreement.

civil litigation: The processes involved with lawsuits filed in court not involving criminal law statutes, such as legal actions for breach of contract or torts.

FIGURE 3.1   Law of Work Framework

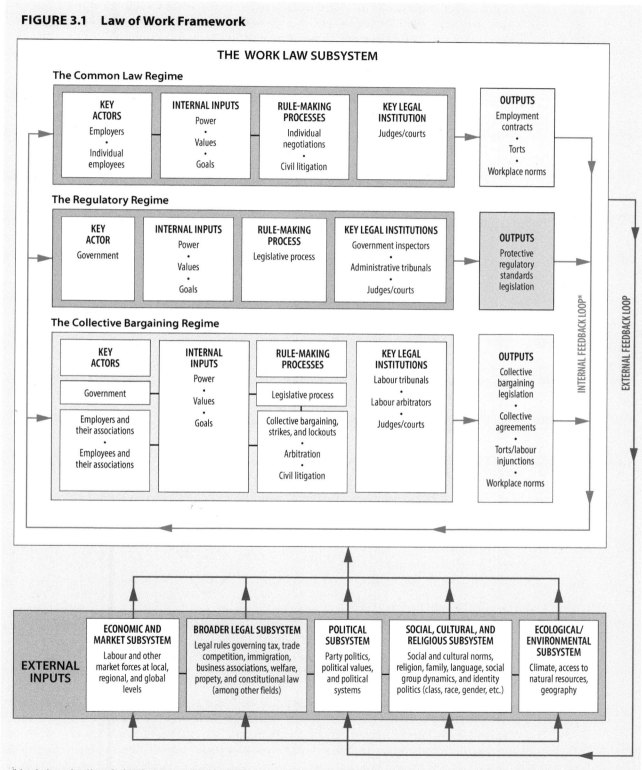

* Legal rules produced by each of the three regimes of work law feed back into the subsystem as information and experience and can provoke changes and adaptations by the actors in all three regimes, which can produce new outputs.

regime. Civil litigation can also produce legal rules in the form of torts, another important output. The courts (and the judges who preside over them) are the *key legal institution*. Judges/courts produce legal rules when they issue the contract interpretation and tort decisions that form the essence of the common law of employment.

An additional output produced by the common law regime is **workplace norms**. These are unwritten rules that nevertheless can have a great influence on how people are expected to behave in given situations.[13] Workplace norms are created over time through common experience that creates expectations. Since things have long been done in a particular way, people expect that those things will continue to be done in those ways. How often can employees take washroom breaks, and do they need to ask permission? Is playful banter and horseplay between workers tolerated or treated as harassment? Does the employer create a climate in which complaints can be raised, or are employees too fearful to speak up? Can workers talk about personal matters or use email or social media during working hours? Who gets first choice in vacation time or overtime? And so on. These are examples of questions and issues that can arise at any workplace, and yet the answers may not be found in any explicit legal rule. However, workplace norms can explain why people behave as they do and ignoring them can create an incomplete picture of how legal rules influence behaviour. Workplace norms are sometimes recognized by judges as "past practices," which can create legally enforceable contractual rights or influence the interpretation of contracts.

Another addition to our framework is *internal inputs*. How the key actors behave—their bargaining strategy, their manner of communication, their propensity to resist or concede points, to pursue conflict or to resist it, and to obey or violate legal rules—depends on their relative power, as well as their values and goals. For example, the employers of recent immigrants in Toronto's Chinatown possess a substantial power advantage. The workers need the piddling wages paid by the employers just to survive. Many of the workers do not qualify for any type of public assistance. Some workers may not legally be able to work in Canada because they do not have a work permit, so they have few other employment options. If they resist the employer, they could be deported. The employers know all of this, and this gives them great power to set working conditions.

Yet not all actors who possess the power to impose their will on others exercise it in an exploitative manner. The decision by an employer to pay a wage rate that is far below subsistence levels (and government-made minimum standards) reflects a value choice. Some employers pay workers more than the market requires because they are guided by a value system based on humane and decent treatment of workers. For example, some companies have adopted a "living wage" policy that sets wage levels at a rate that considers the cost of living in the location where the work is performed, even though they have the bargaining power to insist on lower wages.[14] Actors' goals also shape their decisions. Henry Ford voluntarily adopted eight-hour workdays and doubled his workers' wages in 1914, not only as "an act of social justice" (e.g., values), but also because he believed doing so was necessary "so that the business would be on a lasting foundation." Ford believed that "low wage business is always insecure," and that his business depended on workers having money to buy his cars.[15] If we just assume that terms of employment contracts result from free negotiation shaped by market forces, we would be unable to explain the terms of employment at Ford in the early 20th century. We need to consider how power, values, and goals shape the strategies of the parties who set working conditions.

b. The Regulatory Regime

The regulatory regime, as noted in Figure 3.1, is the domain of the government. It is the *actor* that decides upon the content of the standards and enacts them into law by means of the legislative process (*rule-making process*). Governments, in their law-making function, are also influenced by *internal inputs* in the form of power, values, and goals. A government's perspective on the

---

workplace norms: Norms or expectations that arise in a workplace as a result of past practices or relationships that can influence behaviour at work, even though they are not codified in contracts or statutes.

appropriate role of the state in regulating labour markets often shapes its goals and values as it sets its agenda for regulatory reform, as we discuss in Chapter 4. However, sometimes governments make decisions affecting work laws for more pragmatic political reasons. For example, the federal Conservative government imposed a ban on the use of foreign temporary workers in 2014 by restaurant employers only after the practice attracted considerable public backlash.[16] A government's power is a function of the political climate at a given time and place. The greater the level of support for the government's policy agenda from key stakeholders, including but not limited to the electorate, the greater the capacity of the government to implement that agenda. The *output* of this regime is regulatory standards legislation intended to protect employees, including employment standards, human rights, occupational health and safety, and many other forms of legislation targeting the employment relationship (explained in Part III of the companion volume). The *key legal institutions* responsible for implementing and enforcing that legislation include government inspectors, expert administrative tribunals (e.g., employment standards and human rights tribunals), and judges/courts (which are mostly responsible within the regulatory standards regime for overseeing the administrative tribunals).

c. The Collective Bargaining Regime

Finally, the collective bargaining regime involves two distinct streams or types of *rule-making processes* that produce a range of legal rules (*outputs*):

1. *the legislative process*, through which governments enact collective bargaining legislation that regulates unionization, collective bargaining, industrial disputes, and collective agreement administration; and
2. *the collective bargaining process*, through which unions and employers develop rules through a mix of collective bargaining, sometimes accompanied by industrial conflict, collective agreement administration and labour arbitration, and occasionally civil litigation, involving mostly tort law.

The government is the *key actor* in the legislative process, whereas employees and employers, along with their collective associations, are the *key actors* in the collective bargaining process. Unions are the most common example of collective associations, but there are other non-union forms of employee associations in Canada;[17] employer associations also exist, particularly in industries such as construction and professional sports. As in the case of the common law regime, how the actors in the collective bargaining regime behave and what legal rules are produced through collective bargaining are influenced in large measure by the relative power of the actors and their respective values and goals (*internal inputs*).[18]

The *key legal institutions* in the collective bargaining regime are expert labour tribunals (mostly labour relations boards), labour arbitrators (both **labour arbitrators** and **interest arbitrators**), and judges/courts, which are involved in policing some aspects of collective action, particularly through the use of torts and labour injunctions to restrain strikes and picketing. Finally, the *outputs* of the collective bargaining regime include (1) collective bargaining legislation; (2) collective agreements between unions and employers (and sometimes employer associations), as interpreted by labour arbitrators; (3) court-ordered **torts** and **labour injunctions** that restrict some

---

labour arbitrator: An individual or three-person expert arbitration panel appointed to decide disputes over the application and interpretation of collective agreements.

interest arbitrator: An individual or three-person expert arbitration board tasked with writing the terms of a collective agreement when the union and employer are unable to reach agreement through voluntary collective bargaining.

tort: A type of wrongful act done by one person to another (or to another's property) that judges have recognized as legally actionable. Examples are *nuisance, trespass, negligence,* and *conspiracy.*

labour injunction: An order issued by a judge that prohibits or restricts a union and unionized workers from engaging in some type of collective action, such as a strike or picketing.

forms of collective bargaining–related activities; and (4) the same types of workplace norms we discussed in relation to the common law regime.

2. The Internal Feedback Loop

A key to understanding the framework presented in this chapter lies in paying attention to how its various components interact in an ongoing dynamic process. Two types of **feedback loops** appear in Figure 3.1: (1) an internal feedback loop and (2) an external feedback loop. The internal feedback loop appears in blue, and shows how the *outputs* of each regime "feed back" into the other regimes as information that can influence actors' behaviour and rule-making processes, and eventually produce new outputs.

To demonstrate, consider an obvious example of regime interaction within the work law subsystem. Regulatory standards, such as the minimum wage found in employment standards legislation, regulate both individual employment contracts in the common law regime as well as collective agreements in the collective bargaining regime. Neither type of contract can include a wage clause that provides for less than the statutory minimum wage. Nor can either type of contract include a term that discriminates contrary to human rights legislation, to give another example. In these ways, the outputs from the regulatory standards regime directly influence the behaviour of the key actors and legal institutions in the other two regimes. They also restrict and guide the range of outputs those regimes can lawfully produce. So we cannot fully understand the outputs of the other two regimes without acknowledging the effects of the regulatory standards regime.

Similarly, the legal rules produced by the common law regime affect outputs from the other two regimes. For example, governments have occasionally borrowed concepts from the common law and incorporated them into regulatory standards. The statutory "notice of termination" requirements in Canadian employment standards legislation are an example; they are modelled after the long-standing common law implied contract term requiring "reasonable notice" of termination. More fundamentally, the common law regime acts as the default legal system. Almost every regulatory standard and every collective bargaining law represents the government's response to some perceived inadequacy in the common law model. To fully understand what objective statutory laws are seeking to achieve, we need to understand how the common law would deal with the matter, in the absence of legislation.

Finally, legal rules produced by the collective bargaining regime in the form of collective bargaining laws and collective agreement provisions influence outputs from the other regimes. Canadian collective bargaining legislation imposes many restrictions on the freedom of employers and individual employees to contract that would otherwise prevail in the common law regime. An obvious example: in the common law, a strike by workers is a breach of contract and a tortious conspiracy, but collective bargaining legislation shields workers from those actions by protecting a limited right to strike in some circumstances.[19] Also, many modern-day statutory standards mimic terms that unions and employers had originally included in collective agreements. For example, the roots of present-day maximum hours legislation are firmly embedded in the **Nine-Hour Movement** organized by Canadian unions of the early 1870s, as well as hours of work provisions that appeared later in collective agreements.[20] The three regimes of work law "learn" from one another. See Box 3.2 for another example of how collective bargaining outputs can influence what occurs in the common law regime.

If we study work law in silos, as three distinct regimes that do not interact, we would miss the relationships described in Box 3.2. If we look only at the collective bargaining regime, we will

---

feedback loop: An explanatory device that demonstrates how outcomes produced by a system (e.g., legal rules produced by a legal system) can influence other systems (e.g., the economic system) and also "feed back" into the original system as information in a process of perpetual learning, experience, and change.

Nine-Hour Movement: A social movement peaking in the early 1870s seeking a legislated maximum nine-hour workday.

BOX 3.2 » An Example of the Internal Feedback Loop: The Dofasco Way

Industrial relations scholars have shown that collective agreements, bargained within the collective bargaining regime, influence the terms of individual employment contracts in non-union workplaces (within the common law regime). This is known as the **spillover effect** of collective bargaining.[*]

Some non-union employers pay their employees more than market forces alone would dictate and offer other benefits, including "grievance procedures" that attempt to mirror what unions bargain into their collective agreements, in order to remove or reduce the incentive for their employees to join unions. The spillover effect is an example of the operation of the internal feedback loop: outputs from the collective bargaining regime become inputs in the common law regime, influencing the internal inputs of the actors there, and ultimately the terms of employment contracts and workplace norms within the common law regime. The following excerpt from a recent newspaper story provides a glimpse into this process.

> Robert Perkins thought he had a deal. He gave Dofasco 32 years of his life in the grit and noise of the Hamilton steel mill. In exchange he was to get a secure retirement with a good pension and health benefits.
>
> It was all part of a contract called The Dofasco Way, the package of welfare programs leavened with a healthy dose of fear that kept the company union-free for 75 years, creating what employees always felt was a "family atmosphere" where management really cared about them.
>
> Today, after taking early retirement because of the way his body was worn down in fulfilling his part of that contract, Perkins and several hundred other Hamilton Dofasco veterans fear the old way is dead and the deal has been summarily changed.
>
> "They gave us a package when he retired and now they've decided across the board to take away those

> benefits," said Perkins' wife, Bonnie Hamilton. "Something's just not right here. If they get away with this, what's going to be next?"
>
> Dating back to 1937, The Dofasco Way combined welfare initiatives such as recreation programs, concerts, picnics and a massive Christmas party with one of Canada's first profit-sharing plans. Called The Fund, the plan gave industrial workers an undreamt of promise of security in their old age. That promise, however, was always coupled with a far from subtle threat—join a union and it could all be taken away.
>
> That combination of threat and promise worked for 75 years, but today, many veteran workers fear The Dofasco Way is dying a "death of a thousand cuts," as the steel industry concentrates into a few firms with a global reach. …
>
> The Dofasco Way was rooted in the visceral hatred company founders Clifton and Frank Sherman had toward labour unions—an evil they sought to keep out of their Hamilton plants by creating a sense of mutual interest between workers and management.
>
> "My father felt a union created unrest in a company," Frank Sherman Jr. recalled in a 2008 Spectator interview. "He felt if people working in his company were doing as well as people in unions, why would they need one?"[†]

---

[*] R. Freeman and J. Medoff, *What Do Unions Do?* (New York: Basic Books, 1984); D. Neumark and M. Wachter, "Union Effects on Nonunion Wages: Evidence from Panel Data on Industries and Cities" (1995) 49:1 *Industrial and Labor Relations Review* 20; and L. Kahn, "Union Spillover Effects on Organized Labor Markets" (1980) 15:1 *Journal of Human Resources* 87.

[†] S. Arnold, "The Dofasco Way," *Hamilton Spectator*, June 2, 2012, http://www.thespec.com/news-story/2129793-the-dofasco-way/. Reprinted with permission.

---

not even notice the benefits Dofasco gave its employees as a **union avoidance** strategy and, therefore, the true effects of collective bargaining will be underestimated. If we study only the common law regime, we might wrongly conclude that Dofasco employees used superior negotiating skills to bargain high wages and a generous benefit and retirement package, or that their very high productivity justified these generous contractual entitlements. Only by recognizing that the regimes are interconnected through a process of ongoing information feedback will we discover the full story of how legal rules emerge and influence labour market outcomes.

B. External Inputs and the External Feedback Loop

So far, we have looked only at what goes on *within* the work law subsystem itself, which is concerned primarily with laws that regulate the employment relationship. Now it is time to cast our gaze outward to the broader social system within which the work law subsystem functions. The

---

spillover effect: The effects that collective agreement settlements bargained by unions and employers have on individual employment contracts in non-union workplaces.

union avoidance: A management strategy designed to reduce the risks that employees will join unions.

work law subsystem does not operate in a vacuum. It is influenced by its external environment, and the legal rules it produces can also influence that external environment. These interactions are demonstrated in Figure 3.1 by the black arrows that flow out of the work law subsystem to the external inputs, and from the external inputs back into the work law subsystem. These arrows indicate the *external feedback loop* component of our framework.

1. External Inputs

We can group these external forces into five distinct subsystems (*external inputs*) that function within every advanced society:

- *Economic and market subsystem.* Work law regulates labour markets. Its objective, beyond protecting workers and regulating conflict, is to influence key labour market indicators, such as labour costs, employment levels, labour market skills and training, and labour market adjustment and flexibility. Labour markets are, in turn, influenced by other domestic and foreign markets, including money markets, trade markets, energy markets, transportation markets, product and consumer markets, and securities markets. Changes in these other markets can influence what happens within the work law subsystem.

  For example, as competition for an employer's goods intensifies, the price it can charge for those goods may fall, producing a lower profit margin. This consumer market change may cause the employer to demand wage concessions from employees and influence the amount of wages and benefits the employer can afford to pay its employees. The employers in Toronto's Chinatown, discussed in the excerpt in Box 3.1, are operating in a highly competitive global industry in which profit margins are very low and competition comes from low wage countries such as Bangladesh, Honduras, and China. The market pressure on these employers to keep labour costs low is intense. These market pressures produce a strong incentive for the employers to cheat on compliance with Canadian employment standards laws.

- *Broader legal subsystem.* The work law subsystem is part of a large, complex, and inter-related legal system. It is influenced by developments in many other legal fields, including tax, trade, immigration, competition, business, securities, criminal, intellectual property, social security, privacy, property, constitutional, tort, criminal, and contract law. In a text on the law of work, we are interested in these broader legal fields insofar as they have important effects on how labour markets function.[21]

  Consider some examples. Immigration laws are not specifically concerned with protecting vulnerable employees, but they influence who can have a job in Canada, as well as the conditions under which new immigrants work. Laws that govern privacy in Canada affect the rights of employers and employees even though they have much broader application. Criminal law has played an important role in controlling worker resistance to employer power in Canada. Intellectual property laws regulate ownership of the products of work. Constitutional law determines which levels of government have jurisdiction to enact work laws and restricts the range and substance of laws governments can pass. **Free trade** laws that reduce tariffs and quotas influence the competitiveness of Canadian labour markets and investment decisions in ways that can affect relative bargaining power vis-à-vis employers and workers.[22]

  The preceding examples illustrate how laws that do not specifically target the employment relationship nevertheless have a substantial impact on that relationship and on labour market functioning more generally. We cannot fully understand law's role in regulating

---

free trade: A term used to describe a trade law policy characterized by low or zero trade tariffs and low or zero quotas on the amount of goods that flow between national borders.

labour markets without considering these laws in addition to those that are specifically targeted at protecting vulnerable employees. Therefore, our exploration of regulatory standards in Part III of the companion volume includes (in Chapters 20 and 31-35) consideration of government legislation that affects the behaviour of labour market actors even though protecting vulnerable employees is not its central purpose.

Demonstrators take part in a protest against Quebec's proposed Values Charter in Montreal on September 14, 2013
Source: CP Photo/Ryan Remiorz

- *Political subsystem.* The law of work is a function of the broader political economy within which it functions.[23] The political belief system and the distribution of political power during a particular time shape how a government behaves as a lawmaker and an employer. Proposed changes to work laws are often included in political campaigns as a way to attract voters. Politicians who prefer little regulation of labour markets have vastly different ideas about the role of the state than do politicians who favour greater labour market regulation, and these debates often play out in work law reforms as political winds shift.[24]

- *Social, cultural, and religious subsystem.* Social, cultural, and religious values are powerful determinants of human actions, and they have key implications for the law of work.[25] The rich fields of "sociology of work", "industrial sociology," and "law and society" study how legal rules and the tendency for them to be obeyed (or disobeyed) reflect social norms and values.[26] As noted above, employers of the workers in Toronto's Chinatown are able to ignore employment standards laws in part because the workers lack the language skills and social support mechanisms that would enable them to resist this form of exploitation. The organizations mentioned in Box 3.1 that assist the new immigrants attempt to build up these social networks as part of a broader strategy in pursuit of greater levels of legal compliance. Consider, as another example, the Quebec government's 2013 proposed *Charter of Values* that would have banned public sector employees from wearing religious symbols at work. This proposed law is rooted in cultural and religious tensions within Quebec and cannot be understood without careful consideration of those tensions.[27]

- *Ecological/environmental subsystem.* The types of labour market activities that are feasible are influenced by simple geography (e.g., ocean communities have fisheries and ports, mountain communities have skiing) and access to natural resources (think forestry and mines). Climate can affect the strategies of work law actors in simple ways, such as when a union attempts to coordinate a labour dispute and the accompanying picketing for the balmy summer months rather than the frigid winter months. More fundamentally, climate change poses substantial challenges for labour markets, and work law may need to adapt to respond in the years to come.[28]

These other subsystems are described as *external inputs* in our framework because, although they are not directly related to legal rules that govern the labour relationship, they can each affect the types of work laws governments enact; the perspectives and reasoning applied by tribunals, arbitrators, and judges; and the behaviour, strategies, power, values, and goals of the actors within the work law subsystem. And the influence can flow in both directions, as demonstrated in Figure 3.1 by the *external feedback loop* represented by the black feedback arrows flowing out of the work law subsystem on the right side of the figure to the external inputs, and then back into the work law subsystem.

2. The External Feedback Loop

Consider the history of human rights legislation in Canada. In important early cases within the common law regime, judges refused to recognize a tort of discrimination with the result that, within that regime, it is lawful for employers to discriminate against job applicants and employees.[29] Not surprisingly, an outcome of the common law regime was employment discrimination. Women were paid less than men; people were refused employment because of their religion; Chinese and non-white workers were treated worse than white workers; and so forth.

This output of the common law regime was noted within the broader Canadian society, and it created controversy, social division, unrest, and exclusion. Over time, as social and cultural values evolved, more Canadians came to recognize these blatantly discriminatory practices as unjust. These sentiments eventually were reflected in political discourse, leading to the enactment of "human rights" legislation (within the *regulatory standards regime*). By the 1940s, legislation had been introduced in Canada prohibiting discrimination in employment on the basis of such grounds as race, creed, colour, nationality, ancestry, and place of origin. In the 1950s, gender was added as a prohibited ground, followed by disability and family status in the 1980s.

Sexual orientation was added to Quebec's *Charter of Human Rights* as a prohibited ground of discrimination in 1977, but it was not until 1986 that the next province (Ontario) added sexual orientation to its human rights code. Other provinces followed, but some held out, including Alberta and Prince Edward Island, which continued to permit discrimination in employment against gay and lesbian workers until 1998. In that year, the Supreme Court of Canada decided the case of *Vriend v. Alberta*, in which it ruled that Alberta's human rights legislation violated the *Canadian Charter of Rights and Freedoms* by not including sexual orientation as a prohibited ground.[30] This constitutional law decision effectively required those provinces that had not already done so to add sexual orientation to the list of prohibited grounds of discrimination in their human rights legislation.

This (very simplified) recounting of the history of human rights legislation demonstrates the analytical contribution of the external feedback loop in our framework. For decades, employment discrimination was lawful in Canada. However, changes within the social, cultural, and religious subsystem, in the form of growing intolerance of blatant labour market discrimination, undermined the sustainability of this discriminatory legal model. Politicians picked up on this movement (within the political subsystem) and began calling for government intervention in the labour market in the form of new regulatory standards banning some forms of employment discrimination. However, not all forms of discrimination were considered equally abhorrent. It took much longer for social and political pressures to build for a prohibition on sexual orientation discrimination to be introduced. Not until a major event occurred within the broader legal subsystem did a prohibition on sexual orientation in Canada become universal (see Box 17.4 for a more detailed review of the *Vriend* decision).

The external feedback loop is an analytical tool that draws our attention to the crucial fact that laws are a function of the broader social system in which they exist, and that laws involve an evolutionary process. They are not static. This text will regularly challenge the reader to step back and consider the legal rules in this broader context. This way, we can better understand how we got to the present point, and perhaps also better predict where we are headed.

IV. Chapter Summary

This chapter introduced a framework for analyzing the law of work. This framework represents an important analytical tool and a conceptual model for organizing the content that will follow in the remainder of the text. The key insight is that the laws that govern work are part of a complex system that comprises economic, legal, political, social, cultural, religious, and ecological/environmental subsystems. We need to consider the law of work in this context in order to have a comprehensive understanding of the forces that influence and shape it. This framework will make more sense to you (hopefully!) as we progress through the text.

QUESTIONS AND ISSUES FOR DISCUSSION

1. What are internal inputs, and how do they influence the outputs of the common law and collective bargaining regimes?
2. Give an example of how a legal rule produced by the regulatory standards regime affects the outputs of the common law or collective bargaining regime through the operation of an internal feedback loop.
3. Describe the two rule-making processes within the collective bargaining regime.
4. Explain the relevance of "efficient breach" in the context of work law.
5. The various subsystems identified as external inputs in the Law of Work Framework presented in this chapter have all attracted considerable scholarly attention in their own right. You may have taken other non-law courses that study work and employment. Link the following academic disciplines to an appropriate external subsystem:

   - environmental justice
   - political science/political economy
   - law and society
   - labour market economics
   - sociology of work
   - work and gender
   - labour history

EXERCISE

Using the Law of Work Framework worksheet in Figure 3.2, list factors in the "External Input" boxes that you believe contributed to the poor working conditions experienced by the recent immigrants to Toronto, described in Box 3.1.

UPDATES

Go to emond.ca/lawofworkircb for links to news, author's blog posts, content updates, and other information related to the chapters in this text.

FIGURE 3.2   Law of Work Framework Worksheet

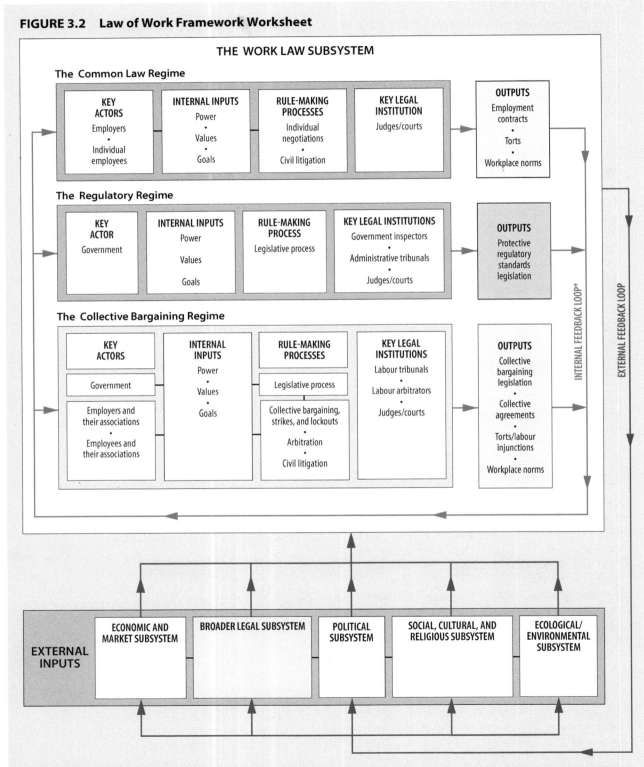

* Legal rules produced by each of the three regimes of work law feed back into the subsystem as information and experience and can provoke changes and adaptations by the actors in all three regimes, which can produce new outputs.

NOTES AND REFERENCES

1. See, e.g., G. England, *Individual Employment Law*, 2nd ed. (Toronto: Irwin, 2008).

2. See, e.g., G. Adams, *Canadian Labour Law*, 2nd ed. (Aurora, ON: Canada Law Book, 1993); and M. Mitchnick and B. Etherington, *Labour Arbitration in Canada* (Toronto: Lancaster House, 2006). It should be noted that the practice of separating the three regimes into "employment law" and "labour law" was not universally adopted in Canada. For example, Professors Harry Glasbeek and, later, Eric Tucker and Judy Fudge of Osgoode Hall Law School long taught and organized their teaching materials on the basis that the three regimes needed to be understood as a coherent web of rules and not as distinct subfields. See H. Glasbeek, J. Fudge, and E. Tucker, *Labour Law* (Toronto: Osgoode Hall Law School, York University, 2007-2008).

3. In Britain and much of Europe, the term *labour law* is used to describe all three regimes that govern employment (common law, regulatory standards law, and collective bargaining law): see, e.g., H. Collins, K. Ewing, and A. McColgan, *Labour Law: Text and Materials*, 2nd ed. (Oxford: Hart, 2005). In Canada and the United States, texts that combine all three regimes are more often entitled "labour AND employment law": see, e.g., Labour Law Casebook Group, *Labour and Employment Law: Cases, Materials, and Commentary*, 8th ed. (Toronto: Irwin, 2011). This is the first book in Canada to adopt the shorter monikers "work law" and "law of work" to describe all three regimes, but authors in other countries have done so: M. Crain, P. Kim, and M. Selmi, *Work Law: Cases and Materials*, 2nd ed. (New Providence, NJ: Lexis-Nexis, 2010); and R. Owens, J. Riley, and J. Murray, *The Law of Work*, 2nd ed. (South Melbourne: Oxford University Press, 2011).

4. *Employment Standards Act, 2000*, SO 2000, c. 41, Part VII ("Hours of Work and Eating Periods"), Part VIII ("Overtime Pay"), and Part IX ("Minimum Wage").

5. The character Forrest Gump in the movie *Forrest Gump* (1994) said: "Stupid is as stupid does." See D. Doorey, "Harry and the Steelworker (or Teaching Labour Law to Non-Law Students)" (2008) 14 *Canadian Labour and Employment Law Journal* 107.

6. Federal Labour Standards Review, *Fairness at Work: Federal Labour Standards for the 21st Century* (Ottawa: Human Resources and Skills Development Canada, 2006), at 192. The problem of high non-compliance with work laws is not a distinctly Canadian problem. On the problem of non-compliance in the United States, see D. Weil, "Implementing Employment Regulation: Insights on the Determinants of Regulatory Performance," in B. Kaufman, ed., *Government Regulation of the Employment Relationship* (Madison, WI: Industrial Relations Research Association, 1997), at 429.

7. Federal Labour Standards Review, supra note 6.

8. Ibid., at 191-92.

9. R. Posner, *Economic Analysis of Law*, 5th ed. (New York: Aspen, 1998), at 131; and C. Goetz and R. Scott, "Liquidated Damages, Penalties, and the Just Compensation Principle: A Theory of Efficient Breach" (1977) 77 *Columbia Law Review* 554.

10. The framework developed in this chapter draws on a long and rich history of systems approaches to law and, in particular, work on industrial relations systems developed by John Dunlop (Harvard University) and later adapted to the Canadian setting by Alton Craig (University of Ottawa): J. Dunlop, *Industrial Relations Systems* (New York: Henry Holt, 1958); and A. Craig and N. Solomon, *The System of Industrial Relations in Canada*, 5th ed. (Scarborough, ON: Prentice Hall, 1996). The influential 1969 Woods Task Force on Labour Relations in Canada adopted the term *industrial relations systems*, assigning it this meaning: "the complex of market and institutional arrangements, private and public, which society permits, encourages, or establishes to handle superior-subordinate relationships growing out of employment and related activities." See *The Report of the Task Force on Labour Relations* (Ottawa: Queen's Printer, 1969), at 9. The industrial relations systems model drew on insights from broader systems theory. See especially T. Parsons and N. Smelser, *Economy and Society: A Study in the Integration of Economy and Social Theory* (London: Routledge, 1956); and N. Luhmann, *The Differentiation of Society* (New York: Columbia University Press, 1982). See also R. Nobles and D. Schiff, *Observing Law Through Systems Theory* (Oxford: Hart, 2013).

11. H. Arthurs, *Law and Learning: Report of the Consultative Group on Research and Education in Law* (Ottawa: Social Sciences and Humanities Research Council of Canada, 1983), at 59. See also Doorey, supra note 5.

12. B. Langille, "Labour Law Is a Subset of Employment Law" (1981) 31 *University of Toronto Law Journal* 200.

13. This is a key insight of *legal pluralism*, a strand of legal theory that draws attention to the many sources of rules and norms that shape behaviour beyond formal contract and state-based law. In the work context, these ideas are reflected in a rich literature on "industrial pluralism." See, e.g., H. Arthurs, "Understanding Labour Law: The Debate over 'Industrial Pluralism'" (1985) 38 *Current Legal Problems* 83; S. Henry, "Factory Law: The Changing Disciplinary Technology of Industrial Social Control" (1982) 10 *International Journal of the Sociology of Law* 365; and Dunlop, supra note 10, at 7-18 for a discussion of the "web of rules" that shape workplace behaviour.

14. A vast literature exists on "living wage" campaigns and policies. For a review, see D. Doorey, "A System of Trans-national Business Interactions: The Case of the Living Wage" (2013) *Osgoode CLPE Research Paper*, No. 37/2013, http://papers.ssrn.com/sol3/papers.cfm?abstract_id=2305623; and L. Glickman, *A Living Wage* (Ithaca, NY: Cornell University Press, 1997). A recent example involves the company Hennes and Mauritz (H&M), the world's second-largest clothing retailer, adopting a plan to implement a "living wage" policy throughout its global supply chain. See "H&M Vows 'Living Wage' for Factory Workers by 2018," *CBC News*, November 25, 2013, http://www.cbc.ca/news/business/h-m-vows-living-wage-for-factory-workers-by-2018-1.2439698.

15. H. Ford, *My Life and Work* (Garden City, NY: Doubleday, 1922), at chapter VIII. The full quotation reads: "Many employers thought we were just making the announcement because we were prosperous and wanted advertising and they condemned us because we were upsetting standards—violating the custom of paying a man the smallest amount he would take. There is nothing to such standards and customs. They have to be wiped out. Some day they will be. Otherwise, we cannot abolish poverty. We made the change not merely because we wanted to pay higher wages and thought we could pay them. We wanted to pay these wages so that the business would be on a lasting foundation. We were not distributing anything—we were building for the future. A low wage business is always insecure."

16. See L. Goodman, "Jason Kenney Suspends Restaurants from Scandal-Plagued Temporary Foreign Worker Program," *National Post*, April 24, 2014, http://news.nationalpost.com/news/canada/canadian-politics/jason-kenney-suspends-restaurants-from-scandal-plagued-temporary-foreign-worker-program.

17. See, e.g., D. Taras and B. Kaufman, "Non-Union Employee Representation in North America: Diversity, Controversy, and Uncertain Future" (2006) 37 *Industrial Relations Journal* 513.

18. See Craig and Solomon, supra note 10, at 8-10; and R. Chaykowski, "Collective Bargaining: Structure, Process, and Innovation," in M. Gunderson, A. Ponal, and D. Taras, eds., *Union-Management Relations in Canada*, 5th ed. (Toronto: Pearson, 2005), 266-69, at 257.

19. Another example involves so-called yellow dog contracts, which are legal under the common law regime based on freedom of contract, but are prohibited by Canadian labour relations legislation. A *yellow dog contract* was a contract term that required an employee to refrain from joining a union as long as he or she was employed with a particular employer, and it permitted the employer to fire the employee if the term was breached. Modern labour legislation prohibits contract terms that prohibit an employee from joining a union.

20. See D. Morton, *Working People*, 5th ed. (Montreal and Kingston: McGill-Queen's University Press, 2007), at 21-25.

21. The argument that "labour law" encompasses the bundle of laws that have important effects on labour markets has been made forcefully by H. Arthurs, "Charting the Boundaries of Labour Law: Innis Christie and the Search for an Integrated Law of Labour Market Regulation" (2011) 34 *Dalhousie Law Journal* 1.

22. See the discussion in A. Jackson, *Work and Labour in Canada: Critical Issues*, 2nd ed. (Toronto: Canadian Scholars' Press, 2009), at 248-53; R. Grinspun and R. Kreklewich, "Consolidating Neoliberal Reforms: 'Free Trade' as a Conditioning Framework" (1994) 43 *Studies in Political Economy* 33; and K. Banks, "Must Canada Change Its Labour and Employment Laws to Compete with the United States?" (2013) 38 *Queen's Law Journal* 419.

23. See Arthurs, supra note 21.

24. F. Martinello, "Mr. Harris, Mr. Rae, and Union Activity in Ontario" (2000) 26 *Canadian Public Policy* 17; D. Doorey, "A Model of Responsive Workplace Law" (2012) 50 *Osgoode Hall Law Journal* 47; and L. Panitch and D. Schwartz, *From Consent to Coercion: The Assault on Trade Union Freedoms*, 3rd ed. (Aurora, ON: Garamond, 2003).

25. See, e.g., H. Krahn, G.S. Lowe, and K.D. Hughes, *Work, Industry, and Canadian Society*, 6th ed. (Toronto: Thomson Nelson, 2011).

26. See, e.g., the periodical *Work, Employment and Society* published by Sage Publications, http://www.sagepub.com/journals/Journal201568/title.

27. See "Charter of Quebec Values Would Ban Religious Symbols for Public Workers," *CBC News*, September 10, 2013, http://www.cbc.ca/news/canada/montreal/charter-of-quebec-values-would-ban-religious-symbols-for-public-workers-1.1699315.

28. See C. Lipsig-Mummé, ed., *Climate@Work* (Halifax: Fernwood, 2013); and D. Doorey, "A Transnational Law of Just Transitions for Labour and the Environment," in A. Blackett and A. Trebilcock, eds., *Handbook on Transnational Labour Law* (Cheltenham, UK: Edward Elgar, 2015).

29. *Christie v. The York Corporation*, [1940] SCR 139; and *Seneca College v. Bhadauria*, [1981] 2 SCR 181.

30. *Vriend v. Alberta*, [1998] 1 SCR 493, 156 DLR (4th) 385.

CHAPTER 4

Key Perspectives That Shape the Law of Work

I. Introduction

According to the *Fortune 500* rankings of American corporations, the fiscal 2013 profits for Wal-Mart Stores (Walmart) were just under US$17 billion, making it one of the most profitable corporations in history.[1] Walmart paid its CEO, Michael Duke, just over $20.6 million in compensation that year.[2] At the same time, the average Walmart retail employee earned between $12 and $13 per hour, or about $20,000 per year.[3] It would take the average Walmart employee 785 years to earn what Mr. Duke earned in one year.[4] The law in both Canada and the United States requires Walmart to pay its employees at least a minimum wage set by the government, even if Walmart would like to pay its employees less, and those employees were prepared to work for less. However, in neither country does the law impose a mandatory *ceiling* on employee wages.

Why do our governments impose legal floors on wages, but not legal ceilings? The answer is probably that minimum wage laws protect "vulnerable workers" who might be taken advantage of by employers owing to their lack of bargaining power. If there were no minimum wage, many employers currently paying that rate would pay their employees less, since they would probably be able to attract workers who need jobs and are willing to work for less. The minimum wage represents a government's rejection of market forces as a mechanism for setting wages for low-income workers. The government is essentially saying, "We don't trust labour market forces and freedom of contract to produce an acceptable wage, given the standard of living we want for our citizens." Governments have not been concerned about maximum wages, because high-income workers have sufficient bargaining power to look after their own interests. Very high income has not been considered a social and economic problem, whereas very low income often has.

However, not everyone agrees that there should be a minimum wage, and some think there should be a maximum wage.[5] Whenever a Canadian government raises the minimum wage, complaints arise from business groups that the move will "cost jobs," countered by worker advocates who reject those claims or argue that the increase is too small. Both sides in this debate point to studies they claim support their position. Others argue that minimum wage policy is about decency and fairness, and not economics. There is no "correct" answer to the question of whether governments should regulate wages. There are only arguments for and against that regulation based on different perspectives.

BOX 4.1 » TALKING WORK LAW

Is the Minimum Wage a Good Policy?

The answer to the question above depends on your perspective. Whether a minimum wage should exist and the level at which such a wage should be fixed are among the many interesting debates that arise within the *law of work*. Attitudes and opinions vary widely. Consider the range of opinions reflected in the following quotations from recent Canadian debates over proposed increases to minimum wage levels:

From the Fraser Institute, a conservative Canadian think tank that advocates for limited government regulation in labour markets:

> Increasing British Columbia's minimum wage to $10.25 an hour could lead to a loss of more than 52,000 jobs. When governments impose high labour costs on businesses, employers react by hiring fewer workers and reducing the number of hours employees work.[*]

From the Wellesley Institute, a think tank that advocates for better health in urban centres:

> An increase in the minimum wage will raise the floor for all Ontario employees. This increase will have a positive impact on those working for minimum wage and other low wage workers. It could also transfer income from shareholders to employees.

The combined impact would reduce income inequality. In a time when governments feel that their budgets are constrained, this is a policy approach to address and reduce income inequality that is crucial and timely.[†]

From "Fairness at Work," a government-commissioned study of federal employment standards laws in Canada:

> In the end, however, the argument over a national minimum wage is not about politics and economics. It is about decency. Just as we reject most forms of child labour on ethical grounds, whatever their economic attractions, we recoil from the notion that in an affluent society like ours good, hard-working people should have to live in abject poverty.[‡]

---

[*] Fraser Institute, "BC's $10.25 Minimum Wage Could Cost More Than 52,000 Jobs and Reduce Opportunities for Young Workers," news release, April 29, 2011, http://www.fraserinstitute.org/research-news/news/display.aspx?id=17461.

[†] S. Block, *Who Is Working for Minimum Wage in Ontario?* (Toronto: Wellesley Institute, October 2013), executive summary, http://www.wellesleyinstitute.com/wp-content/uploads/2013/10/Who-Makes-Minimum-Wage.pdf.

[‡] H. Arthurs, *Fairness at Work: Federal Labour Standards for the 21st Century* (Ottawa: Human Resources and Skills Development Canada, 2006), at 247.

In making decisions about what laws to enact, governments are influenced by their *perspectives* on the role of markets, governments, management, unions, ethics, and power in society and in the workplace. In this way, how a society governs its labour markets is influenced by the political economy in which its legal rules are produced. Do judges and citizens, and the politicians they elect, trust that labour markets will produce desirable outcomes? Do existing legal rules give preference to some interests over others, and, if so, is this distribution of rewards just? Would a different set of preferences be preferable? The answers to these sorts of questions will influence the extent and form of legal rules that emerge to govern work in any society. Therefore, as we learn about these legal rules, we need to be alert to the dominant modes of thinking, or perspectives, used to justify legal rules.

For example, one perspective (perspective A) might view the vast difference between the pay of Walmart's CEO and the average pay of Walmart store employees as a healthy and normal result of market forces. The CEO is "worth" over $20 million annually, while the average retail employee is "worth" $12 per hour (or less if there were not a statutory minimum wage) because that is what the market dictates for these workers. Another perspective (perspective B) might view the vast gap between executive pay and average worker pay as a failure of the market-based

Walmart employees demonstrate in front of the company's head offices, demanding full-time hours.
Source: Marc F. Henning/Alamy.

model. While the CEO can afford to live in a gated mansion with security, yachts, a personal staff, and expensive cars, his employees rely on food banks and public subsidies to feed their children and pay their rent.[6]

If perspective A dominates contemporary social and political thinking, then we should expect few if any new laws to be enacted to address the income gap. However, if perspective B dominates, then the vast difference between executive and average worker pay would be perceived as a recipe for an unhealthy, and economically and politically unstable society. We might therefore anticipate a new law designed to transfer more wealth from executives down to average employees.

The varying perspectives on the appropriate role of law in governing work discussed in this chapter can influence not only the laws governments enact but also the actions, decisions, and strategies of the other actors who help shape work laws (including employees, employers, unions, and employer associations). We need to be alert to the background modes of thinking that shape the actions and laws we will study in this text. Therefore, in this chapter, we introduce the dominant perspectives that have shaped the development of the law of work in Canada. This exercise will give us another important tool through which to analyze the laws we will discuss in the remainder of the text.

II. The Main Perspectives That Shape the Law of Work

Five key perspectives have shaped the debates surrounding the legal regulation of the labour relationship in Canada (and elsewhere):[7]

1. The neoclassical perspective
2. The managerialist perspective
3. The industrial pluralist perspective
4. The critical reformist perspective
5. The radical perspective

The perspectives are summarized in Table 4.1. This taxonomy no doubt oversimplifies the complexity and richness of each of the perspectives, but it is useful for our purposes here. In practice, the boundaries between the perspectives are more blurred. Individuals can move between perspectives from argument to argument, or over their lifetimes. Some laws cannot be neatly fit into just one of the categories. However, our objective is simply to introduce and identify the dominant strands that have prevailed in work law policy debates over the years. As we proceed through the text, we will occasionally note how legal policies have reflected, or been influenced by, shifts in the dominant perspective.

TABLE 4.1   Perspectives on the Law of Work

Perspective	Labour markets	Employment regulation	Unions/collective bargaining
Neoclassical	• Labour markets are presumed to be perfectly competitive and efficient. • Unfettered labour markets produce an optimal allocation of resources.	• Regulation artificially raises costs of labour above optimal market levels and introduces rigidities, with harmful social and economic consequences.	• Unions are a harmful labour cartel that artificially raises labour costs and reduces efficiency, with harmful economic and social consequences.
Managerialist	• Labour market forces alone should not determine working conditions if they result in conditions that do not maximize employee motivation and satisfaction.	• Regulation is largely unnecessary, since employers have an economic interest in treating workers fairly. • If necessary to deal with bad employers, standards should be set at a low enough level that they do not impose undue rigidity and costs on good employers.	• The desire of workers to support collective bargaining indicates a failure of management. • Collective bargaining introduces harmful rigidity and should be resisted. However, if employees choose unionization, the employer should attempt to work with the union.
Industrial pluralist	• Labour markets are imperfect and characterized by a significant imbalance of power between workers and employers.	• Regulation is necessary to protect workers from harsh labour market forces and to ensure a basic and fair level of working conditions. • Regulation is especially important for workers who do not have the protection of collective bargaining.	• Collective bargaining and unions are essential to providing workers with "voice" and balancing bargaining power in the labour relationship. • Collective bargaining is an important tool in combatting income inequality and promoting democracy in the workplace and in society more broadly.
Critical reformist	• Labour markets are imperfect and characterized by a significant imbalance of power between workers and employers, especially with regard to women, youth, visible minorities, and new immigrants, who tend to be the most vulnerable workers.	• Strong regulatory protections are the best way to ensure equitable employment outcomes in a market system.	• Collective bargaining is a strong institution for empowering workers but has failed to reach the most vulnerable workers in society.
Radical	• Labour markets are constructs designed by and for capitalists in order to maintain capitalist control and privilege.	• Regulation is a marginally effective tool for addressing the exploitation of labour that is an inevitable outcome of capitalist relations.	• Unions (and collective bargaining) can be an important and useful means of raising class consciousness, but they will have limited impact unless their focus is on challenging the capitalist model.

A. The Neoclassical Perspective

The **neoclassical perspective** is an economics-based view of work law based on the assumption that labour markets operate generally in the same manner as markets for other goods—labour is a commodity like all other commodities.[8] Neoclassicists assume that labour markets are perfectly competitive, or nearly so. We will leave it to the economists to explain the details of the neoclassical economic model.[9] Here, we are only concerned with introducing at a general level how the neoclassical perspective has influenced the law of work.

However, since neoclassical prescriptions for work law flow from the assumption that labour markets are perfectly competitive, we need to know something about what that means. In a perfectly competitive market, an **equilibrium wage rate** exists for any given job, which is the rate "at which workers are willing to supply exactly the number of hours that employers want to buy."[10] For example, an equilibrium wage rate for baristas of $10 per hour means that every employer in the economy that needs a barista can find one at that rate. The demand for baristas equals the supply of baristas when $10 per hour is offered.

An employer who offers a wage rate lower than $10 per hour will not be able to attract baristas. No barista would accept a rate lower than the equilibrium rate, since other employers offer the equilibrium rate or higher. Workers are assumed to be mobile (able to quit a job and move to a better job whenever they like, or to stop selling their labour altogether) and to possess full information of all alternative job opportunities. No single barista can bargain a wage rate higher than the equilibrium rate, since in a perfectly competitive world the employer can attract all the workers it needs at the equilibrium rate, and all workers are assumed to possess similar skills.

This description of perfectly competitive labour markets obviously does not describe the real world. There is no such thing as a perfectly competitive labour market. However, neoclassicists argue that real-world labour markets "approximate" the theoretical model, so that lessons learned by studying models of hypothetical, perfectly competitive labour markets should still guide labour policy.[11] Since market forces are assumed to operate competitively and to produce the most efficient (optimal) outcomes, attempts to interfere in market forces through the introduction of non-market disturbances, such as regulatory standards to protect workers or the promotion of collective bargaining (and unions), will produce harmful effects, including unemployment.

The neoclassical perspective rejects all of the regulatory standards legislation explored in Part III of the companion volume. For example, if a government introduced a minimum wage of $12 per hour into a perfectly competitive labour market for baristas in which the equilibrium wage rate was $10 per hour, employers would respond by hiring fewer baristas, perhaps replacing them with machines (i.e., substituting capital for labour). Worse still, some employers may simply close or move outside the reach of the law. In this way, a minimum wage is predicted in the neoclassical perspective to cause higher unemployment.[12] This position is reflected in the quotation from the Fraser Institute, a Canadian think tank that espouses the neoclassical perspective (a "think tank" is an institution that conducts research and advocates for certain types of policies), in Box 4.1.

A similar analysis applies to all other wage and non-wage working conditions imposed by government regulation. Since neoclassicists believe market forces alone produce the optimal conditions of employment, any legislation that imposes substantive contract terms is wrong-headed and potentially harmful. If a condition of employment were optimal, then the market would have produced it as a standard term of employment contracts. Hence, employment standards

---

neoclassical perspective: An economics-based view of the law of work based on the ideal of a perfectly competitive labour market. It rejects government intervention in labour markets and collective bargaining, and argues that employers and individual employees should set working conditions under a system of freedom of contract.

equilibrium wage rate: A theoretical wage rate fixed through market forces in which the supply of labour (the number of hours workers are prepared to work) equals the demand for labour (the number of hours purchasers of labour wish to buy).

legislation requiring *notice to terminate an employment contract* is unnecessary, according to neoclassical law and economics scholar Richard Posner (University of Chicago), because if employees and employers valued them, these clauses "would be negotiated voluntarily."[13] Similarly, *occupational health and safety laws* impose costs on employers and are unnecessary, because markets will produce the most efficient level of safety, and employers have "a selfish interest in providing the optimal … level of worker health and safety."[14]

Nor should governments introduce *human rights law* to prohibit discrimination in employment. Market forces alone will take care of any employer dumb enough to discriminate on the basis of factors unrelated to productivity. If women or visible minorities will work for less than men performing similar work, then rational profit-seeking employers will hire only women and visible minorities, and discriminating employers who pay more for white men will be driven out of business or forced to change their discriminatory practices.[15] Richard Epstein (University of Chicago), a scholar in the neoclassical perspective, explains this dynamic as follows:

> [T]he employer who sacrifices economic welfare for personal prejudice will pay for her preferences on the bottom line. By forgoing superior labor in order to hire inferior workers, she will sacrifice resources to indulge consumption choices, and will be at a systematic disadvantage relative to employers whose economic motivations are more rational.[16]

Neoclassicists argue that attempts to "fix" discrimination through legislation will impose unnecessary and inefficient costs on employers and will not help the people the laws are intended to benefit. We considered these arguments against government regulation in Part III of the companion volume.

Finally, the neoclassical perspective also opposes laws that support or legitimize unionization and collective bargaining.[17] They see unions as a form of harmful **cartel**, a combination of workers organized to control the supply of labour in order to artificially raise wages above the equilibrium wage rate.[18] Collective bargaining often results in unionized workers receiving higher wages and better benefits than non-union workers. In the neoclassical perspective, this is a bad thing. Those benefits to unionized workers are said to come at the expense of other non-union workers, employers, shareholders, and consumers, since employers may pay for the costs of collective bargaining by raising their product costs.[19] Thus, in the neoclassical perspective, the laws we considered under Part III of the companion volume are met with suspicion or outright hostility.

The neoclassical perspective prefers the common law regime. This preference makes sense because the foundation of that regime is the notion of "freedom of contract" between individual employee and employer.[20] Law plays a role in this perspective, but a limited one. Judges should enforce the contracts the parties have agreed to, and governments should enact legislation to protect contracts and property rights to restrict anti-competitive practices and, possibly, to promote greater information and mobility in labour markets. Beyond that, the setting of working conditions should be left to contract and market forces. Since the late 1980s, the neoclassical perspective has been very influential in North America in shaping debates about labour policies, especially when politically conservative governments are in power.

B. The Managerialist Perspective

The **managerialist perspective** is closely linked to modern human resource management (HRM). It shares with the neoclassical perspective the belief that government intervention in

---

cartel: A combination of individuals or companies that attempt to use collective force or coordination to fix market prices.

managerialist perspective: A view of the law of work guided by the belief that employers have an economic incentive to treat employees decently and fairly in order to extract commitment and effort. Government legislation of employment should be kept at a minimum. Unionization is a response to poor management and is disruptive.

the labour relationship should be minimal and that, ideally, unions and collective bargaining should not be present at a workplace. However, managerialists put their faith in enlightened management practices rather than theoretically perfect competitive markets. They emphasize that employers and employees share a community of interest: both want the business to be successful. The managerialist perspective draws inspiration from the pioneering work of sociologist Elton Mayo (Harvard University, 1880–1949) and his Hawthorne experiments from the late 1920s to the early 1930s.

Mayo and his researchers concluded that socio-psychological feelings that came from being studied and working as a team caused employees to be more productive.[21] This finding was crucial to the emergence of the "human relations" school (later HRM), which asserts that workers who are treated well on a psychological level will feel more committed to the employer's goals and that this commitment will translate into a more productive labour force. The objective of management should be to foster cooperation and trust with workers. Employers who mistreat their employees will suffer economically, which could result in the failure of their business. Conversely, treating workers decently increases productivity and profits. Therefore, businesses will look out for employees' concerns because it is in their economic interest to do so. This belief is a guiding philosophy of the managerialist perspective.

Magna's "Employee's Charter" in Figure 4.1 is consistent with the managerialist perspective on how employers should treat workers.[22] Magna is a large non-union automobile parts company with its head office in Aurora, Ontario.

In the managerialist perspective, employment regulation should be kept to a minimum, since these laws inject rigidity into the work relationship and impose unnecessary costs on employers.[23] If laws are necessary to deal with the worst types of employers (those who do not perceive the wisdom in treating workers decently), the legal standards should be set at a low level and be flexible enough to not punish or hamstring "good" employers.[24]

Unions and collective bargaining are perceived to be an unnecessary impediment to managerial prerogative and flexibility in the managerialist perspective, so governments should not use law to promote either. Since it is in the economic interest of management to treat workers fairly, workers have no need to look to unions for protection. Managerialists argue that the decision of workers to support unionization reflects a failure of management to address employee needs through progressive HRM policies.[25] However, because unionization is perceived to be a rational response by employees to perceived employer mistreatment, the managerialist accepts, more so than the neoclassicist, that unions have a legitimate role to play in protecting workers from abuse at work. Hence, the managerialist perspective does not call for the legal oppression of unions and collective bargaining, as do the neoclassicists, although it does advocate for the right of employers to resist their employees' attempt to unionize and for a system that permits employees to easily remove a union.[26]

C. The Industrial Pluralist Perspective

The **industrial pluralist perspective** views the work relationship very differently than both the neoclassical and managerialist perspectives. The guiding insight of the industrial pluralist perspective is that an inherent imbalance of power exists between employees and employers that is problematic for both social and economic reasons. In the unfettered labour market model favoured by neoclassicists, individual workers lack the ability to safely voice their concerns or desires for fear of losing their job (they lack "voice"). This lack of voice leaves workers without the means to participate in decisions that can significantly influence their lives.

---

industrial pluralist perspective: A view of the law of work that emphasizes the inequality of bargaining power between employers and employees, and advocates especially for collective bargaining and unions as a means of empowering workers so that they can bargain fairer employment outcomes.

FIGURE 4.1   The Managerialist Perspective Demonstrated in a Corporate "Employee's Charter"

Employee's Charter

Magna is committed to an operating philosophy which is based on fairness and concern for people. This philosophy is part of Magna's Fair Enterprise culture in which employees and management share in the responsibility to ensure the success of the company. It includes these principles:

Job Security
Being competitive by making a better product for a better price is the best way to enhance job security. Magna is committed to working together with you to help protect your job security. To assist you, Magna will provide job counselling, training and employee assistance programs.

A Safe and Healthful Workplace
Magna is committed to providing you with a working environment which is safe and healthful.

Fair Treatment
Magna offers equal opportunities based on an individual's qualifications and performance, free from discrimination or favouritism.

Competitive Wages and Benefits
Magna will provide you with information which will enable you to compare your total compensation, including wages and benefits, with those earned by employees of your direct competitors and local companies your division competes with for people. If your total compensation is found not to be competitive, your total compensation will be adjusted.

Employee Equity and Profit Participation
Magna believes that every employee should share in the financial success of the company.

Communication and Information
Through regular monthly meetings between management and employees and through publications, Magna will provide you with information so that you will know what is going on in your company and within the industry.

The Hotline
Should you have a problem, or feel the above principles are not being met, we encourage you to contact the Hotline to register your complaints. You do not have to give your name, but if you do, it will be held in strict confidence. Hotline Investigators will respond to you.

The Hotline is committed to investigate and resolve all concerns or complaints and must report the outcome to Magna's Global Human Resources Department.

Hotline Number: 1-800-263-1691

Source: Magna Corporation. Reprinted with permission.

Individual workers also lack sufficient bargaining power to negotiate above whatever level of working conditions the employer is prepared to offer. While this lack of power may benefit employers and business owners, industrial pluralists argue that it produces vastly unequal societies in which the wealth created through worker labour tends to gravitate upward to a relatively small proportion of wealthy elite. The resulting income inequality produces an unsustainable and volatile economy, which plants the seeds for political instability. Thus, for the industrial pluralist, addressing the imbalance of bargaining power in the employment relationship should be a central public policy objective of laws governing work. The best approach to rectifying this imbalance is for the law to promote *collective* bargaining in which unions or other employee associations that are independent of the employer negotiate with employers on behalf of workers.

This emphasis on inequality of bargaining power in the capitalist employment relationship, and its perceived harmful effects, is shared with the next two perspectives we will consider (the *critical reformist* and *radical* perspectives). All three dismiss as naive and empirically false the managerialist's claim that employers, through progressive HRM policies, will voluntarily strike an acceptable balance between the competing interests of employees and employers. They also reject the "free market" prescriptions of neoclassicists, arguing that the models on which they are based bear no resemblance to the real world, favour the interests of employers and society's wealthy and powerful elite, and produce vast economic inequality.[27] The differences between these last three perspectives rest primarily on the focus of their critiques and on the types of solutions they prescribe to address the problems.

Industrial pluralists argue that the goal of law in relation to work and employment should be to strike an appropriate balance between the *efficiency* concerns of employers, on the one hand, and the *equity* concerns of workers on the other hand.[28] To achieve this goal, the industrial pluralist supports regulatory labour standards that promote a basic floor of adequate working conditions. However, their main objective is to promote unionization and collective bargaining. Collective employee representation is considered the most effective way to ensure worker voice and promote a healthy distribution of wealth throughout the economy. Collective bargaining, including a legal right to withhold labour (a "strike"), empowers workers by putting them on a more equal footing as they bargain for the sale of their labour. It better ensures that workers can bargain a reasonable share of the economic pie produced by their labour—a result that benefits the economy (by fuelling consumption) and society (by producing a decent standard of living).[29] Box 4.2 features the benefits of collective bargaining according to industrial pluralists.

Industrial pluralists emphasize the link between collective bargaining and income equality. For example, in a 2008 report, the International Labour Organization (ILO), the leading global institution that promotes collective bargaining around the world, stated that international economic evidence demonstrates that income inequality is lower in countries "in which a greater proportion of workers are affiliated with trade unions."[30] Industrial pluralists argue that income inequality is a dangerous social and economic problem, and that laws promoting decent working conditions and protecting workers' right to collective bargaining must be part of the solution. Industrial pluralism was the dominant perspective in Canadian politics from the late 1940s until the late 1980s, with all of the major political parties supporting collective bargaining.[31] Unions represented almost 40 percent of Canadian workers in the mid-1980s, before union coverage began a decline to its current (2013) rate of about 31 percent overall (and only about 17 percent in the private sector).[32]

BOX 4.2 » TALKING WORK LAW

The Benefits of Collective Bargaining

Industrial pluralists argue that collective bargaining is valuable because it promotes several important outcomes:

- *Democracy and voice.* It introduces a form of democracy into the workplace by giving workers the tools and power to participate directly in the development and enforcement of workplace rules and practices.*
- *Distributive fairness.* It empowers workers to bargain a larger share of the economic pie than is possible in the alternative system in which individual employees bargain for the sale of their labour. The result is a stronger middle class and less income inequality, which, according to industrial pluralists, facilitates a healthier economy and more stable society.†
- *Improved productivity.* In a much-cited (and debated) 1984 book entitled *What Do Unions Do?* Harvard University economists Richard Freeman and James Medoff concluded that collective bargaining tends, overall, to improve productivity slightly, although results vary across employers and sectors.‡ The explanations provided for this result included the observation that

unionized workers have lower turnover rates and that collective bargaining "shocks" management into implementing more efficient processes.§

---

* For discussion of the "voice" effects of collective bargaining, see Weiler, supra note 27; R. Freeman and J. Medoff, *What Do Unions Do?* (New York: Basic Books, 1984); G. Davidov, "Collective Bargaining Laws: Scope and Purpose" (2004) 20:1 *International Journal of Comparative Labour Law and Industrial Relations* 81-106, at 86; C. Craver, "Why Labor Unions Must (and Can) Survive" (1998) 1:1 *University of Pennsylvania Journal of Labor and Employment Law* 15-47; K. Klare, "Workplace Democracy and Market Reconstruction" (1988) 38 *Catholic University Law Review* 1. See also Davies, supra note 7, at 183-85; and D. Doorey, "Graduated Freedom of Association: Worker Voice Beyond the Wagner Model" (2013) 38:2 *Queen's Law Journal* 515-48, at 516-20.

† See discussion and sources cited in M. Lynk, "Labour Law and the New Inequality" (2009) 59 *University of New Brunswick Law Journal* 14.

‡ Freeman and Medoff, supra note *. See also J. Bennett and B. Kaufman, *What Do Unions Do? A Twenty Year Perspective* (New Brunswick, NJ: Transaction, 2004).

§ M. Gunderson and D. Hyatt, "Union Impact on Compensation, Productivity, and Management of the Organization," in M. Gunderson and D. Taras, eds., *Canadian Labour and Employment Relations*, 6th ed. (Toronto: Pearson, 2009), 383-429, at 392-94.

D. The Critical Reformist Perspective

As noted above, the **critical reformist perspective** shares much in common with the industrial pluralist perspective. However, the critical reformist perspective is more critical of the outcomes actually produced by collective bargaining in Canada.[33] In practice, collective bargaining has historically benefited certain privileged segments of the working population and not reached the most vulnerable workers. John Godard (University of Manitoba) describes this point:

> [Critical reformists] tend to be highly supportive of labour unions and collective bargaining, but they are at the same time often highly critical of the system within which unions currently operate. Their general argument is that ... unions tend to be least effective in the workplaces where workers are most in need of assistance.[34]

A particularly rich strand of the critical reformist literature involves feminist critiques of collective bargaining in Canada. Professor Judy Fudge (University of Kent) captured the essence of this critique:

> Despite the fact that collective bargaining is gender neutral on its face—at best it assumes a sexless worker, at worst an all male cast. Mostly, it has been done by men for the benefit of men. Its theorists are mostly men, as are its functionaries: arbitrators, board members, union leaders, managers, and lawyers. One of the presumptions of the postwar social consensus was that the labour force was unfragmented; that it was composed of full-time male workers in regular and secure employment. Unions bargained for a family wage for their male members. Until recently, women were ignored.[35]

---

critical reformist perspective: A view of the law of work that supports both collective bargaining and regulatory standards, but emphasizes how both have tended to fail the most vulnerable workers. This perspective focuses on how laws can be reformed to better protect these workers.

Today, more women are union members than men because most unionized workers are in the public sector where women are highly represented.[36] However, reformists emphasize that most vulnerable or precarious jobs in Canada are still filled by women, visible minorities, the disabled, young workers, and new immigrants. These jobs are characterized by low pay, job insecurity, lack of benefits, and greater risk of injury.[37]

Critical reformists are interested in how legal rules and structures have failed to protect Canada's most vulnerable workers. First, the common law model requires workers to "bargain" improvements on their own, but precarious workers lack the bargaining power to do so. Second, although regulatory standards often (although not always) apply to these workers, in practice, government enforcement is wanting, compliance with the law is low, and the workers do not have the means and knowledge to enforce the laws on their own.[38] Third, collective bargaining law remains irrelevant to Canada's most vulnerable workers, since unions lack the desire or capacity (or both) to effectively represent these workers under our existing legal models.

Therefore, the focus of this perspective is on critiquing existing legal structures that fail vulnerable workers—especially women, visible and religious minorities, new immigrants, and young workers—and on proposing legal reforms that would do a better job in this regard. Critical reformists focus on the legal possibilities for more robust and broad-reaching systems of collective representation and resistance than are offered by existing collective bargaining legal models as well as more effective regulatory standards legislation.[39]

E. The Radical Perspective

The focus of the **radical perspective** in relation to work law is on the recurrent "regulatory dilemmas" that by necessity define all capitalist labour markets.[40] This perspective builds on the insights and arguments of Karl Marx. Very briefly, Marx observed that most workers in a capitalist society lack the property necessary to create value through their labour power. Therefore, they must enter a crowded labour market to sell their labour power to those who own property (employers) in order to survive, since few have independent means of wealth.

From the employer's perspective, the worker represents a unit of production (a commodity), and the objective is to extract maximum labour effort from that unit at minimal cost in order to produce profits. However, workers have non-productive needs too; they are humans who seek personal fulfillment and development both at work and in the non-work sphere. They seek earnings from selling their labour to aid in fulfillment of those needs. This dynamic is the source of the regulatory dilemma that confronts all capitalist economies. Employers and workers have conflicting interests. Laws that restrict an employer's ability to extract maximum effort at minimum cost in order to protect workers will come at the expense of the employer's interests in maximizing profits.

Eric Tucker (York University) summarizes the conflict as follows:

> [A]t each phase in the circuit of capital, the need of workers for self-development confronts the logic of capital, which seeks to reduce workers to commodity sellers in competition with each other, to exercise control over their productive capabilities, to shape their needs and to appropriate for themselves the surplus value that is realized in the ... process of production.[41]

The emphasis of the radical perspective is on the various class struggles that arise in a society as workers seek to overcome the inherently exploitive nature of capitalism. This emphasis leads to a different perspective on the role of law in labour markets than the other perspectives we

---

radical perspective: A view of the law of work inspired by Karl Marx's insights and criticism of the capitalist system. It considers regulatory standards regulation and collective bargaining to be helpful but limited in their ability to respond to the exploitive nature of capitalism. This perspective advocates for a more fundamental transformation of the economic model.

have considered. The emphasis in the radical perspective is on either reforming the capitalist model or supplanting it altogether with a different model in which power is more equally distributed throughout society. Radicals are highly critical of both the neoclassical and managerialist perspectives. Both downplay the crucial role that capitalist models and institutions play in creating the power imbalance that so often leads to worker exploitation as employers pursue more and more profits.

The relationship among the radical, industrial pluralist, and critical reformist perspectives is more complex. The radical perspective is generally supportive of regulatory standards and unions and collective bargaining, like the other two perspectives. Regulatory standards can protect workers from the worst types of employer abuses, and unions can be a means of raising class consciousness and of extracting greater benefits from employers through collective action. Therefore, all three perspectives tend to agree on the need for employment regulation and strong unions. All three also recognize that there will be unavoidable conflict in work relations.

However, radicals accuse industrial pluralists (and to a lesser degree critical reformists) of ceding too much to the capitalist model.[42] Industrial pluralists tend to accept that, with effective regulatory standards laws and strong unions, employees' interests can be effectively addressed *within* the capitalist model (albeit occasionally with conflict in the form of strikes or other forms of employee resistance).[43] Radicals argue that, although regulatory standards and laws that protect and promote collective bargaining can serve a useful role, it is a limited role. Capitalism will always work to the advantage of capital; the party that owns the means of production, by virtue of its economic power, will always have greater influence on and access to the political processes that produce legal rules. Therefore, radicals focus much more on the problems of the capitalist model and on class-based resistance to it than do industrial pluralists.

The distinction between the radical and critical reformist perspectives is the most blurred. Both perspectives critique the limited success of unions and collective bargaining in Canada to fundamentally address many types of worker exploitation and mistreatment, yet both are generally supportive of collective bargaining as an institution. However, a belief that exploitation of workers can be fundamentally addressed through the enactment of "better" or different types of regulatory standards than presently exist is a critical reformist argument rather than a radical argument. The radical perspective has less confidence than does the critical reformist perspective in the ability of capitalism to be tamed by protective employment standards regulation.

The radical perspective played an important role in the development of Canadian work law, particularly during the formative years of the Canadian collective bargaining regime. Radical-inspired organizations, such as the Communist Party of Canada, organized unions and led strikes in the early 20th century that contributed to the climate of industrial worker resistance that laid the groundwork for labour legislation that survives to this day.[44] Growing income inequality, large-scale global economic downturns and unemployment, and corporate corruption have spawned renewed interest in the radical perspective and Marx's work.[45]

III. Chapter Summary

The purpose of this chapter is to introduce the main schools of thought, or perspectives, that have tended to guide law of work debates. In practice, the lines between the perspectives are much more blurred than they would appear to be in this chapter; people and organizations can agree with elements of multiple perspectives at once, or they can shift from one perspective to another depending on the issues being debated. However, the categories presented here are nevertheless useful for the journey we have begun.

These perspectives help shape the law of work in a variety of ways. The most obvious is that they influence key policy debates within the political subsystem that produces the legal regulation of work. Often we see reference to the perspectives explicitly in the political speeches and propaganda disseminated by politicians and political parties. Academics and think tanks that research and write about work law often have an allegiance to one or more of these perspectives, and their views and arguments can influence legal developments. Public opinion on the role and form of work laws can reflect one or more of these perspectives, and that opinion in turn influences the beliefs and actions of lawmakers, workers, employers, and associations, as well as judges and adjudicators who enforce legal rules. An understanding of the dominant perspectives will help you recognize their influence as we proceed through the text.

QUESTIONS AND ISSUES FOR DISCUSSION

1. Briefly explain the key components of the five perspectives in work law identified in this chapter.
2. Which of the perspectives are supportive of the regulatory standards regime, and which are not?
3. What are the arguments for and against unions and collective bargaining presented in this chapter?
4. What distinguishes the industrial pluralist, critical reformist, and radical perspectives?
5. What distinguishes the neoclassical and managerialist perspectives?

EXERCISES

1. Locate a media story that considers a debate about work law reform in Canada. Can you identify arguments in the story that can be associated with one of the perspectives discussed in this chapter?
2. Explain which of the five perspectives best represents your present attitude toward law and work, and why.

UPDATES

Go to emond.ca/lawofworkircb for links to news, author's blog posts, content updates, and other information related to the chapters in this text.

NOTES AND REFERENCES

1. "Wal-Mart Stores, Inc.," *Fortune 500*, accessed July 23, 2014, http://fortune.com/fortune500/2013/.

2. "Michael Duke," *Forbes*, accessed November 12, 2014, http://www.forbes.com/profile/michael-duke-1/.

3. "Walmart's Average Employee Would Have to Work 785 Years to Earn CEO's Annual Salary," *Huffington Post*, April 24, 2013, http://www.huffingtonpost.com/2013/04/23/walmart-wages-to-ceo-annual-salary_n_3140618.html.

4. Ibid.

5. See the discussion and sources presented in D. Doorey, "Is It Time to Regulate 'Maximum' Pay in Canada?" *Law of Work* (blog), accessed July 24, 2014, http://lawofwork.ca/?p=4427. See also D. Gruending, "Canadian CEOs Make 171 Times Average, Let's Talk Maximum Wage," *Rabble.ca*, March 2, 2014, http://rabble.ca/blogs/bloggers/dhg/2014/03/canadian-ceos-make-171-times-average-lets-talk-maximum-wage.

6. E. Fox, "Wal-Mart's Low Wages Cost Taxpayers," *CNN Money*, June 5, 2013, http://money.cnn.com/2013/06/04/news/companies/walmart-medicaid/.

7. This is a common taxonomy found in industrial relations textbooks and scholarship, although terminology can vary. See, e.g., J. Godard, *Industrial Relations, the Economy, and Society*, 4th ed. (Concord, ON: Captus Press, 2011), at 9-18; R. Hebdon and T. Brown, *Industrial Relations in Canada*, 2nd ed. (Toronto: Nelson, 2012), at 16-17. See also A. Davies, *Perspectives on Labour Law*, 2nd ed. (Cambridge: Cambridge University Press, 2009); and J. Budd and D. Bhave, "The Employment Relationship," in A. Wilkinson, T. Redman, S. Snell, and N. Bacon, eds., *Sage Handbook of Human Resource Management* (London: Sage, 2010), 51-70.

8. A. Alchian and W. Allen, *University Economics*, 3rd ed. (Belmont, CA: Wadsworth, 1972), at 407-8.

9. Extensive literature exists on the application of the neoclassical economics model to labour markets. Most standard labour market economics texts explain the model. See, e.g., Alchian and Allen, supra note 8; and R. Ehrenberg, R. Smith, and R. Chaykowski, *Modern Labour Economics: Theory and Public Policy* (Toronto: Pearson, 2004), at 44-57. For an excellent discussion on and critique of the neoclassical perspective as applied to labour markets, see B. Kaufman, "Economic Analysis of Labor Markets and Labor Law: An Institutional/Industrial Relations Perspective," in C. Estlund and M. Wachter, eds., *Research Handbook on Economics of Labor and Employment Law* (Northampton, MA: Edward Elgar, 2012), at 52. See also Davies, supra note 7, at 26-32. Other recent critiques of the neoclassical model as applied to labour markets are B. Kaufman, "The Impossibility of a Perfectly Competitive Labour Market" (2007) 31 *Cambridge Journal of Economics* 775; J. Stanford, *Economics for Everyone* (London: Pluto Press, 2008), at 99-110; and J. Stiglitz, "Employment, Social Justice and Societal Well-Being" (2002) 141 *International Labour Review* 9.

10. Davies, supra note 7, at 26. Since no individual employer or employee can influence the market-wide equilibrium wage rate for jobs, neoclassical economists say that everyone is a "price taker" in the labour market. Employers will hire the number of employees they require at the equilibrium wage rate.

11. Kaufman, "Economic Analysis," supra note 9, at 58-61. The assumption that real-world labour markets approximate the perfectly competitive theoretical models is among the mostly hotly contested topics in work law. See Stiglitz, supra note 9.

12. See R. Posner, *Economic Analysis of Law*, 5th ed. (New York: Aspen, 1998), at 361; and Davies, supra note 7, at 139-42. Neoclassicists also argue that the harmful effects of employment regulation are disproportionately experienced by the least advantaged workers. See the video clip of neoclassicist Milton Friedman on the minimum wage at http://lawofwork.ca/?p=6648.

13. Posner, supra note 12, at 359; and R. Epstein, "In Defense of the Contract at Will" (1984) 51 *University of Chicago Law Review* 947.

14. Posner, supra note 12, at 363.

15. G. Becker, *The Economics of Discrimination* (Chicago: University of Chicago Press, 1957); and R. Epstein, *Forbidden Grounds: The Case Against Employment Discrimination Laws* (Cambridge: Harvard University Press, 1992).

16. R. Epstein, *Simple Rules for a Complex World* (Cambridge: Harvard University Press, 1995), at 176.

17. R. Epstein, "A Common Law of Labor Relations: A Critique of the New Deal Labor Legislation" (1983) 92 *Yale Law Journal* 1357.

18. Posner, supra note 12, at 350-58.

19. R. Epstein, "The Case Against the Employee Free Choice Act" (working paper, University of Chicago Law and Economics Olin Working Paper No. 452, 2009), http://papers.ssrn.com/sol3/papers.cfm?abstract_id=1337185.

20. Davies, supra note 7, at 28: "[N]eoclassical economists are strong advocates of the doctrine of freedom of contract. This means that people should be allowed to enter into contracts with whomever they choose, on whatever terms they wish. The law should only interfere where there is evidence that a person has not given his or her genuine consent, for example, in case of duress or undue influence."

21. E. Mayo, *The Social Problems of an Industrialized Civilization* (Abingdon, UK: Routledge, 2007).

22. See the Magna "Employee's Charter" for Canada/USA at the company's website: http://www.magna.com/for-employees/employee's-charter/.

23. Godard, supra note 7, at 15.

24. D. Doorey, "A Model of Responsive Workplace Law" (2012) 50:1 *Osgoode Hall Law Journal* 47, at 67-76; and J. Budd and D. Bhave, "The Employment Relationship," in A. Wilkinson, T. Redman, S. Snell, and N. Bacon, eds., *Sage Handbook of Human Resource Management* (London: Sage, 2010), at 64.

25. The managerialist view that unionization reflects a failure of progressive management practices is demonstrated in the brochure for a seminar on union avoidance prepared by the Human Resources Professionals Association (HRPA) found at this link: http://www.hrpa.ca/ProfessionalDevelopment/Pages/OnDemandWebinarProtectingYourOrganizationfromUnionization.aspx. See also M. Belcourt, G. Bohlander, and S. Snell, *Managing Human Resources*, 6th ed. (Toronto: Nelson Education, 2010), at 556.

26. Doorey, supra note 24.

27. Kaufman, "Economic Analysis," supra note 9; and P. Weiler, *Governing the Workplace: The Future of Labor and Employment Law* (Cambridge: Harvard University Press, 1990).

28. J. Budd, R. Gomez, and N. Meltz, "Why a Balance Is Best: The Pluralist Industrial Relations Paradigm of Balancing Competing Interests," in B. Kaufman, ed., *Theoretical Perspectives on Work and the Employment Relationship* (Champaign, IL: Industrial Relations Research Association, 2004); N. Meltz, "Industrial Relations: Balancing Efficiency and Equity," in J. Barbash and K. Barbash, eds., *Theories and Concepts in Comparative Industrial Relations* (Columbia, SC: University of South Carolina Press, 1989); H. Collins, *Employment Law*, 2nd ed. (Oxford: Oxford University Press, 2010), at 5; and J. Budd, *Employment with a Human Face: Balancing Efficiency, Equity, and Voice* (Ithaca, NY: ILR Press, 2004). Foundational works in industrial pluralism include J. Commons, *Industrial Goodwill* (New York: McGraw-Hill, 1919); S. Webb and B. Webb, *Industrial Democracy* (London: Longmans, Green, 1897); and J. Commons, *A*

History of Labor in the United States (New York: Macmillan, 1919). In Canada, a leading voice in industrial pluralism was Harry Arthurs. See especially H. Arthurs, "Understanding Labour Law: The Debate over 'Industrial Pluralism'" (1985) 38 *Current Legal Problems* 83.

29. See the argument by Professor Robert Reich (University of California, Berkeley), who was formerly US secretary of labor, on how unions and collective bargaining promote a healthy economy in "Why We Need Stronger Unions, and How to Get Them," *Robert Reich* (blog), January 27, 2009, http://robertreich.org/post/257310148.

30. International Labour Organization, *World of Work 2008: Income Inequalities in the Age of Financial Globalization* (Geneva: ILO, 2008), at 83. See also the discussion in the Canadian context by M. Lynk, "Labour Law and the New Inequality" (2009) 15 *Just Labour* 125, http://www.justlabour.yorku.ca/volume15/pdfs/11_lynk_press.pdf.

31. For a discussion of the rise and fall of industrial pluralism in Canada, see L. Panitch and D. Schwartz, *From Consent to Coercion: The Assault on Trade Union Freedoms*, 3rd ed. (Aurora, ON: Garamond, 2003); and H. Arthurs, "Landscape and Memory: Labour Law, Legal Pluralism, and Globalization," in T. Wilthagen, ed., *Advancing Theory in Labour Law and Industrial Relations in a Global Context* (Amsterdam: Koninklijke Nederlandse Akademie van Wetenschappen, 1998), at 21.

32. Statistics Canada, "Table 282-0078—Labour Force Survey Estimates (LFS), Employees by Union Coverage, North American Industry Classification System (NAICS), Sex and Age Group, Annual (Persons)," accessed November 12, 2014, http://www5.statcan.gc.ca/cansim/a26?lang=eng&retrLang=eng&id=2820078&pattern=2820078&csid.

33. A. Forrest, "Organizing Eaton's: Do the Old Laws Still Work?" (1988) 8 *Windsor Yearbook of Access to Justice* 190.

34. Godard, supra note 7, at 15. Godard labels this perspective "liberal-reformist."

35. J. Fudge, "Reconceiving Employment Standards Legislation: Labour Law's Little Sister and the Feminization of Labour" (1991) 7 *Journal of Law and Social Policy* 73, at 77. See also D. Beatty, "Ideology, Politics, and Unionism," in K. Swan and K. Swinton, eds., *Studies in Labour Law* (Toronto: Butterworths, 1983), 299; J. Conaghan, "The Invisibility of Women in Labour Law: Gender Neutrality in Model-Building" (1986) 14 *International Journal of Sociology of Law* 377; and J. White, *Sisters in Solidarity: Women and Unions in Canada* (Toronto: Thompson Educational, 1993).

36. In 2011, 52 percent of union members in Canada were women. See D. Doorey, "Nice Interactive Chart of Canadian Unionization Statistics, 2011," *Law of Work* (blog), accessed July 24, 2014, http://lawofwork.ca/?p=4906.

37. See the collected works in L. Vosko, ed., *Precarious Employment: Understanding Labour Market Insecurity in Canada* (Montreal: McGill-Queen's University Press, 2006); and Law Commission of Ontario, *Vulnerable Workers and Precarious Work* (Toronto: Law Commission of Ontario, 2012), http://www.lco-cdo.org/en/vulnerable-workers.

38. M. Thomas, *Regulating Flexibility: The Political Economy of Employment Standards* (Montreal: McGill-Queen's University Press, 2009).

39. Recent literature from the critical reformist perspective includes C. Cranford, T. Das Gupta, D. Ladd, and L. Vosko, "Thinking Through Community Unionism," in Vosko, supra note 37, at 353; J. Fudge, "After Industrial Citizenship: Market Citizenship or Citizenship at Work?" (2005) 60 *Relations Industrielles* 631; K. Rittich, "Feminization and Contingency: Regulating the Stakes of Work for Women," in J. Conaghan, R.M. Fischl, and K. Klare, eds., Labour Law in an Era of Globalization: Transformative Practices and Possibilities (Oxford: Oxford University Press, 2002); K. Stone, "Rethinking Labour Law: Employment Protection for Boundaryless Workers," in G. Davidov and B. Langille, eds., *Boundaries and Frontiers of Labour Law* (Oxford: Hart, 2006), at 155; and A. Blackett, "Emancipation in the Idea of Labour Law," in G. Davidov and B. Langille, *The Idea of Labour Law* (Oxford: Oxford University Press, 2011).

40. See, e.g., E. Tucker, "Reforming Labour Law: Can We Escape Labour Law's Recurring Regulatory Dilemmas?" (2010) 39:2 *Industrial Law Journal* 99; M. Lebowitz, *Beyond Capital*, 2nd ed. (New York: Palgrave Macmillan, 2003); R. Hyman, "Pluralism, Procedural Consensus, and Collective Bargaining" (1978) 16 *British Journal of Industrial Relations* 16; and H. Braverman, *Labour and Monopoly Capital: The Degradation of Work in the Twentieth Century* (New York: Monthly Review Press, 1974).

41. Tucker, supra note 40, at 108.

42. Tucker, supra note 40, at 113-15. See also, Godard, supra note 7, at 16-17; and R. Hyman, *Industrial Relations: A Marxist Introduction* (London: Macmillan, 1975).

43. Godard, supra note 7. See also Budd, Gomez, Meltz, supra note 28.

44. On the sporadic role of the Communist Party in Canadian labour history, see J. Fudge and E. Tucker, *Labour Before the Law: The Regulation of Workers' Collective Action in Canada, 1900-1948* (Don Mills, ON: Oxford University Press, 2001); and D. Morton, *Working People*, 5th ed. (Montreal and Kingston: McGill-Queen's University Press, 2007).

45. See, e.g., T. Eagleton, *Why Marx Was Right* (New Haven, CT: Yale University Press, 2011); and S. Jeffries, "Why Marxism Is on the Rise Again," *Guardian*, July 4, 2012, http://www.theguardian.com/world/2012/jul/04/the-return-of-marxism.

Selected Cases: Part I

Cases with boldface page numbers appear as Case Law Highlights.

PART II

Industrial Relations and the Collective Bargaining Regime

CHAPTER 5

Mapping the Collective Bargaining Regime

LEARNING OBJECTIVES

After reading this chapter, students will be able to:

- Describe how the common law regime treats collective worker activities, including unionization, collective bargaining, and strikes.
- Describe how early collective bargaining laws modified the common law to both create new rights for workers to act collectively and control unions and employee associations.
- Explain the key legal institutions within the collective bargaining regime and the role they play.
- Identify trends in the composition and quantity of Canadian workers who are governed by the collective bargaining regime.
- Discuss the decline in private sector unionization in Canada and the possible causes of this decline.

CHAPTER OUTLINE

I. Introduction

Mandatory minimum statutory standards such as those explored in the chapters on the regulatory regime that appear in the companion volume to this text[1] are one way governments use law to protect vulnerable workers. Regulatory standards limit freedom of contract in pursuit of the public policy objective of improving working conditions and encouraging wider income distribution. Another method of protecting workers from the harshness of market forces is to "[turn] up the bargaining power valve on the employees' side,"[2] to borrow the words of Professor Brian Langille (University of Toronto), so that employees are negotiating on a more level playing field. This is a principal goal of the collective bargaining regime, which is explored in the chapters that follow.

The collective bargaining regime is concerned with the various legal rules—tort, contract, and legislative—that govern employment relations once workers leave the common law regime of individual employment contracts for **collective bargaining**. This chapter begins with a quick discussion of the common law's historical suspicion of, and hostility toward, collective worker action such as unionization, collective bargaining, and **strikes**. Over time, Canadian governments responded to the common law model by passing laws to further restrain union activity—and

---

collective bargaining: Negotiations between an association of employees and an employer or association of employers aimed at reaching a collective agreement.

strike: Legislation can assign a particular definition to the word *strike*. In Canada, strikes are usually defined to include both (1) a collective refusal by employees to perform work, and (2) a deliberate collective slowdown by workers designed to restrict the output of an employer (commonly known as a *work to rule*).

sometimes to promote unionization and collective bargaining. This chapter introduces some key concepts, processes, and institutions that we need to understand as we move forward in our exploration of Canadian collective bargaining law.

II. A Brief Overview of the Common Law's Treatment of Collective Worker Activities

We learned in the companion volume that the regulatory regime is the government's response to perceived inadequacies with the manner in which the common law regime governs the work relationship. Similarly, to fully understand the laws that inhabit the collective bargaining regime, we need to first observe how the common law deals with collective worker activities. Modern collective bargaining legislation operates in the shadow of common law rules of tort and contract that were often used to crush early attempts by workers to join unions and pressure their employers to engage in collective bargaining.

In the common law, workers may join and form associations, just like you or I can join or form book clubs or a Work Law Students Association. No tort or other common law doctrine prohibits people from associating and forming collective groups. However, the common law does have quite a lot to say about how people *behave when they are acting in association*. It is suspicious of collective action. For example, the right of workers to form and join an employee association does not translate into a common law right of workers to collectively threaten or pressure an employer with economic harm if the employer does not accede to the association's demands or requests. We learned in Chapter 1 in the companion volume that in the common law, freedom of contract reigns supreme, and an employer is free to negotiate—or to refuse to negotiate—with anyone it pleases. Until the mid-1940s, employees could join unions, but their employers could lawfully refuse to recognize and bargain with those unions.[3]

Before Canadian governments legislated a process for union recognition, the only way employees could force an unwilling employer to recognize a union was to engage in what was often an unlawful strike. These work stoppages are known as **recognition strikes**, and some of Canada's most important (and sometimes violent) labour clashes began in this way, before any statutory right to collective bargaining existed. For example, during a recognition strike at Estevan, Saskatchewan in 1931, the RCMP shot and killed three strikers, and it was a 1937 recognition strike at General Motors in Oshawa that produced a landmark collective agreement between the giant automaker and the American-based United Auto Workers Union (see Chapter 6).[4]

Prior to collective bargaining legislation, common law judges treated strikes or threats to strike as torts of **conspiracy to injure** or **intimidation**.[5] Picketing by workers designed to dissuade people from entering a business during a labour dispute could violate torts such as **nuisance**, intimidation, or **inducing breach of contract**.[6] Union organizers who entered employer property to speak with workers were trespassing, and if they encouraged workers to strike and set up picket lines, they could be committing any number of torts (as well as conspiracy or "watching

---

recognition strike: A strike by workers with the aim of pressuring an employer to recognize and bargain with a union on behalf of the employees.

conspiracy to injure: A tort that involves two or more people acting in combination with the intention of causing harm to another party and actually causing that harm.

intimidation: A tort that involves an attempt to coerce another person to do something, or to refrain from doing something they are entitled to do, by the threat of an unlawful act.

nuisance: A tort in which the activities of one person unreasonably interfere with the use or enjoyment of the property of another person.

inducing breach of contract: A tort that involves wrongful acts by a third party that are intended to cause a breach of contract between two other parties.

and besetting" under the *Criminal Code*).[7] A tort or criminal finding could result in the court issuing an **interlocutory injunction** order requiring the activity in question to cease immediately, and a damages award imposed against workers or union leaders. The story of how common law judges used the "labour injunction" to control and restrict collective worker activities is among the most fascinating in all of law.[8]

The employment contracts of employees who strike can also be terminated in the common law model, possibly for cause (Chapter 14 in the companion volume) but certainly with notice (Chapter 13 in the companion volume) because it is an expressed or implied term in employment contracts that employees report to work when scheduled and respect the employer's authority (Chapter 9 in the companion volume).[9] Until protective collective bargaining legislation was passed in the mid-1940s, employees could also be denied employment for joining a union or speaking favourably about unionization, and employers could include terms in employment contracts indicating that support for a union was grounds for summary dismissal (known as **yellow dog contracts**).[10]

This very quick overview of how the common law regime treats collective worker activities is sufficient to demonstrate that, historically, judges have not been sympathetic to unions or collective bargaining, as Professor Harry Arthurs (York University) explained:

> Anglo-Canadian courts have been dealing with issues of individual and collective labour law for at least two hundred years. During that entire period, the courts virtually never, not on any given occasion, created a right which might be asserted by or on behalf of working people.[11]

However, this hostile common law legal environment did not prevent hundreds of thousands of Canadian workers from joining unions in pursuit of collective bargaining in the late 19th and early 20th centuries, as depicted in Figure 5.1. Notice in Figure 5.1 how unionization levels spiked during both World Wars and then again after 1944, the year the first comprehensive collective bargaining legislation was enacted.

Over time, governments intervened in the common law model in a variety of ways and for a variety of policy purposes. Sometimes the intervention was aimed at further controlling unions and workers when the arsenal of torts and hostile contract and criminal law doctrines proved ineffective at stopping collective worker activities that threatened commerce. For example, legislation in the early 20th century sought to reduce strikes by forcing unions and employers to engage in **conciliation** and then wait out a "cooling off" period before a strike could commence.[12] Some legislation was enacted to protect unions and their members from the harshness of common law rules. For example, the Ontario *Rights of Labour Act* excluded union members from liability for the tort of conspiracy when they acted in combination in furtherance of a lawful labour dispute, and in 1932 the *Criminal Code* was amended to remove peaceful labour picketing from the definition of watching and besetting.[13]

But the most dramatic legislative change came in the mid-1940s, when the federal government introduced the legislative model that still acts as the template for collective bargaining across Canada today. The legislation, passed by the federal government in 1944, was known as the *Wartime Labour Relations Order*, or Order in Council **PC 1003**.[14] This legislation, the details of which

---

interlocutory injunction: A temporary court order prohibiting conduct that is potentially unlawful until a decision is released by the court on whether the conduct is unlawful.

yellow dog contract: A contract or contract term that requires an employee to refrain from joining a union or permits termination for cause of an employee who joins a union.

conciliation: A form of mediation in which a neutral collective bargaining expert attempts to assist an employee association (e.g., a union) and an employer or employer association in reaching a collective agreement.

PC 1003: Granted workers collective bargaining rights, including protection from anti-union discrimination by employers and a limited protected right to strike, and imposed on employers a legal "duty to bargain" with unions representing a majority of workers.

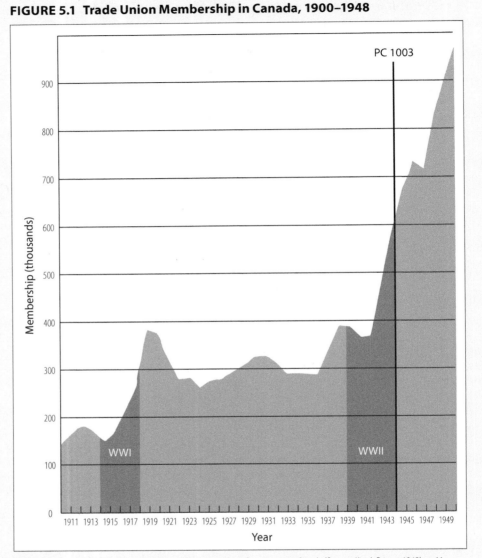

FIGURE 5.1 Trade Union Membership in Canada, 1900–1948

Source: Department of Labour. *Thirty-sixth Annual Report on Labour Organization in Canada* (Ottawa: King's Printer, 1948), at 11.

were adopted by provincial governments in similar legislation after the war, ushered in a new statutory scheme that substantially reduced the reach of the common law over the unionization process, collective bargaining, and labour conflict. Box 5.1 describes the important ways in which the legislative model first created by PC 1003 and later adopted across Canada changed how unionization and collective bargaining was treated under Canadian law.

As we learned in Chapter 19 in the companion volume, jurisdiction over the employment relationship is primarily a provincial matter under the Canadian Constitution, and, therefore, each province in Canada has its own collective bargaining legislation. While there are differences in this legislation across provinces, there is enough similarity that it is common to hear reference to the "Canadian model" of collective bargaining law. The main features of that "model" are those originally mapped out in PC 1003 in 1944.

BOX 5.1 » TALKING WORK LAW

The Wartime Labour Relations Order

The *Wartime Labour Relations Order* (PC 1003), enacted by the federal government in 1944, established a statutory scheme that continues to shape modern collective bargaining legislation. As Table 5.1 demonstrates, the new legal rights introduced by PC 1003 fundamentally altered the legal environment that had regulated collective worker activity under the common law regime.

TABLE 5.1 The Impact of Collective Bargaining Legislation

Legal Rights	Treatment of Collective Worker Activities in the Common Law Regime Before PC 1003	Rules in Collective Bargaining Statutes Beginning in the Mid-1940s
Right to join a union	• Employees could join worker associations. However, an employer could refuse to hire or could terminate a worker who did so, because freedom of contract includes the right to choose with whom you contract.	• PC 1003 introduced a statutory "right to be a member of a trade union or employees' organization" that prohibited employers from refusing employment to, terminating, or discriminating against workers because of their support for collective bargaining. (See Chapter 8.)
Right to collective bargaining	• An employer had no obligation to recognize or bargain with a union that claimed to represent its employees.	• PC 1003 introduced a statutory duty to bargain "in good faith," provided that the union had been "certified" by the government. Certification occurs once a union has satisfied the requirements in the collective bargaining statute, which include proving that a majority of employees wish to be unionized. (See Chapter 10.)
Right to strike and lockout	• A worker could refuse any offer of employment and refuse to work until an acceptable offer was made and accepted. However, an employer could refuse to hire any person who did not accept its offer. • An individual worker who refused to work during the term of an employment contract either had quit or had probably given the employer cause for summary dismissal without notice (see Chapter 14 in the companion volume). • If a group of workers together refused to work for an employer, they were likely engaged in torts such as "conspiracy to injure" the employer or "intimidation." • Organizers of a strike were likely also engaged in "conspiracy to injure" or "intimidation," and could also be committing the tort of "inducing breach of contract." • An employer that "locked out" an employee—refusing to allow an employee to come to work—was committing a fundamental breach of contract that the employee could accept as a constructive dismissal. (See Chapter 15 in the companion volume.)	• PC 1003 introduced a limited, protected right to strike that prohibits an employer from terminating an employee for the reason only that he or she is engaged in a strike that the collective bargaining statute defines as lawful. A lawful strike is one that occurs only after a series of statutorily defined preconditions are satisfied. • Recognition strikes, strikes by non-union workers, and strikes while a collective agreement was in effect remained unlawful. • Employers have a limited right to lock out workers as a bargaining tactic, provided that a series of statutorily defined preconditions are satisfied. (See Chapter 11.)
Right to picket in support of a strike	• Depending on the manner in which it was conducted, picketing could be treated as a tort (i.e., nuisance, inducing breach of contract).	• Picketing was not directly addressed in PC 1003. However, by the mid-1940s peaceful picketing support of a strike was no longer criminal. Picketing could still be tortious, depending on how it was conducted.

III. Labour Relations Legislation, the Outputs of the Collective Bargaining Regime, and Legal Institutions

PC 1003 developed a legislative model that fundamentally altered existing laws governing unions and the processes of collective bargaining, **collective agreements**, strikes, and **lockouts**. Today, those laws have been consolidated in federal and provincial labour relations legislation, such as the federal *Canada Labour Code*, the Ontario *Labour Relations Act*, and the British Columbia *Labour Relations Code*.[15] **Labour relations boards** are responsible for interpreting and enforcing labour relations legislation. We will explore the key elements of labour relations legislation in depth in the chapters that follow.

The "outputs" (or legal rules) produced within the collective bargaining regime include more than just those found in labour relations legislation. For example, unions and employers (sometimes through employer associations) bargain their own legal rules that appear in collective agreements.[16] Disputes about the application and interpretation of collective agreements are resolved by **labour arbitrators**, and a rich body of Canadian labour arbitration jurisprudence exists (see Chapters 13 and 14). Judges continue to play an important, albeit more limited role in the collective bargaining regime than in the common law regime, particularly in the governance of picketing and strikes, where the old tort laws remain important for reasons explained in Chapter 11, and through **judicial review** of the decisions of arbitrators and labour relations boards. Table 5.2 provides a quick overview of the legal institutions responsible for enforcing the legal rules of the collective bargaining regime.

TABLE 5.2 Legal Institutions in the Collective Bargaining Regime

Legal Institution	Primary Role in the Collective Bargaining Regime
Labour Relations Boards	• To interpret and enforce labour relations legislation enacted by governments
Labour Arbitrators	• To interpret and enforce collective agreements negotiated by unions and employers
Courts	• To enforce tort law as applied to collective activities • To provide judicial review of decisions of arbitrators and labour relations boards

IV. A Description of Canadian Employees Governed by the Collective Bargaining Regime

Once employees unionize, they enter a new legal world. The common law rules of employment contracts explored in the companion volume mostly fall by the wayside. For example, common law doctrines like constructive dismissal, repudiation of contract, and wrongful dismissal—

---

collective agreement: A contract between an employer (or employers) and a trade union (or trade unions) that sets out the conditions of employment for a group of employees.

lockout: A tactic whereby an employer refuses to permit employees to report to work and to pay the employees in order to apply pressure on the employees and their union in collective bargaining.

labour relations boards: Expert administrative tribunals responsible for enforcing and interpreting labour relations legislation.

labour arbitrator: An individual or a three-person expert arbitration panel appointed to decide disputes over the application and interpretation of collective agreements.

judicial review: The process through which a decision of an expert administrative tribunal is appealed to a court on the basis that the tribunal exceeded its authority (or jurisdiction) as defined in the statute that created it or that the tribunal's decision was wrong. How much deference a court must give to the expert tribunal's decision is a complex question that is considered in a field of law known as *administrative law*.

crucial legal concepts within the common law regime—no longer apply to an employee governed by a collective agreement and represented by a union. Unionized employees are represented by their union in dealings with the employer, and the collective agreement that the union bargains on behalf of employees supplants any pre-existing individual employment contracts. Therefore, when employees decide to switch from the common law regime to the collective bargaining regime by joining a union, they are electing to fundamentally alter the legal framework that governs their relationship with the employer.

In 2014, approximately 4.6 million Canadian employees had their terms of employment governed by a collective agreement rather than an individual employment contract.[17] That number translates into a **union coverage rate**—the percentage of employees covered by a collective agreement—of 31.5 percent of Canadian employees (down from 34.5 percent in 1998).[18] Table 5.3 presents important details about who Canadian unionized workers are.

TABLE 5.3 Union Representation in Canada, 2011 and 2014

Total union coverage in Canada (2014):	31.5%
Men in unions (2014):	27%
Women in unions (2014):	32%
Union coverage by sector (2011)	
Public sector:	74.7%
Private sector:	17.4%
Union coverage by age (2011)	
15–24:	16.4%
25–44:	32.1%
45–54:	38.3%
55 and older:	36.2%
Union coverage by employment status (2011)	
Full-time:	33.3%
Part-time:	25.1%
Union coverage by workplace size (2011)	
Under 20 employees	14.5%
20–99 employees	32.3%
100–500 employees	42.8%
Over 500 employees	56%

Sources: Employment and Social Development Canada, *Union Coverage in Canada—2014* (Ottawa: Her Majesty the Queen in Right of Canada, 2015), publications.gc.ca/collections/collection_2015/edsc-esdc/Em5-1-2014-eng.pdf; Statistics Canada, *Union Membership and Coverage by Selected Characteristics, 2011*, http://www.statcan.gc.ca/pub/75-001-x/2011004/tables-tableaux/11579/tbl01-eng.htm; and Statistics Canada, "Unionization Rates Falling," http://www.statcan.gc.ca/pub/11-630-x/11-630-x2015005-eng.htm.

union coverage rate: The percentage of employees whose employment conditions are governed by a collective agreement bargained on their behalf by a union.

The union coverage rate in the public sector is more than four times that in the private sector.[19] Publicly provided services such as education, health care, and public administration are very highly unionized, whereas privately provided services such as retail, food services, hospitality, and financial services have very low collective agreement coverage rates. Large workplaces are far more likely to be unionized than small workplaces. There is also a substantial difference in union coverage across provinces. In 2015, Alberta had the lowest union coverage at only 23.5 percent, while Quebec (39.4 percent) and Newfoundland and Labrador (37.3 percent) had the highest (see Table 5.4). Since 2004, a greater percentage of women have been in unions than men.[20] The typical unionized employee in Canada today is a woman working in public services, a sharp contrast to earlier eras in which union members were overwhelmingly male and employed in sectors such as manufacturing, mining, construction, and forestry.[21]

TABLE 5.4 Union Coverage by Province, 2014–2015

	Workers Covered (000's)		Union Coverage (Percentage)	
	2014	**2015**	**2014**	**2015**
Canada	4,587.0	4,649.8	30.4	30.6
Newfoundland and Labrador	81.4	79.8	37.8	37.3
Prince Edward Island	20.3	21.3	32.3	34.1
Nova Scotia	119.3	120.5	30.8	30.9
New Brunswick	88.8	90.8	28.6	29.3
Quebec	1,376.6	1,392.8	39.3	39.4
Ontario	1,572.4	1,564.4	27.0	26.8
Manitoba	192.4	197.4	35.4	35.9
Saskatchewan	153.4	155.9	33.3	33.2
Alberta	418.5	452.9	22.1	23.5
British Columbia	564.0	574.1	30.0	30.3

Source: Statistics Canada, Labour Force Survey (CANSIM, table 282-0220). See Employment and Social Development Canada, *Overview of Collective Bargaining in Canada* (Ottawa: Her Majesty the Queen in Right of Canada, 2016), https://www.canada.ca/en/employment-social-development/services/collective-bargaining/reports/collective-bargaining.html.

Since the 1980s, unionization in the private sector has experienced a steady decline. This is due to a variety of forces that are discussed in Box 5.2. Whether the fall in private sector union representation is a good or bad trend is a matter of *perspective* (see Chapter 4). However, the question of whether governments should be reforming our collective bargaining laws with the aim of expanding private sector collective bargaining has been hotly debated in political elections and policy debates for decades. We will explore these debates in the rest of this text.

BOX 5.2 » TALKING WORK LAW

The Decline in Private Sector Union Coverage

While unionization in the public sector has held strong (nearly 75 percent of public sector employees are unionized), since the 1980s there has been a slow and steady decline in the percentage of private sector workers represented by unions in Canada, as demonstrated in Figures 5.2 and 5.3. Private sector unionization has decreased from about 26 percent in 1984 to about 17 percent today. Changes to collective bargaining laws designed to discourage the spread of collective bargaining provide part of the explanation for this decline. Provincial governments inspired by the *neoclassical perspective* (see Chapter 4) introduced laws that made it more difficult for unions to organize new workers.* However, legislative changes within the collective bargaining regime explain only part of the decline in private sector union representation.

Structural changes in the Canadian economy—in the *economic and market subsystem* (Chapter 3)—over the past four decades are an important part of the story as well. "Structural changes" include *shifts away from heavily unionized* sectors toward sectors with low union representation levels, as well as *changes within sectors*, from unionized workplaces to non-

FIGURE 5.2 Union Membership in Canada of Individuals Aged 17–64, 1981–2014

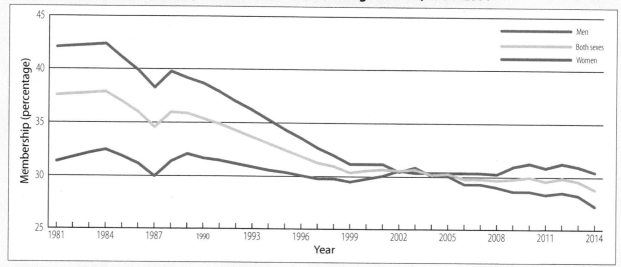

Sources: Statistics Canada, Labour Force Survey, 1997 to 2014; Labour Market Activity Survey, 1986 to 1990; Survey of Union Membership, 1984; Survey of Work History, 1981. http://www.statcan.gc.ca/pub/11-630-x/11-630-x2015005-eng.htm.

FIGURE 5.3 Union Density in Canada, 1997–2015

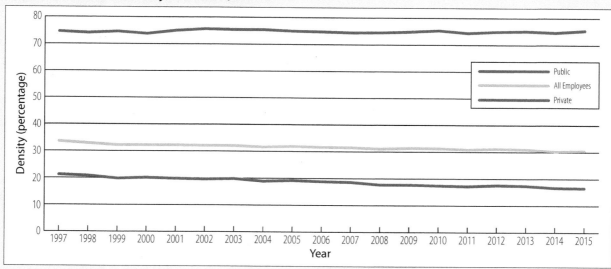

Source: Armine Yalnizyan, Senior Economist, Canadian Centre for Policy Alternatives, based on Statistics Canada data from CANSIM 282-0078.

unionized workplaces.[†] For example, since the 1980s, Canada has lost thousands of unionized manufacturing jobs, aided by "free trade" agreements that encouraged corporations to shed Canadian manufacturing jobs in favour of lower wage and regulation jurisdictions (see Chapter 35 in the companion volume). Although new manufacturing jobs were created, fewer of them have been unionized. The unionization rate in manufacturing fell from 31.2 percent in 1999 to 24.4 percent in 2012.[‡] Unionization levels also fell in other traditionally heavily unionized sectors, including forestry, mining, and construction.[§]

There has also been a shift in the composition of the Canadian workforce from traditionally heavily unionized sectors of the economy (manufacturing especially) toward less unionized sectors (private services) and public sector employment (which is heavily unionized).[#] Between 1984 and 2011, the share of Canadians employed in manufacturing declined from 16.9 percent to 9.2 percent. At the same time, employment in public services such as health care grew substantially. Many of those public sector jobs are unionized, which explains why the public sector unionization rate has remained strong. However, as the labour force trends away from industries with traditionally high levels of union penetration, union representation levels decline.

[*]   S. Slinn, "An Empirical Analysis of the Effects of the Change from Card-Check to Mandatory Vote Certification" (2004) 11 *Canadian Labour and Employment Law Journal* 259; and C. Riddell, "Union Certification Success Under Voting Versus Card-Check Procedures: Evidence from British Columbia, 1978-1998" (2004) 57 *Industrial and Labor Relations Review* 493.

[†]   A. Jackson and S. Schetagne, "Solidarity Forever? An Analysis of Changes in Union Density" (Summer 2004) 4 *Just Labour* 53, at 58, http://www.yorku.ca/julabour/volume4/Jacksonschetagne.pdf.

[‡]   D. Galarneau and T. Sohn, *Long Term Trends in Unionization* (Ottawa: Statistics Canada, 2012), http://www.statcan.gc.ca/pub/75-006-x/2013001/article/11878-eng.htm#n5; and G. Murray, "Unions: Membership, Structures, Actions, and Challenges" in M. Gunderson and D. Taras, eds., *Canadian Labour and Employment Relations*, 6th ed. (Toronto: Pearson, 2009), 74 at 83.

[§]   Ibid.; and R. Morissette, G. Schellenberg, and A. Johnson, "Diverging Trends in Unionization" (2005) 6:4 *Perspectives on Labour and Income*, http://www.statcan.gc.ca/pub/75-001-x/10405/7827-eng.htm.

[#]   D. Galarneau and T. Sohn, *Long Term Trends in Unionization* (Ottawa: Statistics Canada, 2012), http://www.statcan.gc.ca/pub/75-006-x/2013001/article/11878-eng.htm#n5; G. Murray, "Unions: Membership, Structures, Actions, and Challenges" in M. Gunderson and D. Taras, eds., *Canadian Labour and Employment Relations*, 6th ed. (Toronto: Pearson, 2009), 74 at 83; and Statistics Canada, "Portrait of Canada's Labour Force," 2011, https://www12.statcan.gc.ca/nhs-enm/2011/as-sa/99-012-x/99-012-x2011002-eng.cfm#wb-cont.

V. Chapter Summary

This chapter explained how the laws that inhabit the collective bargaining regime should be understood against a backdrop of how collective worker activities have been treated within the common law regime. Many of the legal rules we will explore in the chapters that follow represent attempts to alter the common law approach.

Approximately one-third of Canadian employees have their terms and conditions of employment set through collective bargaining and collective agreements rather than individual employment contracts. Union representation is much higher in the public sector than in the private sector.

QUESTIONS AND ISSUES FOR DISCUSSION

1. Describe how collective bargaining legislation created new legal rights to protect workers who joined unions that did not exist in the common law regime.
2. Is there a common law "right to strike"?
3. Identify the three main legal institutions within the collective bargaining regime and explain what role they play.
4. Using the statistics from Table 5.3, describe the characteristics of a typical employee covered by a collective agreement in Canada. Is that description consistent with your beliefs about what a typical union member looked like before you read this chapter?
5. What factors have contributed to the overall decline in union coverage over the past 30 years in Canada?

EXERCISES

1. Go to a search engine such as Google. Type "Canada" and "the decline of unions."
2. Select a news article from the search results, read it carefully, and then answer the following questions:
   a. What is the story about?
   b. Does the story cite any statistics about union representation in Canada?
   c. Does the story argue or propose that the decline of unions is a positive or negative development for the Canadian economy? For workers? For employers?
   d. Does the article provide any reasons why unions are in decline?
   e. Does the article describe any legal rules that either have contributed to the decline of unions in Canada or could help rejuvenate unions in Canada's private sector?

UPDATES

Go to emond.ca/lawofworkircb for links to news, author's blog posts, content updates, and other information related to the chapters in this text.

NOTES AND REFERENCES

1 D.J. Doorey, *The Law of Work: Common Law and the Regulation of Work* (Toronto: Emond Montgomery, 2016).

2 B. Langille, "Labour Policy in Canada—New Platform, New Paradigm" (2002) 28 *Canadian Public Policy* 133.

3 For a discussion of the common law's treatment of union organizing and collective bargaining, see B. Langille, "The Freedom of Association Mess: How We Got into It and How We Can Get out of It" (2009) 54 *McGill Law Journal* 177, at 188-93.

4 See J. Fudge and E. Tucker, *Labour Before the Law: The Regulation of Workers' Collective Action in Canada, 1900–1948* (Don Mills, ON: Oxford University Press, 2001), at 168-69; and S. Hanson, "Estevan 1931," in I. Aella, ed., *On Strike: Six Key Labour Struggles in Canada, 1919–1949* (Toronto: Lorimer, 1974), 33.

5 In *Quinn v. Leathem*, [1901] AC 495 (HL), the tort of conspiracy to injure was decided; in *Rookes v. Barnard*, [1964] AC 1129, the tort of intimidation was committed when workers threatened to strike (i.e., to breach their employment contracts).

6 *J. T. Stratford & Sons Ltd. v. Lindley*, [1965] AC 269. For a discussion of the application of torts to restrict collective worker activities, see Labour Law Casebook Group, *Labour and Employment Law: Cases, Materials, and Commentary*, 8th ed. (Toronto: Irwin, 2011), at 418-22; Fudge and Tucker, supra note 3; and H. Arthurs, "Labour Law—Secondary Picketing—Per Se Illegality—Public Policy" (1963) 41 *Canadian Bar Review* 573.

7 *Criminal Code*, RSC 1985, c. C-46; and Fudge and Tucker, supra note 4, at 25.

8 H. Arthurs, "Tort Liability for Strikes in Canada: Some Problems of Judicial Workmanship" (1960) 38 *Canadian Bar Review* 346; B. Laskin, "Picketing: A Comparison of Certain Canadian and American Doctrines" (1937) 15 *Canadian Bar Review* 10; and K. Wedderburn, "Strike Law and the Labour Injunction: The British Experience, 1850–1966," in A.W.R. Carrothers, ed., *Report of a Study on the Labour Injunction in Ontario*, vol. 2 (Toronto: Ontario Department of Labour, 1966).

9 *McGavin Toastmaster Ltd. v. Ainscough*, [1976] 1 SCR 718, at 8-9.

10 See Fudge and Tucker, supra note 4, at 2.

11 H. Arthurs, "The Right to Golf: Reflections on the Future of Workers, Unions, and the Rest of Us Under the Charter" (1988) 13 *Queen's Law Journal* 17, at 18.

12 See, e.g., the *Industrial Disputes Investigation Act*, SC 1907, c. 20.

13 That legislation remains in effect as the *Rights of Labour Act*, RSO 1990, c. R33, s. 3(1). On the *Criminal Code* amendments, see Fudge and Tucker, supra note 4, at 165-66.

14 *Wartime Labour Relations Order* PC 1003 is available at http://socserv.mcmaster.ca/oldlabourstudies/onlinelearning/article.php?id=503.

15 *Canada Labour Code*, RSC 1985, c. L-2; *Labour Relations Act*, 1995, SO 1995, c. 1, Sch. A; and *Labour Relations Code*, RSBC 1996, c. 244.

16 Unions are the most common type of employee association. However, many workers are also represented in some manner by non-union forms of employee

associations. For example, employees at WestJet Airlines are represented by a company-sponsored employee association known as Proactive Communication Team (PACT), which negotiates agreements with the employer. Non-union employee associations are usually not covered by labour relations legislation applicable to unions, and employees in those associations continue to be governed by the common law regime's rules of employment contracts. See D. Doorey, "Union Drive at WestJet Highlights Current Tensions in Labour Policy" *Globe and Mail*, August 7, 2015, http://www.theglobeandmail.com/report-on-business/rob-commentary/union-drive-at-westjet-highlights-current-tensions-in-labour-policy/article25865172/; and D. Taras and B. Kaufman, "Non-Union Employee Representation in North America: Diversity, Controversy, and Uncertain Future" (2006) 37:5 *Industrial Relations Journal* 513.

17   Employment and Social Development Canada, *Overview of Collective Bargaining in Canada* (Ottawa: Her Majesty the Queen in Right of Canada, 2016), http://www.labour.gc.ca/eng/resources/info/publications/collective_bargaining/ocba2015-eng.pdf.

18   Employment and Social Development Canada, *Union Coverage in Canada—2014* (Ottawa: Her Majesty the Queen in Right of Canada, 2015), publications.gc.ca/collections/collection_2015/edsc-esdc/Em5-1-2014-eng.pdf. Statisticians use two measures of collective bargaining coverage: (1) "union density" is the percentage of employees who are members of unions; and (2) "union coverage" is the percentage of employees who are covered by a collective agreement. We use the latter in this text. In practice in Canada, the two measures are often close (although not identical). For example, in 2014 the union coverage rate was 31.5 percent (see *Union Coverage in Canada—2014*) compared with a union density rate of 30.4 percent.

19   Statistics Canada, "Unionization Rates Falling," http://www.statcan.gc.ca/pub/11-630-x/11-630-x2015005-eng.htm.

20   Ibid.

21   See A. Jackson and S. Schetagne, "Solidarity Forever? An Analysis of Changes in Union Density" (Summer 2004) 4 *Just Labour* 53, http://www.yorku.ca/julabour/volume4/Jacksonschetagne.pdf for a discussion of changes in representation over time. See also, "How Canadian Unions Are Changing," *CBC News*, March 1, 2012, http://www.cbc.ca/news2/interactives/labour-demographics/.

CHAPTER 6

A Brief History of Labour and the Law*

I. Introduction

Canada has one of the most highly juridical collective bargaining regimes in the world. That means that it has a complex system of laws that regulates how **unions** obtain the right to represent employees (see Chapter 8), the conditions that must be met for unions to enter into bargaining relationships with employers, what unions and employers may and may not do during the course of negotiations (Chapters 9 and 10), and what happens if a union and an employer reach an impasse such that they cannot come to an agreement (Chapter 11). This system of laws was not always in place, however.

The history of the collective bargaining regime is the story of how workers, generally faced with very harsh working conditions and intransigent employers, agitated collectively to better their lot, and how the government and courts responded to this agitation. This chapter will briefly review the main events in Canadian labour movement history that propelled the gradual extension of legal rights to unions, from the emergence of industrial society in the mid-19th century to the adoption of the Wagner model in the mid-1940s, approximately 100 years later.

---

union: An entity that is recognized in law as the exclusive bargaining agent for a particular group of workers.

---

* This chapter was authored by Alison Braley-Rattai, University of Toronto.

II. The Emerging Labour Movement

The first recognized collective labour action in what is now Canada was thought to have occurred as far back as 1794, when employees of the North-West Fur Trading Company went on strike for better wages. However, it does not make sense to speak of a **labour movement** until the dawn of Canadian industrialization, some five decades later. The labour movement is characterized by a series of increasingly coordinated actions on the part of workers in many different occupations who gradually became aware of their common interests as workers, facing similar problems and frustrations.

Therefore, even though workers engaged in collective action to protect their interests throughout the 19th century as productive processes slowly began to change, it was not until about the second half of that century that a discernible labour movement emerged. The development of the labour movement, however, was far from even or linear.[1] For the most part, every action taken by workers was met with strong—often violent—resistance, from both employers and the state.

A. Craft Unionism

The Industrial Revolution that began in Britain in the middle of the 18th century did not arrive in Canada for another 100 years. Until about 1850, Canada was still pre-industrial. Most households lived an agrarian life and produced what goods they needed. Canada's exports were primary resources: predominantly fish, fur, timber, and wheat.[2] There were artisans who produced goods, but as most households were self-sufficient and most people did not work for wages except sporadically, the market for consumer goods was small.

What artisans there were produced items consistent with the master and servant framework discussed in Chapter 5 in the companion volume. As part of the master and servant regime, young boys were oftentimes indentured to a particular **master craftsman** who would take them on as apprentices. The craftsman would teach his craft to the apprentice, who would go through stages of aptitude—**journeyman**, and then a master craftsman in his own right. A master craftsman would set up his own shop and hire a young apprentice, and the cycle would repeat itself.

What characterized the craft era for craftsmen was a strong attachment to the craft itself: pride in the workmanship required, and pride at having a particular skill that others did not possess. Employment relations at this time were marked very often by cruelty and abuse. Nevertheless, there existed a mutuality between the interests of master craftsmen and journeymen, who hoped eventually to become master craftsmen themselves.[3]

Gradually, however, production methods began to change. As full-fledged industrial society gradually emerged during the late 19th century, the mutuality of interests between master craftsmen and their journeymen blurred. Some master craftsmen began to run their shops in line with the large-scale "manufactories" that were the hallmark of early industrialization.[4] The economic insecurity that attended the changed productive processes prompted **craftsworkers** to develop what were known as "friendly societies." Initially, these societies were developed to act as a benefit fund in times of members' need, such as for illness and death. Eventually, though, they evolved

---

labour movement: A general term for the collective organization of working people that evolved to campaign for improved terms and conditions at work, and to contest and challenge various aspects of advanced capitalist society, particularly with regard to social relations of work.

master craftsman: A craftsworker who has attained the highest level of aptitude.

journeyman: A worker who has completed an official apprenticeship in a craft or skill and who is thus qualified to work in that field, under the supervision of a master craftsman.

craftsworker: A worker who applies his or her skills in the context of the craft organizational method of production, which was a precursor to industrial forms of production.

into the early **craft unions** that would represent workers' interests to their employers. These friendly societies were craft-specific, unlike later **industrial unions**, which would try to organize labour *across* occupational lines.

Thus, the first unions in Canada arose to maintain the integrity of the craft system against the onslaught of mechanization. Unlike many of the more militant industrial unions that emerged later, and which will be discussed below, the craft unions did not generally seek to overthrow the impending order. They sought, principally, to assure their place within it. They sought to maintain the respectability of the middle-class life that their status had previously earned them.

Employers generally refused to recognize these early craft unions, however. They often refused to negotiate with them or take their role as **workers' representatives** seriously. The only power unions had at this time was the *economic* power of the strike. Workers could collectively withhold their labour in order to apply pressure on the employer to acquiesce to the union's demands. However, if an employer could withstand the strike, for instance by hiring **replacement workers**, commonly—and derisively—described as "**scabs**" by union members, then the employer need not ever deal with the union. No *legal* mechanism existed at this time to force the employer to recognize or negotiate with the union. Moreover, the law was commonly used *against* unions and workers who engaged in collective action to improve working conditions.

B. Early Legislation Restricting Unions and Collective Worker Action: Pre-1870s

Sometimes government legislation explicitly banned collective worker action, such as organizing ("combining"), attempting to negotiate collectively, striking, and **picketing**. Many examples of such legislation existed in English law. For example, the English *Combinations Acts* of 1799 and 1800 outlawed unions ("combinations") and thus all collective worker action. That legislation was repealed in England in the early 1820s and was never in effect in Canada.[5] However, some early Canadian legislation restricted worker combinations aimed at improving working terms. For example, the *Master and Servant Act*[6] of 1847, for what was then the Province of Canada (consisting of parts of modern day Ontario and Quebec), made it illegal for workers to combine for the purpose of demanding "high or extravagant wages," to breach their employment contracts by refusing to work, and to induce other employees to do the same.[7] Similar legislation existed elsewhere, such as in Nova Scotia.[8]

The *Criminal Code*[9] also played a role in restricting unions and collective worker action. Numerous criminal law provisions protected public order and property. As well, charges for criminal

---

craft union: A union that organizes workers according to their particular skill or trade (such as bricklayers and carpenters) rather than according to their industry. Craft unions first emerged in Canada, in the early to mid-19th century.

industrial union: An organizing ethos in which all workers in a given industry are organized into the same union, regardless of their particular skill or job category. See also *craft union*.

workers' representative: An employee of a company or entity and member of a workers' association who is chosen to defend the interests of fellow employees, usually through an electoral process of the association.

replacement worker: A person who is employed to take the place of another worker who is on strike or locked out. See also *scab*.

scab: A term used to refer to a worker who would otherwise be on strike, but who refuses to strike and instead crosses the picket line. Sometimes "scab" is used to refer generally to any person who crosses a picket line to perform work normally done by workers on strike, including a replacement worker. See also *strikebreaker*.

picketing: A form of protest usually associated with a labour strike, wherein striking workers congregate outside an establishment, usually their place of work, in order to draw attention to their situation, to dissuade others from "scabbing," and to provide mutual solidarity and support.

conspiracy could be invoked for a variety of legal wrongs collectively undertaken. In this regard, the sweeping common law doctrine known as **restraint of trade**, which dates back to 15th-century English courts, could be invoked to restrain many collective worker activities intended to pressure employers for higher wages. The extent to which workers were successfully prosecuted for criminal conspiracy in restraint of trade, however, is uncertain.[10]

At any rate, there appears to have been divergent legal opinions as to the legality of unions per se at this time in Canada.[11] In 1872, a coordinated effort to bring about shorter working days would result in Canada's first legislation to formally legalize unions and to exempt them from common law criminal conspiracy charges associated with restraint of trade.

C. Early Legislation Regulating and Legitimizing Union Activity: 1870s and Beyond

Notwithstanding the hostility that unions faced at the hands of both employers and the legal establishment, workers continued to organize to better their work situations. During the 1860s and early 1870s, workers agitated for a shortened workday, as discussed in Chapter 22 in the companion volume. In 1872, this demand was formally expressed in the context of so-called **Nine-Hour Leagues** that sprang up in various cities and towns. The leagues held public meetings extolling the social virtues of the nine-hour workday: it would permit workers more time to become active in their communities, to become more educated about important civic matters, and to spend more time with their families.[12]

There was no legislation restricting the number of hours in a day a worker could be made to work, and employers were generally unreceptive to the idea of the nine-hour workday. Thus, workers had to use their collective power to force employers to accede to their demands. The various leagues coordinated a series of **general strikes** that would roll across several major cities, beginning in May 1872. However, the Toronto Typographical Union jumped the gun when they went on strike in March against the *Globe*, then owned by George Brown, one of the Fathers of Confederation.

Brown had the strike leaders arrested and charged with criminal conspiracy. Upon a first hearing, Magistrate McNabb relied upon the presumptive illegality of unions as being in restraint of trade.[13] However, a second hearing was ordered. It never occurred because in the meantime, and in response to public disapproval of the treatment of the striking *Globe* workers, then prime minister John A. Macdonald passed the *Trade Unions Act*[14] of 1872 and *An Act to amend the Criminal Law relating to Violence, Threats and Molestation* (*Criminal Law Amendment Act*).[15] Together, these statutes conferred legal credibility upon unions and their central activities.

If there was any doubt as to the legal status of trade unions and their central activities, namely, attempting to negotiate collectively and to strike, the *Trade Unions Act* and the *Criminal Law Amendment Act* were aimed at rectifying that uncertainty. Among other things, the *Trade Unions Act* had the effect of removing all criminal sanctions against union membership by providing that union members could not be prosecuted for criminal conspiracy on the basis only that a purpose of the union was to restrain trade.[16] The *Criminal Law Amendment Act* removed criminal penalties attached to work stoppage, if the strike was peaceful and did not restrict the

---

restraint of trade: An English common law doctrine dating from the 1400s, which states that action or contracts that restrain trade are presumptively non-enforceable and/or illegal.

Nine-Hour Leagues: Organizations active in the late 19th century that attempted to pressure and persuade employers and governments to implement a mandatory maximum nine-hour workday.

general strike: A strike that includes a large number of all workers in a given geographical region and across many industries. A general strike is distinct from a local strike, in which workers in a particular bargaining unit strike during the course of negotiating a collective agreement.

employer from operating the business. However, the provisions of these two Acts were less protective of collective worker action than they may have appeared. First, the *Trade Unions Act* only applied to those unions that chose to register with the government[17]—a precursor of the present certification process. Few unions chose to do so. While the *Criminal Law Amendment Act* had the effect of eliminating some of the *criminal* elements tied to attempting to negotiate and to strike, it added others. In particular, it was now a crime to "watch and beset," which was often interpreted to include picketing by strikers designed to dissuade people from crossing a picket line.[18] The exact scope of this provision was never clear, but when interpreted broadly, which it often was, it had the effect of undercutting the power of strike action by rendering unlawful virtually all peaceful picketing. The labour movement particularly disliked the *Criminal Law Amendment Act*, calling it "harsh and oppressive."[19]

Where legislation did not outlaw collective action, the common law often did. The mere acts of unionizing (combining) and striking (refusing to work) were rarely ruled illegal in themselves.[20] However, judges developed a variety of torts (see Chapter 18 in the companion volume and Chapter 11 in this volume) to, in the words of labour law historians Judy Fudge and Eric Tucker, "protect employers against the kind of harm that strikes were aimed to cause."[21] For example, if striking workers or union leaders attempted to persuade other workers to join the strike or to not cross a picket line, they were committing the tort of "inducing breach of contract." Picketers who obstructed the ingress or egress of an employer's property could be committing the tort of "nuisance," and picketers who stood on private property could be committing the tort of "trespass to property."

As the case in Box 6.1 indicates, since workers have little more than their collective efforts to aid them to achieve their goals, an inability to persuade others to join them seriously undercuts their efficacy.

BOX 6.1 » CASE LAW HIGHLIGHT

Strike at Krug Furniture

Krug Furniture Co. v. Berlin Union of Amalgamated Woodworkers [1903] OJ No. 202

Key Facts: In August 1902, the Amalgamated Woodworkers' International Union passed a resolution ordering a strike of workers known as "finishers" at a factory of Krug Furniture in Berlin (now Kitchener), Ontario. About two weeks later, the woodworkers at Krug Furniture also ceased work in a **sympathy strike** with the finishers. Union members kept a vigil, upon both the trains and the factory, with a view to preventing new workers from taking up work left by the striking workers, and to entice those who continued to work to cease to do so. Additionally, union members had discovered the destination of furniture made by the company with a view to organizing a boycott of these goods. The company filed for an injunction to prevent members of the union from "interfering" with their workmen. The company also sought damages for enticing workmen into breaking their contracts.

Issue: Were the union and its members guilty of the crime of "watching and besetting," and various tortious wrongs including inducing breach of contract as well as intimidation?

Decision: Yes. Justice Meredith ascertained that the union and its members were guilty of the crime of "watching and besetting" as well as various tortious wrongs. The crime of watching and besetting appears to have been made out simply because the purpose of the picketing was "preventing new workmen from entering the plaintiffs' employment, and of constraining their continuing workmen to leave such employment."

Additionally, the union and striking workers were found liable for the tort against inducement to breach contract, something which the government had ceased to view as a crime, but which remained tortious under the common law. Notably, those who actually left their contracts were not charged. Finally, opining that some forms of boycotting were "very obnoxious to the law," Justice Meredith found the union and striking workers liable for intimidation for the attempted boycott. The court concluded that "the result has, in one case at least, been an intimidation of the dealer to such an extent that he is afraid to disclose the facts except secretly." It is never stated, though, what specific actions were found to have been intimidating, leaving open the possibility that the mere fact of organizing a boycott itself may have been the tortious act.

---

sympathy strike: A strike undertaken by workers who do not have an immediate and direct grievance against their own employer, but who strike as a means of showing support and solidarity with other striking workers who do have such a grievance with their employer.

The *Krug* case demonstrates how even peaceful, non-violent picketing could be prohibited by the *Criminal Code* provision against watching and besetting. Justice Meredith noted that some of the ways in which striking workers went about achieving their ends were "offensive" and "highly reprehensible," such things as launching insults and attempting to crowd non-striking workers off of sidewalks.

The *Trade Unions Act*, the *Criminal Law Amendment Act*, and the *Breaches of Contract Act*[22] of 1877, which provided that it was no longer a crime for an employee to quit or breach an employment contract, established the early statutory foundation for collective bargaining rights in Canada.[23] Moreover, although the Nine-Hour Movement fizzled out after the arrest of its striking leaders, it represents a turning point in labour history because it was the first example of labour's coordinated action across various occupational lines. In the words of Professor Craig Heron (York University), the "explosion of broad-based working-class solidarity … encouraged labour leaders to develop a more permanent presence in Canadian public life."[24] Moreover, the legislation that the movement propelled revealed not only the political power of organized labour but also the power of the state to act as a "pacifying force on a militant labour movement."[25] State intervention to quell industrial unrest would become a mainstay of labour's story in the 20th century.

D. Employer Intransigence and Increasing Worker Militancy

Notwithstanding the often opaque legal status of combining, attempting to negotiate, striking, and picketing during the 19th century in Canada, by the dawn of the 20th century, it was clear that government *in*action on behalf of labour—that is, generally allowing workers to fend for themselves—made things little better for the average worker. The legal status of collective worker action in the late 1800s and early 20th century can be summarized as follows:

> Workers who sought to organize a union confronted, first of all, the possibility of economic reprisals by their employer. An employer could, with impunity, refuse to employ unionists, to negotiate with the union, or to abide by any undertakings given to the union. Whether he would, as a matter of prudence actually adopt such a position depended upon the relative power of the parties [see the discussion of "internal inputs" in Chapter 3]. If the employer chose to dismiss unionists or to refuse to recognize a union, the union could respond by calling a strike or imposing other economic sanctions. However, the employer, in turn, could seek relief in the civil or criminal courts against such sanctions and, as the law stood down to the 1940s, be reasonably confident of success. Thus, the freedom to organize often amounted, in practical terms, to no more than the freedom to suffer serious adverse legal and economic consequences.[26]

The economic depression of 1873 had a negative impact upon the burgeoning labour movement. However, employment opportunities improved considerably in the 1880s. By this time, industrialization was moving full steam ahead and with it the motivation to employ **gang bosses** to control and discipline increasingly large workforces. The 1889 Royal Commission on the Relations of Labor and Capital in Canada revealed a system where beatings were administered and workers were easily fired and replaced.[27] This system, which came to be known as the **coercive drive system**, galvanized worker resistance.

Throughout the 1880s, workers organized, forming the first permanent national labour organization, the Trades and Labor Congress of Canada (TLC). For a brief period in the late 19th

---

gang bosses: Workers employed to supervise the increasingly industrializing workforce. They had almost total control over the workers they supervised. Often they were paid based on the productivity of their workers. Thus, the discipline they administered was often harsh and arbitrary.

coercive drive system: A management approach to productivity, most commonly associated with the 19th century, which sought to increase worker output through fear and intimidation.

century, the TLC brought together craft unions and the emerging industrial unionism move-ment, led by the American-based **Knights of Labor**. The Knights of Labor expanded into East-ern Canada in the 1870s and proselytized a new form of unionism that rejected narrow craft-based organizing in favour of a model that organized all workers, skilled and unskilled alike. The idea of industrial unionism threatened the craft unions. As a result, in 1902 the TLC mem-bership ousted the Knights, a move that temporarily stalled the advancement of industrial union-ism in Canada. The TLC existed until 1956 when a merger with the Canadian Congress of Labour led to the founding of the **Canadian Labour Congress**, which today is the only national umbrella labour organization in English Canada.

E. Industrial Disputes Investigations Act, 1907

As workers continued to agitate and strike for better conditions in what were very often unsafe, unsanitary, and exceedingly harsh work environments with long hours and little pay, legislation sprang up that required third-party **conciliation** in industries considered essential for the bur-geoning Canadian economy. The purpose of such legislation was to reduce the amount of time lost to strikes in key sectors by introducing a neutral third party to help resolve disputes, and by imposing a waiting period before a strike (or lockout) could proceed.

One example of such legislation was the *Industrial Disputes Investigations Act* (IDIA) of 1907, enacted by the federal government under the auspices of the then minister of labour William Lyon Mackenzie King. The IDIA was directed to specific industries, namely, mining, communi-cations, transportation, and public utilities, except the railway industry, which, since 1903, had had its own equivalent legislation.[28]

Conciliation boards appointed under the IDIA could neither *prevent* labour action (either strike or lockout) nor impose a settlement upon parties. Rather, conciliation boards provided a means to investigate the dispute in an effort to aid the parties to come to a mutually agreed upon settlement, in the hopes of avoiding work stoppages. King believed that when applied, this model would ensure that the vast majority of collective bargaining disputes would be resolved without a work stoppage. According to a survey from 1912, the majority of parties that underwent con-ciliation arrived at a settlement without any work stoppage.[29]

The IDIA's influence is still felt today. It laid the foundation for two central aspects of our labour relations scheme, namely, the requirement for collective bargaining parties to exhaust government-provided conciliation services and to then wait out a specified period of time (a "cooling-off" period) prior to resorting to labour action (see Chapter 11).[30]

III. Labour in the Early 20th Century and the Interwar Years

By the First World War, Canada had largely left its agrarian mode of production behind. From the early 20th century until the start of the war, Canada experienced spectacular industrial growth for which waves of immigrant labour were necessary. Adults and children worked long days, often in unsanitary, unsafe conditions and for low wages.[31] A 1919 report on labour relations by the Royal Commission on Industrial Relations ascertained that, despite the common excuse that

---

Knights of Labor: An organization formed in the United States in 1869 and that was active in Canada between about 1875 and the early 1900s. The Knights promoted "industrial unionism," the organization of all workers regardless of skill, gender, race, or religion.

Canadian Labour Congress: The largest federal confederation of unions in Canada, representing approximately 3.3 million Canadians. Its main roles are to lobby governments, provide leadership on key issues, and provide training and education resources for its member unions. It holds a national convention every three years.

conciliation: A form of mediation in which a neutral collective bargaining expert attempts to assist an employee association (e.g., a union) and an employer or employer association in reaching a collective agreement.

industrial unrest was organized by "alien" influences who came to rouse an otherwise contented workforce, the real cause was the harsh socio-economic conditions of Canadian workers.[32] The report recommended, among other things, that employers recognize unions as the legitimate representatives of their workers and to negotiate with them. This recommendation fell on deaf ears for another 25 years. Instead, employers resisted union efforts by hiring **strikebreakers**, and employers' efforts to end strikes were often bolstered by government troops. Clashes on picket lines were violent. Troops dealt harshly with strikers who were often maimed and sometimes killed with impunity.

After the First World War, Canada experienced an economic downturn. Soldiers returning home from the war discovered that jobs were scarce and that inflation had considerably outpaced wages. The cost of living was 64 percent over what it had been before the war.[33] People were discontented, remembering the huge profits made by weapons manufacturers. Workers went on strike, demanding increased wages and union recognition, and this labour unrest culminated in what is one of the most famous moments in Canadian labour history, the Winnipeg General Strike of 1919 (see Box 6.2).

BOX 6.2 » TALKING WORK LAW

The Winnipeg General Strike of 1919

What began as a local strike of the building and metal workers in Winnipeg, Manitoba on May 1, 1919, soon amassed a huge following. Two weeks later, an appeal by the Winnipeg Trades and Labour Council for a general strike was met with 30,000 union and non-union workers walking off the job that same morning. Sympathy strikes broke out around the country.

Approximately six weeks later, most of the municipal police, ordered to disperse the crowd, were fired when they refused to sign a "no strike" pledge. They were replaced by "special constables" hired by the business community, whose efforts were supplemented by the North-West Mounted Police. Meanwhile, the Conservative government in Ottawa, under Prime Minister Robert Borden, enacted legislation expanding the scope of criminal sedition, and that law was used as the basis to arrest 12 suspected strike leaders. This event sparked outrage among the strikers and the strike turned violent. On June 21, strikers took to the streets of Winnipeg, where they were met by stampeding police and the special constables. Two strikers were killed, 24 were injured, and 94 were arrested (seven of whom were sentenced to between six months and two years of jail).*

Although the revolt was crushed, the Winnipeg General Strike is viewed as a touchstone event in labour history. According to Professor John Godard (University of Manitoba), it was the first time that workers began to view themselves "as a class" with interests that were divergent from employers' who

Source: Public domain

constituted, thus, a separate class. Also, it sounded the death knell of narrow craft-unionism, since the strike involved large numbers of unskilled workers as well as women.† In the following few decades, demand would be mostly for semi-skilled or unskilled, rather than skilled, labour-power.

---

*   D. Morton, *Working People*, 5th ed. (Montreal: McGill-Queen's University Press, 2007), at 122.
†   John Godard, *Industrial Relations, the Economy, and Society*, 4th ed. (Concord, ON: Captus Press, 2011), at 90–91.

---

strikebreaker: A person who crosses a picket line to work during a strike. Different from a scab, a strikebreaker is generally hired from outside the company.

The interwar years saw the re-emergence and expansion of industrial unionism, the model that had been promoted by the Knights of Labor. Many unions would, throughout these years, agitate not only for better working conditions but also for the replacement of the capitalist economic system, which they viewed as inherently exploitive. Many of these unions were explicitly influenced by **Bolshevism** and other socialist ideas and movements, such as One Big Union (OBU) and the Industrial Workers of the World (called "Wobblies").

A. The Great Depression and the Wagner Act

In 1933, four years after the Great Depression began, about 15 percent of the Canadian population relied on government assistance to survive, and the unemployment rate had reached about 29 percent. Relief camps had been introduced in 1932 by the federal and provincial governments as a temporary measure to keep unemployed men occupied doing manual labour for room and board and 20 cents per day.[34] These camps proved fertile ground for Communist organizers who, in 1935, organized hundreds of relief camp workers to board a train in Vancouver headed to Ottawa to protest conditions in the relief camps and to demand jobs and decent working conditions. The "On to Ottawa Trek" came to an end in Regina, where the RCMP arrested dozens of the "trekkers" and a violent clash left one police officer dead.

In the same year as the On to Ottawa Trek, the US Congress enacted the *National Labor Relations Act*, commonly known as the **Wagner Act**, named for its sponsor, Senator Robert Wagner. The *Wagner Act* sought to bring stability to industry by creating "a process through which an employer could be compelled to recognize a union as the legitimate bargaining agent for its employees."[35] The *Wagner Act* explicitly recognized the unequal bargaining power between employers and employees and that the use of such power to refuse to collectively bargain leads to "industrial strife or unrest."[36]

The *Wagner Act* established employer recognition of unions through three main features. First, it created a legal **certification** process, through which workers could "[designate] representatives of their own choosing."[37] Certification entailed two important principles: **majoritarianism** and **exclusivity**, which will be discussed in greater detail in Chapter 8. The former means that a majority of workers must be in favour in order to organize a union. The latter means that the union so chosen becomes the exclusive bargaining agent for the whole group of workers in what is called the **bargaining unit,** even those that voted against unionization. Second, the Act made **unfair labour practices** illegal. Employers could no longer refuse to hire or choose to fire employees who supported unions, or refuse to negotiate with the duly recognized workers' union. Thus, the Act required employers to bargain collectively with the unions that it certified. An employer's ability to intervene in union organization drives was also significantly curtailed. Third, the Act

---

Bolshevism: The term is derived from the Bolshevik party, which led the Russian Revolution of 1917. Bolshevism refers to the methods, practices, and/or beliefs of the party.

Wagner Act: Collective bargaining legislation enacted in 1935 in the United States, granting workers a legal right to unionize, engage in collective bargaining, and strike. The *Wagner Act* inspired modern Canadian collective bargaining legislation.

certification: The process for legally recognizing a union as the exclusive bargaining agent of a particular group of workers.

majoritarianism: A principle of the Wagner model, it asserts that a union must secure the support of a majority of employees to win the right to act as their representative.

exclusivity: A principle of the Wagner model, it asserts that the union chosen to represent workers becomes the sole or exclusive legal representative for that group of workers.

bargaining unit: A group of workers whose work is similar enough that they are thought capable to be covered by the same collective agreement. Importantly, not all bargaining unit members necessarily choose to join the union.

unfair labour practice: An action undertaken by either the union or the employer that violates one or more articles in the relevant labour relations legislation.

codified the right of workers to strike.[38] These three features of the *Wagner Act* have collectively become known as "the Wagner model." This model is unique to North America. However, it would not come to Canada for nearly a decade after its introduction in the United States.

B. Oshawa General Motors Strike, 1937

In 1937, unlike American workers, Canadian workers still had no legislative provisions requiring employers to negotiate with their unions. Consequently, workers at the General Motors (GM) plant in Oshawa, Ontario who requested and were denied an eight-hour workday, better wages and working conditions, seniority, and recognition of their union (a Canadian affiliate of the American-based United Auto Workers Union [UAW]) had a major confrontation with their employer.[39] Low wages and unsafe working conditions had previously prompted a walkout of most GM employees, in 1928. At that time, the workers won many of their demands. Thus emboldened, many of the workers attempted to organize into a union under the auspices of the Trades and Labor Congress of Canada (TLC). However, the TLC's continued ethos of craft unionism, discussed above, was ultimately rejected by GM employees. Instead, they turned to an industrial union that promised to organize all GM workers—the Communist Auto Workers' Industrial Union of Canada (CAWIUC). However, a struggle between the TLC and the CAWIUC regarding representation for the GM workers meant that Oshawa auto workers would not immediately have union representation.

The GM workers continued to experience speed-ups, few rest periods, and months of only part-time work hours. When yet another speed-up was announced by GM, the workers decided to strike again. In April 1937, 4,000 workers struck against the car manufacturer. The UAW organized the workers under the umbrella of a new competitor to the TLC known as the Canadian Industrial Organization (CIO). The CIO supported industrial unionism—the idea that unions should represent all workers and not just the skilled crafts.

The company ardently opposed the industrial union, with the help of then Ontario premier Mitchell Hepburn, who threatened to use the provincial police to break the strike. The event precipitated a Cabinet crisis when his own minister of labour opposed him, stating that his place was "marching with the workers" and not with GM.[40] The workers did not win formal recognition of their union, but GM agreed to many of the union's proposals. The premier failed in his objective to smash the organizing efforts of the CIO and industrial unionism. The Oshawa General Motors strike stands out in labour history as a "breakthrough for industrial unionism in the mass production industries in Canada," which "stimulated unionization in the auto and other industries."[41]

The General Motors strike of 1937, with workers gathered in Oshawa, Ontario.
Source: Walter P. Reuther Library, Archives of Labor and Urban Affairs, Wayne State University.

IV. Wagner and Rand

A. PC 1003 (1944): The Wagner Model Comes to Canada

The rapid industrialization brought about by wartime growth in the early 1940s, combined with labour shortages as men headed to the front lines of the Second World War, made conditions ripe for organizing. With the economy nearing full employment, workers and their unions enjoyed great bargaining power. Between 1940 and 1945, trade union membership nearly doubled.[42] A nation-wide walkout in the steel industry in 1943, combined with other work stoppages, meant that one out of every three workers was on strike. Meanwhile, a new political party was gaining momentum at both the provincial and federal level: the Co-operative Commonwealth Federation (CCF), the predecessor to the New Democratic Party. The CCF supported a Canadian version of the American *Wagner Act* that would ensure unions a legal right to be recognized with the support of a majority of workers.[43] Unions began to throw their political support behind the CCF.

In 1943, Ontario's Liberal government became the first province to enact legislation modelled after the *Wagner Act*: the *Collective Bargaining Act*.[44] Later that year, the CCF became the official opposition in Ontario, after winning 34 seats in the provincial election. Many of the new MPPs were labour leaders. Growing labour unrest and the threat posed by the growing popularity of the CCF and its new ties to the labour movement finally pushed the federal Liberals, then under the leadership of prime minister Mackenzie King, to introduce its own version of the *Wagner Act*, known as the *Wartime Labour Relations Order*, or Order in Council **PC 1003**.[45] PC 1003 was passed in 1944 pursuant to the *War Measures Act*, which temporarily bestowed jurisdiction over labour relations to the federal government.[46]

PC 1003 enacted the basic framework of the *Wagner Act*, including compulsory union recognition and a duty to bargain with an exclusive union that is supported by a majority of employees. However, PC 1003 also included distinctive Canadian elements, including the practice of mandatory conciliation, which had existed in embryonic form in key Canadian industries since the turn of the century. In addition, unlike the *Wagner Act*, it prohibited strikes during a **collective agreement**, a policy that continues to this day as we will discuss in Chapter 11. As federal wartime legislation, the sun was setting on PC 1003 as soon as it came into being. However, by 1948 virtually every province, as well as the federal jurisdiction, had its own labour relations legislation based on the model introduced in PC 1003. That model dominates Canadian collective bargaining law to this day.

B. The Rand Formula

The Ford strike that took place in 1945 in Windsor, Ontario brought to Canadian labour law its final foundational element—the Rand Formula, alternatively known as mandatory **dues check-off**. The Rand Formula is named for Justice Ivan Rand, who arbitrated a settlement between striking UAW workers and the Ford Motor Company, after the momentous and bitter 99-day strike. At arbitration, the only questions Justice Ivan Rand had to determine were whether to establish a **union-shop**

PC 1003: Granted workers collective bargaining rights, including protection from anti-union discrimination by employers and a limited protected right to strike, and imposed on employers a legal "duty to bargain" with unions representing a majority of workers.

collective agreement: A contract between an employer (or employers) and a trade union (or trade unions) that sets out the conditions of employment for a group of employees.

dues check-off: A "union security" clause whereby all members of a bargaining unit must pay union dues and employers must "check off" these dues from workers' wages and remit them to the union.

union-shop: A "union security" clause whereby all workers in a given job classification are required to join the union. Union-shops are distinct from closed-shops, open-shops, and agency-shops.

and whether to include a mandatory union dues check-off clause in the collective agreement (both of which the union wanted and the company opposed). Rand split the difference (see Box 6.3).

BOX 6.3 » CASE LAW HIGHLIGHT

Justice Ivan Rand and the "Rand Formula"

Ford Motor Company v. United Automobile Workers Union
[1946] OLAA No. 1

Key Facts: In 1945, after a year and a half of failed attempts to reach a collective agreement, unionized workers began a strike at the Ford Motor Company in Windsor. The strike continued peacefully before police were called to clear a path to the boiler room, and the strikers responded by using their cars to block access to the factory and by damaging some company property. The main issues were related to the union's claim for clauses in the collective agreement that would (1) require the employer to deduct union dues from each employee and remit the money to the union; and (2) require all employees covered by the collective agreement to become union members. The strike ended when these issues were referred by the parties to Justice Ivan Rand to issue a binding decision.

Issue: Should the collective agreement require mandatory union membership and mandatory union dues check-off?

Decision: Justice Rand split the difference. He did not require that all workers be required to join the union, but he did require that all workers pay union dues, and that such dues be "checked off" by the employer and remitted to the union.

In accepting the union's claim for a mandatory union dues check-off clause, Rand wrote:

> the employees as a whole become the beneficiaries of union action, and I doubt if any circumstance provokes more resentment in a plant than this sharing of the fruits of unionist work and courage by the non-members. ... I consider it entirely equitable then that all employees should be required to shoulder their portion of the burden of expense for ad-

ministering the law of their employment, the union contract; that they must take the burden along with the benefit. ... It may be argued that it is unjust to compel non-members of a union to contribute to funds over the expenditure of which they have no direct voice; and even that it is dangerous to place such money power in the control of an unregistered union. But the dues are only those which members are satisfied to pay for substantially the same benefits, and as any employee can join the union and still retain his independence in employment, I see no serious objection in this circumstance. The argument is really one for a weak union.

In rejecting the union's claim for a closed "union shop" that would require as a condition of employment that employees become union members, Rand wrote:

> Basing my judgment on the principles which I think the large majority of Canadians accept, I am unable in the circumstances to award a union shop. It would subject the Company's interest in individual employees and their tenure of service to strife within the union and between them and the union ... and it would deny the individual Canadian the right to seek work and to work independently of personal association with any organized group. It would also expose him even in a generally disciplined organization to the danger of arbitrary action of individuals and place his economic life at the mercy of the threat as well as the action of power in an uncontrolled and here an unmatured group.

Although Rand's decision applied only to the parties in the case, union dues check-off clauses soon appeared in collective agreements across Canada, and some provinces enacted laws that effectively required mandatory union dues check-off.[47] For example, as discussed further in Chapter 12, in Ontario, Saskatchewan, Newfoundland and Labrador, and the federal jurisdiction, union dues check-off clauses must be inserted into every collective agreement if the union requests it. In Quebec and Manitoba, union dues are mandatory by law. In other jurisdictions, including Alberta, New Brunswick, Nova Scotia, the law requires employees to authorize a deduction of dues. Whether employees in a bargaining unit are required to become union members is usually left to collective bargaining.

V. Chapter Summary

The development of the labour movement and the gradual extension of the legal rights of workers embodied in the Wagner model and the Rand Formula were the result of a long and arduous (and often violent) process. This process was not linear: where some laws expanded rights, others contracted them. The labour movement continues to evolve as new challenges, such as rising income inequality, global labour markets, and precarious work, throw up new challenges and as anti-union activists, employers, and politicians attempt to erode collective worker rights.

QUESTIONS AND ISSUES FOR DISCUSSION

1. Identify any two historical events discussed in this chapter, and explain their significance.
2. What was the *Industrial Disputes Investigations Act* and in what way does it still resonate in labour law today?
3. Explain the main aspects of the Wagner model of collective bargaining.
4. Explain the difference between a "craft union" and an "industrial union," and identify two Canadian organizations that supported each model.
5. Discuss the basis for Justice Rand's decision. Is it fair to require people to pay union dues if they choose not to belong to a union?

UPDATES

Go to emond.ca/lawofworkircb for links to news, author's blog posts, content updates, and other information related to the chapters in this text.

NOTES AND REFERENCES

1 Workers have never been monolithic, and the labour movement has consistently had to contend with creating solidarity even amidst numerous lines of division.

2 C. Heron, *The Canadian Labour Movement: A Short History*, 2nd ed. (Toronto: Lorimer, 1996), at 1.

3 E. Tucker, "'That Indefinite Area of Toleration': Criminal Conspiracy and Trade Unions in Ontario, 1837-77" (Spring 1991) *Labour/Le Travail* 27, at 28.

4 The differences in the relationship between master and apprentice/master craftsman and journeyman/employer and employee are captured in Charles Dickens's *A Christmas Carol*. There, Ebenezer Scrooge was apprenticed as a young man to Mr. Fezziwig, who is a father figure. He represents the lost traditions that must give way to the new, impersonal, and "every man for himself" ethic that Dickens attributes to the Industrial Age.

5 Supra note 3, at 21.

6 *An Act to Regulate the Duties Between Master and Servant, and for Other Purposes Therein Mentioned*, S. Prov. Can. 1847, c. 23.

7 *Master and Servant Act*, S. Prov. Can. 1847, c. 23; and ibid., at 34.

8 See, generally, D. Hay and P. Craven, eds., *Masters, Servants and Magistrates in Britain and Empire, 1562–1955* (Chapel Hill, NC: University of North Carolina Press, 2004).

9 *Criminal Code*, RSC 1985, c. C-46.

10 Tucker, supra note 3, at 31-32; and P. Craven, "Workers' Conspiracies in Toronto, 1854–72" (Fall 1984) 14 *Labour/Le Travail* 49. In his survey of Toronto courts between 1854 and 1872, Paul Craven (York University) was unable to find a case where workers were convicted on common law conspiracy charges, absent violence or threats of violence.

11 Tucker, supra note 3, at 31-33.

12 Heron, supra note 2, at 14-15.

13 M. Chartrand, "The First Canadian Trade Union Legislation: An Historical Framework" (1984) 16:2 *Ottawa Law Review* 271.

14 *Trade Unions Act*, SC 1872, c. 30.

15 *An Act to amend the Criminal Law relating to Violence, Threats and Molestation*, SC 1872, c. 31.

16 *Trade Unions Act*, supra note 14, s. 2.

17 Ibid., s. 5.

18 *An Act to amend the Criminal Law*, supra note 15, s. 4(c).

19 *Ontario Workman*, May 2, 1872; and *Ontario Workman*, May 23, 1872.

20 See, generally, Craven, supra note 10; J. Fudge and E. Tucker, "The Freedom to Strike in Canada: A Brief Legal History" (2010) 15:2 *Canadian Labour and Employment Law Journal* 333; and Tucker, supra note 3.

21   Fudge and Tucker, supra note 20, at 18.

22   *Breaches of Contract Act, 1877*, SC 1877, c. 35.

23   R. Marsden, "Labour History and the Development of Modern Capitalism," in M. Gunderson and D. Taras, eds., *Canadian Labour and Employment Relations*, 6th ed. (Don Mills, ON: Pearson Education Canada, 2008) 56, at 64.

24   Heron, supra note 2, at 15.

25   Ibid., at 17.

26   H. Arthurs, *Labour Law and Industrial Relations in Canada*, 4th ed. (Deventer, Netherlands: Kluwer, 1993), at 196.

27   J. Rinehart, *The Tyranny of Work: Alienation and the Labour Process*, 2nd ed. (Toronto: Harcourt Brace, 1987), at 35-38.

28   *Railway Labour Disputes Act*, SC 1903, c. 55.

29   M. M. Marks, "The Canadian Industrial Disputes Act" (1912) 44 *The Annals of the American Academy of Political and Social Science* 1.

30   *Labour Relations Act*, 1995, SO 1995, c. 1, Sch. A, s. 18.

31   See, generally, *As Friend and Foe* (Montreal: National Film Board of Canada, 1980), YouTube video, https://www .youtube.com/watch?v=9K9HZ_40H0M.

32   B. Burkett, "The Future of the Wagner Act: A Canadian-American Comparison" (2013) 38:2 *Queen's Law Journal* 363.

33   "Le Canada: A People's History—Voices of Discontent: The Winnipeg General Strike," *CBC*, accessed August 24, 2016, http://www.cbc.ca/history/ EPISCONTENTSE1EP12CH3PA2LE.html.

34   D. Morton, *Working People*, 5th ed. (Montreal: McGill-Queen's University Press, 2007), at 146-47.

35   Burkett, supra note 32, at 364.

36   *National Labor Relations Act*, 1935, 29 U.S.C. § 151 (Findings and declaration of policy).

37   Ibid.

38   Ibid., §163 (Right to strike preserved).

39   See, generally, I. Abella, "Oshawa 1937," in L. Sefton MacDowell and I. Radforth, eds., *Canadian Working Class History* (Toronto: Canadian Scholars' Press, 1992).

40   Morton, supra note 34, at 160.

41   L. Sefton MacDowell, "After the Strike—Labour Relations in Oshawa, 1937–1939" (1993) 48:4 *Relations industrielles/ Industrial Relations* 691, at 691.

42   D. D. Carter et. al., *Labour Law in Canada*, 5th ed. (Deventer, Netherlands: Kluwer, 2002); and *Labour and Employment Law Casebook*, 8th ed. (Toronto: Irwin Law, 2011), at 18.

43   L. S. MacDowell, "The Formation of the Canadian Industrial Relations System During World War Two" (1978) 3 *Labour/Le Travail* 175, at 190.

44   For a review of the legislation, see B. Laskin, "Collective Bargaining in Ontario: A New Legislative Approach" (1943) 21 *Canadian Bar Review* 684.

45   *Wartime Labour Relations Order* (PC 1003) is available at http://socserv.mcmaster.ca/oldlabourstudies/ onlinelearning/article.php?id=503.

46   See Chapter 19 in the companion volume for a discussion of the division of powers (jurisdiction) over labour relations. In 1925, in the case of *Toronto Electric Commissioners v. Snider*, the Privy Council ruled that primary jurisdiction fell to the provinces. The *War Measures Act* temporarily suspended that ruling.

47   See the discussion on and chart of legislative provisions in D. Doorey, "Are Ontario Laws on Union Dues and Membership 'Undemocratic'?" *Law of Work* (blog), April 3, 2013. http://lawofwork.ca/?p=6447.

CHAPTER 7

Why Do Workers Join Unions, and What Effects Do Unions Have on Business?*

LEARNING OBJECTIVES

After reading this chapter, students will be able to:

- Explain the main reasons workers join unions.
- Identify factors that make workers more likely to join unions.
- Discuss the empirical evidence concerning the union effect on firm productivity, profits, employment growth, and innovation.
- Provide a snapshot of the Canadian labour movement.

CHAPTER OUTLINE

I. Introduction

According to Statistics Canada, approximately one in three workers (31.5 percent) in Canada belongs to a trade union.[1] This fact, coupled with the **spillover effect** (see Chapter 3) that unions have on non-unionized workplaces, makes unions an important part of the Canadian economy. Unions provide a number of services to workers. They give workers a collective voice and otherwise provide representation in the workplace; negotiate higher wages and seniority-based job security; and provide access to a third-party grievance process in the event of a dispute with management. On the other hand, unions may affect an employer's competitiveness, especially in industries with non-union firms. This chapter considers important industrial relations questions, such as why workers join unions and the impact of collective bargaining on firm productivity, profits, employment growth, and innovation. It concludes with a brief overview of the Canadian labour movement.

---

spillover effect: The effects that collective agreement settlements bargained by unions and employers have on individual employment contracts in non-union workplaces.

---

* This chapter was authored by Scott Walsworth, Associate Professor of Industrial Relations, Edwards School of Business, University of Saskatchewan.

II. Why Do Workers Join Unions?

In 2004, two University of Calgary professors tricked business students into joining a union, something the students thought they would never do. At about the midpoint of the semester, students were told that their professor had been suspended and a new professor was appointed. The new professor proceeded to unilaterally change the course outline in ways that discounted previous student work, while adding extra assignments. As expected, the students objected. However, the way in which the students went about seeking justice was unexpected, at least to them: almost immediately, they signed a petition, banded together as a group, and proceeded to plan collective action—just like a union.[2]

In this scenario, the students formed a group to address a common problem with a more powerful adversary (the new professor). In essence, they formed a union for the same reasons workers join a union to bargain with their employer. For example, an individual worker may demand a wage increase and threaten to stop working if the employer does not agree. The cost of a single worker refusing to work is relatively small, and the employer would likely respond by refusing to grant the wage increase and perhaps even fire the employee. However, if all of the workers make the same demand with the same threat to withdraw their labour (to strike), the cost to the employer is much greater because production comes to a halt. Once the employer's ability to earn revenue is compromised, the employer is much more likely to begin negotiating a wage increase. In a nutshell, workers join a union to increase their bargaining power to convince their employer to negotiate more favourable employment terms.

Industrial relations and sociology scholars have studied the reasons why people join unions. Their findings are summarized in this section. Sometimes union members want a greater say in how the workplace is run and how their time at work is spent (instrumental reasons). Sometimes union members are looking for better wages, benefits, pensions, or other perks (economic reasons). Most of the time, people join unions because they are interested in both instrumental and economic reasons.

A. *Instrumental Reasons*

What Do Unions Do? is an important book on labour unions that was written over 30 years ago by Harvard professors Richard Freeman and James Medoff. It describes workers' options when faced with unfavourable working conditions as the choice between **exit and voice**.[3] "Exit" refers to a worker's ability to quit if he or she does not like the terms of employment. In the common law regime, "exit" is often the only viable option for employees, since individually they lack the bargaining power to persuade their employer to provide improved contract terms or the inclination to approach their employer with demands for fear of reprisals.

Alternatively, "voice" refers to a worker's ability to communicate discontent to the employer and thereby effect change in the workplace to secure better employment terms (such as a wage increase). Unions are particularly effective at increasing workers' voice in the workplace, because they operate at arm's length from the employers with whom they negotiate. Moreover, they possess the financial resources and expertise to protect employees from employer reprisals when employee concerns are voiced. Many workers join unions to secure a greater level of voice in the workplace, particularly when they feel silenced in the non-union setting. That voice takes the

---

exit and voice: Two options workers have when confronted with an unfavourable employment condition: they can either quit (exit) their job or stay and protest (voice) to effect workplace change.

form of participation in collective bargaining or the **grievance procedure** in a collective agreement, and sometimes in strike action.

Once an employer and a union negotiate a contract, called a *collective agreement*, they are legally bound by the contract while it is in effect (usually between one and four years). To deal with any disputes that arise from the administration or interpretation of the collective agreement, the parties rely on a grievance procedure. For example, an employer who selects workers based on productivity instead of seniority for a training opportunity may violate a **seniority provision** in the collective agreement (see Chapter 12). In a non-union setting, an employee who feels he or she was unfairly denied access to a training opportunity has only one form of redress. That employee can only "exit" (quit) the workplace and pursue an employment standards complaint or sue the employer in common law, depending on the circumstances. A grievance procedure allows a unionized employee to file a grievance alleging the employer violated a clause of the collective agreement. On behalf of the employee, the union will argue the grievance before various levels of management. If a resolution is not found, the grievance will be heard by an arbitrator. Grievance arbitrators are neutral, meaning that they do not favour the employer or the union (they act like judges), and their decisions are binding (meaning they are legally enforced).

B. Economic Reasons

1. Union Wage Premium

If we compare two identical jobs, one performed by a unionized worker and one performed by a non-unionized worker, and we control for all imaginable human capital factors, such as workers' productivity, experience, and education, on average the unionized worker will earn more than the non-unionized worker. This difference is called a **union wage premium** and is the result of the union's ability to bargain higher wages for its members. The size of the union wage premium in Canada, which has been debated in the literature, appears to be shrinking over time. American studies in the 1980s estimated that the union wage premium in the United States was around 18 percent (if a non-union worker earned $20 an hour, a unionized worker would earn 18 percent more, an additional $3.60 for a wage of $23.60 per hour).[4] By contrast, a 2002 study by University of Toronto Professors Tony Fang and Anil Verma found that the union wage premium in Canada was much lower, at around 7 percent.[5] A 2012 Canadian study by Professors Scott Walsworth and Richard Long found the union wage premium to be even lower, at around 4 percent.[6]

2. Seniority-Based Benefits

When employment terms for an employee, such as rate of pay, benefits, access to training, and protection from layoffs, are determined not by merit but instead by seniority (the length of time since being hired), we say the employee is protected by a seniority provision, which has been negotiated by the employee's union. For the employee, the advantage of a seniority provision comes in the form of better employment terms and greater job security as time goes on. Many benefits negotiated into collective agreements improve over time, creating an incentive for

---

grievance procedure: A provision of the collective agreement that permits the union or the employer to allege that the other party violated a clause of the collective agreement. If the dispute is not resolved in-house by meetings of increasingly senior members of management and the union, the dispute is resolved by a neutral arbitrator.

seniority provision: A clause in the collective agreement that allocates employment terms such as rate of pay, promotion, etc. based on length of time since being hired.

union wage premium: The additional wage amount attributed to union membership.

employees to remain with the employer long-term. Seniority provisions also remove potentially unfair or arbitrary measures of performance by employers by creating a clearly defined system for decision-making on such matters as promotions, layoffs, and recalls from layoffs. For the union, the advantage comes in the form of greater solidarity and unity among its members, since workers do not compete with one another to earn better employment terms, such as a pay raise or a promotion. Seniority provisions are standard in most unionized workplaces.

Employers can benefit from seniority provisions because seniority tends to lower turnover rates. On the other hand, some employers are often less enamored with seniority provisions, because they tend to limit employer discretion. A seniority provision may restrict an employer from assigning work to an employee it believes is the most productive by requiring that the work be assigned to the most senior employee. Moreover, since seniority provisions favour longer-serving employees, they can create barriers for young workers and women who experience gaps in service owing to child-rearing and childcare responsibilities. Seniority provisions can also impede an employer's ability to implement an incentive pay program, such as a wage bonus for top performers. For all of these reasons, the utility of seniority provisions has long been a hotly debated subject.

BOX 7.1 » TALKING WORK LAW

Unions as Agents of Social Change

We should be careful not to oversimplify the advantages unions gain for working people. In addition to bread-and-butter issues such as wages, seniority provisions, and grievance procedures, unions also play an important role in promoting broad social issues that affect both unionized and non-unionized workers. When unions go beyond immediate workplace objectives and seek to address the social conditions of workers, they are engaging in social unionism. Read the following passage from the website of UNIFOR, the largest Canadian private sector union in Canada, to get a sense of the social justice areas addressed by the labour movement:

> For decades, union membership (as a share of total employment) had been in steady decline—particu-

larly in the private sector. Running parallel to this decline in union density had been a sharp rise in income inequality, growing threats to retirement security, chronic unemployment and underemployment (particularly for young people) and a noticeable rise in insecure, precarious forms of work, especially among newcomers. The decline of union influence coincided with the rise of grossly imbalanced business-friendly policies, starting in the 1980s, that included tax cuts, labour market deregulation and corporate-led free trade deals.

---

*   UNIFOR, "History & Mission," http://www.unifor.org/en/about-unifor/history-mission.

III. Other Factors That Influence the Likelihood a Worker Will Join a Union

In addition to the instrumental and economic reasons just reviewed, four factors influence the likelihood that a worker will decide to join a union: personal characteristics, socio-economic status, the perceived instrumentality of the union, and the work environment.

A. Personal and Job Characteristics

Workers with greater commitment to a particular employer are more likely to join a union. This makes sense, considering the union wage premium and the seniority provisions discussed above. Older workers are more likely to have intentions to remain with an employer because they find it more difficult to secure a new job. People with dependants (children) are also more likely to want to stay with the same employer because of the risk of a loss of income while they find a new job. Furthermore, unions have been successful in bargaining for greater family benefits and greater job security, which are both important to people with dependants. Workers with firm-specific skills are also more likely to want to remain with the same employer and reap the rewards of a seniority provision. These workers cannot hope to have their skills recognized by a different employer. For example, a worker with years of experience using a one-of-a-kind data software program will have little success of securing a comparable salary with another employer who does not use the same software. Thus, older workers, workers with dependants, and workers with firm-specific skills have more incentive to remain with the same firm and are well placed to take advantage of the seniority provisions and union wage premiums that accompany union membership.

B. Socio-economic Status

In a unionized workplace, the wage rate is determined by a negotiation process between the union and the employer. Subsequent wage increases are assigned based on seniority. This process is most advantageous to workers who are traditionally poorly paid in non-unionized settings. From our discussion of discrimination in Chapter 21, we know that certain groups of people are systematically underpaid. Their experience in the labour market makes them keen to allow a union to negotiate a wage closer to the average. The union wage will almost always be higher than what they could secure on their own. For instance, women, visible minorities, and foreign-trained professionals (on average) earn less than their white, male, Canadian-trained counterparts and therefore stand to benefit the most from a union-negotiated wage, which makes them more likely to join a union if presented with the opportunity.[7]

C. The Work Environment

The level of contact a worker has with co-workers relative to the level of contact with managers and supervisors has an important impact on where a worker's allegiance lies. Workers who feel alienated from their co-workers and close to their supervisor are less likely to turn to a union for representation. By contrast, workers who have a strong bond with co-workers and feel alienated from their supervisor are more likely to join a union. For example, a construction crew that works alongside their supervisor all day, in a positive environment, will be less inclined to join a union compared with the same construction crew that only sees their supervisor once a week for 30 minutes to get instructions.

IV. How Do Unions Affect Business Outcomes?

In their book about Canadian unions, Pradeep Kumar and Chris Schenk observed what they call a "dominant discourse" in the media that portrays unions in an overwhelmingly negative fashion: "[T]here are frequent references in the media that unions are a special interest group, are 'inflexible,' are always demanding more, cause inefficiency."[8] From an empirical perspective, it is interesting to consider whether unions have a negative impact on firm performance.[9] A review of the academic literature on union effects on a company's productivity and profits paints a more nuanced picture.

A. Union Effects on a Company's Productivity and Profits

One of the most straightforward measures of firm success is profits. In industries with unionized and non-unionized workplaces, it would seem that the latter would have an advantage. If it is true that unionized workplaces have greater labour costs, inflexible workplace rules, a reduced ability to attract capital investment, and depressed sales levels, it might be expected that non-unionized workplaces would report higher levels of profits.[10] Alternatively, it is possible that the purported advantages of unions, such as lower rates of employee turnover, greater job security, and higher employee morale, may improve employee productivity so that heightened productivity in unionized workplaces negates the disadvantages commonly associated with unions.

Professors Freeman and Medoff found that the productivity benefits of unions in the US (e.g., greater voice) do not match the added costs of unionization, a point repeated by Freeman in a subsequent publication (see Box 7.2).[11] In fact, a consensus seems to exist among studies from the 1980s and the 1990s that union productivity gains fail to match added cost, and the net productivity effect is negative.[12] Recent US studies, to some degree, repeat this finding. For example, James Swanson and Kim Andrews, as well as Sandra Black and Lisa Lynch, find a negative productivity effect, although Christos Doucouliagos and Patrice Laroche report a small but positive union effect on productivity.[13] To date, only one study has examined the effect of unions on productivity in Canada. Using a small sample of 100 firms, Michel Grant and Jean Harvey found no significant difference between management's perception of workplace productivity in unionized and non-unionized firms.[14]

BOX 7.2 » TALKING WORK LAW

What Do Unions Do? by Richard B. Freeman and James L. Medoff

When published in the mid-1980s, the landmark book *What Do Unions Do?** shocked the business community by providing evidence that supported the beneficial role of unions. Synthesizing ten years of empirical research on the economic impact of unions on the American economy, the authors concluded that "On balance, unionization appears to improve rather than harm the social and economic system." This finding flew in the face of conventional wisdom, which portrayed unions as a cause of workplace conflict and inefficiency, and one of the major causes of the declining competitiveness of American firms. Their conclusion was especially startling since both authors were respected members of the business elite; both were professors in the department of economics at Harvard University.

_____

*   See B. Freeman and J.L. Medoff, *What Do Unions Do?* (New York: Basic Books, 1984).

Studies examining the direct link between union presence and firm profitability in North America are ambiguous. Two older US studies showed that unionized firms experience substantially lower profits, whereas a more recent US study found that union presence is associated with greater profitability, albeit the sample was restricted to newly created firms.[15] Canadian evidence is limited and dated. From a sample of manufacturing industries, Dennis Maki and Lindsay Meredith reported no union effect on profits from 1970 to 1979; whereas Pasquale Laporta and Alexander Jenkins found that union density (i.e., the proportion of workers who are union members in a firm) has a negative effect on firm profitability after analyzing a sample of manufacturing industries from 1986.[16]

B. Union Effects on Employment

Another key firm outcome that has been examined for a union effect is a firm's ability to grow in terms of the number of workers it employs. In theory, it is possible for unions to both increase and decrease employment growth. Unions present employees with "voice" that provides a formal process to channel grievances to management without fear of retribution. This could increase productivity by reducing turnover, enhancing incentives to invest in training, improving communication flows, and increasing employee morale.

The direct link between unionization and employment growth is investigated in only three studies in North America. Studying a sample of 1,798 California manufacturing firms from 1974 to 1980, Jonathan Leonard found that employment in unionized settings grew about 3.9 percent per year slower than in non-unionized settings.[17] There have been no US follow-up empirical studies since Leonard's article. In Canada, Long analyzed a sample of 510 Canadian workplaces from 1980 to 1985 and reported that in the manufacturing sector, union firms grew 3.7 percent more slowly per year than non-union firms; similarly in the non-manufacturing sector, union firms grew 3.9 percent more slowly per year than non-union firms.[18] Also using Canadian data, Walsworth found a smaller negative effect of 2.2 percent per year when the majority of a company's employees are unionized, but no effect when the commonly used "union status" measure is used (where even the presence of a single union member triggers the firm to be coded as "unionized"). In a follow-up study, Walsworth and Long found that only in larger firms in the manufacturing sector do unions have a negative impact on employment growth. By contrast, they found that unions are associated with employment growth in smaller firms in the service sector.[19] All things being equal, an increase in firm productivity will result in firm growth and therefore increase employment.

C. Union Effects on Business Innovation

Innovation may be restricted in a unionized workplace for three reasons. First, with a more formal relationship between workers and managers, it is likely that collaboration between workers in different job areas and collaboration between workers and managers may be limited, making product innovation less probable. Second, workers and managers may be more inclined to view their goals as distinct from each other, leaving workers with reduced incentive to innovate. For example, if a unionized worker is primarily concerned with wage maximization and considers firm profits or market share to be largely the concern of management, there may be limited desire and goodwill to innovate. Third, unions may pursue their goals by appropriating workplace control from management, thus interfering with unilateral management decisions regarding the design, speed, and process of production. In this scenario, it is easy to imagine a management team becoming frustrated with a union that slows or even prevents the implementation of a policy designed to elicit specific employee behaviours, such as a reorganization of the shop floor to encourage collaboration.

On the other hand, there are a number of reasons to suspect that unions promote innovation. The strong preference of unions for seniority-based pay (as opposed to merit-based pay) may encourage higher risk behaviours associated with innovation. In recognizing the separation between pay and productivity, a worker is ensured of less financial consequence for pursuing innovative ideas that may detract from immediate job productivity. For example, a worker is more inclined to temporarily neglect immediate production requirements to experiment with alternative production materials or processes that could significantly alter the final product. Additionally, because union members usually enjoy a wage premium, greater firm-specific loyalty may result, and workers may be more inclined to make contributions toward innovation. Finally, the purported higher cost of union labour and restrictions on outsourcing, via collective agreements, may encourage firms to compete based on product innovation, by offering new products or better quality products instead of competing based on low cost.[20] In this sense, a union-imposed higher production cost makes a low-cost product strategy less viable for unionized firms, and thus potentially promotes alternative product competition strategies that rely more on product innovation.

Only a handful of North American studies examine the direct relationship between unionization and innovation. From a sample of Canadian workplaces studied in 1999, Verma and Fang found no relationship between workplace union density and product innovation.[21] A more recent Canadian study of private sector firms found a small positive union effect on innovation.[22] From a US sample, Koeller found that unionization was significantly lower in firms with high innovation output.[23] Again using a US sample, David Audretsch and J.-Matthias Schulenburg found that high union density in a firm has a negative effect on innovation.[24]

D. Union Effects on Executive Compensation and/or Income Inequality

By way of summary, empirical evidence suggests that unions may have a negative impact on some firm outcomes. However, the evidence is not without exceptions and, especially in the Canadian context, large gaps exist in the industrial relations literature examining union effects on business performance. From an empirical standpoint, then, the effect of Canadian unions on firm performance (as measured by productivity, profit, employment growth, and innovation) is poorly documented in the industrial relations literature and does not provide clear support for the common sentiment that unions are bad for business.

There is a growing body of research that links countries with a strong union presence to higher levels of civic engagement (greater volunteerism or community service), more extensive social programs such as health care and pension plans, and lower levels of poverty.[25] All of these outcomes result in greater income equality, resulting in a society that has more evenly distributed its resources across the population. Union advocates argue that union efforts, such as petitioning government for better social programs or bargaining for more paid time off for community involvement, are partly responsible for greater income equality. Others disagree, and argue that unions do not cause these outcomes. Instead, they say that countries with a more socialist political climate have laws that support a strong union presence and greater income equality.

V. The Canadian Labour Movement: A Snapshot

Canada's close historical, cultural, and economic ties to the United States led US-based "international" unions to play a key role in the establishment of Canadian unions. Indeed, most of the oldest labour organizations in Canada began as small affiliates of much larger US unions. With their larger size and earlier development, US unions provided an attractive option for Canadian workers with few alternatives. US unions often exerted considerable control over their Canadian affiliates. The spread of unionism in the public sector during the 1960s and 1970s brought national (exclusively Canadian) unions to the fore, as international unions were seldom active among Canadian public employees. Since the 1970s, many Canadian unions have seceded from international unions, complaining of a lack of attention from the US leadership. In addition, growing Canadian patriotism and a widening cultural and political gap between Canada and the United States contributed to what is now a strong national labour movement. As a result, the proportion of international union membership declined from more than 70 percent in the mid-1960s to its current level of 5.2 percent.[26]

Most unionized workers in Canada (94.7 percent) belong to unions that have membership in a larger "umbrella" organization, commonly called a **parent union**. Since the 1960s, parent unions have played a key role in organizing non-unionized workers into unions and providing support for affiliated **local unions**—for example, by training of local union representatives, maintaining strike funds, and providing collective bargaining support and legal representation. The largest parent unions in Canada are listed in Table 7.1.

TABLE 7.1 The Largest Parent Unions in Canada

Union	Number of Members (2015)
Canadian Union of Public Employees (CUPE)	635,500
National Union of Public and General Employees (NUPGE)	360,000
UNIFOR	300,152
United Food and Commercial Workers Canada (UFCW)	247,543
United Steel, Paper and Forestry, Rubber, Manufacturing, Energy, Allied Industrial and Service Workers International Union (USW)	190,452
Public Service Alliance of Canada (PSAC)	181,017
Fédération de la santé et des services sociaux (FSSS)	135,527

Source: Statistics Canada, "Labour Organizations in Canada 2015," appendix 5, http://www .labour.gc.ca/eng/resources/info/publications/union_coverage/union_coverage.shtml.

parent union: A larger umbrella organization made up of smaller local unions. It provides service to its member local unions, such as training of local union representatives, maintaining strike funds, and providing collective bargaining support and legal expertise.

local union: A local branch of a union; it is part of and chartered by a parent union.

Public and private sector unions in all Canadian jurisdictions often join a central confederation that provides representation at a national level. Approximately 70 percent of all union members in Canada belong to a union that has membership in a national confederation.[27] The largest and most important confederation is the **Canadian Labour Congress (CLC)**, which represents 44.7 percent of all Canadian union members.[28] At times, the CLC has played an important role on the national front in promoting the agenda of unionized and non-unionized workers. For instance, the CLC was a key figure in the international boycott in support of the anti-apartheid effort aimed at promoting reform in South Africa in the early 1990s, as well as the political campaign to amend the *Canadian Charter of Rights and Freedoms*[29] and provincial human rights codes to legitimize same-sex marriage in 2005. Although the CLC is considered the prominent national representative of organized labour in Canada, it has considerably less power than unions in many other industrialized countries.[30] For example, unlike German unions, it does not engage in collective bargaining or provide direct support for striking affiliates. The CLC's influence is further compromised by its traditional liaison with the socialist federal New Democratic Party (NDP), which has never enjoyed first-party status and rarely achieved second-party status.

VI. Chapter Summary

In this chapter, we explored why workers join unions. Workers join unions for instrumental and economic reasons. Unions are able to promote worker "voice" and can negotiate better employment terms such as a union wage premium, seniority provisions, and a grievance procedure. Certain factors tend to influence the likelihood that a worker will join a union: personal characteristics, such as being an older worker, a worker with dependants, or a worker with firm-specific skills; low socio-economic status; the perceived instrumentality of the union; and a work environment in which workers are alienated from their managers and supervisors. We also reviewed the empirical evidence in search of support for the commonly held perception that unions are uniformly bad for business. Overall, the results were ambiguous and unsupportive.

QUESTIONS AND ISSUES FOR DISCUSSION

1. What is the voice effect? How might it contribute to the productivity of a unionized workplace?
2. How big is the union wage premium in Canada? Why might it be shrinking over time?
3. Conceptually, can you think of reasons why a union might make a worker more productive? Can you also think of ways a union would detract from productivity? Do the same for innovation.
4. Some argue that unions are no longer needed in Canada because we have strong laws that protect workers. Do you agree or disagree? Support your position with topics discussed in this chapter.

EXERCISE

Visit the website of a large parent union (see Table 7.1) and look for web pages aimed at non-unionized workers interested in joining a union. Is the sales pitch effective? After reading the reasons to join a union, do you feel excited about union membership? Using the topics covered in this chapter, write your own sales pitch to convince your classmates to form or join a union.

Canadian Labour Congress (CLC): The largest federal confederation of unions in Canada, representing 3 million Canadians. Its main roles are to lobby governments, provide leadership on key issues, and provide training and education resources for its member unions. It holds a national convention every three years.

UPDATES

Go to emond.ca/lawofworkircb for links to news, author's blog posts, content updates, and other information related to the chapters in this text.

NOTES AND REFERENCES

1 See Statistics Canada, "Labour Organizations in Canada 2015," https://www.canada.ca/content/dam/esdc-edsc/migration/documents/eng/resources/info/publications/union_coverage/UnionCoverage_EN.pdf. This source includes other statistical data on unions, collective bargaining, and industrial relations.

2 D. Taras and P. Steele, "We Provoked Our Students to Unionize: Deception Creates a Lasting IR Message" (2007) 45:1 *British Journal of Industrial Relations* 179.

3 See R. Freeman and J.L. Medoff, *What Do Unions Do?* (New York: Basic Books, 1984).

4 M.L. Blackburn "Are Union Wage Differentials in the United States Falling?" (2008) 47:3 *Industrial Relations* 390-418; and B. Bratsberg and J.F. Ragan Jr., "Changes in the Union Wage Premium by Industry" (2002) 56:1 *Industrial & Labor Relations Review* 65-83.

5 T. Fang and A. Verma, "Union Wage Premium" (2002) 3:9 *Perspectives on Labour and Income* 17.

6 S. Walsworth and R. Long, "Is the Union Employment Suppression Effect Diminishing? Further Evidence from Canada" (2012) 67:4 *Relations Industrielles/Industrial Relations* 654.

7 A. Verma, J.G. Reitz, and R. Banerjee, "Unions, Race, Immigrants and Earnings: A Longitudinal Examination of the Effect of Union Membership on the Income Progression of Immigrants to Canada," *International Migration Review* (Forthcoming).

8 P. Kumar and C. Schenk, "Introduction," in P. Kumar and C. Schenk, eds., *Paths to Union Renewal: Canadian Experiences* (Toronto: University of Toronto Press, 2009).

9 For a complete review of the empirical literature, see S. Walsworth, "What Do Unions Do to Innovation? An Empirical Examination of the Canadian Private Sector" (2010) 65:4 *Relations Industrielles/Industrial Relations* 543.

10 B.T. Hirsch, "Firm Investment Behavior and Collective Bargaining Strategy" (1992) 31:1 *Industrial Relations* 95; J. Godard, "Institutional Environments, Work and Human Resource Practices, and Unions: Canada vs. England" (2009) 62:2 *Industrial and Labor Relations Review* 173; S.G. Bronars, D.R. Deere, and J.S. Tracy, "The Effects of Unions on Firm Behavior: An Empirical Analysis Using Firm-Level Data" (1994) 33:4 *Industrial Relations* 426; and P.B. Voos and L.R. Mishel, "The Union Impact on Profits

in the Supermarket Industry" (1986) 68:3 *Review of Economics and Statistics* 513.

11 Freeman and Medoff, supra note 3; and D.G. Blanchflower and R. Freeman, "Unionism in the United States and Other Advanced OECD Countries" (1992) 31:1 *Industrial Relations* 56.

12 K.B. Clarke, "Unionization and Firm Performance: The Impact on Profits, Growth, and Productivity" (1984) 74:4 *American Economic Review* 893; B. Becker and C.A. Olson, "Unionization and Shareholder Interests" (1989) 42:2 *Industrial & Labor Relations Review* 246; B.T. Hirsch and R.A. Connolly, "Do Unions Capture Monopoly Profits?" (1987) 41:1 *Industrial & Labor Relations Review* 118; M.W. Mitchell and J.A. Stone, "Union Effects on Productivity: Evidence from Western US Sawmills" (1992) 46:1 *Industrial & Labor Relations Review* 135; D. Byrne, H. Dezhbakhsh, and Randall King, "Unions and Police Productivity: An Economic Investigation" (1996) 35:4 *Industrial Relations* 566; and S.G. Bronars, D.R. Deere, and J.S. Tracy, "The Effects of Unions on Firm Behavior: An Empirical Analysis Using Firm-Level Data" (1994) 33:4 *Industrial Relations* 426.

13 J. Swanson and K. Andrews, "Testing the Monopoly Union Model: A Stochastic Frontier Approach" (2007) 46:4 *Industrial Relations* 781; S.E. Black and L.M. Lynch, "How to Compete: The Impact of Workplace Practices and Information Technology on Productivity" (2001) 83:3 *Review of Economics and Statistics* 434; and C. Doucouliagos and P. Laroche, "What Do Unions Do to Productivity? A Meta-Analysis" (2003) 42:4 *Industrial Relations* 650.

14 M. Grant and J. Harvey, "Unions and Productivity: Convergence or Divergence in Perceptions?" (1992) 22:4 *International Studies of Management & Organization* 93.

15 B. Becker and C.A. Olson, "Unions and Firm Profits" (1992) 31:3 *Industrial Relations* 395; Bronars, Deere, Tracy, supra note 12; R. Batt and T.M. Welbourne, "Performance and Growth in Entrepreneurial Firms: Revisiting the Union-Performance Relationship," in J.A. Katz and T.M. Welbourne, eds., *Advances in Entrepreneurship, Form Emergence and Growth, Vol. 5: Managing People in Entrepreneurial Organizations: Learning from the Merger of Entrepreneurship and Human Resources Management* (Bingley, UK: Emerald Group Publishing, 2002).

16 D.R. Maki and M.L. Meredith, "The Effects of Unions on Profitability: Canadian Evidence" (1986) 41:1 *Relations Industrielles/Industrial Relations* 54; and P. Laporta and A. Jenkins, "Unionization and Profitability in the Canadian Manufacturing Sector" (1996) 51:4 *Relations Industrielles/Industrial Relations* 756.

17 J.S. Leonard, "Unions and Employment Growth" (1992) 31:1 *Industrial Relations* 80.

18 R. Long, "The Effect of Unionization on Employment Growth of Canadian Companies" (1993) 46:4 *Industrial & Labor Relations Review* 691.

19 Walsworth and Long, supra note 6.

20 J. Swanson and K. Andrews, "Testing the Monopoly Union Model: A Stochastic Frontier Approach" (2007) 46:4 *Industrial Relations* 781; and S.E. Black and L.M. Lynch, "How to Compete: The Impact of Workplace Practices and Information Technology on Productivity" (2001) 83:3 *Review of Economics and Statistics* 434.

21 A. Verma and T. Fang, "Workplace Innovation and Union Status: Synergy or Strife?" (Proceedings of 55th Annual Meeting, Industrial Relations Research Association, Washington, DC, January 2–5, 2003).

22 Walsworth and Long, supra note 6.

23 C.T. Koeller, "Union Membership, Market Structure, and the Innovation Output of Large and Small Firms" (1996) 17:4 *Journal of Labor Research* 683.

24 D. Audretsch and J.M. Graf von der Schlenburg, "Union Participation, Innovation, and Concentration: Results from a Simultaneous Model" (1990) 146 *Journal of Institutional and Theoretical Economics* 298.

25 G. Sran, M. Lynk, J. Clancy, and D. Fudge, "Unions Matter: How the Ability of Labour Unions to Reduce Income Inequality and Influence Public Policy Has Been Affected by Regressive Labour Laws" (2013), http://www.law.harvard.edu/programs/lwp/papers/CFLR%20Unions%20Matter_2.pdf; M. Lynk, "Labour Law and the New Inequality" (2009) 15 *Just Labour* 125, http://www.justlabour.yorku.ca/volume15/pdfs/11_lynk_press.pdf.

26 See Statistics Canada, supra note 1.

27 Ibid.

28 Ibid.

29 *Canadian Charter of Rights and Freedoms*, part I of the *Constitution Act, 1982*, being Schedule B to the *Canada Act 1982* (UK), 1982, c. 11.

30 For a more complete discussion of the Canadian labour movement in comparison to labour movements in other developed and developing nations, see D. Taras and S. Walsworth, "Employment Relations in Canada," in G.J. Bamber, R.D. Lansbury, N. Wailes, and C.F. Wright, eds., *International and Comparative Employment Relations: National Regulation, Global Changes*, 6th ed. (London: Sage, 2016).

CHAPTER 8

The Unionization Process

LEARNING OBJECTIVES

After reading this chapter, students will be able to:

- Explain the significance of the principles of majoritarianism and exclusivity in the Canadian collective bargaining regime.
- Describe the typical steps in a union organizing campaign.
- Describe the key components of the union certification process and potential issues that can arise during this process.
- Describe how Canadian labour relations boards decide what an "appropriate bargaining unit" is and why this decision is important to the collective bargaining model.
- Explain why certain types of employees are excluded from the right to unionize, including "managerial" and "confidential" employees.
- Compare the card-check model and the mandatory certification vote model for measuring whether a majority of employees support collective bargaining, and identify the jurisdictions that use each model.
- Explain how unions can obtain the legal right to represent workers through voluntary recognition.

I. Introduction

Chapter 8 is longer than most. This is by necessity, owing to the complexity and importance of the subject matter. This chapter describes how non-unionized employees transition from the common law regime to the collective bargaining regime, and explains how unions in Canada obtain the legal right to represent employees. Unions can do so in two ways: by obtaining a government-issued licence (**union certification**) or through **voluntary recognition**, whereby the employer agrees to bargain with a union that has not been certified. The process of unionization varies across Canada's jurisdictions. Our objective in this chapter is to explain common features of the "Canadian model" of unionization, and not to describe every detail of each province's legal model. The term "Canadian model" is used with trepidation because within Canada, a range of occupation-specific models also exist. Construction workers, artists, and agricultural workers are among the types of workers for whom a special and different collective bargaining model exists in some jurisdictions. We will focus on the model of unionization that applies to the vast majority of Canadian employees.

---

union certification: A government-issued licence that entitles a union to represent employees in a defined bargaining unit in their relationship with their employer.

voluntary recognition: An arrangement in which an employer elects to recognize and bargain with a union that has not been certified by the government as the representative of employees.

II. The Pillars of the Canadian Collective Bargaining Model: Majoritarianism and Exclusivity

The American *Wagner Act* of 1935 (see Chapter 6) introduced a model of collective bargaining unlike those developing in Europe and the rest of the world.[1] It included a rule providing that once a union demonstrates that it has the support of a majority of employees in a **bargaining unit**—a defined group of employees of a single employer—then that union becomes the "exclusive bargaining representative" of *all of the employees in the bargaining unit*, even those employees who did not seek the union's representation or join the union.[2] As a result, a collective agreement negotiated by the union covers every employee in a bargaining unit.

The twin concepts of **majoritarianism** and **exclusivity** were borrowed and incorporated into Canadian collective bargaining legislation in the mid-1940s and remain a pillar of the Canadian model to this day. This is an all-or-nothing model of freedom of association. If 100 employees are in the bargaining unit and 50 of them desire union representation, then none of the employees are entitled to collective bargaining, because the union requires majority employee support to acquire the legal right to represent employees.[3] On the other hand, if 51 percent of employees support unionization, then their decision sweeps the remaining 49 percent of employees who rejected unionization into the collective bargaining regime. This legal model encourages a contest for the hearts and minds of employees. That contest begins with a union organizing campaign.

III. The Union Organizing Campaign

A successful union organizing campaign introduces a new dynamic into employment relations that will ultimately restrict the authority and discretion employers enjoy in the common law regime. Not surprisingly, therefore, most employers resist attempts by their employees to unionize.[4] The process by which employees move from the common law regime to the collective bargaining regime is usually an adversarial one. Professor Karen Bentham (University of Toronto) found that 80 percent of Canadian employers actively resist attempts by their employees to unionize through lawful persuasion in the form of arguments against collective bargaining and, sometimes, threats or reprisals against employees who support the union (which violate the **unfair labour practices** provisions in collective bargaining legislation; see Chapter 9).[5]

Employees realize that their employer would prefer to remain non-union, and so they usually keep their interest in a union hidden from the employer for as long as possible. Workers can create their own union, but more often they join established unions.[6] A typical union organizing campaign begins with private meetings between employees and a professional union organizer outside of the workplace, and hushed conversations at the workplace. Sometimes **union organizers** make first contact with employees—for example, by leaving union flyers on car windshields

---

bargaining unit: A group of workers whose work is similar enough that they are thought capable to be covered by the same collective agreement. Importantly, not all bargaining unit members necessarily choose to join the union.

majoritarianism: A principle of the Wagner model, it asserts that a union must secure the support of a majority of employees to win the right to act as their representative.

exclusivity: A principle of the Wagner model, it asserts that the union chosen to represent workers becomes the sole or exclusive legal representative for that group of workers.

unfair labour practice: An action undertaken by either the union or the employer that violates one or more articles in the relevant labour relations legislation.

union organizer: An employee of a union whose principal duties include organizing new workplaces and building union membership.

or approaching employees as they enter or leave the workplace. In other cases, employees contact a union to ask about organizing a union at their workplace.

Once contact is made, union organizers meet with those employees who initially express interest, usually at the union office or another location away from the workplace, such as a coffee shop or restaurant. The organizer will promote the benefits of collective bargaining over individual employment contracts and explain how an organizing campaign works, including the laws that govern the process and the requirement for the union to demonstrate to the government that it represents a majority of the employees. Evidence of this employee support is collected in the form of signed **union membership cards** (similar to the one shown below) or, in some jurisdictions, **union authorization cards**, which indicate that the employee wishes the union to represent him or her in bargaining with the employer.[7] Depending on the jurisdiction, employees may also be

USW Member Card
Reprinted with the permission of United Steelworkers.

required to pay a small fee to the union of between $1 and $5, which is supposed to signal to the employee that he or she is making an important decision and not just signing a petition.[8]

Professional union organizers are rarely permitted on employer property to meet with employees (see Box 8.1), so unions rely heavily on **inside union organizers** to speak to their co-workers at the workplace and ask them to sign union cards.[9] Those cards are then returned to the union organizer. If the union collects sufficient cards to meet the required legislative threshold (see Box 8.3), it can file an **application for certification** with the applicable labour relations board.

---

union membership card: A document that indicates a worker's desire to join and become a member of a union.

union authorization card: A document that indicates a worker's consent and desire to have the union identified on the card represent them in collective bargaining with an employer.

inside union organizer: An employee who assists in efforts to unionize his or her own employer.

application for certification: A formal legal document filed by an employee or union with a labour relations board that commences a process to determine whether the union qualifies to become the legal collective bargaining representative of a group of employees.

Union Access to Workers and Employer Property Rights

In political campaigns, effort is made to ensure voters hear the candidates' messages. The political parties are provided with voters' lists, including home addresses, so that campaigners can knock on doors to persuade voters to vote for their party. Public debates are held in local venues and on television. The media report on what the candidates say, and on the parties' platforms. In the political context, the pursuit of an informed electorate is highly valued.

The unionization process similarly involves a campaign of ideas. Unions seek to persuade employees to support the union, and those opposed to the union, including the employer, advocate remaining non-union. As the Ontario Court of Appeal noted, for the right to organize a union to be meaningful, "it is manifest that employees must have access to union communications and opportunities for organizational activity."*

The most obvious location for discussions about collective bargaining to take place is the workplace. Employers have easy access to employees by virtue of being in control of the workplace. They can order employees to come to meetings during working hours to hear the employer's arguments against unionization (i.e., **captive audience meetings**; see Chapter 9); distribute documents describing the employer's views; engage in one-on-one discussions with employees at work; and contact employees at home by phone, mail, or email.

Unions have a more difficult time reaching employees. Trespass to property legislation protects the right of property owners to exclude union organizers, except in very narrow circumstances, such as when employees work and live on employer property (e.g., a remote mine) or when the entrance

to the workplace is located in a space where the public usually has access (e.g., a shopping mall).† Therefore, unions must rely on "inside union organizers" to speak with their co-workers at work, or attempt to reach employees outside of the workplace and during non-working times.

This inequality of union access to employees has long been a source of controversy, in both Canada and the United States. A number of options exist if Canadian governments wanted to ensure unions are more easily able to communicate their message to workers. For example, in Britain, the law requires that employers allow unions an opportunity to hold meetings at the workplace during working time.‡ In the United States, employers must provide unions with employee phone numbers and email addresses prior to a union certification vote to facilitate discussions outside of work.§ However, Canadian governments have so far declined to adopt similar union access policies.

---

* *Cadillac Fairview Corp. Ltd. v. R.W.D.S.U.* (1989), 71 OR (2d) 206 (Ont. CA), at 208.
† P. Macklem, "Property, Status, and Workplace Organizing" (1990) 40 *University of Toronto Law Journal* 74; and *RMH Teleservices v. BCGEU* (2003), 223 DLR (4th) 750 (BCSC).
‡ See the discussion of the British union access model in D. Doorey, "Union Access to Workers During Organizing Campaigns: A New Look Through the Lens of B.C. Health Services" (2008) 15 *Canadian Labour and Employment Law Journal* 1, at 17–22, http://papers.ssrn.com/sol3/papers.cfm?abstract_id=1285703.
§ National Labor Relations Board, "NLRB Representation Case—Procedures Fact Sheet," https://www.nlrb.gov/news-outreach/fact-sheets/nlrb-representation-case-procedures-fact-sheet.

IV. The Union Certification Process

The "application for certification" initiates a highly complex legal process set out in labour relations legislation. The precise details of what happens next vary across jurisdictions, but in general terms, it is the role of the labour relations board to determine whether the union has satisfied all of the requirements for certification. Those requirements include the following components, each of which can give rise to litigation before a labour relations board.

A. "Trade Union" Status

Most Canadian collective bargaining statutes permit only "trade unions"[10] to apply for certification and not other types of employee associations.[11] Since only a "trade union" can apply for certification, the first thing a labour relations board checks when it receives an application for certification is that a "trade union" filed the application. When the union involved is well

---

captive audience meeting: A meeting that employees are ordered by their employer to attend to listen to the employer's opinions on whether employees should or should not support unionization.

established, its status will not be questioned. But if the organization is newly formed or lacks history before the labour relations board, union status may be challenged. The statutes provide little guidance on what qualifies as a "trade union," beyond a requirement that the organization's objectives include regulating employee relations through collective bargaining and that the organization be independent of the employer.[12] Not every association of workers qualifies as a legally recognized trade union. Labour relations boards have ruled that to qualify as a "trade union," an organization must demonstrate a degree of formality, such as by having bylaws or a constitution, and an executive or officers who have authority to act on its behalf to bargain collective agreements on behalf of employees.[13] A union that is created with the financial support or participation or influence of the employer (known as a **company union**) cannot be certified in Canada.[14] A company union is not illegal in Canada (as it is in the United States), but it lacks legal status to enter into contracts or appear as a party in legal proceedings.[15]

B. Timeliness of Certification Applications

Restrictions exist on *when* a union can apply for certification, so labour relations boards must next ensure that the application is "timely." These restrictions break down generally as follows:

1. If the employer *is not unionized*, then any union can apply to represent its employees. However, there may be a restriction (known as a **statutory bar**) on a union that had previously filed an unsuccessful application for certification relating to the same or similar group of employees rejected in the recent past.[16] The length of the statutory bar is either left to the sole discretion of the labour relations board (e.g., in Nova Scotia, Prince Edward Island) or specified in the jurisdiction's labour relations legislation (ranging from three months in Quebec and British Columbia to one year in Ontario and Saskatchewan), but usually allows the labour relations board some discretion to reduce the period of time.

2. If the employer *is unionized*, then an application for certification by another union to represent the unionized employees (known as a **union raid** or displacement application) can only be filed during an **open period** defined in collective bargaining legislation. A newly certified union is given a grace period of between 6 months (in British Columbia) and 12 months (in most other jurisdictions) to bargain a first collective agreement, during which time no other union can apply to displace it as the representative of the employees in the bargaining unit. When a collective agreement is in effect, open periods arise during the final months of the agreement. For example, in Ontario, if the collective agreement is for less than three years, the open period is during the final three months of the agreement; and if the collective agreement is for greater than three years, the open period is during months 34 to 36 and then the last three months of every subsequent year.[17] Open periods ensure that a union's representation rights can be challenged periodically.

---

company union: An employee association created with the encouragement or assistance of the employer and that is not independent of the employer's control or influence. A company union is often created as a union-avoidance strategy.

statutory bar: A rule found in collective bargaining legislation that prohibits an application from being filed for a defined period of time.

union raid: An attempt by one trade union to organize workers who are represented by another trade union.

open period: A period of time defined in a collective bargaining statute during which a union may apply to displace another union as the representative of a group of employees, or during which unionized employees may file an application to "de-certify" the union.

C. *Required Employee Support for the Union and Collective Bargaining*

Assuming that a "trade union" has filed a "timely" application for certification, the labour relations board then turns to the crucial issue of assessing the level of employee support for the union. This step begins with a review of union membership cards (or union authorization cards, where permitted) submitted by the union to determine the number of employees who support the union and want collective bargaining. To protect employees from possible reprisals, the identity of the employees who sign union cards is not disclosed to the employer, although the employer may learn during the certification process how many or what percentage of employees signed union cards.[18]

In Canada, a simple fraction ultimately determines whether workers have access to the collective bargaining regime. Let's refer to it as "the golden fraction":

$$\frac{\text{Number of employees who want the union to represent them in collective bargaining}}{\text{Number of employees eligible to participate in the decision}}$$

The numerator is the measure of employee support for unionization. It is measured either by a count of union cards or through a government-conducted secret ballot vote. The denominator is the total number of employees eligible to participate in the decision, or the number of **bargaining unit employees**. We know from elementary school math class that a change to either the numerator or denominator without an equal corresponding change to the other will change the quotient, or percentage of union support. The composition of the golden fraction gives rise to a multitude of potential legal disputes that are routinely dealt with at labour relations boards across Canada, a few of which are explored below.

1. Who Is an "Employee" for the Purpose of Union Certification Applications?

In Chapter 2 we discussed the importance of identifying employment status, since most statutes designed to protect workers in fact only apply to "employees." This is true too of collective bargaining statutes. The task of distinguishing between an "employee" and an "independent contractor" is simplified in some jurisdictions (including Ontario and British Columbia) by a broad statutory definition that includes **dependent contractors** (see Chapter 2).[19] A dependent contractor is a worker who exhibits greater autonomy and independence than a typical employee, yet who nevertheless remains economically dependent and largely under the control of one business. For example, Canadian labour relations boards have ruled that taxi and limo drivers, bike couriers, and truck drivers are dependent contractors and entitled to unionize, even though they exhibit far more independence than a typical employee.[20] Even in jurisdictions that do not expressly include "dependent contractor" in the definition of "employees," labour relations boards have applied a broad application of "employee status" that emphasizes economic dependence.[21]

Some employees are expressly *excluded* from the right to unionize in collective bargaining legislation, including various professionals such as lawyers, medical doctors, and engineers.[22] Whether these exclusions violate the *Canadian Charter of Rights and Freedoms*[23] guarantee of freedom of association is an open question (see Chapter 17). Two types of employees that are

---

bargaining unit employee: An employee whose job falls within a bargaining unit that a union either represents or is seeking to represent.

dependent contractor: A worker whose status falls in between that of an employee and an independent contractor. This worker has more autonomy and independence than a typical employee yet remains economically dependent on one customer for income and is subject to considerable control at the hands of that customer.

excluded in every Canadian jurisdiction are employees who exercise managerial functions (**managerial exclusion**) and employees who are engaged in a confidential capacity in matters relating to labour relations (**confidential employee exclusion**). Governments defend these exclusions on the basis that a conflict of interest or loyalties would arise if these employees could unionize, since their allegiance should be to the employer.[24] Employees are divided into two teams, and those who wield real authority and power over subordinates are assigned to the employer's team, as are employees who regularly have access to confidential labour relations information that would be of value to the union's team.

Substantial labour relations board case law explores these exclusions. In applying the managerial exclusion, labour relations boards in Canada have looked for evidence that the employee either (1) holds a senior management position with independent authority to make decisions on policy or the running of the company or (2) exercises real meaningful control over the livelihood of subordinate employees.[25] An employee's job title means very little. Labour relations boards look for evidence that the person actually makes effective decisions about hiring, firing, disciplining, and promoting workers. Simple supervisory tasks like scheduling or directing work are not usually enough to bring a person into the managerial exclusion. The person must have the authority to make decisions that substantially impact employees' wages, job assignments, and job security.[26] The fact that an employee sometimes makes recommendations to management about hiring, firing, promotions, and discipline does not alone signal that the person exercises managerial functions. However, if in fact management always or usually follows those recommendations, then a labour relations board is likely to find that the employee makes "effective managerial decisions" and is excluded. Consider the case presented in Box 8.2.

BOX 8.2 » CASE LAW HIGHLIGHT

The Managerial Exclusion

Langley City Foods Ltd. v. United Food and Commercial Workers International Union, Local No. 1518
2006 CanLII 22075 (BCLRB)

Key Facts: The union applied to be certified for a bargaining unit of employees at a grocery store. It argued that two employees with the job title "assistant store manager" should be excluded because they exercised managerial functions and therefore were not "employees." The assistant store managers supervised the grocery department, which is the largest department at the store; attended management meetings; were responsible for running the store when the owner, Lee, or his wife were away; investigated employee wrongdoing and reported their findings to Lee; and made recommendations to Lee about whether probationary employees should be kept

on, which Lee usually followed. Lee did the hiring, and there was no evidence that the assistant store managers had ever disciplined anyone. The employer argued that notwithstanding their job title, the assistant store managers were really just low-level supervisors with little real authority over the other bargaining unit employees and therefore should be included in the bargaining unit.

Issue: Did the assistant store managers exercise managerial functions such that they fell within the managerial exclusion and therefore were not entitled to be in the bargaining unit?

Decision: The BC Labour Relations Board ruled that the assistant store managers did not exercise sufficient managerial authority over the employees to bring them into the

---

managerial exclusion: A common exclusion from the definition of "employee" in collective bargaining legislation that has the effect of excluding employees who exercise managerial functions from the protected rights to collective bargaining made available to other employees by that legislation.

confidential employee exclusion: A common exclusion from the definition of "employee" in collective bargaining legislation that has the effect of excluding employees who exercise confidential labour relations–related functions from the protected rights to collective bargaining made available to other employees by that legislation.

managerial exclusion. The board summarized its approach to the managerial exclusion:

[T]he Board focuses on whether the person in question exercises effective determination of decisions related to discipline and discharge or whether they provide labour relations input. In addition, the Board considers whether the individual makes decisions regarding hiring, promotion or demotion. The Board has commented that the common theme identified is whether the individual exercises powers that are capable of having a significant impact on the career of an employee. When considering whether an individual makes disciplinary decisions, there is no minimum amount of discipline required. … [R]egardless

of how often the individual imposes discipline, if the individual makes the effective determination of disciplinary decisions that is sufficient to exclude the person as a manager.

In this case, although the assistant store managers effectively ran the store when Lee or his wife were not present, the evidence disclosed that all important decisions relating to hiring, promotion, discipline or dismissal, and wages and benefits were made by Lee. The assistant store managers were conduits of information to Lee about the employees, but they had little real authority to make decisions that affected the working lives of the employees. Therefore, the assistant store managers were included in the bargaining unit, and their ballots in the certification vote were to be counted.

The confidential employee exclusion is very narrow.[27] It excludes from the collective bargaining statute only those employees whose (1) regular, core duties (2) involve handling confidential information of a nature related to industrial relations that is not otherwise available to the union or employees in the bargaining unit, and (3) that would compromise the employer if disclosed to the union.[28] For example, a person whose regular job duties involves participating in management meetings to discuss employer collective bargaining or grievance strategies would be excluded, but a worker who only has incidental contact with collective bargaining information probably would not be excluded under this ground.

2. Who Is the Employer?

Usually the identity of the employer is obvious, but not always. Identifying the employer can prove challenging if control over employees is divided among multiple businesses, such as when work is performed by workers engaged by a subcontractor or supplied by a temporary placement agency. Are workers sent to Company X by a temporary placement agency employees of Company X or the temporary placement agency? The answer can matter greatly to the outcome of a union organizing campaign at Company X. If the "temps" are Company X employees, then their wishes count for the purposes of determining whether the union has majority support. In deciding which business entity is the employer, labour relations boards focus on who exercises control and authority over the employees while they are performing the work.[29] An example is described in Box 8.3.

BOX 8.3 » CASE LAW HIGHLIGHT

Identifying the True Employer

United Food and Commercial Workers International Union, Local 1000A v. Nike Canada Ltd.
2006 CanLII 24724 (Ont. LRB)

Key Facts: The union applied for certification to represent employees at a Nike distribution centre. The certification law in Ontario required the union to demonstrate that at least 40 percent of the employees in the bargaining unit were union members to qualify for a certification vote. When the union filed its application for certification, there were 70 full-time Nike employees in the factory and an additional 180 workers

supplied by Manpower, a temporary employment supplier ("temps"). The contract between Nike and Manpower identified Manpower as the temps' employer. However, in its response to the application for certification, Nike argued that it was the temp's employer. The union argued that Manpower was the employer. If the temps were Nike employees, then they would be employees in the bargaining unit, and the union would not have the requisite 40 percent to obtain a certification ballot.

Issue: Was Nike or Manpower the true employer of the temps for the purpose of the Ontario *Labour Relations Act*?

Decision: The Ontario Labour Relations Board ruled that Nike was the true employer. Citing the leading case on the identification of the employer in Ontario, *York Condominium Corp.* ([1977] Ont. LRB Rep. Oct. 645), the OLRB considered the following factors in its determination:

1. the party exercising direction and control over the employees;
2. the party bearing the burden of remuneration;
3. the party imposing discipline;
4. the party hiring the employees;
5. the party with authority to dismiss the employees;
6. the party who is perceived to be the employer by the employees; and
7. the existence of an intention to create the relationship of employer and employee.

Although Manpower had a representative at the Nike factory, the temps were under the direct control of Nike supervisors in the performance of their work there. Even though the temps were paid by Manpower, Nike effectively determined the rate of pay. Nike supervisors gave warnings to the temps, and Nike could effectively dismiss a temp by instructing Manpower to no longer send that temp to Nike. Manpower hired the temps, but Nike put new temps on a probationary period and could elect not to keep a temp. Therefore, the hiring criteria did not represent a strong indicator in this case. Some longer service temps perceived Nike to be their employer, but many of the temps who had spent less time at Nike perceived Manpower to be their employer. Weighing all of these factors, the Ontario Labour Relations Board decided that the true employer was Nike, since it had ultimate control over the temps at Nike, including disciplinary power and the authority to set the wage rate. With the temps added to the denominator in the golden fraction, the union no longer had membership cards on behalf of 40 percent of the employees, and its application for certification was dismissed.

Collective bargaining legislation grants labour relations boards discretion to declare two or more businesses to be **related employers** for collective bargaining purposes. For a related employer declaration to be made, the board requires that four conditions be met: (1) there must be more than one business entity; (2) the entities concerned must carry on associated or related activities; (3) those activities must be carried out under common control or direction; and (4) there must be a labour relations reason to make the common employer declaration.[30] In the case of *Metro Waste Paper Recovery* in Ontario, Metro used a temporary employee agency (KAS) to supply almost all of its employees at a factory in Whitby.[31] A union applied to represent Metro employees at the factory, but the employer argued that all of the employees worked for KAS. In addition to arguing that Metro was the "true employer," the union also argued that KAS and Metro were related employers. The Ontario Labour Relations Board agreed, finding that the two companies were carrying on related activities at the Whitby factory under common control and direction, and that it would be difficult for the union to bargain with just one of the companies. The union was certified to represent employees of both companies at the Whitby factory.

3. Defining the "Appropriate Bargaining Unit"

The denominator in the golden fraction is the total number of employees eligible to participate in the unionization decision, or the voting constituency. It is the role of labour relations boards to determine who those employees are. They do this by deciding what is an **appropriate bargaining unit**. In general, an appropriate bargaining unit is a grouping of jobs that the labour relations board believes should be bundled together for the purposes of collective bargaining. For example, a union applying to represent employees at a typical Canadian Tire store might propose a bargaining unit like this:

> The Union applies to represent all employees of Canadian Tire at 123 Junction Avenue, in the City of Toronto, except Automotive Service employees, Department Supervisors, and persons above the rank of Department Supervisor.

---

related employers: Two or more companies ruled by a labour relations board to be carrying out associated or related activities under common direction and control and, therefore, to be a single employer for collective bargaining purposes.

appropriate bargaining unit: A grouping of jobs or employees that a labour relations board decides is suitable to be represented together in collective bargaining.

Assume that there are 60 employees that fall within that proposed bargaining unit and the union has signed cards on behalf of 36 of them (or 60 percent). The union looks to be in good shape in a model that requires the union to demonstrate 50 percent or more support to be certified.

However, the employer might argue that the union's proposed bargaining unit is not appropriate. For example, it might claim that an appropriate bargaining unit should include all Canadian Tire stores in Toronto, or all stores owned by the franchisee that owns the store at 123 Junction Avenue, or at the very least it should include the Automotive Service employees and Department Supervisors at the store named by the union. If the employer wins any of those arguments, then the denominator in the golden fraction would increase, and unless the union has supporters among the added employees, the percentage of workers who support the union will decrease. For example, if the labour relations board rules that an appropriate bargaining unit includes the 20 Automotive Service employees at the one store in addition to those the union initially sought, the denominator in the golden fraction increases to 80 and the union's support level falls to 43.7 percent (36/80), which is less than a majority.

BOX 8.4 » TALKING WORK LAW

Appropriate Bargaining Units: Union Organization Versus Viable Collective Bargaining Structures

How a labour relations board defines the bargaining unit is crucial to the potential success of the application for certification, as well as the future viability of the collective bargaining relationship. If a bargaining unit includes only a small subgroup of a company's employees, it may be easier for the union to organize, but once certified, the bargaining unit may have very little bargaining power vis-à-vis the employer. A larger bargaining unit usually has more bargaining power and therefore greater collective bargaining viability than a smaller bargaining unit. However, a larger bargaining unit is also much harder to organize. Professor Brian Langille (University of Toronto) explains this tension:

[T]he bargaining unit serves at least two functions. It serves as the basis for the formation of a long term bargaining structure and it also serves as the basis for organization. Combined with this has been the realization that these two functions often pull in opposite directions, the former in favour of large (broad based) units and the latter in favour of smaller (easier to organize) units. The whole struggle has been to reconcile these conflicting forces.[32]

Labour relations boards seek to balance these competing forces when they determine which bargaining units are appropriate for bargaining.

Sometimes legislation provides direction to the labour relations board on what the bargaining unit should be, or cannot be. For example, it is common for collective bargaining legislation to instruct labour relations boards that a unit consisting solely of "dependent contractors,"[33] "professionals,"[34] or employees with special technical skills ("craft units")—such as electricians or bricklayers[35]—is appropriate, while a unit consisting of "private constables" along with other employees is not.[36] The Ontario *Labour Relations Act* provides that a bargaining unit that comprises security guards and the employees they monitor may be appropriate, but the labour relations board is directed to decide whether placing those two groups of employees in the same unit would create a conflict of interest.[37] The *Saskatchewan Employment Act* prohibits a bargaining unit that includes "supervisors" and the employees they supervise, unless both the employer and union agree otherwise.[38]

In Nova Scotia, the *Trade Union Act* requires two or more "manufacturing" facilities of the same employer to be treated as a single bargaining unit if the facilities are "interdependent."[39] This law is commonly referred to as the "Michelin Amendment" because its purpose was to impede unionization of several large Michelin tire factories.[40] The government was concerned the tire company would leave the province if its workers unionized. The requirement for the union to organize a majority of employees at all of the Michelin plants has proven to be an insurmountable hurdle to collective bargaining.

Situation-specific rules such as these are found in collective bargaining legislation across the country. However, most labour relations boards are given broad discretion to determine what is an "appropriate bargaining unit," and there is a huge body of very important case law explaining how they go about this task.[41] Unions are given wide berth in defining the unit of employees they would like to represent. The legal test is whether the bargaining unit proposed by the union in the application for certification is *an* appropriate bargaining unit, not whether it is the best bargaining unit that the labour relations board could imagine. However, the union does not have carte blanche to decide the type of bargaining unit. Labour relations boards must decide whether the bargaining unit proposed by the union makes good labour relations sense.

For many years, labour relations boards emphasized that an appropriate bargaining unit is one in which employees share a **community of interest**, meaning that their work and employment-related interests and concerns are sufficiently similar that it makes sense for those workers to bargain together as a group. The following factors are relevant in assessing whether a "community of interest" exists among workers in a proposed bargaining unit: (1) similarity of skills, interests, duties, and working conditions; (2) the physical and administrative structure of the employer; (3) functional integration of the work and employees; and (4) geography.[42] Applying the concept of community of interest, labour relations boards historically separated blue-collar factory workers from white-collar office and clerical workers, and part-time from full-time employees, although these distinctions are less rigidly applied today.[43]

More recently, the "nebulous concept of community of interest" has become less important because, to use the words of the Ontario Labour Relations Board, "all employees share a community of interest by virtue of working for the same employer."[44] Labour relations boards prefer larger over smaller bargaining units because, as noted above, they are usually more viable for collective bargaining, but they are also cognizant of the fact that large bargaining units can be difficult for unions to organize. Unions usually prefer the largest bargaining units that they can realistically organize, and therefore labour relations boards tend to give unions the bargaining unit they propose, except when that unit would cause the employer serious labour relations problems.[45] The most common such problems include **undue fragmentation** of bargaining units that could leave the workplace carved up into little pockets of bargaining units, each with their own collective agreement. For example, a unit of six shipping and receiving employees is unlikely to be an appropriate unit, since it makes little labour relations sense to separate them from a larger bargaining unit of all factory workers.

Labour relations boards are also concerned about separating employees into different bargaining units when there is a history of regular interchange of employees in and out of the proposed unit or where there is functional integration of the proposed unit with other parts of the business.[46] In these situations, practical human resources issues arise when employees are covered by a collective agreement some days and not others, or when a strike by workers in one bargaining unit would effectively shut down the work performed by the other bargaining unit. These issues can arise most vividly when there are multiple locations of the same employer within a similar geographical area, as considered in the case discussed in Box 8.5.

---

community of interest: A common test used by labour boards in assessing whether a proposed bargaining unit is appropriate for collective bargaining; it asks whether the workers share sufficient commonality that grouping them together makes industrial relations sense.

undue fragmentation: A legal test used by labour boards to decide whether a proposed bargaining unit is inappropriate because it would carve up the workplace into too many relatively small groups of workers, creating practical business difficulties for the employer.

BOX 8.5 » CASE LAW HIGHLIGHT

What Is an Appropriate Bargaining Unit at Tim Hortons?

United Food & Commercial Workers, Local 206 v. Lynn Management Ltd.

[1999] Ont. LRB Rep. Nov. 19; reconsideration denied 2000 CanLII 1574 (Ont. LRB)

Key Facts: The union (United Food & Commercial Workers, or UFCW) applied to represent employees at one Tim Hortons store in Hamilton, Ontario. The store was a franchise of Tim Hortons Limited and the owner/employer (Lynn Management) also owned ten other Tim Hortons franchises within a 10-kilometre area. The employer argued that the appropriate bargaining unit includes all 11 stores it owns. The union did not have adequate employee support to be certified in any bargaining unit larger than just the one store it had applied to represent.

Issue: Was the union's proposed bargaining unit consisting of one Tim Hortons store an appropriate bargaining unit?

Decision: No. The Ontario Labour Relations Board ruled that a unit of just one store was not appropriate in this case due to the high degree of integration between the various stores owned by the employer. There was a sufficient "community of interest" among employees at individual stores and among employees of all 11 stores to create a viable collective bargaining relationship owing to the similar work and human resources practices that are fairly standard across the Tim Hortons chain. The real issue, therefore, was whether the union's proposed unit of one store would create "serious labour

relations problems" for the employer. The board concluded that it would, and noted:

> [T]he Board must balance the statutory goal of employee self-organization with the goal of promoting certain bargaining structures. The Board judges whether the [union's] proposed unit is *an* appropriate unit rather than *the most* appropriate unit. In that context, the Board may find that its concern for employee access to collective bargaining outweighs the potential for serious labour relations problems. That is the balancing exercise necessitated in judging whether the applicant's single-store unit is an appropriate unit in this case. [emphasis added]

The board ruled that a single-store bargaining unit would "cause undue fragmentation of the employer's functionally integrated enterprise." The employer used common cooking facilities to supply doughnuts to all 11 stores; the stores shared supplies and had a unified management system under the control of the principals of Lynn Management; hiring of employees at the various stores was centralized to a degree by the involvement of Lynn managers; and employees occasionally moved from store to store to pick up or cover shifts. The board ruled that the close integration of the 11 stores rendered a single-store unit inappropriate for collective bargaining, although it acknowledged that absent such integration, a single store may be appropriate. Since the union lacked sufficient support in any unit larger than the single unit it applied for, the board dismissed the application for certification.

The *UFCW* decision presented in Box 8.5 demonstrates the importance of the bargaining unit decision. By deciding that a unit comprising a single store is not appropriate, the OLRB effectively prevented employees at that store from accessing collective bargaining. Those employees could only access the collective bargaining regime if the union could also persuade a majority of employees at the other ten stores to also join the union. The issue of whether a single retail store or a single branch of a large bank or credit union is an appropriate bargaining unit has been hotly contested for decades, and decisions have gone both ways, depending on the facts of each case. Note though while a single store (or branch) may be easier to organize, single-store bargaining units usually lack the bargaining power to achieve strong collective agreements. This basic truism explains in large measure why unions have had great difficulty growing collective bargaining coverage in the private service sector.[47] We will return to this important issue again when we consider collective bargaining and the right to strike in Chapter 11.

4. Measuring Employee Support for Collective Bargaining: The Card-Check Model and the Mandatory Certification Vote Model

Once a labour relations board has sorted out the voting constituency, it directs its attention to testing whether a majority of those employees support collective bargaining. Two models are used in Canada to measure whether a union has majority employee support: (1) the **card-check** model (with a fallback certification vote option) and (2) the **mandatory certification vote** model. Table 8.1 describes in which jurisdictions the models are used.

TABLE 8.1 Proving Majority Support for Collective Bargaining in Canada (Non-Construction Industries)

Jurisdiction	Card-Check Certification	Certification Vote Ballot Details: 1. Required percentage of employees in the bargaining unit who are union members in order to qualify for a certification vote. 2. Vote outcome needed for certification.
Canada (federal)	No.	1. 40% support 2. The union must win the majority of ballots cast.
Alberta	No.	1. 40% support 2. The union must win the majority of ballots cast.
British Columbia	No.	1. 45% support 2. The union must win the majority of ballots cast.
Manitoba	Yes, if 65% or more of employees in the bargaining unit "wish the union to represent them" in bargaining.	A certification vote is ordered if a union applies with the support of between 40% and 64% of employees in the bargaining unit. The union must win the majority of ballots cast.
New Brunswick	Yes, if 60% or more of employees in the bargaining unit are union members. If between 50% and 59% of employees in the bargaining unit are union members, the board "may" certify the union.	A certification vote "may be" ordered if a union applies with the support of between 40% and 60% of employees in the bargaining unit. The union must win the majority of ballots cast.
Newfoundland and Labrador	Yes, but only if the union represents a majority of employees in the bargaining unit AND the employer and union agree to waive requirement for a vote.	A certification vote is ordered if a union submits evidence that at least 40% of employees in the bargaining unit wish the union to represent them. The union must obtain votes on behalf of a majority of employees in the bargaining unit or a majority of employees who cast ballots (provided at least 70% of employees in the bargaining unit cast ballots).
Nova Scotia	No.	1. 40% support 2. The union must win the majority of ballots cast.
Ontario	Available only in the construction sector.	1. 40% support 2. The union must win the majority of ballots cast.
Prince Edward Island	Yes, if more than 50% of bargaining unit employees are union members.	A certification vote "may be" ordered if a union applies with the support of less than 50% of employees in the bargaining unit. The union must win the majority of ballots cast.
Quebec	Yes, if more than 50% of bargaining unit employees are union members.	A certification vote "may be" ordered if a union applies with the support of between 35% and 50% of employees in the bargaining unit. The union must win the majority of ballots cast.
Saskatchewan	No.	1. 45% support 2. The union must win the majority of ballots cast.

card check: A method used in Canadian collective bargaining legislation to measure the level of employee support for unionization that involves counting the number of union membership or authorization cards. If a majority of employees have signed cards, then the union is certified without a certification vote.

mandatory certification vote: A method used in Canadian collective bargaining legislation to measure the level of employee support for unionization that involves the government conducting a secret ballot vote of bargaining unit employees.

In the card-check model, a union can demonstrate majority support *without a vote* by collecting documentary evidence (union cards) demonstrating support for the union on behalf of a specified majority of bargaining unit employees (see Box 8.3). Once the union proves to the labour relations board that it has reached the required majority threshold, the labour relations board can certify the union. In jurisdictions using a card-check model, there is a fallback option for a union to demonstrate majority support by a vote conducted by the labour relations board if the union demonstrates substantial support that nevertheless falls short of the majority threshold. The threshold level of support required for card-check-based certification ranges from a simple majority (Prince Edward Island, Quebec) to 65 percent (Manitoba).

The mandatory certification vote model involves a two-step process. First, the union must collect union cards from a specified percentage (from 35 to 45 percent depending on jurisdiction) of bargaining unit employees in order to qualify for the second step, a mandatory certification vote conducted by the labour relations board. The union must then also win the vote.[48] Even if 100 percent of employees are union members, the labour relations board must still conduct a certification vote. In Canada, unlike in the United States, certification votes are held relatively quickly—in most jurisdictions within seven to ten business days of the date of the union's application for certification.[49] Any issues that require litigation are deferred until after the vote is held, although the vote results may be ordered to remain sealed until that litigation concludes. This "quick vote" model is designed to avoid a protracted, divisive, and disruptive campaign prior to the vote and to limit the opportunity for employers to use their power to pressure employees to turn against collective bargaining.[50]

The decision by Canadian governments regarding which model to use is a highly political one because the choice is not outcome neutral, as explained in Box 8.6.[51] As Professor Paul Weiler (Harvard University) observed, the model a government adopts "tends either to facilitate or to frustrate collective bargaining."[52] Studies demonstrate that union success rates in certification applications are lower under a mandatory certification vote model than under a card-check model. Therefore, governments that desire less collective bargaining coverage and weaker unions favour the mandatory certification vote model, whereas governments that support easier access to collective bargaining prefer the card-check model. Consequently, which model prevails at any moment in time and place depends in large measure on which "perspective" (see Chapter 4) dominates the political landscape.

BOX 8.6 » TALKING WORK LAW

The Politics of Measuring Employee Support for Collective Bargaining

For about four decades prior to the 1990s, governments of all political stripes supported the card-check model of union certification as a sensible and efficient method of testing employee wishes. The industrial pluralist perspective dominated the political climate and prevailing academic sentiments during this period, as discussed in Chapter 4.

The argument in favour of the card-check model ran along the following lines. If a clear majority of employees are union members, then there is little point wasting taxpayers' money and prolonging the start of collective bargaining in order to conduct a second test of majority wishes in the form of a vote. The main effect of requiring a vote is to enable employers to engage in a campaign to defeat collective bargaining. In that campaign, employers enjoy substantial advantages in terms of access (see Box 8.1), control, and power over employees, and many employers cannot resist the temptation to exploit

that power by threatening employees' jobs if they support a union. The card-check model reduces the opportunity for employers to interfere with employees' decisions about whether to try collective bargaining, because unions can often obtain majority membership, or come close to it, without the employer learning of the organizing campaign.

Card-check model advocates also emphasize that union certification simply grants a union a "licence" to try to bargain a collective agreement that a majority of employees would vote for in a ratification vote (see Chapter 10). If a union cannot do that, either it will walk away or the employees will vote it out with their feet. Therefore, as Professor Paul Weiler (Harvard University) argued, employees who decide whether to sign a union membership card are not "making a momentous choice … which should be carefully hedged about with ceremonial trappings, ultimately allowing the employees to make up their minds in the solemnity of the voting booth in the same ways that citizens do about their governmental representatives."*

The card-check model came under increasing attack beginning in the late 1980s and then into the 1990s by employers and politicians, as the neoclassical and managerialist perspectives ascended.† Critics of the card-check model made four basic arguments. First, they argued that the card-check model is "undemocratic" because it does not ensure that every employee has a chance to participate in the unionization decision. Second, they argued that a union membership card is not a guarantee of actual support for collective bargaining because the union organizer may have tricked the employee into signing, or the employee may have signed due to peer pressure or in ignorance of the implications of signing the card. Third, they argued that a mandatory vote is needed to ensure that the employer can present "the other side of the story" to employees, to offset the sales job of union organizers. Finally, proponents of the mandatory certification vote model argued that replacing the card-check model with the mandatory vote model would create new jobs (although how or why it would do so is neither obvious nor fully developed).‡

What is clear is that union success rates in mandatory certification vote proceedings are lower, and certification applications are fewer in jurisdictions using a mandatory certification vote model. For example, Professor Chris Riddell (Queen's University) found that the move to the mandatory certification vote model in British Columbia between 1984 and 1993 led to a 19 percent decrease in union success rates

in certification applications.§ Professor Sara Slinn (York University) found a 10 percent decrease in union success rates after Ontario switched from the card-check model to the mandatory certification vote model.# The relationship between the model adopted and access to collective bargaining is a main driver of government policy in this area. The politics surrounding the choice of model provides a vivid example of the important role the political subsystem plays in shaping the work law subsystem (Chapter 3).

---

* See P. Weiler, *Reconcilable Differences: New Directions in Canadian Labour Law* (Toronto: Carswell, 1980), at 44, and 37-49 more generally.

† For arguments against the card-check model in the United States, see R. Epstein, "The Case Against the Employee Free Choice Act" (working paper, University of Chicago Law and Economics Olin Working Paper No. 452, 2009), http://papers.ssrn.com/sol3/papers.cfm?abstract_id=1337185.

‡ See, e.g., the speech by Ontario Minister of Labour Elizabeth Witmer introducing Bill 7 in 1995; this law introduced the mandatory certification vote for the first time in Ontario: Legislative Assembly of Ontario, Debates (Hansard), October 18, 1995, http://www.ontla.on.ca/web/house-proceedings/house_detail.do?Date=1995-10-18&Parl=36&Sess=1&locale=en#P314_84629.

§ C. Riddell, "Union Certification Success Under Voting Versus Card-Check Procedures: Evidence from B.C." (2004) 57 *Industrial and Labor Relations Review* 493. See also S. Johnson, "Card Check or Mandatory Representation Vote? How the Type of Union Recognition Procedure Affects Union Certification Success" (2002) 112 *Economic Journal* 344.

S. Slinn, "An Empirical Analysis of the Effects of the Change from Card-Check to Mandatory Vote Certification" (2004) 11 *Canadian Labour and Employment Law Journal* 259.

In 1990, all jurisdictions except Alberta and Nova Scotia permitted card-check certification. By 2016, card-check certification was permitted only in Quebec, Manitoba, New Brunswick, Prince Edward Island, and Newfoundland and Labrador (but only if the employer and union agree), and in the construction sector in Ontario.

V. Voluntary Recognition

Most of this chapter was devoted to the union certification process, which nowadays is the most common method by which a union becomes legally entitled to represent employees in collective bargaining. However, prior to the introduction of statutory union certification in the 1940s, unions and employers engaged in collective bargaining after the employer had voluntarily recognized the union. Collective bargaining legislation did not eliminate voluntary recognition, but rather supplemented it by introducing a process to compel employers to bargain with a union that represents a majority of its employees.[53]

In voluntary recognition, the employer agrees to recognize the union as the representative of its employees and to begin collective bargaining. Today, (except in Quebec[54]) an employer and union can bypass the formal union certification process by agreeing to voluntary recognition. This process can avoid the formality, litigation, hostility, and expense often associated with the certification process. On the other hand, voluntary recognition creates the possibility of "sweetheart deals" between employers and friendly unions that do not put the employees' interests first. Moreover, there is no guarantee that a voluntarily recognized union actually has the support of a majority of employees. Therefore, the statutes include checks and balances on voluntarily recognized unions to ensure employees are protected.[55] For example, during the early stages of voluntary recognition, and especially before a collective agreement is concluded, unions may be challenged by affected employees to demonstrate they have majority employee support.[56] Voluntarily recognized unions are not granted the grace period (referred to above under the heading "Timeliness of Certification Applications") provided to certified unions to bargain a first collective agreement.

In some jurisdictions, the right of voluntarily recognized unions (and the employees represented by them) to lawfully strike is also restricted.[57] This restriction results from a requirement for unions to satisfy various preconditions before they can lawfully strike, including exhausting government-mandated **conciliation**. In some jurisdictions, only certified unions are granted the statutory right to access conciliation, with the result that voluntarily recognized unions will never be in a legal strike position. Therefore, it is important to study the applicable statute carefully to learn whether there are differences in the legal rights of voluntarily recognized unions compared with certified unions.

VI. Chapter Summary

This chapter examined the complex process through which Canadian employees can move from the common law regime to the collective bargaining regime. Most of the time, this process involves joining a union, which then must satisfy a list of statutory prerequisites to achieve union certification. However, we noted too that unions can also obtain the right to bargain collective agreements on behalf of employees through voluntary recognition. The chapter also explained some of the big debates that have always surrounded the legal process of certification. Big debates surround the extent to which unions should have access to the employees they are seeking to organize, the importance and role of the bargaining unit description, and the impact of the card-check and mandatory certification vote models on access to collective bargaining. In this chapter, we begin to see the complexity of the collective bargaining regime.

QUESTIONS AND ISSUES FOR DISCUSSION

1. Describe the "card-check" and "mandatory certification vote" models for determining employee support. Under which model do unions have a greater probability of success in an organizing campaign? Which model is in effect in your home province?
2. What are arguments for and against the card-check model?
3. Describe factors that labour boards consider when deciding whether an employee is excluded from collective bargaining legislation because they
   a. exercise managerial functions and
   b. are confidential employees.
4. Explain what factors labour boards consider when deciding whether a bargaining unit is appropriate for collective bargaining. Why is the decision about which bargaining unit is appropriate important in the Canadian collective bargaining model?
5. What concerns arise in relation to voluntary recognition? How are those concerns addressed, if at all, in Canadian collective bargaining law?

UPDATES

Go to emond.ca/lawofworkircb for links to news, author's blog posts, content updates, and other information related to the chapters in this text.

---

conciliation: A form of mediation in which a neutral collective bargaining expert attempts to assist an employee association (e.g., a union) and an employer or employer association in reaching a collective agreement.

NOTES AND REFERENCES

1 For a review of the origins of the American *Wagner Act*, see M. Barenberg, "The Political Economy of the Wagner Act: Power, Symbol, and Workplace Cooperation" (1993) 106 *Harvard Law Review* 1381; and R. Adams, "Union Certification as an Instrument of Labor Policy: A Comparative Perspective" in S. Friedman et al. (eds.), *Restoring the Promise of American Labor Law* (Ithaca, NY: ILR Press, 1994), 260.

2 *National Labor Relations Act*, 1935, 29 U.S.C. § 9(a). See, e.g., C. Morris, *The Blue Eagle at Work: Reclaiming Democratic Rights in the American Workplace* (Ithaca, NY: ILR Press, 2005).

3 *Mounted Police Association of Ontario v. Canada* (2012), 350 DLR (4th) 261, at para. 26. See also D. Doorey, "Graduated Freedom of Association" (2013) 38 *Queen's Law Journal* 511.

4 Not all employers actively resist their employees' efforts to unionize. For example, in 2007, Magna International, a Canadian auto-parts manufacturer, entered into an agreement with the Canadian Auto Workers union called the Framework of Fairness. That agreement granted the union access to the workplace and required the employer to remain neutral and even speak encouragingly about the prospects of employees joining the CAW. In exchange, the union agreed, among other things, to never strike. See M. Malin, "Canadian Auto Workers—Magna International, Inc. Framework of Fairness Agreement: A U.S. Perspective" (2010) 54 *Saint Louis University Law Journal* 525.

5 K. Bentham, "Employer Resistance to Union Certification: A Study of Eight Jurisdictions" (2002) 57 *Relations Industrielles/Industrial Relations* 159.

6 For a recent attempt by employees to form their own union and seek collective bargaining rights through that union, see the story of WestJet Airlines' pilots in T. Johnson and K. Bakx, "WestJet Pilots Vote Against Forming Union," *CBC News*, August 5, 2015, http://www.cbc.ca/news/business/westjet-pilots-vote-against-forming-union-1.3180420.

7 See the Alberta *Labour Relations Code*, RSA 2000, c. L-1, s. 33, on the option of union membership cards or union authorization cards.

8 Jurisdictions that do not require employees to pay a fee to the union at the time of signing a union card are Ontario, British Columbia, Manitoba, Newfoundland and Labrador, and Saskatchewan. See P. Weiler, *Reconcilable Differences: New Directions in Canadian Labour Law* (Toronto: Carswell, 1980), at 42 for a discussion of purposes of the payment requirement.

9 See the discussion in D. Doorey, "The Medium and the Anti-Union Message: Forced Listening and Captive Audience Meetings" (2007) 29:2 *Comparative Labor Law & Policy Journal* 79, http://papers.ssrn.com/sol3/papers.cfm?abstract_id=1010463.

10 The PC 1003 recognized both "employees' associations" and "trade unions," but over time, reference to "employee associations" was dropped from most Canadian collective bargaining legislation: PC 1003, s. 4(1). *Wartime Labour Relations Order* (PC 1003) is available at http://socserv.mcmaster.ca/oldlabourstudies/onlinelearning/article.php?id=503.

11 Some exceptions exist, such as the Ontario *Agricultural Employees Protection Act, 2002*, SO 2002, c. 16, s. 1. This Act protects a right of agricultural workers to join an "employees' association."

12 For example, the Alberta *Labour Relations Code*, supra note 7, s. 1, defines a "trade union" simply as "an organization of employees that has a written constitution, rules or bylaws and has as one of its objects the regulation of relations between employers and employees."

13 See, e.g., *ABC Climate Control Systems*, [2009] Ont. LRB Rep. Sept./Oct. 639; and *United Steel Workers of America v. Kubota Metal Corporation Fahramet Division*, 1995 CanLII 10060 (Ont. LRB), at para. 35. See also D. Doorey, "Graduated Freedom of Association: Worker Voice Beyond the Wagner Model" (2013) 38 *Queen's Law Journal* 511, at 521-26.

14 See, e.g., Ontario *Labour Relations Act, 1995*, SO 1995, c. 1, Sch. A, s. 15; and Manitoba *Labour Relations Act*, CCSM, c. L10, s. 43.

15 Professor Daphne Taras has studied non-union forms of employee representation in Canada. See D. Taras, "Reconciling Differences Differently: Employee Voice in Public Policy Making and Workplace Governance" (2007) 28:2 *Comparative Labor Law & Policy Journal* 167.

16 See, e.g., Ontario *Labour Relations Act, 1995*, supra note 14, s. 10(3) for an example of such a statutory bar. Similar bars appear in every jurisdiction, with some variations in details.

17 Ibid., s. 7(5).

18 Ibid., s. 13 (the identity of union members is not to be disclosed to the employer).

19 See, e.g., BC *Labour Relations Code*, RSBC 1996, c. 244, s. 1 and Ontario *Labour Relations Act, 1995*, supra note 14, s. 1 for statutory definitions of "dependent contractor." For a discussion of the origins of and justification for the "dependent contractor" definition, see H. Arthurs, "The

Dependent Contractor: A Study of the Legal Problem of Countervailing Power" (1965) 16:1 *University of Toronto Law Journal* 89.

20   See, e.g., *Ontario Taxi Workers' Union v. Hamilton Cab*, 2011 CanLII 7282 (Ont. LRB); *Kelowna Cabs (1981) Ltd.*, BCLRB No. 230/85; and *Flash Courier Services Inc. v. National Automobile, Aerospace, Transportation and General Workers Union of Canada (Caw-Canada, Local 114)*, 2002 CanLII 52815 (BCLRB).

21   See, e.g., Teamsters, Local 987 *v. 331001 Alberta Ltd (Barrel Taxi)*, 2011 CanLII 62486 (ABLRB); and *United Cab Ltd.*, [1996] SLRBR No. 24. But see *Federation of Communication, Transport Employees and General Workers of Canada v. 603968 N.B. Inc. (Air Cab)*, 2003 CanLII 64176 (NBLB).

22   See, e.g., Ontario *Labour Relations Act, 1995*, supra note 14, s. 3; and PEI *Labour Act*, RSPEI 1988, c. L-1, s. 7(2). An occupation excluded from one collective bargaining statute might nevertheless be covered by another statute governing collective bargaining in a particular industry or profession.

23   *Canadian Charter of Rights and Freedoms*, part I of the *Constitution Act, 1982*, being Schedule B to the *Canada Act 1982* (UK), 1982, c. 11.

24   *Ontario Utility Foremen's Association v. Borough of Etobicoke (Hydro Electric Commission)*, 1981 CanLII 790 (Ont. LRB); and *Corporation of District of Burnaby*, [1974] 1 CLRBR 1 (BCLRB).

25   *Cottage Hospital (Uxbridge) v. Ontario Nurses' Association*, 1980 CanLII 939 (Ont. LRB); and *United Utility Workers' Association of Canada v. AltaLink Management Ltd*, 2012 CanLII 43190 (ABLRB).

26   *Cowichan Home Support Society*, BCLRB No. B28/97 (leave for reconsideration of BCLRB Nos. B100/95, B179/95, and B217/95, 34 CLRBR (2d) 121); *Alpine Confections Canada, ULC Operating as Dynamic Chocolates v. United Steelworkers of America, Local No. 1-3567*, 2005 CanLII 47795 (BCLRB); *Ontario Utility Foremen's Association v. Borough of Etobicoke (Hydro Electric Commission)*, supra note 24; *United Steelworkers of America v. Ken Bodnar Enterprises Inc.*, 1994 CanLII 9954 (Ont. LRB); *United Food and Commercial Workers Canada Union, Local No. 401 v. Royal Camp Services*, 2016 CanLII 21306 (ABLRB); and *National Automobile, Aerospace and Agricultural Implement Workers Union of Canada (CAW-Canada) v. Reynolds-Lemmerz Industries*, 1995 CanLII 9988 (Ont. LRB).

27   *LRBBC v. Canada Safeway*, [1953] 2 SCR 46; and *Corporation of District of Burnaby*, supra note 24.

28   See recent discussions of the application of the "confidential employee" exclusion in *Gateway Casinos & Entertainment Inc. v. Canadian Office and Professional Employees Union, Local 378*, 2010 CanLII 27987 (BCLRB); *Calgary Board of Education Staff Association v. Calgary Board of Education*, 2013 CanLII 21674 (ABLRB); *Canadian Union of Public Employees v. Peel Children's Aid Society*, 2015 CanLII 57037 (Ont. LRB); *Manitoba Government and General Employees' Union v. Southern Health—Santé Sud*, 2015 CanLII 37991 (MBLRB); and *Saskatchewan Joint Board, Retail, Wholesale and Department Store Union, Local 544 v. Battlefords and District Co-operative Limited*, 2016 CanLII 19983 (SKLRB).

29   See, e.g., *Pointe-Claire (City) v. Quebec (Labour Court)*, [1997] 1 SCR 1015; *United Electrical, Radio and Machine Workers of Canada v. Sylvania Lighting Services*, 1985 CanLII 1016 (Ont. LRB); *Teamsters Local Union No. 938 v. Kraft Canada*, 2007 CanLII 48336 (Ont. LRB); and *Alberta Union of Provincial Employees v. Alberta Health Services*, 2011 CanLII 62488 (ABLRB).

30   See, e.g., *The United Food and Commercial Workers' International Union, Local 175 v. Sobey's Ontario Division of Sobey's Capital Inc.*, 2001 CanLII 10338 (Ont. LRB); *White Spot Ltd. v. British Columbia Labour Relations Board et al.*, 1999 BCCA 93; *RPKC Holding Corporation v. Retail, Wholesale and Department Store Union (AFL-CIO-CLC, Local 414)*, 1986 CanLII 1501 (Ont. LRB); *Penmarkay Foods Ltd.* (1984), 8 CLRBR (NS) 203; and *Etobicoke Public Library Board*, [1989] OLRB Rep. Sept. 935.

31   *Teamsters Local Union No. 419 v. Metro Waste Paper Recovery Inc.*, 2009 CanLII 60617 (Ont. LRB). See also *United Food and Commercial Workers International Union (UFCW Canada) v. PPG Canada Inc.*, 2009 CanLII 15058 (Ont. LRB). Sometimes it is the employer that wants a related employer application in order to expand the size of the bargaining unit and defeat a certification application: *Amalgamated Clothing & Textile Workers Union v. Hornco Plastics*, 1993 CanLII 8031 (Ont. LRB).

32   B. Langille, "The Michelin Amendment in Context" (1981) 8 *Dalhousie Law Journal* 523, at 539.

33   See, e.g., BC *Labour Relations Code*, supra note 19, s. 28.

34   See, e.g., *Canada Labour Code*, RSC 1985, c. L-2, s. 27(3); and Manitoba *Labour Relations Act*, supra note 14, s. 39(3).

35   See, e.g., Ontario *Labour Relations Act, 1995*, supra note 14, s. 9(3).

36   See *Canada Labour Code*, supra note 34, s. 27(6).

37   Ontario *Labour Relations Act, 1995*, supra note 14, s. 14.

38   *The Saskatchewan Employment Act*, SS 2013, c. S-15.1, s. 6(11).

39   Nova Scotia *Trade Union Act*, RSNS 1989, c. 475, s. 26.

40 See Langille, supra note 32.

41 For a fuller discussion of how Canadian labour relations boards determine appropriate bargaining units, see G. Adams, *Canadian Labour Law*, 2nd ed. (Aurora, ON: Canada Law Book, 1993), at chapter 7.

42 *Island Medical Laboratories* (1993), 19 CLRBR (2d) 161.

43 *Canadian Union of Operating Engineers and General Workers (CUOE) v. Red Carpet Food Systems Inc.*, 2001 CanLII 5016 (Ont. LRB); and *Energy and Paperworkers Union of Canada Local 87—M Southern Ontario Newspaper Guild v. Metroland Printing Publishing and Distributing Ltd.*, 2003 CanLII 33962 (Ont. LRB).

44 *United Steelworkers of America v. Burns International Security Services Limited*, 1994 CanLII 9898 (Ont. LRB). See also *National Automobile, Aerospace and Agricultural Implement Workers Union of Canada v. Active Mold Plastic Products Ltd*, 1994 CanLII 9940 (Ont. LRB); *Canadian Union of Public Employees v. Hospital for Sick Children*, 1985 CanLII 899 (Ont. LRB); *Energy and Paperworkers Union of Canada Local 87—M Southern Ontario Newspaper Guild v. Metroland Printing Publishing and Distributing Ltd.*, supra note 43; and *Sodexo Canada Ltd. v. Hospital Employees' Union*, 2012 CanLII 1502 (BCLRB).

45 *Canadian Union of Public Employees v. Hospital for Sick Children*, supra note 44.

46 See, e.g., *United Food and Commercial Workers Canada Union, Local No 401 v. Clean Harbors Lodging Services LP*, 2014 CanLII 38737 (ABLRB); and *United Food & Commercial Workers, Local 206 v. Lynn Management Ltd.*, 2000 CanLII 1574 (Ont. LRB) (one Tim Hortons store is not an appropriate unit when franchisee owns ten other nearby stores).

47 See E. Lennon, "Organizing the Unorganized: Unionization in the Chartered Banks of Canada" (1980) 18 *Osgoode Hall Law Journal* 177; and A. Forrest, "Organizing Eatons: Do the Old Laws Still Work?" (1988) 8 *Windsor Yearbook Access to Justice*.

48 In Newfoundland and Labrador, the statute specifies that the union must either obtain votes on behalf of more than 50 percent of eligible voters (so a person who does not vote counts as a "no" vote) or win the vote provided that at least 70 percent of all eligible voters must have cast ballots: Newfoundland and Labrador *Labour Relations Act*, RSNL 1990, c. L-1, s. 38.

49 Collective bargaining statutes usually include a defined time frame for the conducting of certification ballots, such as in s. 8(5) of the Ontario *Labour Relations Act,*

1995, which directs that votes be held five business days after the application for certification is filed. In Saskatchewan, the statute does not specify a time frame, but in practice the labour relations board has been conducting votes eight days, on average, after the application for certification: http://www .sasklabourrelationsboard.com/pdfdoc/Labour%20 Relations%20Board%202014-15.

50 See the discussion in Weiler, supra note 8, at 44-45.

51 See, e.g., F. Martinello, "Mr. Harris, Mr. Rae, and Union Activity in Ontario" (2000) 26 *Canadian Public Policy* 17; H. Jain and S. Muthu, "Ontario Labour Law Reforms: A Comparative Study of Bill 40 and Bill 7" (1996) 4 *Canadian Labour and Employment Law Journal* 311; and K. Burkett, "The Politicization of the Ontario Labour Relations Framework in the Decade of the 1990s" (1998) 5 *Canadian Labour and Employment Law Journal* 168.

52 Weiler, supra note 8, at 48.

53 See, e.g., Alberta *Labour Relations Code*, supra note 7, s. 42. See the discussion by Chief Justice Laskin (in dissent) in *Beverage Dispensers & Culinary Workers Union, Local 835 v. Terra Nova Motor Inn Ltd.*, [1975] 2 SCR 749.

54 Quebec *Labour Code*, c. C-27, s. 1(b) (only a "certified association" is recognized by the labour relations board). See Adams, supra note 41, at 7.1520.

55 See the discussion of voluntary recognition provisions in Ontario in *Labourers International Union of North America v. Penegal Trim & Supply Ltd.*, 2000 CanLII 12309 (Ont. LRB).

56 See, e.g., Ontario *Labour Relations Act, 1995*, supra note 14, s. 63(1) (a "certified union" is protected from displacement applications for one year after certification); *The Saskatchewan Employment Act*, supra note 38, s. 6-10(3); and Nova Scotia *Trade Union Act*, supra note 39, s. 30 (a voluntarily recognized union that concludes a collective agreement is treated as a certified union, subject to employees challenging whether the union has majority support during the first 30 days of the agreement).

57 *Canada Labour Code*, supra note 34, ss. 48 and 49 (only a certified union or a union that has concluded a collective agreement can give notice to bargain, which is a condition of accessing conciliation, a prerequisite to a lawful strike). In Ontario, a union that enters into a voluntary recognition agreement in writing may access government conciliation and the strike provisions of the legislation: see Ontario *Labour Relations Act, 1995*, supra note 14, s. 18(3).

CHAPTER 9

Unfair Labour Practices and the Right to Organize

I. Introduction

In preceding chapters, we learned that in the common law regime, workers who supported unions and expressed a desire for collective bargaining were frequently targeted for reprisals by resistant employers. Employers could fire employees who supported unions, or refuse to hire them outright. Such behaviour was usually legal in a system based purely on freedom of contract. However, if workers can be fired for joining a union, then they don't have much of a right to unionize. A legal model that permits employers to punish employees who seek collective bargaining is inconsistent with a policy that recognizes collective bargaining as a beneficial, or at least legitimate, method of organizing work relations. Protecting workers from reprisals was also a necessary condition to garner union support for a new legislated model of collective bargaining. Therefore, restrictions prohibiting various forms of **unfair labour practices** were included in 1940s and 1950s collective bargaining legislation and remain a fundamental pillar of the emerging right to organize.

This chapter explores the history and scope of unfair labour practice provisions found in Canadian collective bargaining statutes, focusing on how the law regulates employer behaviour during the period of union organizing campaigns. In later chapters, we will consider how the law regulates the behaviour of unions and employers once a union is legally entitled to represent an employer's workers.

---

unfair labour practice: An action undertaken by someone acting on behalf of either a union or employer, or on their own behalf, that violates one or more provisions in the collective bargaining legislation.

II. Why a Statutory "Right to Unionize"?

Bobby Napora worked as an automotive technician at a company called Marv Jones Honda in Maple Ridge, British Columbia. He had concerns about his working conditions, and on January 21, 2015, he met with a union organizer to learn about the process of organizing a union.[1] At that meeting, Napora signed a union membership card and agreed to act as an **inside union organizer** at the workplace. But a few days later, on January 24, Napora's employment contract was suddenly terminated. The employer argued at a subsequent hearing that the termination was for various performance-related reasons and not Napora's union activities. However, the BC Labour Relations Board disagreed. It ruled that Napora had been fired because he was trying to organize a union and for the purpose of intimidating other employees so that they would not support the union.[2] That action violated the province's unfair labour practice provisions. The board ordered the employer to reinstate Napora to his old job and to pay him for any financial losses he suffered.

Note that nothing in Napora's employment contract prohibited the employer from terminating Napora's employment, either for performance-related reasons or for organizing a union. As a non-union employee, Napora could be fired for any or no reason at all, the only question being whether notice of termination is required (see Chapter 8 in the companion volume). By quickly terminating the main inside union organizer, the employer hoped to bring an abrupt end to a union's burgeoning organizing campaign. If the remaining employees believed that support for collective bargaining would threaten their jobs, they would be less likely to support the union. For an employer desiring to avoid collective bargaining, terminating union supporters or threatening other punishment may make perfect business sense. Unfair labour practices were enacted to protect workers from such reprisals and to reduce industrial conflict that sometimes resulted when workers were fired for supporting collective bargaining.

Almost all employers resist unionization campaigns in some manner, even if most do not resort to firing employees. Professor Karen Bentham (University of Toronto) found that 80 percent of Canadian employers engaged in "actions that unmistakably evince open opposition to

---

inside union organizer: An employee who assists in efforts to unionize his or her own employer.

union certification."[3] And studies have shown that employer opposition, particularly when it includes threats to employee job security, can be effective at thwarting unionization efforts. For example, Professor Terry Thomason found that the probability of a union winning a union certification application fell by 8 to 13 percent when the employer committed an unfair labour practice in Ontario and Quebec, jurisdictions that were using the card-check model of certification at the time of the study.[4] Professor Chris Riddell (Queen's University) found that employer unfair labour practices reduced union success rates in certification applications by 21 percent in British Columbia, where the mandatory certification vote model was in effect.[5]

The Supreme Court of Canada has recognized that in order to exercise the right to organize, employees require statutory protection from employer threats and reprisals.[6] In the 2001 decision of *Dunmore v. Ontario (Attorney General)*, the Supreme Court wrote:

> [H]istory has shown, and Canada's legislatures have uniformly recognized, that a posture of government restraint in the area of labour relations will expose most workers not only to a range of unfair labour practices, but potentially to legal liability under common law inhibitions on combinations and restraints of trade.[7]

The Supreme Court cited with approval a leading Canadian labour law text, which noted that prior to the enactment of modern unfair labour practice provisions, "the freedom to organize would amount 'to no more than the freedom to suffer serious adverse legal and economic consequences.'"[8] By the late 1930s and then into the early 1940s, Canadian governments were finally accepting—albeit often reluctantly and under intense pressure from increasingly militant workers—that employees should have a right to organize and that this right, to be meaningful, needed to be accompanied by government intervention in the form of unfair labour practice legislation that restricted the right of employers to punish employees who supported collective bargaining.

III. The Substance of Unfair Labour Practice Provisions Regulating Employer Behaviour

An amendment to the *Criminal Code* in 1939 criminalized the refusal by an employer to employ a worker who joins an employee association as well as any threat or intimidation by an employer intended to compel a worker to abstain from joining an association.[9] However, prosecutions under that criminal provision were rarely pursued, and the enactment was more symbolic of growing tolerance of collective worker activities than substantive in practice. Recall from Chapter 6 that the Americans had enacted the *Wagner Act* in 1935, which granted employees protection from employer reprisals for associational activity. By the late 1930s, Canadian workers and unions were demanding nothing less for themselves.

The *Wartime Labour Relations Order*, or Order in Council PC 1003, was passed in 1944 in Canada and established the basic framework of the *Wagner Act* in this country (as discussed in Chapter 6). Section 4 of PC 1003 introduced a general statute-based right to associate:

> Every employee shall have the right to be a member of a trade union or employees' organization and to participate in the lawful activities thereof.

To give effect to that general right, PC 1003 also included, among other provisions, a duty to bargain (see Chapter 10), and two categories of restrictions on employer conduct (unfair labour practices) that could impede the right to organize:

1. *Intimidation and coercion prohibition:* It prohibited employers from punishing workers who join or support employee associations, either by refusing to employ them or by imposing conditions in their contracts that seek to restrain the employee from exercising any rights protected by the legislation.

2. *Interference and domination prohibition:* It prohibited employers from providing "financial or other support" to an employee association, and from dominating or interfering with the formation or administration of employee associations.[10]

The first category addressed the reality that employers (usually) have both an interest in seeing an organizing campaign fail and the power to see that it does. The second category was aimed at protecting the right of employees to select their own association that is independent of the employer, and to have that union represent them without meddling from the employer. These elements of PC 1003 remain the fundamental building blocks of the modern day statutory right to unionize. Next, we take a closer look at the sorts of behaviour they proscribe.

A. The Intimidation and Coercion Prohibition and "Anti-Union Animus"

Employees are not making a free choice about unionization if they feel threatened. Threats can take many forms, including physical and **economic threats**. Consider section 96 of the *Canada Labour Code* as an example of a typical non-intimidation clause:

> No person shall seek by intimidation or coercion *to compel a person to become or refrain from becoming or to cease to be a member of a trade union.*[11] [Emphasis added.]

Notice the motive element in that section: it matters *why* the threat was made. The threat must be for the purpose of compelling people to refrain from exercising rights protected by the collective bargaining statute, such as joining a union or engaging in union-related activities.[12] If I threaten to bop a co-worker in the nose unless he gives me $20, I may be committing a crime or giving my employer grounds to fire me, but I am not committing an unfair labour practice. However, if I threaten to bop him if he does not sign a union membership card, then I am violating collective bargaining legislation.

Thankfully, physical threats or violence during union organizing campaigns are relatively uncommon in Canada nowadays. A more frequent problem concerns economic threats. An economic threat includes comments or actions that cause employees to believe that supporting unionization and collective bargaining poses a threat to job security or working conditions. The provisions in collective bargaining legislation that prohibit threats, intimidation, and coercion are intended to police economic threats.

The non-intimidation provisions prohibit employers from disciplining or firing an employee for joining a union or supporting collective bargaining.[13] That is what happened in the *Marv Jones Honda* case described above. In that case, as in many other cases in which an employee is fired or otherwise mistreated during an organizing campaign, the employer claimed that it was unaware of the organizing campaign and of the fired employee's participation in it. The BC Labour Relations Board did not believe the employer. Often there is no direct evidence—no "smoking gun"—that the union can point to that definitively proves that the employer knew that the employee was a union supporter. The union will not usually have a witness who is present when the employer decides to take action against an employee. However, labour relations boards will draw inferences from the circumstances surrounding the events, as the board did in the *Marv Jones Honda* decision. This is what the board wrote on this important point:

---

economic threat: A comment or action intended to signal that economic harm (including job loss or other loss of a work-related benefit) will result unless a specific course of conduct is taken.

I have found it to be more probable than not the Employer terminated Napora due to anti-union animus. While there is no direct evidence his dismissal was motivated by anti-union animus, I find anti-union animus can be pieced together from the circumstances of his termination. The following comments from *Forano Limited*, BCLRB No. 2/74, [1974] 1 Canadian LRBR 13, are instructive in making this decision:

> An employer cannot fire someone for his union membership or activities. That does not mean that employees are immune from discharge during organizational campaigns since they can be fired for proper cause. It does mean that some such legitimate cause must be the actual reason for the discharge … . If the real purpose of a firing was the union involvement, an employer may not search for some arguable justification in the employee's earlier behaviour and advance this as the cause, *ex post facto*. The crux of such an unfair labour practice case is the employer's motivation in the discharge, something which rarely will be disclosed by admissions. Employers don't ordinarily advertise their anti-union activities. Such intention must be pieced together from a pattern of circumstantial evidence.[14]

In some Canadian jurisdictions, labour relations legislation creates a "reverse onus" in cases alleging adverse treatment of union supporters that effectively assumes that the employer acted unlawfully unless it can come forward with a compelling explanation of why its actions were completely free of **anti-union animus**.[15]

This concept of anti-union animus is crucial to the application of the non-intimidation provisions. An employer's actions are said to be "tainted by anti-union animus" if *any part* of the motivation for the action was to avoid unionization or collective bargaining, even if there are also other reasons for the action. The Ontario Labour Relations Board (OLRB) explained this concept as follows in the often-quoted decision of *Pop Shoppe (Toronto) Limited*:

> In order for the Board to find that there has been no violation of the Act it must be satisfied that the employer's actions were not in any way motivated by anti-union sentiment; *the employer's actions must be devoid of "anti-union animus."* The employer cannot engage in anti-union activity under the guise of just cause or under the guise of business reasons. Regardless of the viable non-union reasons which exist the Board must be satisfied that there does not co-exist in the mind of the employer an anti-union motive. The employer best satisfies the Board in this regard by coming forth with a credible explanation for the impugned activity which is free of anti-union motive and which the evidence establishes to be the only reason for its conduct.[16] [Emphasis added.]

Anti-union animus is the term used to describe the motive element of the unfair labour practice.

B. The Interference and Domination Prohibition

Consider section 6 of the BC *Labour Relations Code*, which is typical of the non-interference and domination sections in other Canadian statutes:

> [A]n employer or a person acting on behalf of an employer must not participate in or interfere with the formation, selection or administration of a trade union or contribute financial or other support to it.[17]

These non-interference provisions perform two important functions in the pursuit of a legally protected right to organize.

---

anti-union animus: The motive element of unfair labour practices, it means acting with an intention to defeat or undermine the exercise of lawful activities by a union or union supporters.

1. Encouraging Independent Unions and Preventing Employer Domination

The non-interference provisions protect the right of employees to select representation by an **independent union** of their own choosing. The non-interference provisions operate in tandem with other provisions in the statutes that prohibit associations with employer support from being certified; entering into collective agreements; and acting as a bar to an application for certification by a real, independent union.[18] The legal result is that employee associations that receive employer support contrary to the non-interference provisions are not recognized as "trade unions" and therefore have no legal status under collective bargaining statutes.[19] The objective is to discourage **company unions**, which are associations dominated by the employer and that may not have the employees' best interests in mind. An employer that lobbies employees to support a specific union it perceives to be more friendly than another may also be unlawfully interfering in the selection of a union.[20]

Note, though, that not every instance of employer support of a union is unlawful. Labour relations boards apply what they call a **purposive approach to statutory interpretation**. That means they keep in mind that the purpose of the law is to discourage company unions, and therefore consider whether the employer's support *actually interfered* with the ability of employees to make a free choice to join an independent union. Applying this test, boards have ruled that it was not unlawful for an employer to provide a list of employees to a union seeking to organize its employees, to invite a union to organize its employees, or to permit union organizing at the workplace, provided that the union involved is at arm's-length from the employer and the employer's actions did not interfere with the ability of employees to freely choose whether to support the union.[21]

2. Preventing Employer "Interference" With the Functioning of the Union

The non-interference provisions also prohibit employers from engaging in behaviour that undermines the union's efforts to organize and to represent workers after the union has been certified. For example, labour relations boards have ruled that the following employer conduct unlawfully "interferes" with union activities:

- attempting during the hiring and recruitment process to screen out employees who may be union supporters;[22]
- refusing to provide a certified union with contact information for employees in the bargaining unit and information about their terms of employment;[23]
- bargaining working conditions directly with employees instead of their union;[24]
- refusing to collect and remit union dues to the union in accordance with a union dues clause in a collective agreement; and[25]
- restricting an employee from taking a position as a union official.[26]

The non-interference provisions also give labour relations boards an important tool to deal with employer actions that, *while not motivated by anti-union animus*, nevertheless have a substantial negative impact on unions and the right to organize. Review section 6 of the BC *Labour Relations Code* reproduced above. Notice that unlike the "intimidation and coercion" unfair labour practices discussed earlier in the chapter, the non-interference provision does not include a motive element. If an employer *intends* to interfere with a union, then it is acting with an anti-

---

independent union: A union that is at arm's-length and independent from the control of any employer.

company union: An employee association created with the encouragement or assistance of the employer and that is not independent of the employer's control or influence. A company union is often created as a union-avoidance strategy.

purposive approach to statutory interpretation: An approach to interpreting and applying a statutory provision that is guided by the purpose of the provision.

union animus and is almost certainly in violation of the non-interference provisions, and probably one or more "intimidation and coercion" sections too. However, an employer can violate the non-interference provisions without having a specific intention to undermine a union or its employees' efforts to organize.[27] This type of action is known as a **non-motive unfair labour practice**.

Does this mean that every decision an employer makes that disadvantages unions and employees seeking collective bargaining is unlawful? No, it does not. Labour relations boards have applied a balancing test of sorts to determine when employer actions that lack anti-union animus nevertheless unlawfully interfere with union rights.[28] The OLRB explained the test this way in the case of *Canadian Union of Public Employees, Local 2424 v. Carleton University*:

> [T]he test requires a balancing between the "*business purpose*" behind the employer's conduct and the union's "*protected activity*" which may have been interfered with.[29] [Emphasis added.]

In applying this test, labour relations boards first ask whether employees or union officials were engaged in a "protected activity," including union organizing. If so, then the board considers the "business purpose" behind the employer's decision or rule. If the employer's business purpose is considered weak or unpersuasive, and there is disproportionate harm to the "protected activity" of the union or its supporters, a violation of the non-interference provision may be found, even though the employer's intention was not specifically to interfere with the protected activity.[30]

For example, in the case of *Canadian Paperworkers Union v. International Wallcoverings*, an employer violated the non-interference provision when it fired union-supporting employees based on the mistaken belief that they had engaged in misconduct during a strike.[31] In that case, the employer's business purpose was non-existent, since it had acted on a mistaken belief about employee misconduct. Consider how the OLRB balanced the property rights of a mall owner against the right to organize in the decision discussed in Box 9.1.

BOX 9.1 » CASE LAW HIGHLIGHT

Employer Property Rights Versus the Right to Organize

Cadillac Fairview Corp Ltd. v. R.W.D.S.U.

(1989), 71 OR (2d) 206 (CA)

Key Facts: The Retail, Wholesale and Department Store Union (RWDSU) commenced an organizing campaign of employees of Eaton's, the flagship retail store at the Eaton Centre in Toronto. The only access to the doors where employees entered and exited the workplace were in the mall, which was owned by Cadillac Fairview (CF). Union organizers, some days with the help of then Toronto alderman Jack Layton,* set up at those doors before the store opened and before the public entered the space to distribute literature to employees entering work. Eventually, CF enforced the mall's "no solicitation" policy to exclude all such leafletting and organizing on mall property. It ordered its security guards to remove the union organizers. The union filed an unfair labour practice complaint alleging that CF

Source: Travel Pictures/Alamy

---

non-motive unfair labour practice: A type of unfair labour practice that does not require the presence of anti-union animus.

was "interfering in the formation of a union" contrary to what is now section 70 of the Ontario *Labour Relations Act*. The relevant portion of section 70 reads as follows:

> No employer ... and *no person acting on behalf of an employer or an employers' organization shall participate in or interfere with the formation, selection or administration of a trade union.*† [Emphasis added.]

Issue: Did CF unlawfully interfere in the formation of a union by banning union organizers from the Eaton Centre?

Decision: Yes. The OLRB ruled that CF had violated section 70, and that decision was upheld by the Ontario Court of Appeal. The OLRB ruled that CF was a "person acting on behalf of" Eaton's when it enforced its "no solicitation" policy and, therefore, that section 70 applied to the actions of CF. CF may have valid, business-related reasons for having and enforcing a "no solicitation" rule at its malls that are unrelated to union activity. However, that rule, and property rights in general, are not absolute and must be weighed against the statutorily protected right to organize. The business purpose for the application of the "no solicitation" policy was weak or non-existent here, since the union's organizers were not interfering with any mall business—they were active before the mall opened in an area generally open to the public, but when the public was not present. On the other hand, accessing the mall was essential for the union organizers since it was the only realistic way that the organizers could identify and communicate with workers at this workplace. In the absence of a business justification, the employer's attempt to exclude union organizers from the mall constituted unlawful interference with the formation of a union.

---

* Jack Layton, who would later lead the federal New Democratic Party, was convicted for trespassing because he refused to leave the Eaton Centre when ordered to do so by CF security. Layton was helping the union organizers. His conviction was later overturned: see *R v. Layton*, [1986] CCC (3d) 550 (Ont. Prov. Ct.).

† Ontario *Labour Relations Act, 1995*, SO 1995, c. 1, Sch. A, s. 70.

IV. Employer Expression Rights

Employers are not completely silenced during a union organizing campaign. They do not have to sit idly by while their employees unionize. The unfair labour practice provisions carve out an exception that protects a limited right of employers to campaign against unionization. For example, employers can prohibit union organizing during working hours, when the employees should be performing their jobs.[32] They can enforce their property rights to exclude professional union organizers (with some exceptions, such as when workers live on employer-controlled property or the only access to the workers is by entering employer property, such as in the case of shopping malls[33]). And in general terms, employers are permitted to express opinions about unions and collective bargaining, provided that they do not use threats, intimidation, or coercion (or "undue influence," in most jurisdictions) and do not make promises, such as promising benefits if employees reject collective bargaining. Whether employers should have a protected right to campaign in this way has long been debated, as described in Box 9.2.

BOX 9.2 » TALKING WORK LAW

Should Employers Have a Protected Right to Campaign Against Collective Bargaining?

In 1968, the report of the Task Force on Labour Relations (the Woods Report) examined the state of collective bargaining law and recommended reforms. The report recommended limiting employer speech during union organizing campaigns:

> An employer who opposes certification of a union should be limited to defending his record as employer through the statement of facts, and to rebutting union allegations and promises without threat or promise of future action.*

Professor Paul Weiler (Harvard University), one of Canada's leading labour law scholars and adjudicators, similarly argued that employers should play a limited role in the decision on whether workers are better off unionizing. In his view, employees are deciding who should represent them in their dealing with the employer, and although the employer has an interest in the outcome, it is a decision that should be the employees' alone:

> I have always found it incongruous that the employer should be given a central role in the representation play, even if its campaign is perfectly legal, without a whisper of economic coercion of the employees. ... In making up their minds about union representation, the employees are really choosing

how they will deal with their employer, how they will participate in settling and improving their terms of employment. The employer and the employees have an inherent conflict of interest in that topic. Clearly the employer is affected by the employees' judgment about whether they will be represented by a union. Yet surely that collective employee choice should be as off limits to the employer as the employer's choice of vice-president of industrial relations is off limits to the employees.[†]

However, the argument that employers should be restrained from campaigning on the side of employees who do not want collective bargaining has generally not prevailed under contemporary Canadian law. As discussed in this chapter, the law generally permits employers to campaign against unionization as long as they do not engage in threats, coercion, intimidation, and, in some jurisdictions, "undue influence." Arguments advanced in favour of permitting non-coercive employer campaigning include: (1) the employer's interests are

affected to a substantial degree by the outcome of the campaign, so it should have a right to participate; (2) allowing employers to campaign against unionization contributes to a more informed electorate, since the union will only give "one side of the story"; and (3) freedom of expression is fundamental in Canada and should not be restricted except in exceptional circumstances.[‡]

---

[*] H.D. Woods, A.W.R. Carrothers, J. Crispo, and G. Dion, *Canadian Industrial Relations, Report of the Task Force on Labour Relations* (Ottawa: Queen's Printer, 1968), at 23.

[†] P. Weiler, *Reconcilable Differences: New Directions in Canadian Labour Law* (Toronto: Carswell, 1980), at 45-46. See also P. Alon-Shenker and G. Davidov, "Organizing: Should the Employer Have a Say?" (2016) 17 *Theoretical Inquiries in Law* 63, http://www7.tau.ac.il/ojs/index.php/til/article/viewFile/1373/1439.

[‡] See, e.g., D. McPhillips, "Employer Free Speech and the Right to Trade Union Organization" (1982) 20 *Osgoode Hall Law Journal* 138. See also Canada, Public Works and Government Services Canada, *Canada Labour Code, Part 1, Review: Seeking a Balance, Part 1* (Ottawa: Human Resources Development Canada, 1995), at 63-65 (it recommends a statutorily protected freedom of employers to engage in non-coercive speech).

Section 58(2) of the Nova Scotia *Trade Union Act* is typical of employer expression provisions found in Canadian collective bargaining legislation:

> Nothing in this Act shall be deemed to deprive an employer of his freedom to express his views so long as he does not use coercion, intimidation, threats or undue influence.[34]

Most jurisdictions include similar language. However, there is variation across Canada in terms of how far an employer may go in its efforts to persuade its employees to reject unionization.[35] For example, the Manitoba *Labour Relations Act* includes a freedom of expression provision similar to that of the Nova Scotia *Trade Union Act*, but it also qualifies that an employer may communicate "to an employee a statement of fact or an opinion reasonably held with respect to the employer's business."[36] Together, these two provisions have been interpreted to restrict employers from bad-mouthing unions with claims such as "unions just want your dues" and "employees would be better off without a union."[37] However, in most Canadian jurisdictions, employers are permitted to actively lobby employees to "vote no" and even to say negative things about unions, provided that there are no threats, intimidation, or coercion.[38]

Identifying where the divide lies between lawful expression and unlawful intimidation is not always straightforward. As the OLRB noted in the case of *International Union of Electrical, Radio and Machine Workers v. Lorain Products (Canada) Ltd.*, "the line which separates freedom of expression from undue influence or the other prohibitions [coercion, intimidation, threats] of the *Act* is a thin one which must be drawn having regard to the facts of the particular case."[39] Labour relations boards apply an **objective test** (see Chapter 7 in the companion volume), asking whether an employee of "average intelligence and fortitude" would be intimidated by the employer's expression in the circumstances.[40] In applying this test, labour relations boards consider the context in which the speech is made, as well as the content or substance of the speech itself.[41] For

---

objective test: A legal test used in interpretation of contracts and statutes that asks, What would a reasonable person of normal intelligence think, if told about the circumstances?

example, although employer **captive audience meetings** are usually permitted in Canada, labour relations boards recognize too that the act of forcing non-union, vulnerable employees to listen to the employer's anti-union message can itself be coercive. Therefore, comments made at a captive audience meeting may be ruled to be coercive and intimidating even though in another context the same comments would not be.[42]

Employers enter dangerous waters whenever they make a link between unionization and job security.[43] Thus, an employer that threatens to fire employees, to close the workplace or transfer work, to cut wages or benefits, or to impose any other form of disadvantage on employees if a union is successful is crossing the line into unlawful territory.[44] Bribes, such as a promise to grant a raise or some other benefit if the employees reject unionization, are similarly unlawful.[45] Employers who hire spies or private investigators to infiltrate union supporter groups and report back to the employer, or who use security guards to closely watch union supporters or organizers, have been found to be engaged in unlawful intimidation.[46] In the case considered in Box 9.3, the employer was careful to not make an explicit threat to employees who were considering unionization and yet was still found to have acted unlawfully. Pay attention to the reasoning the labour relations board followed that led it to that conclusion.

BOX 9.3 » CASE LAW HIGHLIGHT

An Employer's Speech During an Organizing Campaign Crosses the Line

United Steelworkers of America v. Wal-Mart Canada, Inc.
1997 CanLII 15529 (Ont. LRB)

Key Facts: In April 1996, the United Steelworkers of America (USWA) commenced an organizing campaign at a Wal-Mart Canada store in Windsor. Within a few weeks, the union had collected union membership cards on behalf of 91 employees out of just over 200 total employees in the bargaining unit sought. The union applied for certification on May 2. A certification vote was held a week later, and the results were 151 votes against unionization and 43 votes in favour. The union filed an unfair labour practice complaint alleging that in the days preceding the vote, the employer had engaged in a campaign of threats and intimidation of employees that tainted the outcome of the vote. The alleged employer conduct included the following:

- telling an employee that a benefit program would be revoked by the employer if the union succeeded;
- inviting employees to ask any question about the union campaign and promising to answer them, but then refusing to answer the one question that concerned employees most: Would Wal-Mart close the store if the union won? When employees asked that, the employer answered that "it would be inappropriate" for the employer to comment on what might happen if the union won;
- permitting an anti-union employee to give a speech against the union at an employee meeting, but not granting a union supporter the same opportunity; and

- not distancing itself from the comment by the anti-union employee at the meeting that Wal-Mart "would not stand for" a union.

Issue: Did Wal-Mart Canada commit an unfair labour practice by its pre-vote actions, and, if so, did those illegal acts taint the outcome of the vote?

Decision: Yes and yes. The OLRB noted that Wal-Mart's response to learning of the union campaign was sophisticated. No one was fired, and there was no direct, overt threat to close the store. However, an explicit threat to remove a benefit was made, and, more importantly, Wal-Mart conveyed to employees the message that there was a real possibility that if the union succeeded, it would consider closing the store. It did this in a number of ways.

First, it permitted an employee to tell co-workers at a store meeting that a vote for the union could threaten their jobs and then did not distance itself from the statement. Second, Wal-Mart planted the seed in the minds of employees that the store could close if the union won. It did this by constantly soliciting questions from employees and then, when asked about the possibility of a store closure, simply refusing to answer. This behaviour would cause "reasonable employees" to conclude a store closure in response to a union win is possible:

[W]e are of the view that the company's failure to answer the questions of associates with regard to the issue of a store closure would cause the average

---

captive audience meeting: A meeting that employees are ordered by their employer to attend to listen to the employer's opinions on whether employees should or should not support unionization.

reasonable employee to conclude that the store would close if the union got in. Given that the inside organizers told management that this was in fact happening, and management did not change its approach, we are satisfied that the company intended employees to draw this conclusion. There is no legal prohibition against answering questions with regard to store closure by saying that the company would not close and would sit down and negotiate with the union if the union was successful. Obviously, it is only illegal for the company to say that the store would close. Therefore, by not alleviating employees' concerns by answering the question, the company was intentionally fueling employee concerns.

Third, the employer's strategy of having five managers circulate around the store for six days straight, repeatedly

engaging employees in one-on-one discussions about the union surpassed simply providing information and crossed the line into "undue influence." The labour relations board ruled that Wal-Mart's unlawful conduct tainted the outcome of the vote:

> We have no doubt that the intentionally generated implied threat to job security which occurred in this case had the result of rendering the representation vote taken meaningless. This case is a classic example of a situation in which the conduct of the employer changes the question in the minds of the employees at the vote from one of union representation to one of "do you want to retain your employment."

Therefore, the board exercised its remedial power to certify the union (see the discussion of remedies, below), leading to the first unionized Wal-Mart store in the world.

The prohibition on "undue influence" covers behaviour that might not otherwise be captured by intimidation, coercion, and threats. Labour relations boards in jurisdictions that prohibit "undue influence"—only British Columbia, Saskatchewan, and Quebec do not[47]—have interpreted the prohibition to involve an unfair exploitation of employer power to pressure employees to accept the employer's views, even if no explicit threat is used.[48] For example, the OLRB ruled in the *Wal-Mart Canada* case (Box 9.3) that by having managers circulate for days engaging employees in one-on-one conversations, the employer engaged in unlawful "undue influence."[49] It was too much for employees to be confronted with constant one-on-one conversations with their bosses.

V. Remedies for Unfair Labour Practices

Recall that the fundamental theory of remedies is to return the aggrieved party to the position he or she would have been in but for the unlawful conduct of the guilty party.[50] Collective bargaining statutes grant labour relations boards broad discretion to design remedies. It is usually pretty straightforward to decide how to compensate an employee who has been stripped of his or her job or benefits: give the job and benefits back to the person. Thus, labour relations boards routinely reinstate employees whose employment was terminated for union activity, usually with full back pay and compensation for lost benefits. In some jurisdictions, including Ontario, the labour relations board also has the power to order a fired employee to return to work on an interim basis, until the person's unfair labour practice complaint is decided (this is known as **interim reinstatement**). An interim reinstatement can help offset the damage done to an organizing campaign by an unlawful termination of a union supporter.

A more challenging remedial question is how to return a union to the position it would have been in but for an employer's unlawful acts. What has a union lost when an employer engages in unfair labour practices? Earlier in the chapter, we cited studies that conclude that when employers act unlawfully during organizing campaigns, the odds of the union winning a certification application fall dramatically. Therefore, the harm to the union is the damage to its organizing campaign, and maybe the opportunity to win the campaign. Labour relations boards have been

---

interim reinstatement: An order by a labour board (or other legal board possessing such authority) that the employer reinstate a terminated employee to their job pending the outcome of litigation that will determine if the employer was within its legal rights to terminate the employee.

creative in their efforts to try and provide a meaningful remedy to unions. For example, they have, among other remedies,

- ordered employers to post and distribute notices to employees explaining how the employer broke the law and will not do so again
- disregarded failed certification votes and ordered second votes, permitting the union to decide the timing
- ordered employers to provide the union with an office or other access to the workplace
- ordered employers to allow the union to make speeches at work during working time, or use company bulletin boards
- ordered employers to provide unions with personal contact information for employees
- ordered that the union be permitted to show pro-union videos at the workplace
- ordered that the employer reimburse the union for organizing costs.

However, these sorts of remedies do not always fully compensate the union for its lost opportunity to organize a workplace. If the unlawful acts by the employer are so serious that they convince employees that supporting the union could cost them their jobs, then the union's chances of obtaining majority employee support may be irreparably damaged. Some governments (Ontario, British Columbia, Manitoba, New Brunswick, Nova Scotia, and the federal jurisdiction[51]) have responded to this reality by empowering labour relations boards to issue **remedial certification**. While some variation exists in the models used across jurisdictions, in essence, remedial certification laws permit a labour relations board to certify a union as the representative of employees as a remedy for unfair labour practices when the board believes that the employer's conduct effectively destroyed the possibility of testing employee wishes through a ballot or card check.

The remedial certification order grants the union a licence to try and bargain a first collective agreement that employees will accept. This was the remedy ordered in the *Wal-Mart Canada* decision discussed in Box 9.3. In that case, the labour relations board described the test for ordering remedial certification as follows:

> [I]n our view the determinative factor … is not whether the employer breaches of the Act are flagrant or egregious but whether or not the employer's breaches of the Act result in the Board concluding that a representation vote does not or would not likely reflect the true wishes of the employees in the bargaining unit about being represented by a trade union. The employer in this case is sophisticated and its response to the union's organizing drive reflects this. We have no doubt that the intentionally generated implied threat to job security which occurred in this case had the result of rendering the representation vote taken on May 9, 1996 meaningless. This case is a classic example of a situation in which the conduct of the employer changes the question in the minds of the employees at the vote on May 9th from one of union representation to one of "do you want to retain your employment."[52]

Remedial certification, where it exists, is an exceptional remedy, and is rarely ordered. It is reserved for cases of serious employer misconduct involving threats to employees' jobs or the firing of union supporters that the board concludes cannot be wiped from the employees' minds. However, the mere threat of remedial certification may act as a strong deterrent to some employers who otherwise may perceive that benefit of breaking the law (avoiding a union certification) to outweigh the cost of any remedial order that might otherwise be ordered (recall the discussion of **efficient breach** back in Chapter 3). Remedial certification is usually accompanied by

remedial certification: An order by a labour relations board certifying a union that may not have established that it has majority employee support as a remedy for seriously unlawful acts by the employer—i.e., convincing employees that supporting a union could cost them their jobs.

efficient breach: A deliberate violation of a contract or government statute owing to the belief that it is more economically efficient to violate the legal rule than to comply with it.

additional remedies that aim to help the union rebuild a relationship of trust with the employees, including access orders that allow union representatives onto employer property.[53]

VI. Chapter Summary

Unfair labour practice provisions modify the common law right of employers to discriminate against employees who support unionization and collective bargaining. Unfair labour practice provisions balance the rights of workers to organize with the right of employers to express opinions about matters that will affect the business. Threats, coercion, and intimidation—both physical and economic—intended to influence employee opinions about unionization are prohibited. Most of the time, unfair labour practices require an intention to undermine union organizing, or a finding that there was anti-union animus. However, Canadian collective bargaining statutes also recognize non-motive unfair labour practices that require a balancing of the employer's legitimate business interests against the right to organize. In order to give meaning to the right to organize, governments have conferred broad remedial powers on labour relations boards to redress employers' unfair labour practices.

QUESTIONS AND ISSUES FOR DISCUSSION

1. In what way do unfair labour practice provisions affect the common law rights of employers?
2. Explain the difference between a motive-based and a non-motive-based unfair labour practice.
3. Should the law permit employers to campaign against unionization? What are arguments for and against a law that would require employers to remain neutral in relation to an attempt by employees to unionize?
4. Write a speech that an employer could read to its employees that argues against unionization, but that does not violate any unfair labour practice provisions in your jurisdiction.
5. What sort of employer conduct is captured by the prohibition on "undue influence"?
6. What is remedial certification, and in what circumstances would it be ordered by a labour relations board?

EXERCISE

In Ontario, British Columbia, Manitoba, New Brunswick, Nova Scotia, Prince Edward Island, and the federal jurisdiction, labour relations boards have the authority to certify a union as the bargaining representative of employees as a remedy for serious unfair labour practices. The theory underlying "remedial certification" is that some illegal acts by an employer will convince employees that joining a union could result in reprisals by the employer. In that case, it is unlikely that the true wishes of the employees could ever be measured by the taking of a representation vote. This exercise involves finding and summarizing a remedial certification case.

1. Go to the CanLII home page: www.canlii.org.
2. In the "Document text" search box, type "remedial certification" and "union." Now undertake the search.
3. Scroll through the decisions and look for a case in which a labour relations board was asked to rule on a union's argument that remedial certification should be ordered. Read the decision and answer the following questions:
   a. What jurisdiction is the case from?
   b. What was the employer's conduct that was alleged to be unlawful?
   c. Did the labour relations board find that the employer committed an unfair labour practice?
   d. If so, did the labour relations board order remedial certification?

e. Describe the labour relations board's reasoning on the question of whether remedial certification should be ordered.

f. What remedies other than remedial certification were ordered, if any?

UPDATES

Go to emond.ca/lawofworkircb for links to news, author's blog posts, content updates, and other information related to the chapters in this text.

NOTES AND REFERENCES

1   These facts are taken from *Marv Jones Honda v. International Association of Machinists & Aerospace Workers District Lodge 250*, 2015 CanLII 5787 (BCLRB). See also *United Food & Commercial Workers, Local 206 v. Swiss Chalet Restaurant #1250*, 2012 CanLII 74380 (Ont. LRB).

2   The OLRB ruled that the termination was for union activity and that the termination had effectively ended the union's campaign. Remedial certification was ordered.

3   K. Bentham, "Employer Resistance to Union Certification: A Study of Eight Canadian Jurisdictions" (2002) 57 *Relations Industrielles/Industrial Relations* 159, at 172. See also M. Campolieti, R. Gomez, and M. Gunderson, "Managerial Hostility and Attitudes Towards Unions: A Canada–US Comparison" (2013) 34 *Journal of Labor Research* 99.

4   T. Thomason, "Managerial Opposition to Union Certification in Quebec and Ontario" (unpublished manuscript, n.d.).

5   C. Riddell, "Union Suppression and Certification Success" (2001) 34 *The Canadian Journal of Economics* 396.

6   See the discussion in D. Doorey, "Graduated Freedom of Association: Worker Voice Beyond the Wagner Model" (2012) 38:2 *Queen's Law Journal* 515, at 528-29. In the 1987 decision *Reference Re Public Service Employee Relations Act (Alta.)*, [1987] 1 SCR 313, at 391, the Supreme Court ruled that "freedom of association" in the *Canadian Charter of Rights and Freedoms* includes a right to form worker associations "without penalty or reprisal."

7   *Dunmore v. Ontario (Attorney General)*, [2001] 3 SCR 1016, para. 20. See also *Delisle v. Canada*, [1999] 2 SCR 989, at para. 32.

8   *Dunmore v. Ontario (Attorney General)*, supra note 7, at para. 22, citing H. Arthurs, et al., *Labour Law and Industrial Relations in Canada*, 4th ed. (Deventer, Netherlands: Kluwer, 1993), at 196.

9   Today the provision is found in *Criminal Code*, RSC 1985, c. C-46, s. 425.

10 To simplify, reference to "employee associations" includes both trade unions and other types of employee associations. However, note that PC 1003 treated unions and employee associations as distinct forms of employee organizations.

11 *Canada Labour Code*, RSC 1985, c. L-2, s. 96. See also BC *Labour Relations Code*, RSBC 1996, c. 244, s. 9; and Ontario *Labour Relations Act, 1995*, SO 1995, c. 1, Sch. A, s. 70.

12 See the discussion in *IBEW, Local 424 v. Flint Canada Inc.*, [1995] Alta. LRBR 48, at 58-59.

13 There are dozens of Canadian cases in which employers have been found to have taken action against union supporters, or threatened to take such action. See *United Food & Commercial Workers, Local 206 v. Swiss Chalet Restaurant #1250*, supra note 1; *Convergys Customer Management Canada Inc. v. B.C. Government and Service Employees' Union*, 2003 CanLII 62911 (BCLRB), at para. 38; *Service Employees International Union Local 2, Brewery, General & Professional Workers' Union v. 3258205 Nova Scotia Ltd*, 2014 NSLB 13; *Common Ground Publishing Corp. v. Communications, Energy and Paperworkers Union of Canada, Local 2000*, 2003 CanLII 63032 (BCLRB); and *White Spot Ltd.* (1993), 21 CLRBR (2d) 146 (BCLRB).

14 *Marv Jones Honda v. International Association of Machinists & Aerospace Workers District Lodge 250*, supra note 1. See similarly, *United Food & Commercial Workers, Local 206 v. Swiss Chalet Restaurant #1250*, supra note 1, at para. 38.

15 See, e.g., Ontario *Labour Relations Act, 1995*, supra note 11, s. 96(5); Manitoba *Labour Relations Act*, CCSM, c. L10, s. 9; BC *Labour Relations Code*, supra note 11, s. 14(7); and *The Saskatchewan Employment Act*, SS 2013, c. S-15.1, ss. 6-32(5).

16 *Pop Shoppe (Toronto) Limited*, [1976] OLRB Rep. June 299; *Barrie Examiner*, [1975] OLRB Rep. Oct. 745; *The Corporation of the City of London*, [1976] OLRB Rep. Jan. 990; *The Labour Relations Code v. United Food and Commercial Workers Canada Union, Local No 401*, 2014 CanLII 31405 (ABLRB); and *United Steelworkers of America v. Plaza Fiberglas Manufacturing Limited*, 1990 CanLII 5659 (Ont. LRB).

17 BC *Labour Relations Code*, supra note 11, s. 6.

18 See, e.g., BC *Labour Relations Code*, supra note 11, s. 31; Ontario *Labour Relations Act, 1995*, supra note 11, ss. 15 and 53. See also the discussion in *Edwards v. Edwards* (1952), 52 CLLC, at para. 17027; and *Tilco Plastics Employee's Association v. Tilco Plastics (1976) Limited*, 1980 CanLII 869 (Ont. LRB).

19 In the United States, it is unlawful per se for an employer to provide any support to an employee association or to recognize and deal with a non-union employee association: see *National Labour Relations Act*, 29 USC s. 158(a)(2). In Canada, it is not unlawful for an employer to establish, aid, or recognize a non-union employee association, unless the employer is engaging in that conduct in order to thwart an organizing campaign by a "real" union: see *Tri-Canada Inc.*, [1981] OLRB Rep. Oct. 1509.

20 See *Christian Labour Association of Canada, Construction Workers Local 52 v. Covertite Eastern Limited*, 1996 CanLII 11156 (Ont. LRB); and *United Electrical, Radio and Machine Workers of America v. Square D Canada Electric Equipment Inc.*, 1980 CanLII 994 (Ont. LRB). However, in British Columbia, the labour relations board has permitted employers to encourage employees to support one union over another: see *Simpe "Q" Care Inc. v. Hospital Employees' Union*, 2007 CanLII 29928 (BCLRB).

21 *Delta Hospital*, [1978] 1 CLRBR 356 (BCLRB) (it is not unlawful for an employer to invite a union to organize its employees); *Canadian Union of Public Employees v. University of Toronto*, 1988 CanLII 3691 (on allowing a union to communicate with employees); *United Steelworkers of America v. Continuous Mining Systems Limited*, 1990 CanLII 5791 (the employer provided the union with a list of employees); *National Automobile, Aerospace, Transportation and General Workers of Canada (CAW-Canada) v. Coca-Cola Bottling Co.*, 2004 CanLII 24945 (Ont. LRB) (the employer allowed the incumbent union to solicit at work but not the union attempting to newly organize its workers); and *665846 B.C. Ltd. v. United Food and Commercial Workers International Union, Local 1518*, 2005 CanLII 17730 (BCLRB).

22 *McGill's Electrical Warehouse*, [1997] Alta. LRBR 385; and *United Food and Commercial Workers Union, Local No. 401 v. Westfair Foods Ltd.*, 2008 CanLII 51092 (ABLRB).

23 *Ontario Secondary School Teachers' Federation District 25 v. Ottawa-Carleton District School Board*, 2001 CanLII 11073 (Ont. LRB); and *The Millcroft Inn Limited*, [2000] OLRB Rep. July/August 665.

24 See *Communications, Energy and Paperworkers Union of Canada v. Rapid Transformers Ltd.*, 1999 CanLII 20142 (Ont. LRB); and *Canadian Union of Public Employees, Local 2424 v. Carleton University*, 1998 CanLII 18245 (Ont. LRB). However, the employer can explain the state of the business or discuss facts with employees that are obvious: see *Board, Retail, Wholesale and Department Store Union v. 101109823 Saskatchewan Ltd*, 2014 CanLII 64280 (SKLRB).

25 *Sandy Bay Ojibway First Nation*, 2009 CIRB 440 (CanLII).

26 See *Canadian Broadcasting Corp. v. Canada (Labour Relations Board)*, [1995] 1 SCR 157.

27 *Canadian Paperworkers Union v. International Wallcoverings*, 1983 CanLII 764 (Ont. LRB), at para. 27.

28 Some statutes include an express provision clarifying that certain actions by an employer do not constitute an unfair labour practice, such as making changes "reasonably necessary for the proper conduct of the business": see BC *Labour Relations Code*, supra note 11, s. 6(4).

29 *Canadian Union of Public Employees, Local 2424 v. Carleton University*, supra note 24, at para. 50. See also *Canadian Paperworkers Union v. International Wallcoverings*, supra note 24; *United Food and Commercial Workers Canada, Local 1288P v. Covered Bridge Potato Chip Company*, 2016 CanLII 20735 (NBLEB); and *Ontario Secondary School Teachers' Federation District 25 v. Ottawa-Carleton District School Board*, 2001 CanLII 11073 (Ont. LRB).

30 See *Canadian Paperworkers Union v. International Wallcoverings*, supra note 29. An employer rule banning union buttons and T-shirts violates non-interference provision: see *Elementary Teachers' Federation of Ontario and Elementary Teachers' Federation of Ontario, Hamilton-Wentworth Local v. Hamilton-Wentworth District School Board*, 2002 CanLII 26879 (Ont. LRB); and *Southern Ontario Newspaper Guild v. Metroland Printing*, 1994 CanLII 9946 (Ont. LRB).

31 *Canadian Paperworkers Union v. International Wallcoverings*, supra note 29.

32 *United Steelworkers of America v. Adams Mine, Cliffs of Canada Ltd.*, 1982 CanLII 978 (Ont. LRB). Some statutes make this right explicit. See, e.g., Ontario *Labour Relations Act, 1995*, supra note 11, s. 77. However, if the employer permits employees to socialize and speak about all subjects except unionization, then a prohibition on discussing unionization may amount to unlawful interference in the formation of a union: see *Union of Bank Employees v. Canadian Imperial Bank of Commerce* (1985), 85 CLLC 16021 (CLRB).

33 See, e.g., Ontario *Labour Relations Act, 1995*, supra note 11, s. 13; and *Cadillac Fairview Corporation Limited v. Retail, Wholesale and Department Store Union*, 1989 CanLII 1116 (Ont. LRB).

34 Nova Scotia *Trade Union Act*, RSNS 1989, c. 475, s. 58(2).

35 Employer speech rights were more restricted in the federal jurisdiction and in Saskatchewan until recently: see, e.g., *Super Value* (1981), 3 CLRBR 412 (SKLRB); and *Bank of Montreal* (1985), CLRBR (NS) 129. Both jurisdictions recently introduced broader employer speech provisions that aligned the approach with that in

other jurisdictions, essentially permitting non-threatening expression: see *Canada Council of Teamsters v. FedEx Ground Package System*, Ltd, 2011 CIRB 614 (CanLII).

36 Manitoba *Labour Relations Act*, supra note 15, s. 6(3)(f).

37 See, e.g., *United Steelworkers, Local 9074 v. Winnipeg Dodge Chrysler Ltd*, 2014 CanLII 36811 (MBLRB).

38 *Service Employees International Union, Local 1 Canada, Applicant v. PRP Senior Living Inc. o/a Sunrise of Aurora*, 2013 CanLII 15847 (Ont. LRB); *Teamsters Local 879 v. Greb Industries Limited*, 1978 CanLII 630 (Ont. LRB); *United Food & Commercial Workers Union, Local 2p6 v. Knob Hill Farms Limited*, 1987 CanLII 3148 (Ont. LRB); *Labourers' International Union of North America, Local 1059 v. West Elgin Construction Ltd.*, 2005 CanLII 19730 (Ont. LRB); *Canadian Hotel and Service Workers Union v. Romzap Ltd (Sheraton Fallsview Hotel & Conference Centre)*, 1995 CanLII 10034 (Ont. LRB); *Cardinal Transportation B.C. Incorporated*, BCLRB No. B344/96; and *Convergys Customer Management Canada Inc. v. B. C. Government and Service Employees' Union*, 2003 CanLII 62911 (BCLRB). The federal jurisdiction used to more tightly restrict employer speech (see *Bank of Montreal* (1985), CLRBR (NS) 129), but after amendments to the *Canada Labour Code* in 2001, the federal labour relations board now permits non-coercive employer campaigning: see *Canada Council of Teamsters v. FedEx Ground Package System*, Ltd, supra note 35.

39 *International Union of Electrical, Radio and Machine Workers v. Lorain Products (Canada) Ltd.*, 1977 CanLII 511 (Ont. LRB), at para. 5.

40 *Excell Agent Services* (2003), 96 CLRBR (2d) 161 (BCLRB); *United Steelworkers of America v. Wal-Mart Canada*, 1997 CanLII 15529 (Ont. LRB); *Board, Retail, Wholesale and Department Store Union v. 101109823 Saskatchewan Ltd*, supra note 24; *Service Employees International Union, Local 1 Canada, Applicant v. PRP Senior Living Inc. o/a Sunrise of Aurora*, supra note 38; and *Saskatchewan Joint Board, Retail, Wholesale and Department Store Union v. Sakundiak Equipment*, 2011 CanLII 72774 (SKLRB).

41 *Excell Agent Services*, supra note 40.

42 See, e.g., *RMH Teleservices International Inc. v. B.C. Government and Service Employees' Union*, 2005 CanLII 24889 (BCLRB); *Peter Ross 2008 Ltd v. United Steel, Paper and Forestry, Rubber, Manufacturing, Energy, Allied Industrial and Service Workers International Union, Local 2009*, 2012 CanLII 12643 (BCLRB); *Labourers' International Union of North America, Local 625 v. Alpine Construction (Windsor) Inc.*, 2011 CanLII 69421 (Ont. LRB); and *United Steelworkers, Local 9074 v. Winnipeg Dodge Chrysler Ltd*, 2014 CanLII 36811 (MBLB). See also D. Doorey, "The Medium and the 'Anti-Union' Message: Forced Listening and Captive Audience Meetings" (2007) 29 *Comparative Labor Law & Policy Journal* 79.

43 *International Union of Electrical, Radio and Machine Workers v. Lorain Products (Canada) Ltd.*, supra note 39; and *UNITE HERE v. Novotel Canada Inc.*, 2012 CanLII 57428 (Ont. LRB).

44 *Peter Ross 2008 Ltd v. United Steel, Paper and Forestry, Rubber, Manufacturing, Energy, Allied Industrial and Service Workers International Union, Local 2009*, 2012 CanLII 26996 (BCLRB); *Hamlet of Kugaaruk*, 2010 CIRB 502 (CanLII); *The Labour Relations Code v. United Food and Commercial Workers Canada Union, Local No 401*, supra note 16; and *Allstar Mechanical Ltd. v. United Association of Journeymen and Apprentices of the Plumbing and Pipefitting Industry of the United States and Canada, Local 170*, 2001 CanLII 33129 (BCLRB).

45 *Canadian Fibre* (2009), 167 CLRBR (2d) 261 (BCLRB); and *United Food and Commercial Workers International Union, Local 175 v. Pharmaphil*, 1994 CanLII 9945 (Ont. LRB).

46 *Convergys Customer Management Canada Inc. v. B.C. Government and Service Employees' Union*, supra note 13; and *United Steelworkers of America v. Radio Shack*, 1979 CanLII 817 (Ont. LRB).

47 Only British Columbia, Quebec, and Saskatchewan do not include "undue influence" among the list of prohibited employer conduct. In British Columbia, this omission has been interpreted to mean employers have broader rights to apply pressure on employees to resist unionization or to select a union of the employer's choosing, provided that overt threats or intimidation are not used: see *Convergys Customer Management Canada Inc. v. B.C. Government and Service Employees' Union*, supra note 13; and *Simpe "Q" Care Inc. v. Hospital Employees' Union*, supra note 20.

48 See, e.g., *K Mart Canada Ltd.*, [1981] OLRB Rep. Jan. 60; *United Steelworkers of America v. Wal-Mart Canada*, supra note 40; and *Service Employees International Union, Local 1 Canada, Applicant v. PRP Senior Living Inc. o/a Sunrise of Aurora*, supra note 38.

49 See similarly *Service Employees International Union, Local 1 Canada, Applicant v. PRP Senior Living Inc. o/a Sunrise of Aurora*, supra note 38.

50 For an excellent review of labour relations board remedies, see J. Andrew, *Labour Relations Board Remedies in Canada*, 2nd ed. (Aurora, ON: Canada Law Book).

51 In Prince Edward Island, there is no express remedial certification, but the labour relations board has found that it has that power: see *Polar Foods v. Prince Edward Island (Labour Relations Board)*, 2002 PESCTD 56.

52 *United Steelworkers of America v. Wal-Mart Canada*, supra note 40, at para. 49. For a discussion of the test applied in British Columbia, see *Cardinal Transportation B.C. Incorporated*, BCLRB No. B344/96 (Reconsideration of BCLRB Nos. B463/94 and B232/95), 34 CLRBR (2d) 1.

53 *Service Employees International Union, Local 1 Canada, Applicant v. PRP Senior Living Inc. o/a Sunrise of Aurora*, supra note 38; and Andrew, supra note 50, at 12:1500.

CHAPTER 10

Collective Bargaining and the Making of a Collective Agreement

I. Introduction

We have seen in preceding chapters that Canadian workers have struggled to access collective bargaining for over a century. In the first half of the 20th century, these struggles occasionally turned violent in the face of employer and government opposition. The Canadian collective bargaining model began to emerge in the mid-1940s. This model borrowed key concepts from the 1935 American *Wagner Act*—including majoritarianism, exclusivity, and union certification. Once a union gained majority employee support within this model, it could obtain a government-issued licence to bargain (a "certification") on behalf of workers. After union certification, a novel legal obligation kicked in: both the union representing employees and the employer were legally required to "bargain in good faith" with the objective of reaching a collective agreement. This chapter examines the content of this duty to bargain.[1]

II. The Effects of Union Certification

The certification of a union marks the beginning of a transition for employers and employees from the *common law regime* to the *collective bargaining regime*. From this point onward, employers are no longer permitted to negotiate terms and conditions of employment directly with employees. A new actor, the union, has entered the scene and our laws require the employer to recognize and bargain with the union as the official, exclusive representative of employees in the bargaining unit.[2] Once a collective agreement comes into effect, all of the common law rules that are applicable to individual employment contracts (see Part II of the companion volume) fall by the wayside and are replaced by a new law of collective agreements (see Chapters 12-14 in this text). The Supreme Court of Canada explained this point in the case of *McGavin Toastmaster Ltd. v. Ainscough*:

> The common law as it applies to individual employment contracts is no longer relevant to employer-employee relations governed by a collective agreement which … deals with discharge, termination of employment, severance pay and a host of other matters that have been negotiated between union and company as the principal parties thereto.[3]

This fundamental shift in legal models marks a transformative moment for both the newly unionized employer and the employees.

One of the most dramatic changes involves the rules regulating the negotiation of contracts. In the common law (non-union) regime, both the employer and employee are free to walk away from a negotiation if they dislike the terms being offered, just as you may walk out of a car dealership if you don't like the price of a car being offered by the salesperson. In the collective bargaining regime, there is a legal obligation imposed on the employer and union to bargain with each other, even if one of them would prefer to walk away or ignore the other party altogether. The imposition on employers of a government-backed "duty to bargain" was a trade-off in the Wagner model, necessary to persuade unions to agree to a model that channelled union recognition disputes into a tightly controlled legal regime. The Wagner model, reflected in Order in Council PC 1003 (1944),[4] put an end to **recognition strikes** by offering unions a means to force employers to the bargaining table. The duty to bargain was central to this statutory scheme.

Canadian governments developed a legal model that was intended to provide a procedural framework through which collective bargaining between unions and employers would produce collective agreements—without work stoppages. Nowadays, the vast majority of collective bargaining (about 95 percent) results in a collective agreement without a work stoppage. Many people are surprised by this statistic, because the media tend to report on collective bargaining only when there is a work stoppage, which can lead to a skewed and mistaken perception that work stoppages in unionized workplaces are common.

III. How Collective Bargaining Works

Canadian collective bargaining is described as being "decentralized," because most bargaining takes place at the level of individual workplaces. Typically, a union is certified to represent employees at a particular location (factory, store, etc.) of a single employer, and the union and employer then bargain a collective agreement that is applicable only to employees who work at that location. This "single employer–single union–single location" **bargaining structure** is by far the most common collective bargaining structure in Canada, but other structures exist.[5] For example, the United Food and Commercial Workers union bargains a single collective agreement with Loblaws that covers multiple unionized stores in a province (single union–single employer–multiple locations). In the construction industry, in some provinces, a union representing a specific trade (e.g., carpenters or bricklayers) may bargain a single collective agreement with multiple employers covering the entire province (single union–multiple employers–multiple locations). In the public sector, it is common for a union to bargain a collective agreement that covers categories of workers (e.g., administrative services or outside workers) who work in a variety of locations.

The collective bargaining process is initiated when one party sends the other a **notice to bargain**. A notice to bargain is a letter that says, essentially, "we would like to begin collective bargaining." Collective bargaining statutes regulate when a notice to bargain can be sent. In the case of the renewal of a collective bargaining agreement, that period varies from two to four months before the end of the expiring agreement. Both the union and the employer select a **chief negotiator** who does the talking on behalf of the party in bargaining. The employer may hire a

---

recognition strike: A strike by workers with the aim of pressuring an employer to recognize and bargain with a union on behalf of the employees.

bargaining structure: A term used to describe the identity and number of parties involved in collective bargaining, and the scope of employees covered by that bargaining.

notice to bargain: A letter from a union or employer to the other party that formally begins the process of collective bargaining.

chief negotiator: The lead spokesperson representing a party in negotiations.

lawyer or appoint a manager, such as the human resources or industrial relations manager, to be their negotiator, or in a smaller workplace, the owner may do the negotiating. Unions are less likely to retain lawyers to do their bargaining, although lawyers may provide advice. Typically, a professional negotiator employed by the union (known as a **business representative** or **staff representative**) acts in that capacity. However, in larger bargaining units, workers may select their own bargaining committee and chief negotiator from among their own ranks. For example, the **local union president** or an elected chair of the union's bargaining committee may assume the task.

Often the union presents its proposals first. However, doing so is not a rule nor is it always the case. It is common practice for the parties to agree on a bargaining protocol. For example, a bargaining protocol may provide that **monetary issues** (wages, benefits, pensions) will be left until after the **non-monetary issues** have been resolved. The protocol might also explain whether the parties will sign off on collective agreement clauses one by one as they are agreed, or whether every clause remains negotiable until agreement is reached on the entire contract. In Ontario and Manitoba, the law requires that collective agreements be **ratified** by a majority of bargaining unit employees before they become legal.[6] Therefore, the parties know that any agreement reached by the negotiating teams is a "tentative" deal only and subject to employee ratification. In other jurisdictions, it is common for the parties to agree at the outset whether agreements are subject to approval by employees or, in the case of the employer, senior executives or a corporate board of directors.

We can think of collective bargaining as having three basic stages. In terms of bargaining strategy, both parties will come to the bargaining table with a list of items they hope to obtain through negotiations. Those items are identified and compiled during a *pre-negotiation stage* of collective bargaining. Unions often compile their bargaining "wish list" by taking a survey of the employees in the bargaining unit, asking them to identify those issues that they most want the union to try to win in negotiations.[7] It is important in collective bargaining for the parties to leave room to make concessions. Therefore, negotiating teams for both parties typically identify their "opening positions," their "preferred outcomes," and their "bottom line" positions. The bottom line position is that point beyond which the party will not move and would accept industrial conflict (strike or lockout) rather than concede more at the bargaining table.

During the *negotiation stage*, the parties will have meetings and attempt to identify and reach agreement on some matters, and search for a "zone of agreement" on more contentious issues.[8] For example, an employer may be prepared, if pushed, to give a 2.5 percent pay raise (employer's bottom line), but may hope to bargain only a 1.5 percent raise (employer's preferred outcome). In that case, the employer's opening position may be a 0 percent raise, and it will argue that it cannot afford a raise. The union may be prepared to accept a 2 percent raise (union's bottom line), but may hope for at least a 2.5 percent raise (union's preferred outcome). The union's opening position may be a 4 percent raise. This scenario is illustrated in Figure 10.1. It shows a potential "zone of agreement" on the issue of wages between 2 and 2.5 percent. That is the range of pay raise that both parties are ultimately prepared to accept.

---

business representative or staff representative: An employee of a union whose job is to negotiate and administer collective agreements.

local union president: A person who leads a subunit of a union, known as a local union. A local union may represent a single workplace or a group of workplaces within a defined geographical area or sector. Local union presidents are usually elected by union members and are (or were) employees of a unionized employer.

monetary issues: Subjects in collective bargaining that impose direct costs on employers, such as wages, benefits, and pensions.

non-monetary issues: Subjects in collective bargaining that relate to contract language, such as the text of a grievance procedure or management rights clause.

ratification (of a collective agreement): A vote by unionized employees in favour of accepting a proposed collective agreement.

FIGURE 10.1 The Potential Zone of Agreement in Collective Bargaining

Employer's opening position	Employer's preferred outcome		Employer's bottom line	
0%	1.5%	2.0%	2.5%	4%
		ZONE OF AGREEMENT		
		Union's bottom line	Union's preferred outcome	Union's opening position

Source: Adapted from R. Walton and R. McKersie, *A Behavioral Theory of Labor Negotiations: An Analysis of a Social Interaction System* (New York: McGraw-Hill, 1965).

The fact that a zone of agreement exists does not guarantee a settlement. In real collective bargaining, a lot of issues are negotiated at once. An agreement on wages may not happen if negotiation is held up on other issues. Personalities and agendas can impede settlement. Moreover, as we discussed in Chapter 3, collective bargaining outcomes are heavily influenced by the relative *power* of the parties.[9] Power is influenced by a large number of factors that act upon the collective bargaining parties at any given time. A union's primary source of power in collective bargaining is the threat of a work stoppage or disruption, but the extent of that threat is affected by a range of forces emanating from within the collective bargaining regime and from outside that regime (*external inputs*). For example, the level of employee support for a strike; the size of the bargaining unit relative to the employer's total workforce; the ability of the employer to operate during a work stoppage; union density in the employer's industry; the state of labour markets and unemployment levels; the level of product competition in the employer's industry; public opinion; and of course the laws that regulate collective bargaining and industrial conflict can all affect relative bargaining power. The *negotiation stage* may reach an impasse that is resolved only through one or both parties resorting to industrial conflict of the types described in Chapter 11.

The final stage is the *settlement stage*, which requires the bargaining committees to write up the agreed-upon collective agreement terms, and often to take them back to be approved (or "ratified") by employees or other stakeholders (see discussion below). If an agreement is subject to approval, and that approval is not forthcoming, the bargaining teams may be required to return to the negotiation stage to try again.

IV. Types of Legal Rules Regulating Collective Bargaining

Three types of legal rules govern the collective bargaining process in Canada (see Figure 10.2). First, statutory freeze provisions "freeze" the terms and conditions of employment during the collective bargaining process. Second, the law imposes on the parties in collective bargaining a "duty to bargain in good faith" and to "make reasonable efforts to conclude a collective

FIGURE 10.2 Types of Legal Rules Regulating Collective Bargaining

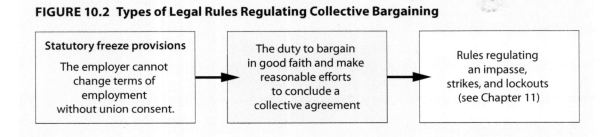

Statutory freeze provisions The employer cannot change terms of employment without union consent.	→	The duty to bargain in good faith and make reasonable efforts to conclude a collective agreement	→	Rules regulating an impasse, strikes, and lockouts (see Chapter 11)

agreement" on both procedural and substantive elements, as we will explore below. Third, complex and extensive rules regulate what happens when negotiations reach an impasse, as well as strikes and lockouts. We will explore this last type of legal rule in Chapter 11.

A. Statutory Freeze Provisions

The statutory freeze provisions are intended to "maintain the prior pattern of the employment relationship in its entirety."[10] During a statutory freeze period, the employer is prohibited from altering any terms and conditions of employment of bargaining unit employees without the union's consent, unless the alteration is consistent with past practice. The legal test is usually referred to as "business as before." Therefore, if an employer has always given employees a holiday bonus or a raise at a specific time, then it could not refuse the bonus or raise because the statutory freeze is in effect. However, if the employer has not given a holiday bonus in the past, then the employer could not do so if a freeze is in effect.[11]

There are two types of statutory freeze: (1) the **certification freeze** and (2) the **collective bargaining freeze**. The two freezes kick in at different times and serve different policy purposes. The details of when the two freezes end vary slightly across jurisdictions. Figure 10.3 depicts how the statutory freeze provisions work in Ontario (see section 86 of the Ontario *Labour Relations Act, 1995*).

FIGURE 10.3 The Statutory Freeze Process in Ontario

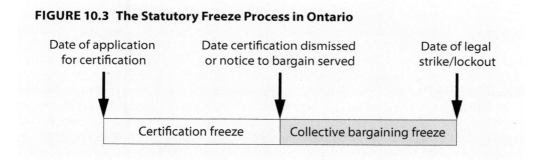

The certification freeze applies from the moment the union serves the application for certification on the employer. It lasts until either (1) the labour relations board dismisses the union's application because the union's organizing attempt failed, or (2) the union wins certification and then serves the employer with a "notice to bargain." That notice triggers both the end of the certification freeze and the beginning of the collective bargaining freeze. In this way, the two freezes blend into each other to create an extended period during which employers must not alter terms of employment without the union's consent that runs from the date of application for certification until the date that the parties are in a legal strike or lockout position (or in some jurisdictions, the date of an actual strike or lockout).[12]

The purpose of the certification freeze is to restrict any advantage the employer might have to start playing around with working conditions in order to influence employees' decisions about whether to support or reject unionization. The purpose of the collective bargaining freeze is slightly different. In 1977, the Canada Labour Relations Board described the purpose of the bargaining freeze in this way:

> The prohibition is imposed on the employer, because Parliament recognizes that in the normal course it is the employer that is in the position to influence the proceedings at the bargaining table

---

certification freeze: A rule found in collective bargaining legislation that prohibits an employer from altering terms of employment without the union's consent during the processing of an application for certification.

collective bargaining freeze: A rule found in collective bargaining legislation that prohibits an employer from altering terms of employment without the union's consent during the period of collective bargaining.

by making decisions affecting its operation without prior consultation with the union. By making such decisions and acting unilaterally, the employer can undermine the authority of the employees' bargaining agent, and also poison the environment within which collective bargaining is being conducted and thereby catalyst avoidable legal or illegal industrial conflict. Such unilateral action is contrary to the cooperative relationship envisioned by and sought to be promoted [by collective bargaining legislation].[13]

The certification freeze applies only during the certification stage, but the collective bargaining freeze applies during each new round of collective bargaining, for as long as the union represents the workers. It is triggered each time either the employer or the union tells the other party that it would like to begin bargaining toward a new collective agreement—each time a new notice to bargain is served.

B. The Duty to Bargain in Good Faith and Make Reasonable Efforts to Conclude a Collective Agreement

How does the law force parties and people to bargain when they have no desire to do so? Take a look at section 17 of the Ontario *Labour Relations Act, 1995*, which essentially mirrors other duty to bargain provisions in Canada:

> The parties shall meet within 15 days from the giving of the notice or within such further period as the parties agree upon and they SHALL BARGAIN IN GOOD FAITH and MAKE EVERY REASONABLE EFFORT TO MAKE A COLLECTIVE AGREEMENT.[14] [Emphasis added.]

Forty words. And most of those words are about when the first meeting takes place. The core of the legal obligation to bargain in Canada is found in the final 14 words requiring the parties to "bargain in good faith" and "make every reasonable effort to make a collective agreement."[15] What meaning to give to those words has been left to labour relations boards, and to the courts reviewing the decisions of those boards. Therefore, in order to understand the substance of the duty to bargain in Canadian collective bargaining law, we need to know how those words have been interpreted. The Supreme Court of Canada has provided some guidance. In the case of *Royal Oak Mines Inc. v. Canada (Labour Relations Board)*, the Supreme Court of Canada explained that the duty to bargain contains both a subjective and objective component:

> Not only must the parties bargain in good faith, but they must also make every reasonable effort to enter into a collective agreement. Both components are equally important, and a party will be found in breach of the section if it does not comply with both of them. There may well be exceptions but as a general rule *the duty to enter into bargaining in good faith must be measured on a subjective standard*, while the *making of a reasonable effort to bargain should be measured by an objective standard* which can be ascertained by a board looking to comparable standards and practices within the particular industry. It is this latter part of the duty which prevents a party from hiding behind an assertion that it is sincerely trying to reach an agreement when, viewed objectively, it can be seen that its proposals are so far from the accepted norms of the industry that they must be unreasonable.[16] [Emphasis added.]

We have considered the difference between objective and subjective tests before (see Chapter 7 of the companion volume). The subjective standard requires the labour relations board to assess the party's motive—is the party making an honest attempt to reach a collective agreement? The objective standard compares the party's behaviour to that of others in the industry. If a party's behaviour substantially veers from the industry norm in a way that impedes the conclusion of a collective agreement, then a labour relations board may determine that the party is not making reasonable efforts to conclude a collective agreement.[17]

We can separate the legal rules that comprise the modern day duty to bargain in good faith into rules that apply to the process of collective bargaining (*how* collective bargaining takes place) and rules that regulate the substance of collective bargaining (*what* is proposed during collective bargaining).

1. The Procedural Duty to Bargain: The *How* of Collective Bargaining

The duty to bargain is primarily concerned with the process of collective bargaining, and labour relations boards have developed rules intended to encourage the parties to engage in a rational and informed discussion about each other's proposals.

a. *The Duty to Meet and Be Prepared to Negotiate*

We can think of this first requirement as the "don't waste the other party's time" rule. The mission of the duty to bargain is to force the parties to come together and engage in a rational, professional discussion about each other's bargaining proposals.[18] With this mission in mind, labour relations boards have imposed a basic requirement on the parties to make themselves available to meet within a reasonable time period. If one party continuously stalls by saying their negotiators are on vacation or too busy with other matters, then they are not "making reasonable efforts to conclude a collective agreement." The parties must also send a person to the bargaining table who is prepared and able to negotiate on behalf of the party. It is a waste of time, and unlawful, for a party to send a junior employee with no authority to the bargaining table merely to sit there and take notes on the other party's submission.

b. *The Duty to Provide Information and Respect the Union's Role as the Employees' Exclusive Representative*

An employer must provide the union with the information it requires to perform its job as the legal bargaining representative of the employees. In the case of a newly certified union, this includes the names, contact information, and terms and conditions of employment of the bargaining unit employees. A failure to provide this information is a violation of the duty to bargain (and perhaps also the prohibition discussed in Chapter 9 on employer interference with the administration of a union).[19] An employer must also not attempt to undermine the union in the minds of employees by, for example, communicating directly with employees about bargaining proposals that have not been discussed first with the union or in a manner that misrepresents the union's bargaining position or that paints the union in a negative light.[20]

c. *The Duty to Be Honest and to Disclose Plans That Will Affect Bargaining Unit Employees*

The duty to bargain requires honesty. Lying to the other party is a violation of the duty to bargain. Therefore, if a party is asked a direct question during negotiations, that party must answer truthfully.[21] An interesting and related issue is whether the duty to bargain requires a party to disclose information that would be of interest to the other party even if it has *not* been asked directly about that information. Does the duty to bargain require "unsolicited disclosure" of relevant information? For example, imagine an employer is considering closing the workplace and firing the workers, but it has not made a final decision yet. Is the employer under an obligation to give the union this information, even if the union does not ask about a possible closure?

It is easy to see why a union would want to know about a possible closure. If the employees are likely to be fired during the term of the collective agreement, then the union's bargaining strategy will change. There would be no point trying to bargain a raise or a new dental plan, for example, if no one will have a job two years later. The union would focus entirely on trying to stop the closure, bargaining higher severance packages or a right to vacant jobs at other locations of the employer if they exist. The employer may not want the union to know its plans, to avoid having to negotiate closure-related issues. Or, the employer's plans may be only hypothetical during negotiations; the closure may never happen. Therefore, the employer may wish to avoid bogging down the negotiations with a hypothetical scenario. Labour relations boards have wrestled with the issue of how much, and when, an employer is obligated to disclose information to the union about its future plans. Box 10.1 describes a leading decision that explores this issue.[22]

BOX 10.1 » CASE LAW HIGHLIGHT

The Duty to Disclose Information in Collective Bargaining

International Woodworkers of America Local 2-69 v.
Consolidated Bathurst Packaging Ltd.
1983 CanLII 970 (Ont. LRB)

Key Facts: The International Woodworkers of America and Consolidated Bathurst Packaging concluded a renewal collective agreement in early 1983 covering employees working at the employer's Hamilton location. In negotiations, the union proposed language that would give employees greater benefits in the case of a plant closure, but eventually dropped that proposal. The employer never mentioned that it was considering or expecting to close the plant. However, soon after the agreement came into effect, the employer announced that it would be closing the Hamilton plant in April 1983. The employer claimed that a decision to close the plant was not made until after the agreement had been concluded. The union filed a bad-faith bargaining complaint, arguing that the employer had decided during the negotiation period to close the plant and had failed to disclose that information to the union.

Issue: Did the employer violate the duty to bargain in good faith by failing to disclose its intention to close the Hamilton plant to the union during collective bargaining?

Decision: Yes. The labour relations board summarized the employer's legal duty to disclose as follows. First, an employer must answer union questions truthfully. Second, an employer must disclose on its own initiative decisions that have already been made and that "will have a significant impact on terms of employment," such as a discontinuance of the workplace. The timing of the announcement on the closure of the plant was an important factor. The board concluded:

> [W]here a decision to close is announced "on the heels" of the signing of a collective agreement, the timing of such a significant event may raise a rebuttable presumption that the decision-making was

sufficiently ripe during bargaining to have required disclosure or that it was intentionally delayed until the completion of bargaining. It can be persuasively argued that the more fundamental the decision on the workplace, the less likely this Board should be willing to accept fine distinctions in timing between "proposals" and "decisions" at face value and particularly when strong confirmatory evidence that the decision-making was not manipulated is lacking. This approach is sensitive to the positive incentive not to disclose now built into our system, and the potential for manipulation. Indeed, a strong argument can be made that the *de facto* decision doctrine should be expanded to include "highly probable decisions" or "effective recommendations" when so fundamental an issue as a plant closing is at stake. Having regard to the facts in each case the failure to disclose such matters may also be tantamount to a misrepresentation.

Here, the board found that the employer had not presented evidence sufficient to "rebut" the presumption that the decision to close the Hamilton plant had ripened during the negotiations, and therefore the employer was under a legal duty to disclose to the union that it was at least contemplating the closure. In terms of remedy, the board declined to order the employer to reopen the plant because the employer had already sold the equipment and instead ordered that monetary damages be paid to the union and employees calculated based on an assessment of the additional severance amounts the union would likely have bargained had it been aware during negotiations that the factory was closing.*

---

*   The decision of the Ontario Labour Relations Board on the remedy is found at *International Woodworkers of America Local 2-69 v. Consolidated Bathurst Packaging Ltd.*, 1984 CanLII 929 (Ont. LRB).

2. The Duty to Bargain and the Substance of Bargaining Proposals: The *What* of Collective Bargaining

Generally speaking, the parties in collective bargaining are left alone to bargain about whatever they like.[23] However, there are exceptions to this "hands off" approach. Sometimes, the content of a bargaining proposal put to the other party can run afoul of the duty to bargain in good faith and make reasonable efforts to conclude a collective agreement.

a. Bargaining Illegal Terms

Neither party can propose an illegal term, such as one that would violate human rights, occupational health and safety, or employment standards legislation.[24] Collective bargaining legislation in Canada also requires that some terms be included in every collective agreement (see Chapter 12), and it is a violation of the duty to bargain for a party to refuse to include such terms. For example, every jurisdiction in Canada requires that collective agreements include a provision providing that all disputes arising under the collective agreement be resolved by final and binding arbitration without a work stoppage (**mandatory arbitration clause**), a requirement that dates back to PC 1003. If a union or employer refuses to agree to a mandatory arbitration clause, then it would be engaging in bad-faith bargaining.

b. Terms That Can Be Proposed, but Not "Bargained to Impasse"

Some types of collective agreement terms may be proposed and discussed in negotiations, but cannot be "bargained to impasse." This means that parties who are unable to agree on a particular term must drop the term from their proposals and cannot use the term as the basis for a strike or lockout. It is up to the labour relations board to determine whether a proposed term has in fact been "bargained to impasse." Bargaining to impasse occurs when the proposed term in dispute holds up a settlement.[25] As an example, changes to the scope of a bargaining unit (the definition of the group of employees covered by a collective agreement) can be proposed, but not bargained to an impasse.[26] A union may propose to expand a bargaining unit to include more jobs than it was originally certified to represent, or an employer may attempt to bargain a smaller bargaining unit. However, if agreement is not reached on the proposed change, neither side can provoke a strike or lockout over the issue. The status quo must prevail.

c. Hard Bargaining Versus Surface Bargaining

A key distincton in collective bargaining law is between lawful **hard bargaining** and unlawful **surface bargaining**. A party engages in "hard bargaining" when it uses its superior bargaining power to insist on a collective agreement that is favourable to its own interests.[27] Hard bargaining is not a violation of the duty to bargain, because the legal model anticipates that collective bargaining is shaped by underlying power relations. The Ontario Labour Relations Board (OLRB) summarized this point: "For whatever else it is, collective bargaining is … a contest of economic power (perhaps only partially masked by polite manners and voluminous statistics)."[28] Collective bargaining legislation grants the parties in collective bargaining a means to pressure the other side to offer more favourable terms, including strikes and lockouts (Chapter 11). The duty to bargain is not intended to aid the weaker party by guaranteeing bargaining outcomes more favourable than that party could obtain on its own.[29]

"Surface bargaining," on the other hand, is a violation of the duty to bargain in good faith. Surface bargaining occurs when a party goes through the motions of collective bargaining without any intention of ever reaching a collective agreement.[30] For example, the party agrees to meet the other party and to engage in cursory discussion of proposals, but the real plan is to avoid the union and a collective agreement.

Distinguishing between hard bargaining and surface bargaining is an extremely difficult exercise. In many cases, where labour relations boards have found that the employer engaged in unlawful surface bargaining, there was also a history of employer unfair labour practices,

---

mandatory arbitration clause: A clause in a collective agreement that requires all disputes arising under the collective agreement to be referred to binding labour arbitration to be resolved.

hard bargaining: A lawful strategy in collective bargaining that involves a party using its superior bargaining power to insist upon collective agreement terms that favour its own interests.

surface bargaining: A strategy in collective bargaining that involves a party going through the motions of bargaining but having no intention of ever concluding a collective agreement. Surface bargaining is a violation of the duty to bargain in good faith.

particularly during the union organizing campaign. The earlier unfair labour practices can taint the employer's later behaviour in collective bargaining and lead the labour relations board to conclude that the employer has no intention of reaching an agreement with the union.[31]

A proposal that includes contract clauses that the proposing party knows the other side will never accept or the refusal to accept clauses that are standard throughout the industry can lead a labour relations board to conclude that a party has no intention to conclude a collective agreement.[32] That was the scenario in the decision described in Box 10.2.

BOX 10.2 » CASE LAW HIGHLIGHT

Proposing Untenable Contract Terms

Royal Oak Mines Inc. v. Canada (Labour Relations Board)
[1996] 1 SCR 369

Key Facts: For 18 months, a bitter strike took place at Royal Oak Mines's Giant Mine in Yellowknife. The employer used replacement workers and hired a security company to deal with violence on the picket line. During the strike, the employer terminated the employment of 49 strikers for alleged picket line misconduct. Four months into the strike, an explosion at the mine killed 9 miners. Following this event, the government assigned senior mediators to help the parties settle their dispute. However, the mediators were unable to produce an agreement. The main stumbling block was the employer's insistence that under no circumstances would it agree to a grievance or arbitration process that would permit the employees who were fired during the strike to challenge their dismissal. The union filed a bad-faith bargaining complaint. The Canada Labour Relations Board ruled that the employer had bargained in bad faith. That decision was reviewed up to the Supreme Court of Canada.

Issue: Did the employer violate the duty to bargain in good faith and to make reasonable efforts to conclude a collective agreement by refusing to agree to a grievance and arbitration process for fired workers?

Decision: Yes. The employer was engaged in unlawful surface bargaining. The requirement to make a "reasonable effort to enter into a collective agreement" is an objective standard, requiring the labour relations board to consider comparable standards and practices in the mining industry. A bargaining position can be "so far from the accepted norms of the industry that they must be unreasonable." That was the case here. The Supreme Court of Canada wrote:

> If a party proposes a clause in a collective agreement, or conversely, refuses even to discuss a basic or standard term, that is acceptable and included in other collective agreements in comparable industries throughout the country, it is appropriate for a labour board to find that the party is not making a "reasonable effort to enter into a collective agreement." … For an employer to refuse an employee a grievance procedure or some form of due process, by which the employee can challenge his or her dismissal on the ground that it was not for just cause, is to deny that employee a fundamental right.

Since no union would accept a collective agreement without an arbitration clause, the refusal of the employer to negotiate that clause indicated a lack of good faith.

When a party has engaged in bad-faith bargaining, the usual remedy is to order the party to go back and engage in lawful bargaining and to send a statement to employees advising them of the unlawful conduct.[33] Labour relations boards can also order that damages be paid to the other party for the wasted cost of negotiation or to employees if they suffered financial losses due to the bad-faith bargaining (e.g., lost wages if the unlawful conduct extended the length of a strike or lockout).[34] In the *Royal Oak Mines* case, the labour relations board ordered the employer to re-table terms that it had offered the union months earlier (which employees had rejected) that included a grievance and arbitration provision applicable to the fired employees.

In *Royal Oak Mines*, the employer's refusal to agree to an arbitration provision was found to be unlawful. However, it is not always unlawful for an employer to use its superior bargaining power to insist on collective agreement terms favourable to its interests. The decision summarized in Box 10.3 describes a famous example of lawful "hard bargaining."

BOX 10.3 » CASE LAW HIGHLIGHT

Lawful Hard Bargaining

Retail, Wholesale & Department Store Union v. T. Eaton Company Limited
1985 CanLII 933 (Ont. LRB)

Key Facts: Eaton's was a large Canadian retailer that had operated mostly non-union for decades prior to an organizing blitz by the Retail, Wholesale & Department Store Union (RWDSU) in the 1980s. That campaign resulted in RWDSU being certified to represent employees at a handful of Eaton's stores around the Greater Toronto Area (GTA). In each of the stores, the OLRB certified separate bargaining units for full-time and part-time employees, as was the practice in the 1980s. That meant that there were over a dozen bargaining units certified to represent Eaton's employees at six GTA stores. The union proposed that the parties negotiate one "master collective agreement" that would apply to all the stores, but the employer insisted on conducting separate negotiations for each bargaining unit and on a process that involved extended discussions of each one of the union's proposals. This meant bargaining would drag on for months, since both employer and union were using the same lead negotiators. The employer took the position that it would not agree to pay the unionized employees any more than what it paid employees in the non-union stores. In November 1984, the union struck at all six GTA stores. Eaton's stayed opened during the strike, using non-striking personnel to run the store. The RWDSU then filed a complaint alleging that the employer had bargained in bad faith.

Issue: Did Eaton's violate the duty to bargain in good faith by, among other actions, insisting on bargaining separate agreements for each of more than a dozen bargaining units and by refusing to offer a raise beyond what non-union workers receive?

Decision: No. The OLRB explained that this was a case of "hard bargaining" by Eaton's. There was nothing improper in Eaton's use of its bargaining power to insist on a collective bargaining process and collective agreement terms that benefit the employer's interests, provided that it was prepared to meet and engage in extended discussions about the union's proposals and that it was prepared to sign a collective agreement. The OLRB's discussion of the issues provides a useful summary of the duty to bargain in Canada:

> [A] major function of the … duty [to bargain] is to oblige the parties to enter into serious negotiations with the shared intent of entering into a collective agreement. This requires that the parties explain their positions to the other side, so as to allow for rational, informed discussions. … An employer cannot enter into negotiations with the intent of ridding itself of the trade union. Neither can it simply engage in "surface bargaining," whereby it "goes through the

motions" of bargaining without any real intent of signing a collective agreement. … [The duty to bargain] does not, however, require that an employer agree to the terms of a collective agreement proposed by a trade union. Neither does it prohibit an employer acting in its own self-interest from engaging in "hard bargaining" so as to obtain an agreement with terms favourable to it. … The fact that the company has not made any major concessions in bargaining relates directly to the type of agreement management is seeking to negotiate. [The duty to bargain] does not … preclude a party from taking a firm position in bargaining.

On the issue of the employer's refusal to offer wages and benefits above what it gives non-union workers, the OLRB wrote:

> Nothing in the *Labour Relations Act* requires an employer to agree to wages and employee benefits for unionized employees that are superior to those being received by non-unionized employees. … Neither is there any provision which prohibits an employer when formulating its bargaining position to take into account the likelihood that improvements in the terms of employment for one group of employees will likely impact on other groups. Indeed, logic suggests that this is a consideration frequently taken into account by employers, since an improvement in the employment conditions of one group of employees will logically lead to calls for similar improvements from other employees of the same employer, whether they be unorganized or included in a different bargaining unit. Further, the fact that an employer refuses to give more to unionized employees, does not, by itself, necessarily mean that the employer is seeking to interfere with the formation of trade unions. Such a conclusion might be justified if the terms being offered to organized employees were inferior to those being enjoyed by comparable non-union employees, for this would indicate an intent to punish employees because they had selected trade union representation. Such, however, is not the case here.

Eaton's did violate the duty to bargain in one respect. It had insisted on a clause prohibiting workers from discussing union matters on employer property, even during non-working time. That prohibition is unlawful interference with the right of workers to engage in union activities, and so insisting on it in bargaining violates the duty to bargain. The union's other arguments were dismissed.

The Eaton's case recounted in Box 10.3 is important for what it tells us about the difficulties unions have had in penetrating the service sector, including retail and banking.[35] While unions are often able to obtain majority support and to organize one or more stores of giant corporations, they have great difficulty bargaining strong collective agreements for those units. RWDSU represented approximately 1 percent of Eaton's 30,000 employees, employed in only six stores. Eaton's was not prepared to give the unionized workers any benefit above what non-union employees receive for the obvious reason that to do so would encourage other workers to join the union. Therefore, the only way that the unionized workers could pressure Eaton's to improve its offer was to strike. They timed the strike for the Christmas shopping rush, hoping to inflict the greatest economic damage. However, the strike had little effect. The stores remained open during the strike and, in any event, the strike affected a very small proportion of the company. Eaton's was prepared and able to withstand a strike at a few stores to ensure unionization did not spread. Unable to win noticeable improvements, the workers decertified the union within a few years.[36]

This basic scenario has played out time and again throughout Canada in industries characterized by large corporations that operate through many scattered stores or branches.[37] The difficultly for workers seeking collective bargaining in these workplaces is that the Wagner model Canada adopted in the mid-1940s was never designed to facilitate collective bargaining in industries that use this business structure.[38] The Wagner model targeted large industrial workplaces, factories, and mines, where hundreds of (mostly male) employees worked regular full-time hours at the same location. The *power* dynamic (see Chapter 3) is very different when 1,000 General Motors employees threaten to strike at a single factory compared with when a handful of employees threaten to strike at a few Eaton's, Walmart, Starbucks, or Scotiabank locations.

Occasionally, governments have sought to address this dynamic by adopting different models of collective bargaining. For example, in Ontario in the 1990s, the New Democratic Party introduced a provision that permitted the labour relations board to "consolidate" multiple bargaining units of the same employer if organized by the same union. That law would have given the union in the Eaton's case the ability to combine the various bargaining units and to thereafter bargain its desired "master" collective agreement. Each new Eaton's store organized by the union would then be swept into the combined bargaining unit, allowing the union to grow over time. In both British Columbia and, more recently, Ontario, government-commissioned studies of the issue have floated the idea of **broader-based bargaining** structures that would enable a union to be certified for sectors of the economy, such as "all employees in the fast-food industry" in a particular city.[39] That model would similarly enable unions to organize store by store but then sweep the organized stores into a single, larger, and potentially more powerful bargaining unit. However, to date, broader-based bargaining (outside of the construction sector) is the exception to the rule in Canada.

V. Chapter Summary

This chapter examined the process and law of collective bargaining in Canada. It demonstrated that the manner of negotiation and the laws that govern the process are dramatically different in the *collective bargaining regime* than in the non-union common law regime. Collective bargaining law, through a duty to bargain in good faith and to make reasonable efforts to conclude a collective agreement, plays a central role in the collective bargaining process. This law is concerned mostly with limiting industrial conflict by encouraging rational and professional discussions between representatives of unions and employers in the hope that collective agreements can be reached without work stoppages. That usually happens. However, sometimes the parties fail to reach a collective agreement. Therefore, a different set of rules is needed to deal with bargaining impasses. Those rules are the subject of the next chapter.

---

broader-based bargaining: A term used to describe collective bargaining structures that involves a broader scope than the one union—one employer—single location structure that dominates Canadian collective bargaining.

QUESTIONS AND ISSUES FOR DISCUSSION

1. What is the difference between monetary and non-monetary issues in collective bargaining? For each type of issue, provide an example of a proposal that might be raised in collective bargaining by either a union or an employer.
2. Describe the three basic stages of collective bargaining and what is involved at each stage.
3. Identify and explain the two "statutory freezes" found in Canadian collective bargaining legislation. What are the policy reasons that explain the two freezes?
4. The duty to bargain includes both a "subjective" and an "objective" component. Explain the meaning of each component.
5. Describe the scope of the "procedural duty to bargain."
6. What is the difference between "hard bargaining" and "surface bargaining"?

EXERCISE

This chapter introduced the difficult distinction between lawful "hard bargaining" and unlawful "surface bargaining." Labour boards have sometimes struggled to distinguish between the two in practice. This exercise challenges you to locate and read a decision in which the distinction is discussed.

1. Go to the CanLII home page: https://www.canlii.org/en/.
2. In the "Document text" search box, type "surface bargaining" and "hard bargaining" and then Search.
3. Locate a decision that involves an allegation that one of the parties (union or employer) engaged in unlawful surface bargaining. Read the decision.
4. Answer the following questions:
   a. On what basis did the complaining party allege that the other party had engaged in unlawful surface bargaining?
   b. Did the labour board (or court if it is a judicial review decision) find surface bargaining had occurred?
   c. How does the decision describe or explain what constitutes the difference between surface and hard bargaining?
   c. Explain the outcome of the case, including which argument won and why.

UPDATES

Go to emond.ca/lawofworkircb for links to news, author's blog posts, content updates, and other information related to the chapters in this text.

NOTES AND REFERENCES

1 For an extensive review of the duty to bargain law in Canada, see G. Adams, *Canadian Labour Law*, 2nd ed. (Aurora, ON: Canada Law Book, 1993), at chapters 10 and 11; and Labour Law Casebook Group, *Labour and Employment Law: Cases, Materials, and Commentary*, 8th ed. (Toronto: Irwin Law, 2011), at chapter 6.

2 See, e.g., Ontario *Labour Relations Act, 1995*, SO 1995, c. 1, Sch. A, s. 17 (duty to bargain in good faith), s. 73(1) (unfair labour practice for unionized employer to bargain directly with employee).

3 *McGavin Toastmaster Ltd. v. Ainscough*, [1976] 1 SCR 718.

4 *Wartime Labour Relations Order* (PC 1003) is available at http://socserv.mcmaster.ca/oldlabourstudies/ onlinelearning/article.php?id=503.

5 See the discussion in R. Chaykowski, "Collective Bargaining: Structure, Process, and Innovation" in M. Gunderson and D. Taras, eds., *Canadian Labour and Employment Relations*, 6th ed. (Toronto: Pearson Education, 2009), at chapter 10.

6 Ontario *Labour Relations Act, 1995,* supra note 2, s. 44; and Manitoba *Labour Relations Act,* CCSM c. L10, s. 69.

7 There is an extensive industrial relations literature studying the conduct and processes of collective bargaining. This book is almost always cited as the leading authority: R. Walton and R. McKersie, *A Behavioural Theory of Labor Negotiations: An Analysis of a Social Interaction System* (New York: McGraw-Hill, 1965). See also Chaykowski, supra note 5; F. McQuarrie, *Industrial Relations in Canada* (Toronto: Wiley, 2003), at 269; and J. Godard, *Industrial Relations, the Economy, and Society,* 4th ed. (Concord, ON: Captus Press, 2011), at 301.

8 Walton and McKersie, supra note 7.

9 See Chaykowski, supra note 5, at 260-64.

10 *Spar Professional & Allied Technical Employees' Association v. Spar Aerospace Products,* [1979] 1 CLRBR 61 (Ont. LRB). See also *D.H.L. International Express Limited,* 2001 CIRB 129 (CanLII).

11 *Canadian Union of Public Employees, Local 3010 v. Children's Aid Society of Cape Breton,* 2009 NSLRB 11 (CanLII).

12 For example, in Ontario, the bargaining freeze ends on the date a strike or lockout would be legal. See Ontario *Labour Relations Act, 1995,* supra note 2, s. 86(1). In British Columbia, the bargaining freeze lasts until the parties actually engage in a strike or lockout, or the union is decertified: see BC *Labour Relations Code,* RSBC 1996, c. 244, s. 45(2).

13 *Canadian Air Pilots Association v. Air Canada, Montreal, Quebec* (1977), 24 di 203 (CLRB). See also *D.H.L. International Express Limited,* supra note 10.

14 Ontario *Labour Relations Act, 1995,* supra note 2, s. 17.

15 Some provinces' legislation does not include the part about making reasonable efforts to make a collective agreement, but the labour relations boards have nevertheless interpreted the duty to bargain as including that obligation.

16 *Royal Oak Mines Inc. v. Canada (Labour Relations Board),* [1996] 1 SCR 369.

17 Ibid.

18 *United Electrical, Radio and Machine Workers of America v. DeVilbiss (Canada) Ltd.* (1976), 76 CLLC, at para. 16009; *Buhler Versatile Inc.,* [2001] MLBD 9 (MLRB); and *Halifax Regional Municipality v. Halifax Professional Firefighters, Local 268,* 2011 NSLB 65 (CanLII).

19 *Professional Institute of the Public Service of Canada v. Treasury Board and Canada Revenue Agency,* 2008 PSLRB 13 (CanLII); *Ontario Public Service Employees Union v. Alcohol and Gaming Commission of Ontario,* 2002 CanLII 40611 (Ont. LRB); *Hotel & Restaurant Employee CAW Local 448 National Automobile, Aerospace, Transportation and General Workers' Union of Canada (CAW-Canada v. The Millcroft Inn Ltd.,* 2000 CanLII 12207 (Ont. LRB); and *United Steelworkers of America, Local 7292 v. Buhler Manufacturing,* 2007 CanLII 81861 (MBLB).

20 *A.N. Shaw Restoration Ltd.,* 1978 CanLII 554 (ON LRB); *British Columbia Automobile Association,* BCLRB No. B498/99; *Cypress (Regional Health Authority) v. Service Employees' International Union-West,* 2016 SKCA 161 (CanLII); and *Egg Films, Inc.,* 2015 NSLB 213 (CanLII).

21 *United Steelworkers of America, Local 4487 v. Inglis Limited,* 1977 CanLII 490 (Ont. LRB); and *International Woodworkers of America Local 2-69 v. Consolidated Bathurst Packaging Ltd.,* 1983 CanLII 970 (Ont. LRB).

22 See also *Ontario Public Service Employees Union v. Ontario (Management Board Secretariat),* 2005 CanLII 8247 (Ont. LRB); *Wray et al. v. Treasury Board (Department of Transport),* 2014 PSLRB 64 (CanLII); *Canadian Union of Public Employees, Local 1251 v. New Brunswick,* 2009 CanLII 74885 (NBLEB); and *United Electrical, Radio & Machine Workers of America v. Westinghouse Canada Limited,* [1980] CanLII 893 (Ont. LRB).

23 *Catholic Independent Schools Diocese of Prince George v. B.C. Government and Service Employees' Union,* 2001 CanLII 32940 (BCLRB), at 26-27.

24 *MacDonalds Consolidated Ltd.,* BCLRB No. 51/76, [1976] 2 CLRBR 292.

25 *Nanaimo Golf & Country Club v. Unite Here, Local 40,* 2015 CanLII 44718 (BCLRB).

26 *Northwood Pulp and Timber Limited* (1994), 23 CLRBR (2d) 298 (BCLRB); United *Brotherhood of Carpenters & Joiners of America Employer Bargaining Agency v. Carpenters Employer Bargaining Agency,* 1978 CanLII 434 (Ont. LRB); *Retail, Wholesale & Department Store Union v. T. Eaton Company Limited,* 1985 CanLII 933 (Ont. LRB); *Coca-Cola Bottling Ltd.* (1999), 52 CLRBR (2d) 203 (BCLRB); and *Brantford Expositor,* [1988] OLRB Rep. July 653. See also *V.I. Care Management* (1993), 19 CLRBR (2d) 153 (employer cannot bargain to impasse a clause that relates to the application of a union's constitution).

27 See, e.g., *Canadian Union of United Brewery, Flour, Cereal, Soft Drink & Distillery Workers, Local No. 304 v. Canada Trustco Mortgage,* 1984 CanLII 1106 (Ont. LRB); *Retail, Wholesale & Department Store Union v. T. Eaton Company Limited,* 1985 CanLII 933 (Ont. LRB); and *Egg Films, Inc.,* 2015 NSLB 213 (CanLII).

28 *United Steelworkers of America, Local 1005 v. Stelco Inc. (Hilton Works),* 2000 CanLII 11075 (Ont. LRB).

29 *Noranda Metal Industries.* BCLRB No. 151/74, [1975] 1 Can. LRBR 145.

30   *Toronto Typographical Union No. 91 v. Daily Times*, 1978 CanLII 507 (Ont. LRB).

31   *United Steelworkers of America v. Radio Shack*, 1979 CanLII 817 (Ont. LRB).

32   Ibid.; and *Royal Oak Mines*, supra note 15.

33   See *United Steelworkers of America v. Radio Shack*, supra note 31 for a discussion of remedies in bad faith bargaining cases.

34   *Buhler Versatile*, supra note 17.

35   See D. Doorey, "Why Unions Can't Organize Retail Workers," *Law of Work* (blog), accessed September 13, 2016, http://lawofwork.ca/?p=7061.

36   See the discussion in A. Forrest, "Organizing Eaton's: Do the Old Laws Still Work?" (1988) 8 *Windsor Yearbook of Access to Justice* 190.

37   The story of attempts to organize bank branches is recounted in E. Lennon, "Organizing the Unorganized: Unionization in the Chartered Banks of Canada" (1980) 18:2 *Osgoode Hall Law Journal* 178.

38   J. Fudge, "The Gendered Dimension of Labour Law: Why Women Need Inclusive Unionism and Broader-Based Bargaining" in L. Brisken and P. McDermott, *Women Challenging Feminism, Democracy, and Militancy* (Toronto: University of Toronto Press, 1993).

39   See Ontario Ministry of Labour, *Changing Workplaces Review: Special Advisors' Interim Report* (Toronto: Queen's Printer for Ontario, 2016), at part 4.6, "Other Models," https://www.labour.gov.on.ca/english/about/cwr_interim/chapter_4_6.php. For a summary of the model proposed in British Columbia in 1992, see D. Doorey, "The Model of Sectoral Bargaining Everyone Is Whispering About," *Law of Work* (blog), accessed September 13, 2016, http://lawofwork.ca/?p=8574.

The Law of Industrial Conflict

I. Introduction

In the vast majority of cases, collective bargaining between employers and unions results in a new collective agreement without any work stoppage or need for government intervention. The parties reach a deal, sign a new collective agreement, and move on. However, while our legal model compels the parties to sit down and bargain with one another, it does not, indeed could not, force them to reach an agreement every time. It is inevitable that sometimes collective bargaining will meet an impasse. The law tightly regulates the industrial conflict that results. As we work our way through this law in this chapter, think about what interests are being promoted by the laws. Do the laws favour one side or the other in the collective bargaining dispute? To what extent do the laws seek to protect third parties—people and organizations that are not directly involved in the dispute—from the effects of industrial conflict?

II. Mapping the Options for Resolving a Collective Bargaining Deadlock

The law of industrial conflict is complicated. The industrial conflict chapter in the leading law school text runs in excess of 100 dense pages![1] We will aim for something considerably shorter here, although there is still a lot to get through. Grab a beverage and a snack. All three regimes of work law (the *common law regime*, the *regulatory regime*, and the *collective bargaining regime*) converge here, each regulating parts of the whole of industrial conflict law. We will focus on the role of the common law and collective bargaining regimes in this chapter, but the regulatory regime also plays a role. For example, the fact that striking or locked-out workers are disqualified from employment insurance benefits in Canada works to the advantage of employers in a collective bargaining dispute.[2] Let's begin with a high-level map of the law of industrial conflict to demonstrate how this chapter is structured.

When collective bargaining reaches an impasse, two legal routes are used in Canada to break the deadlock. First, our legal model permits "economic warfare"—the use of blunt economic pressure to persuade the other party to make concessions in the form of strikes, lockouts, and the unilateral imposition of contract terms by the employer. Second, bargaining disputes can be referred to a neutral third-party arbitrator—an **interest arbitrator**—for resolution. An interest arbitrator is tasked with resolving bargaining disputes by writing the terms of a collective agreement for the parties. These two legal routes, and the source of laws that govern them, are depicted in Figure 11.1.

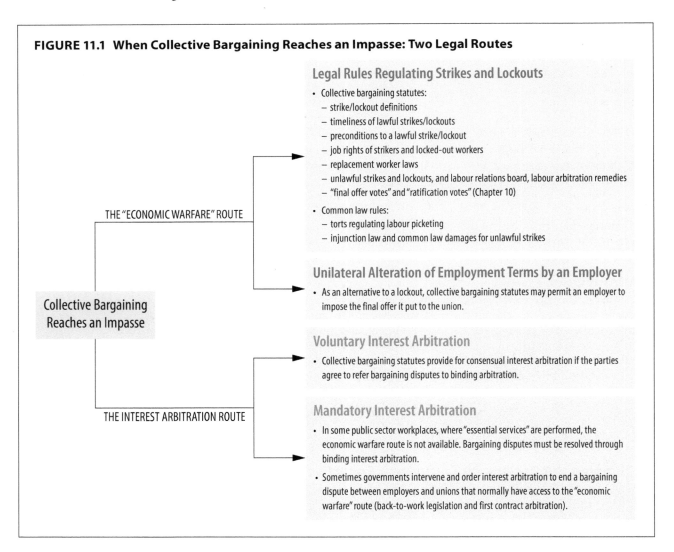

FIGURE 11.1   When Collective Bargaining Reaches an Impasse: Two Legal Routes

Collective Bargaining Reaches an Impasse

THE "ECONOMIC WARFARE" ROUTE

THE INTEREST ARBITRATION ROUTE

Legal Rules Regulating Strikes and Lockouts

- Collective bargaining statutes:
  - strike/lockout definitions
  - timeliness of lawful strikes/lockouts
  - preconditions to a lawful strike/lockout
  - job rights of strikers and locked-out workers
  - replacement worker laws
  - unlawful strikes and lockouts, and labour relations board, labour arbitration remedies
  - "final offer votes" and "ratification votes" (Chapter 10)
- Common law rules:
  - torts regulating labour picketing
  - injunction law and common law damages for unlawful strikes

Unilateral Alteration of Employment Terms by an Employer

- As an alternative to a lockout, collective bargaining statutes may permit an employer to impose the final offer it put to the union.

Voluntary Interest Arbitration

- Collective bargaining statutes provide for consensual interest arbitration if the parties agree to refer bargaining disputes to binding arbitration.

Mandatory Interest Arbitration

- In some public sector workplaces, where "essential services" are performed, the economic warfare route is not available. Bargaining disputes must be resolved through binding interest arbitration.
- Sometimes governments intervene and order interest arbitration to end a bargaining dispute between employers and unions that normally have access to the "economic warfare" route (back-to-work legislation and first contract arbitration).

interest arbitrator: An individual or three-person expert arbitration board tasked with writing the terms of a collective agreement when the union and employer are unable to reach agreement through voluntary collective bargaining.

Most of the legal rules that govern industrial conflict are found in collective bargaining statutes, such as the Ontario *Labour Relations Act, 1995*.[3] Those statutes define what constitutes a strike or lockout and when they are permitted, among other related subjects. It is the responsibility of labour relations boards to enforce collective bargaining statutes, and so labour boards play an important role in the regulation of industrial conflict. The main functions of courts in the regulation of collective bargaining conflicts are (1) to review the decisions of labour tribunals through judicial review; and (2) to apply tort law (see Chapter 18 in the companion volume) to the actions of unions, employers, and especially workers, particularly picket-line behaviour.

III. The "Economic Warfare" Route

Collective bargaining statutes permit each side in the bargaining dispute to exercise legal weapons to pressure the other to make concessions. For the workers and the union, the main weapon is the **strike**. For the employer, it is a lockout or the unilateral imposition of contract terms, both of which are discussed in this chapter. The party that can afford to hold out during a work stoppage the longest usually has a power advantage, giving it an edge in the economic warfare route. As noted in the previous chapter, which party possesses that power is affected by a variety of factors, including the legal rules that govern work stoppages discussed in this chapter, as well as forces produced by *external inputs* (see Chapter 3) such as labour and other market forces and the social and cultural climate in which a work stoppage occurs. An employer in an intensely competitive sector may be less able to withstand a work stoppage than one with few competitors. Workers on strike in a community with deep roots in the labour movement may receive greater public support and sympathy than strikers in a town with little union presence.

Workers lose their wages during a work stoppage and depend on what is usually a relatively paltry **strike pay** stipend from the union, or they look for alternative work. Depending on the extent to which they can continue to operate during a work stoppage by employees, private sector employers may incur lost output and, therefore, lost revenues and profits. As we will see in Chapter 16, the dynamic for public sector employers is different, since governments continue to collect revenues (taxes) during a work stoppage while saving on labour costs. Therefore, the bargaining pressure imposed on government employers is more political than economic.

As we learned in Chapter 10, the duty to bargain in good faith does not prohibit a party from engaging in "hard bargaining" to win the agreement it wants. The laws governing the economic warfare route are not intended to substitute for inequality of power by propping up the weaker party, as explained by the Ontario Labour Relations Board:

> In assessing the economic weapons available the Board must be cautious that it does not become the arbiter as to the parties' choice of economic weapons; *nor is it for the Board to attempt to equalize the economic power available to the parties.* The Board's only concern is to determine whether the activities of the parties exceed the bounds of permissible activity so as to contravene the provisions of *The Labour Relations Act*.[4] [Emphasis added.]

Therefore, the economic warfare route involves the use of blunt power to achieve desired bargaining outcomes.

---

strike: Legislation can assign a particular definition to the word strike. In Canada, strikes are usually defined to include both (1) a collective refusal by employees to perform work, and (2) a deliberate collective slowdown by workers that is designed to restrict the output of an employer (commonly known as a work to rule).

strike pay: A payment made by a union to a union member or person in a bargaining unit during a work stoppage, often as consideration for performing a shift as a picketer.

A. Union and Employee Weapons: The Strike

As noted in Chapter 10, the vast majority of collective agreements are negotiated and settled without a work stoppage. Moreover, as depicted in Figure 11.2, the frequency of strikes in Canada has been trending downward since 1980s.[5] In recent years, most strikes have occurred in the public sector.[6]

FIGURE 11.2 Strike Incidence in Canada and Person-Days Lost, 1991–2015

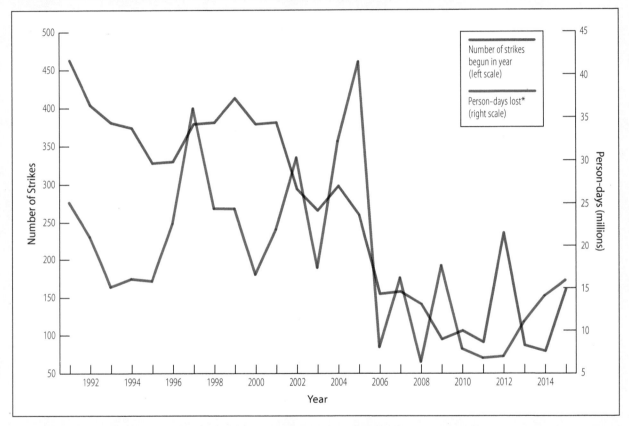

*   Person-days lost = Strike frequency × number of strikers × duration of strikes.

Sources: Labour Canada, "Work Stoppages by Sector and Year," October 5, 2016, http://www.labour.gc.ca/eng/resources/info/datas/work_stoppages/work_stoppages_year_sector.shtml; and M. Gunderson, B. Hebdon, and D. Hyatt, "Strikes and Dispute Resolution" in M. Gunderson and D. Taras, *Canadian Labour and Employment Relations*, 6th ed. (Don Mills, ON: Pearson Education Canada, 2009), at 342.

The right to strike is a fundamental component of the Canadian collective bargaining model, as Justice Abella of the Supreme Court of Canada recently explained in the case of *Saskatchewan Federation of Labour v. Saskatchewan*:

The conclusion that the right to strike is an essential part of a meaningful collective bargaining process in our system of labour relations is supported by history, by jurisprudence, and by Canada's international obligations. As Otto Kahn-Freund and Bob Hepple recognized:

The power to withdraw their labour is for the workers what for management is its power to shut down production, to switch it to different purposes, to transfer it to different places. A legal system which suppresses the freedom to strike puts the workers at the mercy of their employers. This—in all its simplicity—is the essence of the matter.

The right to strike is not merely a derivative of collective bargaining, it is an indispensable component of that right.[7]

The Supreme Court of Canada's recent strong affirmation of the sanctity of the right to strike is at odds with our governments' long-standing efforts to control and restrict strike activity in order to protect both employer interests and the interests of third parties affected by strikes, including other businesses and the public more generally.[8] Collective bargaining laws protect a limited "right to strike," but that is not their central purpose when it comes to regulating industrial conflict. Recall our discussion in Chapters 5 and 6 of the origins of the *Wartime Labour Relations Order*, or Order in Council PC 1003 (1944), and how it came about in large measure as a response to growing industrial unrest and as an attempt to control and limit the number of strikes.[9]

1. What Is a Strike?

The contemporary right to strike appears in our laws as a statutory prohibition on employers from disciplining or terminating employees who engage in a lawful strike. Therefore, it is crucial that we understand what constitutes a strike, and when a strike is lawful. It matters greatly whether worker action is treated as a "strike" or not, because collective bargaining statutes tightly regulate strikes. These laws declare some strikes to be illegal, but also protect striking workers from employer reprisals if the strike satisfies the requirements of a lawful strike. A refusal to work by employees that does not meet the statutory definition of a *strike* falls outside of this web of statutory rules, and so it is dealt with as a matter of contract law rather than statutory strike law.

The statutory definition of strike varies across Canadian jurisdictions. In all jurisdictions, a strike is defined to include a cessation or refusal to work by two or more workers acting *in combination* and *with a common understanding*. The key here is that a strike involves a coordinated act of more than one worker to not work. A single worker who drops his or her tools and stands outside the workplace protesting her employer's low pay is not on strike; if two or more workers agree to drop their tools and picket, they may be. All jurisdictions also include in their definition of *strike* a deliberate slowdown intended to restrict the employer's output, a strategy often described as **work to rule**.

a. The Broad, Objective Definition of Strike

Where definitions of *strike* vary is in regard to what we might call the motive, or subjective, element. This element asks about the motive of the workers. Does it matter *why* workers are refusing to work or are slowing down? Most jurisdictions define *strike* broadly and do not include a motive element. In other words, it does not matter why workers are refusing to work. Consider, for example, the definition of *strike* in the Ontario *Labour Relations Act, 1995*:

> "[S]trike" includes a cessation of work, a refusal to work or to continue to work by employees in combination or in concert or in accordance with a common understanding, or a slow-down or other concerted activity on the part of employees designed to restrict or limit output.[10]

---

work to rule: A form of strike in which workers collectively and deliberately slow down for the purpose of restricting the employer's output.

That definition has two parts. The first refers to concerted refusals to work and the second to a "slow-down" designed to restrict output. Note that the definition does not specify that the refusal to work *be intended to apply pressure on the employer in collective bargaining*. The employees' motive for refusing to work is irrelevant. As long as the employees agreed among themselves to not work, then they are striking, regardless of the motive for their actions. So when employees of General Motors in London, Ontario skipped worked one day in 1995 to attend a political rally protesting provincial government policy, they engaged in a strike.[11] The fact that the intention of the strike was to influence government policy and not General Motors' labour practices did not matter. As long as the workers had a common understanding that they would skip work that day, they engaged in a strike.

The case in Box 11.1 is from BC, where the definition of *strike* similarly does not include a motive element, and it involved the collective refusal by employees to work voluntary overtime.[12] Can that refusal be a strike?

BOX 11.1 » CASE LAW HIGHLIGHT

Is the Refusal to Work Voluntary Overtime a Strike?

Dick's Lumber & Building Supplies Inc. v. United Steelworkers of America, Local No. 1-3567
2006 CanLII 28067 (BCLRB)

Key Facts: The United Steelworkers (the union) represented employees at three separate locations of the employer. Workers at the Surrey location were on strike. Workers at the Burnaby location were not on strike, and there was a standard "no strike" clause in the collective agreement that prohibited them from engaging in a strike. Overtime at the Burnaby location was voluntary (employees were not required to work it), but the employees usually jumped at the opportunity to work overtime to receive the extra pay. However, one day, after the union had reminded them that overtime was voluntary, 18 out of 23 Burnaby employees declined the employer's request to work overtime. The employer filed a complaint with the BC Labour Relations Board, arguing that the refusal to work overtime constituted an illegal strike.

Issue: Was the refusal by the employees to work voluntary overtime a strike?

Decision: Yes. The labour relations board concluded that the workers had collectively agreed, with the encouragement of the union, to refuse overtime. The labour relations board ruled that the union had subtly encouraged the employees to decline overtime when it told them of their right to do so. The fact that the union or some employees believed it was important to support the striking Surrey workers by refusing overtime is irrelevant. There was a collective refusal to work overtime, and that action met the definition of a strike. Since the Burnaby workers were not in a legal strike position, the labour relations board declared the strike to be illegal and ordered the union and employees to cease and desist from refusing to work overtime.

When the statute does not include a motive element—a requirement that the work refusal be intended to influence the employer's bargaining position—then a decision by workers to respect a picket line (a "**sympathy strike**") would also amount to a strike, provided that the refusal is by more than one person acting with a common understanding. If workers refuse to cross a picket line for their own personal reasons, including fear, and there is no evidence they acted with a common understanding, then there is no strike.[13] In British Columbia, the definition of *strike* excludes a work refusal "that occurs as the direct result of and for no other reason" than the workers are respecting a lawful picket line.[14] This language means that in British Columbia, workers who fail to report to work because they are respecting a picket line are not engaged in a strike.[15]

---

sympathy strike: A strike undertaken by workers who do not have an immediate and direct grievance against their own employer, but who strike as a means of showing support and solidarity with other striking workers who do have such a grievance with their employer.

b. The Narrow, Subjective Definition of Strike

Now consider the definition of *strike* in the Manitoba *Labour Relations Act*. The Manitoba definition lists the usual types of conduct included in strike definitions (refusal to work or a slowdown on the part of employees in combination), but then adds a *motive element* that requires those actions to be

> for the purpose of compelling their employer to agree to terms or conditions of employment or to aid other employees in compelling the employer of those other employees to agree to terms or conditions of employment.[16]

Similar language is found in the collective bargaining legislation of Alberta and Nova Scotia. That language requires that the work stoppage or slowdown be intended to influence the employer's position in collective bargaining. It is a narrower definition of *strike* than that which appears in the Ontario and BC statutes. If workers in jurisdictions with a motive element collectively skip work to attend a political protest, they are *not* engaged in a strike because their actions are not intended to influence their employer or their terms of employment.[17] Those workers may be in breach of their employment contract and their duty to report to work, and they may be subject to employer-issued discipline. However, the laws governing strikes do not apply to their actions because they are not striking.

2. When Is a Strike Lawful?

A strike is unlawful unless all of the preconditions for a lawful strike have been satisfied. Those preconditions vary across the country, as depicted in Table 11.1. However, in all jurisdictions, a lawful and therefore protected right to strike exists only for employees whose jobs fall within a bargaining unit of a unionized employer, and then only during a very narrow window of time during collective bargaining and after a series of statutory preconditions have been satisfied. Unionized workers who strike after these legal preconditions have been satisfied experience a limited protection from dismissal or adverse treatment at the hands of the employer (see the next section).[18] Workers who strike before the preconditions have been satisfied are said to have engaged in a **wildcat strike** and may be disciplined by their employer. In some cases, employees who engage in a wildcat strike can be ordered to pay damages to the employer, as can their union if the union encouraged or participated in the strike or did not take reasonable steps to end the strike once it learned about it.[19]

The preconditions for a lawful strike are designed to restrict strikes to those circumstances in which collective bargaining has reached an impasse, and a majority of affected employees have elected to apply pressure on the employer by use of a work stoppage. The requirements for collective bargaining, government conciliation, and a "cooling off" period as preconditions for lawful strikes date to early 20th-century legislation, such as the 1907 *Industrial Disputes Investigation Act*. That legislation was the brainchild of Mackenzie King, who then was the federal minister of labour.[20] These key elements were later incorporated into PC 1003 when King was prime minister, and they remain in some form in all Canadian collective bargaining legislation. Industrial relations scholars have found that some of the legislative preconditions, such as mandatory conciliation and mandatory strike votes, reduce strike incidence in Canada.[21]

TABLE 11.1 Preconditions to a Lawful Strike

Preconditions to a Lawful Strike Found in Canadian Collective Bargaining Legislation	Canadian Jurisdictions Requiring the Precondition
• The workers are unionized. (Non-union employees who strike are probably breaching their individual employment contracts.) • No collective agreement covering the striking employees is in effect. • The union and the employer have engaged in collective bargaining with the intention of reaching a new collective agreement, but failed to reach an agreement. • The union has conducted a strike vote, and a majority of bargaining unit employees' ballots support a strike.	All Canadian jurisdictions.
Mandatory conciliation or mediation and a "cooling off" period: • A government-appointed conciliation officer has met with the parties, but has been unable to assist the parties to reach a new collective agreement. • A mandatory "cooling off" period has passed since a date specified in the statute. Precise details vary across jurisdictions, but in general, the "cooling off" period is from 7 to 21 days after the minister of Labour has notified the parties that no more conciliation will be ordered. (This notification is sometimes called a "no board" report because the minister writes that no conciliation board will be appointed in the report.)	Alberta, Nova Scotia, Ontario, Prince Edward Island, Saskatchewan, New Brunswick
Discretionary conciliation and a "cooling off" period: • The parties must inform the minister of labour that bargaining has reached an impasse. They may request conciliation or the government may require conciliation before a "cooling off" period begins.	Federal, British Columbia, Newfoundland and Labrador, Manitoba
The union must provide notice to the employer of the date of the start of the strike.	• Federal, Alberta, British Columbia: 72 hours' notice • Nova Scotia, Saskatchewan: 48 hours' notice • New Brunswick: 24 hours' notice • Quebec: 7 working days' notice in the public service

wildcat strike: A strike by employees that occurs during a period of time when a strike is not permissible according to collective bargaining laws, such as during the term of a collective agreement.

3. The Legal Rights of Strikers and Replacement Workers

It is an unfair labour practice (see Chapter 9) for an employer to punish workers for exercising rights afforded to them by collective bargaining legislation, including engaging in a lawful strike.[22] This protection from reprisals for engaging in a lawful strike—together with statutory language across Canadian jurisdictions that specifies that workers do not cease to be employees when they go on strike—is how collective bargaining statutes protect the "right to strike."[23] A lawful strike does not end the employment relationship of a unionized employee or give the employer grounds for dismissal, as would be the case for a non-union worker governed by the common law regime. However, an employee can still be disciplined or have his or her employment contract terminated for engaging in an unlawful strike, or for misconduct during a lawful strike (including behaviour on a picket line).[24] For example, in the case of *CAW-Canada and its Local 112 v. Toromont Cat*, the dismissal of a striking employee for throwing a homemade explosive device onto the employer's property was upheld. The Ontario Labour Relations Board ruled that the employer's decision was not motivated by **anti-union animus**.[25]

Everywhere in Canada, employers are entitled to continue to operate during a strike or lockout by assigning work to non-striking employees, including non-bargaining unit employees and bargaining unit employees who elect to continue to work. Moreover, everywhere except in British Columbia and Quebec, employers can also hire new **replacement workers** to perform the work of striking or locked-out employees.[26] The ability to hire replacement workers makes it more feasible for employers to continue to operate during a strike or lockout and thereby empowers employers. For example, during a recent bitter work stoppage at a beer can factory in Toronto that dragged on for nearly two years, the employer bussed in replacement workers each day, past demoralized picketers.[27] Unions routinely lobby governments to prohibit this practice, mostly without success. Whether the government should permit or prohibit replacement workers is one of the enduring debates in this area of law. The two sides of that debate are described in Box 11.2.

BOX 11.2 » TALKING WORK LAW

Should Replacement Workers Be Permitted?

British Columbia and Quebec are the only jurisdictions in Canada today that prohibit employers from using replacement workers to perform the work of striking or locked-out employees. Whether governments should enact anti-replacement worker (ARW) laws is among the most hotly contested issues in collective bargaining law and policy.* The following arguments are usually presented by both sides of the debate.

The arguments in favour of ARW laws include the following:

- The economic warfare route for resolving collective bargaining disputes depends on economic pressure being brought to bear on employees, the union, and the employer. By permitting the employer to hire new workers to do the employees' jobs, the law undermines the economic leverage exerted on the employer during the work stoppage, tilting the power balance in favour of the employer.

- Because the economic pressure on the employer is reduced by the ability to hire replacement workers, employers can hold out longer, and therefore the duration of work stoppages will increase.

- Hostility, anger, and resentment result when replacement workers are bussed across picket lines. This kind of action plants seeds for violence and also poisons the industrial relations climate at the workplace after the work stoppage is over.

The arguments against ARW laws include the following:

- Nothing prevents workers involved in a work stoppage from seeking alternative jobs to supplement their strike pay, and therefore employers should not be prohibited from continuing to produce goods and generate revenues.

---

anti-union animus: The motive element of unfair labour practices, it means acting with an intention to defeat or undermine the exercise of lawful activities by a union or union supporters.

replacement worker: A person who is employed to take the place of another worker who is on strike or locked out. See also *scab*.

- Banning replacement workers will cause more strikes because unions and employees will feel empowered knowing that the employer may not be able to operate during a work stoppage.
- If employers cannot use replacement workers, then they may not be able to operate during a work stoppage and, thus, could lose customers. A loss of customers puts the business at risk, including the future job security of the workers presently on strike or locked out.
- A ban on replacement workers will discourage investment in any jurisdiction that enacts such a law since employers will avoid such a restriction if they can.
- The right to operate their business is a fundamental property right enjoyed by employers that should not be restrained simply because there is a collective bargaining impasse.

Industrial relations scholars have studied the impact of ARW laws on strike incidence and duration. These studies find that ARW laws tend to increase the number of strikes, but they are inconclusive on the question of strike duration. In a 2009 study looking at data covering 1978 to 2003, Professors Paul Duffy and Susan Johnson (Wilfrid Laurier University) found that anti-replacement worker legislation in British Columbia and Quebec caused an increase in the number of strikes, but decreased the length of strikes.[†] Earlier studies using different methodologies and examining data up to 1985 similarly found that ARW laws increase the incidence of strikes, but found the laws also increased the duration of strikes.[‡]

---

[*] Sims Task Force, *Seeking a Balance: A Review of the Canada Labour Code* (Ottawa: Human Resources Development Canada, 1996), at 122.

[†] P. Duffy and S. Johnson, "The Impact of Anti-Temporary Replacement Legislation on Work Stoppages: Empirical Evidence from Canada" (2009) 35:1 *Canadian Public Policy* 100.

[‡] J. Budd, "Strike Replacement Legislation and Collective Bargaining: Lessons for the United States" (1996) 35:2 *Industrial Relations* 245; M. Gunderson, J. Kervin, and F. Reid, "The Effect of Labour Relations Legislation on Strike Incidence" (1989) 22:4 *Canadian Journal of Economics* 779; and M. Gunderson and A. Melino, "The Effects of Public Policy on Strike Duration" (1990) 8:3 *Journal of Labor Economics* 295.

Once the work stoppage ends, could an employer retain replacement workers instead of reinstating the employees who have been on strike or locked out? The short answer is "no." Unlike in the United States, workers who have been involved in a work stoppage in Canada cannot be "permanently replaced."[28] Canadian collective bargaining statutes guarantee striking employees a right to be reinstated to their former jobs once the strike (or lockout) ends.[29] Consider section 87.6 of the *Canada Labour Code* as an example:

> At the end of a strike or lockout not prohibited by this Part, the employer must reinstate employees in the bargaining unit who were on strike or locked out, in preference to any person who was not an employee in the bargaining unit on the date on which notice to bargain collectively was given and was hired or assigned after that date to perform all or part of the duties of an employee in the unit on strike or locked out.[30]

Ontario's law on the reinstatement of striking workers is unusual in the sense that it is restricted to only six months from the date a lawful strike begins. The legislation requires an employer to allow an employee to return to work at any time during or after a strike that lasts six months or less, provided that the employee makes a request in writing and the work the employee does is still being done.[31] If a strike lasts longer than six months, the employer may be permitted to give preference to a replacement worker. However, if the reason the employer refuses to take the striker back is to punish the employee for striking or for being a union supporter, then the employer would be acting with anti-union animus and committing an unfair labour practice.[32]

The Ontario legislation requires the employer to allow a striker to return to work *during a strike* as long as the work is still being done.[33] The legislation permits an employee to cross a picket line staffed by bargaining unit co-workers and return to work. As you might imagine, such an employee will not be very popular with the strikers, especially since any gains won through the strike will also be enjoyed by the bargaining unit employees who chose to return to work. Union members who cross a picket line may experience some form of discipline at the hands of the union, such as a fine, for violating their contract with the union, known as a *union constitution* (see Chapter 15).

4. Labour Picketing

Workers picket for a few key reasons. First, through picketing, workers seek to persuade customers, suppliers, non-striking employees, and replacement workers to stop doing business with the employer, or at least to inform these groups of the issues in dispute and elicit their support (persuasion). Second, through picketing, workers have an opportunity to come together for a common cause and support one another during a difficult and stressful time (solidarity). Third, workers usually receive "strike pay" from the union in exchange for picketing, which is much less than their usual wage but nevertheless provides some income during a work stoppage (income).

The laws governing picketing balance competing interests. The interests of the picketers and the union are to communicate their message and apply economic pressure on the employer. The interests of the employer are to continue operating without disruption and to ensure that a picket line does not obstruct people, supplies, and products from entering and leaving the business's property. Lastly, the interest of other "innocent third parties" is to avoid economic harm from picketing and the presence of a picket line. Imagine, for example, a picket line set up outside a shopping mall or industrial park.[34] Other businesses and mall customers that have no direct involvement in the work stoppage may be economically affected by a picket line, particularly if the picketers make it difficult to enter the mall or park. The manner in which the law has sought to balance these competing interests has evolved over time, and today the law is arguably less restrictive of the right to picket than in the past.

Picketing involves both an expressive component and a physical component. Because picketing involves the expression of ideas, and freedom of expression is an important right in any democratic society, there is a strong argument that workers ought to have a robust right to engage in informational picketing.[35] Picketing also involves a physical component that may include large numbers of people congregating in a small area, possibly with the explicit intention of preventing or impeding the ability of people to cross an area, usually with the intention of causing some inconvenience. There is a signalling element to picketing; people approaching a picket line understand that they are being asked to turn around, and in some instances the mere sight of a picket line may cause some people to do just that.[36] The history and development of picketing law is a story about how courts and governments have balanced the workers' right of expression with concerns about the perceived and actual effects of the physical component of picketing.[37]

Other than in British Columbia, where the *Labour Relations Code* regulates where and when picketing can take place, the law of picketing in Canada mostly involves the courts applying tort law (see Chapter 18 in the companion volume).[38] Judges use torts to regulate what picketers say, where they say it, and, most important, how they behave on the picket line. An employer or third party adversely affected by picketing can file a lawsuit against the picketers (and, in some cases, the union itself), asking a court to restrict or prohibit the picketing. Once the lawsuit has been filed, the party filing it can then go before a judge (by filing a motion) and ask for an **interlocutory injunction** to be ordered that would apply until a full trial can be heard at a later date to decide the lawsuit. However, in reality those lawsuits rarely go to trial because obtaining a quick injunction to restrict picketing is the real objective, and the work stoppage usually ends before a trial date.[39]

The originating lawsuit must allege a proper cause of action; it must point to a legal rule that has been violated. The three types of "causes of action" are (1) breach of contract, (2) breach of statute, and (3) a tort. When picketing is in support of an *unlawful strike*, the cause of action may involve either or both breach of contract and breach of statute. When that is the case, courts have

---

interlocutory injunction: A temporary court order prohibiting conduct that is potentially unlawful until a decision is released by the court on whether the conduct is unlawful.

ordered injunctions to prohibit the unlawful strike and the picketing associated with it.[40] When picketing is in support of a lawful strike or a lockout, the cause of action alleged is normally a tort. As we learned in Chapter 18 in the companion volume, a tort is a judge-made legal wrong. A number of torts could apply to picketing. For example, picketers who engage in intimidation, trespass, defamation, physical obstruction of entry to or exit from a property (nuisance), or violence on a picket line will be committing a tort (and maybe a criminal offence too), and a court will likely order an injunction to restrict that behaviour.[41] Table 11.2 summarizes the most common torts that are applicable to picketing behaviour.

TABLE 11.2 The Most Common Torts Applicable to Picketing Behaviour

Tort	Picketing Behaviour
Nuisance	Picketers physically obstruct or prevent entry to or exit from a property, such as blocking roadways.
Defamation	Picketers make false and disparaging statements about the employer or others.
Trespass	Picketers stand on private property and refuse to leave when asked.
Inducing breach of contract	Picketers knowingly encourage or cause someone to breach a contract they have with the employer. For example, a picket line that prevents a supplier from making a delivery to the employer or encourages employees not on strike to breach their employment contracts by not reporting to work could be inducing breach of contract.

However, sometimes picketing is completely peaceful and involves workers standing around with "On Strike" picket signs and attempting to distribute literature to people who approach the picket line. Even in those cases, judges have sometimes intervened to restrain the picketing. In particular, in mid-20th-century Britain, judges developed a new species of **economic tort** specifically to restrain labour picketing.[42] For example, the tort of "inducing breach of contract" could be applied to almost any situation in which an employee who is not involved in the striking bargaining unit or a supplier to the employer declines to cross a picket line and thereby breaches their contract with the employer. That tort applies when (1) picketers know there is a contract between the employer and a third party and intend by picketing to cause the third party to breach that contract, (2) the third party does breach the contract; and (3) the employer suffers damages as a result.[43]

In carving out a space for lawful picketing, Canadian courts and legislators historically distinguished between **primary picketing** and **secondary picketing**. Primary picketing takes place at the location where the workers involved in the labour dispute work, whereas secondary picketing takes place anywhere else. Primary picketing in support of a lawful strike was usually permitted, provided it was done peacefully. Some jurisdictions enacted laws that specifically declared that it was not unlawful for workers to picket in connection with a lawful strike or lockout, even if that picketing might cause other employees to decline to report to work, creating a limited defence to the tort of "inducing breach of contract."[44] However, those protections were limited to primary picketing, and sometimes to picketing at other locations being used to assist the employer to resist the effects of the work stoppage (known as "allies").[45] In the infamous 1963 case

---

economic tort: A species of tort invented by British judges in the 20th century to restrain collective worker action that is intended to cause economic harm.

primary picketing: Picketing that takes place at the location of the employer directly involved in the labour dispute.

secondary picketing: Picketing that takes place at a location other than the workplace of the employees involved in the labour dispute.

of *Hersees of Woodstock Ltd. v. Goldstein et al.*, the Ontario Court of Appeal ruled that secondary picketing is "illegal per se," meaning that it was afforded no protection by either the common law or statute and courts would routinely order injunctions to prohibit even peaceful, informational secondary picketing.[46] This historical distinction between primary and secondary picketing was revisited and overruled by the Supreme Court of Canada in the landmark 2002 case of *R.W.D.S.U., Local 558 v. Pepsi-Cola Canada*, which is summarized in Box 11.3.

BOX 11.3 » CASE LAW HIGHLIGHT

The Right to Picket and the "Wrongful Action" Model

R.W.D.S.U., Local 558 v. Pepsi-Cola Canada Beverages (West) Ltd.

[2002] 1 SCR 156

Key Facts: During a bitter but lawful work stoppage at a Pepsi-Cola factory in Saskatchewan, employees initially picketed in front of the employer's factory, but then also established picket lines at some managers' homes, at a hotel where replacement workers were staying, and at various retail outlets that sold Pepsi products, hoping to dissuade workers from accepting delivery of Pepsi products. The employer applied to the courts, seeking an injunction to restrain the picketing. Some of the picketing was clearly tortious because it involved violence, intimidation, and trespass. However, the picketing at the retail stores was peaceful. The lower court judge issued an injunction prohibiting not only the tortious picketing but also all picketing at secondary locations. The Court of Appeal overruled the part of the judgment banning peaceful secondary picketing, and the employer appealed that decision to the Supreme Court of Canada.

Issue: Is secondary picketing during a lawful work stoppage illegal per se?

Decision: No. The Supreme Court of Canada overruled the *Hersees* approach. It looked to the robust protection of freedom of expression in the *Canadian Charter of Rights and Freedoms*. Although the Charter does not apply directly to common law rules such as the *Hersees* rule, the Supreme Court of Canada

ruled that the common law should nevertheless evolve in a manner consistent with "Charter values." Picketing is an expressive activity and, therefore, "it engages one of the highest constitutional freedoms: freedom of expression." The Supreme Court of Canada introduced a new "wrongful action model": all labour picketing is lawful unless it is done in a manner that constitutes a tort or violates some other law. It described the sorts of behaviour on a picket line that may be unlawful as follows:

> Picketing which breaches the criminal law or one of the specific torts like trespass, nuisance, intimidation, defamation or misrepresentation, will be impermissible, regardless of where it occurs. Specific torts known to the law will catch most of the situations which are liable to take place in a labour dispute. In particular, the breadth of the torts of nuisance and defamation should permit control of most coercive picketing. Known torts will also protect property interests. They will not allow for intimidation, they will protect free access to private premises and thereby protect the right to use one's property. Finally, rights arising out of contracts or business relationships also receive basic protection through the tort of inducing breach of contract.

No tort or crime had been committed by the Pepsi picketers at the retail stores. Therefore, they were entitled to picket outside of retail stores selling Pepsi.

As a result of the *Pepsi-Cola Canada* decision, labour picketing is lawful, regardless of where it takes place, as long as the manner in which it is conducted is not otherwise illegal. This outcome reserves an important role for tort law. A party seeking to have a court prohibit or limit either primary or secondary picketing must demonstrate that the picketers are committing a crime or tort.[47]

Finally, some jurisdictions have enacted legislation that restricts the right of the courts to issue injunctions to restrain labour picketing. For example, in Ontario, the *Courts of Justice Act* requires that an employer demonstrate that the police were called and that the police were unable to prevent "alleged danger of damage to property, injury to persons, obstruction of or interference with the lawful entry or exit from the premises or breach of the peace" as a precondition to obtaining an injunction.[48] In interpreting this language, courts in Ontario have ruled that an injunction will not be issued to restrain peaceful picketing, even if the picketing has the effect of impeding entry to or exit from a property (i.e., that a nuisance has occurred), provided that the obstruction is not unreasonable. For example, the court refused to grant an injunction to restrain picketing in the case of *Cancoil Thermal Corp. v. Abbott* even though the judge found that "a civil nuisance may have occurred" because picketers were stopping each person who attempted to cross the picket line for at least 15 minutes to discuss the dispute.[49]

B. Employer Weapons: Lockouts and Unilateral Alteration of Terms of Employment

Employers also have weapons at their disposal in the economic warfare route. One option they are granted by collective bargaining legislation is to ask the government, once only, to order a vote by employees on the last offer it put to the union. This option is known as a **final offer vote**.[50] Employers use a final offer vote when they believe they have tabled an offer that a majority of employees would accept, but for some reason, the union is declining to put the offer to the employees. Employers may also lock out their workers or, in some scenarios, impose new employment terms on their employees.

1. Lockouts

Collective bargaining statutes align the timing of a lawful lockout with that of a lawful strike. The moment workers can legally strike, their employer can legally lock them out. A lockout is unlawful if it takes place when the employer is not in a legal lockout position. A lockout involves an employer refusing to allow its employees to report to work. Does that mean that a layoff due to lack of work or a disciplinary suspension of one or more employees is a "lockout"? Both of these scenarios involve an employer telling employees not to report to work. We need to look at the definition of *lockout* in collective bargaining statutes. Here is the definition of *lockout* in the Ontario *Labour Relations Act, 1995*:

Source: CP Photo/Adrian Wyld

"[L]ock-out" includes the closing of a place of employment, a suspension of work or a refusal by an employer to continue to employ a number of employees, *with a view to compel or induce the employees*, or to aid another employer to compel or induce that employer's employees, *to refrain from exercising any rights or privileges under this Act or to agree to provisions or changes in provisions respecting terms or conditions of employment*.[51] [Emphasis added.]

Notice that this definition includes a motive or subjective element: the reason that the employer is not allowing employees to work must be to pressure the employees to agree to terms of employment or to refrain from exercising legal rights.[52] Therefore, a layoff due to a business downturn is not a lockout, provided that the purpose of the layoff is not to compel employees to forgo statutory rights or to gain an edge in collective bargaining.[53]

---

final offer vote: A provision found in collective bargaining legislation that entitles an employer to have the last offer it presented to the union's negotiating team put to a ballot of employees. Employers can only exercise this right once per round of bargaining.

Whether a lockout is a good bargaining strategy for the employer depends on a number of factors. For example, if an employer believes that a strike is inevitable, it may want to control when the work stoppage begins. There are a number of strategic reasons why workers and their union might want to delay the start of a strike, including waiting until winter ends so that picket lines are more bearable, or waiting until a time in the business cycle when the employer is most vulnerable if a work stoppage occurs. The employer can remove that union advantage by locking out the workers earlier. Sometimes, workers and their union would be happy allowing the bargaining to drag on, because the prevailing terms and conditions of employment are superior to what the employer is seeking to obtain in negotiations. Imagine that the employer seeks to cut wages and reduce the pension plan. As long as the employer is abiding by the terms of the old collective agreement during collective bargaining, the employees may be happy with the status quo. In that scenario, the employer may want to lock out the workers quickly in order to put pressure on them to concede to the changes the employer wants.

2. Unilateral Alteration of Terms of Employment

The appendix to this chapter chronicles the collective bargaining between the City of Toronto and the Canadian Union of Public Employees (CUPE) from 2011 to 2012. In 2009, a bitter 40-day "garbage strike" took place in Toronto, and in 2010 Rob Ford was elected as mayor on a promise to, among other things, contract out garbage collection and ensure no "unnecessary strikes." The turning point during negotiations over 2011 to 2012 came when the City of Toronto announced its intention to unilaterally impose the final offer it had tabled to CUPE unless a deal was reached by the date a legal strike or lockout could begin. In another case, in 2014, the University of Windsor imposed the terms of an offer it had made to the Windsor University Faculty Association over the wishes of the union and much of the faculty.[54] In both of these cases, the unions had not taken a strike vote, and therefore the workers were not in a position to strike, which is the weapon the law gives employees faced with an employer's imposition of contract terms, as explained in the case discussed in Box 11.4.

BOX 11.4 » CASE LAW HIGHLIGHT

The Employer's Right to Unilaterally Amend Terms of Employment

United Steelworkers 1-2693 v. Neenah
Paper Company of Canada
2006 CanLII 9888 (Ont. LRB)

Key Facts: The collective agreement between the union and employer, a lumber company, expired on August 31, 2005. The employer told the union that it was losing money and that it would require employees to accept a pay cut. The parties met with a government conciliation officer, but no deal was reached, and as of December 5, 2005, the parties were in a legal strike/lockout position. Prior to that date, the employer sent the union a letter that advised the union that unless a deal was reached before December 5, it intended on that date to implement new terms of employment, including a 6.4 percent wage cut and a substantial change to the pension plan, among other changes. On December 5, the employer began to apply the new terms. The employees continued to work but advised the employer that they did not accept the change. The union filed an unfair labour practice complaint, arguing that an employer was unlawfully bargaining directly with employees, that the

employer could not unilaterally change terms of employment unless and until it has locked out its employees, and that doing so amounted to bad-faith bargaining (see Chapter 10).

Issue: Can an employer unilaterally alter terms of employment without the union's consent, once the parties are in a legal strike/lockout position?

Decision: Yes. Once the legal strike/lockout date has been reached, there is no longer a collective agreement in force, and the collective bargaining freeze (see Chapter 10), which prohibits changes to terms of employment without the union's consent, is over. Therefore, reading the Ontario *Labour Relations Act, 1995* as a whole, an employer is free to treat the old agreement as expired and introduce new terms of employment. The Ontario Labour Relations Board explained that employees are not required to accept the changed terms, because the Act allows them to respond by going on strike:

> In Ontario, the Act is premised on the fact that the parties may engage in economic warfare once the

strike/lock out conditions have been met. Such economic warfare can, so long as it does not otherwise constitute a violation of the Act, take a variety of forms. Unions can legally engage in strikes. They also may engage in other activity which does not amount to a full blown work stoppage, in order to put pressure on the employer. Included in these tactics are rotating strikes, overtime bans, "work to rule" activities etc. The employer has a similar broad range of economic weapons at its disposal (all of which must be exercised subject to the Act's unfair labour practice provisions). It can lock out. It can hire replacement workers to replace locked out or striking workers. I see no reason why, subject to the other provisions of the Act, a unilateral implementation of new terms and conditions (which have been offered to the union in collective bargaining) cannot form part of the employer arsenal. As has already been stated: if the union and the employees do not wish to operate under the new terms and conditions they do not have to.

The union's unfair labour practice complaint was dismissed.

In other jurisdictions, including British Columbia, the right of an employer to unilaterally alter terms and conditions of employment exists only if a lockout or strike has commenced.[55]

IV. The Interest Arbitration Route

The alternative to economic warfare as a means of resolving a collective bargaining impasse is the interest arbitration route. The interest arbitration route is available in four situations.

First, unions and employers may agree to refer a bargaining dispute to arbitration.[56] That process is governed by legislation and is known as **voluntary interest arbitration**. The language in section 79 of the *Canada Labour Code* is typical:

> 79(1) Despite any other provision of this Part, an employer and a [union] may agree in writing, as part of a collective agreement or otherwise, to refer any matter respecting the renewal or revision of a collective agreement or the entering into of a new collective agreement to a person or body for final and binding determination.
> (2) The agreement suspends the right to strike or lockout and constitutes an undertaking to implement the determination.[57]

In some jurisdictions, the parties may agree to be bound by recommendations of a conciliator or mediator rather than referring their dispute to an interest arbitrator.[58] Voluntary interest arbitration is not used all that frequently because one side or the other often believes its interests are best served by sticking with the economic warfare route. Often the party that most fears a work stoppage will propose referring the dispute to arbitration only to be rebuffed by the other party.

Second, the economic warfare route is not available to some unionized public sector workers at all, and bargaining disputes involving these workers are referred by statute to **mandatory interest arbitration**. The most common example is workers who perform "essential services," such as police, firefighters, and medical providers, without whom a real risk to public health and safety would exist.[59] However, in recent years, some governments have, controversially, extended the concept of "essential services" to include services that are important to the economy or would cause inconvenience to the public if interrupted by a work stoppage, such as public transit, mail delivery, and even air travel provided by a lone carrier (Air Canada) within a highly competitive industry.[60]

---

voluntary interest arbitration: A procedure in which a union and employer agree to refer outstanding collective bargaining issues to an interest arbitrator to resolve.

mandatory interest arbitration: Statutorily required interest arbitration to resolve collective bargaining impasses. Replaces the right to strike and lockout.

Some types of essential service workers have a limited right to strike under a system known as the "essential services designation model." In this model, the union and employer must agree on which, and how many, employees are required in order to protect the public from undue risk that could be caused by a work stoppage.[61] That agreement is written into an **essential services agreement**. If the parties cannot agree, then the statute usually provides for the labour board to decide.[62] For example, this model typically applies to ambulance drivers, some health care workers, and prison workers. The determination of the percentage of workers in a bargaining unit that are deemed essential obviously affects the relative bargaining unit of the parties—if a very large percentage of workers are deemed "essential" and therefore are unable to strike, then the threat of a strike is watered down or completely illusory.[63] Because the stakes are high, disputes over essential services agreements are not uncommon.[64] We will consider essential services again in Chapter 16.

Third, parties may end up at interest arbitration as a result of **back-to-work legislation**. A legal strike or lockout may be brought to an end by the government because of concerns that the work stoppage is causing too much disruption, risk, or harm to third parties or the economy. Back-to-work legislation declares a strike or lockout immediately over, orders workers back to work, and refers any outstanding bargaining issues to be decided by interest arbitration.[65] Canadian governments have been very willing to use back-to-work legislation to end work stoppages, particularly public sector strikes involving teachers, college and university staff, transit workers, and municipal workers, such as garbage collectors. The International Labour Organization (ILO) has regularly ruled Canada's back-to-work legislation to be in violation of ILO Convention 87, which (as noted in Chapter 35 in the companion volume) guarantees a robust right to strike.[66] Moreover, in light of the recent Supreme Court of Canada case of *Saskatchewan Federation of Labour v. Saskatchewan*, where it was ruled that the Charter also protects a right to strike, back-to-work legislation is now susceptible to a constitutional challenge. We will explore this issue in Chapter 18.[67]

Fourth, parties may end up at interest arbitration through **first contract arbitration**. As the name suggests, access to interest arbitration through this route is available only in the case of collective bargaining for the first collective agreement after a union has been certified. The basic theory underlying first contract arbitration is that the collective bargaining process is new, the employer and employees are inexperienced, and the bargaining relationship is immature.[68] Together, these factors are a recipe for conflict. According to Professor Paul Weiler (Harvard University), first contract arbitration allows for "a trial marriage, one that could allow the parties to get used to each other and lay the foundations for a more mature and enduring relationship."[69] First contract arbitration is available in some form across Canada except in Alberta, New Brunswick, and Prince Edward Island. The conditions to access first contract arbitration vary.[70] For example, in Manitoba and Quebec, access to first contract arbitration is almost automatic after a period of failed negotiations has passed.[71] In Ontario and British Columbia, the party seeking first contract arbitration must demonstrate that negotiations have failed due to the recalcitrance of the other party, which may involve bad-faith bargaining (see Chapter 10) but need not.[72]

Chapter 16 explores in greater detail the process and criteria used by interest arbitrators. Briefly, in a typical interest arbitration proceeding, both union and employer will attempt to

---

essential services agreement: An agreement between an employer and a union that identifies which and how many employees are "essential" to protect public safety and therefore cannot participate in a work stoppage.

back-to-work legislation: A statute enacted for the specific purpose of bringing an end to a lawful work stoppage by referring outstanding bargaining issues to an interest arbitrator for final resolution.

first contract arbitration: A statutory provision that refers a collective bargaining impasse during negotiations for a first collective agreement to interest arbitration. Conditions for accessing first contract arbitration vary by jurisdiction.

persuade the interest arbitrator (or interest arbitration board consisting of three members) that their proposed collective agreement terms are more reasonable than the other side's proposals. It then falls to the arbitrator (or arbitration board) to decide and impose a final collective agreement on the parties. Legislation ordering mandatory interest arbitration may specify a specific procedure for conducting the arbitration, such as **final offer selection**, and include criteria that the arbitrator must consider in its deliberations.

For example, the 2011 *Restoring Mail Delivery for Canadians Act*, introduced by the federal Conservative Party, ordered a bargaining dispute at Canada Post to interest arbitration, required the union and employer to submit a "final offer" on all outstanding matters, and limited the arbitrator to selecting "either the final offer submitted by the employer or the final offer submitted by the union."[73] The legislation also required the arbitrator to consider the following criteria when deciding which offer to accept:

> 11(2) In making the selection of a final offer, the arbitrator is to be guided by the need for terms and conditions of employment that are consistent with those in comparable postal industries and that will provide the necessary degree of flexibility to ensure the short- and long-term economic viability and competitiveness of the Canada Post Corporation, maintain the health and safety of its workers and ensure the sustainability of its pension plan, taking into account
>
> (a) that the solvency ratio of the pension plan must not decline as a direct result of the new collective agreement; and
>
> (b) that the Canada Post Corporation must, without recourse to undue increases in postal rates, operate efficiently, improve productivity and meet acceptable standards of service.[74]

Legislative directions that restrict the arbitrator's discretion and, like in this language, require special consideration of the employer's economic concerns, may also be subject to a constitutional challenge after the *Saskatchewan Federation of Labour* decision, mentioned above. That decision ruled that where strikes are restricted, a neutral dispute arbitration model must be substituted.[75]

V. Chapter Summary

This chapter is longer than most in this text because the law of industrial conflict is so very complicated. That law weaves statute and common law rules together in often complex ways as it develops the two routes for resolving collective bargaining impasses: (1) the economic warfare route; and (2) the interest arbitration route. In a very general way, we can say that collective bargaining statutes and collective agreements, enforced by labour relations boards and labour arbitrators, regulate the what and when of strikes and lockouts, and the common law courts (mostly through the application of tort law) regulate the how and where of strikes and picketing. However, that does not tell the whole story. As we saw in this chapter, the rules vary across jurisdictions. Moreover, many—about 65 percent or more—Canadians have no legally protected right to strike at all. That is because in Canada, only unionized workers are protected from employer reprisals for striking, and only about 32 percent of Canadians are unionized (see Table 5.3). Included in that 32 percent are many public sector workers who are prohibited from striking because they perform "essential services." Not surprisingly, Canada is often described as having a very narrow right to strike.

---

final offer selection: A form of interest arbitration in which the interest arbitrator is restricted to imposing either the employer's or the union's proposed collective agreement in its entirety.

QUESTIONS AND ISSUES FOR DISCUSSION

1. Explain whether the following scenarios would constitute a strike in a province where the definition of *strike* in the collective bargaining statute (1) includes a motive element and (2) does not include a motive element. If you need more information in order to answer the question, what information do you need?

   a. Three employees do not report to work but call in sick.

   b. Three employees do not report to work because they decided to go to a Toronto Blue Jays playoff game instead.

   c. Three employees refuse to work voluntary overtime because they each have childcare responsibilities that night.

   d. One employee storms out of the workplace after an argument with a supervisor and yells that he is not coming back until the supervisor is "gone."

   e. Three employees miss work to attend a protest about government cuts to welfare rates.

   f. Three employees decide to work slower because their employer is proposing wage cuts in collective bargaining.

2. What is a lockout?

3. Why do workers picket during a strike or lockout?

4. When can an employer unilaterally impose new terms of employment on unionized workers? What options are available to the workers when an employer takes that action?

5. Describe the preconditions that must be satisfied before a strike is lawful in your province.

6. Explain the difference in the approach to picketing in the *Hersees of Woodstock* decision and the *Pepsi-Cola Canada* decision. Provide three examples of picketing behaviour that would likely be ruled to be unlawful after the *Pepsi-Cola Canada* decision and explain why they would likely be unlawful.

7. What is the role of an interest arbitrator? Describe four situations in which a collective bargaining dispute would be resolved through interest arbitration rather than through the economic warfare route.

EXERCISE

The Supreme Court of Canada's 2002 decision in *R. W.D.S.U., Local 558 v. Pepsi-Cola Canada Beverages (West) Ltd.* changed the common law approach to labour picketing. In that decision, the Supreme Court of Canada emphasized the expressive component of picketing and cautioned judges to not easily restrain peaceful labour picketing. Hundreds of picketing cases have been decided since the *Pepsi-Cola Canada* case that have referenced that decision. In this exercise, we "note up" the *Pepsi-Cola Canada* case and describe a case in which the court was asked to impose an injunction restraining picketing.

1. Go to the CanLII home page: www.canlii.org.

2. In the "Noteup" search box, type "Pepsi-Cola Canada" and then find the *R. W.D.S.U., Local 558 v. Pepsi-Cola Canada Beverages (West) Ltd.* case. Select the case.

3. Now, below the "Noteup" search box, you should see a list of over 200 cases that have cited the *Pepsi-Cola Canada* case, but not all will be labour picketing cases.

4. To narrow your search, in the "Document text" search box, type "picketing." You should see a list of over 100 cases.

5. Scroll through the cases and look for one that interests you and that deals with an attempt to obtain an injunction to restrain labour picketing during a work stoppage. Read the case and answer the following questions:

   a. What behaviour by the picketers is alleged to be grounds for an injunction?

b. What "cause of action" is being alleged (i.e., a tort, a crime, a breach of contract or statute)?

c. Is the injunction granted? Why or why not?

d. Why does the court refer to the *Pepsi-Cola Canada* case?

UPDATES

Go to emond.ca/lawofworkircb for links to news, author's blog posts, content updates, and other information related to the chapters in this text.

NOTES AND REFERENCES

1 See Labour Law Casebook Group, *Labour and Employment Law: Cases, Materials, and Commentary*, 8th ed. (Toronto: Irwin, 2011), at chapter 7.

2 *Employment Insurance Act*, SC 1996, c. 23, s. 36(1).

3 Ontario *Labour Relations Act, 1995*, SO 1995, c. 1, Sch. A.

4 *Ontario Hydro*, [1970] OLRB Rep. Dec. 962, at para. 15.

5 M. Gunderson, B. Hebdon, and D. Hyatt, "Strikes and Dispute Resolution" in M. Gunderson and D. Taras, ed., *Canadian Labour and Employment Relations*, 6th ed. (Toronto: Pearson, 2009), at 342.

6 See Employment and Social Development Canada, *Overview of Collective Bargaining in Canada, 2015* (Ottawa: Her Majesty the Queen in Right of Canada, 2016), http://www.labour.gc.ca/eng/resources/info/publications/collective_bargaining/ocba2015-eng.pdf.

7 *Saskatchewan Federation of Labour v. Saskatchewan*, [2015] 1 SCR 245, at para. 3. See also H. Laski, *Liberty in the Modern State* (London: Penguin, 1938), at 128-31.

8 These efforts to restrain strikes during the first half of the 20th century are recounted in detail in J. Fudge and E. Tucker, *Labour Before the Law: The Regulation of Workers' Collective Action in Canada, 1900–1948* (Don Mills, ON: Oxford University Press, 2001) and, in the later decades of the century, in L. Panitch and D. Schwartz, *From Consent to Coercion: The Assault on Trade Union Freedoms*, 3rd ed. (Aurora, ON: Garamond, 2003), especially chapter 4.

9 *Wartime Labour Relations Order* PC 1003 is available at http://socserv.mcmaster.ca/oldlabourstudies/onlinelearning/article.php?id=503.

10 Ontario *Labour Relations Act, 1995*, supra note 3.

11 *General Motors of Canada Limited v. National Automobile, Aerospace and Agricultural Implement Workers Union of Canada (CAW-Canada), et al.*, 1996 CanLII 11152 (Ont. LRB).

12 *Dick's Lumber & Building Supplies Inc. v. United Steelworkers of America, Local No. 1-3567*, 2006 CanLII 28067 (BCLRB); and *Cambridge (City) v. Amalgamated Transit Union (Local 1608)*, 1989 CanLII 3014 (Ont. LRB).

13 See, e.g., *Unilux Boiler Corp. v. United Steelworkers of America, Local 3950*, 2005 CanLII 20765 (Ont. LRB); and *MacMillan Bloedel (Alberni) v. Swanson et al.* (1972), 26 DLR (3d) (BCSC) 641.

14 BC *Labour Relations Code*, RSBC 1996, c. 244, s. 1 (definition of *strike*).

15 *Dollar Thrifty Automotive Group Canada Inc v. Canadian Office and Professional Employees Union, Local 378*, 2013 CanLII 51440 (BCLRB).

16 Manitoba *Labour Relations Act*, CCSM c. L10, s. 1.

17 The BC *Labour Relations Code, BSBC* 1979, c. 212, included a motive element until 1984. In several cases, the board ruled that collective work refusals that were not intended to pressure the employer in bargaining were not "strikes": *British Columbia Hydro and Power Authority and International Brotherhood of Electrical Workers, Local 258 and Local 213*, [1976] 2 CLRBR 410; and *Canex Placer Limited (Endako Mines Division) v. Canadian Association of Industrial, Mechanical and Allied Workers, Local 10*, [1975] 1 CLRBR 269.

18 See, e.g., Ontario *Labour Relations Act, 1995*, supra note 3, s. 1(2) (no person ceases to be an employee for reason only that they stop working owing to a strike or lockout); and s. 5 (every person is free to participate in lawful activities of a union).

19 *Natrel Inc. v. Milk and Bread Drivers, Dairy Employees, Caterers and Allied Employees, Local Union 647*, 2005 CanLII 67419 (Ont. LA); *Mosaic Potash Colonsay ULC v. United Steelworkers Union, Local 7656*, 2012 CanLII 58952 (SKLRB); *King v. Deputy Head (Canada Border Services Agency)*, 2010 PSLRB 125 (CanLII); *General Motors of Canada Ltd. v. National Automobile, Aerospace and Agricultural Implement Workers of Canada (CAW-Canada)*, 2000 CanLII 9564 (Ont. LRB); and *Petrow v. Limo Jet Gold Express Ltd.*, 2009 CanLII 4193 (BC LRB).

20 PC 1003, supra note 9, s. 21. For a discussion of the history of the *Industrial Disputes Investigation Act*, see Fudge and Tucker, supra note 8, at chapter 2.

21 See, e.g., M. Gunderson, A. Melino, and F. Reid, "The Effects of Canadian Labour Relations Legislation on Strike Incidence and Duration" (1990) 41:8 *Labor Law Journal* 512.

22 *Canadian Pacific Railway Co. v. Zambri* (1962), 34 DLR (2d) 654 (SCC); *Chisholm v. Dominion Citrus and Drug*, 1982 CanLII 967 (Ont. LRB); and *Canada v. Graham Cable TV/FM* (1986), 12 CLRBR (NS) 1.

23 Ontario *Labour Relations Act, 1995*, s. 1(2). See also the discussion in G. Adams, *Canadian Labour Law*, 2nd ed. (Aurora, ON: Canada Law Book, 1993), at s. 11(1)(iii); and *McGavin Toastmaster Ltd. v. Ainscough*, [1976] 1 SCR 718.

24 *Canadian Paperworkers Union v. International Wallcoverings*, 1983 CanLII 764 (Ont. LRB), at para. 36 (upholding termination of employees for picket line violence). Often employers and unions agree, as part of the settlement of a strike or lockout, that workers disciplined or terminated for alleged misconduct during a work stoppage can refer a grievance to an arbitrator for review of the employer's decision.

25 *National Automobile, Aerospace, Transportation and General Workers Union of Canada (CAW-Canada) and its Local 112 v. Toromont Cat*, 2001 CanLII 5107 (Ont. LRB).

26 BC *Labour Relations Code*, supra note 14, s. 68; Quebec *Labour Code*, CQLR c. C-27, s. 109. *Canada Labour Code*, RSC 1985, c. L-2, s. 94(2.1), prohibits replacement workers that are used to undermine the "union's representational capacity rather than the pursuit of legitimate bargaining objectives." See L. Vaillancourt, "Amendments to the Canada Labour Code: Are Replacement Workers an Endangered Species?" (2000) 45 *McGill Law Journal* 757.

27 See S. Mojtehedzadeh, "Bitterness Remains as Crown Metal Workers End 2-Year Strike," *Toronto Star*, July 20, 2015, https://www.thestar.com/news/gta/2015/07/20/bitterness-remains-crown-metal-workers-end-2-year-strike.html.

28 For an accessible discussion of American strike law, see P. Secunda, et al., *Mastering Labor Law* (Durham, NC: Carolina Academic Press, 2014), chapters 14-16. In the common law regime, before legislation intervened, an employer could hire replacement workers and retain them over strikers once the strike ended: *Canadian Pacific Railway Co. v. Zambri*, supra note 22, per Locke J.

29 *Canada Labour Code*, supra note 26, s. 87.6; *Saskatchewan Employment Act*, SS 2013, c. S-15.1, ss. 6-37; Manitoba *Labour Relations Act*, supra note 16, s. 12; Quebec *Labour Code*, supra note 26, s. 110.1; Alberta *Labour Relations Code*, RSA 2000, c. L-1, s. 90. In Ontario, the legislation does not include an expressed requirement on employers to reinstate a locked-out employee. However, the board has interpreted the legislation to include a right of employers to hire "temporary" replacements during a lockout: *United Cement, Lime and Gypsum Workers International Union v. Westroc Industries Ltd.*, 1981 CanLII 1034 (Ont. LRB).

30 *Canada Labour Code*, supra note 26, s. 87.6.

31 Ontario *Labour Relations Act, 1995*, supra note 3, s. 80. See *National Automobile, Transportation and General Workers Union of Canada (CAW-Canada) v. Dover Corporation (Canada) Ltd.*, 1997 CanLII 15568 (Ont. LRB); and *Ontario Public Service Employees Union v. Mini-Skool*, 1983 CanLII 973 (Ont. LRB).

32 *United Steelworkers of America v. Shaw-Almex Industries Limited*, 1986 CanLII 1534 (Ont. LRB); also see the discussion in *Ottawa Citizen*, [1999] OLRD No. 1445 (OLRB) (the employer grants jobs to replacement workers over locked-out workers in job posting based on job performance is not tainted by anti-union animus).

33 Ontario *Labour Relations Act, 1995*, supra note 3, ss. 80(1) and (2).

34 See, e.g., *Sobeys Capital Incorporated v United Food and Commercial Workers Canada Union, Local No. 401*, 2011 CanLII 73739 (ABLRB); and *Cadillac Fairview Corp. Ltd. v. R.W.D.S.U. (C.A.)* (1989), 71 OR (2d) 206 (Ont. CA).

35 *R.W.D.S.U., Local 558 v. Pepsi-Cola Canada Beverages (West) Ltd.*, [2002] 1 SCR 156, at para. 32.

36 P. Weiler, *Reconcilable Differences: New Directions in Canadian Labour Law* (Toronto: Carswell, 1980), at 78-85; *Fletcher Challenge Canada Ltd. v. Communications, Energy and Paperworkers Union of Canada*, 1998 CanLII 6528 (BCCA); and *Pollyco (Rupert Square) Shopping Centre Inc. v. Loblaws Companies Ltd.*, 2011 CanLII 4556 (BCLRB).

37 There is a rich academic literature: A.W.R. Carrothers, "Recent Developments in the Tort Law of Picketing" (1957) 35 *Canadian Bar Review* 1005; P. Bergbusch, "Secondary Picketing in Saskatchewan: A Functional Analysis of O.K. Economy v. R.W.D.S.U., Local 454" (1995) 59 *Saskatchewan Law Review* 141; H. Arthurs, "Comments" (1963) 41 *Canadian Bar Review* 573; and H. Arthurs, "Tort Liability for Strikes in Canada: Some Problems of Judicial Workmanship" (1960) 38 *Canadian Bar Review* 346.

38 BC *Labour Relations Code*, supra note 14, ss. 65 and 66. See R. Brown, "Picketing: Canadian Courts and the Labour Relations Board of British Columbia" (1981) 31 *University of Toronto Law Journal* 153. See also *Westfair Foods Ltd. v. United Food and Commercial Workers International Union, Local 1518*, 2000 CanLII 27296 (BCLRB).

39 The test for obtaining an interlocutory injunction was set out in the non-labour case of *RJR—MacDonald v. Canada (Attorney General)*, [1994] 1 SCR 311. Basically, it requires the party seeking the injunction to establish (1) that the lawsuit has established a strong *prima facie* case; (2) that the party will suffer "irreparable harm" if the injunction is not issued; and (3) that the "balance of harm" favours that party.

40 *Gagnon et al. v. Foundation Maritime Ltd.*, [1961] SCR 435; and *St. Anne Nackawic Pulp & Paper v. CPU*, [1986] 1 SCR 704.

41 *Bulk-Lift Systems Ltd. v. Warehousemen and Miscellaneous Drivers' Union Local 419 et al.* (1975), 10 OR (2d) 612 (SC); *Alumicor Limited. v. United Steel, Paper and Forestry, Rubber, Manufacturing*, 2011 ONSC 1707; *Cara Operations v. HRCE & BU, Local No. 40*, 2004 BCSC 1753, [2004] BCTC 1753; *Canadian Pacific Rail Company v. Teamsters Canada Rail Conference*, 2007 BCSC 2020; and *Cascade Aerospace Inc. v. Unifor*, 2014 BCSC 1211.

42 See Labour Law Casebook Group, supra note 1, at 418-22.

43 *D.C. Thomson and Co. Ltd. v. Deaking and Others*, [1952] 2 All ER 361 (CA); and *Prince Rupert Grain Ltd. v. Grain Workers' Union, Local 333*, 2002 BCCA 641.

44 See, e.g., Ontario *Labour Relations Act, 1995*, supra note 3, s. 83.

45 *Consolidated-Bathurst Packaging*, [1982] 3 CLRBR 324.

46 *Hersees of Woodstock Ltd. v. Goldstein et al.*, [1963] 2 OR 81 (Ont. CA).

47 See, e.g., *Prince Rupert Grain Ltd. v. Grain Workers' Union, Local 333*, supra note 43; *Telus Communications Inc. v. Telecommunications Workers Union*, 2005 ABQB 719; and *Brookfield Properties v. Hoath et al.*, 2010 ONSC 6187. B. Adell, "Secondary Picketing After Pepsi: What's Clear and What Isn't?" (2003) 10 *Canadian Labour and Employment Law Journal* 135.

48 *Courts of Justice Act*, RSO 1990, c. C.43, s. 102.

49 *Cancoil Thermal Corp. v. Abbott*, 2004 CanLII 2565 (Ont. SC); *Aramark Canada Ltd. v. Keating*, [2002] OJ No. 3505 (SC); but see also *Industrial Hardwood Products (1996) Ltd. v. International Wood and Allied Workers of Canada, Local 2693* (2001), 52 OR (3d) 694 (Ont. CA); *Ogden Entertainment Services v. United Steelworkers of America, Local 440* (1998), 159 DLR (4th) 340 (Ont. CA); *Canada Post Corporation v. PSAC/UPCE Local 60100*, 2009 NBQB 38; and *Brookfield Properties v. Hoath et al.*, 2010 ONSC 6187.

50 See, e.g., Alberta *Labour Relations Code*, supra note 29, s. 69; and Ontario *Labour Relations Act, 1995*, supra note 3, s. 42.

51 Ontario *Labour Relations Act, 1995*, supra note 3.

52 *Humpty Dumpty Foods*, [1977] 2 CLRBR 248 (Ont. LRB).

53 *Garda Security Screening Inc.*, 2011 CIRB 593; and *Hilton Villa Care Centre Ltd v. Hospital Employees' Union*, 2012 CanLII 68311 (BCLRB).

54 D. Doorey, "University of Windsor's Latest Tactics Raise Intriguing Legal Questions," *Law of Work* (blog), accessed November 1, 2016, http://lawofwork.ca/?p=7564.

55 See, e.g., BC *Labour Relations Code*, supra note 14, s. 45(2); Alberta *Labour Relations Code*, supra note 29, s. 147(3); and *Canada Labour Code*, supra note 26, s. 50(b).

56 See, e.g., Ontario *Labour Relations Act, 1995*, supra note 3, s. 40; and Alberta *Labour Relations Code*, supra note 29, s. 93. For a discussion of a voluntary interest arbitration involving Air Canada and one of its unions, see: D. Doorey, "Explaining the Union's Win in the Air Canada 'Final Offer' Arbitration," *Law of Work* (blog), accessed November 1, 2016, http://lawofwork.ca/?p=3842.

57 *Canada Labour Code*, supra note 26, ss. 79(1) and (2).

58 See, e.g., Manitoba *Labour Relations Act*, supra note 16, s. 106; NS *Trade Union Act*, RSNS 1989, c. 475, s. 72.

59 See, e.g., Ontario *Police Services Act*, RSO 1990, c. P-15; Ontario *Fire Protection and Prevention Act, 1997*, SO 1997, c. 4; and Ontario *Hospital Labour Disputes Arbitration Act*, RSO 1990, c. H.14.

60 See *Toronto Transit Commission Labour Dispute Resolution Act*, SO 2011, c. 2 (banning strikes by all employees of the TTC); *Protecting Air Service Act*, SC 2012, c. 2 (banning strikes by employees of Air Canada); and *Restoring Mail Delivery for Canadians Act*, SC 2011, c. 17 (banning strikes by employees of Canada Post).

61 See, e.g., *Ambulance Services Collective Bargaining Act, 2001*, SO 2001, c. 10.

62 The Saskatchewan *Public Service Essential Services Act*, SS 2008, c. P-42.2 restricted strikes by health care workers and allowed the employer to unilaterally decide which employees were essential. This legislation was struck down as a violation of the Charter's guarantee of freedom of association in *Saskatchewan Federation of Labour v. Saskatchewan*, supra note 7.

63 See the discussion in *Saskatchewan Federation of Labour v. Saskatchewan*, supra note 7.

64 See, e.g., *Ontario v. Ontario Public Service Employees Union*, 2002 CanLII 28309 (Ont. LRB).

65 See, e.g., *York University Labour Disputes Resolution Act, 2009*, SO 2009, c. 1; and *Restoring Mail Delivery for Canadians Act*, supra note 60.

66 See D. Doorey, "Canadian Government Slammed (Yet Again) by ILO for Back to Work Legislation in Canada

Post Dispute," *Law of Work* (blog), accessed November 1, 2016, http://lawofwork.ca/?p=6463.

67   *Saskatchewan Federation of Labour v. Saskatchewan*, supra note 7. For example, a Charter challenge has been launched against legislation prohibiting TTC workers from striking.

68   See S. Johnson, "First Contract Arbitration: Effects on Bargaining and Work Stoppages" (economic research paper, Wilfrid Laurier University, 2008), http://lcerpa.org/public/papers/LCERPA_2009-01.pdf ; C. Riddell, "Labor Law and Reaching a First Collective Agreement: Evidence from a Quasi-Experimental Set of Reforms in Ontario" (2013) 52:3 *Industrial Relations* 702; and J. Sexton, "First Contract Arbitration: A Canadian Invention" (1991) 1 *Labour Arbitration Yearbook* 231.

69   Weiler, *Reconcilable Differences*, supra note 36, at 53.

70   For a review of each jurisdiction's model, see Adams, *Canadian Labour Law*, supra note 23, part 3, s. 13(iii)(g).

71   Manitoba *Labour Relations Act*, supra note 16, s. 87 (access is possible 90 days after certification and failed

conciliation); and Quebec *Labour Code*, supra note 29, s. 93.1.

72   Ontario *Labour Relations Act, 1995*, supra note 3, s. 43. See, e.g., *United Food and Commercial Workers Canada, Local 175 v. Park Lane Chevrolet Cadillac*, 2016 CanLII 65529 (Ont. LRB). See also BC *Labour Relations Code*, supra note 14, s. 55; and *Yarrow Lodge Ltd.* (1993), 21 CLRBR (2d) 1 (BCLRB).

73   *Restoring Mail Delivery for Canadians Act*, supra note 60, s. 11(3).

74   Ibid., s. 11(2).

75   *Saskatchewan Federation of Labour v. Saskatchewan*, supra note 7. See also the comments of Arbitrator Kevin Burkett in the interest arbitration award in *City of Toronto and Toronto Professional Firefighters Association* (2013), noting that legislation that restricts arbitral discretion is constitutionally questionable: http://lawofwork.ca/wp-content/uploads/2013/06/Award-June-2013.pdf.

Timeline of Collective Bargaining Between the City of Toronto and Canadian Union of Public Employees, Local 416, 2011 to 2012

In 2011, a very tense round of collective bargaining began in the City of Toronto. The previous round of bargaining had resulted in a 40-day strike that stopped garbage collection and other public services. This strike became a focal point in the 2010 mayoral election that saw Rob Ford elected mayor, replac-

ing Mayor David Miller. One of Mayor Ford's campaign promises was that he would "contract out" the collection of garbage to a lower-cost private company and fire hundreds of the city's employees currently employed as garbage collectors. The collective agreement in effect in 2010 included a clause preventing contracting out of city services that would result in the dismissal of any employee with ten years or more of service. This language was an obstacle to Mayor Ford's promise to contract out garbage collection and, therefore, amending that language became the city's primary bargaining objective.

The following is a blow-by-blow chronological account of the 2011 to 2012 round of collective bargaining between the City of Toronto and the Canadian Union of Public Employees (CUPE), Local 416 as reported at the time on Professor David Doorey's *Law of Work* blog.[1]

1.   Summer 2009: A 40-Day Strike

Unionized inside and outside workers of the City of Toronto engage in a 40-day strike during the summer of 2009. City Councillor Rob Ford is a vocal advocate during the strike for the Liberal government to enact back-to-work legislation to end the work stoppage.[2] The strike is eventually resolved with an agreement giving the unionized workers a modest raise of between 1.75 and 2.25 percent over three years. The new agreement expires on December 31, 2011. A controversial "sick-day bank" is to be phased out over time. Language that has been in the collective agreement for decades limiting contracting out of public services if doing so will cause a layoff of permanent workers remains in the agreement. That language reads as follows:

> No permanent employee with ten (10) years of seniority shall lose his employment as a result of contracting out or privatization. Employees affected as a result of contracting out shall have access to the Redeployment provisions of Article 28 and the Layoff and Recall provisions of Article 29 ...
>
> The City confirms that during the term of this Collective Agreement and any extension by law, there shall be no new contracting out of work of the Local 416 bargaining unit resulting directly or indirectly in the layoff or loss of employment of permanent employees.

2.   Spring/Summer 2010: The Mayoral Campaign

The mayoral campaign heats up, with most candidates, including Rob Ford, saying they will contract out city services, especially garbage collection, if elected. Ford's website claims that

---

1   See D. Doorey, "Anatomy of a Work Stoppage?" *Law of Work* (blog) http://lawofwork.ca/?p=4495. The entries were edited for brevity in this summary.

2   "McGuinty Not Prepared to Order T.O. Workers Back," *CTV News*, July 8, 2009, http://toronto .ctvnews.ca/mcguinty-not-prepared-to-order-t-o-workers-back-1.414829.

contracting out will save the city "$20 million dollars a year." Also, he promises that if he is elected mayor "taxpayers can have the confidence their garbage collectors won't go on unnecessary strikes." He makes no promises that his government would not instigate a lockout or impose collective agreement terms if collective bargaining reaches an impasse.

3. October 25, 2010: Rob Ford Elected Mayor

Rob Ford is elected mayor of Toronto on a promise to "stop the gravy train" and contract out city services, among other campaign pledges.[3]

4. May 17, 2011: Council Vote

Toronto City Council votes 32 to 13 to contract out garbage collection west of Yonge Street, and consequently to fire some 300 city employees.[4] Mayor Ford claims that savings from contracting out this work will save the city $10 million per year. The city calculates the estimated savings at $7 million per year, while other groups suggest the city is considerably inflating the numbers.

5. October 4, 2011: Collective Bargaining Officially Begins to Renew the Collective Agreement

The formal bargaining begins when one side serves the other with a letter called a notice to bargain. The city serves this notice to the union on October 4. The city claims that its priorities in bargaining are as follows:[5]

- to obtain necessary improvements to modernize its collective agreements to ensure it has the ability to effectively deliver its core services to the public
- to change costly and restrictive collective agreement provisions that hinder the effective management of the city
- to achieve cost containment measures in order to be able to continue to provide its services in the future

6. October to December 2011: Collective Bargaining

The parties engage in some largely unproductive bargaining sessions. No one expects the parties to reach an early collective agreement given that the mayor and to a lesser degree his allies on the employer's Employee and Labour Relations Committee have staked their political credibility on their promise to eliminate or amend the job security provisions in the collective agreement to permit wide-scale contracting out of bargaining unit jobs.

7. December 1, 2011: City Council Rejects a Motion to Require That the Full Council Approve a Lockout

Councillor John Filion files a motion at council that would require that any decision by the city to either lock out or *unilaterally amend the existing terms and conditions of employment* be approved by the full council rather than just the small Employee and Labour Relations Committee, which comprised mostly Rob Ford supporters. The motion fails by a margin of 19 to 18.[6] This means that

---

3   "Rob Ford Elected Mayor of Toronto," *CBC News*, October 25, 2010, http://www.cbc.ca/news/canada/toronto/rob-ford-elected-mayor-of-toronto-1.870381.

4   "Council Votes in Favour of Privatized Garbage Pickup," *CP24*, May 17, 2011, http://www.cp24.com/council-votes-in-favour-of-privatized-garbage-pickup-1.645230.

5   City of Toronto, "HR Facts," http://www1.toronto.ca/wps/portal/contentonly?vgnextoid=8f3ce03bb8d1e310VgnVCM10000071d60f89RCRD.

6   D. Doorey, "City of Toronto Rejects Motion to Require Council Approval of a Lockout of Its Employees," *Law of Work* (blog), accessed November 16, 2016, http://lawofwork.ca/?p=4308.

the Employee and Labour Relations Committee has the power to lock out all of the city's employees without having to take the issue to the full council. The motion foreshadows for the first time that the city may be considering the possibility of unilaterally amending the terms of the collective agreement once the lawful strike/lockout date is reached, a weapon available to the employer (as discussed in Chapter 11) but hardly ever used by a government employer.

8. December 15, 2011: The City Requests That a Conciliation Officer Be Appointed

In order to get to a legal strike or lockout position, government conciliation—an attempt by a professional mediator assigned by the government to get the parties to a deal—must first be exhausted as explained in Chapter 11. The city requests on December 15 that the government appoint a conciliation officer. The countdown to a legal strike/lockout date has now begun.

9. January 2012: Public Exchanges in the Media Are Designed to Influence Public Opinion

In public sector collective bargaining especially, influencing public opinion is a normal part of the bargaining strategy. Each side will claim that it has the public interest in mind and that the other side is being unreasonable and putting those interests at risk. These media campaigns are predictable and largely vacuous, but they can influence public perceptions that in turn can influence relative bargaining power. Throughout the early winter of 2012, both sides along with city politicians engage in public accusations and commentary in the media.

10. January 12, 2012: The City Is Eager to Get to a Legal Strike/Lockout Date

Less than one month after requesting a conciliation officer, the city now informs the minister of labour that it believes bargaining is at an impasse. The next step is for the minister of labour to issue a "no board report" pursuant to section 79(2)(b) of the Ontario *Labour Relations Act, 1995*.[7] A no board report is a step in the process leading to a legal strike and lockout position that involves the minister indicating that further conciliation, in the form of a conciliation board, will not be ordered. In theory, the minister could elect more conciliation with a three-person board (section 79(2)(a)) if that could help get a deal, but that option is virtually never exercised. Seventeen days after the no-board report, the parties will be in position to lawfully strike or lockout, or the employer can unilaterally impose its final offer that was put to the union.

11. January 13, 2012: Union Proposes a Zero Wage Increase Package

The union proposes to settle the collective agreement by agreeing to a wage freeze for the entire term of the new collective agreement. The union is hoping this strategy will put the city on the defensive. No one can claim now the workers are being greedy by offering to accept a loss of real income over three years. Zero percent is less than the national average in the public or private sector, and less than the cost of living. Assuming that the union would have bargained at least a cost-of-living raise, this saves the employer in the range of $10 million per year for the next three years. In normal circumstances, the employer would be able to accept this offer, call it a win, and move on without a work stoppage for another three years. But Mayor Ford has promised his supporters more. He promised he would fire some 7,000 out of 50,000 city employees and replace them with workers employed by third-party contractors. A wage freeze does not achieve this objective,

---

7 *Labour Relations Act, 1995*, SO 1995, c. 1, Sch. A.

because to contract out so many jobs, the city needs revisions to the contracting-out provisions in the collective agreement.

12. January 16, 2012: National Post Doubts Whether the City Can Persuade the Public of the Need for a Work Stoppage

National Post columnists suggest that if the city rejects the wage freeze offer put forward by the union, and a strike or lockout ensues, the public may turn against the city.[8] *National Post* is not a union-friendly publication.

13. January 16, 2012: City Counteroffers, Calls Union Wage Freeze a "Ploy"

As expected, the city negotiators reject the union's offer of a three-year wage freeze. The chair of the employer's bargaining committee, Councillor Doug Holyday (a Rob Ford ally), tells the media that the offer is just a "ploy." The city counteroffers with a "modest lump sum payment" and a concession: the removal of the no contracting out clause is taken off the table in part.[9] Here we have a situation where the employer is responding to a union offer to accept a wage freeze by offering to pay a bonus.

The city says it would agree to keep the job security clause intact for workers with 25 years or more of service. So we see movement. The old language protects "permanent employees with 10 years of seniority" from job loss caused by contracting out of their jobs. The city's new proposal would permit contracting out of bargaining unit jobs leading to the termination of any employee with less than 25 years' service. The city is attempting a classic divide-and-conquer strategy, hoping that it can get sufficient support of employees with greater than 25 years' service to get its proposal ratified in a majority rules ratification vote. It is counting on more senior employees being willing to vote in their interests, even if it means junior employees will lose their jobs.

14. January 18, 2012: No-Board Report Is Issued, and a Strike/Lockout Deadline Is Set

As expected, the minister issues a no-board report, starting the countdown to a work stoppage.[10] The relevant section of the *Labour Relations Act, 1995* that governs this process is section 79(2). Part (b) says that "14 days" after the no-board report, the parties are in a legal strike or lockout (it works out to 17 days because of the way the rules interpret how days are calculated), putting the legal strike/lockout time as midnight on Sunday, February 5. That is the time at which the employer can lock out the workers or the workers can strike. It is also the date on which the city could unilaterally change the terms of employment, such as by cutting wages and benefits.

By way of recap on where the parties stand, the union has offered to roll over the terms of the existing agreement for another three years with no increase in pay or benefits. The employer has offered a lump-sum payment to workers, and the abolition of the job security provisions for all employees except those with greater than 25 years' service.

---

8   "Posted Toronto Political Panel: Wage Freeze Is Bold Gambit," *National Post*, January 16, 2012, http:// news.nationalpost.com/posted-toronto/posted-toronto-political-panel-wage-freeze-is-bold-gambit.

9   D. Rider, "City Offers Longest-Serving Workers Job Security," *Toronto Star*, January 16, 2012, https:// www.thestar.com/news/city_hall/2012/01/16/city_offers_longestserving_workers_job_security.html.

10   D. Dale, "Toronto City Workers Lockout Possible in 17 Days After 'No Board' Report," *Toronto Star*, January 20, 2012," https://www.thestar.com/news/city_hall/2012/01/20/toronto_city_workers_lock-out_possible_in_17_days_after_no_board_report.html.

15. January 19 to 30, 2012: Little News, Parties Continue Talks

After the no-board report is issued, things quiet down for a while. The union's negotiator (Mark Ferguson) tells the media that talks are continuing and that the tone of bargaining has changed in a positive way:[11]

> "For the first time, the city was actually willing, and open, and engaging in the discussions that they had with us. If this tone continues through the bargaining process, that is a very good thing," Ferguson said, calling the shift "a major breakthrough."

We are in the calm before the storm ahead of the February 5 deadline.

16. January 30, 2012: Work Stoppage Deadline Is Days Away, Parties Continue to Bargain

There has been little word from the negotiators, other than the union's spokesperson, who says that talks are moving along. He also expresses unhappiness about the city's unwillingness to promise that it will not lock out workers once the lockout date (February 5) is reached. The city is saying it will assess the situation at that time.

17. February 3, 2012: City Says It Will Unilaterally Alter Conditions of Employment Starting Monday Morning

On February 3, the city tables what it called its "final offer" and publishes a memo outlining its strategy. Nothing is new in terms of the proposals: the union offered to roll over the agreement with a three-year wage freeze, and the city said it would rather give a small pay raise to the employees who remain after they have fired hundreds of workers. So we have the odd situation of an employer offering pay raises, and the union saying it does not want a raise.

The more interesting clarification in the memo is the city's plan to unilaterally impose its final offer on employees once it is in a legal lockout position (Sunday at 12:01 a.m.). Here is what the memo says:

> Given the lack of a settlement and the distance between the parties, I have concluded, in consultation with the City's Executive Director of Human Resources, my Senior Management Team, the City Solicitor's Office, and our external legal counsel, that it would be inappropriate to delay the necessary changes to the collective agreement if we are unable to negotiate a new agreement. To be clear, the Labour Relations Act, 1995 provides the City of Toronto with the ability to implement new terms of employment once the negotiations have broken down and after the 17-day No Board period has expired. Based on those consultations, I have decided, if we do not reach a new agreement by the deadline, that it would be appropriate and necessary to exercise this option.

As explained in Chapter 11, the law gives the employer the legal right to unilaterally impose its final offer once the parties are in a legal strike and lockout position. This strategy has rarely, if ever, been adopted by a government employer.

One reason why the strategy of imposing contract terms is rarely used by employers is that unions and employees often have an obvious countermeasure: they can refuse the terms and begin a strike. That strike can be a complete work stoppage, or it can be a coordinated work-to-rule, partial strike, or rotating strike in which different groups of workers walk off the job at different times. The strategy of imposing contract terms only works if employees are unprepared or unwilling to strike. In this case though, the union had chosen the risky strategy of not taking a strike vote,

---

11 Ibid.

which is required in Ontario as a precondition to a lawful strike. It did so because it wanted to demonstrate to the public that it had no intention of engaging in another work stoppage, and perhaps also because it was not sure what the result of a strike vote would be. In any event, having not taken a strike vote, the union had no weapon available to resist the employer's threat that it would impose its final offer.

18. February 5, 2012: Parties Announce Tentative Deal After All-Night Bargaining

At the last moment, after an all-night bargaining session, the parties reach a tentative four-year collective agreement (which still needs to be ratified by the workers). A *Toronto Star* article published the next day under the headline "Strike Averted" described some of the early details.[12] Note how the headline inaccurately claims that a "strike" was averted, even though the union had insisted from day one that it would not strike and in fact had not even taken the required strike vote. Rather, what was averted was the employer unilaterally imposing its final offer. Pay attention to how language is used in reporting on collective bargaining. For example, often the media call a union proposal a "demand" and an employer proposal an "offer." Does this language suggest that the union is the aggressor in the negotiations? Is that an accurate description of this round of bargaining?

A key change in the collective agreement language relates to contracting out. The new collective agreement permits the employer to contract out bargaining unit work provided only that it does not lead to the dismissal of city employees with 15 or more years' seniority. The employer opened bargaining by insisting on the removal of the clause prohibiting contracting out, then later improved its offer by suggesting that the job security provisions apply only to workers with more than 25 years' service. In the final deal, the city came down to 15 years. In exchange for the concession that would permit the employer to dismiss union members with less than 15 years' service, the employees who will not lose their jobs will receive a 6 percent raise over the four years.

19. February 13, 2012: Unionized Workers Ratify a New Four-Year Agreement

Under our system of labour law, any deal reached by the union's bargaining committee is subject to ratification by the employees governed by the collective agreement. This requirement appears in section 44 of the *Labour Relations Act, 1995*. CUPE held that vote on February 13 and announced that the proposed agreement reached on February 5 had been ratified by a majority of voters. Therefore, a new collective agreement would be in effect for four years, until December 31, 2015.

20. Post-Script: August 2012: Private Garbage Collection Begins in Parts of Toronto

Once the new collective agreement language was in effect, the city moved to contract out garbage collection. The city decided to dismiss hundreds of its own employees and to contract out their work to a private garbage disposal company in the western part of Toronto.

---

12   D. Rider, "Strike Averted: City and Outside Workers Reach Tentative Agreement," *Toronto Star*, February 5, 2012, https://www.thestar.com/news/gta/2012/02/05/strike_averted_city_and_outside_workers_reach_tentative_agreement.html.

The Collective Agreement

I. Introduction

The successful conclusion of collective bargaining is a **collective agreement**, which is a contract between a union and an employer that governs working conditions of employees in jobs that fall within the bargaining unit that the union is legally entitled to represent. As we learned in Chapter 10, unions and employers are afforded considerable latitude in terms of the scope and content of the collective agreements they negotiate. This freedom should not be confused with government indifference to the substance of collective agreements. In fact, governments inject public policy concerns into collective agreements through various legislative mechanisms discussed in this chapter. In addition, labour arbitrators have played a significant role in giving meaning to collective agreement language. A vast body of arbitral case law spanning more than half a century functions in a similar manner to the common law of the individual employment contract. In this chapter, we introduce some important rules of collective agreement interpretation that have played an important role in shaping the rights and duties of unions and unionized employers and employees.

---

collective agreement: A contract between an employer (or employers) and a trade union (or trade unions) that sets out the conditions of employment for a group of employees.

II. The Law and Collective Agreements

Before collective bargaining legislation was enacted in Canada, a collective agreement between a union and an employer could not be enforced in the courts unless it was incorporated into the individual employment contracts of employees. Unions, as unincorporated associations, had no legal status to enter into binding contracts and therefore could not sue or be sued for breach of contract. Moreover, since the parties to collective agreements were employers and unions, individual employees were not able to sue for breach of the agreement in their own right.[1] This lack of legal status did not render collective agreements meaningless in the *common law regime*. The agreements created **workplace norms** (see Chapter 3) that influenced workplace behaviour, and a violation of a collective agreement by the employer would sometimes provoke a strike by aggrieved workers.

It was not until the mid-1940s that Canadian law developed a statutory collective bargaining model that gave legal force to collective agreements. PC 1003 (1944) (see Chapter 6), defined a *collective agreement* as "an agreement in writing between an employer or an employers' organization and a trade union or an employees' organization on the other hand containing provisions with reference to rates of pay, hours of work or other working conditions."[2] Section 10(5) of PC 1003 also provided the following:

> Every party to a collective agreement and every employee upon whom a collective agreement is made binding by these regulations shall do everything he is, by the collective agreement, required to do and shall abstain from doing anything he is, by the collective agreement, required not to do.[3]

Similar provisions exist in modern collective bargaining statutes across Canada that render collective agreements legally binding contracts on the parties to the contract (unions and employers) as well as the employees in the bargaining unit.[4] PC 1003 also required that collective agreements include a dispute resolution procedure to deal with any allegations that the collective agreement has been violated without a work stoppage and other rules relating to the content of collective agreements.[5] This basic model persists today in Canada in various forms.

Most of the common law employment contract doctrines we considered in the chapters on the common law regime in the companion volume to this text—including repudiation, fundamental breach, constructive dismissal, and summary dismissal—do not apply to collective agreements. This much was made clear in the 1975 Supreme Court of Canada case of *McGavin Toastmaster Ltd. v. Ainscough*.[6] In that case, unionized employees engaged in an illegal strike and the employer responded by closing the factory. The union, on behalf of the employees, claimed severance pay as required by the collective agreement. The employer argued that the employees were not entitled to severance pay because they had quit by repudiating the contract (explained in Chapter 5). The Supreme Court of Canada ruled that the common law concept of repudiation of contract did not apply in the *collective bargaining regime*:

> The reality is, and has been for many years now, throughout Canada, that individual relationships as between employer and employee have meaning only at the hiring stage and even then there are qualifications which arise by reason of union security clauses in collective agreements. The common law as it applies to individual employment contracts is no longer relevant to employer-employee relations governed by a collective agreement which, as the one involved here, deals with discharge, termination of employment, severance pay and a host of other matters that have been negotiated between union and company.[7]

---

workplace norms: Norms or expectations that arise in a workplace as a result of past practices or relationships that can influence behaviour at work, even though they are not codified in contracts or statutes.

The legal rules that govern collective agreements sometimes borrow from common law concepts and reasoning, but they comprise a distinct legal regime that we will explore over the next few chapters.

III. State Regulation of Collective Agreement Terms

Governments regulate the content of collective agreements in a variety of ways. We will consider three: (1) mandatory terms; (2) default terms; and (3) prohibited terms.

A. Common Mandatory Collective Agreement Terms

As noted in Chapter 10, Canadian collective bargaining law generally grants unions and employers wide discretion to determine the content of collective agreements, but that discretion is not unlimited. Some terms are required by statutes to be included in all collective agreements (**mandatory collective agreement terms**). Table 12.1 describes some common mandatory collective agreement terms found in Canadian statutes, although other terms are required by some but not other jurisdictions.[8] A **union recognition clause** is needed to clarify which employees the collective agreement covers. It takes the same form as the bargaining unit description we considered in Chapter 8. In fact, the description in the certification issued by the labour relations board that initially grants the union bargaining rights will often just be transposed into the collective agreement and become the recognition clause.

TABLE 12.1 Mandatory Collective Agreement Terms

Collective Agreement Term Required by Statute	What the Term Does
Union recognition clause	Describes the bargaining unit that the collective agreement covers
No strike or lockout clause	Prohibits strikes and lockouts during the term of the collective agreement
Mandatory arbitration clause	Requires that all disputes arising during the collective agreement over the interpretation, application, or enforcement of the agreement be referred to binding labour arbitration
Mandatory union security (only in Manitoba) clause	Requires that the employer deduct union dues from the wages of all bargaining unit employees and remit this amount to the union
Mandatory "just cause" for discipline or dismissal clause (only in British Columbia and Manitoba)	Requires a clause providing that the employer must have "just cause" to discipline or terminate the employment contract of bargaining unit employees

The prohibition on strikes and lockouts during a collective agreement, a distinctive feature of the Canadian collective bargaining model, is implemented by a "no strike or lockout clause" that is required by statute to be included in every Canadian collective agreement.[9] Labour arbitrators can order damages for breach of these clauses caused by a mid-contract strike or lockout. Since mid-contract disputes cannot be settled by strikes or lockouts, an alternative dispute resolution model is needed. The model chosen by Canadian governments was **labour arbitration**, and so every collective bargaining statute in Canada also requires that collective agreements include a

---

mandatory collective agreement term: A term required by statute to be included in every collective agreement. If no such term is included, the statute reads a term into the agreement.

union recognition clause: A clause in a collective agreement that defines the scope of the jobs that are covered by the agreement.

labour arbitration: A binding dispute resolution process used to resolve disputes involving alleged breaches of collective agreements.

clause requiring that disputes relating to the application, interpretation, and enforcement of the agreement be referred to binding labour arbitration.[10] This requirement takes collective agreement disputes out of the courts and into the special world of labour arbitration, which we explore over the next two chapters.

Some provinces require by statute the inclusion of terms that are usually bargained into collective agreements anyway, to avoid bargaining impasses and conflict over these issues. For example, in Manitoba, the *Labour Relations Act* requires that all collective agreements include a **union dues check-off** clause.[11] Other jurisdictions include a default union dues clause provision, as explained below. The BC and Manitoba labour relations statutes require collective agreements to include a **just cause provision**, which requires employers to have a valid reason to discipline or dismiss employees (see Chapter 23 in the companion volume). Other jurisdictions do not require just cause provisions, but unions and employers nevertheless almost always agree to include them in the collective agreement.

B. Default Collective Agreement Terms

A **default contract clause** is one that is read into a contract, unless the parties agree otherwise, or that is read in provided that one party insists on its inclusion.[12] An important example found in many Canadian collective bargaining statutes relates to union dues clauses. In Chapter 6, we considered the famous case of *Ford Motor Company v. United Automobile Workers Union* (Box 6.3) that involved the resolution of a bargaining dispute about the union security clause to be included in a collective agreement. The union wanted a clause requiring both mandatory union membership and union dues check-off, whereas the employer wanted neither. Justice Ivan Rand was appointed to resolve the dispute and decided in favour of a clause that required mandatory union dues check-off, since all employees benefit from the collective agreement, but not mandatory union membership.[13] That trade-off became known as the "Rand Formula."

The Rand Formula is supported (indirectly) in Ontario, Newfoundland and Labrador, and the federal jurisdiction by legislation that creates a default union dues check-off clause.[14] For example, consider the provision in section 47(1) of the Ontario *Labour Relations Act, 1995*:

> [W]here a trade union that is the bargaining agent for employees in a bargaining unit so requests, there shall be included in the collective agreement between the trade union and the employer of the employees a provision requiring the employer to deduct from the wages of each employee in the unit affected by the collective agreement, whether or not the employee is a member of the union, the amount of the regular union dues and to remit the amount to the trade union, forthwith.[15]

This provision effectively grants the union the right to decide whether it wants a union dues check-off clause to be included. The employer can attempt to bargain something different, but it is an unfair labour practice for it to insist on language other than that found in the default statutory language if the union wants the clause included.[16] Similarly, although unions obviously prefer an automatic dues check-off model of the type required in the default clause, if the bargaining unit employees wanted no automatic union dues clause or one requiring employees to personally authorize dues deduction (which is a requirement in several provinces[17]), then they could instruct their union to bargain such a clause. Such changes are possible because the statute does

---

union dues check-off: A "union security" clause whereby all members of a bargaining unit must pay union dues and employers must "check-off" these dues from workers' wages and remit them to the union.

just cause provision: A term in a collective agreement between a union and an employer that requires that the employer demonstrate "just cause," or a good business reason, to discipline or dismiss an employee.

default contract clause: A term that must be included in a contract (including a collective agreement) unless the contracting parties agree otherwise.

not impose a specific union dues check-off clause; instead, it creates a default clause that must be included if the union insists. The purpose is to avoid industrial conflict about union dues check-offs of the sort that led to the original Ford Motor Company dispute.

Another default clause provision found in Canadian collective bargaining legislation deals with the minimum length of collective agreements. In the common law regime, an employer and employee can agree to any length of fixed-term contract, or they can agree to an indefinite term contract of no predetermined length. There is less discretion in the collective bargaining regime. Governments want a minimum period of peace in a unionized workplace during which there can be no work stoppages. Therefore, since it is unlawful to strike or lockout during a collective agreement, all jurisdictions impose a minimum collective agreement term of at least one year from the date the agreement commences "to operate."[18] The parties can agree to a term that is longer than one year, but if they agree to less than one year, or do not include a duration clause at all, the statutes read in a one-year term.[19]

The law requires a defined end date in order to identify the "open periods" during which applications to displace existing unions (union raid) or to decertify the union (see Chapter 15) can be filed. As discussed in Chapter 8, an open period usually commences during the final few months of a collective agreement. The case discussed in Box 12.1 is instructive because it demonstrates the wide scope of government regulation of the unionization and collective bargaining process; it involves a remedial certification, a **final offer vote**, the application of mandatory collective agreement terms, an **open period**, and an application for termination of a union's bargaining rights. The United Steelworkers of America obtained bargaining rights for the group of employees by way of **remedial certification**, after the employer committed serious unfair labour practices (see Chapter 9).

BOX 12.1 » CASE LAW HIGHLIGHT

Minimum Collective Agreement Duration

United Steelworkers of America v. Bennett Chevrolet Geo Oldsmobile Cadillac Ltd.
1999 CanLII 19491 (Ont. LRB)

Key Facts: After the remedial certification order on April 22, 1998, the parties began negotiations for a first collective agreement. Negotiations stalled in October 1998, and Bennett Chevrolet requested a final offer vote on the last offer it had given the union. That offer included a one-year term clause beginning on April 22, 1998 (the date of certification), and concluding on April 21, 1999. The vote was held on November 3, 1998, and a majority of employees voted in favour of the collective agreement. The parties signed the new collective agreement on November 25, 1998. On March 1, 1999, approximately six months after the final offer vote, a group of employees filed an application to terminate the bargaining rights of the union (see

Chapter 15). The union applied to the Ontario Labour Relations Board, arguing that the decertification application was not "timely" because it did not fall within the final three months of the collective agreement, which is the open period during which a termination application can be filed for a one-year collective agreement in Ontario (see Chapter 15). The union argued that the collective agreement had only been "in operation" since November 1998, when the parties executed it, and must therefore operate until November 24, 1999, to satisfy the mandatory minimum one-year requirement in the statute. The mere fact that the term clause was made retroactive to the certification date does not mean that the agreement was actually "in operation" from that date.

Issue: Was the employees' application for termination of the union's bargaining rights "timely"?

---

final offer vote: A provision found in collective bargaining legislation that entitles an employer to have the last offer it presented to the union's negotiating team be put to a ballot of employees. Employers can only exercise this right once per round of bargaining.

open period: A period of time defined in a collective bargaining statute during which a union may apply to displace another union as the representative of a group of employees, or during which unionized employees may file an application to "decertify" the union.

remedial certification: An order by a labour relations board certifying a union that may not have established that it has majority employee support as a remedy for seriously unlawful acts by the employer—i.e., convincing employees that supporting a union could cost them their jobs.

Decision: No. Parties are capable of making a collective agreement retroactive to a date earlier than the contract is actually executed. However, in this case, there was no evidence that any of the contract's terms were applied retroactively back to April 22, 1998. The employer did not start to apply the collective agreement terms until November 25, 1998, after the parties had signed the contract. Section 58 of the Ontario *Labour Relations* *Act, 1995* requires that a collective agreement be "in operation" for at least one year. The labour relations board ruled that the actual start date was November 25, 1998, and therefore it read in a one-year contract term, which meant the contract did not end until November 24, 1999. With that as the end date, the application for termination of the union's bargaining rights did not fall within the open period, and it was dismissed.

C. Prohibited Collective Agreement Terms

Some types of collective agreement terms are prohibited altogether by collective bargaining or other statutes. An obvious example is terms that violate statutes, such as human rights, employment standards, or criminal law statutes.[20] Unions and employers are not exempt from the general public laws that apply to everyone else.

IV. Sources of Collective Agreement Terms and Rules of Interpretation

In Chapter 8 in the companion volume, we considered the sources of individual (non-union) employment contract terms. Three potential sources were identified: (1) expressed contract terms (oral or written); (2) implied contract terms; and (3) ancillary contract terms. We can use the same basic categories to describe the sources of collective agreement terms.

A. Expressed Collective Agreement Terms

In Chapters 8 and 9 in the companion volume, we observed that individual (non-union) employment contracts are often short and sparse in detail. Therefore, implied contract terms play a significant role in the common law regime. Employers usually prefer not to include too much detail in written employment contracts, because judges have conferred broad managerial discretion on employers through the device of standardized implied terms. Recall that in the non-union sector, employers usually draft employment contracts with their own economic interests in mind, and employees infrequently engage in negotiations to vary the standard form contract.

1. Why Collective Agreements Are Usually More Extensive Than Individual Employment Contracts

Collective agreements usually contain much greater written detail than individual (non-union) employment contracts. For example, a collective agreement from 2001 between Stelco in Hamilton and the United Steelworkers Union is 373 pages, including appendixes! There are a number of reasons why collective agreements have so much more detail than individual employment contracts. First, unions employ professional negotiators trained and experienced in the art of negotiating collective agreements that prioritize employee interests. Second, unions (usually) negotiate from a position of greater bargaining strength than individual employees in the non-union setting. That power derives from the threat of a work stoppage (see Chapters 10 and 11), or at least collective non-cooperation. Consequently, it is much more difficult for an employer to simply impose its will and unilaterally set collective agreement terms in the unionized setting. Third, labour arbitrators long ago adopted a principle known as **reserved management rights** (sometimes called *residual management rights*), which encourages unions to bargain contract language that expressly restricts managerial authority.

---

reserved management rights: An interpretive principle applied in labour arbitration that presumes that unionized employers retain the basic rights to run their business as they deem fit, subject to any statutory or contractual restrictions bargained by the union. These rights are sometimes called *residual management rights*.

Reserved management rights is a principle of collective agreement interpretation applied by labour arbitrators. It holds that unionized employers generally retain the implied rights enjoyed by non-union employers to run the enterprise, subject only to statutory and contractual restrictions found in the collective agreement. Until the mid-1960s, there was a lively debate among labour arbitrators over reserved management rights. Some arbitrators, including University of Toronto law professor Bora Laskin, the future chief justice of the Supreme Court of Canada, believed that arbitrators should not be influenced by rules from the common law regime when they are interpreting collective agreements. Laskin explained this position in a 1953 decision involving Peterboro Lock Mfg. Co. Ltd. as follows:

> The introduction of a collective bargaining regime involves the acceptance by the parties of assumptions which are entirely alien to an era of individual bargaining. Hence, any attempt to measure rights and duties in employer-employee relations by reference to pre-collective bargaining standards is an attempt to re-enter a world which has ceased to exist.[21]

In the *Peterboro* case, the employer argued that absent collective agreement language limiting its right to unilaterally change how employees were paid (hourly rate or piece rate), it fell within presumed managerial prerogative to decide. Laskin rejected that argument, finding that the agreement did not grant the employer the unilateral right to decide on a "whim" how employees are paid. The "Laskin approach" required the employer to negotiate managerial prerogatives with the union rather than simply inherit them from arbitrators through the concept of reserved management rights. It was against this background that the famous arbitration case discussed in Box 12.2 came before Professor Harry Arthurs (York University), who was acting as labour arbitrator.

BOX 12.2 » CASE LAW HIGHLIGHT

Reserved Management Rights in the Collective Bargaining Regime

U.S.W.A. v. Russel Steel Ltd.
(1966), 17 LAC 253 (Arbitrator Arthurs)

Key Facts: Russel Steel decided that it no longer wanted to employ its own truck drivers for hauling services, and so it contracted with another company to provide trucks and drivers to perform these services. This is known as **contracting out** bargaining unit work. The employer's former truck drivers were offered a lower-paying job in the warehouse. The union filed a grievance and argued that the collective agreement did not confer on the employer the unilateral right to contract out work normally done by bargaining unit employees. The employer argued that absent a specific restriction on its right to contract out work, it retained that right by virtue of having the reserved right to manage the enterprise.

Issue: Did the employer violate the collective agreement by contracting out the truck driver work?

Decision: No. Arthurs dismissed the union's grievance. He noted that the case provided a classic example of "contracting out" and engaged directly the ongoing "controversy" over the reserved management rights approach in labour arbitration. In

his view, whatever the merits of the two sides of the debate, the collective agreement before him was negotiated within a "climate" of collective bargaining. At the time the parties bargained the collective agreement, that climate included a clear preference by Canadian arbitrators for the reserved rights approach to collective agreement interpretation. Therefore, the parties must have known that an arbitrator was more likely to adopt the reserved management rights approach than the "Laskin approach" and thus more likely to find that the employer can contract out work, absent a clause saying that it cannot. Arthurs wrote:

> The wide notoriety given to labour's protests against [contracting out], the almost equally wide notoriety, especially amongst experienced labour and management representatives, of the overwhelming trend of decisions, must mean that there was known to these parties at the time they negotiated the collective agreement the strong probability that an arbitrator would not find any implicit limitation on management's right to contract out. It was one thing to imply such a limitation in the early years of this

---

contracting out: A practice whereby an employer contracts work formerly performed by its own employees to a third-party business.

controversy when one could not speak with any clear certainty about the expectations of the parties; then, one might impose upon them the objective implications of the language of the agreement. It is quite another thing to attribute intentions and undertakings to them today, when they are aware, as a practical matter, of the need to specifically prohibit contracting out if they are to persuade an arbitrator of their intention to do so.

In this case, the collective agreement included no restriction on the right of the employer to contract out the trucking jobs. Therefore, the employer had the right to do so, and the grievance was dismissed.

The *Russel Steel* decision concerned a very particular set of facts, but it became the leading authority for the reserved management rights approach to collective agreement interpretation and to this day is regularly cited in arbitration decisions.[22] Reserved management rights operate similarly to implied terms in the common law regime (Chapter 9 in the companion volume); they confer a default distribution of contractual rights in favour of the employer that is subject to restrictions bargained into the collective agreement. The practical effect of reserved management rights is that unions seek to bargain extensive collective agreement language that restricts the employer's discretion to make unilateral decisions affecting bargaining unit employees.[23] For example, if a union wants to ensure that its members will not lose their jobs due to the employer contracting out work to a third party, it needs to negotiate a restriction on the employer's right to contract out bargaining unit work.[24] This example helps explain why collective agreements are sometimes so extensive and complex.

2. Common Expressed Collective Agreement Terms

As in the case of individual (non-union) employment contracts, the range of expressed, negotiated collective agreement language is limited only by statute and the creativity and interests of the parties. However, a number of standard types of provisions tend to appear regularly in Canadian collective agreements. A sample collective agreement is included as an appendix to this chapter. In addition to the mandatory collective agreement terms discussed above, most Canadian collective agreements include terms that address the areas identified in Table 12.2.

TABLE 12.2 Common Collective Agreement Terms

Type of Collective Agreement Term	What the Term Does
Management rights clause	Lists subjects over which the employer has discretion and authority to make decisions about the operation of the enterprise, subject to any restrictions appearing elsewhere in the collective agreement
Union security clause	Explains whether employees are required to become union members and/or pay union dues, and the process by which union dues are to be collected from employees
Grievance procedure clause	Describes the procedure and rules governing the filing and processing of grievances filed by employees, the union, or employer
Seniority clause	Explains how "seniority" will be calculated and what rights, entitlements, and obligations are associated with seniority
Job rights clause	Explains the rules for deciding which employees receive promotions, transfers, layoffs, and recalls
"Just cause" clause	Requires that the employer have "just cause" to discipline or dismiss a bargaining unit employee

Type of Collective Agreement Term	What the Term Does
Hours of work and overtime clause	Explains regular hours of work and any rules governing changes to those hours and the assignment and pay required for overtime
Wages, benefits, and leaves (e.g., insurance coverage, vacations, bereavement and other leaves, pensions) clauses	Describe the rates of pay and other benefits coverage and leave entitlements for employees
Duration clause	Defines the term (beginning and end) of the collective agreement

Some important differences exist between collective agreements and individual (non-union) employment contracts that are worth emphasizing. The most obvious difference is that collective agreements usually include a clause requiring the employer to have a good reason (just cause) to discipline or dismiss an employee, and there is no implied contractual term granting employers the right to dismiss employees simply by providing them with notice, as in the common law regime (see Chapter 13 in the companion volume). Therefore, collective agreements usually provide unionized employees much greater job security than do individual employment contracts. Chapter 14 will examine just cause provisions in detail.

Another difference is the importance of **seniority** in the collective bargaining regime.[25] Seniority refers to the length of time that an employee has been employed by the employer, although precise definitions vary from one agreement to the next. For example, seniority might be measured simply from the date of hire, or it might be defined as the length of time employed in the bargaining unit or in a particular department or division of the employer. Collective agreements might also explain what happens to an employee's seniority when the person temporarily leaves the bargaining unit, such as to take a leave or a temporary assignment outside of the agreement.[26] Many rights or entitlements in collective agreements are tied to seniority. For example, more senior employees may be paid at a higher rate, receive greater vacation entitlements, have first access to overtime opportunities, or be given preferential treatment in the event of promotions,[27] transfers, layoffs, and recall from layoffs.[28] Disputes about the application of seniority clauses have led to reams of labour arbitration case law over the years.[29]

Probably the most important application of seniority involves job rights when employers decide to downsize the workforce. Most Canadian collective agreements include some form of **bumping rights** that permit senior employees to "bump" junior employees if temporary or permanent layoffs take place.[30] This entitlement to bump is usually not absolute. Most collective agreements include a requirement that the senior employee possess the skills and ability to perform the job that he or she is seeking to bump into, perhaps with some training. Some agreements go further, and require the bumping employee to possess superior skills to the incumbent he or she is seeking to bump, or to be "relatively equal" to the incumbent in terms of skills or performance. The specific language used is obviously very important. A collective agreement right to bump in the event of layoffs can trigger a complex chain of bumping down through an organization.

A particularly thorny issue relates to the intersection of seniority rights in collective agreements and the duty to accommodate requirement under human rights legislation (see Chapter 29

---

seniority: A measure of an employee's length of service with an employer.

bumping rights: An entitlement found in the terms of a collective agreement that permits a more senior employee to displace a junior employee in the case of a temporary or permanent downsizing of the workforce.

in the companion volume).[31] This issue brings into tension the *regulatory regime* (human rights statutes) and the *collective bargaining regime*. The decision in Box 12.3 considers this tension.

BOX 12.3 » CASE LAW HIGHLIGHT

The Intersection of Collective Agreement Seniority Rights and the Duty to Accommodate

Chatham-Kent Children's Services v. OPSEU, Local 148
(2014), 251 LAC (4th) 313 (Arbitrator Sheehan)

Key Facts: Chatham-Kent Children's Services decided to shut its residential group homes and, as a result, an employee (Elley) was given a notice of layoff. The collective agreement permitted senior employees to bump junior employees in case of a layoff, provided that the senior employee possessed the required "skill, ability, and qualifications" for the position in which she sought to bump. Elley advised the employer that she wanted to bump into the volunteer coordinator position. Elley possessed the necessary qualifications to perform that position. However, the junior employee (Bowen) who held that position at the time suffered from a disability that affected her vision and, as a result, would likely have no position that she could bump into herself if she were displaced from the volunteer coordinator position. Bowen sought to remain in the volunteer coordinator position as a form of accommodation of her disability. The employer and union agreed to refer the dispute to a mediator-arbitrator to resolve the dispute.

Issue: Does the collective agreement entitle Elley to bump Bowen from the volunteer coordinator position even if Bowen's disability may prevent her from bumping into any other position?

Decision: Yes. The Supreme Court of Canada ruled in a decision called *Central Okanagan School District No. 23 v. Renaud** (discussed in Chapter 29 in the companion volume) that the duty to accommodate in human rights legislation requires a

balancing of the right of employees seeking accommodation and the interests of employers, unions, and other employees. The arbitrator summarized this balancing test as follows:

> Accordingly, the relevant test in assessing whether a proposed accommodation measure(s) constitutes undue hardship is whether the impact of such a measure(s) results in a *significant interference with the normal operation of the collective agreement, and the rights of employees under that collective agreement.* While it is clear that the union and other employees may have to "shoulder some of the hardship to facilitate accommodation"; if the interference with the employees' collective agreement rights is significant, then the proposed accommodation measure will be viewed as constituting undue hardship for the other employees. [Emphasis added.]

In this case, if Elley was not able to bump into the volunteer coordinator position, her only option would have been to bump into a lower classification that would result in an annual pay cut of nearly $9,000. That constituted a "significant interference" with her collective agreement rights amounting to undue hardship. Therefore, Elley was entitled to exercise her collective agreement seniority rights to bump into the volunteer coordinator position, even though that could have resulted in Bowen being laid off.

---

*   *Central Okanagan School District No. 23 v. Renaud*, [1992] 2 SCR 970.

Collective agreements define precisely what wages and benefits employees are to receive, and the employer usually has no discretion to veer from those amounts. This is another important difference between the collective bargaining and common law regimes. A non-union employer is usually within its contractual rights to give an employee a raise, introduce new benefits, or reward a hard-working employee with a bonus. Unions usually bargain restrictions on the right of employers to unilaterally decide who gets raises and bonuses. Indeed, a central objective of unions in collective bargaining is often to remove employer discretion in important decisions about wages, benefits, and job entitlements and to replace it with objective standards, such as the application of fixed wage scales and the allotment of other entitlements by seniority. An employer who tries to give an individual employee a special payment not mentioned in the agreement will almost certainly be met with a grievance alleging a collective agreement breach.

B. Implied Contract Terms

In Chapter 9 in the companion volume, we discussed the origins and development of implied terms in the common law regime, including the tests judges apply when deciding whether a term should be implied. In an example of application of the internal feedback loop discussed in Chapter 3, labour arbitrators have learned from the common law regime and applied the same or similar tests to justify the implication of implied collective agreement terms. So, for example, some arbitrators have applied the **business efficacy test** and the **officious bystander test** when asked to imply contract terms.[32] More often, arbitrators make no express reference to these tests, but they look to the "presumed intentions" of the parties in the same manner as do common law judges.

The arbitration decision described in Box 12.4 considers whether an implied term exists in the collective agreement requiring the employer to prevent harassment of its employees.[33] Such an implied term parallels the implied obligation recognized by common law judges on employers to treat employees with civility and decency and in "good faith," which we discussed in Chapter 9 in the companion volume.[34] Other implied terms recognized in the common law regime have also been recognized by labour arbitrators when interpreting collective agreements. An example is the implied obligation for employees to avoid negligent work.[35] On the other hand, important terms implied into individual (non-union) employment contracts by common law judges, such as the implied obligation to provide reasonable notice of termination, have no parallel in the collective bargaining regime. Moreover, some implied terms recognized by labour arbitrators have no equivalent in individual employment contracts, such as the implied obligation imposed on unions to take prompt actions to end illegal strikes.[36]

BOX 12.4 » CASE LAW HIGHLIGHT

Implied Duty of Fairness or Reasonableness in Exercising Management Rights

Toronto Transit Commission v. Amalgamated Transit Union
2004 CanLII 55086 (Arbitrator Shime)

Key Facts: An employee (the grievor) filed a grievance against the Toronto Transit Commission alleging that a supervisor engaged in harassment of the grievor over several years and that the employer failed to take reasonable steps to bring the harassment to an end. The grievor required medical care for anxiety and depression caused by the harassment and related workplace stress, which resulted in periods of absence from work on sick leave. The employer argued that the harassment did not occur. It also objected to the jurisdiction of the arbitrator to hear the grievance on the basis that the union had not identified a collective agreement term that had been violated, since the agreement did not include a "no harassment" clause.

Issue: Did the employer violate the collective agreement by allowing one of its supervisors to engage in prolonged harassment of an employee?

Decision: Yes. Although the collective agreement did not contain an expressed "no harassment" clause, the arbitrator ruled that an implied term required that management exercise its authority in a manner that prevents harassment of employees:

> [E]ven absent an express provision referring to managerial abuse or harassment, and apart from the management rights provision, I determine it is an implied term of the collective agreement that the work of a supervisor must be exercised in a non-abusive, non-harassing manner.

In addition to this general implied term, the arbitrator also referred specifically to collective agreement language that required protection of employees' "safety." The use of that word became the basis for implying an obligation on the employer to exercise its management rights in a manner that protects the physical and psychological safety of employees. The employer's representative (the supervisor) violated these implied terms, and the employer failed to bring the harassment to an

---

business efficacy test: An approach used by common law judges to justify implication of a contract term on the basis that the term is necessary in order to make the contract effective.

officious bystander test: An approach used by common law judges to justify implication of a contract term based on the presumed intention of the parties. The idea is that a contract term is implied if it would be obvious to an uninterested bystander that both parties intended the term to be part of the contract.

end when informed of it by the grievor and the union. A variety of remedial orders were made by the arbitrator, including orders that the employer (1) reimburse the grievor for the difference in his normal pay and the lower amount he received while on sick leave due to the harassment, (2) pay $25,000 to the grievor for "general damages," (3) henceforth ensure that the harassing supervisor had no contact with the grievor at work, and (4) implement a harassment policy and ensure all managers complete anti-harassment training.

In Manitoba, the *Labour Relations Act* expressly reads into every collective agreement a provision requiring the employer, "in administering the collective agreement, to act reasonably, fairly, in good faith, and in a manner consistent with the collective agreement as a whole."[37] Some collective agreements similarly include an expressed term requiring employers to exercise their discretion in a reasonable manner.[38] When such a clause exists, an employee or union could file a grievance challenging an employer action as "unreasonable." For example, an arbitrator applied a reasonableness clause in striking down a rule imposed unilaterally by Thrifty Canada, the car rental company, banning facial jewellery and earrings worn by male employees. Thrifty was unable to demonstrate sufficient business justification for the rule.[39]

However, in most circumstances in Canada, neither a statute nor expressed collective agreement language imposes a general duty on employers to exercise their management rights "reasonably." A controversial and much litigated issue is whether arbitrators should imply a general duty on employers to exercise their managerial rights in a manner that is "reasonable."[40] Whether such an implied term exists is important, because it would enable employees and unions to file grievances challenging employer decisions on a standard of "reasonableness," even though the employer has not violated any expressed term of the collective agreement.

There are two circumstances in which arbitrators imply a requirement for employers to act "reasonably." Firstly, employers must exercise discretion expressly conferred on them by the collective agreement in a manner that is reasonable, and not discriminatory, arbitrary, or in bad faith.[41] The leading Canadian law book on collective agreement arbitration summarizes the extensive case law on the implied obligation on employers to exercise discretion in a reasonable manner in this way:

> [E]ven in the absence of an express requirement of reasonableness, if the [employer's] decision is made pursuant to an express discretionary power, usually that decision will be subject to some level of arbitral review. Indeed, whenever management makes a decision or takes an action in connection with directing its workforce or having an impact on working conditions, it is quite likely that an arbitrator will conclude that a collective agreement provision is affected, and he or she will review that decision for reasonableness, or on the basis that it not be "discriminatory, arbitrary, or in bad faith," or that it further a "legitimate business interest."[42]

To provide just one of dozens of examples, where a collective agreement conferred a discretion on the employer to determine the conditions under which employees would be reimbursed for work-related travel, the arbitrator ruled that discretion was subject to an implied standard of "reasonableness." The employer's condition that workers carpool and share hotel rooms was found to be an unreasonable exercise of managerial discretion.[43]

On the other hand, if the collective agreement simply states a rule without granting the employer discretion over implementation of the rule, then the inference is that the employer has the exclusive right to apply and enforce the rule, and no implied reasonableness standard exists.[44] Also, if the collective agreement includes both a management rights clause and a clause expressly prohibiting an arbitrator from adding to or modifying the expressed terms of the agreement, then an arbitrator may not imply new terms, including a term requiring the reasonable exercise of managerial discretion.[45]

The second circumstance in which an employer's actions will be assessed against a standard of implied "reasonableness" involves the unilateral introduction by the employer of **company rules** while a collective agreement is in force. Company rules must be "reasonable" if violating the rule could lead to employee discipline.[46] The leading case on this point is an old arbitration award from 1965, *Re Lumber and Sawmill Workers' Union, Local 2537 v. KVP Co. Ltd.*, and the test applied to measure the legality of a rules unilaterally introduced by employers is to this day referred to as the "KVP test."[47] That test was described in the *KVP* arbitration award as follows:

> A rule unilaterally introduced by the company, and not subsequently agreed to by the union, must satisfy the following requisites:
>
> 1. It must not be inconsistent with the collective agreement.
> 2. It must not be unreasonable.
> 3. It must be clear and unequivocal.
> 4. It must be brought to the attention of the employee affected before the company can act on it.
> 5. The employee concerned must have been notified that a breach of such rule could result in his discharge if the rule is used as a foundation for discharge.
> 6. Such rule should have been consistently enforced by the company from the time it was introduced.[48]

A new company rule that could lead to employee discipline and that fails to satisfy any one of these requirements may be found by an arbitrator to be unenforceable, although most decisions come down to an analysis of whether the rules are "reasonable." In determining that issue, arbitrators require that the employer demonstrate that the rule in question addresses a legitimate business interest, such as a serious health and safety concern, or some other significant business interest. Hundreds of arbitration decisions consider whether a company rule is "reasonable" applying the KVP test.[49] For example, the introduction of workplace surveillance systems such as cameras, personal searches, and biometric scanning have sometimes been struck down where the employer has been unable to demonstrate that a serious threat of theft or other wrongdoing exists necessitating the infringement on employee privacy.[50] Similarly, dress code and appearance rules unilaterally imposed by an employer must address a pressing business concern or they will be struck down as unreasonable.[51] In the case described in Box 12.5, the union challenged the employer's introduction of mandatory, random alcohol testing as unreasonable.[52]

BOX 12.5 » CASE LAW HIGHLIGHT

Company Rules, Reasonableness, and the KVP Test

Communications, Energy and Paperworkers Union of Canada, Local 30 v. Irving Pulp & Paper, Ltd.
2013 SCC 34, [2013] 2 SCR 458

Key Facts: Irving Pulp & Paper introduced a mandatory alcohol testing policy that subjected 10 percent of employees working in "safety-sensitive jobs" to random alcohol testing over the course of a year. A failed breathalyzer test could result in discipline up to and including dismissal. The union filed a grievance alleging that the requirement to submit to random alcohol testing constituted an unreasonable rule that was not

justified by any pressing business interest and that violated employees' privacy. The arbitrator upheld the grievance, finding that the employer had failed to identify any pressing concern relating to alcohol consumption at the workplace that justified the intrusion on employee privacy. However, on judicial review, the lower court and the New Brunswick Court of Appeal overturned the arbitrator's ruling. The union appealed the matter to the Supreme Court of Canada.

Issue: Was the employer's introduction of mandatory, random alcohol testing a "reasonable" exercise of management rights?

---

company rules: A term used in labour arbitration to describe rules unilaterally introduced by the employer the violation of which can lead to an employee being disciplined or dismissed.

Decision: No. The Supreme Court of Canada upheld the arbitrator's decision that the mandatory testing was "unreasonable," applying the KVP test. The Supreme Court said the following about that test:

> When employers in a unionized workplace unilaterally enact workplace rules and policies, they are not permitted to "promulgate unreasonable rules and then punish employees who infringe them" (*Re United Steelworkers, Local 4487 & John Inglis Co. Ltd.* (1957), 7 L.A.C. 240 (Laskin) …). This constraint arises because an employer may only discharge or discipline an employee for "just cause" or "reasonable cause"—a central protection for employees. As a result, rules enacted by an employer as a vehicle for discipline must meet the requirement of reasonable cause. The scope of management's unilateral rule-making authority under a collective agreement is persuasively set out in *Re Lumber & Sawmill Workers' Union, Local 2537, and KVP Co.* (1965), 16 L.A.C. 73 (Robinson). *The heart of the "KVP test," which is generally applied by arbitrators, is that any rule or policy unilaterally imposed by an employer and not subsequently agreed to by the union, must be consistent with the collective agreement and be reasonable.* [Emphasis added.]

In assessing whether a rule is "reasonable," an arbitrator must consider all of the facts and balance the employer's legitimate business interests and the employees' interest, including their privacy interests. In the case of alcohol testing, an employer may test an employee in a safety-sensitive job when there exists reasonable cause to believe impairment is a risk, such as when an employee demonstrates evidence of impairment, where there has been a serious accident and the employer is seeking its cause, or an employee has a past history of impairment and testing is part of a rehabilitation plan. However, absent such special circumstances, mandatory random alcohol testing would be unreasonable, unless the employer can demonstrate that a serious alcohol problem exists at the workplace and there is no other, less intrusive means available to redress that problem. In this case, the employer identified eight cases of employee impairment over a 15-year period, which the arbitrator found did not meet the threshold required to justify the intrusion on employee privacy that accompanies random alcohol testing. The Supreme Court of Canada upheld that arbitrator's decision that ruled that the union's grievance should succeed.

C. Ancillary Collective Agreement Terms

A third source of collective agreement terms is the various **ancillary documents** that exist in unionized workplaces that are physically separate from the main collective agreement document. Ancillary documents include policy manuals, letters of understanding between the union and employer, insurance plans, and pension documents. Whether these documents are legally enforceable depends on whether they have been incorporated into the collective agreement or constitute separate contracts. In Ontario at least, the latter option is unavailable because the Ontario *Labour Relations Act, 1995* specifies that only one collective agreement can be in effect at a time.[53] Many arbitration cases have considered whether ancillary documents form part of the collective agreement and therefore whether terms and conditions found in them are legally enforceable.

For an ancillary document to be incorporated into a collective agreement, there must be evidence that the parties clearly intended that result.[54] The most obvious evidence is explicit incorporating language in the collective agreement, such as the following collective agreement term:

> The parties agree that the benefits described in Schedule C shall form part of the collective agreement.

---

ancillary documents: Written materials that are physically separate from an employment contract but that include rules that relate to the employment relationship. Examples include employee handbooks, benefits handbooks, and human resources policy manuals.

Even if the ancillary document is not expressly incorporated into the collective agreement, an arbitrator might nevertheless rule that it is inferentially incorporated, based on other evidence demonstrating the parties intended that result.

Many disputes concern the status of employee benefits plans and the denial of benefits under those plans. Here is a typical scenario. The union and employer agree to certain benefits for employees, such as short- and long-term disability wage replacement coverage. One day, employee Stephen becomes very ill and as a result is unable to perform his job for months on end. He files a claim for short-term disability benefits, but he is denied by the insurance company with which the employer contracted to provide the benefits. Stephen believes the denial was improper. Does Stephen file a grievance under the collective agreement against his employer or sue the insurance company for violating the insurance contract his employer entered into to provide the benefits?

The answer depends on a close reading of the collective agreement language and the intention of the parties. Years ago, the leading arbitration text (*Canadian Labour Arbitration*, known simply as "Brown and Beatty" by practitioners, after the names of the text's authors) summarized the case law dealing with this issue and identified the following four categories of collective agreement language:[55]

1. An insurance plan or policy exists, but is not mentioned at all in the collective agreement. *A dispute about the plan is* not arbitrable, since the insurance plan or policy is not incorporated into the collective agreement.
2. The collective agreement provides that employees will be paid a specific benefit if certain conditions are met. *A dispute over the failure to provide the benefit is* arbitrable, since the employer has promised to provide the benefit. The fact that the employer elected to take out insurance does not relieve it of the responsibility to pay the benefit.[56]
3. The collective agreement requires only that the employer pay premiums on an insurance policy. *A dispute over the denial of a benefit by the insurance company is* not arbitrable. However, a dispute over the failure of the employer to pay premiums on a "standard insurance policy" that provides the benefits negotiated by the union is arbitrable.[57] *If an employer fails to obtain insurance that provides the benefits required by the collective agreement, it may be found liable in damages for the unpaid benefits in an arbitration hearing.*
4. A specific plan or policy is incorporated by reference into the agreement. *A dispute is* arbitrable since the terms of the plan form part of the collective agreement.[58]

Countless arbitration decisions have applied these categories (see the exercise at the end of this chapter). For example, in the case of *Kone Inc. v. International Union of Elevator Constructors, Local Union No 82*, collective agreement language stating that the insurance plan "shall be part of this Agreement" was found by a BC arbitrator to constitute an obvious example of category four.[59] Therefore, a denial of benefits by the insurance company could be the subject of a grievance against the employer. In *UPM-Kymmene Miramichi v. Communications, Energy and Paperworkers' Union of Canada, Local 689*, the agreement required the employer to "maintain" the present dental coverage and to reimburse employees for covered expenses, which included "70 percent dentures, crowns and bridges" to a maximum of $1,500 per year. This language in the agreement was found to be an example of category two, so the employer was liable when the insurer refused payment for denture work.[60]

In the often-cited decision described in Box 12.6, the arbitrator considered whether the denial of benefits to an employee by an insurance company was a violation of the collective agreement.

BOX 12.6 » CASE LAW HIGHLIGHT

Is an Insurance Company's Denial of Insurance Benefits a Breach of the Collective Agreement?

Coca-Cola Bottling Ltd. v. U.F.C.W.
(1994), 44 LAC (4th) 151 (Arbitrator Goodfellow)

Key Facts: An employee claimed long-term disability (LTD) benefits but was denied by the insurance company Coca-Cola Bottling had contracted with to provide the benefits. The union filed a grievance under the collective agreement, alleging that the employer was responsible for paying the benefits. The employer objected to the jurisdiction of the arbitrator to hear the grievance, arguing that its only obligation under the collective agreement was to pay premiums on an insurance contract that offered the benefits required by the collective agreement, which it had done. The denial of the LTD benefits by the insurer was a dispute with the insurer and not the employer under the collective agreement.

The collective agreement stated the following: "A new Long Term Disability Plan will be introduced effective Monday, January 6, 1992. Details of this change are set out in a Letter of Agreement attached hereto." The letter of agreement then provided that the employer will introduce "a long term disability insurance program which will include the following features," followed by a detailed list of the features of the insurance program. The letter of agreement also specified that the employer will pay "60% of the LTD premium," and the employee would pay the rest. The employer entered into an insurance contract with an insurance company to provide the benefits required and paid its share of the premiums to maintain the plan. That insurer denied the employee's claim.

Issue: Did the insurer's denial of LTD benefits to the employee violate the collective agreement?

Decision: No. The principal issue in this case is whether the collective agreement required the employer to pay LTD benefits or merely to take out a standard insurance policy providing for LTD benefits. The arbitrator noted that the four categories in

Brown and Beatty are "of assistance," but also concluded that the language in this case did not fit perfectly into any one of them. The key issue to consider was whether the parties intended the employer to bear the cost and risk of liability for LTD benefits, or whether they intended that the employer be permitted to pass on that risk to a third-party insurer by taking out an insurance policy and paying the benefits:

> [I]nsurance plans are normally concluded between an employer and an insurance carrier, and individual employees are not direct parties to those plans, although they appear to have enforceable rights as beneficiaries. But those rights cannot be enforced in the arbitration process, because they do not arise under the collective agreement. The rights may only be enforced against the carrier by the employer, a contracting party to the insurance plan, or by the employee as an individual beneficiary. Thus, the question in all of these cases is whether the employee is left to his or her rights in the courts against the insurance company under the insurance plan, or whether the employee may require the employer to pay the benefits directly, and pursue its own rights against the insurer.

The arbitrator ultimately found that the language in the collective agreement was a hybrid of categories two and three of Brown and Beatty, and that the parties intended that the employer would take out an "insurance" contract that provided the benefits detailed in the letter of agreement and pay the premiums as required. Therefore, the union and the employee could not proceed to arbitration against the employer to dispute the insurer's denial of LTD benefits. The employee could sue the insurance company in court if he believed the insurer violated the insurance contract.

Note that if a benefit plan is found not to be incorporated into the collective agreement, then the employee will usually have the option of suing the insurance company as a beneficiary under the insurance contract. This option is usually less desirable for the employee than filing a grievance against the employer under the collective agreement, since often the union will not fund the private litigation for the employee.

V. Chapter Summary

The collective agreement is a fundamentally different type of contract than the individual (non-union) employment contract (see the companion volume). The legal rules that govern collective agreements are distinct in important ways. A substantial component of public policy is injected into collective agreements through collective bargaining legislation in the form of mandatory, default, and prohibited terms. In addition, labour arbitrators play an important role in giving form and substance to the language negotiated by unions and employers. This chapter introduced the concepts of reserved management rights and implied reasonableness developed by arbitrators. In the next two chapters, we will explore in greater detail the role of labour arbitration and labour arbitrators in the collective bargaining regime.

QUESTIONS AND ISSUES FOR DISCUSSION

1. Who are the parties to a collective agreement?
2. Can a unionized employee be dismissed by the employer, without cause, if the employer provides reasonable notice of that termination? Can a unionized employee be "constructively" dismissed? Explain your answers.
3. Describe an example of a mandatory collective agreement term, a default collective agreement term, and a prohibited collective agreement term.
4. Why are collective agreements often longer and more detailed than individual (non-union) employment contracts?
5. Explain the concept of reserved management rights.
6. Identify and explain two situations in which labour arbitrators have implied an obligation for employers to act "reasonably."

EXERCISE

Dozens of arbitration cases involve disputes over the denial of benefits to employees by an insurance company, and a central issue is whether the collective agreement requires the employer to provide the benefits or simply pay premiums to an insurance company. The answer matters because it decides whether the employee can file a grievance against the employer or has to sue the insurance company in a court. Arbitrators apply the Brown and Beatty "four categories" discussed in this chapter. Try this exercise.

1. Go to the CanLII home page: www.canlii.org.
2. In the "Document text" search box, type the following: "Brown and Beatty" and "four categories." This search should produce dozens of decisions in which the four categories are considered.
3. Scan the case headnotes and select a case that looks interesting and involves a dispute over whether the collective agreement requires the employer to pay benefits. Read the decision and answer the following questions:
   a. What benefit was the employee denied?
   b. What is the collective agreement language in dispute?
   c. Which of the four categories does the arbitrator decide the language falls into? Is the answer that the language is a "hybrid" of more than one category?
   d. What is the arbitrator's decision on the question of whether the insurance company's denial of benefits constituted a breach of the collective agreement?

UPDATES

Go to emond.ca/lawofworkircb for links to news, author's blog posts, content updates, and other information related to the chapters in this text.

NOTES AND REFERENCES

1   See the discussion in *Berry v. Pulley*, 2002 SCC 40, [2002] 2 SCR 493; and *Young v. C.N.R.* (1931), 1 DLR 645. We consider the legal status of unions in the common law in more detail in Chapter 6.

2   *Wartime Labour Relations Order* PC 1003 is available at http://socserv.mcmaster.ca/oldlabourstudies/onlinelearning/article.php?id=503. See s. 1(d).

3   Ibid., s. 10(5).

4   See, e.g., Ontario *Labour Relations Act, 1995*, SO 1995, c. 1, Sch. A, s. 56; and BC *Labour Relations Code*, RSBC 1996, c. 244, s. 48.

5   PC 1003, ss. 17 and 18.

6   *McGavin Toastmaster Ltd. v. Ainscough*, [1976] 1 SCR 718. See also *Syndicat Catholique des Employés de Magasins de Québec Inc. v. Paquet Ltée*, [1959] SCR 206; and *Canadian Pacific Railway Co. v. Zambri*, [1962] SCR 609.

7   *McGavin Toastmaster Ltd. v. Ainscough*, supra note 6, at 725.

8   For example, New Brunswick requires the inclusion of a term requiring employers to provide the union with notice of the introduction of new technology: *Industrial Relations Act*, RSNB 1973, c. I-4, s. 55.1.

9   No strike during a collective agreement. See, e.g., BC *Labour Relations Code*, supra note 4, s. 57; Alberta *Labour Relations Code*, RSA 2000, c. L-1, ss. 73 and 74; and Ontario *Labour Relations Act, 1995*, supra note 4, s. 46. In Quebec and Nova Scotia, there is a limited right to strike or lockout during the term of a collective agreement in the context of mid-term revisions to the contract: NS *Trade Union Act*, RSNS 1989, c. 475, s. 48; and Quebec *Labour Code*, CQLR c. C-27, s. 107.

10   Ontario *Labour Relations Act, 1995*, supra note 4, s. 48.

11   Manitoba *Labour Relations Act*, CCSM c. L10, s. 76. Quebec's *Labour Code* requires union dues check-off too, although it does not expressly require that a union dues clause be included in collective agreements: Quebec *Labour Code*, supra note 9, s. 47.

12   For example, both British Columbia and Manitoba require a collective agreement to include a term establishing a joint consultation committee to discuss workplace issues if one party requests such a term to be included. BC *Labour Relations Code*, supra note 4, s. 53; and Manitoba *Labour Relations Act*, supra note 11, s. 81.

13   *Ford Motor Company v. United Automobile Workers Union*, [1946] OLAA No. 1; and *Syndicat Catholique des Employés de Magasins de Québec Inc. v. Paquet Ltée*, supra note 6.

14   See Ontario *Labour Relations Act, 1995*, supra note 4, s. 47 (non-construction only); *Canada Labour Code*, RSC 1985, c. L-2, s. 70; and Newfoundland and Labrador *Labour Relations Act*, RSNL 1990, c. L-1, s. 87.

15   Ontario *Labour Relations Act, 1995*, supra note 4, s. 47(1).

16   *International Union of Bricklayers and Allied Craftsmen, Local 13 v. United Masonry Construction Ltd.* (1980), 2 CLRBR 416 (SLRB).

17   In Saskatchewan, a union dues check-off provision is not required to be in the collective agreement, but the statute requires dues check-off if both the employee and union so request: *The Saskatchewan Employment Act*, SS 2013, c. S-15.1, s. 32. In Alberta, British Columbia, and Nova Scotia, the statute requires union dues check-off when an employee authorizes it. Prince Edward Island requires an employee authorization for union dues deduction if the collective agreement does not provide for automatic dues deduction: PEI *Labour Act*, RSPEI 1988, c. L-1, s. 45.

18   See *United Steelworkers of America v. Bennett Chevrolet Geo Oldsmobile Cadillac Ltd.*, 1999 CanLII 19491 (Ont. LRB) (a collective agreement must operate for at least one year, and it is not sufficient simply to make the term clause retroactive to a date in the past).

19   See, e.g., BC *Labour Relations Code*, supra note 4, s. 50; and Ontario *Labour Relations Act, 1995*, supra note 4, s. 58.

20   See, e.g., Ontario *Labour Relations Act, 1995*, supra note 4, s. 54 (collective agreement must not discriminate contrary to human rights legislation and Charter). In Manitoba, the statute declares void any collective agreement term that requires an employer to terminate an employee for engaging in activities on behalf of a union: Manitoba *Labour Relations Act*, supra note 11, s. 23(3).

21   *United Electrical, Radio & Machine Workers of America, Local 52 and Peterboro Lock Mfg. Co. Ltd* (1953), 4 LAC 1499 (Laskin).

22   See, e.g., *North Bay Regional Health Centre* (2015), 263 LAC (4th) 316 (Bendel).

23   See *Voice Construction Ltd. v. Construction & General Workers' Union, Local 92*, 2004 SCC 23 at para. 32, [2004] 1 SCR 609.

24   *Essar Steel Algoma Inc. v. United Steelworkers of America, Local 2251*, 2014 CanLII 29950 (Stout).

25   See *Tung-Sol of Canada Ltd.* (1964), 15 LAC 161 (Reville) for an often-cited discussion of the importance of seniority in the collective bargaining regime.

26   See the discussion in D. Brown and D. Beatty, *Canadian Labour Arbitration*, 4th ed. (Aurora, ON: Canada Law Book, 2006), at 6:1,120; and *Children's Aid Society of Cape Breton* (1996), 61 LAC (4th) 70 (La Forest).

27 What constitutes a "promotion" is sometimes a matter of debate. See, e.g., *Canadian Blood Services* (2002), 102 LAC (4th) 223 (Devlin).

28 Whether a layoff has occurred is sometimes a matter of contestation: see *Battlefords and District Co-operatives Ltd. v. RWDSU, Local 544*, [1998] 1 SCR 1118; *Canada Safeway Ltd. v. RWDSU, Local 454*, [1998] 1 SCR 1079; *Crown Ridge Place Nursing Home* (1998), 72 LAC (4th) 232 (Marcotte); and *Colonial Cookies* (1990), 13 LAC (4th) 405 (Foisy).

29 For an extensive discussion of seniority rights in collective agreements, see R. Snyder, *Collective Agreement Arbitration in Canada*, 5th ed. (Markham, ON: LexisNexis, 2013), at chapters 16 and 17; and Brown and Beatty, supra note 26, at chapter 6.

30 *Maloney Electric Corp.* (1985), 22 LAC (3d) 170 (Picher).

31 See *Central Okanagan School District No. 23 v. Renaud*, [1992] 2 SCR 970; *McGill University Health Centre (Montreal General Hospital) v. Syndicat des employés de l'Hôpital général de Montréal*, 2007 SCC 4, [2007] 1 SCR 161; *Bayer Rubber and Communication Energy and Paperworkers Union of Canada, Local 914* (1997), 65 LAC (4th) 261; *Terminal Forest Products (Mainland Sawmill Division) v. USWA, Local 1—1937*, 2016 CanLII 30971 (Coleman); *Canada Post Corp. v. C.U.P.W.* (1993), 33 LAC (4th) 279; and *Lyle v. The Bloom Group (No. 2)*, 2016 BCHRT 45.

32 See, e.g., *McKellar General Hospital and ONA*, [1986] OLAA No. 5. See also *Meadow Park Nursing Home* (1983), 9 LAC (3d) 137 (Swan); and *Greater Toronto Airports Authority* (2010), 191 LAC (4th) 277 (Shime).

33 See also *Canadian Union of Public Employees, Local 227 v. Halifax Regional Water Commission*, 2016 CanLII 32348 (NSLA) (Richardson) (the employer's response to alleged harassment was reasonable).

34 See, e.g., *Lloyd v. Imperial Parking Ltd.* (1996), 25 CCEL (2d) 97 (Alta. QB); and *Boucher v. Wal-Mart Canada Corp.*, 2014 ONCA 419.

35 *New Brunswick v. O'Leary*, [1995] 2 SCR 967.

36 *Polymer Corp. and Oil, Chemical and Atomic Workers' International Union, Local 16-14*, (1958) 10 LAC 31 (Laskin), aff'd 1962 CanLII 3 (SCC).

37 Manitoba *Labour Relations Act*, supra note 11, s. 80.

38 See, e.g., the discussion in *Dalhousie University v. Dalhousie Faculty Association*, 2012 CanLII 51374 (NSLA).

39 *Thrifty (Canada) Ltd. v. O.P.E.I.U., Local 378* (2001), 100 LAC (4th) 162 (Larson).

40 See the discussion in Brown and Beatty, supra note 26, 4:2,320; and M. Mitchnick and B. Etherington, *Labour Arbitration in Canada* (Toronto: Lancaster House, 2006), at 280-84.

41 *Re Council of Printing Industries of Canada and Toronto Printing Pressmen and Assistants' Union No. 10 et al.* (1983), 42 OR (2d) 404 (Ont. CA); *Grain and General Services Union and Viterra Inc.* (2012), 216 LAC (4th) 101 (Pelton); *Re L/3 Communications/Spar Aerospace Ltd. and International Association of Machinists and Aerospace Workers, Northgate Lodge 1579* (2004), 127 LAC (4th) 225 (Wakeling); and *Re Greater Toronto Airports Authority and P.S.A.C., Local 0004* (2010), 191 LAC (4th) 277, 100 CLAS 371 (Shime).

42 Brown and Beatty, supra note 26, at 4:2,326.

43 *Weston School District* (2011), 213 LAC (4th) 129 (Oakley).

44 *Re Metropolitan Toronto Board of Commissioners of Police and Metropolitan Toronto Police Association et al.* (1981), 33 OR (2d) 476 (Ont. CA); *Stelco Inc. v United Steelworkers of America, Local 1005 et al.* (1994), 1994 CanLII 10573 (Ont. SC); *Blue Line Taxi Co. and R.W.D.W.U., Local 1688* (1992), 28 LAC (4th) 280 (Bendel); *Delta School District No. 37 v. CUPE, Local 1091* (1999), 85 LAC (4th) 33 (McPhillips); and *Viterra Inc v Grain and General Services Union (Ilwu Canada)*, 2015 CanLII 70351 (SKLA).

45 *Re Metropolitan Toronto Board of Commissioners of Police and Metropolitan Toronto Police Association et al.*, supra note 44.

46 See the discussion in *Metropolitan Toronto (Municipality) v. C.U.P.E.* (1990), 74 OR (2d) 239 (Ont. CA); *Communications, Energy and Paperworkers Union of Canada, Local 30 v. Irving Pulp & Paper, Ltd.*, 2013 SCC 44, [2013] 2 SCR 458; and *York University v. York University Staff Association*, 2012 CanLII 41233 (Ont. LA).

47 *Re Lumber and Sawmill Workers' Union, Local 2537 v. KVP Co. Ltd.* (1965), 16 LAC 73 (Robinson). See also the discussion in *Communications, Energy and Paperworkers Union of Canada, Local 30 v. Irving Pulp & Paper, Ltd.*, supra note 46; and *Metropolitan Toronto (Municipality) v. C.U.P.E.*, supra note 46.

48 *KVP*, ibid., at 85.

49 For a review of those cases, see Brown and Beatty, supra note 26, at chapter 4 (4:1,500 Company Rules) and, in particular, 4:1,524 (The Reasonableness Requirement).

50 See, e.g., *Woodstock (City) v. Woodstock Professional Firefighters' Association*, 2015 CanLII 20641 (Parmar) (surveillance cameras were unreasonable); *Lenworth Metal Products* (2000), 29 Admin. LR (3d) 258 (OSJ) (cameras); *IKO Industries Ltd.*(2005), 140 LAC (4th) 393 (Tims) (biometric timekeeping system was unreasonable);

and *Gerdau Ameristeel* (2011), 211 LAC (4th) 93 (Tacon) (biometric scanner was not unreasonable).

51   See, e.g., *Ottawa Hospital v. Canadian Union of Public Employees, Local 4000*, 2013 CanLII 643 (Slotnick) (rule banning tattoos and piercings was unreasonable). See also D. Doorey, "Can an Employer Prohibit Tattoos and Piercings?" *Law of Work* (blog), January 15, 2013, http://lawofwork.ca/?p=6119.

52   See also *Trimac Transportation Services-Bulk Systems* (1999), 88 LAC (4th) 237 (Burkett) (mandatory drug and alcohol policy was unreasonable); and *Fording Coal Ltd.* (2000), 88 LAC (4th) 408 (Hope).

53   Ontario *Labour Relations Act, 1995*, supra note 4, s. 55.

54   *Canada Bread Co. Ltd.* (1970), 22 LAC 98 (Christie).

55   Brown and Beatty, supra note 26, at 4:1,400.

56   *UPM-Kymmene Miramichi, Inc. v. Communications, Energy and Paperworkers' Union of Canada, Local 689*, 2002 NBQB 139, 249 NBR (2d) 380; *Wilpark Foods* (1991), 21 LAC (4th) 441 (Ladner); *Cargill Ltd.* (2016), 126 CLAS 172 (McPhillips); and *Morris v. Manufacturers Life Assurance Co.* (2005), 40 CCEL (3d) 65 (Ont. SC) (agreement permitted grievances relating to benefits).

57   See, e.g., *CBC v. Burkett* (1997), 155 DLR (4th) 159 (Ont. CA); *Pavaco Plastics Inc. v. Workers United Canada Council*, 2013 CanLII 7304 (Ont. LA) (Carrier); *Consumers Glass v. United Steelworkers of America, Local 269*, 2000 CanLII 28033 (Ont. LA) (Albertyn); *Sault Area Hospital* (2012), 219 LAC (4th) 105 (Steinberg); and *Nechako Northcoast Construction v. British Columbia Government & Service Employees' Union*, 2010 CanLII 91779 (Hall). The requirement that the insurance policy be of a "standard nature" is an implied obligation read in by arbitrators.

58   *Kone Inc. v. International Union of Elevator Constructors, Local Union No 82*, 2014 CanLII 47211 (BCLRB); *Burns Meats* (1995), 50 LAC (4th) 415 (Hamilton); *TRW Canada* (1991), 19 LAC (4th) 374 (O'Shea); and *Coca-Cola Bottling Ltd.* (1998), 76 LAC (4th) 105 (Christie).

59   *Kone Inc. v. International Union of Elevator Constructors, Local Union No 82*, supra note 58.

60   *UPM-Kymmene Miramichi, Inc. v. Communications, Energy and Paperworkers' Union of Canada, Local 689*, supra note 56.

APPENDIX: SAMPLE COLLECTIVE AGREEMENT

This mandatory term identifies which employees the collective agreement governs. The recognition clause often mirrors the bargaining union description in the certification of the union originally issued by the labour relations board.

Most provinces treat the union dues clause as a default contract clause. The union determines the amount of dues, usually in its constitution. Note that this collective agreement does not include a mandatory union membership clause. Therefore, by requiring mandatory union dues check-off and not mandatory union membership, this clause aligns with the Rand Formula.

This is a typical management rights clause. It explains that the employer reserves the right to manage the enterprise subject to restrictions or limits bargained by the union. As noted in the chapter, arbitrators have sometimes implied a requirement that management exercise its discretion in a "reasonable" manner.

Sample Collective Agreement
between
Beer Workers Union, Local 67 (Union)
and
County Beer Company, Inc. (Employer)

RECOGNITION

1.01 The Employer recognizes the Union as the sole bargaining agent for all employees in Belleville, Ontario, save and except salespersons, office and clerical employees, managers, and persons above the rank of manager.

1.02 In the event that the Employer decides to move its Belleville operations to a new location within 100 kilometers of Belleville, bargaining unit employees displaced by the move shall be given preferential consideration in hiring for the new location.

UNION SECURITY

2.01 The Employer shall deduct, monthly, from the pay of each bargaining unit employee such union dues, fees, and assessments as prescribed by the Union in its Constitution and as directed by the Union. The Employer shall remit the amount so deducted to the Union by direct deposit on the fifteenth day of each month following. The Employer shall also provide the Union with a statement each month indicating the name of each employee from whose pay deductions have been made and the amount deducted.

2.02 The Union agrees to indemnify and save the Employer harmless against all claims or other forms of liability that may arise out of or by reason of deductions made in accordance with this article.

MANAGEMENT RIGHTS

3.01 Subject to the terms of this Agreement, the Union acknowledges that it is the exclusive function of the Employer to manage the enterprise, and to hire, promote, demote, classify, transfer and suspend employees, and to discipline or discharge employees for just cause, provided that a claim by an employee or the Union that the terms of the Agreement have been violated may be the subject of a grievance.

Sample for educational purposes only. Not intended to serve as a template.

Union stewards are usually employees elected by their co-workers to act as the union's representative in the workplace. They assist the union to administer the collective agreement on a day-to-day basis.

A grievance procedure is required by collective bargaining legislation. It usually involves several steps, with each step involving progressively more senior employer and union officials in an attempt to resolve the dispute without an expensive arbitration hearing.

Note that only the employer or union (the "parties") can refer a grievance to arbitration, not an employee. It is common for collective agreements to grant the union "carriage" of the grievance at the point of the decision to refer to arbitration. Since the union pays for the cost of an arbitration (with the employer), the union acts as gatekeeper to avoid frivolous or potentially harmful grievances from moving forward. (For the implications of this gatekeeping role, see Chapter 15.)

UNION STEWARDS

4.01 The Employer acknowledges the right of the Union to appoint 2 Union stewards. The Employer agrees to instruct its managers to co-operate with the stewards in carrying out the terms and requirements of this agreement. The Union agrees to instruct the stewards to similarly co-operate with the managers.

4.02 The Employer agrees that Union stewards are entitled to leave their work posts without loss of pay in order to the perform their Union functions, including to investigate and administer grievances, provided that they first advise a manager and receive permission to leave, which permission will not be unreasonably refused.

GRIEVANCE PROCEDURE

5.01 The Employer, Union, or a bargaining unit employee may file a grievance in accordance with this grievance procedure if they believe a term of the collective agreement has been violated.

5.02 Time lines set forth in this grievance procedure can only be extended with the agreement of the Union and the Employer and an arbitrator may not extend them without such agreement.

5.03 Step One: An aggrieved employee shall either personally or through a steward present a written grievance, signed by the grievor, to a manager. The manager shall consider the grievance and render a decision in writing within 2 working days. If a resolution is not reached, the grievor or the steward shall proceed to the next step of the grievance procedure within 5 days thereafter.

5.04 Step Two: A Union steward may present the written grievance to a manager and within 5 working days, the manager (or a designate) shall meet with the steward in an attempt to resolve the grievance. If the grievance is not resolved, the Union may refer the grievance to Step Three within 5 working days of the Step Two meeting.

5.05 Step Three: The Union may refer the grievance to the Human Resources Manager. Within 5 working days, the HR Manager shall meet with a representative of the Union, including a Union Business Agent, in an attempt to resolve the grievance.

5.06 Employer Grievance: The Employer may file a grievance by serving the grievance on a Union Steward or other Union representative. Within 10 days, the Employer and a Union official shall meet to discuss and attempt to resolve the grievance.

5.07 Step Four: If a grievance is not resolved at or before Step Three, or an Employer grievance is not resolved at the meeting referred to in Article 5.06, either party may refer the grievance to arbitration within 30 days of the Step Three meeting.

The union and employer choose the arbitrator unlike in common law breach of contract lawsuits, where the parties get whatever judge is assigned the file (see Chapter 13).

This clause is a mandatory term that dates back to PC 1003 in 1944 and is a distinctly Canadian addition to the American-based Wagner model of collective bargaining.

"Just cause" provisions such as this are standard in Canadian collective agreements. They mark one of the most substantial differences between non-union employment contracts and collective agreements. A unionized employer subject to a just cause provision must establish it had a good business reason to discipline or dismiss an employee, whereas a non-union employer can usually dismiss an employee without any reason, provided that it gives notice of termination.

ARBITRATION

6.01 The parties agree that the following arbitrators will hear and decide grievances referred to arbitration and that grievances will be referred to the arbitrators in the order in which their names appear:

Professor Elaine Arnott

Mark Alexander

Stacey Markus

Mohammed Llimik

6.02 The decision of the arbitrator is final and binding on the Employer, Union, and affected bargaining unit employees.

6.03 The parties shall share the expense of the arbitrator equally.

NO STRIKE OR LOCKOUT

7.01 There shall be no strike or lockout during the term of this collective agreement.

DISCHARGE AND DISCIPLINE

8.01 No employee shall be disciplined or discharged without just cause.

SENIORITY

9.01 Seniority means length of continuous service with the employer from the date of hire.

9.02 The employee shall post any vacancies on the bulletin board. In the case of job competitions for posted positions within the bargaining unit, the following factors shall be considered: (a) seniority and (b) skill and ability. Where skill and ability of applicants is relatively equal, the more senior employee shall be awarded the promotion.

9.03 Layoffs shall be by order of seniority with more senior employees being laid off last, provided the senior employee has the skill and ability to perform a job in the bargaining unit. More senior employees shall be recalled from temporary layoff first, provided the senior employee possesses the necessary skill and ability to perform a job in the bargaining unit.

9.04 Seniority and employment shall terminate when the employee quits, is discharged for just cause in accordance with this agreement, or is laid-off for a period of 24 months or more.

Seniority rights confer various benefits and advantages on more senior (i.e., longer serving) employees. How seniority is defined and what role it plays vary from agreement to agreement. In this clause, senior employees enjoy preference in job competitions, but that benefit is contingent too on a skill and ability component.

Sample for educational purposes only. Not intended to serve as a template.

This clause is a response to the Russel Steel decision discussed in this chapter. It restricts the employer from contracting out work, but only if doing so will result in a bargaining unit employee losing his or her job.

Canadian occupational health and safety legislation requires joint health and safety committees. Often collective agreements spell out in greater detail than this clause what duties a committee will perform.

Note that the Schedule (an ancillary document) is expressly incorporated into the collective agreement. Also note that the clause explains that the employer's responsibility is to pay premiums on an insurance policy that provides the benefits listed. Provided the employer does so, a denial by the insurance company of a claim will probably not be a breach of the collective agreement and will not be grievable.

CONTRACTING OUT

10.01 The Employer shall not contract out work that will result in the layoff or discharge of a bargaining unit employee.

HEALTH AND SAFETY

11.01 The parties agree to a Safety and Health Committee consisting of 3 members elected or appointed by the Union and 3 members appointed by the Employer who will meet regularly and make inspections of the workplace from time to time.

HEALTH AND WELFARE BENEFITS

12.01 Schedule A to this Agreement provides a description of benefits that shall be provided to employees for the term of this Agreement. Schedule A is incorporated into this Agreement. It is agreed that the Employer will pay the full cost of premiums on an insurance contract through which the described benefits will be provided.

WAGES

13.01 During the term of this Agreement, the parties agree that all payments of wages will be made in accordance with the wage rates set forth in Schedule B which is hereby made part of this Agreement.

PAID VACATION

14.01 All employees who have acquired one year's seniority by July 1 of any year shall be entitled to two weeks' paid vacation to be taken at a time convenient to the employer.

14.02 All employees who have acquired six years' seniority by July 1 of any year shall be entitled to three weeks' paid vacation to be taken at a time convenient to the employer.

14.03 All employees who have acquired twelve years' seniority by July 1 of any year shall be entitled to four weeks' paid vacation to be taken at a time convenient to the employer.

14.04 In determining the timing of vacations, the employer shall consider seniority.

The wage schedule is expressly incorporated into the collective agreement. Unlike an individual employment contract, collective agreement wage clauses cannot usually state unilaterally to give out raises or bonuses to individual bargaining unit employees.

Here is an example of a benefit that increases with accumulated seniority. The requirement for the employer to consider seniority in scheduling vacations is a weaker form of seniority protection than a term that requires that "seniority shall govern."

Another mandatory clause, this duration clause ensures that the collective agreement "operates" for at least one year. No mandatory maximum length of a collective agreement exists. Collective bargaining statutes read into collective agreements an open period during which employees can file an application to decertify the union or another union can raid an existing union (see Chapter 8).

DURATION

15.01 This Agreement shall become effective on December 1, 2017 and terminate on November 30, 2020.

On Behalf of the Union: On Behalf of the Employer:

_____   _____
Jack Dundas   Amanda Wellington
Union Staff Representative   Industrial Relations Manager

_____
Owen Sharpe
Local Union President and Chair,
Bargaining Committee

CHAPTER 13

Grievances and the Labour Arbitration Process

I. Introduction

In earlier chapters, we discussed how a distinctive component of Canadian collective bargaining law is the prohibition on work stoppages during a collective agreement, which dates back to PC 1003 of 1944.[1] Since the parties to a collective agreement cannot resort to "industrial warfare" to settle disputes over the interpretation, application, and enforcement of the collective agreement, a system for resolving disputes without work stoppages is needed. That system is the grievance and arbitration process, the subject of this chapter and the next. Collective bargaining statutes require that all collective agreement disputes be resolved by "final and binding" labour arbitration. Those statutes shift collective agreement disputes from the courts to the specialized legal world of labour arbitration, which has its own procedures, norms, and expansive body of case law that operate like a type of common law of collective agreements. This chapter examines the procedure by which a grievance is filed and processed through to the arbitration stage. It concludes with a discussion of the expanding scope of labour arbitration and the strain this development is placing on the traditional role of labour arbitration as an informal, expedient, and inexpensive alternative to courtroom litigation.

II. The Grievance Procedure

According to the Supreme Court of Canada, the labour arbitration process serves both a private and public function: arbitration resolves private disputes over contract application, and it also serves the important public function of ensuring "the peaceful resolution of labour disputes."[2] The filing of a **grievance** commences a legal process detailed in the collective agreement's grievance procedure. The objective of the grievance procedure is to explore the possibility of resolving the dispute without litigation. There are different types of grievances. The most common is an **individual grievance** filed by an employee (known as the **grievor**), alleging that his or her collective agreement rights have been violated by the employer. A **group grievance** is filed on behalf of two or more employees who allege that they have suffered harm as a result of the same collective agreement violation by the employer. A union may file a **policy grievance** if the employer's alleged wrongdoing is of general interest to the bargaining unit and not specific to an individual employee. Finally, an employer may also file a grievance alleging a breach of the collective agreement by the union or an individual employee (**employer grievance**).[3]

A. Filing a Grievance

Assume that Jessica has worked at County Beer Company for ten years. One day, Amanda, the industrial relations manager, sees Jessica leaving work before the end of her shift by the back factory door. Jessica is carrying a duffle bag that looks heavy. Amanda is suspicious and approaches Jessica near the door. The following conversation ensues:

> AMANDA: Where do you think you are going?
> JESSICA: I have a softball game tonight, and I need to get to the diamond quickly. My car is parked by the back door, so I'm leaving this way.
> AMANDA: Did you punch out?
> JESSICA: Oh crap, I forgot.
> AMANDA: What do you have in the bag?
> JESSICA: Nothing, just personal stuff.
> AMANDA: Can I have a look in the bag?
> JESSICA: No. It's my personal bag.
> AMANDA: Is there something in there you don't want me to see?
> JESSICA: Fine! Take a look. I have to get going.

Jessica unzips the bag, and Amanda finds three full bottles of County Beer ale. Jessica blurts out that she did not know the beer bottles were in the bag and that she must have left them in there after her last softball game. After an investigation, Amanda decides that Jessica stole the beer bottles from her workstation and then concocted the story about the beer bottles being left

---

grievance: A formal complaint lodged under a collective agreement that alleges a contravention of the collective agreement.

individual grievance: A grievance filed by an individual employee alleging their collective agreement rights have been violated by the employer.

grievor: An employee who files a grievance.

group grievance: A grievance filed on behalf of two or more employees who allege the same or a similar breach of the collective agreement.

policy grievance: A grievance filed by a union that raises an issue(s) that are of general interest to all or many employees in the bargaining unit.

employer grievance: A grievance filed by an employer alleging that an employee or the union has violated the collective agreement.

over from a prior baseball game. In Amanda's opinion, the theft, subsequent dishonesty, and leaving work early without punching out amounted to just cause to terminate Jessica's employment contract. Jessica is fired on June 10, 2017. Two days later, she files a grievance alleging that the employer did not have "just cause" to fire her.

Jessica's grievance form would look something like the document in Box 13.1. The grievance activates the grievance procedure in the collective agreement between the employer and Jessica's union. Usually, the grievance procedure requires the employer to respond to the grievance within a defined period of time either by accepting the grievance and granting the remedy sought or by "denying" it. A denial advances the grievance forward to the next stage of the grievance procedure, which typically involves meetings between the employer and union representatives to try and resolve the grievance by either the employee and/or union withdrawing or "dropping" the grievance or the parties reaching some form of settlement. A grievance that is not withdrawn or settled may eventually be referred to arbitration.

BOX 13.1 » TALKING WORK LAW

Example of Completed Grievance Form

UNITED BREWERY WORKERS UNION

STANDARD GRIEVANCE FORM

Employer: County Beer Company

Date: June 12, 2017

Grievance Number: 03-17

Description of the Alleged Breach of the Collective Agreement, Including Article Number(s):

I grieve that the employer has fired me without just cause contrary to Article 8.01 of the Collective Agreement.

What Remedy Are You Seeking?

I seek reinstatement to my job as a bottle sorter, with full back pay, benefits, and without loss of seniority.

Name and Signature of Grievor:
Jessica Willow   *Jessica Willow*

Signature of Union Steward/Representative:
Jack Dundas   *Jack Dundas*

B. Settling or Withdrawing a Grievance

Most grievances are settled or withdrawn (dropped) either during the grievance procedure or at the outset of the arbitration hearing. Sometimes an arbitrator will first help the parties to settle by acting as a mediator and then acting as an arbitrator if a settlement is not reached (a process known as **mediation-arbitration**, or **"med-arb"**). A settlement is in writing and sets out the conditions of the resolution. For example, assume that County Beer Company is concerned that an arbitrator may believe Jessica's explanation for having the beer bottles in her bag, and so, on the morning of the hearing two months later, it decides to settle the grievance on the basis of a reinstatement with a two-month unpaid suspension for bringing alcohol into the workplace and for leaving without punching out her time card. The grievance settlement might look something like the document in Box 13.2. Once a grievance has been settled or withdrawn, it cannot usually be revived unless the parties had agreed otherwise; for example, by agreeing that the settlement or withdrawal is

---

BOX 13.2 » TALKING WORK LAW

A Grievance Settlement

MEMORANDUM OF SETTLEMENT BETWEEN
UNITED BREWERY WORKERS UNION (UNION)

AND

COUNTY BEER COMPANY, INC. (EMPLOYER)

AND

JESSICA WILLOW (GRIEVOR)

In the matter of Grievance No. 03-17 (Termination of Jessica Willow);

Whereas the parties wish to resolve all matters relating to the Grievance;

The parties hereby agree as follows:

1. That the Employer shall reinstate the Grievor effective August 13, 2017, with no loss of seniority.

2. That a disciplinary 2-month unpaid suspension shall be substituted for the termination and that a written record of that suspension will be entered into the Grievor's personnel file for misconduct identified as "bringing alcohol into the workplace and failing to punch out her time card at the end of her shift."

Signed at Belleville, Ontario, on August 12, 2017.

Amanda Wellington   _Jack Dundas_   _Jessica Willow_

---

mediation-arbitration ("med-arb"): A process for resolving grievances in which a neutral expert first acts as a mediator, working with the parties to try to settle the grievance, but failing a settlement the neutral expert sits as an arbitrator and rules on the grievance.

"without prejudice" to the right to raise the issue again in the future. Similarly, once a grievance is withdrawn or settled (or decided by an arbitrator), a new grievance challenging essentially the same alleged breach will not be permitted to proceed. Such a grievance would be blocked by legal doctrines applied in both courts and arbitrations known as **issue estoppel** and *res judicata*.

Some grievances are settled on the basis that an employee will be given "one last chance" to improve his or her behaviour. This type of settlement is referred to as a **last chance agreement**. A last chance agreement specifies future behaviour that will result in the employee's employment termination. If the employee engages in the specified behaviour, and the employer relies on the agreement that states termination will be the automatic consequence, the labour arbitrator will usually limit the inquiry to whether the last chance agreement was violated. If yes, the termination will be upheld.[4] However, interesting questions arise when the last chance agreement permits the employer to fire an employee for behaviour related to a prohibited ground (such as a disability) in human rights legislation. Recall from our discussion of the regulatory regime in the companion volume that it is unlawful to contract out of human rights legislation. What if a last chance agreement permits an employer to automatically fire an alcoholic employee for testing positive in an alcohol test? Is that agreement legally enforceable, even if the employer has not demonstrated that accommodation was possible?[5] Box 13.3 considers these questions.

BOX 13.3 » CASE LAW HIGHLIGHT

Last Chance Agreements and Human Rights Law
Seaspan ULC v. International Longshore & Warehouse Union, Local 400
2014 CanLII 83893 (BCLA) (Arbitrator Lanyon)

Key Facts: The grievor (GH) was a 57-year-old deckhand with a long history of alcoholism and drug use who was working for a shipping company. He entered an employer-sponsored two-year addiction treatment program, which he completed and during which he did not test positive for alcohol or drugs. However, he relapsed on several occasions after that time, while off duty. Eventually, the employer removed him from his duties as a deckhand, which is a safety-sensitive job. The union filed a grievance. The parties settled the grievance by entering into a last chance agreement, which included the following provisions:

- GH will undergo a medical assessment, and the doctor will inform the employer if GH can perform safety-sensitive jobs or, if not, other non-safety-sensitive jobs.
  - If the doctor finds GH can return to work, then GH will be subject to a two-year monitoring agreement that includes "complete abstinence" from alcohol or drugs and random biological testing.
  - If GH can perform only non-safety-sensitive jobs, then the employer will undergo an accommodation search to locate any job GH can perform, but the employer is not required to create a new position.

- Any positive alcohol or drug test "will result in the immediate termination of GH's employment."
- The parties agree that the last chance agreement fulfills the employer's duty to accommodate GH.

The doctor ultimately concluded that GH could return to his deckhand job. However, GH later tested positive for alcohol consumption and was fired. The employer relied on the last chance agreement. The union filed another grievance, this time arguing that the termination amounted to discrimination on the basis of disability (alcoholism).

Issue: Was GH's failed alcohol test and violation of the last chance agreement grounds for the immediate termination of his employment?

Decision: No. The arbitrator noted that there are strong policy reasons why arbitrators should enforce last chance agreements. If employers cannot rely on arbitrators to enforce last chance agreements, then they will not enter into them, and it is desirable to encourage employers and unions to resolve termination grievances without litigation when possible. However, parties cannot enter into a last chance agreement that is inconsistent with human rights legislation. In particular, a last chance agreement cannot contract out of the statutory duty to accommodate employees with a disability. Therefore, the arbitrator is not

---

issue estoppel: A legal principle that prohibits a party from acting in a manner or taking a position that is contrary to a position that party has made in the past and that has been relied on by the other party.

res judicata: A legal principle that prohibits a party from re-litigating an issue that has already been raised in a prior proceeding.

last chance agreement: A type of settlement of a grievance challenging the termination of an employee that includes reinstatement of the employee subject to a condition that if the employee reoffends, then termination will be the consequence.

bound by the clause in the last chance agreement that states that the employer's duty to accommodate has been satisfied. Whether it has or has not is a question the arbitrator must decide, applying human rights law principles (discussed in Chapter 29 of the companion volume).

In this case, GH suffered from a disability, and the termination of his employment was for reasons related to that disability (failing an alcohol test). Therefore, the discussion shifts to whether the employer established that it could not accommodate GH without suffering undue hardship. The arbitrator ruled that four relapses in four years, plus the employer's efforts to offer rehabili-

tation, and its agreement to give GH a last chance agreement had satisfied its duty to accommodate GH in relation to the safety-sensitive job of deckhand. However, in respect to non-safety-sensitive jobs, the employer had not satisfied its duty to accommodate. There was no evidence GH had ever drunk or been intoxicated at work or that his job performance had suffered due to drinking. These "off-duty relapses" should not disqualify him from trying non-safety-sensitive jobs, and the employer had not shown that no such positions were available. Therefore, GH was reinstated to a non-safety-sensitive job, but was still required to continue in rehab and take random tests for substance use.

III. The Labour Arbitration Process

Sometimes there is no settlement and the grievance is not withdrawn. Maybe both parties believe they will win at arbitration, or that regardless of whether they will win, there are good reasons to let a labour arbitrator decide the case. Grievances not settled are either withdrawn (dropped) or referred to arbitration. As discussed in Box 13.4, the decision whether to settle, withdraw, or refer an individual, group, or policy grievance to arbitration usually rests with the union.

BOX 13.4 » TALKING WORK LAW

Who "Owns" the Grievance?

Although collective agreements usually permit individual employees to file grievances on their own behalf, the ultimate authority to settle, withdraw, or refer a grievance to arbitration is usually conferred on the union. Article 5.07 in the sample collective agreement in the appendix to Chapter 12 is typical:

> Step Four: If a grievance is not resolved at or before Step Three, or an Employer grievance is not resolved at the meeting referred to in Article 5.06, *either party* may refer the grievance to arbitration within 30 days of the Step Three meeting. [Emphasis added.]

The "parties" to a collective agreement are the union and the employer, not the employees. The union acts as a "gatekeeper" to the labour arbitration process, because it pays the high costs of arbitration—which can run into tens of thousands of dollars, depending on the complexity of the case—and also because the union needs to be concerned about what is best for the bargaining unit as a whole. An individual grievor may wish that his or her grievance proceed to arbitration, even if it lacks merit or advances a legal argument that could be harmful to other employees. Unions want the discretion to drop a grievance that lacks merit or is not in the interest of the bargaining unit.

Since unions usually have the authority to drop a grievance, even against the wishes of the grievor, collective bargaining statutes require that unions exercise their discretion in a manner that

is not arbitrary, discriminatory, or in bad faith. An employee unhappy with the union's treatment of a grievance may file a **duty of fair representation** complaint with the labour relations board. The tests applied by labour relations boards in those complaints will be explored in Chapter 15. Employers usually like that unions act as a gatekeeper to arbitration, since unions prevent many grievances that lack merit from being referred to arbitration.

Later in this chapter, we will learn that the Supreme Court of Canada has expanded the jurisdiction of labour arbitrators in a manner that requires them to decide disputes involving common law torts, various employment-related statutes (including human rights and employment standards), and *Canadian Charter of Rights and Freedoms** challenges. The fact that unions usually control access to labour arbitration raises interesting access-to-justice concerns in light of these decisions.† For example, if a union withdraws a grievance asserting a tort or Charter violation, the grievor may be prevented from having his or her claim decided. We will consider this issue again in Chapter 15 when we explore the duty of fair representation.

---

*   *Canadian Charter of Rights and Freedoms*, part I of the *Constitution Act, 1982*, being Schedule B to the *Canada Act 1982* (UK), 1982, c. 11.

†   E. Shilton, "Labour Arbitration and Public Rights Claims: Forcing Square Pegs into Round Holes" (2015–2016) 41 *Queen's Law Journal* 275; and B. Adell, "Jurisdictional Overlap Between Arbitrators and Other Forums: An Update" (2000) 8 *Canadian Labour and Employment Law Journal* 179.

---

duty of fair representation: A legal obligation imposed on unions to represent employees who fall within the scope of their representation rights in a manner that is not arbitrary, discriminatory, or in bad faith.

When you file a lawsuit in the courts, you have no choice over which judge is assigned to your case. By contrast, in labour arbitration, the parties can select their own arbitrator, so once a grievance is referred to arbitration, that is the next task.[6] Single arbitrators decide most cases, although **three-person labour arbitration boards** are sometimes appointed. Some collective agreements include a list of agreed-upon arbitrators (see Article 6.01 of sample collective agreement in Appendix to Chapter 12), and the parties select the next available arbitrator on the rotation. Popular arbitrators may not have availability for months. Therefore, to ensure that access to expeditious arbitration is an option, some collective bargaining statutes include provisions for various forms of **expedited arbitration**, which involves the government assigning an arbitrator and imposing specific time limits for the hearing and the issuance of a decision.[7]

Nowadays, as a reflection of the growing legalism in labour arbitration, the vast majority of arbitrators are former lawyers who practised law on behalf of either employers or unions before becoming a "neutral" adjudicator. Some arbitrators are law professors. Other arbitrators are not lawyers, but individuals who have developed expertise in labour arbitration in their former careers as union officials, human resource managers, industrial relations managers, or government mediators. Again, since arbitration has become increasingly legalistic, it is common for the parties to retain lawyers to present their cases. However, human resource managers or industrial relations managers sometimes represent employers, and unions often use their own employees (staff or business representatives) to present the union's case.

The arbitration takes place in a private conference room rather than a courtroom. In many respects, an arbitration hearing resembles a courtroom trial: witnesses testify and the parties' representatives make opening statements and closing arguments like in a trial. The hearing proceeds in the general order described in Box 13.5. However, labour arbitration is also less formal than a trial. For example, Canadian collective bargaining legislation permits arbitrators to accept evidence that would not be allowed by a court,[8] such as **hearsay evidence**, although arbitrators are nevertheless cautious in relying on such evidence and the courts have overturned arbitration awards that relied on hearsay evidence as the basis for critical factual findings.[9] Similarly, arbitrators are not legally bound by the principle of *stare decisis* as are judges (see Chapter 1).[10] However, they nevertheless strive for consistency of legal reasoning and predictability and, therefore, representatives of unions and employers usually reference previous arbitration rulings in their closing arguments in the same manner lawyers in the courts cite case law to judges to bolster their arguments. As a consequence, there is a vast body of labour arbitration decisions that acts as a sort of "common law of the shop".[11]

---

three-person labour arbitration board: An arbitration panel consisting of a person appointed by the employer, a person appointed by the union, and a "neutral," sometimes appointed by the two sides.

expedited arbitration: A form of labour arbitration with strict time deadlines intended to ensure the parties can receive a decision expeditiously.

hearsay evidence: Evidence given by a person based on second-hand knowledge rather than their own direct knowledge or observations.

stare decisis: A Latin term meaning "to stand by a previous decision." It is a guiding principle in the common law regime.

BOX 13.5 » TALKING WORK LAW

The Labour Arbitration Process

Opening Statement

Both parties' representatives briefly describe the issues involved in the grievance and the party's position.

Order of Proceeding and Burden of Proof

The general rule is that the party that filed the grievance proceeds first, and the onus is on that party to prove, on a standard of a proof of "balance of probabilities," that a breach of the collective agreement has occurred.

The main exception to that general rule relates to grievances alleging that there has been discipline or discharge of an employee without "just cause." In those cases, the employer usually must proceed first, even though the union filed the grievance. The rationale for this exception is that the employer is in the best position to explain to the arbitrator its decision to discipline an employee or terminate the employee.

Evidence

Evidence in support of the parties' arguments is presented. Evidence takes three basic forms:

1. Documentary evidence
2. Oral testimony by witnesses
3. Agreed statements of fact

When a party calls a witness, that party asks the witness questions first (**direct testimony**), and then the other party gets to ask the witness questions (**cross-examination testimony**). After cross-examination testimony, the first party is permitted to ask questions to clarify new evidence arising from the cross-examination ("reply evidence"). The arbitrator may also ask questions of any witness.

Closing Argument

Once the parties have finished presenting their evidence, the arbitration hearing concludes with closing statements from the employer and union representatives. Those statements summarize the key evidence the party is relying on and explain the legal rules they want the arbitrator to apply. As noted above, it is common for the representatives of the parties during closing arguments to refer the arbitrator to other arbitration case law involving similar facts and legal issues.

IV. The Labour Arbitration Decision

After the hearing, the labour arbitrator writes a decision and sends it to the parties. In the case of a three-person labour arbitration board, the decision of the majority governs, which in practice often means that the neutral person casts the deciding vote (although sometimes panel decisions are unanimous). That decision will summarize the facts, explain the arbitrator's reasoning, and set out the remedy, if any. As mentioned above, a vast body of labour arbitration decisions has accumulated. Many of those decisions are recorded in the case law reporter known as Labour Arbitration Cases (LAC) and now in free electronic databases such as CanLII, which we have referenced throughout this text.[12] These cases are also summarized in books, including, most notably, *Canadian Labour Arbitration* (known in the field simply as "Brown and Beatty" after the surnames of the original authors).[13] The exercise at the end of this Chapter involves searching for labour arbitration decisions.

An arbitrator's decision is "final and binding" on the parties and employees affected by the decision, subject to the right of the parties to apply to the courts for **judicial review** of the decision (and in British Columbia, a right to "appeal" to the BC Labour Relations Board).[14] Judicial review is the means by which courts supervise the labour arbitration regime. It requires judges to ensure that arbitrators have not exceeded the authority granted them by statute or the parties in the collective agreement. The law of judicial review is complicated and falls within an area of law known

---

direct testimony: Evidence given by a witness called by the party doing the questioning. Leading questions are usually not permitted.

cross-examination testimony: Evidence given by a witness during questioning by the party that did not call that witness.

judicial review: The process through which a decision of an expert administrative tribunal is appealed to a court on the basis that the tribunal exceeded its authority (or jurisdiction) as defined in the statute that created it or that the tribunal's decision was wrong. How much deference a court must give to the expert tribunal's decision is a complex question that is considered in a field of law known as *administrative law*.

as *administrative law*. For our purposes, it is sufficient to note that judges afford arbitrators considerable deference in their interpretations of collective agreements and employment-related statutes, including human rights legislation, because arbitrators are experts in the field.[15] As long as the arbitrator's decision is one that a reasonable arbitrator could come to, a court will usually uphold the arbitrator's decision. The courts give arbitrators less deference on decisions that fall outside the arbitrators' principal area of expertise, such as decisions applying the Charter.[16] This last point provides a good segue into the subject of the expanding scope of labour arbitration and arbitrators' jurisdiction, one of the hot topics in the field.

V. The Expanding Scope of Labour Arbitration

In its early days, back in the 1940s and 1950s, labour arbitration was considered and intended to be a relatively informal, non-legalistic, expedient, and inexpensive alternative to courtroom litigation. The parties often abstained from using lawyers and presented their cases to an arbitrator in an informal manner, sometimes without calling witnesses. Arbitrators wrote brief decisions that were practical and written in plain and simple language. They believed that the scope of their authority was confined to interpreting and enforcing the terms of the collective agreement under which they were appointed. They did not see it as their job to enforce statutes; other administrative tribunals had been assigned that role by the government. Certainly it was not their job to hear cases that raised common law causes of action, such as torts. The common law was the domain of the courts, as we learned in the companion volume. Arbitrators envisioned a solid line between the three regimes of work law (see Chapters 1 and 3), and perceived their role to be a limited one—enforcing the collective agreement.

Early arbitrators recognized that a fundamental difference exists between contract disputes in unionized and non-unionized workplaces. Unlike in the case of individual employees who sue their employers for "wrongful dismissal" in the *common law regime* after the employment relationship has already ended, unions and employers usually must live with one another indefinitely into the future. The ongoing relationship matters, and so arbitrators sometimes acted more like marriage counsellors than divorce court judges, searching for resolutions to conflict that were not overly legalistic, but made practical industrial relations sense and promoted future harmonious relations between employers, unions, and employees.[17]

By the 1970s, labour arbitration had begun to experience what some scholars called "creeping legalism."[18] The parties began to use lawyers more frequently to present their cases. Lawyers are more prone to raise technical legal arguments, which leads to longer (and therefore more expensive) hearings and to more legalistic and lengthy decisions that take arbitrators longer to write. Furthermore, over the past 20 years, the scope of issues that arbitrators are expected to decide has expanded dramatically. Two key Supreme Court of Canada decisions in particular facilitated this expansion: *Weber v. Ontario Hydro* (1995) and *Parry Sound (District) Social Services Administration Board v. O.P.S.E.U., Local 324* (2003).

A. The Weber Decision: Labour Arbitrators' Authority to Enforce the Common Law and the Charter

Mandatory labour arbitration provisions are included in all Canadian collective bargaining statutes. Section 48(1) of the Ontario *Labour Relations Act, 1995* is typical of these provisions. It reads:

> Every collective agreement shall provide for the final and binding settlement by arbitration, without stoppage of work, of all differences between the parties arising from the interpretation, application, administration or alleged violation of the agreement, including any question as to whether a matter is arbitrable.

This language makes clear that if a dispute involves the interpretation or application of a collective agreement, it must go to arbitration and not to the courts.[19] Therefore, if an employee files a lawsuit against his or her employer relating to an entitlement recognized in the collective agreement, the court would dismiss the lawsuit and inform the employee that his or her only recourse is to file a grievance under the collective agreement. In *Weber v. Ontario Hydro*, a unionized employee filed a grievance (which was settled) and also a lawsuit alleging that the employer had engaged in various (common law) torts and violated the Charter (see Box 13.6). The issue before the Supreme Court of Canada was whether that lawsuit should be dismissed because it involved a dispute arising under a collective agreement.

BOX 13.6 » CASE LAW HIGHLIGHT

Labour Arbitrators' "Exclusive Jurisdiction" Over Disputes Arising Under a Collective Agreement

Weber v. Ontario Hydro
[1995] 2 SCR 929

Key Facts: Weber, a unionized employee of Ontario Hydro (OH), suffered from a back disability that left him unable to work and in receipt of sickness benefits provided for in the collective agreement. OH suspected that Weber was malingering, and it hired private investigators to spy on Weber at his home. Using deception, the investigators gained access to Weber's home. Relying on the investigator's report, OH suspended Weber for abusing the sick-leave benefits. Weber filed a grievance challenging the suspension as lacking just cause and the employer's use of private investigators. The grievance was settled during the arbitration process. In addition to the grievance, Weber also filed a lawsuit in court against OH in tort (trespass, nuisance, deceit) and alleging a violation of his Charter rights to be free from unreasonable search (sections 7 and 8 of the Charter). That lawsuit was dismissed by the Court of Appeal on the grounds that the issues it raised arose out of the collective agreement and therefore must be resolved at arbitration and not in the courts. Weber appealed to the Supreme Court of Canada.

Issue: Does the mandatory arbitration provision in the Ontario *Labour Relations Act, 1995* prohibit a lawsuit by Weber against his employer on the basis of torts and Charter violations arising out of the surveillance conducted by investigators on behalf of the employer?

Decision: Yes. The Supreme Court of Canada adopted what it called the "exclusive jurisdiction model." If "the nature of the dispute" can be said to arise under a collective agreement, then labour arbitration is the exclusive forum that must hear and resolve the dispute. A dispute arises from a collective agreement whenever its "essential character" arises "expressly or inferentially" out of the interpretation, application, administration, or violation of the collective agreement. Applying this broad test to the facts, the Supreme Court of Canada ruled that the "essential character" of the lawsuit was a dispute relating to the administration of the collective agreement. That agreement extended the reach of the grievance procedure to "any allegation that an employee has been subjected to unfair treatment or any dispute arising out of the content of this agreement." The collective agreement was the source of the sickness benefits that gave rise to Weber's claim. Therefore, the lawsuit raised issues that stemmed from the collective agreement, with the result that the courts lacked jurisdiction to hear the lawsuit. The Supreme Court of Canada ruled that labour arbitrators have broad remedial authority, including the right to find breaches of the Charter and to order damages for Charter violations as well as to order common law damages for tortious harm. Weber's lawsuit was dismissed.

The *Weber* decision stands for the following proposition: in any dispute that can be said to arise directly or "inferentially" from a collective agreement, unionized employees, unions, and employers have forfeited their rights to sue in the common law courts for torts or bring Charter challenges before courts, and have agreed to be bound by the grievance and labour arbitration process.[20] The principal justification for this extension of labour arbitrators' jurisdiction was to promote a single forum for resolution of disputes in unionized workplaces. However, the vagueness of the legal test—When does the "nature of a dispute" arise "inferentially" from a collective agreement?—spawned hundreds of cases by employers, employees, and unions to sort out exactly when a lawsuit was blocked by the newly expanded exclusive jurisdiction of labour arbitration.[21]

B. The Parry Sound Decision: Labour Arbitrators' Authority to Apply Employment-Related Statutes

The next important decision that expanded the scope of labour arbitrators' jurisdiction was decided in 2003. The *Parry Sound* decision addressed the question of whether arbitrators have the authority—and the legal responsibility—to interpret, apply, and enforce employment-related statutes, such as employment standards and human rights legislation, in the course of interpreting collective agreements. In the case of *McLeod v. Egan* (1975), the Supreme Court of Canada ruled that arbitrators cannot ignore employment-related statutes when they interpret collective agreements.[22] In *McLeod*, an employee filed a grievance alleging that he had been disciplined for refusing to work more than 48 hours in a week. The collective agreement did not restrict the employer's right to assign greater than 48 hours, but the *Employment Standards Act* did, unless the employee consented to work longer hours. The Supreme Court of Canada ruled that management rights, including the right to assign hours of work, must be exercised in a manner consistent with the *Employment Standards Act* and that an arbitrator must decide whether the employer has violated the Act.

The *McLeod* decision clarified that arbitrators must look beyond the "four corners" of the collective agreement and consider whether employers have exercised their management rights in a manner that is inconsistent with employment standards legislation. In the *Parry Sound* decision, the issue before the Supreme Court of Canada was whether a collective agreement incorporates human rights legislation (see Box 13.7). If yes, a complaint by a unionized employee alleging a human rights violation would fall within an arbitrator's jurisdiction.

BOX 13.7 » CASE LAW HIGHLIGHT

Are Labour Arbitrators Required to Apply Human Rights Statutes When They Interpret Collective Agreements?

Parry Sound (District) Social Services Administration Board v. O.P.S.E.U., Local 324
2003 SCC 42, [2003] 2 SCR 157

Key Facts: O'Brien, a counsellor, was dismissed upon returning from maternity leave but within a probationary period defined in the collective agreement. The agreement provided that a probationary employee could be dismissed "at the sole discretion" of the employer and that such action could not be the subject of a grievance. Nevertheless, the union filed a grievance and argued that the decision to dismiss O'Brien was related to her maternity leave and therefore a violation of the Ontario *Human Rights Code*. The arbitrator ruled that since section 48(12)(j) of the *Labour Relations Act, 1995* required arbitrators to "apply human rights and other employment-related statutes" when they interpret the collective agreement, the arbitrator must consider whether the employer violated the *Human Rights Code* when it terminated O'Brien's employment contract. The employer sought judicial review, arguing that since the collective agreement expressly provided that dismissing a probationary employee could not be the subject of a grievance, the arbitrator had no jurisdiction to hear the grievance.

Issue: Are the terms of the *Human Rights Code* effectively incorporated into collective agreements such that an arbitrator must apply the Code to the interpretation of the collective agreement?

Decision: Yes. The Supreme Court of Canada agreed with the arbitrator. It ruled that the prohibition on discrimination in employment in the *Human Rights Code* (see Chapter 26 in the companion book) was incorporated into the collective agreement. Therefore, an allegation that the employer discriminated against O'Brien is an allegation that the collective agreement had been violated, and that dispute falls within the jurisdiction of the arbitrator. The Supreme Court of Canada wrote:

> The obligation of an employer to manage the enterprise and direct the work force is subject not only to express provisions of the collective agreement, but also to the statutory rights of its employees, including the right to equal treatment in employment without discrimination. … [Arbitrators] have not only the power but also the responsibility to implement and enforce the substance rights and obligations of the human rights and other employment-related statutes as if they were part of the collective agreement.

The Supreme Court of Canada ruled that management rights must be exercised in a manner that does not violate a term of the collective agreement or provisions in employment-related statutes. Granting arbitrators the right to apply and enforce statutes that govern employment is consistent with the overriding policy of mandatory labour arbitration, which is to promote industrial peace by allowing for an expeditious and relatively inexpensive dispute-resolution forum. The grievance falls within the jurisdiction of the arbitrator.

The *Parry Sound* decision indicated that employment-related statutes are incorporated into collective agreements, and therefore arbitrators can enforce those statutes in arbitration involving unionized employees covered by a collective agreement.[23] However, this decision does not necessarily mean that unionized employees cannot file complaints directly under a statute rather than file a grievance. That choice depends on an assessment of the nature of the issue in dispute, and whether the government intended that unionized employees be required to pursue their statutory complaints exclusively through the labour arbitration process under a collective agreement. For example, some employment standards statutes (i.e., in Ontario and British Columbia) expressly require unionized employees to pursue the grievance arbitration route rather than file a complaint with an employment standards tribunal.[24] On the other hand, unionized employees usually are not prohibited from filing human rights complaints directly with human rights tribunals, because labour arbitrators and human rights tribunals have "concurrent jurisdiction" (they both have the authority) to hear complaints alleging human rights violations.[25] However, human rights tribunals can refuse to hear a complaint filed by a unionized employee if that complaint has already been dealt with by a labour arbitrator.[26]

C. Is the Expanded Jurisdiction of Labour Arbitrators Undermining the Role Labour Arbitration Was Designed to Play?

The combined effect of *Weber* and *Parry Sound* is that labour arbitration has expanded beyond its original narrow role of interpreting and enforcing collective agreements. The borders between the three regimes of work law have been blurred at the intersection of labour arbitration. Modern labour arbitrators are expected to be experts not only in collective agreement interpretation but also in the common law, statutory law, and even Charter jurisprudence. That is a lot to ask, and there is considerable debate about whether labour arbitration is better or worse for the extended workload it has been asked to carry, as Ontario Chief Justice Warren Winkler discusses in Box 13.8.

BOX 13.8 » TALKING WORK LAW

The Devolution of Labour Arbitration?

In the following excerpt, Warren Winkler, former Chief Justice of Ontario and a former labour lawyer, discusses the changing role of labour arbitrators.* Consider what events Justice Winkler identifies as the cause of this change, and his opinions on whether the changes have been beneficial.

My thesis is that labour arbitration as we know it, that institution that we are all so dependent on in the field of labour relations, has lost its course, has lost its trajectory, has lost its vision. It is at risk of becoming dysfunctional and irrelevant. …

Labour arbitration was intended to be a procedure through which disputes could be resolved in a timely way, on the merits, in an affordable fashion, and with finality. But since the end of what I call the "golden age" of labour arbitration, which spanned the period from roughly 1944 to 1967/68, it has lost its sense, its vision, and has gone off the rails. …

… The parties would appear and present their cases, and this was a non-adversarial, non-acrimonious type of proceeding. The usual process was that the parties would print up their submissions

in a brief; it would be short, and it would contain evidence. This evidence would often conflict, but nobody worried about that. There were frequently no witnesses called, there were no cross-examinations. There was no acrimony because it was non-adversarial. People showed up and presented these cases, which were short and over with quickly.

… While managers represented the interests of employers at collective bargaining, in arbitration they were principally motivated by sound labour relations and a non-adversarial approach. This non-adversarial and non-acrimonious perspective permeated everything and made the system work as successfully as it did. There was none of the litigiousness that followed in later decades; it was most common to have no lawyers involved so that neither the nominee nor the presenter would be a lawyer. I characterize it as something of a "golden age" of labour arbitration, because it was.

Justice Winkler next turns to the reason why this "golden age" of labour arbitration came to an end. The first change was a law passed in 1967 that prohibited judges from acting as labour arbitrators. Judges, who had decided most arbitrations to that point, were replaced in large measure by law professors. Those professors were smart and talented, but they also began a movement toward a more legalistic approach to arbitration. Their decisions were lengthier, read more like court decisions, and took longer to be issued.

The second factor that brought this golden age of labour arbitration to an end was the extension of jurisdiction of labour arbitrators. This was an incremental process; it did not happen all at once; nor did it happen because of any one single event or incident. Even so, there were certain highlights that one can point to that I think are indicators of what happened. These were seminal events in this process of the extension of the jurisdiction of labour arbitrators.

The first of these is the key [1959] case of Polymer Corporation.[†] It involved the unlawful strike of workers at the Polymer plant in Sarnia, and a claim by the employer for damages as a result of the illegal strike. …

The union's argument was that an arbitrator had no jurisdiction to award damages because it was not spelled out in the collective agreement. Professor Bora Laskin [the arbitrator] essentially said that there was a residual jurisdiction in the arbitrator—that if you had a right to hear the case you had the right to formulate a remedy … . That was the thrust of this case, which has affected virtually every single decision in labour arbitration where there is a remedy at issue since that time. …

The next really important case was Weber v. Ontario Hydro in 1995. In this case, Weber had been under surveillance because he was thought to be a malingerer by Ontario Hydro, and finally he sued them. … [T]he Supreme Court said "no." You must look at the nature of the dispute and then look at the four corners of the collective agreement in order to determine whether or not this dispute fits into that employment-related collective agreement. If the answer to that is yes, then it goes there exclusively, and it goes to arbitration; it does not go to the civil courts.

What has been the effect of Weber? It has been enormous … . This was seen as a case that was outside the boundaries—because until this point in time everyone had argued … that arbitrators can deal with issues involving the interpretation, administration, or application of the collective agreement. …

… Weber moved cases such as those related to workplace assaults or defamation into the arbitration process. These were traditionally civil court lawsuits that, until then, no one thought would come within

Warren Winkler, former CJ of Ontario
Source: Reprinted with the permission of the Honourable Warren Winkler.

labour arbitration, with a possible remedy of awarding damages. This was a sea change because it altered the whole concept and notion of labour arbitration. …

The next major development came with Parry Sound Social Services Administration v. OPSEU, which was a case where a probationary employee gets dismissed. There is a probationary employee clause, so that if you are a probationary employee, you cannot seek arbitration. This case goes to the Supreme Court of Canada; they go back and read section 48(12)(j) of the [Ontario] Labour Relations Act that says the Human Rights Act or any other industrial relations–type statute can be arbitrated even if it is inconsistent with the collective agreement. All of a sudden, cases that used to go someplace else go to labour arbitration. …

These three cases effectively created a new world because the sphere of the kinds of cases that, by subject matter, arbitrators could resolve was hugely expanded, and I would say for the better, because it meant a holistic approach. …

The third major factor was a cultural change in the conduct of labour arbitration. Starting in the mid-1960s, the whole idea of an industrial relations–based arbitration process began to shift over to a litigation-based arbitration process.

Originally, the parties worried about whether or not the labour arbitration process would enhance, foster, and benefit industrial relations in the plant. This changed so that now you had the emergence of a group of people who were not worried about that at all; instead, they were worried about winning the case. They did not care whether one party or the other was upset in the workplace. If they were upset, the attitude was "Well, let them be upset." The arbitration process changed from one that was industrial relations based to one that was litigation based. This change drove a wedge between the arbitration process and the labour relations in the plant, and it drove a wedge between the parties in such a way that they did not relate any more. This disconnect proved to be immensely harmful.

The industrial relations practitioners on both sides, who had been such an important part of this community, were displaced by this litigation mentality as the arbitration process was inundated with lawyers. It became a litigation-based arbitration hearing in which the discourse changed from one that was based in industrial relations to one based on law. As a litigation-based process, it was about winning cases, often at any cost. It was also about making technical arguments, taking a different approach to a case, adhering strictly to the rules of evidence, and insisting on the production of documents and on particulars.

The other aspect of this development was that when winning or losing becomes the main focus, the parties then have to be careful about who is chosen as an arbitrator. Each side has to give it their best shot, so the list of who is acceptable becomes a pretty skinny list. Often, this meant choosing the busiest people, because each side felt they needed to have the people who would give them their best chance—even a 1 percent better chance, because winning meant everything. Choosing busy people led, in turn, to significant delays in hearing. This was an incremental, gradual, but steady change in process. …

The outcomes now also reflect the changed trajectory. Now the hearing can take a year and a half or two years, with several adjournments, and it is so technical that nobody can understand the issues, which are not decided on the merits but with decisions thirty-five pages long issued six months later. This is not labour arbitration; it is labour dysfunction.

---

*   W. Winkler, "Labour Arbitration and Conflict Resolution: Back to Our Roots" (lecture, Don Wood Lecture Series, Queen's University, Kingston, ON, 2010), http://irc.queensu.ca/sites/default/files/articles/dwls-2010-warren-k-winkler-labour-arbitration-and-conflict-resolution-back-to-our-roots.pdf. Reprinted with the permission of the Honourable Warren Winkler.

†   *Re Oil, Chemical and Atomic Workers International Union, Local 16-14 and Polymer Corporation Ltd.* (1959), 10 LAC 51; aff'd. 26 DLR LAC 51; aff'd. 26 DLR (2d) 609 (Ont. HCJ).

VI. Labour Arbitration Remedies

Labour arbitrators have broad authority to provide effective remedies for a violation of the collective agreement.[27] That authority derives from the requirement found in collective bargaining legislation that arbitration provide a "final and binding" decision to resolve disputes without work stoppages.[28] According to the Supreme Court of Canada, "[a]rming arbitrators with the means to carry out their mandate lies at the very core of resolving workplace disputes."[29] The same "make-whole" principle considered in our examination of common law remedies for breach of the employment contract (see Chapter 16 of the companion volume) guides the crafting of remedies in labour arbitration. Arbitrators are looking to place the aggrieved party back to the position they would have been in but for the violation, insofar as that is possible.

Therefore, in addition to issuing "declarations" that a collective agreement breach has occurred and ordering the offending behaviour to cease, an arbitrator can order a number of other remedies, including the following:[30]

- damages for harm suffered due to the breach of a collective agreement: for example, lost wages and benefits or, in the case of a union violation (e.g., an unlawful strike), damages for lost profits or revenue[31]
- aggravated damages (for mental suffering) or punitive damages (in narrow circumstances)[32]
- the removal of discipline from an employee's personnel records
- damages for the commission of a tort (when, applying *Weber*, the dispute arises under the collective agreement)[33]

- awarding an employee a job he or she was denied, contrary to the collective agreement
- an apology, in narrow circumstances[34]
- reinstatement for an employee dismissed in contravention of the collective agreement, perhaps with a lesser form of discipline such as unpaid suspension of a fixed duration
- Charter remedies, including declaration that a term in a collective agreement between a government employer and a union violates the Charter; declaration that a statutory provision that violates the Charter is unenforceable insofar as it applies to the collective agreement parties; and damages resulting from a Charter violation (an arbitrator cannot declare legislation invalid, as can a court)[35]

VII. Chapter Summary

This chapter provided a high-level overview of the grievance and labour arbitration process in the collective bargaining regime. Grievance arbitration was intended to provide an expedient, inexpensive, and informal alternative to litigation in the common law courts. This ideal model has been under strain for some time, as arbitration has grown more legalistic and the jurisdiction of arbitrators has expanded exponentially over the years with the encouragement of legislators and the Supreme Court of Canada. The next chapter continues our analysis of labour arbitration by looking more closely at how labour arbitrators interpret the standard requirement found in Canadian collective agreements requiring that employers demonstrate "just cause" to discipline or dismiss a unionized employee.

QUESTIONS AND ISSUES FOR DISCUSSION

1. Describe four types of grievances.
2. What is a "last chance agreement"? Describe a situation in which an arbitrator would refuse to enforce a last chance agreement.
3. Describe three ways in which labour arbitration differs from courtroom litigation.
4. What is "judicial review"?
5. Describe how the Supreme Court of Canada's decisions in *Weber v. Ontario Hydro* and *Parry Sound (District) Social Services Administration Board v. O.P.S.E.U., Local 324* affected the scope of labour arbitrators' jurisdiction.
6. Summarize Ontario Chief Justice Warren Winkler's argument in Box 13.8 in a mini-essay of 500 words or less.

EXERCISE

Labour arbitration deals with mostly private matters between unions and employers. However, most arbitration decisions are made public and reported in various legal case reporters. The most important case reporter in the field is Labour Arbitration Cases (LAC). If you go to a law library, you can probably find these cases in the stacks. Alternatively, if you are a college or university student, you may have access to the electronic version of LAC through your library. You may also have access to the leading labour arbitration textbook, *Canadian Labour Arbitration* (Brown and Beatty), which summarizes arbitration law and links directly to the LAC database in its footnotes. Finally, many arbitration decisions are now available for free on CanLII. To locate them, try this exercise.

1. Go to the CanLII home page: www.canlii.org.
2. From here, you have various options.
   a. If you know the name of the arbitration award, you can search for it in the "Case name" search box.

    b. You can also search a topic in the "Document text" search box. For example, type "just cause," "theft," and "arbitration," which should give you labour arbitration cases from across Canada.

    c. You can also search dedicated labour arbitration databases by province:

        i. Under the "Browse" heading, select a province.

        ii. Under "Boards and Tribunals," select "Labour Arbitration Awards."

        iii. Search for the topic you are looking for within that database by entering a topic in the "Document text" search box.

UPDATES

Go to emond.ca/lawofworkircb for links to news, author's blog posts, content updates, and other information related to the chapters in this text.

NOTES AND REFERENCES

1 *Wartime Labour Relations Order* (PC 1003) is available at http://socserv.mcmaster.ca/oldlabourstudies/onlinelearning/article.php?id=503.

2 *Parry Sound (District) Social Services Administration Board v. O.P.S.E.U., Local 324*, 2003 SCC 42 at para. 30, [2003] 2 SCR 157.

3 See *New Brunswick v. O'Leary*, [1995] 2 SCR 967; and *Shell Canada Ltd. v. United Oil Workers of Canada*, [1980] 2 SCR 181.

4 *Cummins Western Canada v. Teamsters Local Union No. 213*, 2010 CanLII 77035 (BCLA) (Sanderson); *Cameo Inc. v. United Steelworkers of America, Local 3129*, 2000 CanLII 29485 (Ont. LA); *United Steel Workers of America Local 4752 v. Slater Steels Hamilton Specialty Bar Division*, 2003 CanLII 18277 (Ont. SC); *Pepsico Beverages Canada (London) v. United Food and Commercial Workers Canada, Local 175*, 2012 CanLII 35574 (Snow); *Retail, Wholesale and Department Store Union, Local S-955 v. Lilydale Inc.*, 2015 CanLII 57060 (SKLA); and *Toronto Transit Commission v. Amalgamated Transit Union, Local 113*, 2012 CanLII 40324 (Ont. LA).

5 See *Ontario (Human Rights Comm.) v. Gaines Pet Foods* (1993), 16 OR (3d) 290 (SC); *Milazzo v. Autocar and Connaisseur Inc.*, [2005] CHRD No. 3; and *Re: Fantom Technologies* (1998), 70 LAC (4th) 241 (Beck).

6 There are exceptions. For example, in Ontario, grievances involving construction employers must be referred to the Ontario Labour Relations Board, which decides the case as if it were an arbitrator.

7 See, e.g., Ontario *Labour Relations Act, 1995*, SO 1995, c. 1, Sch. A, s. 49; and BC *Labour Relations Code*, RSBC 1996, c. 244, s. 104. See the discussion in G. Adams, *Canadian Labour Law*, 2nd ed. (Aurora, ON: Canada Law Book, 1993), at chapter 12(3)(iii): "Access to Statutory Expedited Arbitration."

8 See, e.g., *Canada Labour Code*, RSC 1985, c. L-2, ss. 60(1) and 16(c); Ontario *Labour Relations Act, 1995*, supra note 7, s. 48(12)(f); Alberta *Labour Relations Code*, RSA 2000, c. L-1, s. 143(2); and BC *Labour Relations Code*, supra note 7, s. 92(1)(b). See the judicial discussion of evidentiary rules in arbitration in *Re City of Toronto and Canadian Union of Public Employees, Local 79* (1982), 133 DLR (3d) 94 (Ont. CA).

9 See *Re Girvin et al. and Consumers' Gas Co.* (1973), 1 OR (2d) 421 (Ont. SC); R. Snyder, *Collective Agreement Arbitration in Canada*, 5th ed. (Markham, ON: LexisNexis, 2013), at 256-63. The courts have also expressed concern over arbitrators' willingness to permit evidence that a court would not have accepted: *Cie minière Québec Cartier v. Quebec (Grievances arbitrator)*, [1995] 2 SCR 1095 (the arbitrator erred in relying on evidence of the employee's post-discharge treatment to overturn the employer's decision to terminate the employee's employment contract).

10 See, e.g., *Isabelle v. Ontario Public Service Employees Union*, [1981] 1 SCR 449, at para. 14.

11 K. Swinton, "Book Review: Canadian Labour Arbitration, by D. J. M. Brown and D. M. Beatty; Collective Agreement Arbitration in Canada, by E. E. Palmer" (1978) 16 *Osgoode Hall Law Journal* 795, at 795.

12 D. Brown and D. Beatty, *Canadian Labour Arbitration*, 4th ed. (Aurora, ON: Canada Law Book, 2006).

13 Ibid. See also Snyder, supra note 9; M. Mitchnick and B. Etherington, *Labour Arbitration in Canada*, 2nd ed. (Toronto: Lancaster House, 2013).

14 BC *Labour Relations Code*, supra note 7, s. 99. British Columbia is unusual in assigning the labour relations board to hear "appeals" of arbitration decisions.

15 See, e.g., *Ontario Public Service Employees Union v. Seneca College of Applied Arts & Technology* (2006), 80 OR (3d) 1 (Ont. CA); *Dunsmuir v. New Brunswick*, 2008 SCC 9, [2008] 1 SCR 190; and *Parry Sound (District) Social Services Administration Board v. O.P.S.E.U., Local 324*, supra note 2. For a nice summary of the law of judicial review of arbitrator's decisions, see Snyder, supra note 9, at chapter 7.

16 The standard of review of arbitrators' application of the Charter is "correctness." See *Cuddy Chicks Ltd. v. Ontario (Labour Relations Board)*, [1991] 2 SCR 5.

17 See P. Weiler, "The Role of the Labour Arbitrator: Alternative Versions" (1969) 19:1 *University of Toronto Law Journal* 16; and D. Beatty, "The Role of the Arbitrator: A Liberal Version" (1984) 34 *University of Toronto Law Journal* 136.

18 P. Weiler, *Reconcilable Differences: New Directions in Canadian Labour Law* (Toronto: Carswell, 1980), at 109-110; K. W. Thornicroft, "Do Lawyers Affect Grievance Arbitration Outcomes? The Newfoundland Experience" (Spring 1994) 49(2) *Relations Industrielles / Industrial Relations* 356.

19 See, e.g., *St. Anne Nackawic Pulp & Paper v. Canadian Paper Workers Union, Local 219*, [1986] 1 SCR 704; *Weber v. Ontario Hydro*, [1995] 2 SCR 929; and *Bisaillon v. Concordia University*, 2006 SCC 19, [2006] 1 SCR 666.

20 A substantial body of literature explores the scope of *Weber v. Ontario Hydro*, supra note 19. See, e.g., R. MacDowell, "Labour Arbitration: The New Labour Court?" (2008) 8 *Canadian Labour and Employment Law Journal* 121; B. Adell, "Jurisdictional Overlap Between Arbitration and Other Forums: An Update" (2000) 8 *Canadian Labour and Employment Law Journal* 179; D. Carter, "Looking at Weber Five Years Later: Is It Time for a New Approach?" (2000) 8 *Canadian Labour and Employment Law Journal* 231; and M. Picher, "Defining the Scope of Arbitration: The Impact of *Weber*—An Arbitrator's Perspective" (1999–2000) 1 *Labour Arbitration Yearbook* 99.

21 Hundreds of court and arbitration decisions apply *Weber v. Ontario Hydro*, supra note 19, in deciding whether courts or arbitrators have jurisdiction over a dispute. Cases finding that arbitration is the exclusive forum include *New Brunswick v. O'Leary*, supra note 3 (the employer claimed that the employee was negligent in use of a leased vehicle); *Cherubini Metal Works Ltd. v. Nova Scotia (Attorney General)*, 2007 NSCA 38, 280 DLR (4th) 235 (an employer's lawsuit against a union, alleging various torts related to the union's filing of many grievances); *Moznick v. Richmond* (2006), 158 LAC (4th) 1 (Joyce) (negligence action for harassment at work); *Giorno v. Pappas* (1999), 42 OR (3d) 626 (Ont. CA) (an employee's defamation lawsuit against a co-worker for an insulting letter sent around the workplace); *Ferreira v. Richmond (City)*, 2007 BCCA 131, 280 DLR (4th) 330 (a tort lawsuit for intentional infliction of mental suffering relating to verbal harassment by co-workers). Cases finding that arbitration is not the exclusive forum and that the lawsuit can continue include *Piko v. Hudson's Bay Co.* (1998), 41 OR (3d) 729 (Ont. CA) (a tort lawsuit relating to an employer's instigation of criminal proceedings against an employee); *Fording Coal Limited v. United Steelworkers of America, Local 7884*, 1999 BCCA 38, 169 DLR (4th) 468 (a defamation lawsuit against a union official for writing that the employer compromised safety in the workplace).

22 *McLeod v. Egan*, [1975] 1 SCR 517. See also the discussion in *Parry Sound (District) Social Services Administration Board v. O.P.S.E.U., Local 324*, supra note 2, paras. 24-30.

23 See also *Brown v. University of Windsor*, 2016 ONCA 431 (the allegation that the employer violated the *Employment Insurance Act* falls within jurisdiction of the arbitrator); *British Columbia Teachers' Federation v. British Columbia Public School Employers' Association*, 2005 BCCA 92, 251 DLR (4th) 497 (the arbitrator has jurisdiction to hear a grievance alleging the employer violated the statute relating to class size). An exception to this general rule is that employment standards rules that are intended to apply only to non-union employees, and therefore are "incompatible" with the collective bargaining regime, are not to be incorporated into a collective agreement (such as the right in employment standards legislation permitting termination with notice alone). *Isidore Garon ltée v. Tremblay; Fillion et Frères (1976) inc. v. Syndicat national des employés de garage du Québec inc.*, 2006 SCC 2, [2006] 1 SCR 27. See the discussion in A. Lokan and M. Yachnin, "From *Weber* to *Parry Sound*: The Expanded Scope of Arbitration" (2004) 11 *Canadian Labour and Employment Law Journal* 1; and S. Luciw, "*Parry Sound* and Its Successors in the Supreme Court of Canada: Implications for the Scope of Arbitral Authority" (2004) 11 *Canadian Labour and Employment Law Journal* 365.

24 See, e.g., Ontario *Employment Standards Act, 2000*, SO 2000, c. 41, s. 99; BC *Employment Standards* Act, RSBC 1996, c. 113, s. 3(7).

25 See, e.g., *Ontario (Human Rights Commission) v. Naraine* (2001), 209 DLR (4th) 465 (Ont. CA); *Quebec (Commission des droits de la personne et des droits de la jeunesse) v. Quebec (Attorney General)*, 2004 SCC 39, [2004] 2 SCR 185; *Northern Regional Health Authority v. Manitoba Human Rights Commission et al.*, 2016 MBQB 89; *Meade v. National Steel Car Limited*, 2016 HRTO 1383; *Canada (House of Commons) v. Vaid*, 2005 SCC 30, [2005] 1 SCR 667; and Brown and Beatty, supra note 12, at 1:4,200.

26   The authority to dismiss a human rights complaint already considered and decided by an arbitrator is either statutory (Ontario *Human Rights Code*, RSO 1990, c. H.19, s. 45.1; BC *Human Rights Code*, RSBC 1996, c. 210, s. 25; and *British Columbia (Workers' Compensation Board) v. Figliola*, 2011 SCC 52, [2011] 3 SCR 422) or derived from the common law doctrine of issue estoppel or abuse of process (*Dick v. The Pepsi Bottling Group (Canada) Co*, 2014 CanLII 16055 (MBHRC)).

27   See *Alberta Union of Provincial Employees v. Lethbridge Community College*, 2004 SCC 28 at para. 41, [2004] 1 SCR 727.

28   See, e.g., Ontario *Labour Relations Act, 1995*, supra note 7, s. 48.

29   *Heustis v. N.B. Elect. Power Commiss.*, [1979] 2 SCR 768.

30   For a full discussion of arbitrators' remedial authority, see Brown and Beatty, supra note 12, at 2:1,500, "Remedial Authority of the Arbitrator."

31   See, e.g., *Re Oil, Chemical and Atomic Workers and Polymer Corp. Ltd.* (1959), 10 LAC 51 (Laskin); aff'd. *Imbleau et al. v. Laskin et al.*, [1962] SCR 338; and *International Union of Elevator Constructors, Local 50 v. Beckett Elevator Company Limited*, 1983 CanLII 960 (Ont. LRB).

32   *Kaiser Aluminum & Chemical of Canada Ltd.*, 2005 CanLII 67217 (Surdykowski); *Greater Toronto Airports Authority v. Public Service Alliance Canada Local 004*, 2011 ONSC 487 (CanLII); *Petrow v. Limo Jet Gold Express Ltd.*, 2009 CanLII 4193 (BC LRB).

33   *British Columbia Nurses' Union v. Health Employers' Association of British Columbia* (2008), 180 LAC (4th) 266 (Taylor).

34   *Prestressed Systems Incorporated v. Labourers' International Union of North America, Local 625*, 2005 CanLII 63785 (Ont. LA). However, apologies are rarely ordered: *Thames Emergency Medical Services Inc. v. OPSEU Local 147*, 2006 CanLII 12300 (Ont. LA).

35   *Weber v. Ontario Hydro*, supra note 19. See Brown and Beatty, supra note 12, at 2:205, "The Charter of Rights and Freedoms." On administrative tribunals (including arbitrators) lacking authority to make general declarations of legislation invalidity, see *Alberta (AG) v. UFCW, Local 401* (2010), 200 LAC (4th) 1 (Alta. QB); and *Cuddy Chicks Ltd. v. Ontario (Labour Relations Board)*, supra note 16.

What Is "Just Cause" for Discipline and Dismissal of Unionized Employees?

I. Introduction

In Part II of the companion volume of this text, we devoted a considerable amount of time exploring how the *common law regime* governs the termination of individual (non-union) employment contracts. We learned that a non-union employer almost always can terminate an employment contract by providing notice, although a lot of disputes take place over how much notice is required. Alternatively, as Chapter 14 in the companion volume explains, a non-union employer can dismiss an employee with no notice, but only if there is cause for **summary dismissal**. In a unionized workplace, the right of the employer to dismiss an employee simply by providing notice does not usually exist. That is because either the collective agreement or the applicable collective bargaining statute require the employer to persuade an arbitrator that it had "just cause" to dismiss the employee. Therefore, unionized employees in Canada have a greater legal claim to continued employment than do non-union employees governed by the common law regime. This chapter examines how labour arbitrators have developed, interpreted, and applied the just cause standard.

---

summary dismissal: Termination of an employment contract by an employer without notice to the employee in response to a serious breach of contract by the employee.

II. The Basic Building Blocks of Just Cause Arbitration Law

In some provinces, the collective bargaining statute imposes an obligation that all collective agreements include a provision requiring the employer to demonstrate "just cause" for discipline or dismissal of an employee.[1] However, even where inclusion of a **just cause provision** is not expressly required by a statute, the parties agree to one almost all of the time.[2] A just cause provision is one of the most important benefits unions negotiate, and it fundamentally transforms the legal treatment of discipline and dismissal that exists in the common law regime. Over time, labour arbitrators have developed an extensive body of jurisprudence that develops the core principles of what constitutes "just cause."

You do realize there's a big difference between dismissal for JUST CAUSE and JUST CUZ, right?

In some respects, the legal tests applied by arbitrators in deciding whether a unionized employer has just cause to discipline or dismiss an employee are similar to the tests applied by the courts in assessing whether a non-union employer has cause for summary dismissal in the common law regime (see Chapter 14 in the companion volume). Sometimes arbitrators directly reference common law decisions. The fact that arbitrators rely on common law decisions should not be surprising, since as we have noted on many occasions throughout this text, the three regimes of work law interact and influence one another (see the discussion of the "internal feedback loop" in Chapter 3). To provide one example, labour arbitrators regularly reference and apply the "proportionality test" recognized by the Supreme Court of Canada in *McKinley v. BC Tel*[3] (described in Box 14.1 in the companion volume) in cases of dishonesty involving unionized employees.[4]

However, for the most part, arbitrators have formed their own legal tests in developing the law of just cause, as Professor Harry Arthurs (York University) explained in a 1967 arbitration award:

> Whatever may have been the early views of labour arbitrators, it is common knowledge that over the years a distinctive body of arbitral jurisprudence has developed to give meaning to the concept of "just cause for discharge" in the context of modern industrial employment. Although the common law may provide guidance, useful analogies, even general principles, the umbilical cord has been severed and the new doctrines of labour arbitrators have begun to lead a life of their own.[5]

In the 50 years since Arthurs made that observation, labour arbitrators have developed more sophisticated and complex legal doctrines, some of which we will now explore.

A. The William Scott Three-Step Analysis

Let's begin with the seminal 1977 case of *Wm. Scott & Company Ltd. v. Canadian Food and Allied Workers Union, Local P-162* (see Box 14.1). In this case, Professor Paul Weiler (sitting then as chair of the BC Labour Relations Board) contrasted the approaches to discipline in the common law courts and labour arbitration, and then set out a three-step analysis for dealing with discipline and dismissal cases under collective agreements with a just cause provision. The legal test developed is more important than the details of the specific facts in the case.

---

just cause provision: A term in a collective agreement between a union and an employer that requires that the employer demonstrate "just cause," or a good business reason, to discipline or dismiss an employee.

BOX 14.1 » CASE LAW HIGHLIGHT

The William Scott Test

Wm. Scott & Company Ltd. v. Canadian Food and Allied Workers Union, Local P-162
(1977), 1 CLRBR 1 (BCLRB)

Key Facts: A unionized employee called a newspaper and alleged that her employer was very inefficient. Wm. Scott & Company, her employer, dismissed the employee, relying on this incident as well as a recent prior one-year suspension for serious misconduct. The termination was upheld by a labour arbitrator, who ruled that the employer had "just cause" to discharge the employee. The union appealed to the BC Labour Relations Board, which had authority to review arbitration decisions to ensure they were consistent with the principles in the BC *Labour Relations Code*. The union argued that the employee's comments to the newspaper were true, that there was nothing vindictive about her actions, and that there wasn't just cause.

Issue: Was the arbitrator's decision to uphold the discharge of the employee inconsistent with the principles guiding the *Labour Relations Code*?

Decision: No. Professor Paul Weiler explained how the approach to discipline and discharge in the collective bargaining regime differs from that in the common law regime:

> Without reviewing the common law ... in any detail, suffice it to say that the [non-union] contract of employment allowed the employer to dismiss an employee without notice for cause (some relatively serious forms of misconduct which, in the eyes of the law, made the continuance of the employment relationship undesirable). But that particular doctrine of the common law can be appreciated only in light of two other features of the master-servant relationship. First of all, even in the absence of cause on the part of the employee, the employer could unilaterally dismiss an employee with reasonable notice, or with pay in lieu of notice. This meant that employees had no legal expectation of continuity of employment even if their performance was satisfactory and work was available. Secondly, if an employee was guilty of some misconduct at work, the employer had no other form of discipline available. The contract of employment did not entitle the employer to suspend the employee, for example.

> [In the collective bargaining regime] an employer no longer retains the unilateral right to terminate a person's employment simply with notice or pay in lieu of notice. Employment under a collective agreement is severed only if the employee quits voluntarily, is discharged for cause, or under certain other defined conditions (e.g. absence without leave for five days; lay-off without recall for one year, and so on). As a result, an employee who has served the probation period secures a form of *tenure*, a legal expectation of continued employment as long as he gives no specific reason for dismissal. ... At the same time, the standard collective agreement also provides the employer with a broad management right to discipline its employees. If an individual employee has caused problems in the work place, the employer is not legally limited to the one, irreversible response of discharge. Instead, a broad spectrum of lesser sanctions are available: verbal or written warnings, brief or lengthy suspensions, even demotion on occasion ... . Because the employer is now entitled to escalate progressively its response to employee misconduct, there is a natural inclination to require that these lesser measures be tried out before the employer takes the ultimate step of dismissing the employee, and thus cutting him off from all of the benefits associated with the job and stemming from the collective agreement.

Weiler then instructed arbitrators to pose the following three distinct questions in a typical discharge grievance:

1. Has the employee given just and reasonable cause for some form of discipline by the employer?
2. If so, was the employer's decision to dismiss the employee an excessive response in all of the circumstances of the case?
3. Finally, if the arbitrator does consider discharge excessive, what alternative measure should be substituted as just and equitable?

In this particular case, Weiler upheld the arbitrator's decision that the employee's misconduct warranted discharge, considering the employee's prior disciplinary record.

The three questions posed by Weiler have guided labour arbitrators dealing with both dismissal and discipline cases ever since. The employer must establish the employee's misconduct on a standard of "balance of probabilities" (that it is more likely than not that the misconduct occurred) by presenting "clear and cogent" evidence that establishes the employee committed the alleged misconduct.[6] In many cases, the answer to question one is fairly straightforward—it is clear that the employee has engaged in misconduct deserving of *some* discipline—but not always. For example, there may be a factual disagreement about whether the employee actually engaged in the conduct alleged at all, or a legal dispute about whether the conduct was actually a violation of the collective agreement. If the answer to question one is "no"—there are no grounds for *any* discipline—then the grievance will be upheld. The remedy from the arbitrator will include an order that the discipline be struck from the employer's records. If the employee had been discharged, probably a reinstatement order will be issued that includes payment of all lost wages and benefits, and accumulation of seniority from the date of the discipline until the date of the reinstatement.

B. Mitigating Factors and Progressive Discipline

If the answer to question one is "yes," then the arbitrator will turn to questions two and three in the *William Scott* test. In deciding whether the employer's chosen response was appropriate, arbitrators consider a range of **mitigating factors/circumstances** that paint a more complete picture of the employee's behaviour and personal circumstances.[7] Those mitigating factors are described in Box 14.2. Among the most important factors are the employee's length of service and prior disciplinary history. A long-service, good employee acquires a stronger claim to his or her job than does a relatively new employee or an employee with prior discipline who has been given an opportunity to improve his or her performance but has failed. As part of their case to the arbitrator, unions and employers will enter evidence of those mitigating factors, which they hope will influence the arbitrator's decision on whether the employer's selected discipline was appropriate and, if not, what lesser penalty should have been imposed.

BOX 14.2 » TALKING WORK LAW

Mitigating Factors in Labour Arbitration

In assessing questions two and three of the *William Scott* test, arbitrators consider a large range of mitigating factors relating to the incident, the employee's work history, and the employee's personal circumstances.

Factors Relating to the Incident

- Was the incident premeditated or an uncharacteristic spur-of-the-moment act?
- Was there an intention to do harm or violate a rule?
- How serious was the incident, in terms of harm to the employer or risk to health and safety?
- Was the employee provoked?
- How has the employer responded to similar behaviour by other employees in the past?
- Was it obvious or known to the employee that the behaviour was unacceptable? (That is, was there a clear employer policy known to the employee?)

Factors Relating to the Employee's Work History

- What is the employee's length of service?

- What, if any, prior discipline has been imposed on the employee, and for what reason?
- Does the employee's previous disciplinary record suggest a high or low risk of reoffending?
- Was there a recent change in job duties or the work environment that played a role in the employee's behaviour?

Factors Relating to the Employee's Personal Circumstances

- Did the employee apologize or express remorse for his or her misconduct?
- Are there any personal factors that might have contributed to or help explain the employee's behaviour (unusual stress, disability, marriage or other family problems, etc.)?
- What would be the personal and economic impact on the employee of losing his or her job? (For example, does the employee have dependants? Is the employee's age and/or skill level such that it will be particularly difficult to find new employment?)

---

mitigating factors/circumstances: Personal or workplace-related factors that, while not directly the cause of an employee's behaviour, help explain or justify an employee's behaviour.

As noted in the *Wm. Scott* decision, **progressive discipline** plays an important role in labour arbitration, along with the associated doctrine of **culminating incident**, a common law doctrine adopted by arbitrators (discussed in Chapter 14 in the companion volume).[8] Unless the employee's misconduct is particularly egregious, arbitrators expect the employer to have exhausted lesser forms of discipline, including warnings and suspensions, before they will uphold a termination. The importance of progressive discipline in labour arbitration motivates many unionized employers to introduce or negotiate clear progressive discipline guidelines. For example, guidelines might specify that a first offence will result in a written warning, the second offence in a one-day suspension, the third offence in a three-day suspension, and the fourth offence in termination. There would usually be an exception for very serious misconduct, permitting the employer to immediately discharge the employee and bypass the progressive steps. Some collective agreements include **sunset clauses**, which require the employer to remove discipline from an employee's file and prohibit the employer from relying on the discipline in the future, after a specified discipline-free period of time has passed.[9]

C. Remedial Authority of Arbitrators in Discipline and Discharge Cases

The third question in the *William Scott* test requires the arbitrator to step into the shoes of the employer and decide what discipline is appropriate in the circumstances. This can involve substituting any lesser form of discipline than that imposed by the employer: a suspension of some length can be substituted for a termination; a shorter suspension can be substituted for a longer suspension; a warning can be substituted for a suspension, and so on. Contrast the right of unionized employers to suspend employees without pay to the situation of the common law non-union employer. In Chapter 15 in the companion volume, we learned that in the common law regime, an unpaid suspension is a breach of contract that an employee can treat as a "constructive dismissal," unless the employment contract grants the employer a right to suspend (and most do not). Collective agreements, in contrast, almost always confer a right to suspend as a form of discipline on unionized employers.

Question three requires the arbitrator to substitute his or her own view for that of the employer. The law did not always permit arbitrators to do so. In the 1968 case of *Port Arthur Shipbuilding Co. v. Arthurs et al.*, the Supreme Court of Canada ruled that once a labour arbitrator decides that an employer had cause to dismiss an employee, the arbitrator could not then substitute his own opinion that a lesser form of discipline was more appropriate.[10] That decision led Canadian governments to amend collective bargaining statutes to grant arbitrators the expressed statutory authority to substitute a lesser form of discipline. Section 48(17) of the Ontario *Labour Relations Act, 1995* is typical:

> Where an arbitrator or arbitration board determines that an employee has been discharged or otherwise disciplined by an employer for cause and the collective agreement does not contain a specific penalty for the infraction that is the subject-matter of the arbitration, the arbitrator or arbitration board may substitute such other penalty for the discharge or discipline as to the arbitrator or arbitration board seems just and reasonable in all the circumstances.

---

progressive discipline: The application in stages by employers of progressively more serious discipline in order to correct performance problems.

culminating incident: The final breach of contract by an employee following progressive discipline that the employer relies on to justify termination of an employee for cause.

sunset clause: A clause in a collective agreement or employment contract that wipes prior discipline from an employee's record after a specified period of discipline-free work.

Note the reference in this section to a "specific penalty" found in the collective agreement. The parties can agree to limit the discretion of the arbitrator by writing into the agreement that for a specific infraction, termination is the automatic penalty and the arbitrator lacks authority to substitute a different penalty.[11]

When the discipline caused the employee to lose wages and benefits (suspensions and terminations), the remedy may also be accompanied by a damage award.[12] It may be months (or longer) between the date of termination and the date of the arbitrator's decision reinstating the employee. In the meantime, a dismissed employee is not working for the employer. For example, if an arbitrator reinstates an employee with a three-month suspension and it has been eight months since the dismissal when the reinstatement takes effect, the damages to the employee include five months' pay and any benefits he or she would have received during that period. Note, however, that the **duty to mitigate** damages applies equally to unionized employees who are dismissed without just cause and non-union employees who are wrongfully dismissed (see Chapter 16 in the companion volume). Therefore, an arbitrator may reduce damages owing to an employee if that employee earned alternative income in the interim, or failed to make reasonable efforts to find alternative employment.[13]

Reinstatement is a common remedy in labour arbitration, which contrasts sharply with the situation in the common law regime, in which courts usually refuse to order **specific performance** (including reinstatement) of individual employment contracts (see Chapter 16 in the companion volume). A study by arbitrator Alan Ponak found that just over half of dismissed unionized employees are reinstated by arbitrators. Of those reinstated, 80 percent receive a substituted lesser form of discipline imposed by the arbitrator, while about 20 percent are reinstated without any substituted penalty.[14] Employees who are reinstated tend to perform well, and only a small proportion end up being dismissed again.[15] Although reinstatement is the normal remedy when a dismissal is ruled to be without just cause, an arbitrator may decide that reinstatement is not an appropriate remedy and order damages instead, similar to how courts remedy wrongful dismissals in the common law.[16] Consider what factors led the arbitrator to take this approach in the decision discussed in Box 14.3.

BOX 14.3 » CASE LAW HIGHLIGHT

When Reinstatement Is Not Ordered in a Case of Dismissal Without Just Cause

United Steelworkers of America, Local 12998 v. Liquid Carbonic Inc.
(1996), 29 OR (3d) 468 (Ont. SC)

Key Facts: The grievor had several instances of discipline on his record, and the employer (Liquid Carbonic) relied on a final culminating incident to justify termination. An arbitrator ruled that although the grievor had a record of discipline, and the culminating incident was deserving of some discipline, the record was not such that termination was justified on a standard of just cause. Much of the prior discipline was for relatively minor offences. However, the arbitrator ruled that reinstatement was not appropriate, because the grievor's record and his demeanour at the hearing demonstrated that he is unwilling or unable to adjust his behaviour and attitude, and animosity was certain to continue if the grievor were reinstated. The arbitrator substituted a 20-day suspension for the termination and instead of ordering reinstatement, he ordered four months' pay. The union applied to the court for judicial review, arguing that the arbitrator effectively permitted the employer to dismiss the grievor by giving notice, which is not permitted in the collective bargaining regime.

duty to mitigate: A legal obligation on the victim of a breach of contract by the other party to make reasonable efforts to limit the amount of damages suffered as a consequence of the breach.

reinstatement: A legal remedy issued by a court or administrative tribunal (including an arbitrator) ordering an employer to re-employ an employee it had terminated in violation of a contract of service.

specific performance: An order by a court requiring a party found to have breached a contract to carry out its obligations as specified in the contract.

Issue: Did the arbitrator make an error in ordering damages based on four months' pay rather than reinstatement of the grievor?

Decision: No. Nothing in the collective agreement, the collective bargaining statute, or arbitration case law requires that an arbitrator always reinstate an employee who is dismissed without just cause. Rather, arbitrators have discretion to order an appropriate lesser penalty to dismissal if they find no just cause for dismissal. If the arbitrator believes reinstatement is not appropriate owing to the particular circumstances of the case, it is within the arbitrator's authority to order damages in lieu of reinstatement. The arbitrator's decision was upheld.

III. Specific Grounds for Discharge and Discipline

Having described the basic principles applied by arbitrators to discharge and discipline grievances, we can now consider their specific application to a variety of types of (alleged) employee misconduct. Not surprisingly, the types of mischief that can lead to discipline of unionized employees mirror those that get non-union employees into trouble (see Chapter 14 in the companion volume). Thousands of arbitration decisions involve employee discipline and discharge. The exercise at the end of this chapter explains how to search such decisions using CanLII.

A. Dishonesty

Dishonesty—such as **time theft**[17] (including surfing the web for personal use at work instead of working[18]), property theft, falsification of records, and outright lying to the employer (including on an application form[19])—is considered a serious workplace infraction because trust and confidence are at the core of the employment relationship.[20] At the same time, the Supreme Court of Canada noted in *McKinley v. BC Tel* (Box 14.1 in the companion volume) that not every incident of dishonesty is so serious that it irreparably ruptures an employment relationship and arbitrators have adopted that reasoning.[21] Arbitrators consider all of the surrounding circumstances, including whether the dishonesty was premeditated; whether there is a pattern of dishonesty; whether there was harm to the employer; how serious the dishonesty was; whether the employee admitted the misconduct and expressed remorse;[22] and whether any other mitigating factors of the sort listed in Box 14.2 above apply, especially length of service and the employee's disciplinary record.[23] If the arbitrator finds that the dishonest behaviour occurred or the employee admits it, then questions two and three of the *William Scott* test will focus on mitigating factors. Consider the case described in Box 14.4.

BOX 14.4 » CASE LAW HIGHLIGHT

Is Theft of a Pack of Cigarettes Just Cause for Termination?

Canada Safeway Limited v. United Food and Commercial Workers Union, Local No. 832
2012 CanLII 97767 (MBLA)

Key Facts: The grievor was a 36-year-old cashier at Canada Safeway in Manitoba. A co-worker reported to the employer that the grievor was behaving suspiciously and that she believed he was stealing cigarettes. The employer conducted surveillance of the grievor, which led the employer to believe the grievor had been deliberately slipping cigarettes into his work apron. The grievor initially denied that he had done so when confronted by the employer, but later he claimed to have found a pack of cigarettes in his apron when he got home. He claimed that he must have put the cigarettes in his apron with the intention of returning them to the correct spot in the store but then forgot they were there and mistakenly brought the cigarettes out of the store. He was dismissed for theft. The union filed a grievance alleging that the employer lacked just cause to dismiss the grievor.

Issue: Did the employer have just cause to dismiss the grievor for theft of a pack of cigarettes?

---

time theft: When an employee falsely claims wages for time not actually worked.

Decision: Yes. The arbitrator indicated that since the parties presented different stories, credibility of the witnesses was important. The arbitrator cited the leading court decision on assessing a witness's credibility, *Faryna v. Chorny*,* in which the court stated: "the real test of the truth of the story of a witness … must be its harmony with the preponderance of the probabilities which a practical and informed person would readily recognize as reasonable in that place and in those conditions." The arbitrator ruled that the employer had satisfied on a balance of probabilities that a theft occurred. The grievor's story that he placed the cigarettes in his apron and then forgot about them was not credible. His demeanour in the hearing was that of a person making up a story, and the employer's witnesses' and video evidence, while not conclusive that the grievor stole the cigarettes, was consistent with the employer's theory that the grievor engaged in deception to first hide the cigarettes behind a cash register and then later place them into his apron.

Having found that a theft occurred, the arbitrator then considered whether dismissal was an appropriate penalty. Theft was a serious concern for a retailer like Canada Safeway, and employees knew it. For cashiers especially, the opportunity for theft is high and it is important that the employer be able to issue stiff penalties to deter it. The grievor had nine separate disciplinary incidents on his employment record, the most serious resulting in a three-day suspension. The fact that the grievor failed to confess and apologize and instead fabricated a story caused the arbitrator to conclude that reinstatement would be inappropriate. The dismissal was upheld.

---

* *Faryna v. Chorny*, [1951] BCJ No. 128 (QL) (CA).

A pack of cigarettes is worth only about $10, but it was enough to cost the employee in the *Canada Safeway* case his job.[24] However, in another Canada Safeway case, an arbitrator reinstated an employee who had consumed a drink from the store shelf, noting that the employee had a clean service record for 35 years, that the theft was a "momentary aberration," that there would be "severe economic consequences" for the employee if the termination was upheld, and that the employee admitted his guilt and apologized.[25] The contrast in the outcomes of these similar cases demonstrates the importance of mitigating factors in cases of employee dishonesty.

B. Poor Performance and Incompetence

An employee's performance may fall short of the employer's expectations for any number of reasons. Arbitrators have long distinguished between "culpable" (blameworthy) poor performance and "non-culpable" incompetence. Poor performance is culpable if it is due to carelessness, laziness, inattentiveness, deliberate neglect or disregard, or neglect of safety rules. Discipline may be an appropriate employer response to culpable performance problems, and in dealing with grievances challenging such discipline, arbitrators have applied the usual *William Scott* test.[26] Arbitrators look for a pattern of culpable performance problems, accompanied by progressively more serious warnings and discipline issued by the employer, before they will affirm a termination for poor performance. Arbitrators accept that, in addition to written warnings and termination if there is just cause, a temporary **disciplinary demotion** is a possible response by an employer to culpable poor performance.[27] A temporary disciplinary demotion has the corrective objective of bringing home to the employee the urgency of improving his or her performance to avoid dismissal if improvement does not occur.

Poor performance is considered non-culpable if it is due to the employee's lack of physical or mental capacity to perform the job at the standard the employer requires (often referred to as **incompetence**); the employee is trying, but he or she just cannot meet the standard. Arbitrators consider discipline to be an inappropriate response to non-culpable incompetence. Yet, an employer is nonetheless entitled to insist that employees meet reasonable performance standards.

---

disciplinary demotion: A form of discipline in which an employee is transferred to a position of less prestige, responsibility, or pay.

incompetence: Poor work performance by an employee that is non-culpable and due not to any deliberate malfeasance by the employee, but to an inability to perform the job to a reasonable standard of competence.

Therefore, arbitrators recognize the right of employers to respond to non-culpable incompetence by imposing a non-disciplinary demotion or transfer to put the employee in a job he or she is capable of performing, or (ultimately) by dismissing an employee who is unable to perform any available job.[28] However, before employers can take such actions, they must satisfy criteria initially spelled out in the 1982 arbitration decision of *Re Edith Cavell Private Hospital*, as discussed in Box 14.5. These criteria roughly parallel the (non-union) "duty to warn" recognized by judges (see Chapter 14 in the companion volume) in the common law regime, and are intended to ensure that the employee is given a fair chance to learn the job and to improve before he or she is demoted or dismissed.

BOX 14.5 » TALKING WORK LAW

When Can an Employer Dismiss an Incompetent Employee?

Sometimes employees lack the physical or mental capacity to competently perform their job. Arbitrators have developed standards to measure when termination of an incompetent employee is a "just" termination. The leading case, still regularly cited in cases involving non-culpable incompetence, is called *Re Edith Cavell Private Hospital v. Hospital Employees' Union, Local 180*.* In his decision, Arbitrator Hope set out the following criteria that an employer must satisfy before a dismissal for incompetence will be considered "just":

It is not open to an employer alleging a want of job performance to merely castigate the performance of the employee. It is necessary that specifics be provided. An employer who seeks to dismiss an employee for a non-culpable deficiency must meet certain criteria:

(a) The employer must define the level of job performance required.

(b) The employer must establish that the standard expected was communicated to the employee.

(c) The employer must show that it gave reasonable supervision and instruction to the employee and afforded the employee a reasonable opportunity to meet the standard.

(d) The employer must establish an inability on the part of the employee to meet the requisite

standard to an extent that renders her incapable of performing the job and that reasonable efforts were made to find alternate employment within the competence of the employee.

(e) The employer must disclose that reasonable warnings were given to the employee that a failure to meet the standard could result in dismissal.

Arbitrators have applied these criteria to both dismissals and demotions for incompetence, and in recent years, arbitrators have also sometimes required employers to satisfy the criteria as a precondition to imposing a "disciplinary demotion" as well as dismissal for "culpable" poor performance. This development was endorsed by the Supreme Court of Canada in *Alberta Union of Provincial Employees v. Lethbridge Community College*,† in which the Supreme Court of Canada questioned whether arbitrators should persist with the distinction between demotions and dismissals for culpable and non-culpable performance problems, since what really matters is the disruption to the employment relationship when an employee fails to perform his or her job adequately.

---

* *Re Edith Cavell Private Hospital v. Hospital Employees' Union, Local 180* (1982), 6 LAC (3d) 229 (Hope).

† *Alberta Union of Provincial Employees v. Lethbridge Community College*, 2004 SCC 28, [2004] 1 SCR 727.

C. *Insubordination and the "Work Now, Grieve Later" Rule*

An employee who refuses to comply with an order of a superior may be committing the serious disciplinary offence of **insubordination**. Insubordination is considered a serious infraction because it undermines the fundamental presumption in work law that the employer is the boss and the employee a subordinate.[29] In order to find that insubordination has occurred, arbitrators require the employer to establish the following: (1) that there was a clear order that the employee understood; (2) that the order was given by a person in authority; and (3) that the

---

insubordination: A breach by an employee of the implied or expressed term of an employment contract requiring the employee to obey an employer's orders and instructions.

employee disobeyed the order. Each of these requirements can give rise to controversy at an arbitration hearing, and failure by the employer to establish any of them can result in the discipline being overturned.[30]

Sometimes, employees may believe that the employer is ordering them to do something prohibited by the collective agreement, and they may refuse to obey on that basis. For example, an employer may order an employee to perform work that he or she does not usually perform, and the employee may genuinely believe the collective agreement entitles him or her to refuse to do the work. Can the employee refuse in that case?[31] The answer is determined by a rule developed by labour arbitrators known as **work now, grieve later**. According to this rule, an employee who believes an employer's direction violates the collective agreement must nevertheless comply with the direction and then file a grievance to challenge it afterward. The basis for the rule was explained in the often-cited 1944 American arbitration decision in *Ford Motor Co.* as follows:

> *[A]n industrial plant is not a debating society.* Its object is production. When a controversy arises, production cannot wait for exhaustion of the grievance procedure. While that procedure is being pursued, production must go on. And some one must have the authority to direct the manner in which it is to go on until the controversy is settled. That authority is vested in Supervision. It must be vested there because the responsibility for production is also vested there; and responsibility must be accompanied by authority. *It is fairly vested there because the grievance procedure is capable of adequately recompensing employees for abuse of authority by Supervision.*[32] [Emphasis added.]

Since an employee is required to comply with an order and then file a grievance challenging the right of the employer to issue the order, it is possible that an employee could be "justly" disciplined for refusing to comply with the order even though an arbitrator later decides that the order itself violated the collective agreement.[33]

As the concluding sentence in the *Ford Motor Co.* passage indicates, the "work now, grieve later" rule is justified on the basis that the employee can file a grievance and, if successful, obtain a remedy from an arbitrator if the employer's order was improper. A variety of exceptions have been recognized by arbitrators over the years, most of which deal with situations in which the harm to the employee could not adequately be remedied in a future arbitration hearing. The most commonly recognized exceptions to the "work now, grieve later" rule include the following:

- *Health and safety.* The employee has a genuine belief that complying with the employer's order will put him or her or someone else in danger, the employee advised the employer of this concern, the concern was a reasonable one, and the danger was sufficiently serious to justify the refusal.[34] See Box 14.6 for an example.
- *Illegal employer orders.* An employee cannot be punished for refusing to comply with an order to perform an illegal act that would expose the employee to sanctions.[35] For example, an employee could refuse to comply with an order to drive a vehicle or transport dangerous goods without the proper licence.[36]
- *Union officials.* An employee who is also a union official may refuse an employer's order when it is necessary to do so in order for the official to perform legitimate union functions. There must be some urgency to the union business such that obeying the employer's order would cause irreparable harm to the employees the official is obliged to represent. At a general level, employees who are also union officials (e.g., union stewards) are given greater latitude to defy or challenge management when acting in their role as union officials, which sometimes requires them to take an adversarial position.[37]

---

work now, grieve later: A rule developed by labour arbitrators that requires an employee who believes the employer is ordering him or her to do something in contravention of the collective agreement to do as directed and then file a grievance later challenging the employer's direction. There are some exceptions to this rule.

- *Personal appearance.* An employee may refuse to comply with a company rule regulating personal appearance in cases where complying with the rule would unduly prejudice the employee. For example, a rule requiring an employee to cut his beard or hair (particularly if the hair is associated with religious beliefs) or to remove a tattoo would have a substantial impact on the employee beyond the workplace, and related adverse effects on the employee could not easily be remedied by an arbitrator. Therefore, an employee may be permitted to refuse to comply pending the outcome of a grievance.[38]
- *Medical examinations and privacy.* Employees cannot be disciplined for insubordination for refusing to subject themselves to medical exams ordered by the employer or to disclose private medical information to the employer. However, in some instances a refusal to provide the employer with medical information may justify the employer in refusing to permit an employee to return to work.[39]

BOX 14.6 » CASE LAW HIGHLIGHT

Is Refusal to Perform Dangerous Work Insubordination?

Lennox Industries (Canada) Limited v. United Steelworkers of America, Local 7235
1999 CanLII 20394 (Ont. LA)

Key Facts: The grievor worked on a production line at Lennox Industries (Canada), and he was seen speaking to a co-worker down the line, away from his workstation. A supervisor ordered the grievor to return to his workstation and start working because the line was being held up. The supervisor then stood about one foot away from the grievor, and intensely ordered him to get back to work. The grievor told the supervisor he could not work with the supervisor so close and hollering at him because it was making him nervous, that his hands were shaking, and that his job involved dealing with very sharp metal that could cut off his fingers if he was not careful. He requested a health and safety representative to assess the situation. The supervisor refused that request because he did not perceive any unusual danger. When the grievor refused to start working, the supervisor suspended the grievor without pay for two days for insubordination. The union filed a grievance asserting a lack of just cause as well as a violation of the *Occupational Health and Safety Act* for penalizing the grievor for exercising the right to refuse unsafe work under the legislation.

Issue: Did the employer violate the *Occupational Health and Safety Act* and/or the collective agreement when it suspended the grievor?

Decision: Yes. First, the employer violated the *Occupational Health and Safety Act* when it punished the grievor for exercising the right to refuse unsafe work (see Chapter 24 in the companion volume). The test to exercise that right in the legislation is whether the grievor had a "subjective belief of danger." Clearly the grievor believed he was at risk of being cut in the circumstances. The legislation required the employer to request a health and safety representative once the grievor raised his concerns to the risk, and by refusing to do so and then punishing the grievor, the employer violated the *Occupational Health and Safety Act*. Second, the employee's refusal to work fit within the health and safety exception to the "work now, grieve later" rule. The grievor honestly believed he was in danger; he communicated this concern to the employer; and the concern of being cut or having a finger cut off was reasonable under the circumstances and sufficiently serious to justify the refusal. Therefore, the arbitrator rescinded the suspension because the employer did not have just cause.

D. Harassment, Violence, and Threats of Violence in the Workplace

Arbitrators treat harassment, violence, and threats of violence[40] in the workplace as serious infractions, for obvious reasons. Employers have a legal obligation to ensure a safe workplace that is free from harassment and fear of violence, and therefore arbitrators accept that discipline, up to and including dismissal, may be warranted. However, as you should expect by now, context matters. Not every instance of harassment, violence, or threat of violence warrants discipline or dismissal. Arbitrators consider all of the circumstances surrounding the incident(s), including the seriousness of the incident, and the usual mitigating factors such as length of service and past disciplinary record. They also consider whether the grievor was provoked; whether the incident was a one-off event that was an uncharacteristic outburst by the grievor; and whether the grievor apologized and demonstrated remorse.[41] In the case of harassment, workplace culture may be relevant. If rough language or sexual banter is common, and the alleged victim has participated in the past or not previously objected, an arbitrator is more likely to accept an argument that the grievor was unaware that his or her comments were unwanted and offensive.[42]

Sometimes, as in the case considered in Box 14.7, both the grievor who has been disciplined for harassment or violence and the victim are unionized employees *in the same bargaining unit*. This can put the union in an uncomfortable position, since it needs to be sympathetic to the victim, but it also has a legal obligation to represent the grievor if a grievance is filed to challenge the discipline. How unions balance these competing interests is considered in Chapter 15.

BOX 14.7 » CASE LAW HIGHLIGHT

Is a Fight in the Workplace Just Cause for Termination?

Re Ontario Store Fixtures and United Brotherhood of Carpenters & Joiners of America, Local 1072
(1993), 35 LAC (4th) 187 (Arbitrator MacDowell)

Key Facts: The grievor was a union steward and a representative on the workplace health and safety committee at Ontario Store Fixtures. In this latter capacity, he asked a co-worker to remove a cart from an aisle because blocking aisles was a safety hazard. The co-worker responded angrily, telling the grievor to mind his own business and get lost. When the grievor insisted that the cart be moved, a loud argument ensued that led the co-worker to shove the grievor, who responded by punching the co-worker in the face. The employer dismissed the grievor and gave the co-worker a written warning. The grievor alleged that he had been dismissed without just cause.

Issue: Did the employer have just cause to dismiss the grievor for punching another employee in the face?

Decision: No. The arbitrator explained that underlying the requirement for just cause in the collective bargaining regime "is a fairly simple notion: 'fairness' in both procedural and substantive terms." He continued: "There must be a sensible balance between the employer's legitimate interest in the efficient operation of his business, and the employee's equally legitim-

ate interest in a continued livelihood with a degree of job security. The real question is: where to strike the balance?"

In answering that question, arbitrators emphasize the need for employers to take a "corrective approach" to employee misbehaviour that applies "progressive discipline." In this case, the grievor engaged in misconduct deserving of discipline. However, in relation to question two in the *William Scott* test—Was the employer's decision to dismiss the employee an excessive response in all of the circumstances of the case?—there were numerous mitigating factors to consider. Those factors included the following: the grievor had 12 years' seniority without any prior discipline; he did not instigate the physical altercation, although he overreacted to the shove by punching the co-worker; the incident began when the grievor was attempting to address an issue the employer admits raised safety concerns; the incident lasted only seconds, and involved a spontaneous and provoked outburst; the co-worker was not seriously harmed, and there was no weapon involved; the grievor had no past problems with violence or aggression, and there was no reason to believe the grievor would reoffend; and the grievor was apologetic, remorseful, and admitted what he did was wrong. In light of these findings, the arbitrator ruled that dismissal was an excessive response. He reinstated the grievor and substituted a six-week unpaid suspension.

E. Absenteeism and Lateness

Like employees in the common law regime, unionized employees in the collective bargaining regime have a contractual obligation to attend work as scheduled. Therefore, if an absence is without a good reason or the employee failed to advise the employer of the absence where there was an opportunity to do so, the absence will usually be considered "culpable" and deserving of some discipline.[43] Unionized employers usually apply progressively more serious forms of discipline before dismissing an employee for poor attendance in the hopes that the employee will get the message and improve his or her attendance. Indeed, since arbitrators expect employers to apply progressive discipline (as discussed above), an employer that fails to provide a tardy employee with a clear warning and chance to improve his or her attendance will almost certainly have its decision to dismiss the employee overturned. Many employers introduce "attendance management policies" that set out the progressive discipline that will be applied to employees who are late or absent for culpable reasons.

For discipline to be justified, it must be "culpable." That means the employee's absence must be blameworthy, and it must have been within the employee's power to attend work. Therefore, if the absence is for reasons beyond the employee's control, such as illness, an accident, or, for example, the sudden death of a loved one or serious family issue, an arbitrator is unlikely to find that the absence was culpable. Similarly, if the absence is related to disability, religion, or some other reason related to a prohibited ground of discrimination in human rights legislation, it is considered to be **innocent absenteeism**, and the employee cannot be disciplined.[44] The employer's legal right to dismiss the employee for absence related to human rights grounds is now governed by human rights law, including the duty to accommodate (explored in Chapters 28 and 29 in the companion volume). As noted in the previous chapter, arbitrators are required to apply human rights statutes when they interpret collective agreements. Therefore, most unionized employees take their human rights issues to labour arbitrators rather than human rights tribunals. Many of the leading Supreme Court of Canada decisions dealing with the duty to accommodate workers began as labour arbitration decisions that were judicially reviewed to the courts.

When deciding whether an employer has just cause to dismiss an employee for "innocent" or non-culpable absenteeism, arbitrators (and human rights tribunals) consider two questions:

1. Is the employee's absenteeism excessive relative to an average employee in the work establishment?
2. If yes, then is there a reasonable prospect of the employee being able to return to work in the foreseeable future, considering any potential accommodation to the point of undue hardship if the reason for the absence is related to human rights grounds?[45]

This test was affirmed by the Supreme Court of Canada in the 2008 case of *Hydro-Québec v. Syndicat des employé-e-s de techniques professionnelles et de bureau d'Hydro-Québec, section locale 2000 (SCFP-FTQ).*[46]

F. Off-Duty Conduct

At a general level, how employees behave during their non-working time is none of the employer's business, except when that behaviour interferes with the ability of the employee to perform his or her job or could harm the employer's reputation or other business interests. The leading arbitration decision setting out the test employers must satisfy in order to justify discipline or dismissal for off-duty conduct is the 1967 case of *Re Millhaven Fibres Ltd. v. Atomic Workers Int'l Union, Local 9-670*, in which the arbitrator proclaimed the following test:

[I]f the discharge is to be sustained on the basis of … justifiable reasons arising out of conduct away from the place of work, there is an onus on the Company to show that:

(1) the conduct of the grievor harms the Company's reputation or product;

(2) the grievor's behaviour renders the employee unable to perform his duties satisfactorily;

(3) the grievor's behaviour leads to refusal, reluctance or inability of the other employees to work with him (that is based on a legitimate fear of injury or harm, and not just a dislike of the grievor[47]);

(4) The grievor has been guilty of a serious breach of the *Criminal Code* and thus rendering his conduct injurious to the general reputation of the Company and its employees; or

(5) Places difficulty in the way of the Company properly carrying out its function of efficiently managing its works and efficiently directing its working forces.[48]

---

innocent absenteeism: An employee's absence from work due to reasons that are not blameworthy, such as illness, injury, or disability.

The employer need only establish that one of the criteria is met, although as in each just cause case, all of the circumstances will be considered in assessing whether the employer's response was appropriate, including the mitigating factors discussed previously. In particular, arbitrators balance the harm to the employer against the right of employees to live their private lives without employer supervision.[49]

In measuring harm to the employer's reputation, arbitrators apply an "objective test" (see Chapter 7 in the companion volume), asking, "What would a reasonable person of normal intelligence think, if told about the circumstances?" In this instance, Would a reasonable person aware of the employee's off-duty conduct believe the conduct would cause real injury to the employer's reputation?[50] Evidence of actual harm is not necessary. Since there must be a nexus between the employee's behaviour and harm, or potential harm, to the employer's reputation or other business interests, it matters what the employee's job entails and the line of business the employer is in. For example, teachers, law enforcement employees, and other employees in positions of authority and trust may be held to a higher standard of integrity in their off-duty behaviour than are labourers who do not work with the public or young people.[51]

In recent years, the question of whether an employee's use of social media outside of working hours can give rise to discipline or dismissal has arisen. The *Millhaven* test is applied in these cases, with a focus on the potential harm to the employer's reputation. Box 14.8 contrasts two recent arbitration awards involving the dismissal of firefighters for offensive Tweets, which were exposed in a *National Post* article.[52] What explains the different outcomes?

BOX 14.8 » CASE LAW HIGHLIGHT

Can Off-Duty Tweeting Be Grounds for Dismissal of a Unionized Employee?

	Toronto Professional Fire Fighters' Association, Local 3888 v. Grievance of Lawaun Edwards [Edwards Grievance] 2014 CanLII 62879 (Arbitrator Misra)	Toronto (City) v. Toronto Professional Fire Fighters' Association, Local 3888 [Bowman Grievance] 2014 CanLII 76886 (Arbitrator Newman)
Key facts:	The grievor, who had 2.5 years of discipline-free service, was dismissed for the following Twitter exchange: Other person: Just stood behind a girl who used the word "like" roughly 300 times to order her coffee. Stay in skool, kidz Grievor: Would swat her in the back of the head be considered abuse or a way to reset the brain? Other person: Maybe foreplay? Grievor: Unlikely, intelligence and a vocabulary is sexy. Saying "like" that amount of times means you have none	The grievor, who had 2.5 years of discipline-free service, was dismissed for a series of Tweets, including the following: Grievor: Reject a woman and she will never let it go. One of the many defects of their kind. Also weak arms. Grievor: I'd never let a woman kick my ass. If she tried I'd be like HEY! You get your … ass back in the kitchen and make me some pie. Grievor: If you were deaf I would rape you and then break your fingers so you can't tell anyone … The grievor claimed he thought his Tweets were private and readable only by his "followers." The grievor wrote a lengthy apology to the employer, acknowledging that his Tweets were inappropriate.
Decision:	The Twitter exchange was inappropriate and deserving of some discipline because it was disrespectful to women. The grievor's Twitter account identified him as a firefighter, and the *National Post* story had harmed the employer's reputation. However, dismissal was too harsh a	The employer had just cause for termination. The arbitrator referred to the *Millhaven* test criteria and concluded that criterion four should be updated to recognize serious breaches of human rights legislation that harm the employer's reputation. The question an arbitrator should ask when considering potential harm to an employer's reputation is this: Would a reasonable and fair-minded member of the public, if apprised of all the facts, consider that the

	Toronto Professional Fire Fighters' Association, Local 3888 v. Grievance of Lawaun Edwards [Edwards Grievance] 2014 CanLII 62879 (Arbitrator Misra)	Toronto (City) v. Toronto Professional Fire Fighters' Association, Local 3888 [Bowman Grievance] 2014 CanLII 76886 (Arbitrator Newman)
Decision: *continued*	consequence? The Tweet was directed at an anonymous person, no one at work had complained, and the grievor had a clean disciplinary record. The employer had a social media policy, but it had not done a good job of disseminating it.	grievor's continued employment would so damage the reputation of the employer as to render that employment untenable? Here, the grievor made comments on Twitter that were highly offensive. In fact, he made many offensive comments over a two-year period. The comments were sometimes violent and certainly sexist. The Tweets caused reputational harm to the employer after they were widely reported in the media. Although the grievor apologized, the arbitrator doubted his apology was sincere and that he fully grasped how offensive his comments were. The arbitrator did not accept the grievor's argument that he thought Tweets were private. She wrote: "When engaging in social media use … the user must accept responsibility when the content is disseminated in exactly the manner promoted by the social media provider."
Outcome:	The grievor was reinstated with a three-day suspension.	The dismissal of the grievor was upheld. The grievance was dismissed.

G. Intoxication at Work

Drinking or taking mind-altering drugs at work, particularly when a job is safety sensitive, is considered a serious disciplinary offence.[53] Reporting to work intoxicated is also a serious offence, although the employer must establish that the employee is impaired; for example, an employee who had a beer at some point before his or her shift began may not be impaired.[54] As discussed in Chapters 27 and 29 of the companion volume, different considerations may apply if the employee has a drug and/or alcohol addiction, which are considered disabilities. An employer who disciplines an alcoholic or drug-addicted employee for reporting to work intoxicated may be required to demonstrate that it had accommodated that employee's disability by, for instance, allowing the employee to take a leave of absence to attend an addiction program.[55]

IV. Chapter Summary

This chapter explored in some detail the law of "just cause" for discipline and dismissal in the collective bargaining regime. The right of unionized employees not to be subjected to discipline or dismissal without a good reason is among the most significant differences between the common law regime and the collective bargaining regime. Another difference is that unionized employers usually have a greater range of disciplinary options short of dismissal available to them. For example, whereas a suspension without pay is usually a breach of contract that the employee can treat as a "constructive dismissal" in the common law regime (see Chapter 15 in the companion volume), in the collective bargaining regime arbitrators expect an employer to consider a suspension before jumping to the ultimate sanction of a dismissal as part of progressive discipline. Another important difference between the two regimes in their treatment of termination for cause is that labour arbitrators, in contrast to courts, regularly order that unionized employees who have been dismissed without just cause be reinstated to their jobs. On the other hand, as this chapter explained, arbitrators' tests for just cause in many respects parallel the tests applied by the common law courts in considering whether employers had cause for "summary dismissal" without notice (see Chapter 14 in the companion volume).

QUESTIONS AND ISSUES FOR DISCUSSION

1. Explain the *William Scott* test applied by arbitrators in "just cause" grievance arbitrations.
2. If an arbitrator rules that an employer did not have just cause to dismiss an employee, what remedies can that arbitrator order?
3. What is the "work now, grieve later" rule? Describe five exceptions to that rule.
4. Describe mitigating factors that might persuade an arbitrator to substitute a lesser penalty in a case involving dismissal of an employee for theft.
5. Compare the approaches of courts and labour arbitrators to discipline and dismissal for off-duty conduct by reviewing the discussion of the topic in this chapter and the discussion of the common law approach in Chapter 14 of the companion volume. Are the legal tests different in the two regimes? If so, how are they different?

EXERCISE

There are a variety of excellent legal digests that compile and summarize labour arbitration case law dealing with just cause for discipline and dismissal. Most university libraries have these books, and students may have access to electronic versions through their university or college. Leading books include the following:

- D. Brown and D. Beatty, *Canadian Labour Arbitration*, 4th ed. (Aurora, ON: Canada Law Book, 2006).
- M. Mitchnick and B. Etherington, *Labour Arbitration in Canada*, 2nd ed. (Toronto: Lancaster House, 2013).
- R. Snyder, *Collective Agreement Arbitration in Canada*, 5th ed. (Markham, ON: Lexis-Nexis, 2013).

The leading publication in which to find labour arbitration case law is *Labour Arbitration Cases* (LAC). This series can be found in many academic libraries and is available electronically with a licence that many university and college libraries purchase. In recent years, CanLII has begun to post labour arbitration decisions. Try this exercise to locate arbitration decisions that involve disputes over whether an employer had just cause to discipline or dismiss a unionized employee.

1. Go to the CanLII home page: www.canlii.org.
2. Under the "Browse" heading, select a jurisdiction.
3. Under "Boards and Tribunals," select "Labour Arbitration Awards."
4. In the "Document text" search box, search for cases involving employee theft. For example, type "just cause" and "theft."
5. Scroll through the decisions and find a case in which an employee was disciplined or dismissed for theft. Read the case and answer the following questions:
   a. Did the arbitrator find that there were grounds for discipline?
   b. Did the arbitrator agree that the employer's discipline was appropriate in all the circumstances?
   c. Did the grievance succeed, and if so, what remedy did the arbitrator order?

UPDATES

Go to emond.ca/lawofworkircb for links to news, author's blog posts, content updates, and other information related to the chapters in this text.

NOTES AND REFERENCES

1   See, e.g., Manitoba *Labour Relations Act*, CCSM c. L10, s. 79, which requires that every collective agreement "contain a provision requiring that the employer have just cause for disciplining or dismissing any employee" in the bargaining unit. See also BC *Labour Relations Code*, RSBC 1996, c. 244, s. 84.

2   Sometimes the collective agreement does not include a just cause provision or excludes the term's application to some employees, such as probationary employees. For a discussion of how arbitrators have dealt with the absence of just cause provisions, see the discussion in D. Brown and D. Beatty, *Canadian Labour Arbitration*, 4th ed. (Aurora, ON: Canada Law Book, 2006), at 7:1,200.

3   *McKinley v. BC Tel*, 2001 SCC 38, [2001] 2 SCR 161.

4   See, e.g., *United Steelworkers, Local 3950-65 v. Metal Koting (Continuous Colour Coat Limited)*, 2012 CanLII 63726 (Ont. LA) (Hayes); *Hamilton Health Sciences v. Canadian Union of Public Employees CUPE Local 4800*, 2006 CanLII 50484 (Ont. LA) (Surdykowski); and *Sysco Food Services of Ontario v. National Automobile, Aerospace, Transportation and General Workers Union of Canada (CAW-Canada), Local 414*, 2004 CanLII 54978 (Ont. LA) (Gray).

5   *Port Arthur Shipbuilding Co.* (1967), 17 LAC 109 (Arthurs).

6   See *F.H. v. McDougall*, 2008 SCC 53, [2008] 3 SCR 41 for a discussion of the "balance of probabilities" standard in civil cases, especially paras. 45-46; and *Edmonton (City)* (2013), 232 LAC (4th) 376 (Jolliffe).

7   Many cases discuss these mitigating factors. Some often-cited authorities include *Steel Equipment Co. Ltd.* (1964), 14 LAC 356 (Reville); *Wm. Scott & Company Ltd. v. Canadian Food and Allied Workers Union, Local P-162* (1977), 1 CLRBR 1 (BCLRB); and *Galco Food Products* (1974), 7 LAC (2d) 350 (Beatty).

8   See discussion in R. Snyder, *Collective Agreement Arbitration in Canada*, 5th ed. (Markham, ON: LexisNexis, 2013), at 532-36; M. Mitchnick and B. Etherington, *Labour Arbitration in Canada*, 2nd ed. (Toronto: Lancaster House, 2013), at 182-83.

9   See, e.g., *O. I. Canada Corp v. United Steelworkers of America*, 2009 CanLII 27269 (Ont. LA) (Chauvin).

10 *Port Arthur Shipbuilding Co. v. Arthurs et al.*, [1969] SCR 85.

11 *Region of Peel v. Canadian Union Of Public Employees, Local 966*, 2011 CanLII 7758 (Ont. LA) (Brownlee); *Workers Canada Union, Local No. 401 v. Aviscar Inc*, 2015 CanLII 20440 (ABGAA) (Wallace); and *T.T.C.* (2010), 193 LAC (4th) 273 (Harris). The language must be specific and clear. See the discussion in *Warehousemen and Helpers Union, Local 979 v. Brink's Canada*, [1983] 1 SCR 382.

12 The authority of arbitrators to award damages for breach of a collective agreement was affirmed in *Imbleau et al. v. Laskin et al.*, [1962] SCR 338.

13 Mitigation: see, e.g., *Toronto Association for Community Living v. Canadian Union of Public Employees*, 2006 CanLII 50487 (Ont. LA) (Surdykowski); and *Canada Post Corporation v. Canadian Union of Postal Workers*, 2010 CanLII 86707 (BCLA) (Gordon).

14 A. Ponak, "Discharge Arbitration and Reinstatement: An Industrial Relations Perspective" (1992) 2 *Labour Arbitration Yearbook* 31.

15 Ibid.

16 *United Steelworkers of America, Local 12998 v. Liquid Carbonic Inc.* (1996), 29 OR (3d) 468 (Ont. SC); *George Brown College of Applied Arts and Technology v. Ontario Public Service Employees Union*, 2011 CanLII 60727 (Ont. LA) (Bendel).

17 *U.F.C.W., Local 2000 v. Canada Safeway* (2002), 108 LAC (4th) 161 (Chertkow); *Alberta Union of Provincial Employees v. Lethbridge Community College*, 2004 SCC 28, [2004] 1 SCR 727.

18 See *Unite Here Local 75 v. Fairmont Royal York Hotel*, 2012 CanLII 3872 (Ont. LA) (Trachuk) (an employee was reinstated with suspension for surfing the web for personal use at work).

19 *Re Gould Manufacturing of Canada Ltd. and United Steelworkers of America* (1973), 33 DLR (3d) 527 (Ont. Div. Ct). The test for assessing discipline for mistruths on application forms is similar to that in the non-union setting, discussed in Chapter 6 in the companion volume. The employer must demonstrate the dishonesty, that it affected the employer's hiring decision, and that it suffered some prejudice. See the discussion in Brown and Beatty, supra note 2, at 7:3,324.

20 See *Re Phillips Cable Ltd. and International Union of Electrical, Rad* (1974), 6 LAC (2d) 35 (Adams): "Honesty is a touchstone to viable employer-employee relationships."

21 *McKinley v. BC Tel*, supra note 3.

22 See the discussion of the importance of accepting responsibility for misconduct in *British Columbia Hydro and IBEW Local 258* (2001), 94 LAC (4th) 305 (Kinzie).

23 See Brown and Beatty, supra note 2, at 7:3,300. Cases where a dishonest employee was reinstated include the following: *Sobeys West Inc. (Safeway) v. United Food And Commercial Workers, Loc. 1518*, 2015 CanLII 68542 (BCLA) (Kondopulos); *Women's College Hospital v. Service*

Employees International Union, Local 1 Canada, 2011 CanLII 26325 (Ont. LA) (Stout); and *Overwaitea Food Group v. United Food & Commercial Workers Union, Local 1518*, 2014 CanLII 11427 (BCLA) (Doyle). Cases where dismissal of a dishonest employee is upheld by the arbitrator include the following: *Sysco Food Services of Ontario v. National Automobile, Aerospace, Transportation and General Workers Union of Canada (CAW-Canada), Local 414*, supra note 4; *Hamilton Health Sciences v. Canadian Union of Public Employees CUPE Local 4800*, supra note 4; *Toronto (City) v. Canadian Union of Public Employees, Local 5089*, 2014 CanLII 87075 (Ont. LA) (Sheehan); *Surrey (City) v. Canadian Union of Public Employees, Local 402*, 2012 CanLII 66328 (BCLA) (Brown); *Protrans BC Operations Ltd v. BC Government and Service Employees' Union*, 2012 CanLII 97717 (BCLA) (Jackson); *Capitol Regional District v. Canadian Union of Public Employees, Local 1978*, 2013 CanLII 54957 (BCLA) (Nichols); *Shaw Cablesystems G.P. (North Shore) v. International Brotherhood of Electrical Workers, Local 213*, 2010 CanLII 37096 (BCLA) (Kinzie); *Government of the province of British Columbia v. British Columbia Government and Service Employees' Union*, 2000 CanLII 29378 (BCLA) (Lanyon) (the termination of an alcoholic for stealing alcohol was upheld).

24 See also *Labatt Brewing Company v. International Union of Operating Engineers, Local 796*, 2001 CanLII 25965 (Ont. LA) (Surdykowski) (upholding dismissal of an employee who stole a $10 promotional baseball cap). But see *Teamsters Local 847 v. Maple Leaf Sports and Entertainment*, 2016 CanLII 70978 (Ont. LA) (Jesin) (reinstatement with suspension of employee who helped himself to pop from the soda fountain machine).

25 *Canada Safeway Ltd. v. United Food and Commercial Workers Union, Local 1518* (2011), 210 LAC (4th) 173 (Glass).

26 See, e.g., *Toronto (City) v. Canadian Union of Public Employees, Local 79*, 2013 CanLII 72336 (Ont. LA) (Randall) (poor performance due to laziness, reinstatement with one-month suspension); and *Madawaska Doors* (2004), 127 LAC (4th) 378 (Dumoulin).

27 *Toronto Transit Commission v. Amalgamated Transit Union, Local 113*, 2011 CanLII 52245 (Ont. LA) (Slotnick); *Kingston Independent Nylon Workers Union v. Invista (Canada) Company*, 2014 CanLII 27444 (Ont. LA) (Steinberg); *Re London (City)*, [2009] OLAA No. 317 (Williamson); and *Re Steel Co. of Canada Ltd. and U.S.W.A., Local 1005* (1976), 7 LAC (2d) 132 (Beatty).

28 *Re Edith Cavell Private Hospital v. Hospital Employees' Union, Local 180* (1982), 6 LAC (3d) 229 (Hope); *Re Peelle Co. and United Steelworkers of America, Local 6457* (1994), 39 LAC (4th) 370 (Kennedy); *Telus*

Communications Company v. Telecommunications Workers Union, 2016 CanLII 61445 (Ont. LA) (Hornung); *George Brown College of Applied Arts and Technology v. Ontario Public Service Employees Union*, 2010 CanLII 65077 (Ont. LA) (Bendel); *CUPE, Local 2348 v. Winnipeg Regional Health Authority—Midwives*, 2014 CanLII 22979 (MBLA) (Gibson); *Calgary Board of Education v. International Brotherhood of Electrical Workers (Local Union 254)*, 2008 CanLII 88120 (ABGAA) (Sims); and *Dr. John Gillis Memorial Lodge v. Prince Edward Island Union of Public Sector Employees*, 2013 CanLII 101338 (NSLA) (Slone). See also the discussion in R. Snyder, *Collective Agreement Arbitration in Canada*, 5th ed. (Markham, ON: LexisNexis, 2013), at 676-80.

29 There are hundreds of arbitration decisions involving insubordination. Those available on CanLII include the following: *Senior Flexonics (Canada) Limited v. Sheet Metal Workers' International Association, Local Union 540*, 2010 CanLII 13639 (Ont. LA) (Gray); *Waterloo Region District School Board v. Custodial and Maintenance Association*, 2012 CanLII 42060 (Ont. LA) (Stout); *British Columbia Maritime Employers Association v. International Longshore and Warehouse Union, Local 500*, 2011 CanLII 85130 (BCLA) (McPhillips); *British Columbia (Children & Family Development) v. British Columbia Government & Services Employees Union*, 2009 CanLII 88302 (BCLA) (Korbin); *Teck Coal Limited v. United Steelworkers, Locals 9346*, 2014 CanLII 37907 (BCLA) (Kinzie); and *Canada Post Corporation v. Canadian Union of Postal Workers*, 2010 CanLII 86367 (BCLA) (Gordon).

30 See Brown and Beatty, supra note 2, at 7:3,612.

31 See, e.g., *Tenneco Canada Inc. v. United Steelworkers, Local 2894*, 2014 CanLII 46059 (Ont. LA) (Wilson).

32 *Matter of Ford Motor Co.*, 3 LA 779 (1944) (Shulman). See also *Re USW and Lake Ontario Steel Company Ltd.* (1968), 19 LAC 103 (Weiler).

33 See the discussion in *York Farms Ltd.* (1981), 2 LAC (3d) 112 (Chapman).

34 See, e.g., *Toronto East General Hospital* (2004), 131 LAC (4th) 220 (Reilly) (refusal not based on reasonable risk concern); and *Lennox Industries (Canada) Limited v. United Steelworkers of America, Local 7235*, 1999 CanLII 20394 (Ont. LA) (Knopf).

35 *Re National Starch & Chemical Co. (Canada) Ltd. and Canadian Union of Distillery Workers* (1976), 11 LAC (2d) 288 (Rayner).

36 *Re Thibodeau-Finch Express Inc. and Union des Chauffeurs de Camions, Local 106* (1987), 30 LAC (3d) 58 (Frumkin).

37 *Robertshaw Controls Canada Inc. v. United Electric, Radio and Machine Workers of America, Local 512* (1982), 5 LAC (3d) 142 (Egan); *Re Firestone Steel Products of Canada v. U.A.W. Local 27* (1975), 8 LAC (2d) 164 (Brandt); *Burns*

Meats Ltd. v. Canadian Food & Allied Workers, Local P139 (1980), 26 LAC (2d) 379 (Picher); *Natrel Inc. v. Milk and Bread Drivers, Dairy Employees, Caterers and Allied Employees, Local Union 647,* 2005 CanLII 67419 (Ont. LA) (Surdykowski); and *Re National Steel Car Ltd. and U.S.W.A.* (2001), 101 LAC (4th) 316 (Shime).

38   *Dominion Stores* (1972), 31 LAC (3d) 257 (Brandt).

39   *Monarch Fine Foods Co. Ltd. and Milk and Bread Drivers, Dairy Employees, Caterers and Allied Employees, Local 647* (1978), 20 LAC (2d) 419 (Picher).

40   See *Communications, Energy and Paperworkers Union of Canada, Local 1178 v. Hood Packaging Corp.,* 2013 CanLII 35534 (Ont. LA) (Trachuk), observing that Ontario's *Occupational Health and Safety Act* imposition of a legal duty on employers to maintain workplaces free from threats increases the seriousness of workplace threats.

41   *Re Natrel Inc. v. C.A.W.—Canada, Local 462* (2005), 143 LAC (4th) 233 (Knopf); *Re Ajax-Pickering Transit Authority* (2003), 123 LAC (4th) 51 (Craven); *Re Dominion Glass Co. and United Glass & Ceramic Workers, Local 203* (1975), 11 LAC (2d) 84 (Linden); *Amalgamated Transit Union, Local 113 v. Toronto Transit Commission,* 2013 CanLII 90055 (Ont. LA) (Shime); *Black & McDonald Ltd. v. Labourers' International Union of North America,* 2016 CanLII 4952 (Ont. LA) (Slotnick); *Coca-Cola Bottling Company v. National Automobile, Aerospace, Transportation and General Workers Union of Canada,* 2009 CanLII 70988 (Ont. LA) (Chauvin); *Re McMaster University and S.E.I.U., Local 532* (1993), 33 LAC (4th) 33 (Brunner).

42   *Regional Municipality of Niagara Police Services Board v. Niagara Region Police Association,* 2009 CanLII 16288 (Ont. LA) (Snow); and *Vale Canada Ltd v. United Steelworkers of America, Local 6500,* 2012 CanLII 81310 (Ont. LA) (Johnson).

43   *Goodyear Canada Inc. v. United Steelworkers of America, Local 834L,* 2004 CanLII 54975 (Ont. LA) (Gray); *Sysco Central Ontario, Inc. v. Teamsters, Local Union 419,* 2013 CanLII 76889 (Ont. LA) (McNamee); and *Stelco* (1987), 28 LAC (3d) 90 (Lucas).

44   *Pharma Plus Drugmarts Ltd. v. United Food & Commercial Workers Canada, Local 175,* 2013 CanLII 34835 (Ont. LA) (Marcotte); and *Re United Automobile Workers and Massey-Ferguson Ltd.* (1969), 20 LAC 370 (Weiler).

45   *St. Joseph's General Hospital, Elliot Lake v. Ontario Nurses' Association,* 2006 CanLII 7155 (Ont. LA) (Luborsky); *Re Maple Leaf Meats* (2001), 98 LAC (4th) 40 (Whitaker); *AirBC Ltd. and Canadian Airline Dispatchers Association* (1995), 50 LAC (4th) 93 (McPhillips); and *Loblaws Companies Limited v. United Food & Commercial Workers, Local 247,* 2014 CanLII 9496 (BCLA) (Brown).

46   *Hydro-Québec v. Syndicat des employé-e-s de techniques professionnelles et de bureau d'Hydro-Québec, section locale 2000 (SCFP-FTQ),* 2008 SCC 43, [2008] 2 SCR 561.

47   *Re Port Moody (City) v. C.U.P.E., Local 825* (1997), 63 LAC (4th) 203 (Laing).

48   *Re Millhaven Fibres Ltd. v. Atomic Workers Int'l Union, Local 9-670,* [1967] OLAA No. 4, 18 LAC 324 (Anderson). The employer must demonstrate that at least one of the criteria is satisfied: *Re Air Canada and International Association of Machinists, Lodge 148* (1973), 5 LAC (2d) 7 (Andrews). There are hundreds of cases applying *Millhaven Fibres* in off-duty conduct discipline scenarios.

49   *Cape Breton-Victoria Regional School Board v. Canadian Union of Public Employees, Local 5050,* 2011 NSCA 9, 298 NSR (2d) 258.

50   See, e.g., *Ottawa-Carlton District School Board* (2006), 154 LAC (4th) 387 (Goodfellow); *Re British Columbia (Workers' Compensation Board) and E.C.E.U. (Campbell)* (1997), 64 LAC (4th) 401 (Glass); *Sun Country Regional Health Authority v. Canadian Union of Public Employees, Local 5999,* 2013 CanLII 94436 (SKLA) (Ish); *Canada (Attorney General) v. F.J.T.,* 2008 FC 740, [2008] FCJ No. 932 (QL); *Canadian Union of Public Employees, Local 787 v. First Student Canada (Cardinal Coach Lines Ltd),* 2012 CanLII 70257 (ABGAA) (Wallace); *Ontario Public Service Employees Union v. Ontario (Natural Resources),* 2008 CanLII 32797 (Ont. GSB) (Jackson). See also *Emergency Health Services Commission and Ambulance Paramedics of British Columbia, C.U.P.E., Local 873* (1987), 28 LAC (3rd) 77 (McColl), warning that arbitrators should be careful not to accept employer concerns about potential harm too lightly and should require the harm to be of a serious nature.

51   *Grand Erie District School Board v. Ontario Secondary School Teachers' Federation, District 23,* 2016 CanLII 72391 (Ont. LA) (White) (teachers are held to a high standard of integrity); *Ottawa-Carleton District School v. Ontario Secondary School Teachers' Federation, District 25 Plant Support Staff,* 2006 CanLII 60956 (Ont. LA) (Goodfellow); *Ontario (Transportation) v. Ontario Public Service Employees Union,* 2013 ONSC 7227 (the dismissal of a transportation officer for an indecent act was upheld); and *Maritime Employers' Association v. International Longshoremen's Association, Local 1654,* 2013 CanLII 65439 (Ont. LA) (Hayes) (a fight between two longshoremen at a union hall was not grounds for termination).

52   See P. Kuitenbrouwer, "Two Toronto Firefighters Terminated over 'Unacceptable' Sexist Tweets, Third Reportedly Fired over Facebook Post," *National Post,* September 16, 2013, http://news.nationalpost.com/toronto/two-toronto-firefighters-terminated-over

-unacceptable-sexist-tweets-third-reportedly-fired-over
-facebook-post.

53 See, e.g., *Bullmoose Operating Corporation v. Communication, Energy and Paperworkers Union, Local 443*, 1999 CanLII 20292 (BCLA) (Greyall); *Horizon Plastics Company Limited v. United Food & Commercial Workers Canada, Local 175*, 2010 CanLII 29972 (Ont. LA) (Stout); *Bombardier Transportation v. CAW-Canada*, 2002 CanLII 61259 (Ont. LA) (Harris); and *Labatt Alberta Brewery v. Unifor Local 250A*, 2015 CanLII 98936 (ABGAA) (Seveny).

54 *Toronto Transit Commission v. Amalgamated Transit Union, Local 113*, 2012 CanLII 453 (Ont. LA) (Slotnick).

55 *Domtar Inc v. Communications, Energy and Paperworkers Union of Canada, Local 74*, 2011 CanLII 52247 (Ont. LA) (Albertyn); *Calgary (City) v. Canadian Union of Public Employees (Cupe 37)*, 2015 CanLII 61756 (ABGAA) (Hodges); *Goldcorp Canada Ltd v. United Steel Workers, Local 7580*, 2013 CanLII 89968 (Ont. LA) (Kennedy); *British Columbia v. British Columbia Crown Counsel Association*, 2012 CanLII 51827 (BCLA) (Germaine); and *Shaw Cablesystems GP v. Telecommunications Workers' Union*, 2014 CanLII 16663 (BCLA) (Fleming). See also *Lakeport Brewing LLP v. Teamsters Local Union 938*, 2006 CanLII 71519 (Ont. LA) (Surdykowski) (alcoholism was not accepted as an excuse for alcohol theft by an employee); *British Columbia (Public Service Agency) v. British Columbia Government and Service Employees Union*, 2008 BCCA 357, 298 DLR (4th) 624.

CHAPTER 15

The Regulation of Unions: Legal Status, the Duty of Fair Representation, and Decertification

I. Introduction

This chapter carves out several special issues in the law of unions not previously explored in any length elsewhere in this text, but that are deserving of attention in our exploration of the collective bargaining regime. The first issue raises a fundamental question: What exactly is a union under the law? This is a deceptively complex question. Stripped to the basics, a union is really just a combination of individual workers who have joined together for the purpose of trying to improve working conditions. Does the union itself have a legal existence separate and apart from those workers in the same way that a corporation is recognized as a "legal person" separate from its shareholders and employees? The issue of a union's legal status is important because it determines whether unions can bring lawsuits and be sued as parties in the *common law regime*.

As we have seen throughout Part II, collective bargaining statutes confer legal rights and responsibilities on unions and so, *within* the collective bargaining regime, unions clearly do have legal status. An important example of a legal obligation imposed on unions is the **duty of fair representation** (DFR) owed by unions to the workers that they are legally entitled to represent. The scope of that duty is explored in this chapter. Finally, just as collective bargaining legislation

---

duty of fair representation: A legal obligation imposed on unions to represent employees who fall within the scope of their representation rights in a manner that is not arbitrary, discriminatory, or in bad faith.

closely regulates the process through which workers transition from the common law regime to the collective bargaining regime (Chapter 8), it also regulates how workers can remove their union and return to the common law regime. That process is commonly referred to as **decertification**, and is explored later in this chapter.

II. What Is the Legal Status of a Union to Sue and Be Sued in the Common Law Regime?

We learned in Chapter 6 that for many years, combinations of workers were considered unlawful conspiracies, and that workers who joined unions could face liability in tort, or even criminal law. In the common law regime, unions were considered unincorporated associations that lack legal status, similar to, say, a book club.[1] Since they were not "legal persons," unions could not enter into enforceable legal contracts, including collective agreements, and they could not sue others or be sued. Individual union members and union officials could be sued if they personally committed a legal wrong, but the union itself lacked any legal status within the common law regime.

In the 1957 case of *Orchard v. Tunney*, the Supreme Court of Canada ruled that although a union does not have an independent legal status, each individual union member, upon joining the union, notionally enters into a contract with each other member, the terms of which are set out in the union's constitution. This conception of unions became known as the "web of contracts" theory. If a union member suffered harm due to a breach of the union constitution, that member could sue union executives involved in the decision and recover damages from the union's assets, and each individual union member could sue other union members for breach of the union constitution that bound them all together in contract law. The web of contracts theory was based on a legal fiction, since it ignored basic elements of contract law that we considered in Chapter 7 of the companion volume, including the need for offer, acceptance, and mutual consideration as conditions of a binding contract between two persons. However, more recently, the Supreme Court of Canada abandoned the notion that a web of contracts exists between union members in the case presented in Box 15.1.

BOX 15.1 » CASE LAW HIGHLIGHT

Are Unions Legal Persons?

Berry v. Pulley
2002 SCC 40, [2002] 2 SCR 493

Key Facts: Pilots working for Air Canada and Air Ontario were members of the same union, the Canadian Air Line Pilots Association (CALPA). When the two employers commenced merger discussions, a process in CALPA's constitution was triggered that required the two groups of pilots to negotiate a method for deciding how seniority would work once the two groups of pilots worked for the same employer. The Air Canada pilots argued that the Air Ontario pilots' seniority list should be placed at the bottom of the Air Canada seniority list (end tailed), while the Air

Ontario pilots argued that the two seniority lists should be merged (dovetailed). When the two groups could not agree, the dispute was referred, as required by the CALPA constitution, to binding arbitration. The arbitrator issued a decision that effectively merged part of the two seniority lists. The CALPA executive accepted the decision, but the Air Canada pilots took exception, voted not to implement the arbitrator's seniority list, and eventually left CALPA and formed their own union (Air Canada Pilots Association), which was certified as the pilots' new union. Air Ontario pilots launched a class action lawsuit in the common law courts against individual Air Canada pilots, arguing that when they refused to accept the arbitrator's award merging

---

decertification: The legal process through which unionized workers remove their union as their legal representative and transition from the collective bargaining regime to the common law regime.

part of the seniority list, they breached the CALPA constitution that bound all of the pilots in a contract.

Issue: Could the Air Ontario pilots sue individual Air Canada pilots for breaching the CALPA constitution by refusing to abide by the arbitrator's decision?

Decision: No. The court ruled that it no longer made sense to pretend that there was a "web of contracts" between each individual union member. Since collective bargaining legislation grants unions extensive legal rights and imposes legal obligations on unions, it was time to recognize that unions have legal status to enter into a contract with their members. Therefore, unless a statute provides that a union cannot be sued, when a person becomes a union member, he or she enters into a contract with the union, and the union can be sued in its own name "at least for the purposes of discharging their function and performing their role in the field of labour relations." Therefore, in this case, the lawsuit filed against individual Air Canada pilots was dismissed, since there was no contract between the Air Ontario pilots and the Air Canada pilots. The union (CALPA) had complied with the constitution by referring the dispute to arbitration and accepting the arbitrator's ruling.

Berry v. Pulley found that unions have a legal existence separate from their members and union officials because modern collective bargaining statutes confer that existence on them by granting them extensive legal rights and imposing on them legal obligations. Therefore, unions can now sue and be sued in the common law courts in relation to matters not arising directly from the collective agreement (resolved by arbitration) or an employment-related statute (resolved by an administrative tribunal). For example, unions have sued and have been sued by their members for alleged breaches of the union's constitution and by their own employees for breach of their employment contracts as well as for alleged torts committed by union officials.[2]

Note that an important exception is stated in *Berry v. Pulley*. The court indicated that a statute might also expressly provide that a union cannot sue or be sued in its own name. Such a statute exists in Ontario. According to the *Rights of Labour Act*, "a trade union shall not be made a party to any action in any court unless it may be so made a party irrespective of this Act or of the *Labour Relations Act*."[3] That is confusing language, but what it means in practice is that unions that exist solely because the Ontario *Labour Relations Act, 1995* gives them legal powers still cannot be sued in the common law courts in Ontario.[4] As a result, lawsuits filed in courts against unions certified under Ontario law are usually dismissed because of the *Rights of Labour Act*.

III. A Union's Duty of Fair Representation (DFR)

We learned in Chapter 6 that the central principles of union certification under the Wagner model of collective bargaining are exclusivity and majoritarianism. Based on these principles, if a union can establish that it has majority employee support in a bargaining unit found to be appropriate by the labour relations board, then it may be "certified," which means it is granted a legal licence to represent *all of the employees in the bargaining unit*, even those employees who are not union members and who may not have wanted union representation at all. As a trade-off for granting the union "exclusive" bargaining rights, a DFR is imposed on unions to ensure that they represent all bargaining unit employees fairly, without arbitrariness, discrimination, or bad faith. The DFR struggles to balance protecting the individual employee from injustice and unfair or unprofessional treatment at the hands of the union, while also respecting the right of unions to take into account the interests and will of the majority in a legal model based on collectivity.[5]

A. The History of the Duty of Fair Representation

The origins of the DFR date to a 1944 decision of the US Supreme Court, *Steele v. Louisville & Nashville Railroad*. A union had denied membership and seniority rights to black workers in the bargaining unit at a time before human rights laws prohibited such discriminatory actions. The court ruled that exclusive representation carried with it an obligation on unions to exercise their authority fairly on behalf of all employees they represent, without discrimination.[6] Two decades later, in 1967, the US Supreme Court defined the substance of the DFR to include avoidance of behaviour that is "arbitrary, discriminatory, or in bad faith."[7] In 1968 in Canada, the federal government's Task Force on Labour Relations (the Woods Report), which included an important review of Canadian collective bargaining laws, recommended the adoption of the American DFR in Canadian law.[8]

Ontario was the first province to take this step in 1971, introducing a statutory DFR, which now appears as section 74 of the Ontario *Labour Relations Act, 1995*. That section reads as follows:

> A trade union ... so long as it continues to be entitled to represent employees in a bargaining unit, shall not act in a manner that is arbitrary, discriminatory or in bad faith in the representation of any of the employees in the unit, whether or not members of the trade union or of any constituent union of the council of trade unions, as the case may be.[9]

Other jurisdictions followed thereafter with similar statutory provisions. Today, all but two Canadian jurisdictions have codified the DFR into their collective bargaining statute. In New Brunswick and Prince Edward Island, where no statutory DFR exists, the courts have recognized a parallel common law duty on unions to represent bargaining unit employees fairly, without arbitrariness, discrimination, or bad faith.[10] In these latter jurisdictions, employees with a DFR complaint rely on this common law duty and may sue their union in court. In jurisdictions with a statutory DFR, employees must file a DFR complaint with the labour relations board.[11]

B. The Scope of the Duty of Fair Representation

The union's DFR applies to *all employees in the bargaining unit*, and not just union members. Bear in mind that an important difference exists between union members and bargaining unit employees. Only employees who sign a union membership card and thereby join the union are union members, whereas any employee who works in a job that is included in the bargaining unit description that the union represents is a bargaining unit employee. Unless the collective agreement includes a **mandatory union membership clause**, some employees in a bargaining unit may not be union members. The DFR is intended to ensure that unions do not give preference to union members over non-union members. Also, the DFR applies to the manner in which unions represent bargaining unit employees *in their relationship with their employer*.[12] It does not regulate internal union affairs, such as the election of union officials, the amount or use of union dues, or the discipline of union members by the union. These sorts of internal union disputes are contract matters governed by the union's constitution and do not fall within the scope of the DFR.[13]

The DFR provisions found in collective bargaining statutes vary in scope, so it is important to look at the language they use. The provision in the Ontario *Labour Relations Act, 1995*, cited above, is an example of a broadly worded DFR obligation that applies generally to "the representation" of bargaining unit employees. That language applies both to collective agreement administration, including the handling of grievances, and to collective bargaining, including the decisions unions make during the bargaining process about prioritizing bargaining proposals. British Columbia, Nova Scotia, Saskatchewan,[14] and the federal jurisdiction apply a similarly broad DFR.[15] In Alberta, Manitoba, Newfoundland and Labrador, and Nova Scotia, the DFR applies more narrowly to the handling of grievances and collective agreement administration

---

mandatory union membership clause: A clause in a collective agreement that requires that every employee covered by the collective agreement (every bargaining unit employee) become a member of the union that negotiated the collective agreement.

issues, and not to the collective bargaining process.[16] For example, section 153(1) of the Alberta *Labour Relations Code* provides as follows:

> No trade union or person acting on behalf of a trade union shall deny an employee or former employee who is or was in the bargaining unit the right to be fairly represented by the trade union with respect to the employee's or former employee's rights *under the collective agreement*.[17] [Emphasis added.]

In the provinces with a narrower DFR scope, employees cannot challenge decisions unions make about what terms to include (and not include) in collective agreements.

C. The Substance of the Duty of Fair Representation

Both the statutory and the common law versions of the DFR in Canada require unions to avoid the following types of behaviour in their treatment of bargaining unit employees:

- *Arbitrariness.* Unions must turn their attention to the issues involved, investigate them, and make reasonable decisions based on their investigation. The Supreme Court of Canada has described this branch of the DFR obligation as follows: "A union cannot act arbitrarily, disregarding the interests of one of the employees in a perfunctory matter. Instead, it must take a reasonable view of the problem before it and arrive at a thoughtful judgment about what to do after considering the various relevant and conflicting considerations."[18] Negligent actions by a union, such as missing a mandatory time limit for proceeding with a grievance, can also amount to arbitrary conduct.[19]
- *Discrimination.* Unions must not violate human rights statutes, such as by discriminating on the basis of the prohibited grounds found in those statutes, or make decisions based on personal favouritism or biases.[20]
- *Bad faith.* Unions must not make decisions based on personal animosity, revenge, pettiness, or dishonesty.

Most DFR complaints relate to the union's conduct either in collective bargaining or in the processing of grievances—in particular, decisions by unions to not file a grievance or to settle or withdraw a grievance against the wishes of the grievor.

1. The Duty of Fair Representation and Decisions on Whether to Proceed to Arbitration with a Grievance

Most collective agreements permit employees to file grievances if they believe the employer has violated their collective agreement rights. However, as noted in Chapter 13, the decision whether to refer grievances to labour arbitration is usually reserved to the union and not the individual grievor. Therefore, a union may elect to drop a grievance rather than proceed to arbitration, against the wishes of the grievor. The implications for employees of the union making this decision can be significant. Consider a typical termination grievance. An employee is dismissed for alleged theft and files a grievance, denying the theft. The union investigates and concludes that the employer will be able to prove the theft and that an arbitrator will uphold the grievance, so it drops the grievance. At that point, the employee cannot bypass the union's decision and proceed to arbitration directly, since the collective agreement gives the union the exclusive right to decide which grievances can move forward. Nor can the employee bypass the arbitration process altogether and sue the employer in a court for wrongful dismissal, since, as we have learned, unionized employees do not have that option. Therefore, the union's decision to drop the grievance effectively ends the employee's options for challenging the employer's decision to dismiss him or her.

When a union drops an employee's grievance, the employee's only legal recourse is to pursue a DFR complaint alleging that the union's decision was arbitrary, discriminatory, or made in bad faith. Scholars have long debated whether granting unions the unilateral right to drop employee grievances is a just model. Two alternative models proposed by leading Canadian labour law scholars are described in Box 15.2.

BOX 15.2 » TALKING WORK LAW

Should Unions Have the Right to Drop an Employee's Grievance Contrary to the Wishes of the Employee?

Collective agreements usually confer the right to decide whether a grievance proceeds to arbitration on the union, rather than the individual grievor. As a result, an employee's right to challenge an employer's decision may be subrogated to the union's right to decide which grievances are worthy of litigation. Some Canadian legal scholars have questioned whether this union right is just.

Professor Bernie Adell (Queen's University) argued that employees should have a legal right to proceed to arbitration with any grievance that their union declines to arbitrate. This position is sometimes called *individual rights theory*. Adell argued that "whenever the law gives a substantive right to someone, as it does an individual employee to enjoy the fruits of collective bargaining as contained in a collective agreement, it ought (in the absence of compelling reasons to the contrary) to provide a procedural means of enforcing that substantive right."[*]

In Canada, individual rights theory in relation to grievances has not prevailed for a couple of key reasons. First, in industrial relations, there is value in having unions act as gatekeepers to the grievance procedure. Employers expect unions to drop grievances lacking merit so that employers do not incur unnecessary legal and arbitration costs. If every employee can take their grievance to arbitration, even if they have to pay the union's share of the cost themselves, the employer would still be left paying its share. Second, if the employer is not guaranteed that a resolution reached with the union on a grievance will be enforced, then it will be less willing to engage in good-

faith efforts to settle grievances, and the law should encourage reasonable settlements.

Professor Paul Weiler (Harvard University) proposed that unions be permitted to settle or drop grievances, subject to the right of employees to challenge the union's decision as being arbitrary, discriminatory, or made in bad faith using DFR law.[†] However, he believed that an exception should be made for grievances that challenge dismissals. Weiler argued that employees should have a unilateral right to proceed to arbitration with dismissal grievances, at their own expense, even if the union refuses to move forward, due to the critical importance of the grievance to the employee and also because termination grievances rarely give rise to fundamental conflicts of interest among different groups of bargaining unit employees. In response to the complaint that employers might end up defending frivolous dismissal grievances in expensive arbitration hearings that a union would otherwise have dropped, Weiler was unmoved. He wrote: "I just think that there are limits to the sacrifice which can be made to individual rights in the pursuit of decent collective bargaining relationships, and that that limit is reached here."[‡]

---

* B. Adell, "Collective Agreements and Individual Rights: A Note on the Duty of Fair Representation" (1985-86) 11 *Queen's Law Journal* 251, at 255.
† P. Weiler, *Reconcilable Differences: New Directions in Canadian Labour Law* (Toronto: Carswell, 1980), at 137-39.
‡ Ibid., at 139.

In the 1984 case of *Canadian Merchant Service Guild v. Gagnon et al.*, the Supreme Court of Canada described the principles that must be applied when assessing whether a union's decision to drop a grievance violates the DFR:

1. The exclusive power conferred on a union to act as spokesperson for the employees in a bargaining unit entails a corresponding obligation on the union to fairly represent all employees in the unit.
2. When, as ... is generally the case, the right to take a grievance to arbitration is reserved to the union, the employee does not have an absolute right to arbitration and the union enjoys considerable discretion.
3. This discretion must be exercised in good faith, objectively and honestly, after a thorough study of the grievance and the case, taking into account the significance of the grievance and of its consequences for the employee on the one hand and the legitimate interests of the union on the other.
4. The union's decision must not be arbitrary, capricious, discriminatory or wrongful.

5.   The representation by the union must be fair, genuine and not merely apparent, undertaken with integrity and competence, without serious or major negligence, and without hostility towards the employee.[21]

The key point to note is that, in applying these principles, labour relations boards and courts grant unions wide discretion to make what are often difficult decisions. As long as the union turned its mind to the facts and issues raised by the grievance, did a fair investigation, and came to a rational decision not tainted by discrimination or bad faith, the DFR complaint will usually be dismissed, even if the judge or labour relations board might have come to a different decision had it been making decisions for the union. Given this standard, most DFR complaints challenging a union's decision to drop a grievance fail. However, they do not all fail. Consider what the union did wrong in the case described in Box 15.3.

BOX 15.3 » CASE LAW HIGHLIGHT

The Duty of Fair Representation in the Administration of a Collective Agreement

Mwemera v. United Brotherhood of Carpenters and Joiners of America, Local Union No. 2010

2016 CanLII 8866 (Alberta Labour Relations Board)

Key Facts: Approximately one year into his employment, Mwemera was assigned to take a forklift training course. On the first day of the course, he twice fell asleep and was awakened by the instructor. The employer learned of these incidents, called him to the office, and issued a written warning. Mwemera returned to the class, but a few minutes later he was told to return to the office where he was informed that his employment was terminated. The employer relied on its "Rules of Conduct," which listed "sleeping while on duty" as an offence that "may result in immediate dismissal." Mwemera called the union representative (Orrel) to seek help. Orrel asked Mwemera if he had fallen asleep, and Mwemera said yes but that so had others who had not been dismissed. Mwemera told Orrel that he believed the supervisor was out to get him. Orrel told him that "there is not much I can do," since Mwemera admitted to falling asleep. Mwemera became angry and accused Orrel of not doing his job and taking the side of the employer. No grievance was filed, but Mwemera filed a DFR complaint against the union.

Issue: Did the union violate the DFR by not investigating the termination and advocating on Mwemera's behalf?

Decision: Yes. The labour relations board ruled that it should have been obvious to Orrel that Mwemera was seeking the union's assistance to challenge the termination through the filing of a grievance, even though Mwemera never said the words "file a grievance." The fact that Mwemera eventually became angry with Orrel and was rude did not relieve Orrel of the duty to investigate the circumstances of the termination. Labour relations boards will closely scrutinize a union's decision not to grieve or proceed with a grievance that relates to termination of employment given the critical importance of the issue. Here, Orrel did very little to investigate the circumstances of the termination. He did not challenge the employer on why Mwemera was dismissed and not the other employees who had fallen asleep. He did not ask the employer for any documentary evidence. Instead, he had a short conversation with Mwemera on the phone, and quickly concluded that since he had fallen asleep, there was nothing the union could do. The DFR requires the union to fully investigate the circumstances and come to a reasoned conclusion on the merits. Here, the union's cursory investigation fell fall short of that standard and was therefore "arbitrary." As a remedy, the labour relations board ordered that a grievance be filed and be referred directly to arbitration. Further, Mwemera was entitled to select his own lawyer whose fees would be paid for by the union.

What does the employee "win" if his or her DFR complaint challenging the union's decision to drop their grievance is successful? As always, the purpose of a remedy is, as much as possible, to return the victim to the situation he or she would have been in but for the illegal conduct. What harm has an employee suffered when a union refuses to move forward with a grievance? In the case of a termination grievance, that harm is not the loss of employment, because the termination may have been upheld had it gone to arbitration. The harm caused by the union's breach of the DFR is *loss of the opportunity to challenge the employer's termination decision before an arbitrator*. Therefore, the usual remedy in a successful DFR complaint over a union's decision to drop a grievance is an order by the labour relations board to "revive" the grievance and send it to arbitration, sometimes with an accompanying order that the union pay for an independent lawyer to represent the employee. That is what was ordered in the *Mwemera* decision. If an arbitrator later reinstates the employee, the union may be ordered to pay a portion of the damages owing to the employee that were caused by the delay associated with the DFR proceedings.[22]

2. The Duty of Fair Representation and Collective Bargaining

As noted earlier, some jurisdictions include broad DFR provisions in their collective bargaining statutes that apply to collective bargaining and collective agreement administration. Unions are hardly ever able to obtain every improvement they initially set out to negotiate through collective bargaining. As bargaining progresses, they must give up some items in order to secure other items deemed to be more important. However, reasonable employees can disagree on what is most important, and some collective agreement items are zero-sum games—one group of employees gain at the expense of another group of employees.

For example, in the City of Toronto collective bargaining that was described in the appendix to Chapter 11, the employer (the city) initially sought the outright removal of collective agreement language that restricted its right to dismiss employees and contract out their jobs. The union sought to keep that protective language and proposed a 0 percent raise to win the employer over. After months of difficult negotiations, the union agreed to language that protected employees with 15 years' seniority or more from losing their jobs to contracting out and gave those employees a small raise. However, employees with less than 15 years' seniority could thereafter be dismissed by the employer and their jobs contracted out to a private contractor.[23] Should the union be faulted for making that agreement? Clearly the outcome is unfair to the employees whose jobs are no longer protected. On the other hand, in a very hostile climate, the union managed to protect the continued employment of a large portion of the bargaining unit when the employer had threatened to eliminate far more jobs and to impose its final offer on the employees if they did not accept the employer's proposal.

Because unions routinely must make difficult decisions in the face of competing employee interests, they are given a wide latitude to decide what course of action is best. Union decisions that benefit one group of employees over another do not violate the DFR, unless that decision was arbitrary, discriminatory, or made in bad faith. In the case described in Box 15.4, the union was confronted with a decision about how to treat the seniority rights of two groups of employees following the merger of two job classifications into one. No matter what decision the union made, one group of employees would be unhappy. Note how the BC Labour Relations Board assessed the union's decision-making process. When unions run into DFR trouble in relation to collective bargaining conduct, it is usually because union officials were dishonest to the membership in the hope of pushing through a settlement, the union's own rules or procedures were ignored, or preference was given to one group of employees over another for no rational reason.[24]

BOX 15.4 » CASE LAW HIGHLIGHT

The Duty of Fair Representation in the Collective Bargaining Process

Ormerod v. Unifor, Local Union No. 333-BC
2016 CanLII 36389 (BCLRB)

Key Facts: The union represented a bargaining unit comprising both large bus drivers ("transit operators") and community shuttle operators (CTOs). Under the collective agreement, transit operators were paid more than CTOs and accumulated seniority from their date of hire. CTOs accumulated seniority from their date of hire while they were CTOs. However, if they later became transit operators, they did not carry their seniority with

them but rather started over at the bottom of the transit operator seniority list (they were end tailed). Over time, about 75 CTOs became transit operators under this scheme. In 2015, the employer and union agreed to eliminate the CTO classification and treat all drivers as transit operators based on the premise that "a bus is a bus." The union agreed that the 65 CTOs who would now be required to become transit operators would have their seniority merged (dovetailed) with the existing transit operator seniority list, rather than end tailed. As a result, some of the CTOs being newly transferred into the transit operator position would have greater seniority than existing transit operators who had lost their CTO seniority when they became transit operators under the old model. The employees overwhelmingly (89 percent) voted to accept the new collective agreement. However, a group of former CTOs who had become transit operators and not been given credit for their CTO seniority filed a DFR complaint against the union.

Issue: Did the union act arbitrarily, in a discriminatory manner, or in bad faith by agreeing to merge the seniority lists of the CTOs and transit operators in the circumstances?

Decision: No. The decision of the labour relations board began by noting that it "has long taken the position that it takes a 'hands off' approach to collective bargaining" because the parties generally know best how to balance the many competing interests involved in a typical bargaining relationship. It then cited approvingly an often quoted passage from *Seagrams Employees v. Distillery, Winery, Soft Drink & Allied Workers*, a 1978 decision by the BC Labour Relations Board:

> A trade-union is the legal bargaining agent for the entire unit of employees—often a large, all-employee unit which has been designed to minimize industrial unrest. … The simple fact of the matter is that not all of the interests of these employees can be entirely satisfied in any one set of negotiations. The union chosen by the employees to be their exclusive bargaining agent must have the authority … to make the critical choices about which contract items will be negotiated with the employer: e.g. whether to pursue healthy trade adjustments in lieu of a slightly higher across-the-board wage increase; or whether to emphasize pension benefits instead of longer, paid vacations. As these examples indicate, the union's decisions will favour some employees and others may not like them. But it would be quite inconsistent with a system of free collective bargaining if the Labour Board, later on, were entitled to make the judgment that such choices were unreasonable, unfair, and thus illegal.*

The BC Labour Relations Board ruled that there was no evidence of bad faith: the union had explained to the employees that the seniority list would be dovetailed and held meetings with employees to discuss the issue. There was no evidence of dishonesty or an attempt to hide the agreement. Moreover, the union did not act in a *discriminatory* manner: there was no evidence that the union acted out of personal favouritism for the CTOs being transferred to the transit operators group. There was also no evidence that the union's decision to agree to the merged seniority list was arbitrary. The union explained that many of the CTOs did not want to become transit operators and perceived the elimination of their job as a hardship. The union believed that it would be doubly difficult on them to strip them of their seniority when they became transit operators. The BC Labour Relations Board accepted that the union's decision was rational under the circumstances: no matter what solution the union agreed to regarding the treatment of seniority, some employees would be disadvantaged. The DFR complaint was dismissed.

---

* *Seagrams Employees v. Distillery, Winery, Soft Drink & Allied Workers,* [1978] 1 CLRBR 375 (BCLRB).

IV. The Decertification of Unions

Chapter 8 explained **union certification**, the legal process by which employees move from the non-union common law regime to the unionized collective bargaining regime. A labour relations board can certify a union as the legal representative of all employees in a bargaining unit if it is satisfied that a majority of employees wish to be represented by the union. Proof of majority support is proffered through one of two models. In the **card-check** model, the union must collect union membership cards from a specified majority of bargaining unit employees. In the **mandatory certification vote** model, the union must first collect union cards from a specified percentage in order to qualify for the second step, a mandatory certification vote conducted by the labour relations board. Once certified, the union is responsible for representing the bargaining

---

union certification: A government-issued licence that entitles a union to represent employees in a defined bargaining unit in their relationship with their employer.

card check: A method used in Canadian collective bargaining legislation to measure the level of employee support for unionization that involves counting the number of union membership or authorization cards. If a majority of employees have signed cards, then the union is certified without a certification vote.

mandatory certification vote: A method used in Canadian collective bargaining legislation to measure the level of employee support for unionization that involves the government conducting a secret ballot vote of bargaining unit employees.

unit employees in collective bargaining and collective agreement administration until the employees decide that they no longer wish to be represented by the union.

In a system based on majority employee wishes, rather than an individual right to move back and forth freely between collective bargaining and individual employment contracts, there must be a process by which a majority of employees can escape the collective bargaining regime if they desire. That process is known as *terminating collective bargaining rights*, or sometimes just **decertification** for short, and it is governed by specific rules found in collective bargaining statutes. There are a variety of circumstances that can lead a labour relations board to "decertify" a union.

A. *Decertification Due to Loss of Majority Employee Support*

Most commonly, a union is decertified because it is no longer supported by a majority of bargaining unit employees. A bargaining unit employee can file an "application to terminate bargaining rights" with the labour relations board, which triggers an inquiry by the board into the union's level of support. However, as with applications for certification, decertification applications can only be filed during narrow windows of time defined in the collective bargaining legislation. For example, a newly certified union is protected from decertification applications for between ten months and two years, depending on the jurisdiction, in order to give the union a chance to negotiate an agreement and also to ensure a period of peace during which there is no campaigning for and against unionization.[25] During the term of a collective agreement, decertification applications can only be filed in the **open period** near the end of the collective agreement, which we discussed in Chapter 8.[26] In some jurisdictions, applications for decertification are also restricted while the union and employer are in conciliation to reach a new collective agreement (Ontario) or during all or part of the length of a strike or lockout (Alberta, Manitoba, New Brunswick, Ontario, and the federal jurisdiction).

The decertification process is similar in design to the certification process in that the labour relations board is tasked with measuring the level of employee support for the transition from one regime to another. In the case of decertification, no professional union organizers are running the show, so employees need to take the lead themselves. Usually one or more employees initiate the campaign. They research the process and get forms from labour relations board websites (and/or speak to a lawyer or other knowledgeable person) and begin to collect the signatures of bargaining unit employees on a document known as a **decertification petition**. The petition requires employee names and signatures (dated and witnessed). By signing the petition, employees declare that they no longer wish to be represented by the union. After employee names and signatures are collected, the petition is submitted to the labour relations board as part of the application to terminate the union's bargaining rights. Neither the employer nor the union is supposed to learn the names of employees who have supported the petition.

The labour relations board reviews the decertification application to ensure that it is "timely" (filed during a period in which decertification applications can be filed). If so, it begins the process of assessing the level of employee support. This assessment requires a measure of the number of bargaining unit employees who signed the decertification petition as well as the total number of eligible voters (employees in the bargaining unit) to produce a percentage of employee support. The details of how Canadian governments measure employee support for decertification are presented in Table 15.1. A majority of bargaining unit employees must express a desire to remove the union in order for the decertification application to be successful.

---

decertification: The process by which members of a collective bargaining unit disassociate from the union that represents them. It is also referred to as *terminating collective bargaining rights*.

open period: A period of time defined in a collective bargaining statute during which a union may apply to displace another union as the representative of a group of employees, or during which unionized employees may file an application to "decertify" the union.

decertification petition: A form, signed by employees who no longer desire to be represented by a union, that is used as evidence of employee support in an application to terminate the representational rights of a union.

TABLE 15.1   How Canadian Governments Measure Employee Support for Decertification

Jurisdiction	Level of Employee Support Needed to Apply for Decertification	Test of Majority Support
Federal	40% plus one or more bargaining unit employees sign the petition	A vote, and the majority of ballots cast
Alberta	40% or more bargaining unit employees sign the petition	A vote, and the majority of ballots cast
British Columbia	45% or more bargaining unit employees sign the petition	A vote, and the majority of ballots cast
Manitoba	50% plus one or more bargaining unit employees sign the petition	A vote, and the majority of ballots cast
New Brunswick	40% or more bargaining unit employees sign the petition	A vote, and the majority of ballots cast by eligible voters, which excludes employees absent from work on the day of the vote
Newfoundland and Labrador	40% or more bargaining unit employees sign the petition	A vote, and the majority of ballots cast
Nova Scotia	50% plus one or more bargaining unit employees, or a "significant number" of union members, sign the petition	A vote, and the majority of ballots cast
Ontario	40% or more bargaining unit employees sign the petition	A vote, and the majority of ballots cast
Prince Edward Island	50% plus one or more bargaining unit employees sign the petition	A vote, and the majority of ballots cast OR If the labour relations board is satisfied based on petition evidence that a majority of employees no longer wish to be represented by the union based on this evidence, it may decertify a union without a vote
Quebec	50% plus one or more bargaining unit employees sign the petition	A vote, and the majority of ballots cast OR Support evidence; if the labour relations board is satisfied based on petition evidence that a majority of employees no longer wish to be represented by the union based on this evidence, it may decertify a union without a vote
Saskatchewan	45% or more bargaining unit employees sign the petition	A vote, and the majority of ballots cast

Importantly, employers must play no role in initiating, encouraging, supporting, or facilitating a decertification application. The decision whether to leave the collective bargaining regime by decertifying the union is to be made voluntarily by the employees, and employer participation may be considered unlawful employer interference in the administration of the union (see Chapter 9). The requirement that a decertification campaign be free of employer involvement parallels the requirement that union certification be free of employer involvement.[27] If the employer makes threats or uses coercion to pressure employees into applying to decertify the union, or if it makes promises of rewards if they do so, such actions would amount to unfair labour practices that would cause the labour relations board to dismiss the decertification application. However, even if the employer's participation is only supportive or encouraging, the labour relations board may consider the application to be tainted. As a consequence, the labour relations board may dismiss the application on the basis that the application does not reflect the true wishes of the employees. Many decertification applications are dismissed by labour relations boards for this reason.

Employer support can include granting employees time off work; providing employees with resources such as office space, materials, copiers, and fax machines to help them prepare the decertification application; making promises to employees about working conditions should a decertification application be successful; referring employees to a lawyer to help with the decertification; or paying all or part of any legal fees incurred by employees who initiated the application.[28] Consider what role the employer played in decertification in the case discussed in Box 15.5.

BOX 15.5 » CASE LAW HIGHLIGHT

Employer Interference in Decertification Efforts

Unionized Employees of Tenaquip v. Teamsters, Local Union 419
1997 CanLII 15586 (Ont. LRB)

Key Facts: A group of employees filed an application for decertification of the union. The union filed a response with the labour relations board arguing that the employer had initiated and supported the application and, thus, requested that the application be dismissed. Two employees drove the campaign. They posted a notice at work inviting employees to talk to them about decertifying the union, and when no one responded, they summoned each employee to a company boardroom during working hours and presented them with a petition to sign in support of the application. The two employees claimed they had not asked the employer's permission to use the boardroom. On the day the application was signed, the two employees left work for two hours to file the application to decertify. The employees claimed they never gave the employer a reason for their absence.

Issue: Did the employer initiate the decertification application by giving support to the two employees and if so, should the Ontario Labour Relations Board (OLRB) dismiss the application?

Decision: Yes and yes. The OLRB summarized the evidence as follows:

> It is clear that signatures on the petitions were solicited during working hours; employees were summoned to leave their work areas and to attend at the boardroom for the purposes of a series of short individual meetings. The two lead petitioners spent a cumulative total of close to an hour each away from

their work duties. Each of the employees spent up to 5 minutes attending in the boardroom in addition to the time travelling to and from the boardroom. The petitioners' open and notorious approach to the solicitation of petition signatures may have created something of a parade appearance for any observer.

The OLRB concluded that the employer must have been aware of the employees' efforts to campaign for decertification at the workplace and condoned it:

> I am persuaded that the employer made a contribution to the application. That contribution was two-fold. First, it permitted the petitioners' activities and thereby contributed resources (license to the petitioners to come and go during their working hours, use of the boardroom, access to employees during their working hours) which were significant to facilitating the application. But more importantly in this case, the employer, through its cooperation with and toleration of the petitioners' activities, communicated an explicit and important message to employees that it supported the application.

The fact that no employees responded to the initial notice about decertification but then most signed the petition when summoned to the boardroom is evidence that the employees believed that the employer was involved. Without the employer's contribution in permitting the two lead employees to use company time to solicit support, the campaign may not have gotten off the ground. Therefore, the OLRB dismissed the decertification application, finding that the employer effectively initiated the campaign.

In some jurisdictions, a failed decertification application results in a bar being imposed that prohibits further applications for a defined period of time.[29]

B. Other Reasons for Decertification

Depending on the jurisdiction, collective bargaining legislation grants labour relations boards discretion to order a union decertified for a variety of other reasons, including the following:

- *The union failed to commence collective bargaining (Ontario and New Brunswick).* If a union fails to give the employer a "notice to bargain" or otherwise fails to commence bargaining after a defined period of time (60 days in Ontario, 30 days in New Brunswick), then a labour relations board can decertify the union for "sleeping on" its bargaining rights.[30]
- *The certification was obtained by fraud (Ontario, Manitoba, New Brunswick, Saskatchewan, and federal).* If a union's application for certification was obtained by reliance on fraudulent statements or documents, such as forged union membership cards, the labour relations board can terminate the union's certification.[31]
- *The union "abandoned" its bargaining rights (Manitoba, British Columbia, Saskatchewan, Alberta, and Ontario[32]).* If a union takes no steps to bargain a collective agreement or to administer a collective agreement, a labour relations board may rule that the union has "abandoned" or "slept on" its bargaining rights and decertify the union.
- *The union was displaced by another union in a union raid.* As discussed in Chapter 8, a union can apply for certification of employees represented by a different union during the open period. If a raiding union is successful, then the union that previously represented the employees is decertified and the new union replaces the old union as the employees' legal representative.

C. The Effects of a Successful Application for Decertification

What happens when a union is decertified? The short answer is that the union ceases to represent the employees any longer, any collective agreement that was in effect ceases to operate, and the employees are suddenly thrust back into the common law regime.[33] One moment, the employees exist within the collective bargaining regime. The next moment, they have an individual employment contract with their employer and all the rules of the common law govern that relationship (see Part II of the companion volume). What are the terms of that employment contract?

One option is that the employee and employer return to a situation akin to a new common law hiring, so that the terms of the individual employment contract must be bargained anew, with a new offer, an acceptance, and mutual consideration (see Chapter 7 of the companion volume). However, that approach would be unworkable in practice, since the work itself must continue seamlessly, and there would not usually be time for the employer to bargain new individual employment contracts with the entire group of formerly unionized employees.[34] Another option is that the former terms of the collective agreement simply carry over and become implied terms (see Chapter 9 of the companion volume) of the new individual employment contract. This option has the benefit of allowing a seamless transition from the collective bargaining regime to the common law regime. If an employee was earning $30 per hour and was entitled to a health and dental plan and 15 days of paid vacation under the old collective agreement, then those entitlements become implied terms of the new individual employment contract. If the (now non-union) employer subsequently cuts the employee's pay to $20 per hour or cancels the health and dental plan, the employee could bring a lawsuit in court for breach of contract, including perhaps constructive dismissal (see Chapter 15 of the companion volume).

But how much of the old collective agreement should be implied into the new individual employment contracts? For example, if the old collective agreement that governed the employment relationship before decertification required the employer to have "just cause" to dismiss an employee, does that requirement carry over to the individual employment contract, effectively ousting the normal common law right of employers to dismiss non-union employees simply by giving notice of termination? Is the grievance and arbitration provision of the old collective agreement implied into the employment contract, so that a dismissed employee must proceed to arbitration rather than file a wrongful dismissal lawsuit in court?[35] The case in Box 15.6 wrestles with these questions.

BOX 15.6 » CASE LAW HIGHLIGHT

What Happens When Employees Decertify Their Union?

OSSTF v. Muskoka Board of Education

[1996] OLRD No. 3369 (Ont. LRB), aff'd. OJ No. 1354 (Ont. Ct. J. (Gen. Div.))

Key Facts: The custodial employees of the Muskoka Board of Education were represented by the Service Employees Union (SEU) until September 25, 1995, when a majority of the employees voted to decertify the union. Shortly thereafter, in early October 1995, a new union (Ontario Secondary School Teachers' Federation, or OSSTF) successfully applied to be certified for the same employees. That certification triggered the statutory collective bargaining freeze (see Chapter 10), during which time the employer could not alter any terms or conditions of employment without the union's consent. In November 1995, still during the statutory freeze period, an employee named Blundell was dismissed for innocent absenteeism due to a prolonged absence related to a disability. Blundell filed a grievance challenging the termination as lacking just cause. The employer replied that since the old collective agreement between SEU and the employer was no longer in effect, the just cause provision in it no longer applied and Blundell's terms of employment were governed by the common law of the individual employment contract. OSSTF filed a complaint with the labour relations board on behalf of Blundell, arguing that the just cause term of the old collective agreement carried over into the new individual employment contract of Blundell, so that when the employer fired Blundell without just cause, it effectively altered a condition of employment and therefore violated the statutory freeze provisions in the *Labour Relations Act, 1995*.

Issue: Did the just cause provision in the old collective agreement become an implied term of Blundell's individual employment contract with the employer after the SEU was decertified? If so, did the employer violate the statutory freeze provisions by dismissing Blundell without just cause?

Decision: No and no. From the moment SEU was decertified, the employment relationship changed from one in which the employer was legally required to deal with the union as Blundell's bargaining representative to one governed by the common law of the individual employment contract. The terms of the expired collective agreement "which relate directly to the individual employer-employee relationship" are implied into the individual employment contract "unless there is an agreement to the contrary, or other circumstances from which there may be implied terms and conditions of employment different from those set out in the collective agreement." However, terms in the collective agreement that confer collective rights and rights on the union (as opposed to the employee) cannot be implied into an individual employment contract.

Therefore, the terms of the expired collective agreement that applied to Blundell's individual employment contract, and that were "frozen" when the OSSTF applied for certification, were those that related to individual employee rights but not to collective rights. The OLRB ruled that the expired collective agreement conferred a right on the *union* to challenge terminations as lacking just cause, but not on individual employees, as explained in the following passage:

> In our view, "just cause" protection in the collective agreement between SEU and the MBE confers rights of a collective nature ON THE [SEU], not of an individual nature on the individual bargaining unit employee. This "just cause" protection does not survive the termination of the collective agreement. After [SEU was decertified], the employees, including Mr. Blundell, correspondingly lost the right [to] file a grievance and to request the union to pursue a challenge to the employer's assertion of "just cause" for discharge, through the grievance and arbitration process. ... Mr. Blundell's right to challenge his dismissal was governed by the common law, and the appropriate procedure for remedying any breach of the common law was a [wrongful dismissal] action in the Courts ... [where] the court would apply the common law standard of "cause."

Since Blundell's employment contract did not include a term stating that he could only be dismissed for just cause, the employer did not violate the statutory freeze provisions in the *Labour Relations Act, 1995*, even if it had dismissed Blundell without just cause. The complaint was dismissed.

In the *OSSTF v. Muskoka Board of Education* decision, the OLRB ruled that parts of the collective agreement that regulate the relationship between individual employees and the employer are implied into the employment contract after decertification, absent agreement to the contrary, but not those parts that deal with the collective relationship between the union and the employer. Since the collective agreement conferred the decision whether to arbitrate a matter of just cause on the union and not the employee, the just cause provision did not carry over as an implied term of the employee's individual employment contract. Had the collective agreement granted employees a personal right to challenge their dismissal as lacking just cause, then the just cause term may have been implied into the contract.[36] In most cases, employees immediately forfeit the just cause protection that existed under the collective agreement once the union is decertified and instead become subject to the common law rules regulating termination of employment contracts, discussed at length in Part II of the companion volume.

V. Chapter Summary

With this chapter on decertification, we have come full circle in this text. We have learned how employees transition from the common law regime to the collective bargaining regime and then back again. Because unions may possess significant institutional powers, the courts and governments recognized the need to regulate unions to ensure that they can be held responsible for their conduct. In the common law regime, although judges have long held individual union officials personally responsible for their deeds through tort and sometimes criminal law, the courts have struggled in assigning a distinct legal personality to unions. Recently, the courts have overcome this challenge by ruling that, by imposing extensive legal rights and responsibilities on unions, collective bargaining statutes have effectively given unions the legal status to act in their own capacity. A significant legal responsibility imposed on unions in Canada is the duty of fair representation. This chapter explored the scope of that obligation and noted that unions have been given considerable deference to make difficult decisions, provided that those decisions are based on a fair consideration of facts and issues and not tainted by discrimination or bad faith.

QUESTIONS AND ISSUES FOR DISCUSSION

1. Describe the basis on which the Supreme Court of Canada ruled that unions have legal status to sue and be sued in their own right in *Berry v. Pulley*. Had the original union (CALPA) violated the union constitution in that case? Why or why not?
2. In your home province, is the source of the DFR imposed on unions statutory (found in a statute) or common law (judge made)?
3. Describe the substance of the DFR (the three types of behaviour that unions are required to avoid). Provide an example of each type of behaviour.
4. Is it a violation of the DFR for a union to make a decision that disadvantages one of its members? Explain your answer.
5. Describe the process by which employees can decertify their union in your home province.
6. What happens to employees' terms and conditions of employment when the union that had represented them is decertified?

UPDATES

Go to emond.ca/lawofworkircb for links to news, author's blog posts, content updates, and other information related to the chapters in this text.

NOTES AND REFERENCES

1 *Orchard v. Tunney*, [1957] SCR 436; and *Berry v. Pulley*, 2002 SCC 40, [2002] 2 SCR 493.

2 See, e.g., *Birch v. Union of Taxation Employees*, 2008 ONCA 809, 93 OR (3d) 1 (a union lawsuit against members for breach of constitution for crossing a picket line was dismissed because the contract clause was unconscionable); *McNairn v. United Association of Journeymen and Apprentices of the Plumbing and Pipe Fitting Industry of the United States and Canada, Local 179*, 2004 SKCA 57, 240 DLR (4th) 358; *Williams v. Telecommunications Workers Union*, 2012 ABCA 284; *Hokanson v. Sheet Metal Workers International Association, Local 280*, [1985] BCJ No. 550 (QL) (BCSC); *Kiewning v. Communications, Energy and Paperworkers Union of Canada*, 2011 ONSC 712; and *Fullowka v. Pinkerton's of Canada Ltd.*, 2010 SCC 5, [2010] 1 SCR 132.

3 *Rights of Labour Act*, RSO 1990, c. R.33, s. 3(2).

4 See *Nipissing Hotel Ltd. et al. v. Hotel & Restaurant Employees & Bartenders International Union et al.*, [1963] 2 OR 169 (Ont. HCJ); *Seafarers International Union of Canada et al. v. Lawrence* (1977), 15 OR (2d) 226 (Ont. SC); and *Choice Environmental Ltd v. Tri-Phase Environmental Inc*, 2011 CanLII 84637 (Surdykowski). But see *Public Service Alliance of Canada v. Canada (Attorney General)* (2002), 62 OR (3d) 682 (Ont. CA) (unions certified under federal collective bargaining legislation are not barred from civil actions by *Rights of Labour Act* because they do not depend on Ontario *Labour Relations Act, 1995* for their existence); and *Kiewning v. Communications, Energy and Paperworkers Union of Canada*, supra note 2. See also *Labour Relations Act, 1995*, SO 1995, c. 1, Sch. A.

5 This tension has long been the subject of academic debate. See, e.g., B. Adell, "Collective Agreements and Individual Rights: A Note on the Duty of Fair Representation" (1985-86) 11 *Queen's Law Journal* 251.

6 *Steele v. Louisville & Nashville Railroad*, 323 U.S. 192 (1944). See the discussion of the development of the American duty of fair representation law in P. Secunda et al., *Mastering Labor Law* (Durham, NC: Carolina Academic Press, 2014), at chapter 18.

7 *Vaca v. Sipes*, 386 U.S. 171 (1967).

8 H.D. Woods, A.W.R. Carrothers, J. Crispo, and G. Dion, *Canadian Industrial Relations, Report of the Task Force on Labour Relations* (Ottawa: Queen's Printer, 1968), at 104. See the discussion of the evolution of the Canadian DFR in *Rayonier Canada (BC) Ltd. v. IWA, Local 1-217*, [1975] 2 CLRBR 196 (BCLRB), at 200.

9 Ontario *Labour Relations Act, 1995*, supra note 4, s. 74.

10 See *Burns et al. v. National Automobile, Aerospace, Transportation and General Workers Union of Canada (CAW-Canada, Local 219 et al.)*, 2012 NBCA 13, 383 NBR (2d) 245; *Hedges v. National Automobile, Aerospace and Agricultural Implement Workers Union of Canada* (1996), 145 Nfld & PEIR 189 (PESCTD); and *Lanigan v. PEITF*, 2015 PESC 36.

11 *Gendron v. Supply and Services Union of the Public Service Alliance of Canada, Local 50057*, [1990] 1 SCR 1298; and *Bakaluk et al. v. Western Star Trucks Inc. et al.*, 2004 BCSC 417, 27 BCLR (4th) 359.

12 *Smith v. United Food and Commercial Workers' International Union, Local 1518*, 2004 CanLII 65553 (BCLRB). See also *Elliott v. Canadian Merchant Service Guild et al.*, 2008 PSLRB 3 (DFR does not apply to union's conduct during representation of employee before workers' compensation tribunal); and *Legault v. AEFO*, 2001 CanLII 17634 (Ont. LRB).

13 *Interior Systems Contractors Association of Ontario*, [1995] OLRB Rep. Aug. 1082; and *Petingola v. United Food & Commercial Workers Union, Local 1000A*, 2010 CanLII 56878 (Ont. LRB).

14 The Saskatchewan DFR language was recently amended in a manner that appears to broaden the scope of the DFR from a duty to represent employees fairly in "grievance or rights arbitration" in the old language to a more general duty to represent employees fairly with regard to rights "pursuant to a collective agreement or this Part" of the *Saskatchewan Employment Act*, SS 2013, c. S-15.1. At the time of writing, the board had not elaborated on the significance of this change. See the discussion in *C.B. v. Canadian Union of Public Employees, Local 21*, 2015 CanLII 90524 (SKLRB).

15 The Canada Industrial Relations Board has ruled that the DFR provision in the *Canada Labour Code* (RSC 1985, c. L-2) applies to collective bargaining as well as contract administration. See *George Cairns et al*, 2001 CIRB 111 (CanLII).

16 A good discussion of the differences in DFR scope appears in *Complainant 6226 v. Canadian Auto Workers, Local 4600*, 2011 CanLII 21920 (NSLB).

17 Alberta *Labour Relations Code*, RSA 2000, c. L-1, s. 153(1).

18 *Gendron v. Supply and Services Union of the Public Service Alliance of Canada, Local 50057*, supra note 11. See also *Judd v. Communications, Energy and Paperworkers Union of Canada, Local 2000*, 2003 CanLII 62912 (BCLRB); and *Caddy v. B.C. Government and Service Employees' Union*, 2004 CanLII 34983 (BCLRB) (the union's failure to

investigate facts and make an informed assessment amounts to arbitrary conduct).

19 *Anonymous Applicant v. National Automobile, Aerospace, Transportation and General Workers Union of Canada (CAW-Canada, Local 40)*, 2012 CanLII 34216 (Ont. LRB); *Coppins v. United Steelworkers, Local 7689*, 2016 CanLII 79633 (SKLRB); and *Toronto Transit Commission*, [1997] OLRD No. 3148.

20 See *Rayonier Canada (BC) Ltd. v. I.W.A., Local 1-217*, supra note 8; and *Caddy v. B.C. Government and Service Employees' Union*, supra note 18.

21 *Canadian Merchant Service Guild v. Gagnon et al.*, [1984] 1 SCR 509. See also *Noël v. Société d'énergie de la Baie James*, 2001 SCC 39, [2001] 2 SCR 207.

22 *Anonymous Applicant v. National Automobile, Aerospace, Transportation and General Workers Union of Canada (CAW-Canada, Local 40)*, supra note 19.

23 D. Dale and T. Boyle, "City Workers to Get 6% Pay Hike over Four Years," *Toronto Star*, February 13, 2012, https://www.thestar.com/news/city_hall/2012/02/13/city_workers_to_get_6_pay_hike_over_four_years.html.

24 See, e.g., *Diamond Z Association*, [1979] OLRB Rep. Oct. 791; and *Ahokas v. Canadian Union of Public Employees, Local 87*, 1983 CanLII 895 (Ont. LRB).

25 Most jurisdictions ban decertification applications for between 10 and 12 months from the date of certification. Saskatchewan bars applications for two years from the date of certification: see *Saskatchewan Employment Act*, supra note 14, s. 6-17(4).

26 See, e.g., Ontario *Labour Relations Act, 1995*, supra note 4, ss. 63 and 67.

27 See, e.g., Ontario *Labour Relations Act, 1995*, supra note 4, s. 15.

28 See, e.g., *Fleischmann v. Universal Workers Union, L.I.U.N.A. Local 183*, 2014 CanLII 12266 (Ont. LRB); *Empco-Fab*, [1982] OLRB Rep. 1162 (the employer paid the legal fees of employees initiating the decertification campaign); *George Stinson v. International Brotherhood of Electrical Workers Local 105*, 2016 CanLII 53492 (Ont. LRB) (the employer worked closely with decertification application organizers to assure employees that nothing

bad would happen if the union were decertified); and *Unionized Employees of Tenaquip v. Teamsters, Local Union 419*, 1997 CanLII 15586 (Ont. LRB) (the employer provided time off and office time to help the campaign).

29 See, e.g., Ontario *Labour Relations Act, 1995*, supra note 4, s. 111(2)(k); and BC *Labour Relations Code*, RSBC 1996, c. 244, s. 33(3).

30 See Ontario *Labour Relations Act, 1995*, supra note 4, s. 65; and NB *Industrial Relations Act*, RSNB 1973, c. I-4, s. 24.

31 See, e.g., Ontario *Labour Relations Act, 1995*, supra note 4, s. 64; *Saskatchewan Employment Act*, supra note 14, s. 6-109; *Canada Labour Code*, supra note 15, s. 40; Manitoba *Labour Relations Act*, CCSM c. L10, s. 52; and NB *Industrial Relations Act*, supra note 30, s. 26.

32 The Ontario *Labour Relations Act, 1995* does not expressly recognize "abandonment" as a statutory basis for ordering decertification, but the OLRB has read in that authority. See *J.S Mechanical*, [1979] 2 CLRBR 87 (Ont. LRB).

33 See, e.g., Ontario *Labour Relations Act, 1995*, supra note 4, s. 63(18) (collective agreement ceases to operate upon a board order decertifying a union); and *Canada Labour Code*, supra note 15, s. 42.

34 *Isidore Garon ltée v. Tremblay; Fillion et Frères (1976) inc. v. Syndicat national des employés de garage du Québec inc.*, 2006 SCC 2 at para. 27, [2006] 1 SCR 27.

35 See the discussion in *Re Telegram Publishing Co. Ltd. v. Zwelling et al.* (1975), 11 OR (2d) 740 (CA) (the terms of an expired collective agreement that relate to the individual employment relationship become implied terms of the employment contract); *Mental Health Hospital v. Alberta Union of Provincial Employees*, 1986 ABCA 117; *Sullivan v. Victoria Golf Club*, 1994 CanLII 2622 (BCSC); and *Isidore Garon ltée v. Tremblay; Fillion et Frères (1976) inc. v. Syndicat national des employés de garage du Québec inc.*, supra note 34.

36 In *Sullivan v. Victoria Golf Club*, supra note 35, the court ruled that the grievance and arbitration provisions of the collective agreement carried over into the individual employment contract after the union was decertified.

Public Sector Labour Relations*

I. Introduction

In many respects, the labour laws that govern the public and private sectors are the same or similar. For example, the laws governing union certification, unfair labour practices, and grievance arbitration (all considered elsewhere in this text) are mostly the same in the two sectors. However, in other respects, important differences exist in the labour laws that apply to the public service. Those differences are the focus of this chapter, and they relate to the following areas:

- the rules concerning essential services;
- strike and picketing rules;
- the limits on topics that can be collectively bargained;
- the use of interest arbitration instead of strikes and lockouts;
- the composition of bargaining units; and
- the implications of the duty of fidelity of public servants to the Crown.

Why does the public sector require a special legal regime? What makes the public service exceptional? Generally, there are three reasons for this exceptionalism.

The first reason is the government's need to protect the public. The government's overriding responsibility is to the public interest, and the public interest needs to be taken into account when

---

* This chapter was authored by Christopher C. Rootham, partner with Nelligan O'Brien Payne.

determining the collective bargaining rights of employees.[1] The need to protect the public is particularly pertinent when considering the right of public servants who work in essential services to strike. Public service strikes can greatly inconvenience the public without causing economic harm to the government. Therefore, essential services legislation is in place to protect the public interest.[2]

The second reason is that the locus of bargaining authority is more diffuse in the public sector than it is in the private sector. In the private sector, it is common for a single person (or a small committee of people) to have the ultimate authority to bind the employer in collective bargaining. In the public sector, by contrast, it is difficult to find a single person with authority because governments are, by their nature, consultative bodies where decisions are made after input from a number of different people and interests.

The third reason is the sovereign nature of the state as employer. The government, or the **Crown**, has sovereign authority in Canada. Some consider it a mistake for the Crown to voluntarily limit its sovereign authority through collectively bargaining with its employees. As Quebec Premier Jean Lesage put it back in the early 1960s: "The Queen does not negotiate with her subjects."[3]

These three reasons are often unsatisfactory in explaining the differences between public and private sector collective bargaining law. Nevertheless, they are the commonly stated reasons for these differences, and the actual differences can often be drawn from one or more of these three reasons.

II. Terminology: What Is the "Public Service"? Who Is "the Employer"? Who Is a "Public Servant"?

The first step in this chapter is to define key terms and identify the employer in public sector collective bargaining.

A. What Is the "Public Service," and Who Is "the Employer" in Public Service?

What is the "public service"? The public service needs to be distinguished from the "public sector" (commonly referred to as the *broader public sector*). The easiest way to think of the public sector is as a series of concentric circles (see Figure 16.1). The innermost circle is the core **public service**. The public service is controlled directly by the central financial planning agency for the particular government being considered—for example, the **Treasury Board** federally, or the Management Board of Cabinet in the province of Ontario. This central financial planning agency is responsible for all of the human resource functions within this inner-most core. Federally, this inner-most core is called the *core public administration*.

The next concentric circle comprises those agencies or organizations that have authority over their own human resources, but are still controlled to some extent by the central financial planning agency. These agencies sign their own collective agreements, design their own staffing rules, and have their own human resource policies; however, those collective agreements, rules, and

---

Crown: The Crown in Canada is Her Majesty in right of Canada or in right of a province. The Crown is a synonym for the government.

public service: The public service comprises those departments and agencies that are controlled and managed directly by a central financial planning agency of the Crown. It is distinct from the public sector, which receives funding from the government but is responsible for its own management.

Treasury Board: A committee of the Queen's Privy Council (i.e.. Cabinet) comprising the minister of finance and four other Cabinet ministers. The actual work of the Treasury Board is done by its administrative arm—the Treasury Board Secretariat. The Treasury Board Secretariat essentially manages the public service, including its collective bargaining and other human resource functions.

FIGURE 16.1 Map of the Public Sector

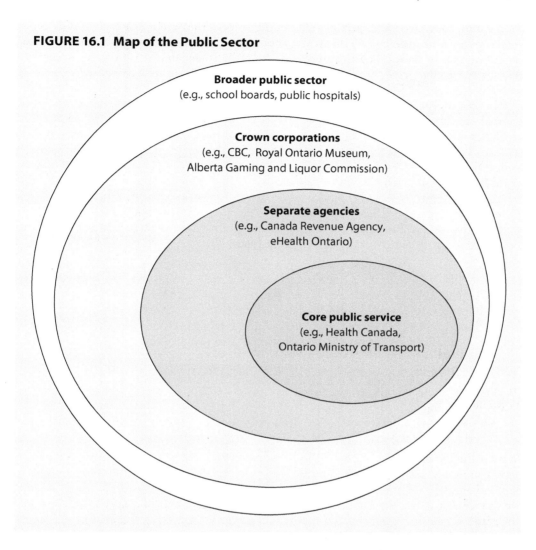

policies are still reviewed and, to some extent, approved by the central financial planning agency. Federally, these agencies are called *separate agencies*; in Ontario, they are called *public bodies*, and they have other names in some other provinces. For example, Canada Revenue Agency is a separate agency in the federal government; and eHealth Ontario is a public body in Ontario. Not every province uses this concentric circle: British Columbia, for example, has one collective agreement for all ministries and agencies. In other words, British Columbia only has its equivalent of the core public service.

The next concentric circle comprises **Crown corporations**. Crown corporations are corporations wholly and directly owned by the government. They are responsible for their own collective bargaining and human resource management and are run by an independent board of directors; however, they are still responsible to their shareholder—the government. The Canadian Broadcasting Corporation, the Alberta Gaming and Liquor Commission, and the Royal Ontario Museum are three examples of the hundreds of Crown corporations across Canada.

Crown corporation: A corporation wholly and directly owned by the provincial or federal Crown.

The outermost circle is commonly referred to as the **broader public sector**. Public sector employers are funded entirely by the federal or provincial government, but collective bargaining typically occurs at the local or organizational level. Health care and education are sectors with public sector employers. In both of these sectors, provincial governments are still experimenting with the degree of centralization that should be used for collective bargaining. Ontario, for example, uses a form of two-tiered bargaining for its teachers: some issues are negotiated at the school-board level, and other issues (including wages) are negotiated on a province-wide basis.

This chapter will address collective bargaining by organizations in the two innermost concentric circles only; that is, organizations where the employer is either the central financial planning agency (e.g., the federal Treasury Board) or a separate agency designated by the government. Typically the third and fourth circles are governed by private sector labour laws or sector-specific statutes (e.g., in education, policing, and health care).[4]

B. Who Is a "Public Servant"?

The final preliminary issue is, Who is a **public servant**? In Chapter 2, the common law tests for distinguishing between an employee and an independent contractor in the private sector were explored. Those tests apply to public service workers as well. In addition, however, the various statutes governing the public service in each jurisdiction set out certain formalities of appointment before a person becomes a public servant. In the absence of those formalities, an individual is not a public servant, no matter how much control is being exercised over that individual or how dependent he or she is on the public service. See Box 16.1.

BOX 16.1 » CASE LAW HIGHLIGHT

Defining "Public Servant"

Canada (Attorney General) v. Public Service Alliance of Canada
[1991] 1 SCR 614

Key Facts: The federal government (the Solicitor General) had hired a number of teachers to provide educational programs for prison inmates. Those teachers were public servants and in a bargaining unit represented by the union Public Service Alliance of Canada (PSAC). However, in 1984, the Solicitor General decided to privatize these services and entered into a contract with a private educational company named Econosult to provide these programs through teachers hired by Econosult. Through its contract with Econosult, the Solicitor General set the pay rates for the teachers, set their hours of work, provided their equipment, and otherwise controlled their employment. However, the contract also specified that the teachers were not employees of the government. PSAC filed an application with the Public Service Relations Board arguing that the teachers were in fact employees of the government, applying the usual tests for determining whether a worker was an employee or a contractor (see Chapter 2). The employer challenged that decision in the courts, arguing that since the teachers had not

been formally appointed to the public service, they could not be government employees.

Issue: Were teachers who were under the control of the government but not formally appointed to the public service considered to be government employees?

Decision: No. Despite the fact that the government exercised control over the teachers, the Supreme Court of Canada concluded that the teachers were not "employees" because they had not been formally appointed by the Public Service Commission in accordance with the *Public Service Employment Act.* The Supreme Court of Canada stated:

> The positions in the Public Service are determined by the Treasury Board and appointments to the public service are within the exclusive rights and authority of the Public Service Commission. Exceptions are carefully spelled out in the Employment Act. ... In the scheme of labour relations which I have outlined above there is just no place for a species of de facto public servant who is neither fish nor fowl.

---

broader public sector: Those sectors of the economy that are funded predominantly or exclusively through taxpayer money, and that have management that is independent from the government.

public servant: An employee formally appointed to the public service following the requirements of legislation.

III. Distinguishing Features of Public Sector Collective Bargaining Law and Policy

As noted above, while much of the law that governs the public service is the same as or similar to that governing private sector employees, there are important differences. The remainder of this chapter examines those key distinguishing features.

A. Essential Services

An important difference between the public and private sectors is that **essential services** are prevalent in the public sector. We briefly considered essential services in Chapter 11 in relation to interest arbitration. While private sector labour laws can recognize essential services,[5] essential services provisions are an integral part of the law governing the public service. There are, broadly speaking, three models for dealing with strikes in essential services:

1. the "no strike" model, where strikes and lockouts are illegal;
2. the "unfettered strike" model, where the standard strike/lockout regime applies; and
3. the "designation" model, where strikes are permitted but certain workers or positions are designated as essential to ensure that enough workers remain at work during a strike to ensure that essential services are continued.

In Canada, the "no strike" model is used in certain circumstances where any strike would unduly impact essential services. For example, police officers and firefighters are prohibited from striking throughout Canada. The "unfettered strike" model is used typically for the third and fourth concentric circles discussed above (Crown corporations and, sometimes, the education sector). In most other situations, however, the "designation" model prevails. The first step in applying the designation model is to determine what an essential service is. While the definition of *essential service* varies slightly from jurisdiction to jurisdiction, the core concept is that an essential service is one that affects the safety or security of the public. For example, the Alberta *Labour Relations Code* defines *essential services* as those services

> (a) the interruption of which would endanger the life, personal safety or health of the public,
or
> (b) that are necessary to the maintenance and administration of the rule of law or public security.

Unions and employers have argued for definitions of health, safety, and security that are either extremely narrow or very broad, respectively. For example, unions have often taken the position that safety and security means only circumstances of imminent physical danger, while employers have argued that safety and security encompasses emotional as well as physical well-being. Labour relations boards and the courts have typically taken a midway point between those two extremes: "safety and security" has been interpreted as more than simple economic inconvenience, but less than imminent national danger. Essential services legislation does not immunize the government or the country from economic harm from a strike, nor does it permit the government to carry on business as usual. However, it does guard against the probability or even the possibility of harm or injury to the health or physical well-being of individuals.

---

essential services: Services that are essential to protect the health, safety, or security of the public. For example, police officers, firefighters, and medical practitioners perform essential services. Some governments consider services that are important to the public, such as public transit or mail delivery, as essential services as well.

Some examples of essential and non-essential services are listed in Table 16.1.

TABLE 16.1 Essential and Non-essential Services

Essential Services	Non-essential Services
	Law librarians
Data processors for welfare programs the withdrawal of which is likely to create a risk or hazard to the health of the recipient	Data processors for other welfare programs
Veterinarian inspectors at federally regulated abattoirs	Veterinarian inspectors at provincially regulated abattoirs
Border officers who conduct inspections and decide appropriate actions to maintain border security	Border officers who assess and collect duties, taxes, fees, and fines
Parks Canada workers who monitor forest fires, coordinate search-and-rescue operations, pilot search-and-rescue vehicles, ensure the integrity of the water supply within parks, and ensure proper handling and storage of garbage (to reduce the risk of bear attacks)	

The burden of proof in each case rests with the employer. The employer must place evidence before the labour relations board to convince it that a reasonable basis exists for finding that a service is essential.[6]

One of the significant issues in essential services is whether employees must perform their "whole job" during a strike, or whether they only have to perform the part of their job that is found to be essential. A similar issue is whether the government has the unilateral authority to dictate the level of service that needs to be provided once the service has been found to be essential. In most jurisdictions, these issues are negotiated between the employer and the union, who enter into an **essential services agreement** that governs these and other issues relating to essential services. The federal government, by contrast, has reserved the right to dictate the level of service that needs to be provided by its employees, and the Supreme Court of Canada has upheld that rule.

BOX 16.2 » CASE LAW HIGHLIGHT

Determining Which Employees Are Essential Employees

C.A.T.C.A. v. The Queen
[1982] 1 SCR 696

Key Facts: In 1980, unionized air traffic controllers threatened a strike. The minister of transport decided that commercial airlines must maintain their normal operations in the event of a strike. Therefore, the Treasury Board attempted to designate all 1,782 air traffic controllers as essential. There was no dispute that air traffic control was an essential service to ensure safe air travel. However, the union argued that the employer could not designate all (or nearly all) of the bargaining unit employees as essential and thereby effectively eliminate the right to strike. Rather, the union argued that only those employees necessary to protect the safety and security of the public by ensuring that emergency flights continue, such as medical and emergency air evacuations, mercy missions, military operations and the like, are essential. The Public Service Staff Relations Board agreed with the union and declared that only 272 employees (and 151 alternates) were essential. The employer challenged that decision to the courts.

Issue: Did the Public Service Staff Relations Board exceed its authority by deciding how many air traffic controllers were essential to ensure that emergency flights could continue, rather than deciding how many employees were essential to maintain all air travel at its pre-strike levels?

---

essential services agreement: An agreement between an employer and a union that identifies which and how many employees are "essential" to protect public safety and therefore cannot participate in a work stoppage.

Decision: Yes. On eventual appeal to the Supreme Court of Canada, that court decided that under the *Public Service Staff Relations Act*, the employer (i.e., the federal government)—not the Public Service Staff Relations Board or the union—determines the level of essential service that must be performed in the event of a strike. The Supreme Court of Canada wrote:

> As I see it, the task of the [Public Service Staff Relations] Board … is to consider those employees and classes of employees in the bargaining unit who have been designated by the employer, and to decide whether the performance of their stipulated duties as employees is necessary for public safety or security. … I can find nothing in the section to indicate that the function of the Board is to determine … what services normally provided by employees in the bargaining unit are, in the event of strike action, necessary to be continued in the interest of public security or safety. …

Counsel for the [union] also contended that the [decision that the government can unilaterally decide what services are essential] would reduce the effectiveness of legitimate strike action. The result of the Court's decision is certainly to impair the impact of a strike by employees in the bargaining unit involved here but that does not mean that the decision is wrong. The members of the bargaining unit involved in this case are nearly all persons the nature of whose duties brings them within the definition of designated employees and Parliament has decided that designated employees are not permitted to strike.

Therefore, the union's appeal was dismissed.

In the years immediately after the *C.A.T.C.A.* decision, 60 percent of federal public service bargaining units had over half of their members designated as essential, and 35 percent had all or virtually all of their members designated as essential.

Another issue that arises in essential services is the notion of "job bundling." Imagine that there are three employees, each of whom spends a third of his or her time performing essential services. In this scenario, are all three employees expected to work full-time during a strike, or must the essential components of the jobs be "bundled" so that only one employee is declared essential and works full-time? Job bundling in this limited sense is typically permitted, subject to the terms of an essential services agreement. Job bundling does not extend beyond this basic concept. For example, an employer is not expected to require some employees to work overtime so that others can strike. An employer is also not expected to reassign managers or other employees excluded from the bargaining unit to perform these essential duties.

Finally, the interaction between replacement workers and essential services varies from province to province. In British Columbia, the labour relations board has concluded that an employer cannot require essential services workers to attend work while at the same time hiring replacement employees;[7] in Ontario, by contrast, the labour relations board concluded that it did not have the jurisdiction to prevent an employer from hiring replacement workers at the same time as preventing other essential services employees from striking.[8]

B. *Public Sector Strike and Picketing Rules*

If an essential services regime is in place and the parties have been unsuccessful in bargaining, the union may call a strike on behalf of its members. Most of the rules concerning strike activity (discussed in Chapter 11) in the private sector are similar in the public sector and spelled out in detail in the labour legislation of each jurisdiction. For example, public sector strike rules address the timing of a strike vote, notice to the employer, and whether a strike vote can be combined with a ratification vote. They also address limits on the right to strike while Parliament or the legislature is not in session and other government-specific concerns.

Picketing is more restrictive during public sector strikes than it is in private sector strikes. Striking public servants may not impede or restrict access to essential services. Therefore, picketing in public sector strikes is constrained in a way that is different from private sector strikes. This issue has played out most frequently in regulating picket lines at courthouses. The rule of law in Canada requires unimpeded access to the courts. Therefore, obstructing persons officially connected with the court and preventing access by the public to courts of law is a form of criminal contempt. A courthouse picket line has exactly that effect: it impedes court officers and members of the public from attending court. Therefore, picket lines at courthouses are typically prohibited or, at the very least, extremely limited.[9] For other government buildings, some level of delay is acceptable: it will depend upon how urgently the essential service must be performed.

Finally, there is some dispute over whether public sector strikes are primarily economic or political in nature. In the private sector, a strike is ultimately an economic weapon: a strike causes (or at least is intended to cause) the employer to lose money, and so the question of when or how to settle a strike is largely an economic question. Public sector strikes are different. The government does not lose money during a strike—on the contrary, it saves money by not having to pay its striking employees while it continues to collect taxes.[10] Strikes in the public sector are ultimately political battles. The real question is this: Will a strike put enough political pressure on the government to resolve the strike on terms favourable to the union, or will public sympathy and votes remain with the government?

Despite the inherently political nature of public sector strikes, many courts have been reluctant to characterize such strikes as inherently "political" instead of "economic" in nature. The courts have tended to focus on the actual issues at stake in the strike. If the issues relate primarily to working conditions, then the strikes are economic;[11] if the issues are about the content of legislation or government policy, then the strikes are more political.[12]

C. Limits on Topics That Can Be Collectively Bargained

In the private sector, there are few limits to the topics on which a union and employer may choose to bargain (see Chapter 11). While a limited number of bargaining proposals are illegal, and some collective agreement provisions are mandated by statutes, the parties are otherwise only constrained by their imagination when it comes to the topics of bargaining. Not so in the public sector. In the public sector, several topics are excluded from collective bargaining.

The federal *Public Service Labour Relations Act*, for example, prohibits bargaining on any issue that is established by legislation.[13] This restriction has the impact of preventing bargaining on the following topics:

- *Pensions:* Pensions in the federal public service are created by statute; therefore, there is no collective bargaining about the funding or benefits of pension plans in the federal public service.
- *Appointments (including seniority):* The appointment process in the core public administration is set out in legislation and, therefore, may not be collectively bargained. Setting out this process in legislation has the practical effect of removing any seniority-based rules for filling vacant positions in the federal public service.
- *Job classifications*
- *Assignment of duties*
- *Layoffs:* While unions may negotiate the amount of severance a laid-off employee will receive, the decision to lay off employees and the selection of which employees to lay off are outside the scope of collective bargaining.

While legislation varies from jurisdiction to jurisdiction,[14] bargaining in the public sector is generally on a more limited set of topics than in the private sector.

D. Interest Arbitration

While interest arbitration is sometimes used in the private sector, as discussed in Chapter 11, it is more generally used in the public sector. Public sector employees who do not have the right to strike—such as police officers and firefighters—always have a bargaining dispute resolved by way of interest arbitration. Other public sector unions sometimes "opt in" to interest arbitration, either by statutory right or with the agreement of the employer. The rules for interest arbitration may vary from jurisdiction to jurisdiction, and may even vary within jurisdictions, depending on the employees involved. A complete description of the interest arbitration regime in Canada would fill an entire book. This chapter aims to provide a basic overview of interest arbitration as it relates to the public sector.

Interest arbitration, unlike grievance rights arbitration, usually (although not always) occurs before a panel of three people. Two members of the panel are "nominees"—individuals selected by the union and employer, respectively. These nominees cannot be directly affiliated with the employer or the union (e.g., a union cannot select its lawyer as a nominee); however, the nominees are expected to advocate their interests.[15] The third member of the panel is truly neutral, and ends up being the de facto decision-maker in an interest arbitration case. If the parties cannot agree on the neutral chair of the arbitration panel, then the appointment is made by a labour relations board or a minister, as long as the selection results in someone who is broadly acceptable by virtue of the person's training and expertise.[16] An **interest arbitrator** must of course not be biased in favour of either party,[17] and he or she must also have the necessary qualifications to be an effective arbitrator (including, where necessary, the ability to conduct the hearing in both official languages).[18]

There are two types of interest arbitration in Canada. The first, and predominant, type is straightforward: the parties make submissions on each of their proposals, and the arbitration panel is free to select one or the other proposal on each issue, or construct its own answer to the issues raised. For example, if the union proposes a 3 percent wage increase and the employer proposes a 1 percent wage increase, the arbitration panel is free to decide upon a 2 percent wage increase (or some other percentage between 1 and 3).

The second type of interest arbitration is called **final offer selection**, or "baseball," arbitration.[19] In final offer selection arbitration, both sides submit their complete final offer; the arbitration panel then has to select one of the two final offers, without amendment. The theory is that this approach forces the parties to compromise when putting in their final offers, making it easier to reach an agreement once the parties have seen how close they are in their final offers.[20] However, final offer selection arbitration becomes more difficult when a large number of issues are involved. An arbitrator will have a hard time selecting a final offer when one side is aggressive on all issues while the other party has compromised on every issue except one where it has been incredibly aggressive (to the point of including a "poison pill" proposal).

Each statute that establishes an interest arbitration regime lists a number of factors that the interest arbitration panel must consider when rendering its decision. However, regardless of the wording of the statute, interest arbitrators retain their discretion to make a fair and impartial award. In doing so, interest arbitrators tend to follow five principles when making their decision:

- The **replication principle**: Interest arbitrators intend to replicate an agreement that conventional bargaining (with a strike or lockout) would have produced. Interest arbitrators are not there to apply an abstract notion of social justice, but instead to replicate the result

---

interest arbitrator: An individual or three-person expert arbitration board tasked with writing the terms of a collective agreement when the union and employer are unable to reach agreement through voluntary collective bargaining.

final offer selection: A form of interest arbitration in which the union and employer submit a complete final offer for a collective agreement, and then the arbitration panel selects either the union's or the employer's final offer in its entirety.

replication principle: The principle that since interest arbitration is a substitute for free collective bargaining, the interest arbitrator should seek to replicate, to the extent possible, an agreement that the parties would have likely reached had they had recourse to the economic sanctions of a strike or lockout.

of collective bargaining. In doing so, interest arbitrators look for objective factors that predict the results of collective bargaining, including the terms of freely negotiated collective agreements in the same industry; the terms of collective agreements in the same community; the terms contained in the expired collective agreement; and the bargaining history between the parties.

- The **conservatism principle**: Interest arbitration is an inherently conservative exercise. As a general rule, interest arbitrators are reluctant to award major breakthroughs; they see major breakthroughs as reserved for negotiations. This does not mean that an arbitrator will never award a significant pay increase;[21] however, for the most part, interest arbitrators see themselves as a stop-gap measure pending the next round of bargaining.

- The **necessity principle**: Governments have to be able to attract and retain quality employees. Interest arbitrators will assess proposals with a view to whether particular terms are necessary to meet those goals.

- The **comparability principle**: Interest arbitrators seek to maintain comparable terms and conditions—especially pay—between comparable jobs in the public and private sectors. Interest arbitrators are also concerned about internal comparability—in other words, treating similar public servants similarly. Where two bargaining units have been compared with each other for a long period of time—for example, where police officers and firefighters have received comparable wage increases for decades—interest arbitrators will tend to follow those comparable agreements.

- The **ability to pay principle**: Among interest arbitrators, considerable controversy exists over whether arbitrators should consider the government's "ability to pay" when making an award. Interest arbitrators have, traditionally, been reluctant to consider "ability to pay"—recognizing that a government rarely truly has an inability to pay, but instead has an unwillingness to pay (or an unwillingness to tax).[22] In response, some legislation establishing interest arbitration contains provisions permitting or requiring interest arbitrators to consider "ability to pay"; virtually all such legislation permits or requires interest arbitrators to consider the general state of the economy and the government's fiscal position when making their awards. When assessing economic circumstances, arbitrators consider what "a majority of fair-minded, well-informed taxpayers would consider to be a fair and reasonable award."[23] Interest arbitrators also examine the evidence carefully to ensure that there is a true inability to pay instead of just an unwillingness to pay (or an unwillingness to cut service levels). For example, on December 16, 2009, an interest arbitrator awarded an interim award (instead of a final award) for firefighters in Windsor that did not approve a reduction to a 42-hour workweek that would normally be justified on the basis of comparative analysis.[24] The interest arbitrator made that decision in light of the disproportionate impact the 2008–2009 recession was having in Windsor. The firefighters eventually received their 42-hour workweek effective December 31, 2014. By contrast, when the City of Toronto argued that it had an inability to pay its firefighters in 2013 because of a short-term budget deficit, the same interest

---

conservatism principle: The principle that interest arbitrators should not impose significant changes on the parties to a collective agreement, and should instead reserve those big changes for freely negotiated agreements.

necessity principle: The principle that interest arbitrators should order the terms (e.g., wages and other benefits) necessary to attract and retain employees for the employer.

comparability principle: The principle that interest arbitrators should maintain comparable terms and conditions (e.g., pay) between comparable jobs in the public and private sectors.

ability to pay principle: The principle that where provided by statute, interest arbitrators may (or must) consider the government's ability to pay when deciding the terms of their award.

arbitrator was unimpressed and made an award based upon the long-standing comparable agreement with police officers.[25]

Whether interest arbitration is a suitable process for resolving bargaining disputes is a matter of ongoing debate. Some commentators are concerned about what industrial relations scholars call the "corrosive and narcotic" effect on bargaining: corrosive in that it decreases the number of collectively bargained settlements, and narcotic in the sense that the parties become addicted to interest arbitration.[26] Evidence of the corrosive effect (sometimes called the "chilling effect") and narcotic effect on interest arbitration is mixed.[27] There is some evidence of it in certain sectors, but less in others. Some public sector employers also complain that the interest arbitration system leads to higher wage increases; this allegation is much more controversial, and there is very little evidence that interest arbitration leads to higher wage increases than negotiated agreements.[28]

E. Bargaining Unit Composition

As Chapter 8 noted, a bargaining unit serves at least two functions: it is the basis for organization and the basis for a long-term bargaining structure. Thus, labour relations boards must balance two different policy considerations when determining the "appropriate bargaining unit": they must create a unit that is not so large or disparate as to make union organizing impossible, and they must ensure that the unit is not so small as to make collective bargaining unfeasible. In the public sector, the second policy consideration usually outweighs the first. Public sector employers are "not merely tolerant of collective bargaining, but rather anxious for it to get under way."[29] Therefore, bargaining units in the public sector tend to be much larger than in the private sector.

Another reason for larger bargaining units in the public sector is that legislation often defines the appropriate bargaining unit instead of simply leaving the labour relations board to determine whether a particular group of employees shares a community of interest. In Ontario, for example, the *Crown Employees Collective Bargaining Act*[30] designates seven bargaining units:

- administrative employees;
- correctional employees;
- institutional and health care employees;
- office administration employees;
- operational and maintenance employees;
- technical employees; and
- a residual bargaining unit, mainly comprising lower-level managers.

The first six bargaining units are represented by the same union: the Ontario Public Service Employees Union (OPSEU). The legislation requires OPSEU to negotiate one central agreement for its six bargaining units over seven issues, and then separate agreements to deal with other issues. In practice, OPSEU only negotiates a separate agreement for correctional employees, and it negotiates on behalf of the other five bargaining units at a central bargaining table.

The federal public service has a larger number of bargaining units than Ontario. Rather than define bargaining units, the federal *Public Service Labour Relations Act* creates a presumption that bargaining units will follow classification lines.[31] This presumption means that, with the exception of dockyard workers who have separate bargaining units for the east and west coast, no regional or geographical-based bargaining units exist in the federal public service: all employees of a particular classification are covered by the same collective agreement across Canada.[32] The federal government made a policy decision when collective bargaining was introduced that employees performing the same work would be paid the same, regardless of where they work. While there are a small number of regional pay differences,[33] this policy has remained in place to the present day.

IV. Implications of Public Servants' Duty of Fidelity

As discussed in Chapter 9 of the companion volume, every employee owes his or her employer a duty of fidelity. This duty has a number of unique features in the federal public service. First, the duty of fidelity is owed to the government, not to the political party in power at any given time. Public servants are therefore required by statute to swear or affirm an oath of loyalty to the Crown before becoming a public servant. For example, federal public servants are required to swear the following oath:

> I, [name], swear (or solemnly affirm) that I will faithfully and honestly fulfil the duties that devolve on me by reason of my employment in the public service of Canada and that I will not, without due authority, disclose or make known any matter that comes to my knowledge by reason of such employment.[34]

In the Province of Ontario, public servants must give an oath of allegiance and loyalty to the Queen.[35] This duty of fidelity to the Crown (as opposed to a duty to any particular political party) exists because of the public interest in an impartial public service. The Canadian tradition of the public service emphasizes the characteristics of impartiality, neutrality, fairness, and integrity— as opposed to a "spoils" system that is more prevalent in other countries (and was, historically, used in Canada).

The duty of fidelity is balanced against the right of public servants to criticize the government. Public servants have the right to criticize the government, just as every citizen has a right to do so. However, this right of public criticism must be balanced against the public servant's duty of fidelity to the Crown. This means that public servants must act with some restraint when criticizing the government publicly. The degree of restraint depends upon the position occupied by the public servant, the visibility of the public servant, the nature of the criticism, and the topics of the criticism. For example, a data-entry clerk has greater latitude to criticize the government than a deputy minister; a public servant also has latitude to criticize the government about policies that jeopardize the life, health, or safety of the public.

Linked to the concept of the duty of fidelity is the obligation of political neutrality. Public servants have a constitutional right to participate in political activity; however, this right is limited by their obligation to perform—and be seen to perform—their duties in a politically neutral manner. In most jurisdictions, the balance between these two obligations is set out in statute. Federally, for example, public servants below the rank of deputy minister have the right to engage in political activity as long as doing so "does not impair, or is not perceived as impairing, the employee's ability to perform his or her duties in a politically impartial manner."[36] This provision means that an employee, for example, cannot help a political party during working hours or using work equipment. If a public servant wants to run for political office, he or she needs to obtain permission from the Public Service Commission. If the political office is federal, provincial, or territorial, the public servant must take a leave of absence during the election period and may be asked to take a leave of absence prior to the election period; if the public servant is running for municipal office, a leave of absence is not mandatory but may be required, depending on the nature of the election, the nature of the public servant's duties, and the visibility of the public servant. Finally, the Public Service Commission has the right to refuse to grant permission to a public servant who wants to run for political office.

Finally, special rules apply to **whistle-blowers** in the public service. Most jurisdictions have legislation that provides a forum, person, or body to whom whistle-blowers can make their disclosure; this legislation also protects whistle-blowers from reprisals for having disclosed wrongdoing (or what they thought, in good faith, was wrongdoing).[37] Sometimes, public servants have

---

whistle-blower: An employee who discloses information about harmful or illegal conduct of his or her employer or co-workers.

gone directly to the media or the public to disclose wrongdoing, either before or after reporting the wrongdoing internally or to this whistle-blowing forum. Most of the time, public whistle-blowing is prohibited: a public servant is expected to go "up the ladder" instead of directly to the public. Public whistle-blowing is only permitted in the most serious cases, when there is insufficient time to go "up the ladder" or to the whistle-blower protection forum and the subject-matter of the disclosure involves an imminent risk of danger to the life, health, and safety of people or the environment.

V. Chapter Summary

In *Vaughan v. Canada*, Justice Binnie of the Supreme Court of Canada wrote:

> The terms and conditions of employment of the federal government's quarter of a million current workers are set out in statutes, collective agreements, Treasury Board directives, regulations, ministerial orders, and other documents that consume bookshelves of loose-leaf binders. Human resources personnel are recruited into the system, spend a career attempting to understand it and die out of it.[38]

This pronouncement, while somewhat demoralizing on its face, captures the public's view of the public service as rule-driven and fastidious in the application of those rules. However, these rules—particularly when they depart from the normal approach to labour law in the private sector—are there as a result of the unique qualities of the government as employer. The government is accountable to citizens, not shareholders; public sector unions correspondingly advocate to the public as much as to their employer. This fundamental fact means that the laws are different in the public service.

QUESTIONS AND ISSUES FOR DISCUSSION

1. Should labour law be any different in the public service than in the private sector? Explain your answer.
2. Where should labour boards draw the line between protecting essential services and allowing public servants to go on strike?
3. Describe three models for dealing with strikes in Canadian essential services.
4. Should public servants be allowed to run for elected office or engage in other forms of political activity? Why or why not?
5. When and why should whistle-blowers be protected?

UPDATES

Go to emond.ca/lawofworkircb for links to news, author's blog posts, content updates, and other information related to the chapters in this text.

NOTES AND REFERENCES

1 J. Finkelman and S. Goldenberg, *Collective Bargaining in the Public Service: The Federal Experience in Canada* (Montreal: Institute for Research on Public Policy, 1983), at xxvii and 7.

2 Advisory Committee on Labour-Management Relations in the Federal Public Service, *Working Together in the Public Interest: Second Report* (Ottawa: Treasury Board Secretariat, 2001), at 14.

3 Or, more accurately, "La Reine ne négocie pas avec ses sujets."

4 For further information about Crown corporations, see I. Bernier and A. Lajoie, *Regulations, Crown Corporations and Administrative Tribunals* (Ottawa: Minister of Supply and Services Canada, 1985). A number of books have been written about collective bargaining in the broader public sector. In education, for example, I recommend in particular S. Slinn and A. Sweetman, *Dynamic*

Negotiations: Teacher Labour Relations in Canadian Elementary and Secondary Education (Montreal: McGill-Queen's University Press, 2012).

5   For example, *Canada Labour Code*, RSC 1985, c. L-2, s. 87.4.

6   *Public Service Alliance of Canada v. Parks Canada Agency*, 2008 PSLRB 97, at para. 180.

7   *Beacon Hill Lodge v. BCNU and HEU* (1986), No. 2/86 (BCLRB), aff'd. *Beacon Hill Lodge v. British Columbia*, [1987] BCJ No. 713 (CA).

8   *Ontario (Management Board Secretariat)*, [1998] OLRD No. 3050.

9   *B.C.G.E.U. v. British Columbia (Attorney General)*, [1988] 2 SCR 214, at para. 29. See also *Ontario Public Service Employees Union v. Ontario (Attorney General)* (2002), 58 OR (3d) 577 (CA).

10 We all still have to pay our taxes even if there is a public sector strike, after all.

11 *Grain Workers' Union, Local 333 v. B.C. Terminal Elevator Operators' Assn.*, 2009 FCA 201, [2010] 3 FCR 255.

12 *British Columbia Teachers' Federation v. British Columbia Public School Employers' Assn.*, 2009 BCCA 39.

13 *Public Service Labour Relations Act*, SC 2003, c. 22, s. 113.

14 For example, Ontario's *Crown Employees Collective Bargaining Act, 1993*, SO 1993, c. 38 is much more permissive than the *Public Service Labour Relations Act*.

15 *Yorkton (City) v. Yorkton Professional Fire Fighters Association, Local 1527*, 2001 SKCA 128, 207 DLR (4th) 651.

16 *C.U.P.E. v. Ontario (Minister of Labour)*, 2003 SCC 29, [2003] 1 SCR 539.

17 *Canadian Union of Postal Workers v. Canada Post Corporation*, 2012 FC 975.

18 *Canadian Union of Postal Workers v. Canada Post Corporation*, 2012 FC 110.

19 Major League Baseball is the most famous employer to use final offer arbitration.

20 See, e.g., E. Black and J. Silver, "Contradictions and Limitations of Final Offer Selection: The Manitoba Experience" (1990) 45 *Relations Industrielles/Industrial Relations* 146; and J. Rose, "Legal Challenges to Interest Arbitration: Evidence from Canada" (2015) 66:3 *Labor Law Journal* 177.

21 One of the most famous examples is *Association of Law Officers of the Crown v. Ontario (Management Board of Cabinet)*, [2000] OLAA No. 790, where arbitrator Kaplan ordered a 30 percent wage increase for Ontario Crown lawyers.

22 M. Teplitsky, "Ability to Pay and the Independence of Arbitration: An Arbitrator's Perspective," in W. Kaplan et al., eds., *Labour Arbitration Yearbook* (1998) (Toronto: Lancaster House, 1998), at 357.

23 *Niagara (Regional Municipality) Police Services Board and Niagara Police Association* (1997), 78 LAC (4th) 42, at 58.

24 *Windsor (City) v. W.P.F.F.A.* (2009), 100 CLAS 246 (Burkett); and *Re: Windsor (City) and W.P.F.F.A. (Renewal Collective Agreement)* (2013), 117 CLAS 353.

25 *Toronto (City) and I.A.F.F., Local 3888 (Renewal Collective Agreement)* (2013), 116 CLAS 117 (Burkett).

26 J. Rose, "The Leech, the Tortoise and the Owl: The World of Interest Arbitration in Ontario" *Labour Arbitration Yearbook* (1994–1995) (Toronto: Lancaster House, 1995), at 393; and G. Adams, "The Ontario Experience with Interest Arbitration: Problems in Detecting Policy" (1981) 36:1 *Relations Industrielles/Industrial Relations* 225.

27 R. Hebdon, "Public Sector Dispute Resolution in Transition" in D. Belman, M. Gunderson, and D. Hyatt, eds., *Public Sector Employment in a Time of Transition* (Madison, WI: Industrial Relations Research Association, 1996), 85-125.

28 See, e.g., T. Kochan, D. Lipsky, M. Newhart, and A. Benson, "The Long-Haul Effects of Interest Arbitration: The Case of New York State's Taylor Law" (2010) 63:4 *Industrial and Labor Relations Review* 565.

29 *Insurance Corp of British Columbia and CUPE, Local 1695* (1974), 1 CLRBR 403 at 407.

30 *Crown Employees Collective Bargaining Act, 1993*, supra note 14, s. 23. The bargaining units are more fully defined in the OPSEU collective agreement: "Collective Agreements with Respect to Working Conditions, Employee Benefits and Salaries between the Ontario Public Service Employees Union and the Crown in Right of Ontario Represented by Management Board of Cabinet, January 1, 2015 to December 31, 2017," https://opseu.org/sites/default/files/2015-2017_opseu_central_unified_agreement_-_final.pdf.

31 *Public Service Labour Relations Act*, supra note 13, ss. 57, 70, and 91.

32 Ibid.

33 For example, employees working in isolated communities receive a special isolated post allowance. Lawyers working in Toronto also have a regional rate of pay.

34 *Public Service Employment Act*, SC 2003, c. 22, ss. 12, 13, and 54.

35 *Public Service of Ontario Act, 2006*, SO 2006, c. 35, Sch. A, ss. 5-6; and *Oaths and Affirmations*, O. Reg. 373/07, ss. 1-3.

36 *Public Service Employment Act*, supra note 34, s. 12.

37 See, e.g., the *Public Servants Disclosure Protection Act*, SC 2005, c. 46, which applies to federal public servants; the *Public Interest Disclosure (Whistleblower Protection) Act*, SA 2012, c. P-39.5, in Alberta; or *The Public Interest Disclosure (Whistleblower Protection) Act*, CCSM c. P217, in Manitoba.

38 *Vaughan v. Canada*, 2005 SCC 11 at para. 1, [2005] 1 SCR 146.

Selected Cases: Part II

Cases with boldface page numbers appear as Case Law Highlights.

PART III

The Canadian Charter of Rights and Freedoms and the Law of Work

The Charter and Regulatory Standards

I. Introduction

April 17, 1982 was a momentous day in Canadian law. That was the day the *Canadian Charter of Rights and Freedoms* came into force.[1] In the hierarchy of government regulation, the Charter is perched at the top. The Charter is part of the *Constitution Act, 1982*, and its purpose is to regulate government action. The Charter imposes checks and balances on what governments can and cannot do by guaranteeing Canadians a bundle of fundamental rights and freedoms. Governments cannot impede the exercise of these rights and freedoms by Canadians, unless they can establish pressing and substantial reasons for doing so. In short, every government action, including every statute and regulation enacted, must be consistent with the Charter; otherwise, it is unlawful. Therefore, it makes sense to consider the role that the Charter plays in the law of work.

The influence of the Charter will be examined in this chapter and in Chapter 18.[2] This chapter introduces the structure of the Charter, explains how it restrains government in terms of the regulation of work, and examines how the Charter has influenced the development of the *common law regime* and the *regulatory standards regime*. In Chapter 18 we address the complex question of how the Charter's guarantee of "freedom of association" has impacted the development of collective bargaining laws in Canada.

Prime Minister Pierre Elliott Trudeau (left) and Queen Elizabeth II sign the Proclamation of the Constitution Act, 1982, *which includes the* Canadian Charter of Rights and Freedoms, *on April 17, 1982.*

Source: Library and Archives Canada/National Archives of Canada fonds/e002852801

II. What or Whom Does the Charter Govern?

The Charter came into force after much political debate and wrangling over its contents. What resulted was a compromise document, sparse in text, yet deceptively complex in its meaning and application. The first important point to understand about the Charter is that it only applies to government action.[3] Its purpose is to regulate the relationship between governments and citizens, not the relationships between private citizens and private companies. It is essential to understand this crucial distinction. The Charter sets limits on government actions.

How do governments *act*? First, they enact and administer laws and regulations. And second, they act in the capacity of the employer of their own employees. When a Canadian government acts in either of these two capacities, it must not do so in a manner that is inconsistent with the Charter. Most Charter cases are targeted at government legislation that is alleged to violate the Charter. However, occasionally complaints arise that the government, acting as an employer, has contravened Charter rights in the manner in which it has treated its employees.

The fact that the Charter applies directly to government employers but not private sector employers can be confusing. It means that if my employer is the City of Toronto, the Province of British Columbia, or the Government of Canada, then my employer and my employment contract must comply with the Charter. So, if a Canadian government had a policy of paying its male employees more than its female employees for the same jobs, that policy could be directly challenged as a violation of section 15 of the Charter, which protects the right to equal treatment on the basis of sex. However, if Walmart, General Motors, or Tim Hortons had such a discriminatory policy, the Charter would *not* apply. Employees of those private sector employers could challenge the policy by filing a complaint under a human rights, pay equity, or employment standards statute, but the Charter would not help them.

Often it is obvious whether an employer is "the government," but not always. Occasionally, the courts have been asked to decide whether an employer is "the government" on the basis that it receives significant government funding, for example, or is highly regulated by the government. Consider colleges, for example. They are not "the government" in an obvious sense, but because they receive a significant amount of public funding and are under significant control of a provincial government, the Supreme Court of Canada has treated colleges as government actors for the purposes of the Charter.[4] Therefore, in the case of *Lavigne v. Ontario Public Service Employees Union*, the Supreme Court of Canada ruled that the Charter applied directly to a collective agreement between a union and a community college.[5] However, the courts have ruled that universities are not government actors because although universities also receive public funding, governments have far less direct control over universities than they do colleges.[6]

III. Understanding the Charter Challenge

Now that we know that the Charter regulates only government conduct, we can begin our exploration of the substance of the Charter. First, let's examine how the Charter operates in practice. Governments must consider the Charter whenever they are proposing and drafting new laws. Usually, a government that receives legal advice that a proposed law (a bill) will infringe the Charter is expected to revise the bill to bring it into Charter compliance or withdraw the bill.[7] Once legislation is enacted into law, it can be challenged by anyone who believes that the law violates a right or freedom protected by the Charter. This type of legal proceeding is described as a **Charter challenge**. The Supreme Court of Canada has created a two-step process to analyze Charter challenges.

Charter challenge: A legal proceeding that alleges that government action contravenes the *Canadian Charter of Rights and Freedoms*.

A. Step One: Has Government Infringed a Charter Right or Freedom?

The first step in the analysis is to decide whether some government action contravened a Charter-protected right or freedom. If it does not, then the Charter does not apply, the Charter challenge is dismissed, and the government's action is confirmed as lawful.

Sometimes, it is obvious that the government has violated a Charter right or freedom. For example, until 2006, the Ontario *Human Rights Code* prohibited discrimination on the basis of "age," but then defined "age" as between 18 and 64 years old. This definition meant that it was perfectly legal for employers to discriminate against workers who were under 18 or over 64, but that discrimination in employment against people between the ages of 18 and 64 was illegal. Age was defined in this way in order to permit **mandatory retirement**, a practice in which employees are required to leave their jobs upon attaining a specific age. Whether you were protected from discrimination depended entirely upon your age, and therefore the definition of "age" clearly contravened section 15 of the Charter. The Supreme Court of Canada decided as much in the 1990 case of *McKinney v. University of Guelph* (see Box 17.3), in which eight University of Guelph professors challenged their forced retirement at age 65.[8] In the *McKinney* case, the real dispute related to the second part of the Charter's two-step analysis, which is discussed in the next section.

Other times, it is not at all clear whether government action has infringed a Charter-protected right or freedom, so complex arguments take place at this first step of the analysis. For instance, as we will discuss later in this chapter, the Supreme Court of Canada has recognized prohibited grounds of discrimination under section 15 of the Charter that are not expressly listed in that section; these grounds are referred to as **analogous grounds**. A landmark Charter challenge based on analogous grounds is the 1995 case of *Egan v. Canada*. That case involved a Charter challenge against legislation that denied Old Age Security spousal benefits to same-sex couples. In its decision, the Supreme Court of Canada ruled that section 15 protects against discrimination on the basis of "sexual orientation," even though that ground is not listed in section 15.[9] The case also involved a very complicated set of arguments at the step-one stage.

B. Step Two: If an Infringement Exists, Is It Justified in a Free and Democratic Society?

If a court or tribunal rules that government action has interfered with a Charter right or freedom, then it moves to the second step of the analysis: the section 1 analysis. That step is described in section 1 of the Charter, which reads:

> The *Canadian Charter of Rights and Freedoms* guarantees the rights and freedoms set out in it subject *only to such reasonable limits prescribed by law as can be demonstrably justified in a free and democratic society*. [Emphasis added.]

Section 1 explains that sometimes it is justifiable for a government to violate a Charter right or freedom. It requires a balancing of interests. In certain instances, in order to protect or pursue an important public interest, it may be necessary to impinge upon Charter rights and freedoms. Section 1 provides the legal mechanism to enable courts and tribunals to engage in that complex balancing exercise.

---

mandatory retirement: A legal rule in a statute or contract that terminates an employment contract upon the employee reaching a specified age.

analogous grounds: Prohibited grounds of discrimination in equality legislation that are not enumerated (listed) in the legislation, but which the courts have read into the legislation because of their similarity to the enumerated grounds that are protected (e.g., sexual orientation, marital status, and citizenship).

The language in section 1 is very vague. However, in one of the earliest cases after the Charter was enacted, the Supreme Court of Canada developed a section 1 "test" that must be applied whenever this balancing of interests takes place. The test became known as the *Oakes* **test** because the case in which it originated is called *R v. Oakes*.[10] That case was not itself about work, but the *Oakes* test applies to all Charter challenges that engage section 1. The *Oakes* test is a "proportionality test," which means that it guides judges in their assessment of whether the benefit to society of allowing a Charter violation outweighs the harm to the individual of having his or her Charter right violated. The components of the *Oakes* test are described in Box 17.1.

BOX 17.1 » TALKING WORK LAW

Analysis of Section 1 of the Charter: The *Oakes* Test

Section 1 of the Charter requires courts and tribunals to weigh the harm to individual Canadians of having a Charter right or freedom restricted by government action against the interests of the broader Canadian society. If the greater good is served by permitting the government to violate a Charter right or freedom, then section 1 permits a court or tribunal to allow that violation. In the 1986 decision in *R v. Oakes*, the Supreme Court of Canada developed a test for applying section 1 to a case of Charter infringement. That test became known as the *Oakes* test. The *Oakes* test has two parts, each of which the government must prove:

Part One: The Pressing and Substantial Concern Test

Part one requires that the objective of, or reason for, the limitation on the Charter right must relate to "a pressing and substantial concern." This means, essentially, that the government must persuade the court or tribunal that its actions, which were found to impinge on Charter rights or freedoms, were taken to address a serious public concern. Usually, the government passes part one of the *Oakes* test without much difficulty, but not always, as we will see when we look at the case of *Vriend v. Alberta* later in the chapter.

Part Two: The Proportionality Test

If the court or tribunal accepts that the purpose of the government action is to address a pressing and substantial concern, then the court will move on to part two of the *Oakes* test, which is known as the "proportionality test." Most Charter challenges are won or lost based on the outcome of the proportionality test. The Supreme Court of Canada described the proportionality test in the *Oakes* decision as follows:

First, the measures adopted must be carefully designed to achieve the objective in question. They must not be arbitrary, unfair or based on irrational considerations. In short, *they must be rationally connected to the objective* [the "rational connection" test]. Second, the means, even if rationally connected to the objective in this first sense, *should impair "as little as possible"* the right or freedom in question [the "minimal impairment" test] ... . Third, there must be a *proportionality* between the effects of the measures which are responsible for limiting the Charter right or freedom, and the objective which has been identified as of "sufficient importance" [the "balance of harm" test]. [Emphasis added.]

In order to justify a violation of a Charter right or freedom, a government must satisfy all three components of the proportionality test: (1) rational connection; (2) minimal impairment; and (3) balance of harm or "proportionality." If the government fails to prove any of these elements, the government's actions will be ruled unconstitutional. When a government satisfies the *Oakes* test, we say that the Charter violation was "saved by section 1."

In the case of a statute that violates the Charter, the remedy can include striking down the entire statute or just the part of the statute that violated the Charter. Sometimes the courts have provided the government with a period of time before the law becomes invalid, during which the government can develop and enact a new, replacement law that is Charter compliant.

In dozens of court cases in which a Charter right was infringed by the government, the government's actions were "saved by section 1." Some of those cases have related to workplace law. The *McKinney v. University of Guelph* decision discussed in Box 17.3 is one example.

***Oakes* test:** The test applied by courts and tribunals when interpreting section 1 of the *Canadian Charter of Rights and Freedoms*. The test requires courts and tribunals to balance the interests of individuals in having their Charter rights and freedoms protected against any broader social benefits that would result from allowing a restriction of a Charter right or freedom. Named after the case *R v. Oakes*, the test was formulated by the Supreme Court of Canada.

IV. What Rights and Freedoms in the Charter Are Important to the Law of Work?

Now that we have a basic idea of how the Charter works, we need to look more carefully at what rights and freedoms it protects. In addition to section 1, the two sections of the Charter that are most important to the law of work are section 2 (fundamental freedoms), especially "freedom of thought, belief, opinion and expression" and "freedom of association," and section 15 (equality rights). Section 6 (mobility rights) is also important, as it grants Canadians the right to work in any province. The text of these sections appears in Box 17.2.

BOX 17.2 » TALKING WORK LAW

The Sections of the Charter That Are Most Important to the Law of Work

Guarantee of Rights and Freedoms

1. The *Canadian Charter of Rights and Freedoms* guarantees the rights and freedoms set out in it subject only to such reasonable limits prescribed by law as can be demonstrably justified in a free and democratic society.

Fundamental Freedoms

2. Everyone has the following fundamental freedoms:

(a) freedom of conscience and religion;

(b) freedom of thought, belief, opinion and expression, including freedom of the press and other media of communication;

(c) freedom of peaceful assembly; and

(d) freedom of association.

Mobility Rights

6(1) Every citizen of Canada has the right to enter, remain in and leave Canada.

(2) Every citizen of Canada and every person who has the status of a permanent resident of Canada has the right

(a) to move to and take up residence in any province; and

(b) to pursue the gaining of a livelihood in any province.

Equality Rights

15(1) Every individual is equal before and under the law and has the right to the equal protection and equal benefit of the law without discrimination and, in particular, without discrimination based on race, national or ethnic origin, colour, religion, sex, age or mental or physical disability.

(2) Subsection (1) does not preclude any law, program or activity that has as its object the amelioration of conditions of disadvantaged individuals or groups including those that are disadvantaged because of race, national or ethnic origin, colour, religion, sex, age or mental or physical disability.

Section 2(d), "freedom of association," has produced an extensive body of case law relating to the extent to which governments can regulate and restrict the rights of workers to unionize, engage in collective bargaining, and strike. Section 2(b), "freedom of thought, belief, opinion and expression," has played a role in the development of the law's treatment of the right of workers to picket and leaflet during labour disputes. We will leave discussion of these issues to Chapter 18, where we will examine the Charter's role in the context of the *collective bargaining regime*. In the remainder of this chapter, we will consider the Charter's role in the development of the common law regime and the regulatory standards regime.

A. *The Charter and the Common Law Regime of Work Law*

We can deal with the Charter's impact on the common law regime relatively quickly.[11] First, recall that the Charter only regulates government action, not the actions of private citizens and organizations. Therefore, insofar as a lawsuit is between two private (i.e., not government) actors, the Charter does not directly apply. As a result, the Charter has played a very limited role in the development of the common law of employment. However, the Supreme Court of Canada decided in 1986 that, even though the Charter does not apply directly to judges deciding contract and tort disputes between private actors, common law judges should nevertheless be guided by "Charter values" as they develop and apply common law rules.[12] In this way, the Charter can indirectly influence the development of the common law.

Probably the clearest example of the "Charter values" approach is the 2002 case of *RWDSU, Local 558 v. Pepsi-Cola Canada Beverages (West) Ltd.*, where the Supreme Court of Canada ruled that tort law should develop in a manner consistent with "Charter values," and overruled a long-held common law rule that placed heavy restrictions on the right of expression of workers involved in a labour dispute. The case involved striking Pepsi employees who were distributing literature at retail stores that sold Pepsi products, asking shoppers to support them by boycotting Pepsi products during the strike.

That sort of peaceful **secondary picketing** has been treated as a tort in the Canadian common law since the pre-Charter 1963 decision of the Ontario Court of Appeal in *Hersees of Woodstock Ltd. v. Goldstein et al.*[13] However, in the *RWDSU* decision, the Supreme Court of Canada ruled that an absolute ban on peaceful picketing and leafleting by workers was inconsistent with "Charter values" since "picketing ... always involves expressive action" and "it engages one of the highest constitutional values: freedom of expression."[14] The Supreme Court of Canada introduced a new rule, which essentially made all forms of information leafleting lawful under the common law, provided that it was not done in a manner that was unlawful, such as by taking place on private property (illegal trespass) or involving the commission of a crime or tort (such as assault, battery, or nuisance).

B. The Charter and the Regulatory Standards Regime

While the Charter was never intended to have a substantial impact on the common law regime, it was expected to influence the development of the regulatory standards regime. In fact, government regulation was the central target of the Charter. The Charter's section 15 equality rights provision has attracted the most judicial attention. That section states that "[e]very individual is equal before and under the law and has the right to the equal protection and equal benefit of the law without discrimination." It then lists various **enumerated grounds**: "race, national or ethnic origin, colour, religion, sex, age or mental or physical disability."

Not every legislative distinction violates section 15. There are two important provisos. First, the distinction must negatively impact individuals in ways that undermine their human dignity by, for instance, perpetuating negative stereotypes, prejudices, and historical disadvantages.[15] Second, the distinction must be based on one of the "enumerated grounds" listed expressly in section 15 or on an analogous ground. Analogous grounds have been added to the enumerated list by courts over time on the basis that they reflect a personal characteristic that is unchangeable (immutable), or involve a characteristic that a person ought not to be expected to change in order to achieve equality, and people who share the characteristic have been subjected to historical disadvantage, stereotypes, and prejudice. To date, the Supreme Court of Canada has added "sexual orientation,"[16] "marital status,"[17] and "citizenship"[18] as analogous grounds under section 15.

In a series of Charter challenges launched against legislation that excluded agricultural and health care workers from coverage under collective bargaining statutes, lawyers argued that "occupational status" should be recognized as a new analogous ground. They argued that by excluding workers employed in specific industries (e.g., agriculture and health care) from the

---

secondary picketing: Picketing in a labour dispute that takes place at a location other than the workplace where the workers engaged in the dispute are employed.

enumerated grounds: The characteristics listed in equality legislation (including the *Canadian Charter of Rights and Freedoms*) upon which discrimination is prohibited, such as sex, age, skin colour, and religion.

full scope of protections offered most other occupations under collective bargaining statutes, the government was making a distinction that undermined the dignity of these workers and perpetuated the stereotype that some classes of low-wage work are less deserving of legal protection than others. However, the Supreme Court of Canada has so far rejected this argument on the basis that section 15 does not apply to a distinction based on which segment of the labour market a person elects to work in.[19]

The most effective way to demonstrate the influence of the Charter on the regulatory standards regime is to look at important work-related Charter decisions. The case summarized in Box 17.3 provides an example of a Charter challenge in which a violation of section 15 equality rights is "saved by section 1."

BOX 17.3 » CASE LAW HIGHLIGHT

Mandatory Retirement and Age Discrimination "Saved by Section 1"

McKinney v. University of Guelph
[1990] 3 SCR 229

Key Facts: McKinney was forced to retire at age 65 pursuant to the University of Guelph's mandatory retirement policy. He launched a Charter challenge against the university's policy and the Ontario *Human Rights Code*, which protected against age discrimination, but only for persons aged 18 to 64. McKinney asserted that both the policy and the Code violated section 15 of the Charter by discriminating against him on the basis of his age. The Supreme Court of Canada ruled that the Charter did not apply to the university's mandatory retirement policy because the university was not "the government." However, the Charter clearly did apply to the *Human Rights Code*.

Issue: Does the definition of age (18 to 64) in human rights legislation violate the protection against age discrimination in section 15 of the Charter? If so, is that violation saved by section 1 of the Charter?

Decision: Yes. The Code's definition of "age" makes a distinction based solely on the enumerated ground of age, and this distinction imposes a burden on those 65 and older by taking away a benefit available to those not in the class of workers who are aged 18 to 64.

However, the violation of section 15 is "saved by section 1." The Supreme Court of Canada applied the *Oakes* test as follows:

- *The pressing and substantial concern test*: The objective of the legal rule was to permit the continuance of the widespread practice of mandatory retirement and to address the government's concern that abolishing mandatory retirement would have serious negative ramifications for Ontario's labour market and the operation of pension plans.
- *The proportionality test*:
  1. Rational connection test: The "age" definition maintains stability and predictability in pension arrangements and permits mandatory retirement.
  2. Minimal impairment test: The issue of whether to permit mandatory retirement is complex, with broad social and economic consequences. Governments should be given latitude in addressing complex problems. The government had a reasonable basis for concluding that the age definition impaired the rights of older workers as little as possible.
  3. Balance of harm test: The aim of prohibiting age discrimination was to protect those workers who are most vulnerable (18- to 64-year-olds). Workers 65 and older can access public and private pensions. Governments should be given leeway in making these tough policy decisions.

Since the government satisfied all parts of the *Oakes* test, the definition of age in the *Human Rights Code* was permitted to remain and McKinney lost his Charter challenge.

The discriminatory definition of age (18 to 64) in the Ontario *Human Rights Code* survived the Charter challenge in *McKinney*. This meant that it continued to be lawful for an employment contract to include a requirement that the employee retire at any age older than 64, and that the employee subject to such a requirement would have no human rights complaint available to challenge it. About 50 percent of Canadian workers were subject to a mandatory retirement requirement in the late 1990s, most of whom were in well-paid jobs covered by a pension plan that kicked in upon retirement.[20] In recent years, Canadian governments have moved to abolish the practice of mandatory retirement. For example, the definition of age in the Ontario *Human*

Rights Code at issue in *McKinney* was amended in 2006 to read "18 years or more."[21] Other provincial governments made similar amendments.[22] Today, with some exceptions, it is unlawful in Canada for an employer to force an employee to retire for no reason other than the employee's age. The reasons for this change of heart are addressed in our discussion of human rights statutes in Chapter 25 of the companion volume.

In *McKinney*, the Ontario government successfully argued a section 1 defence to its violation of section 15 of the Charter. In *Vriend v. Alberta*, discussed in Box 17.4, the Alberta government failed in its attempt to defend its refusal to protect gay and lesbian workers from discrimination in their employment. As you read the summary of the *Vriend* decision, pay close attention to the government action that is found to violate the Charter, keeping in mind that it was Vriend's private sector employer who fired him and not the government.

BOX 17.4 » CASE LAW HIGHLIGHT

Charter Requires Governments to Prohibit Discrimination in Employment on the Basis of Sexual Orientation

Vriend v. Alberta
[1998] 1 SCR 493

Key Facts: Vriend was employed by an Alberta college until the employer learned that he was gay, at which point Vriend was fired on the basis that being gay was inconsistent with the college's policies. Vriend attempted to file a complaint under the province's *Individual's Rights Protection Act*, but he could not because, unlike most provinces, Alberta did not prohibit discrimination in employment on the basis of "sexual orientation." Vriend then filed a Charter challenge asserting that the omission of sexual orientation from human rights legislation violated his section 15 Charter right to equality.

Issue: Does the omission of "sexual orientation" from the list of prohibited grounds in human rights legislation violate section 15 of the Charter?

Decision: Yes. First, government action can take the form of a positive action or an omission. An underinclusive protective statute can violate the Charter. Second, the deliberate decision of the Alberta government to not prohibit discrimination on the basis of sexual orientation amounted to a distinction that denied equal protection to gays and lesbians. The Supreme Court of Canada had already ruled in the 1995 case of *Egan v. Canada* that "sexual orientation" was an analogous ground to those expressly included in section 15. Therefore, the government's omission of sexual orientation from its human rights legislation was an omission that created a distinction contrary to section 15 of the Charter.

Section 1 did not save the violation of section 15. The omission of the analogous ground of sexual orientation from Alberta's human rights legislation failed every element of the *Oakes* test: it did not address a pressing and substantial concern; it was not rationally connected to the objective of protecting Albertans from discrimination (in fact, the omission was "antithetical" to that objective); it did not impair the rights of gays and lesbians as little as possible; and the harm to gays and lesbians from the exclusion far outweighed whatever benefit the omission was intended to achieve. To remedy the Charter violation, the Supreme Court of Canada ordered that "sexual orientation" was to be immediately "read into" the Alberta *Individual's Rights Protection Act*.

The *Vriend* decision forced Alberta to protect workers from discrimination in employment based on sexual orientation against the wishes of the province's elected government.[23] The decision provoked a heated debate within Alberta about how the government should respond, as discussed in Box 17.5.

The Law of Work Framework: The *Vriend* Decision and Tensions Between External Subsystems

We can map the tensions that led "sexual orientation" to be added to the Alberta *Individual's Rights Protection Act* by referring back to the Law of Work Framework presented in Chapter 3. By the time *Vriend v. Alberta* reached the Supreme Court of Canada in 1997, most provinces—Quebec (1977), Ontario (1986), Manitoba (1987), Nova Scotia (1991), British Columbia (1992), New Brunswick (1992), and Saskatchewan (1993)—and the federal government (1996) had already added "sexual orientation" to the grounds of prohibited discrimination in their human rights legislation. However, the notion of using law to protect gays and lesbians from employment discrimination remained unpopular in Alberta, at least among the elected politicians tasked with making laws as well as many constituents in the government's political base.*

Within the *political subsystem* of Alberta in the 1990s, the Progressive Conservative government was strongly resistant to legislating protections against labour market discrimination for gays and lesbians. The extent to which these political values reflected the attitudes of Alberta's citizens (i.e., the *social, cultural, and religious subsystem*) rather than just its elected politicians is a question that interests sociologists and political scientists. Certainly, conservative religious organizations in Alberta were resistant to advancing legislative protections to gays and lesbians. The *political subsystem* and the *social, cultural, and religious subsystem* interacted in a manner that produced resistance to recognizing sexual orientation as a protected ground. This relationship is depicted in Figure 17.1 by the black arrow lines (1). Ralph Klein, who was Alberta's premier at the

FIGURE 17.1 The *Vriend* Decision Within the Law of Work Framework

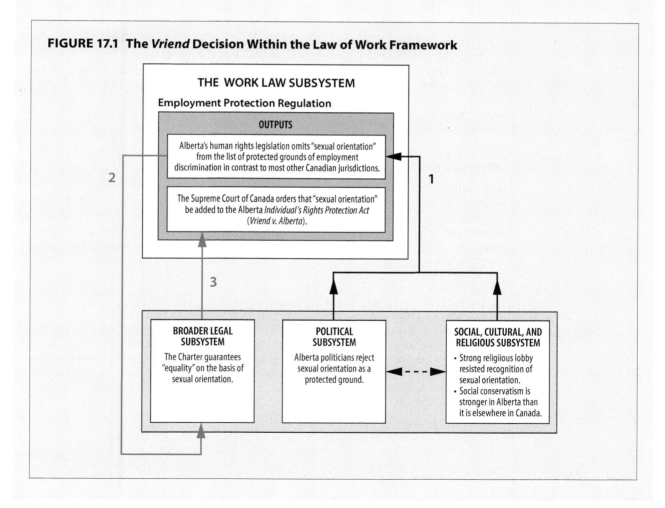

time *Vriend* was decided, explained the government's opposition to legislating protections for gays and lesbians by noting that most Albertans, whom he described as "severely normal," were opposed to the move.[†]

The Alberta legislature debated whether to include sexual orientation as a protected ground in its human rights legislation in the 1980s and decided against it. The path of this initial decision is depicted by the black arrow lines in Figure 17.1. The absence of sexual orientation as a protected ground provoked Vriend's decision to launch a Charter challenge (in the figure, see the blue external feedback loop arrow line [2]), which put the *political subsystem* and the *social, cultural, and religious subsystem* on a collision course with the *broader legal subsystem*, which includes the Charter. The result of this clash was the decision of the Supreme Court of Canada to read in sexual orientation as a prohibited ground of discrimination in Alberta's human rights legislation (see the red arrow line [3]). This is an example of how developments in the broader legal subsystem (constitutional law) can directly impact outputs within the *work law subsystem*.

The *Vriend* decision ended the legal debate over whether Alberta should prohibit discrimination on the basis of sexual orientation, but not the political debate. Many citizens, organizations, and some politicians were so angered by the decision

that they called on the government to exercise the rarely used section 33 Charter provision known as the "notwithstanding clause."[‡] Section 33 permits a government to override Charter rights for renewable five-year periods. In the end, then premier Ralph Klein and the Alberta government he led elected not to use the notwithstanding clause. However, in a show of symbolic defiance, the government also did not formally revise the *Individual's Rights Protection Act* to expressly include sexual orientation until 2010, some 12 years after *Vriend* was decided.

The story of how sexual orientation came to be included as a protected ground in Alberta's human rights legislation requires an understanding of the broader social and political context and the tensions that sometimes result when the dominant political, cultural, or religious orthodoxy collides with the Charter's fundamental rights and freedoms.

---

[*]   G. Filax, *Queer Youth in the Province of the "Severely Normal"* (Vancouver: University of British Columbia Press, 2006).

[†]   See T. Macklem, "*Vriend v. Alberta*: Making the Private Public" (1999) 44 *McGill Law Journal* 197, http://lawjournal.mcgill.ca/userfiles/other/7854438-44.1.Macklem.pdf.

[‡]   B. Cossman, "Canadian Same Sex Relationship Recognition Struggles and the Contradictory Nature of Legal Victories" (2000) 48 *Cleveland State Law Review* 49, at 51.

V. Chapter Summary

The *Canadian Charter of Rights and Freedoms* is part of Canada's Constitution. It regulates the relationship between governments and citizens, not the relationships between private citizens and private companies. It sets limits on government conduct and also regulates how governments can treat their own employees. All of the statutes and regulations must comply with the Charter. This chapter considered some of the most important ways that the Charter has influenced the development of the common law regime and the regulatory standards regime.

QUESTIONS AND ISSUES FOR DISCUSSION

1. Winifred was dismissed from her job at Microsoft in Ottawa. She believes that the reason is related to her boss's intolerance of her religion. She wants to launch a Charter challenge against her employer, alleging that her section 15 equality rights have been violated. Would you advise her to go ahead with that lawsuit?

2. Explain the meaning of *enumerated grounds* and *analogous grounds* in the context of the Charter. Provide two examples of analogous grounds.

3. Describe the steps of the *Oakes* test.

4. What happens to legislation that is found to be in violation of the Charter?

5. Why has the Charter had relatively little influence on the development of the common law regime of work law?

6. Section 15 of the Charter protects the right of Canadians to be treated equally, without regard to sex, age, religion, disability, and other grounds. Why then do we also need human rights codes in Canada that also prohibit discrimination on similar grounds?

NOTES AND REFERENCES

1. *Canadian Charter of Rights and Freedoms*, part I of the *Constitution Act, 1982*, being Schedule B to the *Canada Act 1982* (UK), 1982, c. 11.

2. This chapter draws on material originally published in D. Doorey, "The Charter and the Law of Work: A Beginner's Guide," September 21, 2012, http://papers.ssrn.com/sol3/papers.cfm?abstract_id=2150279.

3. Charter, supra note 1, s. 32.

4. *Lavigne v. Ontario Public Service Employees Union*, [1991] 2 SCR 211.

5. Ibid.

6. *McKinney v. University of Guelph*, [1990] 3 SCR 229.

7. A former government lawyer has filed a lawsuit against the federal government in Ottawa, asserting that the government is failing to meet its legal duty to ensure that new legislation is Charter compliant. See J. Ling, "What Are the Odds?" *Canadian Bar Association National Magazine*, December 2014, http://www.nationalmagazine.ca/Articles/December-2014-Web/What-are-the-odds.aspx.

8. Ibid.

9. *Egan v. Canada*, [1995] 2 SCR 513.

10. *R v. Oakes*, [1986] 1 SCR 103.

11. See G. England, "The Impact of the Charter on Individual Employment Law in Canada: Rewriting an Old Story" (2006) 13 *Canadian Labour and Employment Law Journal* 1.

12. *RWDSU v. Dolphin Delivery Ltd.*, [1986] 2 SCR 573; and *Hill v. Church of Scientology of Toronto*, [1995] 2 SCR 1130.

13. *Hersees of Woodstock Ltd. v. Goldstein et al.*, [1963] 2 OR 81 (CA). This decision was among the most controversial and criticized labour law decisions of the 20th century. See H. Arthurs, "Comments" (1963) 41 *Canadian Bar Review* 573, http://www.cba.org/cba_barreview/Search.aspx?VolDate=12%2f01%2f1963. Arthurs' comments explain how the Court of Appeal misapplied tort law in order to reach the conclusion that all secondary picketing is per se illegal.

14. *RWDSU, Local 558 v. Pepsi-Cola Canada Beverages (West) Ltd.*, 2002 SCC 8 at para. 32, [2002] 1 SCR 156.

15. The "test" for section 15 equality cases is described in the non-labour cases *Law v. Canada*, [1999] 1 SCR 497 and *Andrews v. Law Society of British Columbia*, [1989] 1 SCR 143. See also *Ontario (Attorney General) v. Fraser*, 2011 SCC 20 at paras. 114-116, [2011] 2 SCR 3. It is a difficult test, and for our purpose we do not need to analyze it in detail since section 15's influence on work law has been limited. See also *Ontario Nurses' Association v. Mount Sinai Hospital*, 2005 CanLII 14437 (ONCA), which struck down exclusion from statutory severance pay due to "frustration of contract" that arises from disability.

16. *Egan v. Canada*, supra note 9; and *Vriend v. Alberta*, [1998] 1 SCR 493.

17. The Supreme Court of Canada ruled that laws or employment practices by government employers that treat married people differently than non-married people would violate section 15, since "marital status" was an analogous ground: *Miron v. Trudel*, [1995] 2 SCR 418.

18. *Andrews v. Law Society of British Columbia*, supra note 15.

19. See *Health Services and Support—Facilities Subsector Bargaining Assn. v. British Columbia*, 2007 SCC 27 at paras. 162-167, [2007] 2 SCR 391; and *Dunmore v. Ontario (Attorney General)*, [2001] 3 SCR 1016. In the *Dunmore* decision, Justice L'Heureux-Dubé, in dissent, said that the occupational status of an agricultural worker should be recognized as an analogous ground; see paras. 165-170.

20. M. Gunderson, "Banning Mandatory Retirement: Throwing Out the Baby with the Bathwater" (2004) *Backgrounder* [C.D. Howe Institute] 79, at 3, http://web.umoncton.ca/umcm-sitesgr/retraite/D22.pdf.

21. *Human Rights Code*, RSO 1990, c. H.19, s. 10.

22. Quebec and Manitoba have protected workers older than 64 from age discrimination since the 1980s. Other provinces followed Ontario and amended their human rights laws so that mandatory retirement clauses in employment contracts would violate the prohibition on age discrimination: British Columbia (in 2008), Saskatchewan (in 2007), Nova Scotia (in 2009), and Newfoundland and Labrador (in 2007). The federal government revised the *Canadian Human Rights Act* (RSC 1985, c. H-6) in 2011 in a similar manner. See the discussion in "Mandatory Retirement Fades in Canada," *CBC News*, August 20, 2009, http://www.cbc.ca/news/business/mandatory-retirement-fades-in-canada-1.799697.

23. The *Vriend* decision provoked a huge body of academic commentary on the scope of a government's right to decide which personal characteristics are deserving of protection from employment discrimination. See, e.g., F.C. DeCoste, "Case Comment: *Vriend v. Alberta*: Sexual Orientation and Liberal Polity" (1996) 34 *Alberta Law Review* 950; and L. Gotell, "Queering Law: Not by *Vriend*" (2002) 17 *Canadian Journal of Law and Society* 89.

CHAPTER 18

The Charter and the Collective Bargaining Regime*

I. Introduction

Collective bargaining involves a group of workers coming together to advance their workplace goals by negotiating on more equal terms with their employer. In this way, collective bargaining is a quintessential example of freedom of association in action. Historically, however, exercising this freedom has proven to be perilous for workers. As noted in Chapter 6, in the common law regime, employers could discipline or dismiss employees who exercised their freedom of association by joining a union, and there was no legal obligation on employers to recognize unions, much less bargain with them. This state of affairs often resulted in conflicts, sometimes violent, between employers and unions, as workers were forced to rely on strike action to gain recognition for collective bargaining and to enforce the terms of any collective agreement with employers.

The Wagner model, discussed throughout this volume, was designed to protect and structure the freedom of association of employees. It was also designed to obviate the need for "union recognition strikes" and, in its Canadian variant (introduced in 1944 by Order in Council PC 1003), strikes to enforce collective agreement terms.[1] Wagner model legislation created protections for workers against retribution, intimidation, and discrimination by employers; detailed mechanisms for the certification of unions, triggering an associated duty to bargain on employers; and

---

* This chapter was co-authored by Benjamin Oliphant and David Doorey. Mr. Oliphant is a lawyer with Gall Legge Grant & Munroe LLP in Vancouver, and an adjunct professor in the Faculty of Law at the University of British Columbia.

created grievance mechanisms through which disputes about the application and interpretation of collective agreements could be quickly (and peacefully) resolved.[2] As Brian Langille observed, the Wagner model of collective bargaining is how freedom of association is "instantiated" in the Canadian workplace.[3]

Statutory collective bargaining rights have proven to be important to workers in promoting and protecting collective action and associational freedom in the workplace. However, because these rights are statutory, they are only as valuable as legislatures make them. Governments sometimes exclude entire groups of workers from the protective legislative scheme altogether. Alternatively, they may eliminate these rights on an ad hoc basis through back-to-work orders during otherwise lawful strike action (see Chapter 11) or by legislating collective agreement terms without the assent of workers. Governments can also restrict the scope of collective bargaining rights; for example, by narrowly defining permissible strike action or limiting the topics over which the parties can bargain, which can diminish the ability of workers' associations to collectively achieve workplace goals. It is in this context that workers and their unions turned to the constitutional protections available in the *Canadian Charter of Rights and Freedoms*, which, as we learned in Chapter 17, imposes restrictions on the scope of *government action*.

Chapter 17 introduced the Charter and outlined the two-step process followed in analyzing Charter claims. As you may recall, the first step is to decide whether some government action has infringed upon a Charter-protected right or freedom. If it has, then the second step is to analyze whether that infringement is "demonstrably justified in a free and democratic society" under section 1 of the Charter. The section 1 "test" that must be applied whenever this balancing of interests takes place—the *Oakes test*—was described in Box 17.1.[4]

Chapter 17 explored the application of the Charter to the common law regime and regulatory regime. However, the Charter has had its greatest impact on the collective bargaining regime. This chapter examines that impact, focusing on the scope of freedom of expression (section 2(b) of the Charter) and freedom of association (section 2(d)), along with a brief summary of the (so far unsuccessful) attempts to argue that some collective bargaining legislation violates equality rights under section 15. (To review those provisions of the Charter that are most relevant to the collective bargaining regime—sections 1, 2, and 15—see Box 17.2.)

II. Freedom of Expression (Section 2(b))

The Supreme Court of Canada has interpreted freedom of expression very broadly.[5] In essence, if an act conveys or attempts to convey meaning in a non-violent manner, it has usually been found to fall within the scope of protected expression in section 2(b) of the Charter. As a result of the broad definition of protected expression, most legal disputes involving freedom of expression take place at step two of the Charter analysis, under section 1. The question becomes whether a government restriction on freedom of expression is "demonstrably justified in a free and democratic society." For example, employers have occasionally challenged labour legislation restricting their right to speech during union organizing campaigns. Although statutory restrictions on employer speech violate employers' section 2(d) freedom of speech, those restrictions have been found to be justified under section 1 as necessary to protect vulnerable workers from coercion at work during organizing campaigns.[6]

An important line of cases involving freedom of expression in the collective bargaining regime relates to the rights of workers to engage in picketing against their employers. In an early Charter case, *RWDSU v. Dolphin Delivery Ltd.* (1986), the Supreme Court of Canada ruled that peaceful labour picketing is a protected "expression" under section 2(b) of the Charter because it conveys meaning.[7] However, the following question remained: When, and under what circumstances, could picketing be restrained or limited by the state? In undertaking this analysis, the courts considered the fact that picketing conveys meaning beyond the actual words stated or written on a placard. That is, picketing also has a **signalling effect**: it can provoke "an automatic reflex response from workers, suppliers, and consumers," which the Supreme Court felt "may discourage some people from making rational choices based on persuasive discourse."[8] In other words, when people see a picket line, they "hear" *Don't you dare cross this line.*

In some cases, the courts expressed concern over this "signalling effect," suggesting that it could constitute coercion rather than expression intended to persuade. In the 1999 case of *U.F.C.W., Local 1518 v. KMart Canada Ltd.*, the Supreme Court of Canada said the following about the signalling effect associated with labour picketing:

> The decision for people, whether employees, suppliers or consumers, not to cross the picket line may be based on its coercive effect rather than the persuasive force of the picketers. As the Board noted, "picketing is both a signal and the exercise of freedom of expression." It is the "signal" component of conventional picketing which attracts the need for regulation and restriction in some circumstances.[9]

In that case, the Supreme Court of Canada ruled that a statutory definition restricting picketing violated freedom of expression of the picketers insofar as it went *beyond* restricting the signalling effect of picketing and prohibited mere peaceful informational leafletting as well. However, in the Charter challenge described in Box 18.1, the Supreme Court defended the importance of picket-line activities that seek "to dissuade people from crossing the picket line" other than through rational persuasion, such as informing those crossing a picket line that videos of them might be posted online.[10] In so doing, the Supreme Court signalled broader constitutional protection for picket-line tactics of importance to unions in the course of lawful strikes.

BOX 18.1 » CASE LAW HIGHLIGHT

Is Filming Employees Crossing a Picket Line a Protected Freedom of Expression?

Alberta (Information and Privacy Commissioner) v. United Food and Commercial Workers, Local 401
2013 SCC 62, [2013] 3 SCR 733

Key Facts: The Alberta *Personal Information Protection Act* (PIPA) prohibits the collection, use, and distribution of "personal information" about an individual without that person's consent. In the context of lawful picketing, members of the United Food and Commercial Workers union filmed the picket line and used the images of identifiable persons crossing the picket line for promotional and training material. The Privacy Commissioner of Alberta found that notwithstanding the impact on freedom of expression, the union had breached PIPA by collecting and distributing images of identifiable individuals without their consent.

Issue: Do statutory restrictions on the use by organizations of photos and videos without a person's consent violate the freedom of expression of unions seeking to use such photos during a lawful labour dispute?

Decision: Yes. This violation was not saved by section 1 of the Charter. The Supreme Court of Canada found that filming the

picket line was constitutionally protected expression, both with respect to the signalling effect (i.e., to dissuade individuals from crossing the picket line) and to the subsequent use of the videos collected for expressive purposes. Based on the *Oakes* test, the Supreme Court ruled that while PIPA embodied a pressing and substantial objective by protecting important interests that are "intimately connected to … individual autonomy, dignity and privacy," the Alberta legislation was significantly overbroad, as it contained no mechanism to accommodate the expressive activities of unions engaged in strike action. In finding that the restrictions imposed by PIPA could not be justified under section 1, the court emphasized the significance of freedom of expression in the context of labour disputes, given the relatively limited privacy interests engaged in this context (i.e., the filming occurred in public and did not reveal intimate details of the individuals filmed). Thus, although recognizing that some limitations on picket-line activity may be justifiable in furtherance of individual privacy rights, PIPA did not achieve a reasonable or proportionate balance, and therefore the restrictions in PIPA were not justified under section 1 of the Charter.

---

signalling effect: A phrase used by courts to describe the psychological, perhaps unspoken, message conveyed to a person confronted by labour picketing that the picketers desire that person to not cross the picket line.

In Chapter 11, we examined the courts' historical distinction between **primary picketing** and **secondary picketing**. While primary picketing was given broad legal protection, secondary picketing at locations other than the struck workplace was treated in the common law as "illegal per se."[11] However, that distinction was dissolved in the 2002 Supreme Court of Canada decision of *R.W.D.S.U., Local 558 v. Pepsi-Cola Canada Beverages (West) Ltd.* (see Box 11.3). The Supreme Court decided that informational picketing, whether primary or secondary in nature, "engages one of the highest constitutional values: freedom of expression."[12] Therefore, it ruled, even though the Charter does not apply directly to individuals in the context of private disputes, the common law governing those disputes should nevertheless evolve in a manner consistent with Charter values. A common law rule that treats picketing as automatically unlawful based simply on where it takes place is inconsistent with Charter values. As a result, today all labour picketing associated with a lawful strike (or lockout) is legal, unless the manner in which it is done is illegal for some reason.

This decision does not mean that limitations cannot be placed on union expression, on the picket line, or elsewhere. Legislation that restricts peaceful picketing will now likely violate section 2(b) of the Charter, as will legislation that substantially interferes with incidental (but important) elements of picket-line expression (see Box 18.1). However, some limitations on the right to expression through picketing will still likely be upheld, or "saved," under section 1. For example, in the 1988 case of *B.C.G.E.U. v. British Columbia (Attorney General)*, the Supreme Court of Canada ruled that a restriction on picketing in front of courthouses violated section 2(b), but was saved by section 1, because the need to ensure access to justice was pressing and substantial and justified a restriction on expression.[13] Overall, however, it is fair to say that there has been a recent movement by the Supreme Court toward recognizing broader expressive rights for unions and workers, particularly in the context of otherwise lawful picketing and strike action.

III. Freedom of Association (Section 2(d))

Section 2(d) of the Charter says simply that everyone has "freedom of association." What meaning to attribute to those three words has proven to be a mystifying task. After more than 30 years of section 2(d) litigation, the courts are still sorting out what precisely this freedom encompasses. As we will see, the Supreme Court of Canada's meandering and sometimes contradictory decisions in developing the scope of freedom of association have made this area of the law of work among the most complex. Table 18.1 summarizes key Supreme Court of Canada decisions on section 2(d). We can divide the development of the meaning of freedom of association under the Charter into three periods: the early years, which includes the "First Labour Trilogy" (1987); the middle period, in which the court began loosening restrictions imposed by the First Trilogy; and the modern era, embodied by the judgments in the "Second Labour Trilogy" of 2015.

---

primary picketing: Picketing that takes place at the location of the employer directly involved in the labour dispute.

secondary picketing: Picketing that takes place at a location other than the workplace of the employees involved in the labour dispute.

TABLE 18.1 Key Supreme Court of Canada Cases on Freedom of Association

1987: **"First Labour Trilogy"**	Three Supreme Court of Canada cases decided that the Charter's "freedom of association" provision (section 2(d)) protects a right to form and join employee associations, and to exercise with others the rights and freedoms that individuals enjoy. The Supreme Court also decided that freedom of association does not protect a right to strike. The three cases in the First Labour Trilogy were *Reference Re Public Service Employee Relations Act (Alta.)*; *PSAC v. Canada*; and *RWDSU v. Saskatchewan*.
1990	*Professional Institute of the Public Service of Canada v. Northwest Territories (Commissioner)*: Applying the same reasoning as in the First Labour Trilogy, the Supreme Court of Canada ruled that freedom of association does not protect a right to collective bargaining.
2001	*Dunmore v. Ontario (Attorney General)*: The exclusion of farm workers from the Ontario *Labour Relations Act, 1995* violated the freedom of association of farm workers. Section 2(d) protects the ability to engage in certain collective activities, such as making "collective representations" to an employer. Because farm workers are excluded from the protections provided in the collective bargaining statute, they have been unable to engage in these activities. If a government enacts protective legislation, such as collective bargaining legislation, but then excludes some workers from its protections, it violates section 2(d) if the exclusion "substantially interferes" with the ability of the excluded workers to exercise their freedom to associate.
2007	*Health Services and Support—Facilities Subsector Bargaining Assn v. British Columbia ("BC Health Services")*: Freedom of association protects a right to collective bargaining after all, and the government violated section 2(d) by passing legislation that negated terms of previous collective agreements and imposed other terms without consulting or bargaining with the affected workers. That violation was not saved by section 1 of the Charter. The right to collective bargaining includes an obligation on employers to consider collective representations from employee associations in good faith and to engage in "a meaningful dialogue" with the association about those representations.
2011	*Ontario (Attorney General) v. Fraser*: After *Dunmore*, the Ontario government enacted the *Agricultural Employees Protection Act* (AEPA), applicable only to farm workers. The AEPA grants farm workers protection from reprisals for forming or joining employee associations and requires employers to listen to representations on behalf of employees presented through an association. However, it does not provide a right to collectively bargain in good faith, a right to strike, or other key protective elements provided in the Ontario *Labour Relations Act, 1995*. In *Fraser*, the Supreme Court ruled that the AEPA does not violate section 2(d) since it protects a right to associate and requires employers to listen to and consider "in good faith" collective representations made by employee associations. That satisfied the requirements established in *Dunmore* and *BC Health Services*.
2015: **"Second Labour Trilogy"**	*Mounted Police Association of Ontario v. Canada (Attorney General)*: A law that excludes RCMP members from the general labour relations legislation and imposes a collective bargaining representative violated freedom of association. It deprived RCMP members of the right to select their own employee association that is independent from the employer and to make representations to their employer through that association. *Saskatchewan Federation of Labour v. Saskatchewan*: The Supreme Court overruled the First Labour Trilogy decisions and, inspired by Chief Justice Dickson's dissent in *Re Alberta Reference* (see Box 18.2), ruled that freedom of association protects a right to strike as a necessary component of meaningful collective bargaining. *Meredith v. Canada (Attorney General)*: A law that temporarily fixed the level of wage increases for RCMP members did not violate section 2(d), because the restrictions were minor (the wage rates imposed reflected what other unions had bargained elsewhere in the public service), they were time-limited (three years), and the statute still permitted the workers' association to bargain additional allowances for members.

A. The Early Years: The "First Labour Trilogy" (1987) and Professional Institute of the Public Service of Canada (1990)

Very early on in the life of the Charter, in a set of three decisions released in 1987 (known collectively as the "First Labour Trilogy"), the Supreme Court of Canada explained that freedom of association is to be interpreted narrowly to include only the following:

- a freedom to form and to join associations, including unions; therefore, a law prohibiting people from forming or joining a union or other employee association would infringe section 2(d) of the Charter;
- a freedom to engage collectively in the exercise of constitutional rights; and
- a freedom to engage in activities through an association that individuals are legally entitled to do; for example, since individuals are legally entitled to play golf, the government would violate section 2(d) by prohibiting golf associations.[14]

That was a relatively narrow reading of the scope of "freedom of association," and applying it in the First Labour Trilogy cases, the Supreme Court of Canada ruled that section 2(d) did *not* include a "right to strike." It found that striking was an inherently "collective" activity, and, therefore, since the Supreme Court considered that individual workers do not have a legal right to strike, there was no Charter-protected right to strike.[15] The Supreme Court also encouraged deference to governments in striking a complex balance between competing interests in relation to labour policy matters. Applying the same logic in the 1990 case of *Professional Institute of the Public Service of Canada v. Northwest Territories (Commissioner)*, the Supreme Court ruled that section 2(d) also does not protect a right to collective bargaining.[16]

Litigation under section 2(d) of the Charter quieted down after those early cases. However, before moving forward, it is worthwhile to pause and consider the most famous dissent in work law history. It was penned by Chief Justice Brian Dickson of the Supreme Court of Canada in one of the First Labour Trilogy cases, *Reference Re Public Service Employee Relations Act (Alta.)* ("*Re Alberta Reference*"), which is discussed in Box 18.2.[17] As we will see, that dissent proved highly influential in convincing the Supreme Court of Canada to overrule the First Labour Trilogy approach years later.

BOX 18.2 » TALKING WORK LAW

Chief Justice Dickson's Famous Dissent in Re Alberta Reference

As described previously, in the First Labour Trilogy cases decided in 1987, the Supreme Court of Canada ruled that "freedom of association" in section 2(d) of the Charter was not broad enough to protect a right of workers to strike. In the lead decision of the trilogy, *Re Alberta Reference* (1987), Chief Justice Brian Dickson argued for a more robust scope of freedom of association that recognized rights to collective bargaining and to strike.

Widely regarded as one of Canada's finest judges, Chief Justice Dickson was also among its finest judicial philosophers. His lyrical conception of freedom of association has had an enduring influence over this area of the law. Here are some passages from his famous dissent in *Re Alberta Reference*:

> Freedom of association is the freedom to combine together for the pursuit of common purposes or the

Brian Dickson, Chief Justice of the Supreme Court of Canada from 1984 to 1990.
Source: CP Photo/Ron Poling

advancement of common causes. It is one of the fundamental freedoms guaranteed by the Charter, a *sine qua non* of any free and democratic society, protecting individuals from the vulnerability of isolation and ensuring the potential of effective participation in society. In every area of human endeavour and throughout history individuals have formed associations for the pursuit of common interests and aspirations. Through association individuals are able to ensure that they have a voice in shaping the circumstances integral to their needs, rights and freedoms.

Freedom of association is the cornerstone of modern labour relations. Historically, workers have combined to overcome the inherent inequalities of bargaining power in the employment relationship and to protect themselves from unfair, unsafe, or exploitative working conditions. ...

If freedom of association only protects the joining together of persons for common purposes, but not the pursuit of the very activities for which the association was formed, then the freedom is indeed legalistic, ungenerous, indeed vapid.

In my view, while it is unquestionable that s. 2(d), at a minimum, guarantees the liberty of persons to be in association or belong to an organization, it must extend beyond a concern for associational status to give effective protection to the interests to which the constitutional guarantee is directed. ...

The purpose of the constitutional guarantee of freedom of association is, I believe, to recognize the profoundly social nature of human endeavours and to protect the individual from state-enforced isolation in the pursuit of his or her ends. ...

As social beings, our freedom to act with others is a primary condition of community life, human progress and civilized society. Through association, individuals have been able to participate in determining and controlling the immediate circumstances of their lives, and the rules, mores and principles which govern the communities in which they live. ...

Freedom of association is most essential in those circumstances where the individual is liable to be prejudiced by the actions of some larger and more powerful entity, like the government or an employer. Association has always been the means through which political, cultural and racial minorities, religious groups and workers have sought to attain their purposes and fulfil their aspirations; it has enabled those who would otherwise be vulnerable and ineffective to meet on more equal terms the power and strength of those with whom their interests interact and, perhaps, conflict. ...

What freedom of association seeks to protect is not associational activities *qua* particular activities, but the freedom of individuals to interact with, support, and be supported by, their fellow humans in the varied activities in which they choose to engage.*

---

* *Reference Re Public Service Employee Relations Act (Alta.)*, [1987] 1 SCR 313.

B. Cracks in the First Labour Trilogy: Dunmore (2001), BC Health Services (2007), and Fraser (2011)

Despite Chief Justice Dickson's strong dissent, calling for a broader interpretation of section 2(d) of the Charter that protects the right to collective bargaining and to strike, the narrower scope of freedom of association adopted by the majority of Supreme Court judges in the First Labour Trilogy appeared to have won the day. The practical result was that governments could, for example, continue to ban or restrict strikes and to exclude specific groups of workers altogether from collective bargaining statutes that granted other workers a robust set of legal entitlements intended to bolster their right to collective bargaining.

However, as the 21st century dawned, cracks began to appear in the First Labour Trilogy as the Supreme Court of Canada shifted toward a broader interpretation of section 2(d) of the Charter. The first sign of change came in the 2001 case of *Dunmore v. Ontario (Attorney General)*, which challenged the exclusion of farm workers from the Ontario *Labour Relations Act, 1995* as a violation of their freedom to associate.[18] The exclusion of farm workers from the collective bargaining statute and its protections from unfair labour practices meant that farm workers were effectively left in the common law regime. Consequently, they could be dismissed or discriminated against by employers if they attempted to unionize or exercise other collective labour rights (such as striking).

The Supreme Court of Canada ruled in *Dunmore* that Chief Justice Dickson was right in his dissent when he found that freedom of association must include protection of some activities that are inherently collective, such as "making collective representations to an employer."[19] The history of farm workers' attempts to associate showed that while unionization was not prohibited by law, farm workers were nevertheless effectively unable to associate because they had no legal rights protecting them from employer reprisals for unionizing.[20] On that basis, the Supreme Court found that while section 2(d) of the Charter did not provide a right to full-fledged Wagner model–style collective bargaining, the legislature must at least provide workers with protections against unfair labour practices when the absence of those protections effectively stifles their ability to unionize.[21]

Dunmore is a tricky case because it was not obvious what the government action being challenged was. Recall that the Charter only directly regulates governments. The farm workers' claim in *Dunmore* was that they could not join unions and make collective representations to employers because their (private sector) employers might threaten or dismiss them, and there was no law stopping their employers from doing so. In other words, the argument was that the government action consisted of a *failure* of the government—an omission—to apply to farm workers the unfair labour practice sections in the *Labour Relations Act, 1995* that apply to most other workers. The Supreme Court of Canada got around the "state action" limitation in *Dunmore* by holding that when a government creates a protective legal regime (such as the *Labour Relations Act, 1995*), it cannot then exclude *some* workers from the protections if doing so "substantially interferes" with the ability of those workers to exercise the rights protected by freedom of association.[22] The finding in *Dunmore* that a Charter violation can be based on the failure of a government to protect workers from the harmful acts of private actors demonstrates a conceptual complexity associated with section 2(d) related to the difference between freedoms and rights, as discussed in Box 18.3.

BOX 18.3 » TALKING WORK LAW

Rights Versus Freedoms in Section 2(d) Analysis

One of the complicating factors with respect to the constitutional protection of labour rights is that they are just that: rights. We can say that a legal "freedom" is the individual's ability to act or not act in a certain manner as he or she sees fit. However, a legal "right" places a duty or obligation on others, either to act in a certain way (positive rights) or to not act in a certain way (negative rights).*

Often, the Charter's section 2 fundamental freedoms are conceived of as "legal freedoms"; that is, they may require that the government not coerce or constrain a party's choice to engage in a particular activity, but they need not act to facilitate or protect it. "Freedom" cases involve the government prohibiting conduct (e.g., making participation in certain associations unlawful or limiting expressive activities such as picketing), and the claim is that the government cannot do so. However, such claims do not place a duty on others, for example, to join your association or to listen to your expression, even if the refusal of others to join or listen would render your freedom less meaningful. Conceived of as a freedom, section 2(d) simply requires the government to not unduly limit your activities, leaving you with the freedom to engage in the activities or not. Cases involving legislative or common law restrictions on picketing, for

example, are prototypical freedom cases; unions are seeking to have a legal obstruction removed in order to allow them the freedom to express themselves, or not, as they choose.

Other cases are what we might call "rights" cases. The claim here is not only that the government cannot act to restrict the exercise of a freedom, but that the government has an obligation to actively advance, facilitate, or otherwise protect the party's exercise of the freedom from restrictions imposed by third parties. In the context of freedom of association, unions do not always request to be entirely unrestrained from state regulation. Sometimes, they look to the government to require other private parties to act in such a way as to not unduly undermine associational activities. It is this imposition of duties on third parties that makes these rights cases more controversial.

Questions regarding the constitutional obligations of governments to actively facilitate or protect the exercise of freedoms are particularly salient in the context of labour relations, as the entire Wagner model is dependent on the imposition by the state of legal duties on others, most notably, but not exclusively, employers. A *right* to collective bargaining, for example, may place a *duty* on employers to "bargain in good faith," because without this duty, the *freedom* to collectively bargain for workers may be meaningless if the employer chooses to simply ignore the union. Similarly, a *right to strike* may impose a *duty* on employers to not fire the strikers or to hire permanent replacement employees. This disconnect between the labour relations realities embodied in the Wagner model and the traditional conception of section 2 of the Charter as a bulwark only against government interference in the exercise of a "freedom" has complicated section 2(d) case law in a way that does not often arise with respect to the other fundamental freedoms.

In his famous dissent in *Re Alberta Reference*, Chief Justice Dickson acknowledged the conceptual difference between rights and freedoms, but noted that nevertheless the two are

often used interchangeably. He then observed that the conception of freedom as simply an obligation not to interfere "may be too narrow," since it ignores the situation "where the absence of government intervention may in effect substantially impede the enjoyment of fundamental freedoms."[†] This observation proved prophetic years later in the *Dunmore* decision.

* W. Hohfeld, *Fundamental Legal Conceptions as Applied in Judicial Reasoning* (New Haven, CT: Yale, 1946). See also B. Langille, "Why the Right-Freedom Distinction Matters to Labour Lawyers—And to All Canadians" (2011) 34 *Dalhousie Law Journal* 143.
† *Reference Re Public Service Employee Relations Act (Alta.),* [1987] 1 SCR 313, at para. 77.

The next big step in the development of section 2(d) of the Charter occurred in 2007, when the Supreme Court of Canada released its decision on *Health Services and Support—Facilities Subsector Bargaining Assn v. British Columbia* ("*BC Health Services*").[23] In this case, unionized health care workers brought a Charter challenge against a new law (*Health and Social Services Delivery Improvement Act*) that suspended collective bargaining in the health sector, unilaterally imposed new collective agreement terms and cancelled others, and prohibited unions from bargaining about certain topics. According to the government, the Act was adopted to deal with a crisis in relation to the high medical costs in the province. To the surprise of many in the labour law community, the Supreme Court ruled that it was time to recognize a right to collective bargaining under section 2(d). Expressly rejecting the logic of its previous holdings, the Supreme Court found that this new constitutional right to collective bargaining imposes an obligation on government employers to bargain in good faith and to consult with unions before passing laws that negatively impact collective bargaining and collective agreements.

Next came the 2011 case of *Ontario (Attorney General) v. Fraser*, which arose after the Ontario government responded to *Dunmore* by passing the *Agricultural Employees Protection Act* (AEPA).[24] The AEPA did precisely as the Supreme Court had ordered in *Dunmore*, and nothing more.[25] It provided protections against unfair labour practices and the ability to make "collective representations," but it did not include an expressed "duty to bargain in good faith," nor did it provide any protections for strike action or any alternative dispute resolution mechanism (such as impartial binding arbitration). In 2011, a majority of the Supreme Court of Canada ruled that the AEPA did not violate section 2(d).

In *Fraser*, the Supreme Court of Canada held that section 2(d) of the Charter does not require that every worker be given access to the key elements of the Wagner model found in the *Labour Relations Act, 1995*. The Supreme Court ruled that it was implied in the AEPA that agricultural employers hear and consider "representations" by workers' associations and that they do so "in good faith," and that this was sufficient to fulfill the constitutional right to collectively bargain, even though it fell far short of the full-fledged "duty to bargain in good faith" found in collective bargaining legislation (see Chapter 10). In other words, as long as the law requires employers to listen and consider collective employee representations, it satisfies section 2(d). The Supreme Court emphasized that under section 2(d), "no particular type of bargaining is protected." Rather, "[i]n every case, the question is whether the impugned law or state action has the effect of making it impossible to act collectively to achieve workplace goals."[26]

C. The "Second Labour Trilogy" (2015)

If *Fraser* showed the Supreme Court of Canada hitting the brakes on the constitutional right to collectively bargain after *BC Health Services*, the court shifted back into high gear in 2015, releasing another trilogy of decisions (the "Second Labour Trilogy"). In these cases, the Supreme Court reaffirmed and broadened its rulings in *Dunmore* and *BC Health Services*, and confined whatever remained of the First Labour Trilogy and, arguably, *Fraser*, to the dustbin of past section 2(d) decisions.

In the first case in the Second Labour Trilogy, *Mounted Police Association of Ontario v. Canada (Attorney General)*,[27] the Supreme Court of Canada affirmed that the freedom to associate entails both the freedom to create an employee association that is independent from the employer and the right to engage in a process of meaningful collective bargaining through that chosen association. The problem with the model of collective bargaining provided in the legislation that was at issue was that the collective bargaining representative it imposed on RCMP members was "plainly not independent of RCMP management. Rather, it is squarely under its control."[28] As a result, excluding RCMP members from the general labour relations legislation and imposing this alternative bargaining regime violated section 2(d), and was not saved by section 1.

A few weeks later, in *Saskatchewan Federation of Labour v. Saskatchewan*, the Supreme Court of Canada definitively overturned the rulings in the First Labour Trilogy when it decided that freedom of association protects a limited right to strike.[29] See Box 18.4.

BOX 18.4 » CASE LAW HIGHLIGHT

Does the Charter Protect a Right to Strike?

Saskatchewan Federation of Labour v. Saskatchewan
2015 SCC 4, [2015] 1 SCR 245

Key Facts: Saskatchewan enacted the *Public Service Essential Services Act*, which prohibited "essential services employees" from striking. It defined "essential services" broadly and granted the employer the unilateral right to determine which and how many employees were "essential." The legislation effectively permitted the employer to ensure that large numbers of public sector workers could not engage in a strike. Moreover, the legislation did not provide for a neutral substitute mechanism (such as interest arbitration) for determining bargaining disputes in the event of an impasse. The Saskatchewan Federation of Labour challenged the legislation as a violation of section 2(d) of the Charter.

Issue: Does legislation that prohibits employees designated by the employer as "essential services employees" from striking infringe section 2(d) of the Charter by substantially interfering with the Charter right to meaningful collective bargaining?

Decision: Yes. By a majority of 5 to 2, the Supreme Court of Canada ruled that "freedom of association" protects the right to strike, thereby overturning the rulings in the First Labour

Trilogy of 1987. Justice Abella, for the majority, ruled that the time had come for the right to strike to be given the Supreme Court's "constitutional benediction." The Supreme Court wrote that striking was "the 'powerhouse' of collective bargaining" that promotes equality in collective bargaining in a system in which there exists a fundamental power imbalance between employers and employees. A right to meaningful collective bargaining necessarily requires a right to strike: "the ability to engage in the collective withdrawal of services is a necessary component of the process through which workers can continue to participate meaningfully in the pursuit of their collective workplace goals." The Saskatchewan legislation violated section 2(d) of the Charter by banning the right to strike at the conclusion of a collective agreement, and the law was not saved by section 1 because it went further than needed to protect the public through the continuance of true essential services. Many of the employees that the employer could unilaterally designate as "essential services employees" were not essential at all. Moreover, even for employees who were essential, the legislation failed to provide any meaningful alternative mechanism for resolving bargaining impasses, such as interest arbitration. The Supreme Court ruled that the Saskatchewan legislation was unconstitutional.

The final decision in the Second Labour Trilogy, *Meredith v. Canada (Attorney General)*, involved circumstances similar to *BC Health Services*, in that collective agreement entitlements (wage raises, in this case) for RCMP members had been limited by legislation.[30] *Meredith* arose out of the *Expenditure Restraint Act*, which rolled back scheduled wage increases across the federal public sector in light of the financial crisis, provoking a flurry of section 2(d) litigation across the country.[31] The Supreme Court of Canada held that, on the facts of that case, the legislation did not "substantially interfere" with a meaningful process of collective bargaining and did not violate section 2(d). The reasoning in *Meredith* is scanty. However, it appears to have turned on the fact that the wage rates imposed were generally in accordance with wage rates bargained elsewhere in the public service, the imposed wage rates were time-limited (three years), and the employee association could still negotiate additional monetary allowances for its members.[32]

D. Where We Are Now on the Charter Freedom to Associate

As you can see, the development of the scope of freedom of association under the Charter has been a slow and laboured exercise. Even seasoned lawyers have difficulty explaining to their clients what it all means and what the Supreme Court of Canada is likely to do next. However, it is fair to say that, currently, there are effectively three core (and interrelated) rights protected under section 2(d), which closely mirror the key statutory protections in the Wagner model: (1) the right to join, form, and belong to a union; (2) the right to collective bargaining; and (3) the right to strike. Table 18.2 provides a quick summary of the content of each set of rights as they stand at the time of writing.

TABLE 18.2 A Snapshot of the Present (2016) Scope of Freedom of Association

Collective Activity	State of Section 2(d) Jurisprudence
The right to join, form, and belong to a union	• Laws that prohibit workers from forming or joining associations that are independent of the employer and that represent the employees' interests violate section 2(d) of the Charter. See First Labour Trilogy; *Dunmore v. Ontario (Attorney General)* (2001); and *Mounted Police Association of Ontario v. Canada (Attorney General)* (2015). • Government employers that discriminate against workers for exercising the right to associate violate section 2(d). See *Delisle v. Canada (Deputy Attorney General)* (1999). • If governments exclude a type of worker from protective collective bargaining legislation and as a result those workers are effectively unable to join and form unions, then the omission from the protective legislation violates section 2(d). See *Dunmore v. Ontario (Attorney General)* (2001).
The right to collective bargaining	• A law or other government action that prohibits or suspends collective bargaining or that cancels collectively bargained contract terms infringes upon section 2(d) if (1) the matter involved is sufficiently important to employees that the government's actions amount to a "substantial interference" with a meaningful process of collective bargaining; and (2) the government failed to "bargain" or "consult" in good faith. See *BC Health Services* (2007). • A legal model that imposes an association on employees that is not independent of the employer and mandates the employer to consult or bargain only with that association violates section 2(d). See *Mounted Police Association of Ontario v. Canada (Attorney General)* (2015).
The right to strike	• A law that explicitly bans the right of workers to strike at the conclusion of a collective agreement, or that renders that right to strike effectively meaningless, violates section 2(d). See *Saskatchewan Federation of Labour v. Saskatchewan* (2015). • A law that bans a strike by truly essential services workers and that does not provide a substitute neutral alternative dispute resolution process such as interest arbitration violates section 2(d) and is unlikely to be saved by section 1. See *Saskatchewan Federation of Labour v. Saskatchewan* (2015).

E. Freedom to NOT Associate?: Lavigne (1991) and Advance Cutting & Coring Ltd. (2001)

Two additional cases are noteworthy in this section because they raise the difficult question of "negative freedom of association"—the freedom to *not* associate. That is, does section 2(d) of the Charter protect against "forced" association, in the same way that freedom of expression protects against *compelled* speech,[33] and freedom of religion protects freedom *from* religion?[34]

Two common practices in labour law have been challenged as amounting to "forced" association contrary to section 2(d) of the Charter. The first arose in the 1991 case of *Lavigne v. Ontario Public Service Employees Union*, in which an employee of a college was covered by a collective agreement that required all bargaining unit employees to pay union dues, a common collective agreement term in Canada that has legislative support (Chapter 6).[35] Lavigne argued that his employer (the government[36]) had violated his freedom of association by agreeing to a provision that obliged him to pay union dues, a portion of which were then used by the union to fund some causes with which Lavigne did not agree, including funding the New Democratic Party.

The Supreme Court of Canada ruled that the collective agreement clause did not violate the Charter rights of Lavigne, although the judges disagreed on why. Four of the judges ruled that the requirement for Lavigne to pay money toward causes he did not agree with did violate section 2(d), but that the violation was "saved" by section 1, because unions serve an important function in society in contributing to public debate. Another three judges ruled that section 2(d) was not violated at all, since freedom of association does not include a freedom not to associate.

The second case that raised the issue of the freedom to not associate is *R v. Advance Cutting & Coring Ltd.*[37] In 2001, this case challenged Quebec legislation that required construction workers to join one of five unions. Did this "compulsory unionism" violate a freedom not to associate? The judges decided that it did not, but as in *Lavigne*, there was profound disagreement on why. Eight of the nine Supreme Court judges ruled that section 2(d) of the Charter includes a "right not to associate." Five of the nine judges ruled that this right was violated in this case. However, by a score of five to four, the Supreme Court ruled ultimately that the violation was saved by section 1, on the basis that there were important characteristics of the Quebec construction industry that justified the infringement.

It is not clear whether and how this approach has changed following the various twists and turns over the past decade and a half in section 2(d) jurisprudence. On the one hand, the Supreme Court clearly held in *Mounted Police* that in order for the freedom of association to be meaningful, employees must have the ability to choose their bargaining representative and, presumably, the ability to choose no representative at all.[38] However, and apparently unlike the other fundamental freedoms, this choice is not necessarily cast in individual terms. As the court explained in *Mounted Police*, "[b]y necessity, a collective framework not only serves employees' interests, but imposes limits on individual entitlements in order to permit the pursuit of collective goals"; in this way, the Wagner model involves "trade-offs of individual rights to gain collective strength."[39] The more the Supreme Court relies on the Wagner model as the prototypical framework within which meaningful collective bargaining takes place, the more difficult it becomes to argue for a freedom to not associate.

IV. Equality Rights (Section 15)

Section 15 of the Charter sets out fundamental equality rights. For a distinction in a statute to violate section 15, it must be shown that (1) it is discriminatory on the basis of an **enumerated ground**

---

enumerated grounds: The personal characteristics that are expressly listed in section 15(1) of the *Canadian Charter of Rights and Freedoms*, namely race, national or ethnic origin, colour, religion, sex, age, or mental or physical disability.

or **analogous ground**; and (2) it "fails to respond to the actual capacities and needs of the members of the group and instead imposes burdens or denies a benefit in a manner that has the effect of reinforcing, perpetuating or exacerbating their disadvantage."[40]

Unions have argued that section 15 equality rights should protect vulnerable workers who have been excluded from protective labour legislation. For example, it was argued in the *Dunmore* and *Fraser* cases that the exclusion of farm workers from the protections afforded most other workers in the Ontario *Labour Relations Act, 1995* violated section 15, as well as section 2(d) (freedom of association). The argument was that "vulnerable workers" should be recognized as a new analogous ground. If that were the case, then it would be a breach of section 15 for a law to treat farm workers differently from anyone else. However, the courts have consistently found that occupational status is not an analogous ground.[41]

A different tack was taken in *BC Health Services*, where the union did not argue that the objective of the law was discriminatory, but rather that the legislation had a disproportionate effect based on a number of intersecting grounds, and in particular, gender.[42] In essence, the allegation was that the law was discriminatory because women were disproportionately employed in the health care sector, and therefore legislation harming the interests of workers in that sector disproportionately harmed women.[43] The Supreme Court of Canada again dismissed this argument, largely out of hand.

Some Canadian labour law scholars have criticized the position of the courts that section 15 does not apply to laws that distinguish among occupations. For example, Brian Langille[44] and Diane Pothier[45] have argued that once a government elects to confer labour rights on some employees—such as a right to collective bargaining or to strike—it should be considered a violation of section 15 for the government to then exclude those same rights from other workers.[46] In other words, they argue that the government does not necessarily have to grant any workers a legal right to strike, but once it elects to create a right to strike, it cannot just pick and choose which employees get it. To date, the courts have rejected that argument.

V. Chapter Summary

As you have no doubt concluded, this attempt to simplify the Charter's influence on labour and law has proven a challenge. What is clear is that over the past decade and a half, the courts have been increasingly aggressive in scrutinizing legislative attempts to directly undermine the freedom of workers and to avoid providing workers with a sufficiently robust foundation of rights that would allow them to have a meaningful impact on working conditions. In doing so, *context* has been the keyword, and section 2(d) in particular has developed on its own unique labour relations track, focused on the pragmatic realities of labour relations instead of on abstract logic or ensuring that section 2(d) applied uniformly regardless of the type of association at issue.[47] We might conclude that the Supreme Court of Canada has taken to heart the old dictum of Oliver Wendell Holmes that "[t]he life of the law has not been logic: it has been experience."[48] The result of this contextual, pragmatic approach is sensitivity to the experience of workers and the realities of the Wagner model. It is difficult to argue with the Supreme Court's conclusion in *Saskatchewan Federation of Labour* that in the context of the Charter, "the arc bends increasingly towards workplace justice."[49]

---

analogous grounds: Personal characteristics that are not expressly listed in section 15(1) of the Charter, but are sufficiently similar in nature to the enumerated grounds to be considered protected, such as sexual orientation, marital status, and citizenship.

QUESTIONS AND ISSUES FOR DISCUSSION

1. Describe the elements of picketing that are protected by section 2(b) of the Charter, and the possible limits on that freedom.
2. Explain how the interpretation of section 2(d) of the Charter in the "First Labour Trilogy" differs from the interpretation offered in the "Second Labour Trilogy."
3. Describe the state of jurisprudence in relation to the right to collective bargaining under section 2(d) of the Charter.
4. Describe the freedom to *not* associate. How was this matter addressed in *Lavigne v. Ontario Public Service Employees Union* (1991) and *R v. Advance Cutting & Coring Ltd.* (2001)? What is the significance of these decisions?
5. Describe arguments that have been used in cases alleging that a collective bargaining law violated section 15 of the Charter.

UPDATES

Go to emond.ca/lawofworkircb for links to news, author's blog posts, content updates, and other information related to the chapters in this text.

NOTES AND REFERENCES

1 See, generally, J. Fudge and E. Tucker, "The Freedom to Strike in Canada: A Brief Legal History" (2010) 15:2 *Canadian Labour and Employment Law Journal* 333; and B. Langille, "What Is a Strike?" (2009–2010) 15 *Canadian Labour and Employment Law Journal* 355. The *Wartime Labour Relations Order* (PC 1003) is available at http://socserv.mcmaster.ca/oldlabourstudies/onlinelearning/article.php?id=503.

2 See, generally, B. Langille and B. Oliphant, "The Legal Structure of Freedom of Association" (2014) 40 *Queen's Law Journal* 249, at 258-62.

3 B. Langille, "Why Are Canadian Judges Drafting Labour Codes—And Constitutionalizing the Wagner Act Model?" (2010) 15 *Canadian Labour and Employment Law Journal* 101, at 108.

4 *R v. Oakes*, [1986] 1 SCR 103.

5 See, generally, P.W. Hogg, *Constitutional Law of Canada*, 5th ed. [looseleaf] (Toronto: Carswell, 2012), at §43.5.

6 *Cardinal Transportation BC Inc.* (1997), 34 CLRBR (2d) 1 (BCLRB). See also comments in *Wal-Mart Canada Corp. v. United Food and Commercial Workers, Local 1400*, 2004 SKCA 154 at para. 53, 247 DLR (4th); *Bank of Montreal* (1985), 10 CLRBR (NS) 129; and S. Slinn, "Captive Audience Meetings and Forced Listening: Lessons for Canada from the American Experience" (2008) 63:4 *Relations Industrielles/Industrial Relations* 694.

7 *RWDSU v. Dolphin Delivery Ltd.*, [1986] 2 SCR 573. We will focus primarily on picketing in this section of the chapter. However, freedom of expression comes up in other aspects of labour law as well. One example is in the case of *Lavigne v. Ontario Public Service Employees Union*, [1991] 2 SCR 211, discussed below. In this case, the Supreme Court ruled that Lavigne's freedom of expression was not infringed when he was forced to pay money toward causes he disagreed with, because he was still able to express himself as he saw fit.

8 *U.F.C.W., Local 1518 v. KMart Canada Ltd.*, [1999] 2 SCR 1083. See also *Fletcher Challenge Canada Ltd. v. Communications, Energy and Paperworkers Union of Canada* (1998), 155 DLR (4th) 638 (BCCA).

9 *U.F.C.W., Local 1518 v. KMart Canada Ltd.*, supra note 8, at para. 42.

10 *Alberta (Information and Privacy Commissioner) v. United Food and Commercial Workers, Local 401*, 2013 SCC 62, [2013] 3 SCR 733. The images were posted on the provocatively titled website www.casinoscabs.com (the site is no longer active).

11 *Hersees of Woodstock Ltd. v. Goldstein et al.*, [1963] 2 OR 81 (Ont. CA). This case is a fine example of the historical animosity between the courts and organized labour, and it is not the only one. See B. Langille and B. Oliphant, "From Rand to Rothstein: Labour Law, Fundamental Values and the Judicial Role," in I. Entchev and L.M. Kelly, eds., *Judicious Restraint: The Life and Law of Justice Marshall E. Rothstein* (Toronto: LexisNexis Canada, 2016), 259-60, and the sources cited therein.

12 *R.W.D.S.U., Local 558 v. Pepsi-Cola Canada Beverages (West) Ltd.*, 2002 SCC 8 at para. 32, [2002] 1 SCR 156.

13 *B.C.G.E.U. v. British Columbia (Attorney General)*, [1988] 2 SCR 214.

14 The 1987 First Labour Trilogy comprises *Reference Re Public Service Employee Relations Act (Alta.)*, [1987] 1 SCR 313; *PSAC v. Canada*, [1987] 1 SCR 424; and *RWDSU v. Saskatchewan*, [1987] 1 SCR 460.

15 As a number of scholars have pointed out, this position is difficult to defend. For example, legal strike action in the context of Wagner model collective bargaining legislation occurs at the end of a collective bargaining term, and can be seen as an example of individuals doing collectively what each is free to do alone: refuse to work at the conclusion of a contract, unless and until an agreement is reached. See D. Beatty and S. Kennett, "Striking Back: Fighting Words, Social Protest and Political Participation in Free and Democratic Societies" (1988) 13 *Queen's Law Journal* 214; D. Pothier, "Twenty Years of Labour Law and the Charter" (2002) 40 *Osgoode Hall Law Journal* 369, at 376-77; and B. Oliphant, "Exiting the Freedom of Association Labyrinth: Resurrecting the Parallel Liberty Standard Under 2(d) & Saving the Freedom to Strike" (2012) 70:2 *University of Toronto Faculty of Law Review* 36.

16 *Professional Institute of the Public Service of Canada v. Northwest Territories (Commissioner)*, [1990] 2 SCR 367.

17 See D. Doorey, "A Good Day to Revisit the Most Famous Dissent in Labour Law History," *Law of Work* (blog), January 29, 2015, http://lawofwork.ca/?p=7852.

18 *Dunmore v. Ontario (Attorney General)*, 2001 SCC 94, [2001] 3 SCR 1016. See also *Labour Relations Act, 1995*, SO 1995, c. 1, Sch. A.

19 *Dunmore v. Ontario (Attorney General)*, supra note 18, at para. 17.

20 See, generally, the collection of essays in F. Faraday, J. Fudge, and E. Tucker, *Constitutional Labour Rights in Canada: Farm Workers and the Fraser Case* (Toronto: Irwin Law, 2012). In *Dunmore v. Ontario (Attorney General)*, supra note 18, the Supreme Court distinguished the farm workers' circumstance from that of others without access to Wagner model–style collective bargaining. For example, it referred to the case of *Delisle v. Canada (Deputy Attorney General)*, [1999] 2 SCR 989, where the Supreme Court found that the exclusion of police officers from collective bargaining legislation did not violate section 2(d) because the police had nevertheless been able to effectively organize themselves.

21 *Dunmore v. Ontario (Attorney General)*, supra note 18, at para. 17 ("This is not to say that all such activities are protected by s. 2(*d*), nor that all collectivities are worthy of constitutional protection; indeed, this Court has repeatedly excluded the right to strike and collectively bargain from the protected ambit of s. 2(*d*)").

22 The other basis upon which the Supreme Court rested this finding is that the statutory exclusion had a "chilling" effect on associational activities. See the discussion in Langille and Oliphant, supra note 2, at 262-65.

23 *Health Services and Support—Facilities Subsector Bargaining Assn v. British Columbia*, 2007 SCC 27, [2007] 2 SCR 391 ("*BC Health Services*").

24 *Ontario (Attorney General) v. Fraser*, 2011 SCC 20, [2011] 2 SCR 3.

25 *Agricultural Employees Protection Act, 2002*, SO 2002, c. 16.

26 *Ontario (Attorney General) v. Fraser*, supra note 24, at para. 46. *Fraser* was widely considered a retrenchment from the holding in *BC Health Services* (supra note 23), narrowing the scope of section 2(d) protection for labour rights. See, e.g., S. Barrett, "The Supreme Court of Canada's Decision in *Fraser*: Stepping Forward, Backward or Sideways?" (2012) 16:2 *Canadian Labour and Employment Law Journal* 331; A. Braley, "'I Will Not Give You a Penny More Than You Deserve': *Ontario v Fraser* and the (Uncertain) Right to Collectively Bargain in Canada" (2011–2012) 57:2 *McGill Law Journal* 351; and J. Fudge, "Constitutional Rights, Collective Bargaining and the Supreme Court of Canada: Retreat and Reversal in the Fraser Case" (2012) 41:1 *Industrial Law Journal* 1.

27 *Mounted Police Association of Ontario v. Canada (Attorney General)*, 2015 SCC 1, [2015] 1 SCR 3.

28 Ibid., at para. 113.

29 *Saskatchewan Federation of Labour v. Saskatchewan*, 2015 SCC 4, [2015] 1 SCR 245.

30 *Meredith v. Canada (Attorney General)*, 2015 SCC 2, [2015] 1 SCR 125.

31 In addition to the *Meredith* case, ibid., see also *Federal Government Dockyard Trades and Labour Council v. Canada (Attorney General)*, 2013 BCCA 371, 376 DLR (4th) 318; *Canada (Procureur général) c. Syndicat canadien de la fonction publique, section locale 675*, 2014 QCCA 1068; and *Association of Justice Counsel v. Canada (Attorney General)*, 2012 ONCA 530, 117 OR (3d) 532. And the fun might not be over quite yet: see *Federal Government Dockyard Trades and Labour Council v. Canada (Attorney General)*, 2016 BCCA 156, 387 DLR (4th) 172; *Gordon v. Canada (Attorney General)*, 2016 ONCA 625; and *Canada (Procureur général) c. Syndicat canadien de la fonction publique, section locale 675*, 2016 QCCA 163. See also *Expenditure Restraint Act*, SC 2009, c. 2, s. 393.

32 The decision in *Meredith v. Canada (Attorney General)*, supra note 30, is sparsely reasoned, and it appears to exhibit signs of section 2(d) fatigue; as a result, it may not have any enduring significance.

33   See, e.g., *RJR-MacDonald Inc. v. Canada (Attorney General)*, [1995] 3 SCR 199, at para. 124, citing *Slaight Communications Inc. v. Davidson*, [1989] 1 SCR 1038.

34   See, e.g., *Mouvement laïque québécois v. Saguenay (City)*, 2015 SCC 16, [2015] 2 SCR 3, at paras. 70-76.

35   *Lavigne v. Ontario Public Service Employees Union*, supra note 7.

36   The Supreme Court ruled that colleges are "government" for the purposes of the Charter because of the degree of control governments exercise over colleges.

37   *R v. Advance Cutting & Coring Ltd.*, 2001 SCC 70, [2001] 3 SCR 209.

38   At least viewed in collective terms, the "choice" imperative in relation to collective bargaining includes the right to "dissolve existing associations." See *Mounted Police Association of Ontario v. Canada (Attorney General)*, supra note 27, at para. 86.

39   *Mounted Police Association of Ontario v. Canada (Attorney General)*, supra note 27, at paras. 92 and 85.

40   See *Kahkewistahaw First Nation v. Taypotat*, 2015 SCC 30 at paras. 18-21, [2015] 2 SCR 548.

41   See *Delisle v. Canada (Deputy Attorney General)*, supra note 20, at para. 44; *Baier v. Alberta*, 2007 SCC 31 at paras. 63-66, [2007] 2 SCR 673. *BC Health Services*, supra note 23, at para. 165; *Ontario (Attorney General) v. Fraser*, supra note 24, at paras. 114-16; and *Reference re Workers' Compensation Act, 1983 (Nfld.)*, [1989] 1 SCR 922. For an interesting discussion of this issue, see R. Elliot and M. Elliot, "The Addition of an Interest-Based Route into Section 15 of the Charter: Why It's Necessary and How It Can Be Justified" (2014) 64 *Supreme Court Law Review*, 2nd series, 461.

42   See *BC Health Services*, supra note 23, at paras. 163-66. See also the discussion of the BC Court of Appeal in *Health Services and Support—Facilities Subsector Bargaining Assn. v. British Columbia*, 2004 BCCA 377 at paras. 122-40, 243 DLR (4th) 175.

43   For an elaboration on this argument, see M. Buckley and F. Sampson, "LEAF and the Supreme Court of Canada Appeal of *Health Services and Support—Facilities Subsector Bargaining Assn. v. British Columbia*" (2005) 17 *Canadian Journal of Women & the Law* 473.

44   See B. Langille, "The Freedom of Association Mess: How We Got into It and How We Can Get out of It" (2009) 54 *McGill Law Journal* 177.

45   D. Pothier, "Twenty Years of Labour Law and the Charter" (2002) 40 *Osgoode Hall Law Journal* 369.

46   See also Elliott and Elliot, supra note 41.

47   The Supreme Court's "contextual" approach to section 2(d) is not without its occasional detractors. See J. Cameron, "Due Process, Collective Bargaining and s 2(d) of the Charter: A Comment on B.C. Health Services" (2006) 13 *Canadian Labour and Employment Law Journal* 233; Oliphant, supra note 15; and Langille and Oliphant, supra note 2, at 285-88.

48   E. Fuller, "Oliver Wendell Holmes, Jr.," *Encyclopedia Britannica*, accessed February 17, 2017, https://www.britannica.com/biography/Oliver-Wendell-Holmes-Jr.

49   *Saskatchewan Federation of Labour v. Saskatchewan*, supra note 29, at para. 1.

Selected Cases: Part III

Cases with boldface page numbers appear as Case Law Highlights.

Glossary

ability to pay principle: The principle that where provided by statute, interest arbitrators may (or must) consider the government's ability to pay when deciding the terms of their award.

analogous grounds: Personal characteristics that are not expressly listed in section 15(1) of the Charter, but are sufficiently similar in nature to the enumerated grounds to be considered protected, such as sexual orientation, marital status, and citizenship.

ancillary documents: Written materials that are physically separate from an employment contract but that include rules that relate to the employment relationship. Examples include employee handbooks, benefits handbooks, and human resources policy manuals.

anti-union animus: The motive element of unfair labour practices, it means acting with an intention to defeat or undermine the exercise of lawful activities by a union or union supporters.

application for certification: A formal legal document filed by an employee or union with labour relations board that commences a process to determine if the union qualified to become the legal collective bargaining representative of a group of employees.

appropriate bargaining unit: A grouping of jobs or employees that a labour relations board decides is suitable to be represented together in collective bargaining.

back-to-work legislation: A statute enacted for the specific purpose of bringing an end to a lawful work stoppage by referring outstanding bargaining issues to an interest arbitrator for final resolution.

bargaining structure: A term used to describe the identity and number of parties involved in collective bargaining, and the scope of employees covered by that bargaining.

bargaining unit: A group of workers whose work is similar enough that they are thought capable to be covered by the same collective agreement. Importantly, not all bargaining unit members necessarily choose to join the union.

bargaining unit employee: An employee whose job falls within a bargaining unit that a union either represents or is seeking to represent.

binding precedent (or binding decision): An earlier decision by a court of higher ranking dealing with the same legal issue in a case that comes before a lower court judge. The lower court judge is required to apply the same reasoning and legal test applied by the higher court.

Bolshevism: The term is derived from the Bolshevik party, which led the Russian Revolution of 1917. Bolshevism refers to the methods, practices, and/or beliefs of the party.

breach of contract: Occurs when a party to a contract violates one or more terms of a legally binding contract.

broader-based bargaining: A term used to describe collective bargaining structures that involves a broader scope than the one union–one employer–single location structure that dominates Canadian collective bargaining.

broader public sector: Those sectors of the economy that are funded predominantly or exclusively through taxpayer money, and that have management that is independent from the government.

bumping rights: An entitlement found in the terms of a collective agreement that permits a more senior employee to displace a junior employee in the case of a temporary or permanent downsizing of the workforce.

business efficacy test: An approach used by common law judges to justify implication of a contract term on the basis that the term is necessary in order to make the contract effective.

business representative or staff representative: An employee of a union whose job is to negotiate and administer collective agreements.

Canadian Labour Congress: The largest federal confederation of unions in Canada, representing approximately 3.3 million Canadians. Its main roles are to lobby governments, provide leadership on key issues, and provide training and education resources for its member unions. It holds a national convention every three years.

captive audience meeting: A meeting that employees are ordered by their employer to attend to listen to the employer's opinions on whether employees should or should not support unionization.

card check: A method used in Canadian collective bargaining legislation to measure the level of employee support for unionization that involves counting the number of union membership or authorization cards. If a majority of employees have signed cards, then the union is certified without a certification vote.

cartel: A combination of individuals or companies that attempt to use collective force or coordination to fix market prices.

certification: The process for legally recognizing a union as the exclusive bargaining agent of a particular group of workers.

certification freeze: A rule found in collective bargaining legislation that prohibits an employer from altering terms of employment without the union's consent during the processing of an application for certification.

Charter challenge: A legal proceeding that alleges that government action contravenes the *Canadian Charter of Rights and Freedoms*.

chief negotiator: The lead spokesperson representing a party in negotiations.

civil litigation: The processes involved with lawsuits filed in court not involving criminal law statutes, such as legal actions for breach of contract or torts.

coercive drive system: A management approach to productivity, most commonly associated with the 19th century, which sought to increase worker output through fear and intimidation.

collective agreement: A contract between an employer (or employers) and a trade union (or trade unions) that sets out the conditions of employment for a group of employees.

collective bargaining: Negotiations between an association of employees and an employer or association of employers aimed at reaching a collective agreement.

collective bargaining freeze: A rule found in collective bargaining legislation that prohibits an employer from altering terms of employment without the union's consent during the period of collective bargaining.

commercial contract: A contract between two businesses, including a business in the form of an independent contractor.

common law: A system of judge-made rules originating in England around the 12th century, and inherited by Canada as a British colony, that uses a precedent-based approach to case law. Earlier decisions dealing with similar facts or legal issues guide later decisions in an attempt to create legal predictability. However, common law rules can and often do evolve as social values change.

company rules: A term used in labour arbitration to describe rules unilaterally introduced by the employer the violation of which can lead to an employee being disciplined or dismissed.

company union: An employee association created with the encouragement or assistance of the employer and that is not independent of the employer's control or influence. A company union is often created as a union-avoidance strategy.

comparability principle: The principle that interest arbitrators should maintain comparable terms and conditions (e.g., pay) between comparable jobs in the public and private sectors.

conciliation: A form of mediation in which a neutral collective bargaining expert attempts to assist an employee association (e.g., a union) and an employer or employer association in reaching a collective agreement.

confidential employee exclusion: A common exclusion from the definition of "employee" in collective bargaining legislation that has the effect of excluding employees who exercise confidential labour relations—related functions from the protected rights to collective bargaining made available to other employees by that legislation.

conservatism principle: The principle that interest arbitrators should not impose significant changes on the parties to a collective agreement, and should instead reserve those big changes for freely negotiated agreements.

conspiracy to injure: A tort that involves two or more people acting in combination with the intention of causing harm to another party and actually causing that harm.

contract: A legally binding agreement consisting of reciprocal promises between two or more parties.

contracting out: A practice whereby an employer contracts work formerly performed by its own employees to a third-party business.

craft union: A union that organizes workers according to their particular skill or trade (such as bricklayers and carpenters) rather than according to their industry. Craft unions first emerged in Canada, in the early to mid-19th century.

craftsworker: A worker who applies his or her skills in the context of the craft organizational method of production, which was a precursor to industrial forms of production.

critical reformist perspective: A view of the law of work that supports both collective bargaining and regulatory standards, but emphasizes how both have tended to fail the most vulnerable workers. This perspective focuses on how laws can be reformed to better protect these workers.

cross-examination testimony: Evidence given by a witness during questioning by the party that did not call that witness.

Crown: The Crown in Canada is Her Majesty in right of Canada or in right of a province. The Crown is a synonym for the government.

Crown corporation: A corporation wholly and directly owned by the provincial or federal Crown.

culminating incident: The final breach of contract by an employee following progressive discipline that the employer relies on to justify termination of an employee for cause.

decertification: The legal process through which unionized workers remove their union as their legal representative and transition from the collective bargaining regime to the common law regime. It is also referred to as *terminating collective bargaining rights*.

decertification petition: A form, signed by employees who no longer desire to be represented by a union, that is used as evidence of employee support in an application to terminate the representational rights of a union.

default contract clause: A term that must be included in a contract (including a collective agreement) unless the contracting parties agree otherwise.

dependent contractor: A worker whose status falls in between that of an employee and an independent contractor. This worker has more autonomy and independence than a typical employee yet remains economically dependent on one customer for income and is subject to considerable control at the hands of that customer.

direct testimony: Evidence given by a witness called by the party doing the questioning. Leading questions are usually not permitted.

disciplinary demotion: A form of discipline in which an employee is transferred to a position of less prestige, responsibility, or pay.

distinguish: To explain how a prior legal decision dealt with facts or legal issues that are different from the facts or issues in the current case.

dues check-off: A "union security" clause whereby all members of a bargaining unit must pay union dues and employers must "check off" these dues from workers' wages and remit them to the union.

duty of fair representation: A legal obligation imposed on unions to represent employees who fall within the scope of their representation rights in a manner that is not arbitrary, discriminatory, or in bad faith.

duty to mitigate: A legal obligation on the victim of a breach of contract by the other party to make reasonable efforts to limit the amount of damages suffered as a consequence of the breach.

economic threat: A comment or action intended to signal that economic harm (including job loss or other loss of a work-related benefit) will result unless a specific course of conduct is taken.

economic tort: A species of tort invented by British judges in the 20th century to restrain collective worker action that is intended to cause economic harm.

efficient breach: A deliberate violation of a contract or government statute owing to the belief that it is more economically efficient to violate the legal rule than to comply with it.

employee: A worker who is in a position of subordination to an employer and subject to rules and entitlements set out in an employment contract.

employer grievance: A grievance filed by an employer alleging that an employee or the union has violated the collective agreement.

employment: An organizational form through which a person (employee) sells his or her labour power to a buyer of labour (employer) in exchange for value and in which the relationship is governed by an employment contract.

employment contract: A contract between an employer and an individual employee that defines the conditions under which the employee will provide labour to the employer in exchange for a monetary benefit (wages, salary), and sometimes other benefits (e.g., health benefits). An employment contract may be written or oral.

enumerated grounds: The personal characteristics that are expressly listed in section 15(1) of the *Canadian Charter of Rights and Freedoms*, namely race, national or ethnic origin, colour, religion, sex, age, or mental or physical disability.

equilibrium wage rate: A theoretical wage rate fixed through market forces in which the supply of labour (the number of hours workers are prepared to work) equals the demand for labour (the number of hours purchasers of labour wish to buy).

essential services: Services that are essential to protect the health, safety, or security of the public. For example, police officers, firefighters, and medical practitioners perform essential services. Some governments consider services that are important to the public, such as public transit or mail delivery, as essential services as well.

essential services agreement: An agreement between an employer and a union that identifies which and how many employees are "essential" to protect public safety and therefore cannot participate in a work stoppage.

exclusivity: A principle of the Wagner model, it asserts that the union chosen to represent workers becomes the sole or exclusive legal representative for that group of workers.

exit and voice: Two options workers have when confronted with an unfavourable employment condition: they can either quit (exit) their job or stay and protest (voice) to effect workplace change.

expedited arbitration: A form of labour arbitration with strict time deadlines intended to ensure the parties can receive a decision expeditiously.

expert administrative tribunals: Decision-making bodies created by a government statute and given responsibility for interpreting and enforcing one or more statutes and any regulations pursuant to that statute.

feedback loop: An explanatory device that demonstrates how outcomes produced by a system (e.g., legal rules produced by a legal system) can influence other systems (e.g., the economic system) and also "feed back" into the original system as information in a process of perpetual learning, experience, and change.

final offer selection: A form of interest arbitration in which the union and employer submit a complete final offer for a collective agreement, and then the arbitration panel selects either the union's or the employer's final offer in its entirety.

final offer vote: A provision found in collective bargaining legislation that entitles an employer to have the last offer it presented to the union's negotiating team put to a ballot of employees. Employers can only exercise this right once per round of bargaining.

first contract arbitration: A statutory provision that refers a collective bargaining impasse during negotiations for a first collective agreement to interest arbitration. Conditions for accessing first contract arbitration vary by jurisdiction.

free trade: A term used to describe a trade law policy characterized by low or zero trade tariffs and low or zero quotas on the amount of goods that flow between national borders.

gang bosses: Workers employed to supervise the increasingly industrializing workforce. They had almost total control over the workers they supervised. Often they were paid based on the productivity of their workers. Thus, the discipline they administered was often harsh and arbitrary.

general strike: A strike that includes a large number of all workers in a given geographical region and across many industries. A general strike is distinct from a local strike, in which workers in a particular bargaining unit strike during the course of negotiating a collective agreement.

grievance: A formal complaint lodged under a collective agreement that alleges an contravention of the collective agreement.

grievance procedure: A provision of the collective agreement that permits the union or the employer to allege that the other party violated a clause of the collective agreement. If the dispute is not resolved in-house by meetings of increasingly senior members of management and the union, the dispute is resolved by a neutral arbitrator.

grievor: An employee who files a grievance.

group grievance: A grievance filed on behalf of two or more employees who allege the same or a similar breach of the collective agreement.

hard bargaining: A lawful strategy in collective bargaining that involves a party using its superior bargaining power to insist upon collective agreement terms that favour its own interests.

hearsay evidence: Evidence given by a person based on second-hand knowledge rather than their own direct knowledge or observations.

incompetence: Poor work performance by an employee that is non-culpable and due not to any deliberate malfeasance by the employee, but to an inability to perform the job to a reasonable standard of competence.

independent contractor: A worker who is in business for himself or herself and who, therefore, is not an employee.

independent union: A union that is at arm's-length and independent from the control of any employer.

individual grievance: A grievance filed by an individual employee alleging their collective agreement rights have been violated by the employer.

inducing breach of contract: A tort that involves wrongful acts by a third party that are intended to cause a breach of contract between two other parties.

industrial pluralist perspective: A view of the law of work that emphasizes the inequality of bargaining power between employers and employees, and advocates especially for collective bargaining and unions as a means of empowering workers so that they can bargain fairer employment outcomes.

industrial union: An organizing ethos in which all workers in a given industry are organized into the same union, regardless of their particular skill or job category. See also *craft union*.

injunction: A legal order issued by a judge prohibiting a person from engaging in a particular course of action, such as breaching a contract, committing a tort, or violating a statute.

innocent absenteeism: An employee's absence from work due to reasons that are not blameworthy, such as illness, injury, or disability.

inside union organizer: An employee who assists in efforts to unionize his or her own employer.

insubordination: A breach by an employee of the implied or expressed term of an employment contract requiring the employee to obey an employer's orders and instructions.

interest arbitrator: An individual or three-person expert arbitration board tasked with writing the terms of a collective agreement when the union and employer are unable to reach agreement through voluntary collective bargaining.

interim reinstatement: An order by a labour board (or other legal board possessing such authority) that the employer reinstate a terminated employee to their job pending the outcome of litigation that will determine if the employer was within its legal rights to terminate the employee.

interlocutory injunction: A temporary court order prohibiting conduct that is potentially unlawful until a decision is released by the court on whether the conduct is unlawful.

intimidation: A tort that involves an attempt to coerce another person to do something, or to refrain from doing something they are entitled to do, by the threat of an unlawful act.

issue estoppel: A legal principle that prohibits a party from acting in a manner or taking a position that is contrary to a position that party has made in the past and that has been relied on by the other party.

journeyman: A worker who has completed an official apprenticeship in a craft or skill and who is thus qualified to work in that field, under the supervision of a master craftsman.

judicial review: The process through which a decision of an expert administrative tribunal is appealed to a court on the basis that the tribunal exceeded its authority (or jurisdiction) as defined in the statute that created it or that the tribunal's decision was wrong. How much deference a court must give to the expert tribunal's decision is a complex question that is considered in a field of law known as *administrative law*.

jurisdiction: The scope of authority over which a government, court, or expert administrative power has the power to govern.

just cause provision: A term in a collective agreement between a union and an employer that requires that the employer demonstrate "just cause," or a good business reason, to discipline or dismiss an employee.

Knights of Labor: An organization formed in the United States in 1869 and that was active in Canada between about 1875 and the early 1900s. The Knights promoted "industrial unionism," the organization of all workers regardless of skill, gender, race, or religion.

labour arbitration: A binding dispute resolution process used to resolve disputes involving alleged breaches of collective agreements.

labour arbitrator: An individual or a three-person expert arbitration panel appointed to decide disputes over the application and interpretation of collective agreements.

labour injunction: An order issued by a judge that prohibits or restricts a union and unionized workers from engaging in some type of collective action, such as a strike or picketing.

labour movement: A general term for the collective organization of working people that evolved to campaign for improved terms and conditions at work, and to contest and challenge various aspects of advanced capitalist society, particularly with regard to social relations of work.

labour relations boards: Expert administrative tribunals responsible for enforcing and interpreting labour relations legislation.

last chance agreement: A type of settlement of a grievance challenging the termination of an employee that includes reinstatement of the employee subject to a condition that if the employee reoffends, then termination will be the consequence.

local union: A local branch of a union; it is part of and chartered by a parent union.

local union president: A person who leads a subunit of a union, known as a local union. A local union may represent a single workplace or a group of workplaces within a defined geographical area or sector. Local union presidents are usually elected by union members and are (or were) employees of a unionized employer.

lockout: A tactic whereby an employer refuses to permit employees to report to work and to pay the employees in order to apply pressure on the employees and their union in collective bargaining.

majoritarianism: A principle of the Wagner model, it asserts that a union must secure the support of a majority of employees to win the right to act as their representative.

managerial exclusion: A common exclusion from the definition of "employee" in collective bargaining legislation that has the effect of excluding employees who exercise managerial functions from the protected rights to collective bargaining made available to other employees by that legislation.

managerialist perspective: A view of the law of work guided by the belief that employers have an economic incentive to treat employees decently and fairly in order to extract commitment and effort. Government legislation of employment should be kept at a minimum. Unionization is a response to poor management and is disruptive.

mandatory arbitration clause: A clause in a collective agreement that requires all disputes arising under the collective agreement to be referred to binding labour arbitration to be resolved.

mandatory certification vote: A method used in Canadian collective bargaining legislation to measure the level of employee support for unionization that involves the government conducting a secret ballot vote of bargaining unit employees.

mandatory collective agreement term: A term required by statute to be included in every collective agreement. If no such term is included, the statute reads a term into the agreement.

mandatory interest arbitration: Statutorily required interest arbitration to resolve collective bargaining impasses. Replaces the right to strike and lockout.

mandatory retirement: A legal rule in a statute or contract that terminates an employment contract upon the employee reaching a specified age.

mandatory union membership clause: A clause in a collective agreement that requires that every employee covered by the collective agreement (every bargaining unit employee) become a member of the union that negotiated the collective agreement.

master craftsman: A craftsworker who has attained the highest level of aptitude.

mediation-arbitration ("med-arb"): A process for resolving grievances in which a neutral expert first acts as a mediator, working with the parties to try and settle the grievance, but failing a settlement the neutral expert sits as an arbitrator and rules on the grievance.

mitigating factors/circumstances: Personal or workplace-related factors that, while not directly the cause of an employee's behaviour, help explain or justify an employee's behaviour.

monetary issues: Subjects in collective bargaining that impose direct costs on employers, such as wages, benefits, and pensions.

necessity principle: The principle that interest arbitrators should order the terms (e.g., wages and other benefits) necessary to attract and retain employees for the employer.

negotiation: Discussion between two or more people aimed at reaching an agreement.

neoclassical perspective: An economics-based view of the law of work based on the ideal of a perfectly competitive labour market. It rejects government intervention in labour markets and collective bargaining, and argues that employers and individual employees should set working conditions under a system of freedom of contract.

Nine-Hour Leagues: Organizations active in the late 19th century that attempted to pressure and persuade employers and governments to implement a mandatory maximum nine-hour workday.

Nine-Hour Movement: A social movement peaking in the early 1870s seeking a legislated maximum nine-hour workday.

non-monetary issues: Subjects in collective bargaining that relate to contract language, such as the text of a grievance procedure or management rights clause.

non-motive unfair labour practice: A type of unfair labour practice that does not require the presence of anti-union animus.

notice to bargain: A letter from a union or employer to the other party that formally begins the process of collective bargaining.

nuisance: A tort in which the activities of one person unreasonably interfere with the use or enjoyment of the property of another person.

Oakes **test:** The test applied by courts and tribunals when interpreting section 1 of the *Canadian Charter of Rights and Freedoms*. The test requires courts and tribunals to balance the interests of individuals in having their Charter rights and freedoms protected against any broader social benefits that would result from allowing a restriction of a Charter right or freedom. Named after the case *R v. Oakes*, the test was formulated by the Supreme Court of Canada.

objective test: A legal test used in interpretation of contracts and statutes that asks, What would a reasonable person of normal intelligence think, if told about the circumstances?

officious bystander test: An approach used by common law judges to justify implication of a contract term based on the presumed intention of the parties. The idea is that a contract term is implied if it would be obvious to an uninterested bystander that both parties intended the term to be part of the contract.

open period: A period of time defined in a collective bargaining statute during which a union may apply to displace another union as the representative of a group of employees, or during which unionized employees may file an application to "de-certify" the union.

own account self-employed workers: Independent contractors who have no employees.

parent union: A larger umbrella organization made up of smaller local unions. It provides service to its member local unions, such as training of local union representatives, maintaining strike funds, and providing collective bargaining support and legal expertise.

PC 1003: Granted workers collective bargaining rights, including protection from anti-union discrimination by employers and a limited protected right to strike, and imposed on employers a legal "duty to bargain" with unions representing a majority of workers.

picketing: A form of protest usually associated with a labour strike, wherein striking workers congregate outside an establishment, usually their place of work, in order to draw attention to their situation, to dissuade others from "scabbing," and to provide mutual solidarity and support.

policy grievance: A grievance filed by a union that raises an issue(s) that are of general interest to all or many employees in the bargaining unit.

precarious work: Work that is defined by characteristics such as job insecurity; short job tenure; low pay; few benefits; low collective bargaining coverage; and sporadic, limited, or unpredictable work hours.

precedent: An earlier decision by a judge that dealt with the same, or very similar, facts and legal issues as those before a judge in the current case.

primary picketing: Picketing that takes place at the location of the employer directly involved in the labour dispute.

progressive discipline: The application in stages by employers of progressively more serious discipline in order to correct performance problems.

protective standards regulation: Government regulation designed primarily to protect employees by imposing mandatory standards, such as minimum contract requirements and safety rules.

public servant: An employee formally appointed to the public service following the requirements of legislation.

public service: The public service comprises those departments and agencies that are controlled and managed directly by a central financial planning agency of the Crown. It is distinct from the public sector, which receives funding from the government but is responsible for its own management.

purposive approach to statutory interpretation: An approach to interpreting and applying a statutory provision that is guided by the purpose of the provision.

radical perspective: A view of the law of work inspired by Karl Marx's insights and criticism of the capitalist system. It considers regulatory standards regulation and collective bargaining to be helpful but limited in their ability to respond to the exploitive nature of capitalism. This perspective advocates for a more fundamental transformation of the economic model.

ratification (of a collective agreement): A vote by unionized employees in favour of accepting a proposed collective agreement.

recognition strike: A strike by workers with the aim of pressuring an employer to recognize and bargain with a union on behalf of the employees.

regulations: Government-made detailed rules introduced as a supplement to, and pursuant to authority created in, a statute. For example, the Ontario *Employment Standards Act, 2000* requires that employers pay at least "the prescribed minimum wage," but does not say what that wage rate is. That Act gives the government the right to introduce regulations (in s. 144), and one regulation (O. Reg. 285/01) sets out the precise amount of the minimum wage.

reinstatement: A legal remedy issued by a court or administrative tribunal (including an arbitrator) ordering an employer to re-employ an employee it had terminated in violation of a contract of service.

related employers: Two or more companies ruled by a labour relations board to be carrying out associated or related activities under common direction and control and, therefore, to be a single employer for collective bargaining purposes.

remedial certification: An order by a labour relations board certifying a union that may not have established it has majority employee support as a remedy for seriously unlawful acts by the employer—i.e. convincing employees that supporting a union could cost them their jobs.

replacement worker: A person who is employed to take the place of another worker who is on strike or locked out. See also *scab*.

replication principle: The principle that since interest arbitration is a substitute for free collective bargaining, the interest arbitrator should seek to replicate, to the extent possible, an agreement that the parties would have likely reached had they had recourse to the economic sanctions of a strike or lockout.

res judicata: A legal principle that prohibits a party from re-litigating an issue that has already been raised in a prior proceeding.

reserved management rights: An interpretive principle applied in labour arbitration that presumes that unionized employers retain the basic rights to run their business as they deem fit, subject to any statutory or contractual restrictions bargained by the union. These rights are sometimes called *residual management rights*.

restraint of trade: An English common law doctrine dating from the 1400s, which states that action or contracts that restrain trade are presumptively non-enforceable and/or illegal.

scab: A term used to refer to a worker who would otherwise be on strike, but who refuses to strike and instead crosses the picket line. Sometimes "scab" is used to refer generally to any person who crosses a picket line to perform work normally done by workers on strike, including a replacement worker. See also *strikebreaker*.

secondary picketing: Picketing that takes place at a location other than the workplace of the employees involved in the labour dispute.

seniority: A measure of an employee's length of service with an employer.

seniority provision: A clause in the collective agreement that allocates employment terms such as rate of pay, promotion, etc. based on length of time since being hired.

signalling effect: A phrase used by courts to describe the psychological, perhaps unspoken, message conveyed to a person confronted by labour picketing that the picketers desire that person to not cross the picket line.

specific performance: An order by a court requiring a party found to have breached a contract to carry out its obligations as specified in the contract.

spillover effect: The effects that collective agreement settlements bargained by unions and employers have on individual employment contracts in non-union workplaces.

standard employment relationship: A model of employment characterized by stable, long-term job security, full-time hours, decent benefits, and wage rates that rise steadily over time.

stare decisis: A Latin term meaning "to stand by a previous decision." It is a guiding principle in the common law regime.

statute: A law, or legislation, produced by a government that includes rules that regulate the conduct of business and people. An example is the Ontario *Employment Standards Act, 2000.*

statutory bar: A rule found in collective bargaining legislation that prohibits an application from being filed for a defined period of time.

strike: Legislation can assign a particular definition to the word *strike*. In Canada, strikes are usually defined to include both (1) a collective refusal by employees to perform work, and (2) a deliberate collective slowdown by workers designed to restrict the output of an employer (commonly known as a *work to rule*).

strike pay: A payment made by a union to a union member or person in a bargaining unit during a work stoppage, often as consideration for performing a shift as a picketer.

strikebreaker: A person who crosses a picket line to work during a strike. Different from a scab, a strikebreaker is generally hired from outside the company.

subsystem: In legal sociology, a self-contained system within the broader social system that possesses its own rules, norms, and modes of communication. Examples include economic and market; legal; political; social, cultural, and religious; and ecological/environmental subsystems.

summary dismissal: Termination of an employment contract by an employer without notice to the employee in response to a serious breach of contract by the employee.

sunset clause: A clause in a collective agreement or employment contract that wipes prior discipline from an employee's record after a specified period of discipline-free work.

surface bargaining: A strategy in collective bargaining that involves a party going through the motions of bargaining but having no intention of ever concluding a collective agreement. Surface bargaining is a violation of the duty to bargain in good faith.

sympathy strike: A strike undertaken by workers who do not have an immediate and direct grievance against their own employer, but who strike as a means of showing support and solidarity with other striking workers who do have such a grievance with their employer.

three-person labour arbitration board: An arbitration panel consisting of a person appointed by the employer, a person appointed by the union, and a "neutral," sometimes appointed by the two sides.

time theft: When an employee falsely claims wages for time not actually worked.

tort: A type of wrongful act done by one person to another (or to another's property) that judges have recognized as legally actionable. Examples are *nuisance, trespass, negligence,* and *conspiracy.*

Treasury Board: A committee of the Queen's Privy Council (i.e.. Cabinet) comprising the minister of finance and four other Cabinet ministers. The actual work of the Treasury Board is done by its administrative arm—the Treasury Board Secretariat. The Treasury Board Secretariat essentially manages the public service, including its collective bargaining and other human resource functions.

unfair labour practice: An action undertaken by someone acting on behalf of either a union or employer, or on their own behalf, that violates one or more provisions in the collective bargaining legislation.

union: An entity that is recognized in law as the exclusive bargaining agent for a particular group of workers.

union authorization card: A document that indicates a worker's consent and desire to have the union identified on the card represent them in collective bargaining with an employer.

union avoidance: A management strategy designed to reduce the risks that employees will join unions.

union certification: A government-issued licence that entitles a union to represent employees in a defined bargaining unit in their relationship with their employer.

union coverage rate: The percentage of employees whose employment conditions are governed by a collective agreement bargained on their behalf by a union.

union dues check-off: A "union security" clause whereby all members of a bargaining unit must pay union dues and employers must "check-off" these dues from workers' wages and remit them to the union.

union membership card: A document that indicates a worker's desire to join and become a member of a union.

union organizer: An employee of a union whose principal duties include organizing new workplaces and building union membership.

union raid: An attempt by one trade union to organize workers who are represented by another trade union.

union recognition clause: A clause in a collective agreement that defines the scope of the jobs that are covered by the agreement.

union-shop: A "union security" clause whereby all workers in a given job classification are required to join the union. Union-shops are distinct from closed-shops, open-shops, and agency-shops.

union wage premium: The additional wage amount attributed to union membership.

unpaid intern: A term used to describe a person who performs work for a business or receives training by a business, but who is not paid for that work.

vicarious liability: A legal rule under which an employer is liable for damage caused to a third party by one or more of its employees.

voluntary interest arbitration: A procedure in which a union and employer agree to refer outstanding collective bargaining issues to an interest arbitrator to resolve.

voluntary recognition: An arrangement in which an employer elects to recognize and bargain with a union that has not been certified by the government as the representative of employees.

Wagner Act: Collective bargaining legislation enacted in 1935 in the United States, granting workers a legal right to unionize, engage in collective bargaining, and strike. The *Wagner Act* inspired modern Canadian collective bargaining legislation.

whistle-blower: An employee who discloses information about harmful or illegal conduct of his or her employer or co-workers.

wildcat strike: A strike by employees that occurs during a period of time when a strike is not permissible according to collective bargaining laws, such as during the term of a collective agreement.

work now, grieve later: A rule developed by labour arbitrators that requires an employee who believes the employer is ordering him or her to do something in contravention of the collective agreement to do as directed and then file a grievance later challenging the employer's direction. There are some exceptions to this rule.

work to rule: A form of strike in which workers collectively and deliberately slow down for the purpose of restricting the employer's output.

workers' representative: An employee of a company or entity and member of a workers' association who is chosen to defend the interests of fellow employees, usually through an electoral process of the association.

workplace norms: Norms or expectations that arise in a workplace as a result of past practices or relationships that can influence behaviour at work, even though they are not codified in contracts or statutes.

yellow dog contract: A contract or contract term that requires an employee to refrain from joining a union or permits termination for cause of an employee who joins a union.

Index